CURRENT BUSINESS AND LEGAL ISSUES IN JAPAN'S BANKING AND FINANCE INDUSTRY

2nd Edition

CURRENT BUSINESS AND LEGAL ISSUES IN JAPAN'S BANKING AND FINANCE INDUSTRY

2nd Edition

Mitsuru Misawa

University of Hawai'i At Mānoa

World Scientific

NEW JERSEY · LONDON · SINGAPORE · BEIJING · SHANGHAI · HONG KONG · TAIPEI · CHENNAI

Published by

World Scientific Publishing Co. Pte. Ltd.

5 Toh Tuck Link, Singapore 596224

USA office: 27 Warren Street, Suite 401-402, Hackensack, NJ 07601

UK office: 57 Shelton Street, Covent Garden, London WC2H 9HE

British Library Cataloguing-in-Publication Data
A catalogue record for this book is available from the British Library.

ISBN-13 978-981-4291-01-9
ISBN-10 981-4291-01-3

Printed in Singapore.

To my two daughters,
Anne Megumi Misawa and Marie Lei Misawa

Preface to the 2nd Edition

This book is about Japanese business and law. Since the release of the 1st edition, it has been widely used as both a professional reference and an academic text suitable both for business and legal professionals, and for upper-level undergraduate or graduate courses at business and law schools. The objective of this book is to provide relevant and in-depth information on the current state of business and law in Japan. The 2nd edition contains four new chapters added to reflect the most current changes in the economy and law that have taken place in Japan since the release of the 1st edition:

Chapter 11: A Recent Reform of Banking Law — US and Japanese Comparative Study on Creation of Legal System for Banking Agencies

Recently, an enactment designed to create a legal system for banking agencies in Japan to improve depositors' benefits based on the required structural changes of Japanese financial and capital markets was approved and promulgated. I compare the U.S. and Japanese banking law systems, detailing the provisions of the Banking Law reform, and offering analysis and commentary on the current state of Japanese banking law. (Originally published in The Banking L. J., January 2006, 123(1), Mitsuru Misawa, Comparative Study of US and Japanese Bank Director's Duty of Disclosure.)

Chapter 12: Japanese Shareholders' Lawsuits Concerning Political Donations

In Japan, there has been an increased scrutiny of companies' general participation in the political process, particularly in political campaign contributions. Over the past decade, Japan has placed new restrictions on companies' political giving and required greater disclosure of campaign contributions. Shareholders have increasingly sought to hold companies accountable for their campaign contributions. The lack of transparency and the ineffectiveness of enforcement mechanisms have led to many lawsuits, such as the Yawata Steel Shareholders' Derivative Suit and the Kumagaigumi Shareholders' Derivative Suit. (This article originally appeared in Colum. J. Asian L., Colum. University, Spring 2008, 21(2), Mitsuru Misawa, An Overview of Problems Concerning Political Donations in Japan, pp. 162–181.)

Chapter 13: Financing Japanese Investments in the United States: Case Studies of a Large and a Medium-Sized Firm

This is the true story of the opening of Japanese Nissan Motor's factory in Smyrna, Tennessee in 1983. I worked for this project as an investment banker at the Industrial Bank of Japan. We used financial engineering techniques to get the required $400 million for the project as efficiently as possible. This was the first successful case of a Japanese company using these advanced techniques. As a model case, these financing methods are still studied by many Japanese companies when they are considering their investments in US. (Originally published in Financial Management, The Financial Management Association, 14(4), Winter 1985, Mitsuru Misawa, Financing Japanese Investments in the United States: Case Studies of a Large and a Medium Size Firm, pp. 5–12.)

Chapter 14: New Japanese-Style Management in a Changing Era

This article was written in 1987. At that time, there was a growing interest in defining and implementing characteristic Japanese management techniques. The causes and new directions of the changes in the Japanese economy due to increased globalization were explored.

It was predicted at that time that Japanese management methods would be Americanized and would converge with their American counterparts. However, reality proved otherwise. Japanese managers have honored the traditional decision-making processes of their organizations. While the globalization of the Japanese economy has advanced at an astounding pace since then, significant differences still remain between the management philosophy and techniques used within traditional Japanese companies and those which exist within Anglo-American companies. Thus, although my article was written many years ago, it remains relevant today. (This article was published in <u>Colum. J. World Business</u>, Vol. XXII, Mitsuru Misawa, New Japanese-Style Management in a Changing Era, pp. 9–17, Copyright Elsevier 1987.)

Chapter 15: Successful Japanese Management Cases as a Contrarian

Again, when the world economy is facing serious difficulties, the management of Japanese corporations is attracting attention from all over the world. Many of these corporations have been successful in the marketing, production, financing, and allocation of their resources in today's borderless environment. However, these success stories are only partially known in the West.

I recently conducted case constructions of 11 Japanese companies from field studies consisting of numerous visits to and interviews with managers of those corporations. Analyses of these cases revealed an interesting and noteworthy common principle as the basis of their success, which was their position as a "contrarian." "Contrarian" refers to someone who moves in opposition to others. As two of the most successful companies in this context, a full analysis of the cases of Tokyo Disneyland and Ina Food Industry is provided.

(This article is abstracted from the author's previously published articles:

1. A Case Study, Asian Case Research Centre, The University of Hong Kong, Ref. 05/254C, August, 2005, Mitsuru Misawa, Tokyo Disneyland — Joint Venture vs. Licensing.
2. A Case Study, Asian Case Research Centre, The University of Hong Kong, Ref. 06/305C, November, 2006, Mitsuru Misawa, Ina Food Industry: A New Management Philosophy For Japanese Businesses.)

As shown in this book, Japanese businesses have already entered a new era in which they must modify major traditional management practices, such as corporate solidarity, homogeneity, and commitment, in order to succeed. They must introduce the concepts of individualism and the merit system into their management practices. They must also maintain the advantages of their present legal and regulatory system while at the same time discarding its weak points. They have realized the necessity of shifting away from their conventional system and adopting some new practices. Japanese businesses are aware that the economy can take new steps toward progress only when a new style of Japanese business and legal system is established. Today, Japanese businesses feel the necessity of maintaining their positive assets while at the same time nurturing management techniques oriented towards entrepreneurship and high-technology industries.

In coping with rapid changes in the environment, Japanese management techniques and legal practices continue to change. In the era of internationalization, Japan and foreign countries have followed a path of convergence, despite differing traditions. By following this course, businesses both in Japan and abroad are expected to achieve greater progress in productivity, cost efficiency, and profit maximization, while maintaining good quality control. Professionals must be open-minded in evaluating these techniques and practices, regardless of the source country, and must try to be both flexible and aggressive in experimenting with innovations, in order to refine and polish the traditional techniques and practices of their own styles of business. An analysis of these techniques and practices, based on a wide range of actual case studies, would be invaluable for anyone seeking to improve his or her business practices. The efficacy and practicality of any management technique is put to the test only when transplanted from the soil in which it was nurtured to a new and different environment.

There is a great deal to be learned from such a study by both Japanese and foreign professionals. In this sense, the management techniques and legal practices newly adopted by Japan, and the Japanese management techniques and legal practices adopted by foreign countries are an area of research that fully deserves the attention of scholars and experts both in Japan and foreign countries. These studies should serve as valuable test cases for the theory and practice of modern business. It is hoped that this book will be used as a starting point for such studies.

Finally, I would like to express my deep appreciation to my two daughters, Anne Megumi Misawa and Marie Lei Misawa, who have provided me with continued support and encouragement during the writing of this book.

Mitsuru Misawa
Honolulu, Hawaii

Preface to the 1st Edition

As a finance professor in a US university, I have not noticed many books on Japan, especially books written by Japanese authors. I have 30 years of experience as an investment banker in Tokyo and New York. Over these years I have gained tremendous insight into both Japanese and American issues in finance, law and business. My expertise in these three areas contributes to a unique perspective, as shown in this book. Because I am from Japan, this book was written from an insider's perspective.

Japanese corporate behavior and practice raise a number of issues for international businessmen, accountants and lawyers. In today's globally developed economy, it is important that Japan's current law, system and way of thinking are easily and accurately comprehended by those in foreign countries whose structures differ from those in Japan. Japan's economy is the second largest in the world, but there are many things that outsiders find difficult to understand. Their interest in the Japanese law, market and economy is significant and increasingly prominent. This book on Japan is surely relevant to their interests.

This book includes a number of citations as footnotes that show the readers how they may begin to collect vital information from Japan. The data here are pertinent to any understanding of the Japanese markets but are difficult for people outside the Tokyo markets to obtain.

The book is based on ten articles on Japanese finance and law that have already been published in respected journals. For each chapter, I have included additional and introductory comments regarding Japan's banking and finance industry. I would like to thank the journals for permitting me to use my articles, copyrights of which are held by them.

Financial support from the Center for Japanese Global Investment and Finance at the University of Hawaii, is gratefully acknowledged. To know more about the Center, please see the Appendix of the book. I also greatly acknowledge the support and understanding of my family, which has helped complete the book.

Contents

About the Author

Dr. Misawa received his LLB from Tokyo University Law School in 1960, LLM from Harvard Law School in 1964, MBA from the University of Hawaii as an East-West Center grantee in 1965 and Ph.D. from the University of Michigan (International Finance) in 1967.

He is Professor of finance (International Finance and International Banking) and Director of the Center for Japanese Global Investment and Finance at the University of Hawaii, which was established in 1997 under the sponsorship of Japanese Keidanren (Japanese Federation of Economic Organizations). His tenure at the University of Hawaii was granted in June, 1998.

Before joining the University of Hawaii in August 1996, he was with the Industrial Bank of Japan (now Mizuho Financial Group, the world's largest bank) for 30 years. His career included assignments as an investment banker in New York and Tokyo for 15 years each. During his career at IBJ, he served as the Executive Vice President at IBJ Trust Bank (NY), Deputy General Manager of the Loan Department at IBJ (Tokyo), the General Manager of the International Headquarters at IBJ (Tokyo), and the President of IBJ Leasing (NY) as a member of the Board of Directors of IBJ Leasing (Tokyo). One of the financial arrangements he conducted as an investment banker at IBJ was the Nissan Motor's direct investment to manufacture trucks and cars in Smyrna, Tennessee in 1983. For total financing of $400 million, he employed "global financial engineering" techniques. Since then, these techniques have been widely used by other Japanese investment to the US.

His researches have been published in numerous academic and professional journals, including Sloan Management Review, Financial Management, Columbia Journal of World Business, Vanderbilt Journal of Transnational Law, Banking Law Journal, Temple International and Comparative Law Journal, Columbia Journal of Asian Law, Journal of International Law and Business (of the Northwestern University School of Law), Penn State International Law Review (of the Dickinson School of Law), and many cases developed at Asian Case Research Centre at the University of Hong Kong.

His 14 cases on Japanese companies are listed at the Asian Case Research Center, University of Hong Kong (http://www.acrc.org.hk/) for sales in Asia, at Harvard Business Online (http://cb.hbsp.harvard.edu/cb/search/misawa?Ntk=HEMainSearch&N=0) for sales in the US and at the European Case Clearing House (http://www.ecch.com/) for sales in Europe.

Through this network, 5500 copies of his cases were sold in the last 3 years to a number of universities, companies, investment banks and consulting firms throughout the world.

His recent book on *"Cases on International Business and Finance in Japanese Corporations"*, (November 2007, Hong Kong University Press, ISBN: 978-962-209-891-6; British Library Cataloguing -in-Publication Data) is currently used as a text book of international business and finance by various universities of the world.

Dr. Misawa is a consultant for a number of international institutions such as IBJ (Japan) and OSG Corporation (Japan). From 1989 to 1996, he served as the US Counselor on the Keidanren's "Council for Better Corporate Citizenship." From 1993 to 1996, he served as a member of the Business School's Visiting Committee of the University of Michigan, which was composed of global business executives. Dr. Misawa was appointed "Colonel of the State of Kentucky" in 1984 and "Arkansas Traveler" in 1985 in recognition of his achievements in soliciting Japanese investments for these states.

Chapter 1

Introduction

The book is about Japan's Banking and Finance with special emphasis on current business and legal issues.

The Commercial Code was transplanted from Germany to Japan in 1899 as a part of the general acceptance of Western law in the Meiji period. The post-war corporate laws in Japan were modeled after those in the United States. For example, the Securities Exchange Law of Japan enacted in 1948 was based upon the laws of 1933 and 1934 in the United States and was imposed by the occupation authorities as a condition for the reopening of the securities exchanges. This Japanese law contained disclosure provisions substantially similar to the requirements of the American law. Germany is a civil law country, while the United States is a country of the common law. Any confusion in the legal concepts in Japan may be attributed to the slight difference in the rules and practices of the two source countries.

The basic assumption of occupation authorities in suggesting the new corporate practice and legislation appears to have been that what worked well in the United States would also work in Japan. No question was raised as to the congeniality of the environment into which the new legislation was being transplanted. If transplanted control methods and corporate practices of Anglo-American origin should not be well adapted to Japanese procedures, then Japanese economy and markets would be prevented from performing their functions as efficiently as required.

On this basis material revisions of laws have been made since then in order to improve and enhance the financial system focusing on its market

1

functions. Many changes were also made to accommodate new trends occurring in the markets.

About 55 years have passed since the end of World War II and it is now appropriate to evaluate the efficacy of the transplanted systems, practices and laws from the US. The hypothesis established by the occupation authorities at that time is tested in various areas in light of the congeniality of the Japanese environment into which the American system was transplanted. You will see them all in the following chapters.

Chapter 2 is an introduction to Tokyo as the international market. A current subject of debate in the international business world is whether the Tokyo international capital market has what it takes to emerge as a leader in the world's capital market. This article attempts to evaluate whether the Tokyo international capital market can play a major role in the realm of international finance and what it must do to get there. The historical development and relevant laws and regulations governing the operation of this market are discussed.

There are many problems to be resolved. First and foremost is the internationalization of the yen. Secondly, concomitant with the internationalization of the yen is the further internationalization of the Tokyo market as an intermediary in the money supply field. This highlights the disclosure problem. Because of the uniqueness of Japanese accounting standards and the emergence of the International Financial Reporting Standards (IFRS), three different types of disclosures have been created in the Japanese market: (1) those based on the Japanese accounting standards; (2) those based on accounting standards of foreign countries; and (3) those based on the IFRS. As a result, questions arise: How should Japanese authorities handle disclosures? Should all three standards be accepted as legitimate? What are the conditions of acceptance?

Chapter 3 describes Japan's big bang reform. Although ten years have passed since the bubble economy burst, and ¥7.2 trillion in public funds were poured into most of the Japanese banks in 1999 in order to beef up their net worth capital, the profit figures of 131 major banks in 2003 did not show signs of the financial market's complete recovery from the damage incurred by the bursting of the bubble economy. In 1996, ¥685 billion of tax money was used to liquidate the special housing loan companies (Jusen) that were burdened by enormous debts. At that time, it looked as though that would settle the banks' bad debts, but it turned out that it was only the start.

The August 1995 annual report of the International Monetary Fund (IMF) criticized Japan's Banking Policy Administration for failing to take effective measures against the deterioration of its banking system. The Board asked Japan to take speedy action to correct problematic banks. The report also stated that the market mechanisms that are supposed to help depositors and investors select banks are not working due to the insufficient disclosure about the operating information of banks, and that it is necessary to establish a clear-cut rule specifying how the necessary funds for cleaning up the bad debts of problem banks, including public funds, are to be born by the stakeholders.

In August 1999, it was revealed that the net asset deficiency of the Long Term Credit Bank of Japan, Ltd. (LTCB) at term's end (March 31, 1999) was ¥2.78 trillion. The report also pointed out that the government of Japan established the Financial Revitalization Law to pave the way for nationalization of an asset deficient bank and subsequent transfer of its business to other banks. On September 28, 1999, the Financial Reconstruction Commission (FRC) decided to transfer LTCB to "partners" led by Ripple Wood Holdings, L.L.C. of the United States. A sum of almost ¥4 trillion of public funds was poured into the bank to cover its bad loans, including its secondary losses.

Upon the announcement of the examination results of 19 major banks by the Financial Services Agency (FSA), and immediately after the enactment of the Financial Revitalization Law, the Nippon Credit Bank, Ltd. (NCB) was suddenly nationalized by the FSA on the grounds that the bank was net asset deficient. It is important to note that the net worth ratios of LTCB and NCB were published at 10% and 8% respectively.

As a result, criticisms against Japanese banks, such as claims that they were not disclosing their operations accurately, were heard all over the world. Japan's economy is the second largest in the world, next to that of the United States, and its financial and banking market is one of the major markets in the world. International interest in the Japanese market and economy is ever-increasing. But Japanese corporate behavior and practice have raised a number of issues. One of the major issues involves Japan's accounting and reporting systems. This article investigates the methods of processing bad loans and the disclosures practiced by Japanese banks. It also studies the legal requirements and accounting standards behind them. It seems that there are systems, as well as rules and regulations, unique to Japan that are substantially dissociated from international standards. On October 17, 1996, the Economic Council, an advisory organization the Prime Minister, to presented a report including a restructuring plan entitled "For the Revitalization of the Financial System of Our Country." The restructuring plan was based on the recognition of the severe crises: while reformation of financial sector is moving at accelerated rates in the United States and European countries, as well as some Asian countries, the move toward reformation of the financial system in Japan is still very slow; Japan is clearly lagging behind in the competition among global markets and systems; and its position in the world financial system and industry is deteriorating relative to those countries. The report stated, "In order to overcome this relative deterioration of our position and make it possible for the users to benefit from more efficient and better financial services, it is necessary for the government to get rid of the excessively protective attitude toward the financial institutions and the traditional convoy system provided under the guidance of the Ministry of Finance; in particular, it is necessary to implement various policies geared toward building a system designed for the benefits of the users, which is based on the market mechanism and the principle of their own risks. It is not enough for the new financial system to be sound and stable; it must be also efficient and revolutionary."

It also stated, "Therefore, the reform must not be gradual or phased; it must be done in one big stroke; the quicker, the better, if Japan is to compete with various countries of the world and it should be done by the end of 1999 in one big change, in the manner of a Big Bang."

This proposal should be given proper consideration because it seeks the reform within a defined time limit, it was not drafted in coordination with any of the related ministries and agencies, and it put forth a clear image of how the Japanese financial system should be in the future. One noteworthy factor is that it emphasizes the importance of mandating liberalization in order to allow the competition principle to operate and minimizes the use of administrative discretion by specifying by law all the regulative items as exceptions.

The outline of this reform plan is as follows:

Realization of Broader Competition

In order to facilitate the entry of not only the financial institutions but also non-financial institutions into the financial market from the standpoint of promoting competition among financial institutions, all entry restrictions and limitations related to the types of businesses and methods used, as well as approval or permit procedures, will be abolished.

Liberalization of Asset Transactions

In order to improve the functions of the capital market, it is necessary to liberalize the commissions for selling and buying securities, completely revamp the securities taxation system, which include abolishing the securities transaction tax, to liberalize further transactions outside the regular stock exchange, to promote the introduction of new financial technologies, to reform the markets for issuing and trading corporate bonds, and to introduce the stock option system.

Reevaluation of Regulating and Monitoring System

It is mandatory for the Japanese financial system to overhaul its system of regulation and administration in order to survive in the international "inter-system competition." Therefore, it is necessary to refurbish the system's foundation concerning the handling of failing financial institutions, change the administrative practices from the ones in the past which relied heavily on the individual administrator's discretion and were heavily protective of the financial institutions to one based on established rules honoring the market function, and enforce the policy of competition in the financial businesses.

Chapter 4 describes bad loans of Japanese banks. In this chapter, three subjects are discussed on bad loans in Japan. Part One is for "Bad

Loans: A Comparative Study of US and Japanese Regulations Concerning Loan Loss Reserves", Part Two is for "Bank Director's Decisions on Bad Loans: A Comparative Study of US and Japanese Standards of Required Care" and Part Three is for "Case Study of the Long Term Credit Bank of Japan."

Japan's banking policy administration is in the midst of criticism, accused of failing to take effective measures against the deterioration of its banking system. Claims that Japanese banks were not disclosing their operations accurately were heard all over the world.

According to the current accounting rule in Japan and by request of the United States, financial statements of some Japanese corporations written in English must have notations or legends that verify that the statement was prepared in accordance with the Japanese Securities Exchange Law and accounting standard, and not under the accounting standards of any other country. What this means is that the Japanese accounting process is no longer trusted internationally.

This article investigates the methods of processing bad loans and disclosures practiced by Japanese banks. It also studies the legal requirements and accounting standards behind them. The recent bankruptcy case (The Long-term Credit Bank) is closely examined. It seems that there are systems as well as rules and regulations unique to Japan that are substantially dissociated from international standards. In this article, the author compares the differing US and Japanese legal regulations and business practices.

Based on this analysis, the author concludes that it is important for Japan to appropriate the necessary minimum reserves against loan losses through more stringent evaluations of bad loan risks and that Japanese banks must improve their shortcomings to regain their international credibility. He points out that various rules and regulations concerning loan loss reserves in Japan significantly lag behind those of the United States. According to the author, identifying the true status of bad loans and determining how to deal with them can only be accomplished by a thorough examination of the accounting standards in their entirety.

As a result of the extensive failures of financial institutions that have occurred since 1995 in Japan, legal action against previous bank directors is expected to increase in the future. The question is, what should be the duty of care for a bank director, and in particular, what should be the court standard for determining if the duty of care has been breached by the director. This article examines the laws related to bank directors' responsibilities and discusses some Japanese court cases. The differences in legal systems and the court rulings in Japan and the United States also are compared.

During the second half of the 20th century, the banking business in Japan was under the so-called Convoy System by the Ministry of Finance (MOF). During that time not a single bank failed, which created the myth that "financial institutions never go under." Japan's financial institutions have gone through drastic changes as a result of the fundamental changes in the financial market including the financial relaxation after the "Japanese Financial Big Bang" and the deflation after the "Bubble" burst. In today's environment financial institutions are expected to be managed with tighter controls based on the directors' own responsibilities.

Due to the rampant failures of financial institutions that occurred since 1995 when the Bubble Economy collapsed, the Resolution and Collection Corporation (RCC) was created by the Deposit Insurance Corporation of Japan, a government organization, as the major shareholder in order to expedite the cleanup of defaulted loans. The RCC's responsibilities include:

1. Receiving the defaulted financial institutions' assets and collecting them;
2. Reestablishing bankrupt corporations; and
3. Pursuing the directors involved in the defaulted financial institutions for violating their duties of care.

So far the RCC has received the assets of 172 defaulted financial institutions and has taken 122 legal actions against 86 defaulted financial institutions seeking damages for violations of the duty of care. The issue in each of these legal actions is whether the loan execution judgments of the previous management team constituted violations of the duty of care for directors under the Commercial Code.

Actions against the previous directors are expected to increase in the future. The question is: What is the duty of care for a director of a bank and, in particular, what should be the criterion for a court in determining whether or not a director of a financial institution has violated that duty. This article discusses the direction Japan should take in the future by examining the Japanese laws related to bank directors' responsibilities and some actual cases in Japan, referencing the bank directors' responsibilities in the United States as well.

The fact that so many questionable loans were made by Japanese banks suggests a strong possibility that the Japanese standard for violations of bankers' duty of care is far too lenient as compared to that of the United States, which has overcome its own bad loan problem. The following analysis is based on the hypothesis that the lenient duty of care standard is the main cause of the large number of bad loans in Japan. Thus the comparison of the legal systems and the court judgments of Japan and the United States is appropriate. Also, this analysis is significant because the GDP of Japan is the second largest in the world and Japanese banks are receiving large sums of money from around the world to operate funds internationally. How the directors of these Japanese banks are operating and whether they are paying full attention to their duty of care should be a matter of grave concern to the international banking world. The total amount of overseas funds Japanese banks have taken in (liabilities) as $523 billion, while the total amount of funds they have discharged (claimable assets) is $564 billion as of June 2004. The reason that such large amounts of funds are flowing into Japanese banks is because foreign lenders trust Japanese banks. However, it is doubtful if those same lenders would continue to trust Japanese banks if they knew that the standard of duty of care required of Japanese Bank Directors is much lower than those required of bank directors in the United States.

Chapter 5 examines disclosure issues in Japan. Part One is for "A Comparative Study of US and Japanese Bank Directors' Duty of Disclosure" and Part Two is for "Case of Seibu Group — Recent Problems on Japanese Corporate Disclosure System."

As a publicly-held company, a bank is required to make timely and appropriate disclosures of corporate information to the public, including investors. In this article, the author studies what a Japanese bank is required to disclose in regard to its important management information including bad debts in terms of its timing and contents under the Japanese Commercial Law, Securities Exchange Law, Banking Law, and Financial Revitalization Law. After explaining comparable obligations under US law, the author suggests changes to the Japanese policies. It is important to better understand how Japanese banks operate and their required disclosure, if US banks are to compete with their Japanese counterparts, the second largest GDP country in the world. This advance knowledge is critical not only for US investors in Japanese banks but also for US institutional investors involved in transactions with Japanese banks.

The code of ethics of the Japanese Banking Association defines the importance of disclosure by its member banks as follows:

A bank, in consideration of its social responsibility and public mission, is required to obtain broad understanding and trust from the society, in particular, from its shareholders and investors. Fair disclosure of management information for being selected and judged by the market and users should contribute to not only the promotion of the society's understanding of and trust on the bank but also to its own self-cleaning capability in order to achieve healthier management. Such management information disclosures should be geared toward timely and appropriate provisions of various types of information required for rational judgments by shareholders, investor, and users.

Generally speaking, it is not a desirable thing for a bank to disclose all corporate information. It is analogous to individuals disclosing their bookkeeping information, the amount of money they carry in their wallets or the amount of their pay check. However, if we consider that a bank is constantly involved in financial activities on a large scale, we can easily understand why those who are on the opposite side of those deals want such disclosures. It is also not difficult to understand that a bank wants to disclose positive information but negative information as well, because the latter will probably benefit the bank in the long run. Persons on the other side of a bank transaction who want information about the bank include:

1.   the "government agency" who is to control the bank's operation;

2. the "auditor" of a company who is to monitor the bank's operation;
3. the shareholder (Incidentally, the shareholder wants such information not necessarily for its desire to participate in the management of the bank but rather for judging the optimum timing for trading the bank's shares.); and
4. the bank's "transaction partner."

The transaction partner wants information in order to decide whether to participate in a deal with the bank or what to do with a deal already in existence. Such information is important for the bank's creditors and the bank's customers (depositors).

However, it is not unusual for a bank to be unwilling to disclose information voluntarily or to want to disclose only beneficial information. Various laws and regulations are set up to prevent banks from controlling information disclosure to their advantage, and those laws and regulations specify the types of information to be disclosed and who should receive them.

For Part Two, the recent Seibu Scandal is introduced as a Japanese disclosure case study. The Seibu case in Japan, has given the investors of the world some reason to doubt the Japanese disclosure system. Seibu, one of the leading Japanese listed companies, had disclosed incorrect information as to its shareholdings by affiliated companies for some 40 years. It is considered to be the Japanese "Enron" Case, as the scandal sent a large shockwave through the Japanese business community and the international investors to Japan.

Yoshiaki Tsutsumi, the former chairman of the board of Kokudo Corp., who led the Seibu Group as the owner in a practical sense, was arrested by the Tokyo District Public Prosecutors Office on March 3, 2005, and subsequently indicted by the same on March 24, 2005, on a charge of violations of the Security Exchange Law concerning the stocks of Seibu Railway Co., Ltd. owned by Kokudo Corp.

There are two parts to the alleged charge. First is that while in fact Kokudo owned approximately 64 percent of the outstanding shares of Seibu, it hid a portion of its shares and reported to the Ministry of Finance (MOF) its outstanding shares of stock as 43 percent. The second part is a charge of insider trading for selling a portion of the Seibu stocks without disclosing the fact that such falsified numbers had been submitted year after year, "an important fact concerning the business," which Tsutsumi was well aware of.

Chapter 6 considers the difference of sales recognition existing between US and Japan. Trading companies are institutions unique to Japan; nonetheless their importance is recognized internationally. Marked changes have been noted in their amounts of sales. The changes appeared in the list of top 500 corporations of the world in the July 2003 issue of *Fortune* magazine. In the rankings based on the amount of sales for corporations, the Japanese trading companies took a nose dive from their usual high ranking positions. For example, Mitsubishi, which held 10th place a year ago, plummeted to 389th and Mitsui from 11th a year ago to the 171st position.

The five major trading companies had been using the US standard for disclosure, except in regard to sales amount, for which they used the Japanese standard. This was because their position in the industry worldwide was based on the amount of sales. However, when they saw the US standard had adopted a stricter definition, they started to use the US standard for the sales amount.

The problem with the accounting system of Japanese companies is that such an important change is made haphazardly. The definition of amount of sales under the Japanese accounting standard is not clear and is left to each industry's custom. Not providing a set standard that would facilitate a better comparison.

Chapter 7 studies Japanese issues and perspective on the convergence of international accounting standards. While the business activities of corporations are becoming more international every year, the accounting system of individual countries seem to remain very local, differing from country to country. Recently, a cry was heard for the need for an international standardization of the accounting system so that investors can understand and properly compare the performance of corporations of other countries when they seek financing overseas. As a result of these concerns, international accounting standards are gradually taking shape.

The Norwalk Agreement was the result of a joint meeting between the US Financial Accounting Standards Boards (FASB) and the International Accounting Standards Board (IASB) in September 2002. The agreement sought convergence between the International Financial Reporting Standards (IFRS) and US standards, and laid the foundation for further convergence of various international accounting standards. It was decided that the IFRS is to be adopted officially in 2005 as the financial reporting standard for corporations in the European Union whose stocks are traded in markets.

The European Union has asked non-EU entities operating in the European Union to disclose information based on the "IFRS or an equivalent standard" starting in 2005. Currently, more than 250 Japanese corporations and Japanese local governments have issued stocks and bonds in the European Union. Most of these Japanese corporations disclosed financial information using Japanese accounting standards.

Japanese efforts may be successful because Japan is negotiating diligently with the European Union and is asking for its approval of the Japanese accounting standard as an equivalent to the IFRS. If the Japanese accounting standard fails to be recognized as an equivalent of the IFRS, disclosure by Japanese companies based on the Japanese accounting standard currently in the European Union would not be allowed, severely affecting the financing activities of Japanese companies seeking to raise funds in the European Union. Japanese corporations are also concerned about the possibility that Japanese accounting standards could be branded as inferior to the European or US Accounting Standards, thus causing a general mistrust among investors in Japanese capital markets.

There have been divergent opinions from both government and private sectors about the adoption of the IFRS in Japan and no consensus has yet been reached. In the midst of this, on June 24, 2004, the Corporate Accounting Rule Council of the Japanese Government Ministry of Finance (MOF)," published a memorandum titled "Adoption of International Accounting Standards in Japan" (MOF Memorandum). The purpose of the MOF Memorandum was to canvass and compile various arguments about what should be done in Japan, from an official standpoint, regarding adopting international accounting standards to coincide with the European Union's adoption of the IFRS in 2005.

The Japanese Corporate Accounting Rule Council (the Council) was given the responsibility of setting up the business accounting system and auditing standard. In the MOF Memorandum, as a first step, the Council made a general observation of the international trends surrounding the IFRS, summarized the arguments and comments about the IFRS from a legal standpoint, and provided the Council's comment about future tasks. The Council also provided its opinions regarding the application of the IFRS to foreign as well as domestic corporations.

This article summarizes various arguments existing in Japan on the current issue of standardization as well as the official position of the Japanese government expressed in the MOF Memorandum. The Japanese government's position as expressed in the MOF Memorandum is extremely important to investors in foreign countries. The author analyzes the government's positions and makes comments on the problems and issues indicated in the MOF Memorandum.

Chapter 8 examines shareholders' derivative action in Japan. The New York Daiwa Bank scandal in 1995, which involved Daiwa Bank's concealment of the $1.1 billion in losses from the illegal funding of US Treasury bonds, resulted in the most severe economic penalties ever imposed by the United States on Japan. These penalties included the termination of Daiwa Bank's US operations and a substantiated international distrust of Japanese financial institutions, including their closely aligned governmental regulators, the Ministry of Finance.

In September 2000, a Japanese court handed down a decision in this shareholders' representative action that ordered the defendants, 12 directors of Daiwa Bank, to pay bank damages totaling $775 million (approximately 82.9 billion yen). These damages ranged from $530 million (approximately 56.7 billion yen) to $70 million (approximately 7.5 billion yen) per person, and shocked the international society because of the size of the penalties. The award raised many basic legal and economic issues regarding the shareholders' representative action system in Japan, which was first introduced to Japan by the United States in 1950. Because of the importance of the Japanese economy to the world, the representative action system's behavior is expected to have a tremendous effect on the international economic society.

The Daiwa decision examined the duties assumed by the directors of a financial institution, which require them to establish an internal control system for monitoring risks and for enforcing laws and regulations, the differences in the duties of care among the directors, and the objectives of the responsibilities, as well as the scope of damages. The court decision also sounded a very important alarm about how Japanese corporations are managed. The environment that allowed Japanese companies to be run so loosely seemed to be the fact that the supervising authorities and the legal system failed to rigorously pursue the lack of risk management and the concealment of responsibilities. The Daiwa case made the point that it is extremely dangerous for Japanese financial institutions to try to operate overseas in this same lax manner. Another such incident could invite international mistrust of the entire Japanese financial system.

In this article, the author compares the differing United States and Japanese reactions to the New York Daiwa Bank scandal on legal, economic, and sociological levels. Based on his analysis, the author concludes that cultural differences between the United States and Japan lie at the heart of the scandalous proportions of the Daiwa Bank incident in New York. Furthermore, the author believes that the Daiwa Bank case offers an important lesson for US and Japanese companies with international operations: "When in Rome, do as the Romans do."

Chapter 9 considers the recent trend in Japanese securities regulations. The Commercial Code was transplanted from Germany to Japan in 1899 as part of the general acceptance of Western law in the Meiji period. The post-war methods of corporate disclosures in Japan were modeled after those adopted by the United States in 1933 and 1934. The Securities Exchange Law of Japan enacted in 1948 was imposed by the occupation authorities as a condition for the reopening of the securities exchange. This Japanese law included disclosure provisions substantially similar to the requirements of the US law.

The basic assumption of the occupation authorities in suggesting the new corporate and securities legislation appears to have been that what worked well in the United States would work in Japan. No question was raised as to the receptiveness of the environment into which the new legislation was being transplanted. If transplanted control methods and corporate practices of Anglo-American origin should not be well adapted to Japanese procedures, then Japanese markets would be prevented from performing their functions as efficiently as desired.

The original Securities Exchange Law was established under the guidance of General Headquarters (GHQ) after WWII and the securities system operated under the tight guard of the United States. For example, the securities business of securities companies were protected and nurtured by the Securities Exchange Law. However, the guard provided by the United States was removed in accordance with the Peace Treaty of 1951 between Japan and the United States. Arrival of freer financial and securities activities, which took off in the latter half of 1960s, introduced various problems that had never been thought of and that could not be dealt with by the existing Securities Exchange Law. The introduction of foreign securities dealers in Japan was one of those problems, which was eventually addressed by the enactment of the "Law Concerning Foreign Securities Dealers," a special law of the Securities Exchange Law.

Domestically, an inter-industrial problem developed relating to over-the-counter sales of government bonds at banks, which led to the revision of the Banking Law. Stock price index future trading, which is unrelated to securities, was introduced in 1988, which was then followed by option trading introduced in 1989, the latter being useful economically but more problematic as it is difficult to deal with from a legal standpoint. In 1992, banking operations and securities operations came to be entered mutually through subsidiaries as a reform of the entire financial system across the boarder of the Securities Exchange Law.

When Japan became the world's second largest economic power, internationalization of Japan advanced with a tremendous momentum. In the Japanese stock market, the number of shares held by non-Japanese investors is about 20 percent and the sales volume held by that 20 percent is about 50 percent. When such a fast change occurs in any economy, laws often lag behind.

A material revision of the Securities Exchange Law of Japan was made in 2004 in response to the changes occurring in domestic and foreign economic and financial trends. The Securities Exchange Law has gone through scores of changes, but the recent change was extensive, in order to improve and enhance the financial system focusing on its market functions, such as enhancement of market monitoring and enrichment of marketing venues for securities.

More specifically, it modified the basic stance taken in the original law, for example, it approved banks' participation in securities business. The changes were also made to accommodate new trends in the market, such as the Takeover Bid (TOB) process, the Proprietary Trading System (PTS), the Green Sheet Market, and the Best Execution Policy of the securities companies. Enhancement of market monitoring through the Securities Exchange Surveillance Committee was another major change in the securities regulation.

Chapter 10 introduces M&A for Foreign Investments in Japan. It discusses M&A climate for foreign investments in Japan. M&A plays an important role in promoting investment in Japan. It takes place in the form of a merger, transfer of business and stock acquisition. Compared to starting a company from scratch, M&A is advantageous in that it allows the founder to effectively use existing business resources; it is also a common practice around the world. In Japan, however, there are few M&As in terms of value and number of cases compared to industrialized nations in Europe and the United States. In particular, there are extremely few M&As of a Japanese company by a foreign company.

M&A should be viewed in a positive light as a means of corporate management to carry out strategic restructuring. For a small or medium sized company or a venture company with strong technology, it should be seen as an important technique for obtaining the necessary financing or business resources to take over or to further develop a business. In addition, the activation of M&A would also enable to introduce a new checking function for business management from outside, which would promote the efficiency of the business.

Activation of M&A in Japan, in macro terms, will rejuvenate the Japanese economy by transferring business resources and introducing new technology and systems. Employment will also be created. In addition, it will broaden the alternatives for business management and employment formats in Japan and make the Japanese economic and social systems and business practices more transparent in the globalized economic society, thereby helping it be a system that is acceptable to the rest of the world.

There are a few factors that make it difficult for a foreign company to carry out an M&A in Japan.

1. The information on M&A is not sufficient in the market.. Although it is vital to properly collect necessary information regarding firms, when one looks for the appropriate firms as the M&A target, that kind of information is not easily available in Japan. As for information regarding sale of firms, due in part to the negative image, the information rarely appears or circulates widely in the market.

There exists negative image against M&A. In certain cases, employees fearing dismissal put up a protest when their company becomes the target of an M&A but turns out to be abortive. Sometimes the mere rumor of an acquisition is enough for a client to suspend business with the company. The sensitiveness of resistance is even stronger if the buyer is a foreign company. At the root of this issue is the present situation of corporate governance in Japan. Stockholders have little power over management and little awareness of their rights. Consequently, the judgment of management takes precedence. This trend is fueled by interlocking stockholding among Japanese companies. Administrative and legal procedures concerning M&A businesses are not efficient. It is said that M&A professionals there aren't many good as yet in Tokyo.

Chapter 2

The Tokyo International Capital Market for Foreign Issuers and Required Disclosure[a]

This article evaluates whether the Tokyo international capital market can play a major role in the realm of international finance and what it must do to get there. The historical development and relevant laws and regulations governing the operation of this market are discussed. In addition, this article summarizes various arguments existing in Japan on the current issue of accounting standardization as well as the official position of the Japanese government expressed in the Ministry of Finance Memorandum.

In September 2005, Citigroup, Inc. issued a total of ¥230 billion ($2.3 billion) in Samurai Bonds, a figure eclipsing the record 220 billion yen issued in 2002 by Daimler Chrysler AG. Citigroup, Inc. is said to issue a total of $20 billion of Samurai Bonds in 2005. Samurai Bonds are yen-denominated bonds issued in Japan by nonresidents such as foreign banks, governments and companies. Citigroup, the largest US financial services company, is expected to use proceeds from the issuance for investment activity and system upgrade work in Japan and the United States. The Samurai Bond market has been active of late, with recent issuers including the Korea Development Bank and the Polish government.[1]

---

[a] This chapter is based on the author's previously published article:
Mitsuru Misawa, "The Tokyo International Capital Market for Foreign Issuers and Required Disclosure," *The Journal of Payment Systems Law*, published by A.S. Pratt & Sons, the same publisher as *The Banking Law Journal*, November/December 2005, November 7, Volume 1, pp. 699–753.

[1] *See Japan Today*, "Citigroup to Issue Y230 Bil in Samurai Bonds," September 5, 2005. (http://www.japantoday.com/e/?content=news&id=648225).

A current subject of debate in the international business world is whether the Tokyo international capital market has what it takes to emerge as a leader in the world's capital market. This article evaluates whether the Tokyo international capital market can play a major role in the realm of international finance and what it must do to get there. The historical development and relevant laws and regulations governing the operation of this market are discussed.

Many problems exist that need to be resolved. First and foremost is the internationalization of the yen. Secondly, concomitant with the internationalization of the yen is the further internationalization of the Tokyo market as an intermediary in the money supply field. This highlights the disclosure problem. Because of the uniqueness of Japanese accounting standards and the emergence of the International Financial Reporting Standards (IFRS), three different types of disclosures have been created in the Japanese market: (1) those based on the Japanese accounting standards; (2) those based on accounting standards of foreign countries; and (3) those based on the IFRS. As a result, questions arise: How should Japanese authorities handle disclosures? Should all three standards be accepted as legitimate? What are the conditions of acceptance?[2]

This article summarizes various arguments existing in Japan on the current issue of accounting standardization as well as the official position of the Japanese government expressed in the Ministry of Finance (MOF) Memorandum. The author analyzes the government's positions and makes comments on the problems and issues indicated in the MOF Memorandum.

Economic Aspects of the Tokyo International Capital Market

Although the Japanese capital market launched in 1955, for quite some time the market served only as a source of foreign capital needed to cover the deficits in the nation's balance of payments. It was not until after 1970, when the Japanese balance of payments began generating a steady surplus, that the Japanese market could accommodate the full

---

[2] *See* infra n.69.

scale issue and acquisition of foreign securities. It was at that time that Tokyo became an international capital market. This trend, however, proved to be short-lived, as the steep rise in the cost of oil imports had forced the Japanese government to revert to its pre-1970 policy, requiring the government to take measures to reduce the deficit in the nation's long-term capital payments balance.

Since then, the Japanese balance of payments has improved tremendously reporting a positive overall net surplus over the last 20 years. It is important to examine Japan's recent position on the international balance of payments, and the impact the yen's internationalization will have on Tokyo's development as an international market.

Recent Position of Japan's International Balance of Payments

Reaching ¥140 billion, the trade surplus increased substantially in 2004. The current account balance added to the service income totaled ¥186 billion. At the same time, however, the capital account balance remained in a minor ¥5 billion deficit, resulting in a substantial overall balance surplus of ¥172 billion (see Table 1).

For a number of years, Japan has shown patterns of a substantial trade surplus, a small capital account balance, and a whopping overall balance surplus; a stark contrast to the US pattern of a large trade deficit, a large capital account balance, and a mild overall deficit balance.

Consequently, the foreign currency reserve of Japan reached an historical high in 2004 with $819 billion, significantly surpassing the mere $84 billion of the United States. This really demonstrates how enormous Japan's current foreign currency reserve is in view of the fact that Japan's GDP was $4170 billion as compared to the $10,894 billion of the United States (see Table 2).

Reflecting this strong international balance of payments of Japan, the yen's exchange rate against the US dollar has been comparatively strong, maintaining a level of ¥100-110/US dollars. This is a large appreciation from the fixed rate of ¥360/US dollars that existed until 1973.

Table 1 — Japanese Balance of Payments

Year	(Current Account)	Goods & Services	Trade Balance	Exports	Imports	Services
(1997)	114,363	57,680	123,103	495,190	372,087	-65,423
(1998)	155,278	95,229	159,844	488,665	328,820	-64,546
(1999)	130,522	78,650	140,155	457,948	317,793	-61,505
(2000)	128,755	74,298	125,634	495,257	369,622	-51,336
(2001)	106,523	32,120	85,270	465,835	380,564	-53,150
(2002)	141,397	64,690	117,333	494,797	377,464	-52,643
(2003)	157,668	83,553	122,596	519,342	396,746	-39,043
(2004)	186,184	101,961	139,022	582,951	443,928	-37,061

Unit: 100 Million Yen
Source: MOF, Japan, http://www.mof.go.jp/1c004.htm

Table 1 — Japanese Balance of Payments (Cont.)

Year	Income	Current Transfers	(Capital & Fin. Account)	Financial Account	Capital Account	(Changes in Res. Assets)
(1997)	67,396	-10,713	-148,348	-146,445	-4,879	-7,660
(1998)	71,442	-11,463	-170,821	-151,508	-19,313	9,986
(1999)	65,741	-13,869	-62,744	-43,655	-19,088	-87,963
(2000)	65,052	-10,596	-94,233	-84,287	-9,947	-52,609
(2001)	57,007	-9,604	-61,726	-58,264	-3,462	-49,364
(2002)	82,665	-5,958	-84,775	-80,558	-4,217	-57,969
(2003)	82,812	-8,697	77,341	82,014	-4,672	-215,288
(2004)	92,731	-8,509	17,370	22,504	-5,134	-172,675

Unit: 100 Million Yen
Source: MOF, Japan, http://www.mof.go.jp/1c004.htm

Table 2 — Official Foreign Reserves and GDPs In 2004

	Official Foreign Reserves	GDP
Japan	8,192 4,454	41,700
China		12,300
Germany	936	2,300
USA	821	109,839
Unit: Millions of US dollars		
Source: IMF, http://www.imf.org/external/np/sta/ir/usa/eng/curusa.htm		

With the second largest GDP, next only to the United States, a strong international balance of payments, and the world's largest foreign currency reserve, there is no question that the economic fundamentals of Japan are extremely strong. These are clear indicators that Tokyo has the potential to become one of the strongest international capital markets in the world.

Internationalization of the Yen

The successful internationalization of the yen relies on its credibility with the rest of the world. As long as the fundamentals of the Japanese economy remain healthy and the trading value of the yen tabled for a prolonged period, the potential to successfully internationalize the yen is promising.

The internationalization of the yen made a sharp expansion after the US-Japan Yen-Dollar Rate, Financial/Capital Market Special Conference [3] held in May 1984. The general concept of "internationalization" of the yen encompassed a rise in yen usage in international trades or the holding of yen. More specifically, it included an increase in the following: (1) use of the yen in import/export trade settlements (normal trades), (2) use as a means of financing and financial operations in the international financial market (capital trades), and (3) amount of yen held by monetary authorities of each country as a reserve for external trade settlements. The internationalization of the yen was

---

[3] http://www.meti.go.jp/hakusho/tusho/soron/S62/00-01-06.html.

meaningful domestically for several reasons: (1) it alleviated exchange risks in international trades conducted by Japanese companies; (2) it enhanced the competitive strengths of Japanese financial institutions having rich yen funds; and (3) it increased the size and efficiency of Japanese financial and capital markets because of an expansion of nonresident participation in those markets. It was meaningful from the international standpoint because (1) it made it easier for non-residents to divert risks; and (2) it complemented the US dollar as a key currency. The report of the Foreign Exchange Council Related to Internationalization of Yen[4] held in March 1985 stressed the importance of financial liberalization, liberalization of Euro-Yen trade, and internationalization of the Tokyo market in order to promote the internationalization of the yen. The internationalization of the yen has since been securely moving forward as forecasted in the aforementioned report.

The most notable incident was the creation of the Tokyo Offshore Market in December 1986. An offshore market accommodated non-resident fundraising and fund operations by nonresidents (so-called external-external transactions) as free trades with minimum restrictions in terms of financing and taxation. The Tokyo Offshore Market provided facilities for foreign exchange banks to set up offshore accounts (special international financial transaction accounts) in order to separate domestic transactions from offshore accounts of other banks. The size of the total transaction reached $404.2 billion as of December 2003.[5]

In order for the Tokyo market to function as an international financial center, linking with London and New York, via the Tokyo Offshore Market, further internationalization of the yen was essential. At the time, there were various restrictions on the offshore market that prevented the transfer of funds from an offshore account to a domestic account, although removal of such restrictions was gradually sought in accordance with the liberalization of the domestic market.

However, the internationalization of the yen was still far from its desired outcome. The use of the yen in international financing operations

---

[4] http://www.meti.go.jp/hakusho/tusho/soron/S62/00-01-05.html.
[5] Gaikokukawase Jouhousha "Gaitame Nenkan (2004)" p. 136.

remained but a distant goal and vision (see Table 3). Despite the fact that Japan's GDP totaled approximately 15 percent of the world's total GDP, the status of the yen in the international market remained relatively low. The yen-based balances in international bonds-outstanding was 4 percent, yen-based offshore assets of banks was 5.2 percent, and share of yen in official holdings of foreign exchange by IMF member countries was 3.9 percent, as of the end of the year 2004.

Table 3 — Various Statistics Concerning Internationalization of Yen

Share of National Currencies in Official Holdings of Foreign Exchange by IMF Member Countries (%)				
	1995	1996	1997	1998	1999
Yen	6.8	6.7	5.8	6.2	6.4
USD	59.0	62.1	65.2	69.4	71.0
Euro ----		--	--	17.9

Source: International Monetary Fund Home Page, http://www.imf.org/.

Ratio (%) of Yen-Based Balances in Foreign Trades of Japan (Worldwide)				
Import	22.7	20.6	22.6	21.8	23.5
Export	36.0	35.2	35.8	36.0	36.1

Source: Home Page of Ministry of Finance, Japan,
http://www.mof.go.jp/singikai/siryou/a140912/21.pdf.

Currency Breakdown of BIS Reporting Banks' Cross Border Positions (%)				
Yen	4.0	6.5	6.9	5.7	6.6
USD	47.4	49.2	52.2	49.1	47.2
Euro	--	--	--	--	--

Source: BIS Quarterly Reviews, 1995–2004, Bank for International Settlements (BIS) Home Page, http://www.bis.org.

International Bonds and Notes (Amounts Outstanding) By Currency (%)				
Yen	15.8	16.7	15.6	11.7	10.5
USD	34.2	37.6	41.0	45.2	46.5
Euro	--	--	--	--	--

Source: BIS Quarterly Reviews, 1995–2004, Bank for International Settlements (BIS) Home Page, http://www.bis.org.

Table 3 — Various Statistics Concerning Internationalization of Yen (Cont.)

Share of National Currencies in Official Holdings of Foreign Exchange by IMF Member Countries (%)				
	2000	2001	2002	2003	2004
Yen	6.3	5.2	4.5	4.1	3.9
USD	70.5	70.7	66.5	65.8	65.9
Euro	18.8	19.8	24.2	25.3	24.9

Source: International Monetary Fund Home Page, http://www.imf.org/.

Ratio (%) of Yen-Based Balances in Foreign Trades of Japan (Worldwide)				
Export	34.2	35.6	36.7	--	--

Source: Home Page of Ministry of Finance, Japan,
http://www.mof.go.jp/singikai/siryou/a140912/21.pdf.

Currency Breakdown of BIS Reporting Banks' Cross Border Positions (%)				
Yen	7.3	5.2	5.3	5.3	5.1
USD	63.1	64.3	60.9	58.2	58.5
Euro	16.7	18.1	20.9	23.6	23.6

Source: BIS Quarterly Reviews, 1995–2004, Bank for International Settlements (BIS)
Home Page, http://www.bis.org.

International Bonds and Notes (Amounts Outstanding) By Currency (%)				
Yen	9.8	5.8	5.5	4.4	4.0
USD	47.4	50.8	47.7	40.5	36.7
Euro	--	32.2	35.7	43.5	46.9

Source: BIS Quarterly Reviews, 1995–2004, Bank for International Settlements (BIS)
Home Page, http://www.bis.org.

Although the ratio of trades conducted by all major industrial countries, each in its own currency, is more than 50 percent, the share of yen-based trades conducted by Japan is less than 40 percent for exports and less than 30 percent for imports. The share of yen in the world's total foreign currency reserves has been slightly more than 5 percent during the last several years. The size of the issuing market of the Samurai

Bonds is gradually increasing due to the relaxing of regulations govern-ing issuing conditions and the improvement in issuing procedures. However, the increase of Samurai Bonds is still only about one-sixth of the Euro-Yen nonresident bonds.

Why so little progress in the internationalization of the yen? It has been said that the law of inertia applies to currency used in international trade. It may be interpreted to mean that once a specific currency is used in international trade, it will not easily be replaced by another currency.

The US dollar was and remains the key currency, sustaining more significant usability, efficiency, and reliability than any other currency. Furthermore, other reasons for the faltering progress to internationalize the yen include the lack of trust in the Japanese economy, the need to seek feasible economic reasons in selecting currencies for international trades, problems concerning the differences in the customs of foreign trades, government regulations, etc. There is no question how critical the internationalization of the yen is to promoting Tokyo as a full-fledged player in the international capital market.

Historical Development of the Tokyo International Capital Market

During the 1980s and 1990s, national restrictions on cross-border money flow were gradually eased under pressure from the Organization for Economic Cooperation and Development (OECD),[6] a consortium of most of the world's industrial countries. Liberalization of European securities markets was accelerated because of the European Union's efforts to develop a single European market without barriers. For international companies, gaining access to global capital markets should lower their marginal cost of capital and increase their availability of capital. What about globalization of Japanese markets? Did they follow suit to the trend and need of the world?

---

[6] The OECD groups 30 member countries sharing a commitment to democratic government and the market economy. It plays a role in fostering good governance in the public service and in corporate activity. *See* the details at http://www.oecd.org/home/.

In Japanese markets, there are five possible ways for foreign governments and companies to raise funds:

- Yen-Denominated Publicly Offered Foreign Bonds (Samurai Bonds);
- Foreign Currency Denominated Bonds (Shogun Bonds);[7]
- Issues of Foreign Stocks in Japan;
- Syndicated Loan; and
- Euro-Yen Bond.

Foreign Bonds and Yen Bonds in the Japanese Market

Foreign bonds in the Japanese market are bonds whose currency, issuing site, or issuing body (issuer of the bond) are not Japanese. The possible types of Japanese foreign bonds (see Table 4) include:

- Foreign currency-denominated foreign bonds. The issuing currency is foreign currency and the interest and redemption are both paid in foreign currency. Those that are issued publicly by foreign issuers in Japan are called Shogun Bonds.
- Yen-denominated foreign bonds. The issuing currency, interest, and redemption payments are all in yen. (Case 1 in Table 4.) Those that are issued by foreign issuers in Japan are called yen-denominated foreign bonds (so-called Samurai Bonds) and those that are issued overseas are called Euro-Yen bonds. (Case 3 in Table 4.)

Foreign Currency Denominated Bonds

Bonds that are issued in denominations of US dollars, German marks, Canadian dollars, Australian dollars, and other foreign currencies in Japan by foreign governments and corporations as well as Japanese corporations are called Shogun Bonds. (See Case 2 in Table 4.)

---

[7] "Shogun" was the practical ruler of Japan for most of the time in Japanese history. For Shogun, *see*
http://search.netscape.com/ns/search?fromPage=NSCPTOP&query=shogun&x=8&y=12.

Table 4 — Financing in Japanese Markets

	Currency	Issuing Market	Issuers/Borrowers
Case 1:	Yen	Japan	Foreign
Yen-Denominated Foreign Bonds (Samurai Bonds)	(1) *Standard Bonds*: Issuing currency is yen and interest and redemption payments are all paid in yen. (2) *Dual Currency Bonds*: Issuing currency is yen and interest payment is paid in yen, while redemption payment is paid in a foreign currency. (3) *Reverse Dual Currency Bonds*: Issuing currency is yen and redemption payment is in yen, while interest payment is paid in a foreign currency.		
Case 2:	Foreign Currency	Japan	Currency Bonds:
Foreign Currency-Denominated Foreign Bonds (Shogun Bonds)	(1) *Standard Bonds*: (issuing currency and interest and redemption payments are all in foreign currencies) (2) *Dual Currency Bonds*: (redemption payment is in yen) (3) *Reverse Dual Currency Bonds*: (interest payment is in yen)		
Case 3: Euro Bonds	Yen	Overseas	Foreign, Japanese
Case 4: Foreign Stocks	Yen	Japan	Foreign
Case 5: Syndicated Loans	Yen	Japan	Foreign

Concurrent with the public offering in the Japanese market of yen-denominated foreign bonds, moves to float privately placed foreign currency bonds in Japan started in July 1972, with the issue of 20 million dollars worth of bonds by the European Investment Bank. In 1974, such bonds had totaled $906.8 million in 46 issuances. In addition, there were instances when a portion of the bonds floated in a public offering or a private placement basis in overseas capital markets were sold in Japan in the form of private placements. An example of such an issue under this type of sale is the North American Rockwell Overseas Corporation bond issue in May 1972.

Two cases of World Bank bonds ($200 million, private offerings) totally underwritten by life insurance companies were issued in April and May of 1988, and a convertible bond ($175 million) by the same issuer was issued as well in August of the same year for the first time. Starting in November, a series of reverse dual bonds of high coupons denominated in Australian dollars were issued, so that the year 1989 ended with a total of eight cases amounting to ¥2,238 million.

Table 5 — Bonds Issues by Non-Japanese Residents in the Japanese Domestic Market

	Total		Foreign Currency-Denominated Bonds (in yen value)		Yen-Denominated Bonds	
	Number	Amount	Number	Amount	Number	Amount
1987	33	6,307	8	1,332	25	4,975
1988	42	8,099	1	127	41	7,972
1989	59	12,228	8	2,238	51	9,990
1990	70	12,360	39	6,610	31	5,750
1991	37	7,045	17	2,010	20	5,035
1992	35	11,750	0	0	35	11,751
1993	55	16,934	2	350	53	16,584
1994	62	12,307	9	1,003	53	11,304
1995	72	16,165	28	6,400	44	9,765
1996	163	39,337	106	26,125	57	13,212
1997	133	21,762	57	14,560	76	7,202
1998	57	4,123	11	1,525	46	2,598
1999	88	10,368	2	145	86	10,223
2000	133	29,190	12	623	121	28,567
2001	112	20,190	46	3,185	66	17,005
2002	225	21,187	117	8,205	108	12,982
2003	223	23,910	154	9,708	69	14,210
2004	174	27,743	109	9,273	65	18,470

Unit: 100 Million Yen
Source: Ministry of Finance, http://www.mof.go.jp/shoutou/monthsty.htm

In 2000, reverse dual bonds of World Bank (¥30 billion) were issued in July and regular bonds of International Finance Corporation (Washington, D.C.) (¥10 billion) were also issued. The year 2000 had a total of 12 cases amounting to ¥62 billion and in 2004, there were 109 issuances totaling ¥927.3 billion. Issuance of foreign bonds in the Japanese market was quite active over the past three year period (see Table 5).

Yen-Denominated Publicly Offered Foreign Bonds

Samurai Bonds are yen-denominated and are publicly offered by non-residents in the Japanese market. (See Case 1 in Table 4.) They are paid in Japanese yen as the issuing currency (standard bonds). Samurai Bonds can be issued as dual currency (redemptions are paid in foreign currency) and as reverse dual currency (interests are paid in foreign currencies).

In 2003, the total amount of bonds issued was $15,409 million and the total number of bonds issued was 70 (see Table 6). The standard for qualified bonds was eliminated as of Jan. 1, 1996, and any issuer, regardless of its credit, was able to issue the bonds. It is expected that bonds below investment grade will be offered more and more.

Old issuing records for this type of bond show that the internationalization of the Tokyo capital market started in December of 1970, with the issuance of yen-denominated publicly offered bonds in the amount of ¥6 billion by the Asian Development Bank. However, because Japanese banks purchased approximately 80 percent of the bonds, they almost could have been considered privately placed bonds. In a way, this first issue served as a test of Tokyo's maturity as a major international financial center. In 1971, the World Bank issued two yen-denominated bonds, ¥11 billion in June and ¥12 billion in October. This was a noteworthy issuance because the portion purchased by Japanese banks was approximately one-third of the total; moreover, the issue terms were consistent with the prevailing market conditions. Encouraged by the World Bank's success, the Asian Development Bank decided to undertake a full scale issue of publicly offered bonds; ¥10 billion in November of 1972. The success of the World Bank and the Asian Development Bank prompted many foreign organizations to follow suit. These organizations consisted of international institutions, national governments, local public bodies, public corporations, and private enterprises running the gamut of the public and private sectors. In March 2003, the World Bank issued yen-denominated bonds of ¥80 billion successfully (see Table 6).

Table 6 — List of Recent Yen-Denomination Foreign Issues (Publicly Offered);
Samurai Bonds

	When Issued	Amt. Issued (¥ billion)	Int. Rate (%)	Issue price (%)
The Republic of South Africa	July 2001	600	2.00	100.00
Andes Development Corp (Brazil)	July 2001	250	1.17	100.00
The Korean Development Bank (Korea)	July 2001	500	1.15	100.00
Republic Brazil	Aug. 2001	2000	3.75	100.00
Royal Thailand	Dec. 2001	90	0.80	100.00
Korean Gas Group (Korea)	Sept. 2002	100	0.93	100.00
European Investment Bank (EU)	Dec. 2002	200	(See *1)	100.00
Citigroup, Inc. (USA)	Dec. 2002	450	0.47	100.00
Seoul Special City (Korea)	Dec. 2002	125	0.39	100.00
International Bank for Reconstr-uction and Development (World Bank)	Mar. 2003	80	(See *2)	100.00

(*1) For the first year, the rate is 3.6%. The following years' % will be determined according to market price. Therefore, the subscriber's yield is not available. (*2) For the first year, the rate is 3.5%. The following years' % will be determined according to market price. Therefore, the subscriber's yield is not available. Source: Mizuho Financial Group, "Shoken Manual", 2002–2004, pp. 398–401.

Table 6 — List of Recent Yen-Denomination Foreign Issues (Publicly Offered);
Samurai Bonds (Cont.)

	Life (yrs)	Subscriber's Yield (%)	Commissioned Company	Under-writer
The Republic of South Africa	6	2.000	Fu, T-M, IBJ	Miz, T-M, JP
Andes Development Corp.	5	1.170	T-M	Miz, T-M
The Korean Development Bank	5	1.150	IBJ	Miz, IBJ
Republic Brazil	2	3.750	Fu, T-M, IBJ	No
Royal Thailand	3	0.800	M-S	Miz, ML
Korean Gas Group	3	0.930	Miz	Miz, No
European Investment Bank	30	n/a	T-M	Nichi
Citigroup, Inc.	3	0.470	T-M	Nichi, No, Dai
Seoul Special City	1	0.390	Miz	No
World Bank	30	n/a	T-M	No

Source: Mizuho Financial Group, "Shoken Manual", 2002–2004, pp. 398–401.
Commissioned Banks: Underwriters:
IBJ-Industrial Bank of Japan No-Nomura Securities Co.
T-M-Tokyo-Mitsubishi Bank Nichi-Nikkou Securities Co.
Fu-Fuji Bank Dai-Daiwa Securities Group Inc.
M-S-Mitsui-Sumitomo Bank ML-Merrill Lynch
Miz-Mizuho Financial Group JP-JP Morgan

The main target of the Tokyo international capital market at the time was to handle issues of yen-denominated publicly offered foreign bonds, with an emphasis on high grade yen-denominated bonds floated by well known international issuers, such as international institutions and foreign governments.[8] The reason for this was two-fold: First, because the internationalization process had not yet been fully attained, the market was not yet fully consolidated in Japan. Second, investors had relatively little knowledge of international markets, as well as an underdeveloped sense of risk and a poor grasp of proper interest rates. Thus, it was considered best to focus on issues that were sure to foster the growth of a first-rate capital market. Consistent with this goal, the market considered good issuers with established international reputations to be those that have made international issuances publicly in the United States and Europe at least three times during the past five years or at least 10 times during the past 20 years.[9]

In addition to World Bank and Asian Development Bank bonds, Australian Government bonds were issued in July 1972, and Quebec (Canada) bonds in the following September. The Australian bonds were the first to be floated by the Australian Government in 55 years and represented a revitalization of the yen-denominated bond market, which had been dormant since the World War I era when the British, French, and Russian Governments turned to the Japanese market for short-term war financing. Hence it could be said that the issuances by the Australian Government on the Tokyo capital market were the first long-term yen-denominated publicly offered government bonds of its kind. For this reason, the float of the Australian Government bonds and of the Quebec bonds on the Japanese capital market were significant events as they, in effect, inaugurated the full-scale internationalization of the Japanese capital market.

The first private corporation bond was the Sears bond offered in 1979 (the principal underwriter was Nomura Securities). In 1989, the first reverse dual bond was issued by the government of Denmark, and a vari-

---

[8] Ministry of Finance, Okurasho Shokenkyoku Nenppo, 1973 Nenban (Annual Report-Ministry of Finance, 1973) 52 (Kinyu Zaisei Jijyo Kenkukai 1973).
[9] *Id.*

able interest bond by Inter-American Development Bank as well as convertible bonds by Glaxo, as a private issuer, was introduced in 1991, with Nomura Securities acting as the principal underwriter for both of them. Samurai Bond issuances peaked in the year 2000 with total issuances at ¥2,857 billion. During 1997 and 1998, the issuances slumped to a total of less than ¥1,000 billion. However, issuances of Samurai Bonds have recently been quite active. In 2004, they amounted to ¥1,467 billion, which constituted an 81 percent increase from the previous year. The issuers included Merrill Lynch (USA) for ¥201 billion, Bank of America (USA) for ¥180 billion, General Motors Acceptance Corp. (USA) for ¥70 billion, and Korean Electric Power Corp. (Korea) for ¥20 billion. In September 2005, Citigroup Inc. issued a total of ¥230 billion in Samurai Bonds,[10] a figure eclipsing the record ¥220 billion issued in 2000 by DaimlerChrysler AG. Citigroup, the largest US financial services company, is expected to use the proceeds from the issuance for investment activity and system upgrade work in Japan. The recent recovery may be attributed to the regained trust by foreign issuers in Japanese institutional investors.[11]

Although there were problems within the distribution markets (corporate bond registration system and poor fluidity) common to all the securities markets in Japan, they were nonetheless growing, offering merchandise, and accommodating the needs of both the issuing bodies as well as investors. Because Samurai Bonds are Japanese bonds, they are controlled by Japanese law. Disclosure documents had to be prepared according to the Securities Exchange Law of Japan,[12] and the bonds had

---

[10] "Samurai" (or bushi) were the members of the military class, the Japanese warriors. For Samurai, *see* http://www.japan-guide.com/e/e2127.html. For Samurai Bonds, *see* Table 4. In September, 2005, Citigroup issued six tranches of samurai bonds with maturities ranging from five to 30 years. The issuance of 30-year samurai bonds is said to be the first in the market. Even among straight corporate bonds issued in Japan, 30-year instruments are a rarity. Nikko Citigroup Ltd., a joint venture of Nikko Cordial Corp. and Citigroup, will lead-manage the issuance. Citigroup issued a total of about $20 billion, or roughly ¥2.2 trillion, of bonds in 2005 with nearly half denominated in nondollar currencies, such as the yen and the euro. For the details, see Nikkei, Sept. 5, 2005 (http://www.nni.nikkei.co.jp/AC/TNKS/Nni20050904D04JFF01.htm).
[11] For the details, see Nikkei, http://www.nikkei.co.jp/news/main/20041219.
[12] Law No. 25 of April 13, 1948 (Japan). Subsequent amendments to the law reflected US developments. Most recently the law was amended on March 3, 1971. Law No. 4 of

to be placed under the control of managing companies established for that purpose.

Euro-Yen Bonds

This is a type of yen bond issued in the Euro Market (overseas market) for which international underwriter groups are formed, as is true for other Euro bonds, offered and issued mainly in Europe. (See Case 3 in Table 4.) This issuance is executed outside of the Japanese market, thus putting the yen to use overseas, which is part of the long-term goal to internationalize the Tokyo Market.

The benefits to the issuer are, if issued by a resident, (1) there is no foreign exchange risk; (2) it can be issued with no collateral; and (3) it can be issued at a more advantageous condition than in the domestic market. On the other hand, the investor's merits include owning yen bonds when the yen rate is appreciating strongly.

Although the issuing of Euro-Yen bonds had grave consequences on the financial policies of Japan in the beginning, its regulations were gradually loosened as it contributed to the internationalization of the yen. As it happened, the Euro-Yen bond issuances by nonresidents were first restricted to international organizations and national governments and no issuing by private institutions was allowed. The first such issuance was made in the amount of ¥10 billion by the European Investment Bank (EIB) in April 1977, the peak year of 1988 generated 4,167 issuances totaling ¥11,086 billion (see Table 7). However, complete relinquishment of the issuing standards for Euro-Yen bonds by nonresidents, as a result of the agreement of the Japan-US Yen-Dollar Committee held in May 1984, removed the volumetric restriction and allowed foreign provincial or state governments and government institutions as well as qualifying private firms to issue Euro-Yen bonds. Moreover, starting in April 1984, the standard for a qualified bond for issuing by private firms was further relaxed, increasing the number of companies eligible for issuing Euro-Yen bonds by more than three times,

---

1971 [hereinafter cited as Securities Exchange Law]. For details, see http://www.houko.com/00/01/S23/025.HTM.

and variable interest bonds as well as zero coupon bonds came to be included as Euro-Yen bonds in June 1984.

Table 7 — Euro-Yen Bond Issuances by Non-Residents

Year	No. of Issuances	Amount
1972	151	29,939
1973	224	22,130
1974	395	35,579
1975	512	49,809
1976	314	32,904
1977	250	33,280
1978	638	51,021
1979	2,024	101,942
1980	2,509	108,845
1981	4,777	129,099
1982	6,074	178,726
1983	3,264	123,286
1984	3,963	139,182
1985	4,165	167,719
1986	5,201	172,567
1987	4,414	123,223
1988	4,167	110,857
1989	477	44,587
1990	442	42,769
1991	270	30,611
1992	319	43,387
1993	747	48,691
1994	2,253	109,760
1995	3,041	115,837
1996	5,345	149,374
1997	5,492	169,522
1998	2,979	109,304
1999	4,321	156,256
2000	4,151	159,922
2001	5,069	159,238
2002	4,549	129,224
2003	3,882	105,433
2004	2,790	96,368

Unit: ¥100 Million
Source: Ministry of Finance,
http://www.mof.go.jp/shoutou/month-sty.htm

In April 1984, it became possible for qualifying domestic corporations to freely issue Euro-Yen bonds. Moreover, the tax-withholding obligation for interest to be collected by nonresidents was removed for Euro-Yen bonds issued after April 1985, and a relaxation of the standard for qualified bonds was implemented in October 1985. A total of 270 brands of the publicly offered Euro-Yen bonds issued with a total amount of ¥ 3,061 billion in 1991. This market has become more active with the total number of Euro-Yen issuing cases in 2004 at 2,790 and the total amount to reach ¥9,636.8 billion (US $96.4 billion) (see Table 7).

Foreign Stocks in Japan

Similar to the development of the foreign bond market, the issue of foreign stocks in Japan began with the private placement of stocks by L'Air Liquide S.A. of France in May 1972. (See Case 4 in Table 4.) The first foreign issuer to make a public offering in Japan was General Telephone & Electronics Corporation, a US corporation, in October 1972. Thus far, there have been 30 foreign stock issuances totaling $102.8 million, three of which were public offerings totaling $50.81 million (see Tables 8 and 9). Besides the above-cited domestically issued foreign securities, the regulation of the acquisition of previously issued securities via foreign securities exchanges was liberalized in July 1971 for the benefit of the investing public with the inclusion of such foreign securities in investment trust portfolios in February 1970. The foreign securities acquired through foreign securities exchanges consisted of stocks valued at ¥54.8 billion and bonds at ¥69.5 billion as of December 1973, both showing a marked gain.

In the wake of such increased investment in foreign securities, six shares: (1) FNCC; (2) Dow Chemical; (3) FirstChicago; (4) GTE; (5) I.U. International Corp. (USA); and (6) Paribas (France) were listedon the Tokyo Stock Exchange in December 1973. Further, in February of 1974 Cie Française des Petroles, S.A. joined the list.

The number of foreign companies traded at the Tokyo Stock Exchange declined after having peaked at 125 in 1991. The decline was because of the fact that investment in overseas stocks lost its luster as a result of the appreciation of the yen, as well as various cyclical economic factors such as the general decline of world stock markets since 1990 (see Tables 8 and 9).

Table 8 — The Numbers of Listed Foreign Companies

Year	Newly Listed	Delisted	Total
1973	6		6
1974	8		14
1975	2		16
1976	1		17
1977		2	15
1982		3	12
1983		1	11
1984	1	1	11
1985	10		21
1986	31		52
1987	36		88
1988	25	1	112
1989	10	3	119
1990	7	1	125
1991	3	3	125
1992		6	119
1993	1	10	110
1994	?	17	93
1995	?	16	77
1996	2	12	67
1997	1	8	60
1998	3	11	52
1999		9	43
2000	3	5	41
2001	1	4	38
2002		4	34
2003		2	32
2004		2	30

Source: Compiled from Tokyo Stock Exchange Manual, 1996–2004.

Table 9 — Foreign Stocks Listed in Tokyo (Price Changes for Sept. 3, 2004, to Sept. 17, 2004)

Asia	High	Price Low	Final	Sales Unit	Profit/ Share	Annual Dividend
Henders on Land Develop ment Co. Ltd. (8990)	520	515	515	500	HK$ 1.300	HK$ 0.80
National Australi an Bank, Ltd. (8637)	2120	2070	2120	100	A$ 2.488	A$ 1.63
Westpac Banking Corp. (8641)	1350	1330	1330	100	A$ 1.156	A$ 0.78
Source: 2004 Tokyo Stock Exchange, Inc. Annual Report.						

Table 9 — Foreign Stocks Listed in Tokyo (Price Changes for Sept. 3, 2004 to Sept. 17, 2004) (Cont.)

North America	High	Price Low	Final	Sales Unit	Profit/ Share	Annual Dividend
Pepsi Co. Inc. (2953)	5300	5300	5300	50	US$ 2.05	US$ 0.64
Dow Chemical Co. (4850)	--	--	--	10	US$0.99	US$1.34
IBM (6680)	9450	9210	9310	10	US$4.40	US$0.64
Motorola, Inc. (6686)	--	--	--	50	US$0.38	US$0.16
Apple Computer, Inc. (6689)	4000	3761	3910	50	US$ 0.19	--
Boeing Co. (7661)	5820	5820	5820	50	US$ 0.86	US$ 0.68
Bank of America Corp. (8648)	4900	4900	4900	50	US$ 7.13	US$ 3.04
Merrill Lynch (8675)	--	--	--	10	US$ 4.05	US$ 0.64
AFLAC, Inc. (8686)	4400	4350	4350	50	US$ 1.52	US$ 0.33
Toronto-Dominion Bank (8640)	--	--	--	100	C$ 1.51	C$ 1.20
Source: 2004 Tokyo Stock Exchange, Inc. Annual Report.						

Table 9 — Foreign Stocks Listed in Tokyo (Price Changes for Sept. 3, 2004 to Sept. 17, 2004) (Cont.)

Europe	High	Price Low	Final	Sales Unit	Profit/ Share	Annual Dividend
BP Amoco g.l.e. (5051)	1000	686	1000	100	US$ 0.46	US$ 0.26
Aegon N.V. (8689)	--	--	--	10	EUR 1.15	EUR 0.20
Telefoni ca, S.A. (9481)	1547	1517	1547	50	EUR 0.44	EUR 0.25
Vokswa gen AG (7659)	4710	4500	4500	10	EUR 2.84	EUR 1.30
Daimler Chrysler AG (7663)	4600	4600	4600	10	EUR 0.44	EUR 1.50
Deutsche Bank AG (8651)	7900	7610	7900	10	EUR 2.44	EUR 1.30
Deutshe Telecom AG (9496)	1950	1903	1903	50	EUR 0.30	--
Alcatel (6687)	1516	1347	1516	10	EUR 1.46	--
Société Générale (8666)	9600	9600	9600	10	EUR 0.18	EUR 2.10
Source: 2004 Tokyo Stock Exchange, Inc. Annual Report.						

With the focus still aimed at revitalizing the market, the Tokyo Stock Exchange lowered the initial listing fees and the minimum trading unit for offshore stocks as of January 2004. However, the initial listing requirements of the Tokyo Stock Exchange are still considered severe compared to those of the New York Stock Exchange (see Table 10).

Table 10 — Comparison of Japanese and US Listing Standards

	Tokyo SE	NYSE*	Nasdaq
Minimum No. of Shareholders	20,000	5,000	400
No. of Stocks Held by General Shareholders	Qualitative Judgment**	2.5 million (1.1 million)	1.1 million
Before Tax Profit	¥400 million (about $4 million)	$25 million ($2.5 million)	$1 million
*The figures in the parentheses for NYSE represent the standards for US companies.			
**It prohibits a small number of shareholders from owning a large amount of stocks.			
Source: Tokyo Stock Exchange, Fact Book, 2003.			

Moreover, in an effort to minimize the disclosure costs for foreign companies, the requirement for translation of annual reports was eliminated and the required items of the financial statements simplified as of January 2004. It is questionable whether the offshore stock section of the Tokyo Stock Exchange will be revitalized as a result of these measures.

Syndicated Loans

Syndicated loans to non-resident borrowers are a type of loan in which multiple banks offer loans under the same contract arranged by a leader bank in Japan. (See Case 5 in Table 4.) Because a standardized contract is used, loan making and transferring after lending are simplified for participating banks.

Since 1972, syndicated loan activities utilizing dollars acquired from the Eurodollar market and from Japan's foreign reserve surplus[13] have been very brisk. The total loan sum reached five billion dollars by the end of 1973.[14] Borrowers of these loans included international oil companies, financial institutions, and public organizations.[15] Syndicated loans are typically yen denominated; their total annual size was ¥11 trillion in 2002 (about US $110 billion) (see Table 11). The market grew 20 times in 30 years from 1973 to 2002.

---

[13] This is based on foreign currency deposits held by the Ministry of Finance at Japanese commercial banks.

[14] The Euro credit market expanded at a fairly rapid pace. In 1973, the volume grew to $23 billion, of which $5.3 billion (26.5 percent) was estimated to be syndicated by Japanese banks. See EUROMONEY 35 (Euromoney Publication Limited, Feb. 19, 1974); Nihon Kogyo Shinbun (Daily Industrial Paper), March 12, 1974, at 3.

[15] The borrowers' names are not usually disclosed. Among the borrowers for whom Japanese banks acted as a manager in syndicated loans, the following names are included: Republic of Columbia, Instituto Mobiliare Italiano, National Iranian Tanker Co., Comision Federal de Electricided, National Bank of Hungary and Deutsce Aussenhandelsbank.

Table 11 — Yen-Denominated Syndicated Loans to Non-Resident Borrowers

Year	1999	2000	2001	2002
Amount	3.0	8.0	9.7	10.9
Unit: ¥1,000 billion Source: Bank of Japan, http://www.boj.or.jp/seisaku/03/moo0309a.htm				

One of the benefits for borrowing companies is that they can use various funding channels and do not have to depend heavily on the performance of the main bank, allowing them to raise large amounts of funds expeditiously.

The benefits for financial institutions are:

- Credit risk management. In other words, it is possible to participate in syndicated loans and manage lending portfolios.
- Increased commission income. As an arranger, it is possible for a financial institution to increase commission income without increasing debts.
- Efficient operation of lending business. The lending business can be streamlined to increase the profit ratio by standardizing contracts, rationalizing borrower's risk evaluation, and centralizing principal and interest collection operations to an agent bank.

An even more important benefit is the improvement of the price finding function. This means the lending interest can be normalized as a whole by promoting prices that match with risks through the expansion of the syndicated load credit trading market.

Legal Aspects of the Tokyo International Capital Market

Regulatory Structure

The Japanese Securities Exchange Law of 1948[16] is applicable to the proposed securities issuances by foreign entities. The Securities Exchange Law was enacted at the insistence of the occupation authorities as a condition for the reopening of the Japanese securities exchanges.

---

[16] *See supra* n.12.

The Japanese law was a modified version of the US law, requiring the disclosure of corporate information and covering the regulation of the securities markets.[17] However, securities regulation in Japan differs somewhat from that of the United States because of the differences in the basic legal systems and the social structures of the two counties.

In Japan the supervision of the securities markets is entrusted to the Ministry of Finance.[18] The MOF exercises executive, quasi-judicial, and quasi-legislative powers similar to those of the Securities and Exchange Commission in the United States. Consistent with the policy underlying US securities regulation, Japanese law requires the disclosure of corporate information through the registration system when securities are to be sold to the public.[19] Public corporate securities issues are generally subject to the law, but all bond issues, bank securities, and small issues under ¥100 million (approximately $1 million) are exempt from the registration requirement.[20] Registration statements must include adequate information for the benefit of the investors,[21] but if the MOF finds that a registration statement includes false information, fails to include information covering important matters, or is misleading, it reserves the right to deny registration.[22] Before the MOF issues a formal "stop order," however, the company is entitled to a hearing at which it is allowed to present clarifying information and amend its registration statement.[23] If the MOF deems the amendment appropriate and

---

[17] For the detail of securities regulation in Japan see Mitsuru Misawa, "Securities Regulations in Japan," Vanderbilt Journal of Transnational Law, Vol. 6, No. 2, Spring 1973, at 447–510.

[18] The Ministry of Finance ("MOF") was reorganized on January 6, 2001. The name was changed from Okurasho to Zaimucho in Japanese, but the English name still remains the same. For more information about the reorganization, see http://www.mof.go.jp. The Financial Services Agency (FSA) was created as of July 1, 1997, with the integration of the Banking Supervisory Agency and the Financial System Planning Bureau of the Ministry of Finance. See MOF Web site at http://www.fsa.go.jp/news/newsj/15/singi/f-20040624-1/01.pdf.

[19] Securities Exchange Law art.4.

[20] Japan Ministry of Finance Regulation, Registration of Offers and Sales of Securities No. 32, art. 1 (1972). This regulation was promulgated pursuant to the 1972 amendments in the Securities Exchange Law.

[21] Securities Exchange Law art. 5.

[22] *Id.*, art. 10.

[23] *Id.*, art. 10.

satisfactory, it can permit the registration of the issuance,[24] which is a sine qua non for the offering of securities to the public. Moreover, the law also requires that a prospectus, containing essentially the same information as the registration statement, be presented to every subscriber of the corporate issue.[25] Included in the prospectus is all information that the MOF deems essential and appropriate to the public interest, or for the protection of investors.[26] In addition to its jurisdiction over securities registrations, the MOF has authority to regulate the trading of securities, and to conduct studies and investigate matters in the public interest covering the entire field of securities issuance and trading. For example, the MOF may choose to investigate securities dealers,[27] securities exchanges, [28] securities dealers associations, [29] issuing companies and companies submitting securities reports[30] as well as examine corporate books, require submission of reports on business or property, and require the attendance of witnesses.[31] Further, the MOF can go to the courts and seek injunctive relief to proscribe the conduct of those engaged, or about to engage, in any act violative of the securities law.[32]

Registration Requirements

Under the Japanese Securities Exchange Law, the following are classified as securities: government bonds, local government bonds, bonds issued by a juridical entity established under a special law, stocks, warrants, beneficiary certificates of an investment trust or loan trust, securities or certificates issued by foreign countries or foreign juridical

---

[24] *Id.*, art. 10.
[25] *Id.*, art. 13.
[26] *Id.*, art. 13.
[27] *Id.*, art. 55.
[28] *Id.*, art. 154.
[29] *Id.*, art. 76.
[30] *Id.*, art. 26.
[31] *Id.*, arts. 182–184, 186.
[32] *Id.*, art. 187.

entities, and such other securities or certificates as may be prescribed by Cabinet Order.[33]

An important difference between the exemption provisions under the Japanese Securities Exchange Law and those in the United States and other countries is that, in Japan, domestic bonds that are guaranteed and those secured with property are exempt from registration.[34] There are three primary reasons for exempting bonds from the registration requirements of the Securities Exchange Law: (1) the primary purchases of bonds are made by financial institutions capable of investigating the financial condition of the issuing companies; (2) almost all of the companies issuing bonds are listed companies that provide current public information concerning the status of the issuing company; and (3) it is believed that disclosure of financial information about a company is less essential to bondholders than to stockholders because the former is secured by liens on specific company properties. These liens are said to offer bondholders sufficient protection in the event of financial difficulties. However, the real reason for exempting bond issues from registration is probably that the buying and selling that occur in the relatively undeveloped bond market are done by institutions that are not in need of extensive protection. Nevertheless, registration has always been required of publicly offered foreign bond issues because these bonds have not been secured with property.

Disclosure Required for Offerings of Securities

Prior to the enactment of the Securities Exchange Law in 1948, the Commercial Code[35] served as the only law regulating security issues in Japan. Under the Commercial Code, the corporate promoters had to disclose the required information at the time of incorporation by publishing the articles of incorporation in the official Gazette or in a daily newspaper.[36] Therefore, the disclosure requirements of the

---

[33] *Id.*, art. 2.

[34] *Id.*, art. 4.

[35] Law No. 48, enacted on March 9, 1899, amended 18 times (hereinafter cited as the "Commercial Code"). For details, *see* http://www.ron.gr.jp/law/law/syouhou1.htm.

[36] Commercial Code arts. 166, 173, 175, 183, 184, & 188.

Commercial Code provided insufficient investor protection. In comparison to the Commercial Code, the Securities Exchange Law was a great advance, requiring publicity and detailed information concerning publicly held companies whose securities did not meet the requirements of "exempted securities" or "exempted transactions."

Under the Japanese Securities Exchange Law, the registration statement filed with the MOF, in conjunction with the prospectus that summarized the more detailed registration statement, acts as the required disclosure mechanism. A registration statement becomes effective on the 30th day after it is filed or on the 30th day after the filing of an amendment, during which period the MOF reviews the statement and determines whether full and fair disclosure has been provided.[37]

Although the MOF examines registration statements, it does not guarantee the security nor does it make a judgment as to its quality. Rather, the law requires the disclosure of sufficient and accurate facts to enable the investing public to make a reasonable assessment of investment. The criteria for determining the relevancy of the required information are provided by MOF ordinance,[38] but the ultimate responsibility for adequate and accurate disclosure lies with the issuer[39] and in the event of a deficiency in the registration statement, amendments are required, after which the registration statement becomes effective at the lapse of the pre-effective period designated by the MOF.[40] This interval between filing and effective registration enables underwriters, prospective purchasers, and other interested parties to familiarize themselves with the nature of the offering. On or after the effective date, the registered securities can be offered to the public, but each purchaser has to receive a prospectus at or before the sale or delivery of the securities, or at the time of confirmation of purchase.[41]

---

[37] Securities Exchange Law art. 8. The effective date may be accelerated by order of the MOF, if information about the issuer is adequately available for the protection of investors.

[38] *Id.*, art. 5. The matters necessary and appropriate for the protection of public interest or investors are prescribed by a MOF ordinance.

[39] *Id.*, arts. 16–18.

[40] *Id.*, art. 9.

[41] *Id.*, art. 15.

During the waiting period that precedes the effective date, however, offers using a temporary prospectus are permitted.[42]

Disclosure Requirements Applicable only to Foreign Securities Flotation

With the growing internationalization of the Tokyo capital market, came the regular practice of foreign enterprises, foreign governments, and foreign public entities of placing their securities in Japan on a public offering basis. Japan was, therefore, faced with the urgent need to institute a well-regulated system that would provide for sufficient disclosure by foreign entities when issuing their securities in Japan.

Disclosure Required of Foreign Governments and Foreign Public Organizations

The disclosure requirements of the Securities Exchange Law are generally applicable to the securities floated by foreign governments or foreign public organizations. To regulate this disclosure system the Ministerial Ordinance Concerning Notification of Offering or Secondary Distribution of Foreign Securities was promulgated in 1972.[43] The securities falling under this ordinance are defined as government bonds, municipal bonds, securities issued by corporations in accordance with special legislation, and those whose investment certificates are issued by corporations established in accordance with special legislation.[44] Collectively these are characterized as foreign securities.

When foreign securities are offered up for sale in Japan, those who issued such securities are required to submit a registration statement. Additionally, because the issuers are based abroad, they are required to appoint an agent or proxy domiciled in Japan who is duly authorized to

---

[42] *Id.*, art. 15.

[43] Japan, Ministry of Finance Ordinance No. 26 (April. 2, 1972) [hereinafter cited as Ministry of Finance No. 26]. In accordance with this Ministerial Ordinance, Australian Federal Government Bonds for ¥10 billion were floated in July 1972 and Quebec Provincial Bonds for ¥10 billion were floated on a public offering basis in September 1972.

[44] Ministry of Finance Ordinance No. 26, art. 1.

represent the issuer in connection with any and all acts relevant to soliciting securities subscriptions.[45] The registration statement is to provide the investing public with all the information necessary to enable a reasoned judgment on the investment in the securities. Therefore, the registration statement contains all requisite information for the protection of the investors as well as information necessary to enable investors to make sound and legitimate decisions on the investment.[46]

Issuers of foreign securities are diverse, including governments, public organizations, international institutions, and government-affiliated agencies. In the registration statement, the classification of the issuer is outlined in the section entitled, General Description of Issuers. The sections for Basic Matters Relating to Offered Securities, Purposes of Fund Raising and Uses of Funds, and Legal Opinions are required for the protection of investors. In particular, the subsections "Matters Concerning Mortgages and Guarantees," "Duties of Commissioned Banks,"[47] "Matters Concerning Meeting of Creditors," "Treatment of Taxes," and "Applicable Laws and Court of Jurisdiction" are established under the section Basic Matters Relating to Offered Securities with a view toward protecting the investors. The registration statement is divided into Part I dealing with information to be disclosed to the investing public in the prospectus and Part II containing information that needed not be disclosed in the prospectus.[48]

It is stipulated that the documents attached to the registration statement cover such areas as the proxy letter, various agreements, including the underwriting agreement, written legal opinions, and pertinent articles of related laws and regulations mentioned in the written legal opinions.[49] Of these accompanying documents, two are thought to

---

[45] *Id.*, art. 4.

[46] *Id.*, art. 5.

[47] The duties of commissioned banks in Japan are to perform an originating role in the flotation of bonds; to inform the issuers of current market conditions; to advise them as to the amount of bond issues, the term and timing of offerings; and to hold securities for the creditors.

[48] For a concrete example see The Industrial Bank of Japan, Ltd., Memorandum-Papua New Guinea, Japanese Yen Gon Von Bonds, Series A (1973/1985), Guaranteed by the Commonwealth of Australia 3-19 (The Industrial Bank of Japan, Ltd. Dec. 1973).

[49] Ministry of Finance Ordinance No. 26, art. 7.

be of particular importance from the viewpoint of protecting the investing public: (1) "agreement concerning a contract on entrusting care of securities for the creditors,"[50] and (2) "written legal opinions prepared by the proper legal experts on the legality of subscription to and sale of the said securities and the pertinent articles of the laws and regulations mentioned in the said legal opinions."[51]

The Japanese Commercial Code does not apply to securities floated by foreign governments or foreign local public organizations.[52] Accordingly, there is no option except to protect the interests of investors by means of an agreement until satisfactory legal regulations are firmly established. To achieve this end, it is generally requested that an agreement between issuers and commissioned banks, entrusted with the care of securities for the creditors, be accompanied with the registration statement.

Because the issuers of foreign securities are foreign governments and foreign public organizations, legal questions such as applicable laws and jurisdiction are involved. Therefore, the MOF made it mandatory for issuers to attach a written legal opinion to insure the protection of investors. The matters required in the legal opinion include:

- whether the issue has any legal merit;
- whether the elements of the contract, under which the issuer entrusted the care of the securities for the creditors, are legal and whether it is admitted by international private law of the issuer's country to designate the applicable laws and court of jurisdiction;
- whether the elements of the contract relative to the repayment of principal and payment of interest are legal; and
- whether the provisions for compulsory execution (in the event of default) are legal; especially whether a foreign judicial decision will be considered valid; whether or not it is possible to carry out execution on the basis of a judgment passed down by a Japanese court of justice or by a foreign court of justice.

---

[50] *Id.*, art. 7(3).

[51] *Id.*, art. 7(5).

[52] According to article 482 of the Commercial Code only a foreign company that establishes its principal office in Japan or its chief objective is to carry on business in Japan shall comply with the provisions in the Commercial Code.

Disclosure Required of Foreign Corporations

To establish a well-regulated reporting system for foreign corporations,[53] inviting subscriptions to stocks or corporate bonds in Japan, the revision of Ministerial Ordinance Concerning Offering or Secondary Distribution of Securities was promulgated in 1973.[54] When a foreign corporation files its securities registration statement, it appoints a person domiciled in Japan and duly authorized to represent the foreign corporation to execute any and all acts relevant to offering the invitation.[55] When a foreign corporation attaches the necessary documents to its securities registration statement, such documents, unless written in Japanese, have to be properly translated into Japanese.[56]

Statements explaining that the effect on operations as a result of changes in the exchange rate[57] are common in the compilation of a prospectus prepared by a foreign corporation. When foreign corporations file registration statements, in addition to the many other documents required of a Japanese corporation, it is also necessary for them to attach a letter evidencing the right of representation, a letter evidencing the right of proxy, and a written legal/expert opinion.[58]

Financial Information and Accounting Principles

Although a foreign corporation is required to file a registration statement, a prospectus, and a securities report similar to those required of Japanese corporations, a foreign corporation is allowed some discretion in making

---

[53] For the purpose of floating 7.5 million shares of common stock in Japan on a public offering basis, General Telephone & Electronics Corp. (GTE), as a first foreign corporation, filed a registration statement with the MOF on Aug. 19, 1972. The public offering price per share was set at $28.25, and total subscription payments for ¥6,400,740,000 were completed on Oct. 7, 1972. This is the first stock ever issued in Japan by a foreign corporation on a public offering basis.

[54] Japan, Ministry of Finance Ordinance No. 26 (Apr. 1972), as amended, Japan, Ministry of Finance Ordinance No. 5 (Jan. 30, 1973) [hereinafter cited as Ministry of Finance Ordinance No. 5].

[55] Ministry of Finance Ordinance No. 5, art. 7.

[56] *Id.*, art. 4(3).

[57] *Id.*, art. 14.

[58] *Id.*, art. 10.

entries on its materials provided that the information presented is not misleading. [59] For instance, when a foreign corporation maintains accounting principles and standards different from those used by a Japanese corporation, it is requested that the exact differences be specified, and the affected amounts and figures be properly disclosed. The emergence of the International Financial Reporting Standards (IFRS) has raised a difficult question for the Japanese MOF as to whether it will accept these applications based on the IFRS as legitimate. Additionally, foreign corporations are required to include disclosure of consolidated financial statements. [60]

International Financial Reporting Standards

While the business activities of corporations are becoming more international every year, the accounting systems of individual countries seem to remain very local and differ from country to country. Because of these differences, a cry went out for an international standardization of the accounting system so that investors could understand and properly compare the performance of corporations of other countries when seeking financing overseas. In answer to these concerns, international accounting standards are gradually taking shape.

The Norwalk Agreement, in September 2002, was the result of a joint meeting between the US Financial Accounting Standards Boards (FASB)[61] and the International Accounting Standards Board (IASB).[62]

---

[59] *Id.*, arts. 9, 12, 15.

[60] *Id.*, art. 10(2).

[61] "The mission of the Financial Accounting Standards Board is to establish and improve standards of financial accounting and reporting for the guidance and education of the public, including issuers, auditors, and users of financial information." Financial Accounting Standards Board, Mission Statement, available at http://www.fasb.org/.

[62] In June 1973, the International Accounting Standards Committee was established by the joint efforts of 10 countries, including the United States, Japan, England, France, and Germany. This committee was reorganized as the IASB in April 2001.

The agreement sought convergence between the IFRS[63] and US standards, and laid the foundation for further convergence of various international accounting standards.[64] It has been decided that the IFRS is to be adopted officially in 2005 as the financial reporting standard for corporations in the European Union (EU) whose stocks are traded in EU markets.

The EU has asked non-EU entities operating in the EU to disclose information based on the "IFRS or an equivalent standard" starting in 2005. As of now, more than 250 Japanese corporations and Japanese local governments have issued stocks and bonds in the EU. Most of these Japanese corporations disclosed financial information using Japanese accounting standards.[65]

Japan is diligently negotiating with the EU for its approval of the Japanese accounting standard as an equivalent to the IFRS. If the Japanese accounting standard fails to be recognized as an equivalent of the IFRS, disclosure by Japanese companies based on the Japanese accounting standard will not be allowed in the European Union markets. This would severely affect the financing activities of Japanese companies seeking to raise funds in the European Union. Japanese corporations also

---

[63] This is a collective name for accounting standards established by the International Accounting Standards Board (IASB) with the purpose of being approved and observed internationally. International Accounting Standards (IAS) were issued by the International Accounting Standards Committee (IASC) from 1973 to 2000. The IASB replaced the IASC in 2001. Since then, the IASB has amended some IAS, has proposed to amend other IAS, has proposed to replace some IAS with new International Financial Reporting Standards (IFRS), and has adopted or proposed certain new IFRS on topics for which there were no previous IAS. *See* generally the Web site of the IASB at http://www.iasb.org.

[64] In October 2002, SEC Chairman Harvey C. Pitt applauded the decisions by the FASB and the IASB to work together toward greater convergence between US Generally Accepted Accounting Principles ("US GAAP") and international accounting standards. He said, "This is a positive step for investors in the United States and around the world. It means that reducing the differences in two widely used sets of accounting standards will receive consideration by both boards, as they work to improve accounting principles and address issues in financial reporting." Press Release, US Securities and Exchange Commission, Actions by FASB, IASB Praised (Oct. 29, 2002), available at http://www.sec.gov/news/ press/2002-154.htm.

[65] Kazuo Hiramatsu and Shigeo Naruse, Kaikei Kijun — Nichi Ou Sougo Shounin WoNikkei [Accounting Standards — Hoping for Mutual Acceptance between Europe and Japan], NIKKEI, July 27, 2004, at 27.

are concerned about the possibility that Japanese accounting standards could be branded as inferior to the European or US Accounting Standards, thus causing a general mistrust among investors in Japanese capital markets.[66]

There have been divergent opinions from both government and private sectors about the adoption of the IFRS in Japan and no consensus has been reached. In the midst of this, on June 24, 2004, the Corporate Accounting Rule Council[67] of the Japanese MOF,[68] published a memorandum entitled "Adoption of International Accounting Standards in Japan" (MOF Memorandum).[69] The purpose of the MOF Memorandum was to canvass and compile various arguments about what should be done in Japan, from an official standpoint, regarding adopting

---

[66] Japanese Ministry of Economy, Trade and Industry, Report on the Internationalization of Business Accounting in Japan, available at http://www.iasplus.com/resource/0406ifrsjapangaap.pdf. (July 21, 2004).

[67] The mandate of the Corporate Accounting Rule Council is defined as: "the Corporate Accounting Rule Council shall investigate and examine the processes of the establishment of business accounting and auditing standards, the standardization of cost calculation and refurbishments or improvements of corporate accounting systems as well as to report the results of such investigations and examinations to the Prime Minister, the Commissioner of Financial Services Agency, and related organizations and consult with them." *See* Japanese Government Ministry of Finance, Organizational Ordinance, Article 24, No. 392 (1998), available at http://www.soumu.go.jp/s-news/2002/pdf/021017_3_06.pdf [hereinafter Organizational Ordinance].

[68] The Ministry of Finance was reorganized on Jan. 6, 2001. The name was changed from "Okurasho" to "Zaimucho" in Japanese, but the English name still remains the same. For more information, see the Ministry's Web site at http://www.mof.go.jp [hereinafter MOF Web site]. The Financial Services Agency (FSA) was created on July 1, 1997, with the integration of the Banking Supervisory Agency and the Financial System Planning Bureau of the Ministry of Finance. The new FSA has integral responsibility over supervision of the financial system, and supervision and inspection of financial institutions. In view of the rapid changes in the environment surrounding the economy and financial markets, the planning of the financial system focused on building a stable and vigorous financial system, and securing the efficiency and fairness in the financial markets. In the supervision and inspection of financial institutions, further efforts to maintain and improve the soundness of financial institutions were made. Coordination with foreign financial authorities was strengthened in order to cope adequately with the globalization of finance. Details on the FSA, available at http://www.fsa.go.jp [hereinafter FSA Web site].

[69] Memorandum from the Ministry of Finance on the Adoption of International Accounting Standards in Japan (June 24, 2004), available at http://www.fsa.go.jp/news/newsj/15/singi/f-20040624-1/01.pdf [hereinafter MOF Memorandum].

international accounting standards to coincide with the EU's adoption of the IFRS in 2005.

The Japanese Corporate Accounting Rule Council was given the responsibility of setting up the business accounting system and auditing standard.[70] In the MOF Memorandum, as a first step, the council made a general observation of the international trends surrounding the IFRS, summarized the arguments and comments about the IFRS from a legal standpoint, and provided the council's comment about future tasks. The council also provided its opinion regarding the application of the IFRS to foreign as well as domestic corporations.

Differences between Japanese Accounting Standard and IFRS

It is important to see how the Japanese Accounting Standards and the IFRS differ. Since 1998, Japan has been aggressively working on renovating its accounting standard, i.e., the so-called Accounting Big Bang, including reviewing the scope of consolidation, tax effect accounting, retirement benefits accounting, financial instruments accounting, asset-impairment accounting and others, mainly to provide international alignment in consideration of the IFRS and the US Accounting Standard.

The Accounting Big Bang placed big burdens on the balance sheets of companies through market price evaluations of financial products and estimations of pension liabilities. For example, the special losses of 400 major Japanese companies used to be several trillion yen, yet the same came to exceed 10 trillion yen since 1999.[71] On the other hand, the Accounting Big Bang caused many corporate realignments and led to healthier corporate balance sheets, thus contributing to a structural renovation of the Japanese economy.

---

[70] Organizational Ordinance, n.67 *supra* at art. 24. The council decided on Feb. 20, 2002, to take up the issue of IFRS and discuss the issue in the light of accounting and auditing standards.

[71] Editorial, NIKKEI, July 27, 2004, at 27.

In late March 2004, when the major elements of the IFRS were made clear, the Ministry of Economy, Trade and Industry (METI)[72] of Japan did a comparison of the Japanese Accounting Standard against the IFRS and the US Accounting Standard, in particular, 23 major items including expressions of financial reports, accounting for retirement benefits, financial instruments accounting and asset-impairment accounting. [73] The METI report stated:

> With respect to the standards for recognizing impairment losses of fixed assets, Japanese accounting standards, which will be enforced in Japan from the end of March 2006, as well as US accounting standards, use undiscounted cash flows as the basis whereas the IFRS uses the recoverable amount as the basis. Regarding the standards for the measure of impairment losses, however, both Japanese accounting standards and the IFRS use the recoverable amount. Therefore, no significant difference exists between the two. With respect to the treatment when the recoverable amount bounces back, the IFRS permits reversing, whereas neither the Japanese accounting standards nor the US accounting standards permit a reversal. Thus, Japanese accounting standards can thus be said to be more conservative.[74]   (See Table 12).

Based on such an analysis, METI concluded that, despite minor technical differences, the Japanese standard is equal to or better than the IFRS.[75]

---

[72] *See* Ministry of Economy, Trade, and Industry, at http://www.meti.go.jp. METI is in charge of international trade and industry in the Japanese government.

[73] Japanese METI, Report Concerning Internationalization of Japan's Business Accounting, at 14, available at http://www.meti.go.jp/english/report/downloadfiles IBAreporte.pdf.

[74] *Id.* at 12.

[75] *Id.* at 13.

Prospects for the Tokyo International Capital Market

The Nature of the Market

The Tokyo capital market has been moving steadily toward internationalization. To fully measure Tokyo's progress in internationalization, it is necessary to briefly examine current international capital markets.[76]

The various international capital markets differ considerably due to the varying economic powers, historic backgrounds, and policies of their respective countries. In terms of function, they are divided into three categories. The first category is the type of market that exports the capital accumulated by the country in which it is located. A prime example is Frankfurt. Secondly, are the Euro markets, such as London, which do not always have exportable capital but carry on intermediary functions in the international movement of money through price mechanisms. These intermediary markets flourish because the governments of these countries encourage their development by allowing the free flow of money, by creating a favorable market climate, and by granting financial institutions freedom to use their sophisticated know-how. Thirdly, there is the New York market, which performs the functions of both the first and second types. Although New York formerly served as a typical capital export market, this function was curtailed by the adoption of a series of monetary restrictions initiated by the United States in the 1960s, including the institution of an interest equalization tax, aimed at countering the huge deficits in the US international payments balance. In early 1974, however, the US government abolished the interest equalization tax as a result of an improvement in its payments balance. Encouraged by improved conditions, the New York market is increasing its functions as an intermediary in the supply of money.

---

[76] The presently functioning international capital markets are New York, London, Frankfurt, Paris, Amsterdam, Zurich, Brussels and Hong Kong. In addition, Beirut and Singapore have been noticed as oil dollar market and Asian dollar market, respectively.

Table 12 — Accounting for Impairment under Japanese, US and International Standards

Item	Japanese Standards	US Standards	International Accounting Standards
Criteria for recognition of impairment	Impairment loss is recognized when the sum of undiscounted future cash flows is less than the book value.	Impairment loss is recognized when the sum of undiscounted future cash flows is less than the book value.	Impairment loss is immediately recognized when the recoverable amount is less than the book value.
Criteria for measurement of impairment	The recoverable amount is used as the basis for the measurement of impairment loss. The difference between the book value and the recoverable amount is recognized as impairment loss.	The fair value is used as the basis for the measurement of impairment loss. The difference between the book value and the fair value is recognized as impairment loss.	The recoverable amount is used as the basis for the measurement of impairment loss. The difference between the book value and the recoverable amount is recognized as impairment loss.
Impairment loss of goodwill	(1) When there is an indication of impairment, testing for impairment loss is performed on a unit that is large enough to include both a group of assets that are associated with the operation to which the good will is attributed, and good will. Any increase in the amount of impairment loss that is computed by adding good will is	Testing for the recognition of impairment loss relating to goodwill is performed in two steps, as follows: Step 1: The fair value and the book value of the reporting unit are compared. If the fair value of the reporting unit	(1) Good will is allocated to a cash-generating unit at the time it is acquired as the result of business combinations. When it cannot be allocated, a comparison is made between the book value excluding good will and the recoverable amount of the cash-generating unit being examined. (2) When the book

	allocated to good will as a general rule. (2) When it is possible to allocate the book value of goodwill to groups of assets that are associated with the attributed operation on a reasonable basis, the book value of good will is allocated to individual asset groups first, and then the recognition of impairment loss is tested. Recognized impairment loss is allocated to good will first, and the remainder is allocated over individual component assets using a rational method, such as allocation that is proportionate with book values.	is less than its book value, Step 2 is performed. Step 2: The fair value of goodwill is computed by deducting from the fair value of the reporting unit the fair value of all recognized and unrecognized assets and liabilities. The excess of the carrying amount of goodwill over this amount is recognized as impairment loss. Only when a group of assets is a reporting unit or includes a reporting unit, goodwill is included in the group of assets for testing of impairment loss recognition.	value of good will can be allocated to a cash-generating unit, it is allocated to the cash-generating unit being examined. A comparison is made between the book value after goodwill allocation and the recoverable amount, either annually or whenever there is an indication. In connection with (1) and (2) mentioned above, if the recoverable amount is less than the book value, impairment loss is recognized at the level of the smallest unit to which good will can be allocated. The impairment loss thus recognized is allocated to goodwill first, and the remainder is allocated over individual component assets using a rational method, such as allocation proportionate with book values.

Source: Japanese METI, Report Concerning Internationalization of Japan's Business Accounting, at 8, available at http://www.meti.go.jp/english/report/downloadfiles/ IBAreporte.pdf, Table of Contents.

Up to the present, Japan has emphasized making Tokyo an export-type capital market. Therefore, appropriate measures have not been initiated to foster Tokyo's growth as an intermediary money market. To accomplish this important function, the Tokyo market needs to cooperate with Asian international markets, including, Singapore, which serves as the hub of the Asian dollar market. In view of Japan's economic and financial power as well as its firmly established market standing, Tokyo should play a leading role in international cooperation in Asia.

In considering the development of the Tokyo market, most noteworthy is the close working relationship between the Japanese government and private enterprise, as well as the relationship between Japanese government policies and the Japanese capital market. In pursuit of the sound development of the Japanese capital market, the Japanese government has actively implemented numerous policies designed to improve the market environment and is expected to continue its efforts in this direction. It is quite natural for money to flow into a safe, fully controlled market, provided that such money can be managed as effectively and at better interest rates elsewhere. Therefore, the Tokyo market with its safeguards and favorable status will very likely play a larger role in Asia in the future.

Application of International Accounting Standards in Japan

The Japanese Securities Exchange Law is applicable to all proposed securities issuances by foreign entities on the Japanese markets.[77]   As long as foreign entities submit financial documents prepared according to Japanese accounting standards, these documents are regarded as "not compromising the protection of public interests or investors" by the MOF.

Foreign entities that want to conduct business in Japan or intend to raise funds in Japan must submit their financial statements to the MOF prepared in accordance with Japanese accounting principles. This creates a heavy burden on foreign entities because the Japanese accounting system is so different from international standards, both culturally and

---

[77] See *supra* n.12 at art. 127-4.

functionally. Thus, companies also have to separately prepare their financial documents in accordance with the standards of their home country, resulting in a duplication of effort. Consequently, foreign companies would rather try to raise funds in markets other than the Japanese markets.

In consideration of these problems, it seems best that the Japanese accounting standards move toward closer alignment with international standards. However, the Japanese accounting standards are a long standing tradition in the Japanese business world rooted in a deep history and intimately entangled with other critical regulations, such as the Commercial Code, the Securities Exchange Law, and the Tax Law. Other factors slowing the adoption of the International Accounting Standards in Japan are the vast cultural differences, traditions, and value systems. It is expected that the acceptance of international standards will occur slowly and gradually with much consideration placed on the over-all process to internationalize the Japanese economy.

Conclusion

The development of Tokyo as a mature international financial market will take a considerable amount of time; many problems still need to be resolved. Japan needs to cultivate a long-range plan toward the internationalization of the yen. Currently, the yen plays a very small role in international transactions but there is considerable potential for increased use of the yen as a settlement or trade currency. Along with the internationalization of the yen is the further internationalization of the Tokyo market as an intermediary money market.

After World War II, Japan enacted the Securities Exchange Law based on two US statutes-(1) the Securities Act of 1933 and (2) the Securities Exchange Act of 1934 — which called for detailed disclosure to ensure the protection of investors. The disclosure system in Japan, however, has some material defects in comparison with its US counterparts.

One basic issue that needs to be addressed is the accounting standards. Now is the time for Japan to seriously consider the adoption of the IFRS.

However, the stark cultural differences and value system will make a quick adoption of the IFRS unlikely. The economic recovery of Japan, the country with the second largest GDP in the world, will lead to the economic recovery of the world. For Tokyo to be a real world market, it is necessary to aim for building a more efficient disclosure system and to support the overall restructuring of the socioeconomic system.

During the reformation of the financial system presently under way in Japan, it is essential to promote "new financial flow" and to normalize the risk of distribution as well as to improve efficiency in the economic society as a whole in order to seek further development. As a premise to this, a renewal of financial services to support such a reform is indispensable. The strengthening of the disclosure system, such as the accounting standards, is the most essential part. Such a refurbishment of the system will enable users of Japanese financial services from around the world to select combinations of risks and returns more securely.

Bibliography

Bank of Japan, http://www.boj.or.jp/seisaku/03/moo0309a.htm

BIS Quarterly Reviews, 1995–2004, Bank for International Settlements (BIS) Home Page,http://www.bis.org.

Commercial Code, Law No. 48, enacted on March 9, 1899, amended 18 times. For details, see http://www.ron.gr.jp/law/law/syouhou1.htm.

Commercial Code, Law No. 48, arts. 166, 173, 175, 183, 184, & 188.

EUROMONEY 35 (Euromoney Publication Limited, Feb. 19, 1974); Nihon Kogyo Shinbun (Daily Industrial Paper), March 12, 1974, at 3.

FSA, at http://www.fsa.go.jp [hereinafter FSA Web site].

Financial Accounting Standards Board, Mission Statement, available at http://www.fasb.org/.

Gaikokukawase Jouhousha "Gaitame Nenkan (2004)" p. 136.

Hiramatsu, K., Naruse, S. Kaikei Kijun — Nichi Ou Sougo Shounin WoNikkei [Accounting Standards — Hoping for Mutual Acceptance between Europe and Japan], NIKKEI, July 27, 2004, at 27.

IASB at http://www.iasb.org.

IMF, http://www.imf.org/external/np/sta/ir/usa/eng/curusa.htm

International Monetary Fund Home Page, http://www.imf.org/.

Japan Organizational Ordinance, http://www.soumu.go.jp/s-news/2002/pdf/021017_3_06.pdf at art. 24.

Japan Today, "Citigroup to Issue Y230 Bil in Samurai Bonds," Sept. 5, 2005, available at http://www.japantoday.com/e/?content=news&id=648225.

Japanese Ministry of Economy, Trade and Industry, Report on the Internationalization of Business Accounting in Japan, available at http://www.iasplus.com/resource/ 0406ifrsjapangaap.pdf. (July 21, 2004).

Ministry of Economy, Trade and Industry, Japan, http://www.meti.go.jp/hakusho/tusho/soron/S62/00-01-05.html.

Ministry of Economy, Trade and Industry, Japan, http://www.meti.go.jp/hakusho/tusho/soron/S62/00-01-06.html.

Ministry of Economy, Trade and Industry, Report Concerning Internationalization of Japan's Business Accounting, at 13, available at http://www.meti.go.jp/english/report/downloadfiles IBAreporte.pdf.

Ministry of Economy, Trade, and Industry, website at http://www.meti.go.jp.

Ministry of Finance Ordinance No. 26 (Apr. 2, 1972) [hereinafter cited as Ministry of Finance No. 26].

Ministry of Finance Ordinance No. 26, art. 1.

Ministry of Finance Ordinance No. 26, art. 4.

Ministry of Finance Ordinance No. 26, art. 5.

Ministry of Finance Ordinance No. 26, art. 7(3).

Ministry of Finance Ordinance No. 26, art. 7(5).

Ministry of Finance Ordinance No. 26, art. 7.

Ministry of Finance Ordinance No. 5 (Jan. 30, 1973) [hereinafter cited as Ministry of Finance Ordinance No. 5].

Ministry of Finance Ordinance No. 5, art. 10(2).

Ministry of Finance Ordinance No. 5, art. 10.

Ministry of Finance Ordinance No. 5, art. 14.

Ministry of Finance Ordinance No. 5, art. 4(3).

Ministry of Finance Ordinance No. 5, art. 7.

Ministry of Finance Ordinance No. 5, arts. 9, 12, 15.

Ministry of Finance, Japan Home Page, http://www.mof.go.jp/singikai/siryou/a140912/21.pdf.

Ministry of Finance, Memorandum on the Adoption of International Accounting Standards in Japan (June 24, 2004), available at http://www.fsa.go.jp/news/newsj/15/singi/f-20040624-1/01.pdf [hereinafter MOF Memorandum].

Ministry of Finance, Okurasho Shokenkyoku Nenppo, 1973 Nenban (Annual Report — Ministry of Finance, 1973) 52 (Kinyu Zaisei Jijyo Kenkukai 1973).

Ministry of Finance, Organizational Ordinance, Article 24, No. 392 (1998), available at http://www.soumu.go.jp/s-news/2002/pdf/021017_3_06.pdf [hereinafter Organizational Ordinance].

Ministry of Finance, website at http://www.fsa.go.jp/news/newsj/15/singi/f-20040624-1/01.pdf.

Ministry of Finance, website at http://www.mof.go.jp/1c004.htm.

Ministry of Finance, website at http://www.mof.go.jp/shoutou/monthsty.htm.

Misawa, M (1973). "Securities Regulations in Japan," Vanderbilt Journal of Transnational Law, Vol. 6, No. 2, Spring 1973, at 447–510.

Misawa, M. (2005). "The Tokyo International Capital Market for Foreign Issuers and Required Disclosure," The Journal of Payment Systems Law, published by A.S. Pratt & Sons, also the same publisher of The Banking Law Journal, Nov./Dec. 2005, Volume 1, pp. 699–753.

Mizuho Financial Group, "Shoken Manual", 2002–2004, pp. 398–401.

NIKKEI, Editorial, July 27, 2004, at 27.

Nikkei, Sept.5, 2005 (http://www.nni.nikkei.co.jp/AC/TNKS/Nni20050904D04JFF01.htm).

Nikkei, http://www.nikkei.co.jp/news/main/20041219.

Securities Exchange Law, Law No. 25 of April 13, 1948 (Japan) art. 127-4. Subsequent amendments to the law reflected US developments. Most recently the law was amended on March 3, 1971. Law No. 4 of 1971. For details, see http://www.houko.com/00/01/S23/025.HTM.

Securities Exchange Law, art. 4.

Securities Exchange Law, art. 5.

Securities Exchange Law, art. 8.

Securities Exchange Law, art. 10.

Securities Exchange Law, art. 13.

Securities Exchange Law, art. 15.

Securities Exchange Law, art. 154.

Securities Exchange Law, art. 187.

Securities Exchange Law, art. 2.

Securities Exchange Law, art. 26.

Securities Exchange Law, art. 55.

Securities Exchange Law, art. 76.

Securities Exchange Law, art. 9.

Securities Exchange Law, arts 16–18.

Securities Exchange Law, arts. 182–184, 186.

The Industrial Bank of Japan, Ltd., Memorandum-Papua New Guinea, Japanese Yen Gon Von Bonds, Series A (1973/1985), Guaranteed by the Commonwealth of Australia 3–19 (The Industrial Bank of Japan, Ltd. Dec. 1973).

Tokyo Stock Exchange, Inc. Annual Report, 2004.

US Securities and Exchange Commission Press Release, Actions by FASB, IASB Praised (Oct. 29, 2002), available at http://www.sec.gov/news/ press/2002-154.htm.

Chapter 3

Japan's Big Bang Reform[a]

Before the Big Bang

Despite the fact that it has been 10 years since the bubble economy burst and that public funds in the total sum of 7.2 trillion yen were poured into most of the banks in Japan early 1999 with the intention of beefing up their net worth capital, the financial figures of major banks including the 17 major city banks at the end of March 1999 did not show signs of complete recovery from the damage the financial market incurred due to the burst of the bubble economy. Prior to this, 685 billion yen of tax money was used in 1996 to liquidate the special housing loan companies (Jusen) which were burdened with enormous amounts of debts. At that time, it looked as though that sufficed to settle the problem debts of banks, but it turned out that we were only at the start of the problem settlement.[1]

---

[a] This chapter is based on the author's previously published articles:
1. Mitsuru Misawa, "Revitalization of Japanese Banks: Japan's Big Bang Reform". In: Frenkel, Michael/Hommel, Ulrich/Rudolf, Markus (Eds.): Risk Management, 2nd Revised and Enlarged Edition, Berlin: Springer, 2005, pp. 801–820. Reprinted with kind permission of Springer Science + Business Media.
2. Mitsuru Misawa, "Bad Loans of Japanese Banks –Directors' Civil and Criminal Liabilities–," 18 Temp. Int'l & Comp. L. J. 101 (2004), pp. 101–127.

[1] As to the details of the Jusen (special housing loan companies) problems, see Mitsuru Misawa, "Lenders' Liability in the Japanese Financial Market — A Case of Jusen, the Largest Problem Loan in Japan," Management Japan, Vol. 30, No. 2, Autumn 1997, pp.18–28 and Vol. 31, No. 1, Spring 1998, pp.19–28.

Let us now look at the recent figures of these banks. Without an exception, the ordinary profits of all 17 major banks were in red, and the aggregate loss amount was about 6 trillion yen. Their current term profits after tax amounted to a loss of 3.6 trillion yen. On the other hand, the total amount of bad debts[2] still amounts to about 20 trillion yen and the write-down amount[3] for settling them reached an amount of about 10.4 trillion yen.

The deposit and loan amounts decreased about 25 trillion and 24 trillion yen respectively, showing a sign that the banks are heading toward a diminishing equilibrium. (Table 1)

Demise of the High Growth Period and Birth of the Bubble Economy

After realizing almost twenty years of prosperity with an average annual growth rate of 10% or higher, the Japanese economy started to stagnate in the beginning in the mid-1970s. In particular, in 1974 and 1975, the so-called "oil shock" triggered the first and most serious recession since World War II.

In the meantime, based upon "misunderstanding" that a high rate of economic growth is the norm, the Japanese government and industries pushed further for economic growth. This resulted in the creation of hefty domestic demands helped by a large volume of government bond issues and a torrential flow of exports to overseas markets.

---

[2] As to the definition of "bad debt" (classified debts), see "Severity of the Crisis as Indicated in Key Words," Shukan Toh-yo Keizai (Weekly Oriental Economist), Feb. 2, 1998, p.46. As to its reality, see "Reality of Banks' Bad Debts," Shukan Toh-yo Keizai, April 4, 1998, pp.38–40.

[3] As to the definition of the "write-down amount for bad debts," see *Supra* note 2 of 1998.2.7 at p.46.

Table 1 — Financial Figures of Major 17 Banks, March 1999

(Unit: ¥100Million, %, Δ=loss)

| | Ordinary Profit | | Current Term Profit After Tax | | Bad Debt | | Increase/ Decrease of Deposits (less CD) | Increase/ Decrease of Loans | Bad Debt Lending Ratio | Profit from Selling Stocks/Bonds | | Latent Profit on Listed Securities | | BIS Ratio of Owned Capital | Public Funds Infusion Amount |
	Mar. '99 Term	Comp. w/ Prev. Term	Mar. '99 Term	Comp. w/ Prev. Term	Balance	Write-off Amount				Stocks	Bonds	Balance	Comp. w/ Prev. Term		
DKB	Δ6,045	Δ4,495	Δ3,762	Δ2,298	22,048	9,720	Δ33,146	Δ18,893	6.7	1,024	603	1,773	523	11.46	9,000
Sakura	Δ7,542	Δ3,370	Δ3,753	Δ1,548	17,605	10,234	Δ27,150	Δ27,925	5.5	125	511	Δ1,560	Δ1,154	12.38	8,000
Fuji	Δ5,889	Δ126	Δ3,929	1,258	13,617	7,121	Δ43,527	Δ22,373	4.6	Δ1,160	796	1,132	3,406	11.21	10,000
Tokyo Mitsubishi	Δ223	8,952	454	9,460	20,776	8,895	Δ45,554	Δ36,031	5.3	3,054	1,038	8,417	Δ2,077	11.87	0
Asahi	Δ4,075	Δ2,177	Δ2,200	Δ360	9,201	6,521	Δ5,174	Δ1,228	4.4	1,045	131	819	Δ32	11.90	5,000
Sanwa	Δ6,534	Δ2,401	Δ3,944	Δ535	16,862	10,030	Δ21,741	Δ16,578	4.3	Δ496	983	3,344	23	11.06	7,000
Sumitomo	Δ7,410	Δ1,236	Δ3,741	2,476	19,599	10,725	Δ52,999	Δ22,134	5.8	Δ376	494	4,099	895	*10.95	5,010
Daiwa	Δ2,500	Δ988	Δ1,165	Δ636	7,434	3,687	Δ6,907	Δ10,076	7.2	132	543	Δ2,095	Δ112	12.73	4,080
Tokai	Δ3,393	Δ2,948	Δ1,857	Δ1,914	4,760	5,776	Δ13,768	Δ16,334	2.5	647	389	1,954	Δ572	12.60	6,000
Total of city banks	Δ43,611	Δ8,789	Δ23,897	5,903	131,902	72,709	Δ249,966	Δ171,572	5.1	3,995	5,488	17,883	900	11.60	54,090
IBJ	Δ3,519	58	Δ1,957	1,462	18,442	9,243	Δ14,675	Δ3,695	8.2	3,181	559	123	Δ4,652	11.30	6,000
Mitsui Trust	Δ1,966	Δ2,010	Δ1,440	Δ1,515	7,622	4,298	Δ2,626	Δ18,596	9.9	1,242	71	Δ1,085	Δ2,103	15.40	3,502
Mitsubishi Trust	Δ1,938	Δ1,994	Δ1,196	Δ1,298	13,007	5,035	Δ1,729	Δ18,157	12.1	348	719	3,591	Δ667	11.66	3,000
Yasuda Trust	Δ3,304	Δ1,791	Δ3,758	Δ2,163	5,511	3,148	4,879	Δ9,654	9.1	Δ2,081	14	112	1,938	12.42	0
Toyo Trust	Δ2,253	Δ2,413	Δ1,277	Δ1,362	8,994	3,719	990	Δ5,262	12.5	450	Δ15	Δ133	Δ651	*13.83	2,000
Chuo Trust	Δ602	Δ693	Δ487	Δ610	2,031	981	11,972	3,776	5.0	Δ79	Δ34	Δ436	163	13.18	2,000
Nihon Trust	Δ837	1,171	Δ841	163	2,393	871	514	Δ3,166	24.1	Δ26	Δ115	Δ1	Δ1	8.16	0
Sumitomo Trust	Δ1,875	Δ940	Δ1,071	Δ354	9,464	4,156	Δ2,362	Δ12,876	8.6	50	492	1,030	99	12.52	2,000
Total of trust banks	Δ12,775	Δ8,670	Δ10,070	Δ7,139	49,022	22,208	10,610	Δ63,935	11.6	Δ96	1,132	3,078	Δ1,222	12.46	12,502
Total	Δ59,905	Δ17,401	Δ35,924	226	199,366	104,160	Δ254,031	Δ239,202	8.3	7,080	7,179	14,928	Δ4,974	11.79	72,592

Source: Compiled from "Ekonomisuto" (Economist), June 8, 1999, p. 27.

As a result, a phenomenal bubble economy of historic proportions was created by the end of the 1980s. The root causes of this were: 1) an enormous amount of funds were accumulated in industry; 2) with the advancement of financial liberalization and internationalization, the financial and capital markets grew to such huge sizes that it became easier for industry to acquire funds from such markets and its reliance on banks reduced; 3) faced with this "loss of loyalty" to the banks by their traditional customers, the banks increased loans to the real estate industry and investment in stocks.

During the high growth period preceding this period, the huge demand for capital investment funds was met by loans from banks because the securities market, the essential function of which is to meet such demands, was not fully developed. When high growth terminated, the demand for capital investment itself receded, and what little demand for funds existed, could be satiated by the securities market, particularly oversea markets much more cheaply. This led to a substantial reduction of customers for the banks to lend to. Moreover, during the bubble economy period, the industry was able to borrow money at super low rates from the markets to pay back the moneys they owed to the banks. Thus, it became vital for the banks to find profitable lending targets for the sake of their own survival. What they found was real estate financing using land, which at that time was valuable collateral, as security.

After the bubble period, enormous bad debts amounting to 80 trillion yen were created. Perhaps we should not be too critical of the banks profiting from increasing loans backed by real estate when the land price was increasing. The truth of the matter is that nobody could foresee that the land price could drop that much[4].

However, as a matter of practicality, they cannot just sit doing nothing and hope that the market mechanism will take care of the enormous bad debts of the financial institutions by itself, and even if it is possible to do so, it would take too long and the financial system may not survive. Thus, infusing public funds in some manner became unavoidable.

---

[4] As to the details of the land price drop in Japan, see "Why Banks Made Big Mistakes?" Shukan Toh-yo Keizai, March 28, 1998, pp.30–34.

Consequently, the infusion of public funds to the banks became a national imperative. In other words, the financial instability and the economic downturn went hand in hand to bog down the Japanese economy. It recorded negative growth rates two years in a row in 1997 and 1998, and the jobless rate got stuck near 5%.

In 1997, the public's concern for instabilities of some of the major banks' operations heightened. Many banks became unhealthy under the burden of huge debts. The latent profit of stocks owned by the banks that can be counted as a part of the bank's net worth reduced due to the drop in stock prices, and the banks accelerated the compression of assets such as the lending balance that constitute the denominator for the BIS ratio of owned capital[5] that represents the healthiness of the banks, in order not to reduce such ratio. This caused a sharp credit contraction through the bank's reluctance to lend and collection of loans, resulting in an abnormal situation in which the total loan balance of the banks across the nation decreased compared to the previous year.[6]

At this point, even some good industrial corporations experienced temporary fund shortages. Without an influx of funds, the industry cannot initiate any new capital investments. Therefore, the entire economy headed toward a diminishing equilibrium. The basic cause for the long economic downturn was the banks' contraction of credit.

In order to escape from this new form of "compound recession" led by the recession in the financial world, it was inevitable to seek a turnaround in the financial world, and what was hampering the recovery in the financial sector were the huge bad loans that were encumbering the financial institutions. To wipe out the bad debts from the books of the financial institutions by whatever means necessary came to be recognized by the general public as an inevitable premise for the fundamental recovery of the economy, the Japanese Big Bang[7] which is

---

[5] As to "BIS Ratio of Owned Capital," see *Supra* note 2 of 1998.2.7 at p.43.
[6] As to the details of the "reluctance to lend" phenomenon, see *Supra* note 2 of 1998.2.7 at p.49.
[7] As to the "Japanese Big Bang," see Shukan Toh-yo Keizai, July 25, 1998, p.43. As to its reality, see "Big Bang Seeing the First Sign of Realization with the Public Fund Infusion," February 2, 1998, pp.10–13.

internationally sought and the various reforms of the financial systems accompanying it.

Thus, as of March 1999, a sum of 7.3 trillion yen[8] of taxpayers' money[9] was infused into the 17 major banks. (Refer to Table 1)

The Japanese Big Bang (Financial Overhaul)

On October 17, 1996, the Economic Council, an advisory organization for the Prime Minister, presented a report including a restructuring plan entitled "For the Revitalization of the Financial System of Our Country."

The restructuring plan was based on the severe recognition of crises: while reformation of financial sector is moving at accelerated rates in the U.S. and European countries as well as some Asian countries, the move toward reformation of the financial system in Japan is still very slow; Japan is clearly lagging behind in the competitions among global markets and systems; and its position in the world financial system and industry is deteriorating relative to those countries. The report stated, "In order to overcome this relative deterioration of our position and make it possible for the users to benefit from more efficient and better financial services, it is necessary for the government to get rid of the excessively protective attitude toward the financial institutions and the traditional convoy system provided under the guidance of the Ministry of Finance; in particular, it is necessary to implement various policies geared toward building a system designed for the benefits of the users, which is based on the market mechanism and the principle of their own risks. It is not enough for the new financial system to be sound and stable; it must be also efficient and revolutionary."

---

[8] There area several conflicting opinions about how much public funds are needed. See "Betrayal in the Bank Rescue Plan — Uncertainty That Can Not Be Wiped Out Even with Public Fund Infusion of 30 Trillion Yen," <u>Shukan Toh-yo Keizai</u>, March 28, 1998, pp.14–16.

[9] See "Ineffective Public Fund Infusion," <u>Shukan Toh-yo Keizai</u>, January 1, 1998, pp.10–14 for a negative opinion for the infusion of public funds, and "Bank's Public Fund Infusion Requests Lack Sincerity," <u>Shukan Toh-yo Keizai</u>, March 28, 1998, pp.22–23 for a questioning opinion.

It also stated, "Therefore, the reform must not be gradual or phased; it must be done in one big stroke; it is the quicker, the better, if Japan should compete with various countries of the world and it should be done by the end of 1999 in one big change, in the manner of a Big Bang."

This proposal should be given a proper consideration because it seeks the reform within a defined time limit, it was not drafted in coordination with any of the related ministries and agencies, and it put forth a clear image of how the Japanese financial system should be in the future. One noteworthy factor is that it emphasizes the importance of mandating liberalization in order to allow the competition principle and minimizing rooms for the use of administrative discretion by listing in laws all the regulative items as exceptions. This is all because of the urgency of the need for restructuring the Japanese financial and capital markets.

Let us now examine the outline of this reform plan.

Realization of Broader Competition

In order to facilitate the entry of not only the financial institutions but also non-financial institutions into the financial market from the standpoint of promoting competition among financial institutions, all entry restrictions and limitations related to the types of businesses and methods used, as well as approval or permit procedures, will be abolished.

Liberalization of Asset Transactions

In order to improve the functions of the capital market, it is necessary to liberalize the commissions for selling and buying securities, completely revamp the securities taxation system, which include abolishing the securities transaction tax, to liberalize further transactions outside the regular stock exchange, to promote the introduction of new financial technologies, to reform the markets for issuing and trading corporate bonds, and to introduce the stock option system.

Reevaluation of Regulating and Monitoring System

It is mandatory for the Japanese financial system to overhaul its system of regulation and administration in order to survive in the international "inter-system competition." Therefore, it is necessary to refurbish the system's foundation concerning the handling of failing financial institutions, change the administrative practices from the ones in the past which relied heavily on the individual administrator's discretion and were heavily protective of the financial institutions to one based on established rules honoring the market function, and enforce the policy of competition in the financial businesses.

Reforming the Financial System

In the midst of these changes toward the Big Bang, the banks themselves became to believe that it is becoming increasingly important for them to reform the system.

While the banks were eliminated after the World War II from the securities business according to Article 65 of the "Securities Exchange Law",[10] the banks provided necessary funds for the industry because the securities market was relatively underdeveloped.

The banks, particularly major banks, were resisting, at least on the surface, the exclusion from the corporate bond underwriting business, claiming that the exclusion is a deprivation of an established right dating back to the days before the World War II; however, they were not feeling much pain at that point because they knew they were the only ones able to satiate the strong demand for funds from industry.

However, the situation changed completely with the demise of the high growth period. Because the industrial companies were able to accumulate enormous amounts of internal reserves and depreciation allowances during the high growth period, they were able to use the internal funds for capital investment with ease as the economy shifted gear to more stable growth. Now they did not have to depend on bank loans which they once needed to satisfy their needs quickly and easily.

---

[10] Law No. 25 of 1948 (Japan).

On top of that, the domestic securities market, which was only a limited source of funds in the early days of the high growth period, had also grown sufficiently by then. At the same time, securitization, which became popular in the international financial market, particularly in the European market, provided another means of obtaining funds for the corporations easily and at extremely low costs.

All of this contributed to the loss of good lending customers for the banks, and created serious concern regarding the survival of the banks. At this point, the banks finally realized with seriousness the significance of their being excluded from the securities business according to Article 65 of the "Securities Exchange Law." Thus, they came to believe that they must obtain the legalization for handling securities. Although they were allowed to handle public bonds, they considered they could not regain the customers they once had without being able to handle industrial financing such as underwriting of stocks and bonds.

Shift Toward the "Business-Category Subsidiary" System

On June 19, 1992, a bill titled "Law concerning reconditioning of the related laws for reforming financial and securities exchange systems" passed the Diet and the new law was issued on June 26, 1992. The gist of the law is to allow banks and securities brokerage firms to participate in each other's business through the establishment of subsidiaries for each business category and to look for the creation of healthy competitive capital markets.

While both types of institutions were allowed to participate in each other's business with the implementation of the law ("System Reform Law" for the sake of simplicity), of all the banks, only the subsidiaries of the long-term credit banks, trust banks and government financial institutions were allowed to conduct securities-related businesses. Thus, The Industrial Bank of Japan, The Long-Term Credit Bank of Japan, and The Central Bank of Agriculture and Forestry established securities brokerage subsidiaries and started operations on July 26, 1993.

Since these companies were not allowed to enter the stocks brokerage business, their businesses were limited to underwriting and selling straight corporate bonds. A policy was laid down that "consideration would be given to allowing within one year" for the participation in the new business of city banks, which were left behind the long-term credit and trust banks.

On October 1, 1993, the trust bank subsidiaries of Nomura Securities, Daiwa Securities, Nikko Securities, and Yamaichi Securities started their banking businesses. As the securities subsidiaries of the banks were not allowed to enter the stock brokerage business for the time being, the trust banks were not allowed to enter main trust businesses such as loan trusts, pension trusts, and special money trusts. This was done in order not to apply too much pressure to the existing business of the trust banks.

Such was the way in which the financial system reform was introduced with the main thrust being the introduction of the banks into securities business through their subsidiaries. The securities subsidiaries of the banks have been expanding since then backed by the negotiation powers of the parent banks with the clients.

Legalization of Financial Holding Companies

In the flow toward the Big Bang, the banks began to realize that they were not quite satisfied with the Subsidiary by Business Category Plan and came to request the legalization of financial holding companies which would give them full capability to conduct a wide range of financial businesses to compete against international pressures.

A bill for revising the "Anti-Monopoly Law,"[11] which contained a section for the legalization of financial holding companies, was passed by the Diet on June 11, 1997. There were three types of holding companies, which were still prohibited because they can create over-concentrations of business control power; a "zaibatsu" type business group whose total asset exceeds 15 trillion yen, a holding company formed by uniting a large scale financial company and a general business company, and a holding company formed as a combination of major companies belonging to related industry fields. The detailed guidelines on this matter in this law was left to be developed by the Fair Trade Commission.

---

[11] Law No. 54 of 1947 (Japan).

On July 9, 1997, the Fair Trade Commission disclosed its guidelines for the scope of pure holding companies to be legalized by the revised "Anti-Monopoly Law." It stated that holding companies containing a financial institution with total assets exceeding 15 trillion yen and a general business company with total assets exceeding 300 billion yen are not allowed. The Ministry of Finance further established a rule that, in case of a holding company whose center pillar is a bank, the business companies owned by such a holding company should be limited to specific types of financial businesses such as leasing and credit corporations, and any subsidiaries operating in general businesses, even if they are smaller than 300 billion yen in total assets, are prohibited based on the principle of preventing banks from having excessive controlling power over general industries.

Also, they eased a rule which had hitherto prevented any financial institution from owning more than 5% of the stock of another company. The new rule stated that said restriction would not be applied to cases of owning the stocks issued by financial institutions, the stocks of subordinate companies 50% of whose incomes are dependent on the parent financial institution, and the stocks of companies or holding companies who operate in financial businesses specific to financial institutions such as liability guaranty companies.

As a result of this loosening of the 5% rule, it became possible for a city bank to bring under its roof, not as a subsidiary by business category, a company which operates in financial businesses specific to quasi-financial institutions in addition to the existing financial institutions of various kinds.

As to how these special financial holding companies[12] should be, the Financial System Research Committee, which is a consulting body of the Ministry of Finance, comments as follows:

"How they should develop their businesses and what organizational forms they should take are matters to be decided by each financial institution as the responsibility of its own management. However, from the standpoint of the optimal financial system, it is preferable that they

---

[12] "Reaction to the New Development of Financial Intermediary Function," a report dated May 26, 1995.

be allowed to select organizational forms most suitable to their own management strategies from a broad range of choices as the range of businesses that can be handled by financial institutions are widening due to new developments in financial intermediary functions.

It is also preferable that they be allowed to select a financial institution form that enables them to split a financial business into a separate entity so that they can offer total financial services more effectively as a financial group as a whole, as well as to prevent the risks caused by having multiple varieties of business from affecting depositors or settlement services."

The merits of financial holding companies are as follows:

1. While it provides a variety of financial services in a complex manner as a group, it is easier to prevent management risks of its subsidiaries from spreading to other subsidiaries or conflicts of interest among subsidiaries.
2. While the risk profile of each business unit is made apparent, it is also possible to make a unified decision; moreover, it is possible to make the business and organizational operation of each unit more efficient and maneuverable by bringing each business unit as a separate entity under a holding company.

However, there are several problems with the financial holding company system as follows:

1. When a financial holding company is established, it should not be allowed to have general business companies under it. In the U.S., the separation of banking businesses and commercial and industrial businesses has become established as a fundamental rule. There should not be capital relations between general business companies and financial institutions in Japan as well.
2. Since a financial holding company provides general financial services to its clients, the chance of causing conflicts of interest is undeniable. A strict firewall must be established between a financial holding company and its subsidiaries and among the subsidiaries themselves to secure fairness and transparency in financial transactions.
3. If all of the constituent companies of a holding company are 100% subsidiaries of the holding company, there is a possibility

that profits and losses of the holding company can be distributed among the subsidiaries to conceal the management conditions as a corporate group, thus interfering with the benefits of the stockholders of the holding company. In order to prevent such demerits from occurring, various regulations have to be implemented. At the same time, there will be a need for legal measure, to enforce substantial disclosure of the holding company's operations. Therefore, it will be necessary to amend systematically the "Commercial Law", [13] the "Securities Exchange Law",[14] and the "Tax Law"[15] to provide consistency among these laws in relation to this problem.

4. In order to maintain fairness, the enforcement of the "Anti-Monopoly Law" must be emphasized and monitoring and control over financial transactions must be enriched and enhanced.

Revitalization Through Coordination and Consolidation in 1990s

The Tokyo Financial Market has been tormented all through the 1990s by lingering illness in the form of huge losses attributed to bad debts created by the collapse of the huge bubble economy. The loss of its prestige, which was once considered comparable to those of New York and London, is unbelievable. There is no doubt, as it stands now, that the Japanese financial institutions will be engulfed by the waves of worldwide financial competition.

On top of that, with the legalization of pay-off (deposit guaranty up to a principal of 10 million yen only), which is scheduled to occur in April 2001,[16] at hand, fierce competition is occurring on all sides in the domestic market. Moreover, the Japanese Big Bang (financial overhaul) is in progress. It may not be possible for even the biggest bank to win this survival game alone.

In order for the Japanese banks to end the "cleanup of the past" and strengthen themselves in order to survive in the worldwide financial competition, it is necessary for them to consider reorganization as an

---

[13] Law No. 48 of 1947 (Japan).

[14] *Supra* note 10.

[15] For example, Corporate Income Tax Law (Law No. 34 of 1965, Japan).

[16] As to the details of "pay-off," see *Supra* note 2 of 1998.2.7, at p. 40.

alternative management plan, as the above-mentioned task will require restructuring and a huge amount of system investment. Since the infusion of public funds in March 1999, the strengthening of Japanese banks has become the national imperative and the Financial Revitalization Committee of the Japanese Government has been seeking "reorganizations that would create banks that can compete in the worldwide market."

In the midst of such a trend, the Japanese financial institutions are seeking the possibilities of partial, overall and total consolidations. (See Table 2) Of all these moves, a move of the largest scale was revealed recently.

On August 20, 1999, The Industrial Bank of Japan, The Dai-Ichi Kangyou Bank and The Fuji Bank, three major banks in Japan, reached an agreement to establish a financial holding company by the fall of 2000 and integrate their businesses across the board. The corporation group to be controlled by this joint holding company will be divided and reorganized into a retail bank for individuals, a wholesale bank for corporations, an investment bank and others to be established according to the type of business.[17]

As a result of the integration of these three banks, the total asset will reach about 141 trillion yen based on simple addition, and an "ultra-mega bank" will be created which will truly the biggest bank in the world, exceeding in size the Tokyo-Mitsubishi Bank (total assets of about 70 trillion yen) and the Deutsche Bank (total asset of about 97 trillion yen). The group will be joined not only by the securities companies under the three banks, but also insurance companies such as The Dai-Ichi Mutual Life Insurance, so that it will be a great financial reorganization of an unprecedented scale across the borders of banking, securities and insurance. (See Table 3)

---

[17] For the details of the announcement, see <u>Nihon Keizai Shimbun</u> (Japan Economic Journal), August 20, 1999, pp. 1–2.

Table 2 — Alliances Formed by Japanese Financial Institutions in the late 1990s

Announcement	Contents of Merger
Aug '99	IBJ, DKB and Fuji Bank reached an agreement to establish a financial holding company by 2000.
Mar '99	Nippon Life Insurance formed alliance with Hitachi. New Japan Securities and Wako Securities announced to merge by April 2000. Nomura Securities requested subordinated loan from Sakura, Sanwa and IBJ. Sanwa obtained Universal Securities' stocks from Daiwa Securities.
Feb '99	Sakura and Tokai requested Toyota increase of capital. Yokohama Bank transferred its securities division to Tokai Bank.
Jan '99	Taiyo Life and Daido Life went formed overall alliance aiming for a holding company. Mitsui Trust and Chuo Trust announced merger in April 2000. Mitsubishi, Sumitotomo, IBJ and Nomura formed alliance. Fuji reorganized Yasuda Trust as a subsidiary. Sanwa became the leading stockholder of Toyo Trust forming alliance with the latter.
Dec '98	Temporary nationalization of Nippon Credit Bank decided.
Nov '98	GE Credit, U.S., announced the purchase of Leasing Div. of Japan Lease. Nippon Life Insurance established J.V. with Deutshe Bank in asset management.
Oct '98	Nippon Life Insurance joined force with Patnum, U.S., to develop new merchandises. Mitsui Trust established J.V. with State Farm, U.S., in trust field. Temporary nationalization of Long Term Credit Bank decided. IBJ and First Life Insurance formed overall alliance through capital enforcement, etc. Sumitomo Bank merged Kansai Bank as a subsidiary. Yasuda Trust transferred asset management division to the subsidiary of DKB and Fuji. Daiwa Bank announced its decision to become a large regional bank. DKB and JP Morgan, U.S., formed alliance in asset management field.
Sep '98	Tokai and Asahi formed overall alliance aiming for holding company. 4 financial companies of Mitsubishi group formed alliance in pension field.
Jul '98	Tokyo Mitsubishi made a large investment in Tokyo Mitsubishi Securities. GE Credit, U.S., announced to buy out Lake's consumer financing division. Sumitomo and Daiwa Securities formed J.V. , Daiwa becoming a holding company.
May '98	DKB made Kankaku Securities its subsidiary. Citibank, U.S., formed a J.V. with Nikko Securities becoming a top stockholder of Nikko. IBJ and Nomura formed partial alliance in asset management area.

Source: Compiled from Shukan Toh-yo Keizai (Weekly Oriental Economist), April 17, 1999, p. 30.

Such a grand scale reorganization is necessary because, first of all, the world financial market is heading toward an oligopolistic market at an alarming rate. It is believed that there will be only 15 banks or so left worldwide that can offer a broad range of services internationally.

The wave of huge mergers and acquisitions of financial institutions started late 1997 with the merger of Union Bank of Switzerland (UBS) and Swiss Bank (SBC), followed one after the other by the merger of Citicorp and Travelers Group, and Deutsche Bank's buyout of Bankers Trust since then each time the newly formed alliance declaring the birth of the world's largest group.

There are three major currents that are the prime movers of these huge conglomerations of financial institutions. The first is a trend towards "one stop financing" which is one financial institution providing everything the customer wants, breaking down the boundaries between banking, securities and insurance. The second is the globalization that seek business activities and money across country borders. The third is the Internet Revolution that accelerates the other two trends.

Of these trends, the most interesting one is the third item, the Internet Revolution, which makes it easier to exchange and analyze enormous amounts of customer data so that the synergistic effect of the integration across business categories can be fully expected. Globalization reached another phase with cross-boarder transaction costs drastically reduced due to the popularization of the Internet. As a result, it is expected that the trend toward huge integration will continue for the foreseeable future.

In the midst of these trends, it is quite abnormal to have as many as 17 "major banks" in Japan. Integration of banks in Japan is inevitable. First of all, as is evident from the return on equities (ROE) of Japanese banks being substantially lower than those of the US banks, the international competitiveness of the Japanese banks is low.[18] If the banks withdraw from overseas markets, having been beaten in competition, it will certainly affect the Japanese industrial companies operating in those markets. The Financial Revitalization Committee of

---

[18] It is necessary for Japanese banks to secure at least about 2% of profit margin if they wish to meet the international standards for the "BIS ratio of Owned Capital" of 8% and the ROE of 10%. For details, see Nihon Keizai Shimbun, August 29, 1999, p. 13.

the Japanese Government says, "the number of major banks that conduct overseas operations should be limited to about four."

Table 3 — Organizational Chart of Financial Holding Company

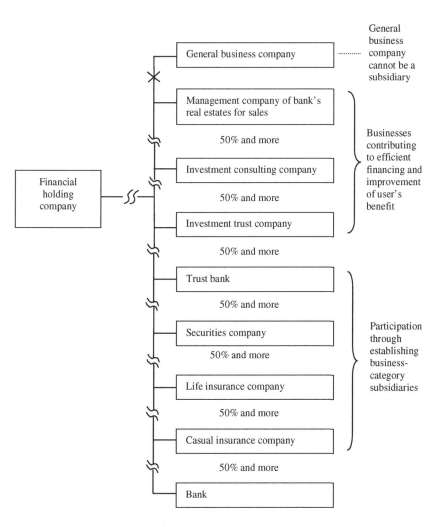

Note; ⌇ indicates "firewall" to be established.

Secondly, with the legalization of pay-off scheduled for April 2001, it is necessary to speed up the strengthening of the management bases for the complete stabilization of the financial system. It inevitably involves some reorganization in order to improve efficiency. Meanwhile, the bad debt problem is expected to linger on. It is strongly hoped for that the 17 major banks which received the infusion of public funds this spring tighten their belts through reorganizations for the sake of proper repayment of those funds as well.

Thirdly, the competition with financial institutions other than banks is getting fiercer. For example, GE Capital, the world's largest non-bank institution, is steadily increasing its inroad. Japanese finance companies for consumers and small companies are also growing. The future threat will be the banks and securities brokers using the Internet. They are acquiring substantial numbers of customers in the US. For the traditional banks in Japan to be able to compete with these "cyber financial institutions," whose strongest forte is the cost competitiveness, they must slim down their organizations by reducing the number of branches and staff members.

Given these reasons, banks other than the three mentioned earlier will have to make plans for large scale cooperation and mergers.[19] It goes without saying that the people who are involved will have to go through painful decisions and efforts to achieve results through such a large scale integration.

The first task will be to reduce the number of branches and employees to improve asset efficiency. The window operation for individual customers, which provides such a low return on assets, has been mechanized. However, it is a difficult decision for a bank with a branch in a prestigious metropolitan location to make a drastic change. But, it must be done to restructure high cost areas of the organization, including integration of branches.

Another task would be to review each business sector from the standpoint of efficiency. The key to success would be to reduce

---

[19] As to the possibilities of further integration of Japanese banks and their combinations, see "Curtailment of Financial Institutions — Last Decision (Disappearing Banks, Remaining Banks)," Shukan Toh-yo Keizai, April 17, 1999, pp. 30–33.

overlapping activities. It will be also important to weed out some of the overlapping subsidiaries and to integrate computer systems.[20]

The reorganization through integration of IBJ, Dai-Ichi and Fuji can be viewed as an eruption of "huge magma," or frustration, which has been accumulating deep in the Japanese financial market for the last ten years, and as a firm farewell to the "distressful past" and to fly out to a "challenging future." In that sense, it is an epoch-making attempt to put an end to the post-war financial history of Japan, and can even be called "a brilliant attempt."

What we should note here is the integration of IBJ, Dai-Ichi and Fuji is going to be achieved through a formation of a holding company, which is really the direction indicated in the reform plan for the financial system under the Japanese Big Bang, and it means that the reorganization of the Japanese financial system entered into a new phase. The Japanese banks, struggling under the heavy load of bad debts, had realized that they could not survive alone and they have insisted that "equal partner mergers" would not result in the elimination of inefficiency and their agony has thus persisted. The three banks recognized this "deficiency in reorganization," and chose to rely on the global standard of establishing a holding company and various subsidiaries, where each business can be more clearly defined.

Mr. Nishimura, the president of the Industrial Bank of Japan, stated during a press conference the reason for a holding company over a merger as follows:

"We thought the formation of a holding company to control subsidiary companies is the most effective approach from the standpoint of the optimum distribution of financial resources, speedier decision making, realization of efficient management, and quick response to customer needs."[21]

Thus the "Mega Bank" that is to be born as a result of the integration of the three banks is a grand experiment for the revitalization of the

---

[20] As to the content of the rationalization plans presented by Japanese banks associated with their public fund infusion request, see "Amounts of Funds 21 Banks Are Receiving and Their Rationalization Plans," Shukan Toh-yo Keizai, March 28, 1998, pp. 20–21.
[21] *Supra* note 18.

Japanese banks, and whether the Japanese financial institutions can survive or not depends on the result of this great experiment.

Japanese banks in the 2000s

Although ten years had passed since the bubble economy burst, and ¥7.2 trillion in public funds were poured into most of the Japanese banks in 1999 in order to beef up their net worth capital,[22] the profit figures of 131 major banks in 2003 did not show signs of the financial market's complete recovery from the damage incurred by the burst of the bubble economy (see Table 4). In 1996, ¥685 billion of tax money was used to liquidate the special housing loan companies (Jusen) that were burdened by enormous debts.[23] At that time, it looked as though that would settle the bad debts of banks, but it turned out that they were only at the start of the problem settlement.

Table 4 — Profits of 131 Japanese Banks from 2001-2003[24]
(Unit: 100 million yen)

	March 2001	March 2002	March 2003
Current Term Profit After Tax	41,989	48,515	7,799

The August 1995 annual report of the International Monetary Fund (IMF) criticized Japan's Banking Policy Administration for failing to take effective measures against the deterioration of its banking system.[25] The Board asked Japan to take speedy action to correct problematic banks. [26]   The report also stated that market mechanisms that are

---

[22] As to the details of the special housing loan companies' problems and public funds infusion, see Mitsuru Misawa, Lenders' Liability in the Japanese Financial Market — A Case of Jusen, the Largest Problem Loan in Japan, 31 Management Japan 19, 19–28 (1998).

[23] *Id.*

[24] Japanese Bankers Association, Statistical Data, available at http://www.zenginkyo. or.jp/stat/kessan/stat0503.html (Japanese) (last visited Dec. 27, 2004).

[25] Int'l Monetary Fund, 1996 Annual Report of the Executive Board 28 N.4, 30 (1997) (Citing Int'l Monetary Fund, International Capital Markets: Developments, Prospects, And Policy Issues (Aug. 1995)).

[26] *Id.* at 56.

supposed to help depositors and investors select banks are not working because of insufficient disclosures about the operating information of banks, and that it is necessary to establish a clear-cut rule specifying how the necessary funds for cleaning bad debts of problematic banks, including public funds, are to be born by the stakeholders.[27]

In August 1999, it was revealed that the net asset deficiency of the Long Term Credit Bank of Japan, Ltd. (LTCB)[28] at term's end (March 31, 1999) was ¥2.78 trillion. [29]   The report also pointed out that the government of Japan established the Financial Revitalization Law[30] to pave the way for nationalization of an asset deficient bank and subsequent transfer of its business to other banks.[31]   On September 28, 1999, the Financial Reconstruction Commission (FRC) [32] decided to

---

[27] *Id.* at 30, 55–56; see also Japanese Disclosures Not Showing Real Pictures, Nihon Keizai Shimbun [Nikkei Weekly] (Japan), Jan. 25, 1995 (discussing a way to solve the bad debts, referring also to the IMF's Aug. 1995 report).

[28] "Following the selection of the preferred acquirer of the Bank [LTCB]on March 1, 2000, all common shares of the LTCB were transferred to Partners [New LTCB Partners C.V., an investment group comprised of leading U.S. and European financial institutions and other investors], and as a result the temporary nationalization came to an end." Shinsei Bank, 2000 Annual Report 6 (Aug. 2000), available at http://www.shinsei-style.com/investors/en/ir/report/report_1999/pdf/ar00eng.pdf (last visited Nov. 9, 2004) [hereinafter Shinsei Bank 2000].   On June 5, 2000, the LTCB changed its name to Shinsei Bank, Limited.   With the name change, a new beginning was forged. To emphasize this, the Bank selected the name "Shinsei," because in Japanese it means "new birth."   It began operations anew as a private bank under new management.   *Id.* at 2.   Shinsei Bank, Limited is now located at 1–8, Uchisaiwaicho 2-chome, Chiyoda-Ku, Tokyo, Japan with ¥451.2 billion of capital and with 2,122 employees.   Shinsei Bank, Ltd., Company Profile, at http://www.shinsei-style.com/investors/en/about/ company/profile.html (citing information as of Mar. 31, 2004) (last visited Nov. 28, 2004).

[29] Shinsei Bank 2000, *Supra* note at 3.

[30] Law Concerning Emergency Measures for the Reconstruction of the Functions of the Financial System, No. 132 (1998), available at http://www.dpj.or.jp/seisaku/zaisei/BOX2192.html (Japanese) (last visited Dec. 27, 2004).

[31] Shinsei Bank, 2000, *Supra* note at 4; see also Shinsei Bank, 1999 Annual Report 1 (Sept. 1999), available at http://www.shinseibank.com/investors/en/ir/report/report_1998/pdf/ar99eng.pdf (last visited Nov. 28, 2004) [hereinafter Shinsei Bank 1999].

[32] The FRC was merged into the Financial Services Agency (FSA) on January 6, 2001. Financial Services Agency, Pamphlet 2, at http://www.fsa.go.jp./info/infoe/pamphlet_e.pdf (showing that the FRC was merged into the FSA on Jan. 6, 2000 (last visited Nov. 28, 2004).
The FRC had been working to restore stability and vitality in the financial system through quick resolution of failed financial institutions under the Financial Revitalization Law

transfer LTCB to "partners"[33] led by Ripple Wood Holdings, L.L.C. of the United States.[34] A sum of almost ¥4 trillion of public funds was poured into the bank to cover its bad loans, including its secondary losses.[35]

Upon the announcement of the examination results of nineteen major banks by the Financial Services Agency (FSA),[36] and immediately after the enactment of the Financial Revitalization Law, the Nippon Credit Bank, Ltd. (NCB)[37] was suddenly nationalized by the FSA on the

---

and capital injection into viable institutions using public funds under the Financial Function Early Strengthening Law [Law No. 143, 1998]. With these efforts, the environment surrounding financial institutions had on the whole regained stability.

Hideyuki Aizawa, Statement on Financial Policy for the Finance Committee, House of Representatives (Aug. 8, 2000), at http://www.fsa.go.jp/frc/infoe/ie004.html (last visited Nov. 9, 2004).

[33] Partners was established as a partnership by Ripplewood Holdings, L.L.C., of the United States, and other leading international financial institutions and investors, with the aim of acquiring LTCB. All investor groups participating in Partners have a long-term view of the Bank's development and most plan to sustain their investment for ten to fifteen years or longer. Shinsei Bank 2000, *Supra* note 7, at 6.

[34] Shinsei Bank 1999, *Supra* note 31 at 3.

[35] Shinsei Bank 2000, *Supra* note 28 at 6.

In view of the large amount of losses incurred in the disposal of nonperforming assets, at the time of the termination of temporary nationalization [LTCB] made an application for Special Financial Assistance (a monetary grant and a supplement to offset losses incurred in the conduct of the activities of a bank under temporary nationalization) to the Deposit Insurance Corporation (DIC) . . . . The total amount of this assistance was ¥3,588.0 billion.

Id.

[36] See Aizawa, *Supra* note 32. Aizawa states:

[T]he Financial Services Agency was created as of July 1, [2000,] with the integration of the Financial Supervisory Agency and the Financial System Planning Bureau of the Ministry of Finance. The new FSA has integral responsibility over planning of the financial system and supervision and inspection of financial institutions. In view of the rapid changes in the environment surrounding the economy and financial markets, the planning of the financial system . . . focus[ed] on building a stable and vigorous financial system and securing the efficiency and fairness in the financial markets. In the supervision and inspection of financial institutions, further efforts to maintain and improve the soundness of financial institutions will be made. Coordination with foreign financial authorities will be strengthened in order to cope adequately with the globalization of finance.

Id.; see also http://www.fsa.go.jp (providing further details of FSA).

[37] Takuya Fujii, President's introduction to Nippon Credit Bank, Ltd., 1999 Annual Report (July 1999), available at http://www.aozorabank.co.jp/en/company/ir/library/annual/download/annual1999/1999_1.pdf (last visited Nov. 28, 2004). On December 13,

grounds that the bank was net asset deficient.[38] It is important to note that the net worth ratios of LTCB and NCB were published at ten percent (10%) and eight percent (8%) respectively.[39]

As a result, criticisms against Japanese banks, like claims that they were not disclosing their operations accurately, were heard all over the world.[40] Japan's economy is the second largest in the world, next to that of the United States, and its financial and banking markets are one of the major ones in the world. International interest in the Japanese market and economy is ever-increasing. But Japanese corporate behavior and practice are raising a number of issues. One of the major issues involves Japan's accounting and reporting systems. This article will investigate the methods of processing bad loans and the disclosures practiced by

---

1998, the Prime Minister notified NCB of his decision to initiate Special Public Management of NCB pursuant to the Financial Revitalization Law (Law No. 132, 1998). *Id.* As a result, NCB was nationalized and the DIC acquired all of its shares on December 17, 1998. *Id.* The DIC appointed a new management team, effective December 25, 1998. *Id.* Then:

[o]n September 1, 2000, [NCB] ended its period of special public management that began on December 13, 1998 upon the closing of a Share Purchase Agreement dated June 30, 2000 for the transfer of the Bank's stock by the [DIC] to an investment group consisting of SOFTBANK CORP., ORIX Corporation, the Tokio Marine and Fire Insurance Co., Ltd., and other financial institutions. Operations of the new privately owned bank started on September 4, 2000. On September 5, [2000, NCB] applied for an enhancement of capital in accordance with the Financial Early Stabilization Law [Law No. 143, 1998] and submitted a Business Improvement Plan to the Financial Reconstruction Commission.).

Nippon Credit Bank, Ltd., 2000 Annual Report 1 (Oct. 2000), available at http://www.aozorabank.co.jp/en/company/ir/library/annual/download/annual2000/2000_ 1.pdf (last visited Nov. 28, 2004). NCB changed its name to Aozora Bank, Ltd. on January 4, 2001. Aozora Bank, Ltd. is located at 3-1, Kudan-minami 1-chome, Chiyoda-ku, Tokyo, Japan with ¥419.8 billion of capital and 1,345 employees. See generally Aozora Bank Online, at http://www.aozorabank.co.jp/en/company/ (last visited Nov. 28, 2004).

[38] John Choy, Nationalization of Nippon Credit Bank Fails to Quell Bad-Loan Fears, Japan Econ. Inst. Rep., Jan. 8, 1999, available at http://www.jei.org/Archive/ JEIR98/9847w1.html.

[39] See the announced financial figures for NCB and LTCB on http://www.nikkei. com (Japanese), on June 26, 1998 (LTCB's seventy-fourth term) and June 27, 1998 (NCB's sixty-fifth term). These ratios were calculated from the disclosed data for these banks. *Id.*

[40] Mitsuru Misawa, Daiwa Bank Scandal in New York: Its Causes, Significance and Lessons in the International Society, 29 Vand. J. Transnat'l L. 1023 (1996) (discussing the differences in disclosure systems existing between the United States and Japan).

Japanese banks. It will also study the legal requirements and accounting standards behind them. It seems that there are systems, as well as rules and regulations, unique to Japan that are substantially dissociated from international standards. With the world's second largest Gross National Income (GNI),[41] Japan is still an economic giant, making it important for the world to see a full recovery of its economy. Proper disposal of bad loans held by Japanese banks is critical to the recovery of the Japanese economy. The IMF, as well as the entire world, is watching to see how Japan plans to take care of this problem.

Bad Loans Under Prolonged Business Stagnation in Japan

The Economic Planning Agency (EPA)[42] strongly asserted that the major cause of the current deep downturn of the Japanese economy was the delay in the disposal of bad loans of financial institutions.[43] This was primarily caused by the private sector and the government which, as a result, aggravated the after effects of the burst of the "bubble" economy.[44] It is said that reasons for delaying the disposal of bad loans were: (1) optimism that merchandise and land prices would eventually go up again; (2) banks' failure to take necessary action because they waited to see what others would do as a result of their traditional conservatism;

---

[41] World Bank Group, Total GNI 2003, Atlas Method (Sept. 2004), available at http://www.worldbank.org/data/databytopic/GNI.pdf. The World Bank now uses GNI in constant dollars instead of Gross National Product (GNP), "which differs from GNP in that it also includes a terms of trade adjustment; and gross capital formation which now includes a third category of capital formation: net acquisition of valuables." World Bank, Change in Terminology, at http://www.worldbank.org/data/ changinterm.html (last visited Nov. 27, 2004).

[42] In 1997, the Economic Planning Agency (EPA) was absorbed into the Cabinet Office of the government due to the restructuring of Japanese government agencies. Most of the information about the EPA can be found in the website of the Cabinet Office at http://www.cao.go.jp/index-e.html.

[43] Research Bureau, EPA, The Japanese Economy in 1998: A review of events and challenges for the future: Recovering from the aftereffects of the bubble's collapse, Analysis of Economic Situations (Dec. 28, 1998), at http://www5.cao.go.jp/99/f/kaiko-e/kaiko-e.html.

[44] *Id.*

and (3) financial institutions' failure to sufficiently disclose information.[45]

Simultaneous to the EPA's announcement, the FSA published the results of its thorough inspection conducted on major banks. The result of the inspections conducted over the nineteen major banks (including LTCB and NCB) during the period of July 1998 through September 1998, indicated that even inspections of bad loans conducted by major banks were generally loose. A shortage of loan loss reserves totaling ¥5.40 trillion was revealed.[46]

In an April 2001 article, the Nikkei Weekly stated that, according to an FSA estimate, a sum of approximately ¥150 trillion was loaned to questionable borrowers.[47] In essence, it revealed that in addition to a sum of ¥81 trillion in questionable loans, previously identified by the FSA, ¥70 trillion continued to be lent out to questionable borrowers.[48] Their contents are as follows:

Table 5 — Breakdown of Loans Outstanding to Financial Institutions as of March 2000[49]
(Unit: trillions of yen)

	FSA's new statistics	Newly published questionable loans	Previously published questionable loans
Normal loans	522	N/A	N/A
Loans needing cautions	117	117	64
Loans with concerns of failures	21	21	11
Failed or essentially failed loans	13	13	6
Total	673	151	81

---

[45] *Id.*

[46] See Financial Services Agency Online, Loss on Disposal of Bad Loans of All Japanese Banks (1998), available at http://www.fsa.go.jp/p_fsa/news/newse/ne_002b. html (last visited Nov. 9, 2004) (charting nationwide bank loss figures for bad loans as of Sept. 1998).

[47] 22% of Loans Said Nonperforming, Nikkei Weekly (Japan), Apr. 23. 2001.

[48] *Id.*

[49] For statistics on bad loans according to the specific class of bank, see Financial Services Agency Online, Risk Management Loans of All Japanese Banks as of the End of March 2000 (2001), available at http://www.fsa.go.jp/news/newse/e20000728-1b.html (last visited Nov. 9, 2004).

In September 2001, Japanese retailer Mycal Corporation [50] was reportedly classified by its main banks as a borrower requiring caution since their loan loss provisions were believed to be no more than three to five percent. [51]   Mycal Corporation was a failed business from all practical standpoints.   With a debt of ¥1.74 trillion, the corporation applied for court mandated protection under the Civil Rehabilitation Law. [52]   The provision rate of three to five percent was obviously too low. [53]   Although the financial institutions claimed that this provision rate was estimated based upon the past records of businesses going down together, it was a questionable undertaking in light of the following facts: (1) past records had little significance when faced with an incredibly large amount of bad loans, which they had never previously experienced; and (2) the uncollectible amount was basically an estimate of the future amount and should have been evaluated on a case-by-case basis. [54]   As can be seen from this example, all parties involved (the FSA, financial institutions, and auditors) in the issue of reserves for bad debts were governed by old corporate accounting principles.

A closer look at NCB showed an asset deficiency of ¥94.4 billion as of March 1998 year-end.   The net asset deficiency included the unrealized loss of negotiable securities at ¥274.7 billion as well as its net worth ratio of zero, according to FSA's inspection result released in December 1998 (see Table 6). [55]   Since the bank announced in its closing public statement for fiscal year 1998 that its net worth ratio was 8%, it is

---

[50] Mycal Corporation, Company Profile, at http://www.mycal.co.jp (Japanese) (last visited Dec. 27, 2004). At the time of the application, Mycal Corporation was located in Osaka, Japan with capital of ¥74 million and 20,178 employees.

[51] See Mycal Goes Belly-Up After Banks Refuse to Extend Further Support, Nikkei Weekly (Japan), Sept. 17, 2001; Hajime Matsuura, Foreign brokers upset at stricter inspections, Nikkei Weekly (Japan), Sept. 25, 2001.

[52] Minjisaisei-ho [Civil Rehabilitation Act], Law No. 225 (1999) (Japan).

[53] See Bickering Continues over Bad-Loan Disposals, Nikkei Weekly (Japan), Oct. 9, 2001.

[54] Big Firms Going Under in Alarming Numbers, Nikkei Weekly (Japan), Nov. 5, 2001; see Banks Struggle To Master Risk Management, Nikkei Weekly (Japan), Nov. 19, 2001.

[55] Makoto Sato, Nationalization Threatens Convoy System: Supervisory Agency Faces Test in Closure of Nippon Credit Bank, Nikkei Weekly (Japan), Dec. 21, 1998, Finance, at 12.

clear that there is a significant difference between its own publicized value and the net value based on the inspection.

Table 6 — Correction for the NCB's Closing Statement for FY 3/98[56]

Net worth = A	¥467.1 billion
Deficiency in loan loss amortization and reserves = B	¥561.5 billion
Asset deficiency = (A-B)	¥94.4 billion
Unrealized loss of negotiable securities = C	¥180.3 billion
Net asset deficiency = (A-B-C)	¥274.7 billion

More importantly, it was reported that NCB, which was under special state control (temporary nationalization), had approximately ¥3 trillion of asset deficiency as of December 1998 (the point at which the bank was placed under the state special control). [57] This ¥3 trillion of asset deficiency was indeed ten times larger than the publicized ¥274.7 billion (see Table 6) asset deficiency at fiscal year-end March 1998. This indicates a large discrepancy between the publicized data and the actual data.

Realizing this ¥3 trillion asset deficiency, the Japanese government decided to infuse a sum of approximately ¥3.5 trillion of public funds and to transfer NCB to domestic financial institutions including SOFTBANK Corporation[58] and ORIX Corporation[59] (see Table 7).

---

[56] *Id.*; Asako Ishibashi, Another Bank Nationalization Looms: Government Deems Nippon Credit Bank Insolvent, Moves To Put Institution Under Temporary State Control, Nikkei Weekly (Japan) Dec. 14, 1998, at 1.

[57] NCB's Debts Exceed Assets by 3.04 Trillion Yen, Nikkei Weekly (Japan), June 21, 1999, at 10 [hereinafter NCB's Debts].

[58] Softbank Corporation, Corporate Profile, at http://www.softbank.co.jp/english/index.html (providing corporate information) (last visited Dec. 27, 2004).

[59] Orix Corp., Corporate Outline, at http://www.orix.co.jp/grp/co_e/index.htm (providing corporate and other general information) (last visited Dec. 27, 2004).

Table 7 — Infusion of Public Funds to NCB March 2002[60]

Reason for Infusion	Amount of Public Funds
To cover the asset deficiency	Approx. ¥3.2 trillion
Infusion for enhancing the capital after the transfer (preferred stock)	¥240 billion
Public funds infused in March 1998	¥60 billion
Burden sharing if a substantial loss occurs with the borrower after the transfer	Undetermined
Total	At least ¥3.5 trillion

Bibliography

"22% of Loans Said Nonperforming," Nikkei Weekly (Japan), Apr. 23. 2001.

Aizawa, H. Statement on Financial Policy for the Finance Committee, House of Representatives (Aug. 8, 2000), available at http://www.fsa.go.jp/frc/infoe/ie004.html (last visited Nov. 9, 2004).

"Amounts of Funds 21 Banks Are Receiving and Their Rationalization Plans," Shukan Toh-yo Keizai, March 28, 1998, pp. 20–21.

"Analysis of Economic Situations," Dec. 28, 1998, http://www5.cao.go.jp/99/f/kaiko-e/kaiko-e.html.

Aozora Bank Online, at http://www.aozorabank.co.jp/en/company/ (last visited Nov. 28, 2004).

"Bank's Public Fund Infusion Requests Lack Sincerity," Shukan Toh-yo Keizai, March 28, 1998, pp. 22–23.

"Banks Struggle To Master Risk Management," Nikkei Weekly (Japan), Nov. 19, 2001.

"Betrayal in the Bank Rescue Plan — Uncertainty That Can Not Be Wiped Out Even with Public Fund Infusion of 30 Trillion Yen," Shukan Toh-yo Keizai, March 28, 1998, pp. 14–16.

"Bickering Continues over Bad-Loan Disposals," Nikkei Weekly (Japan), Oct. 9, 2001.

"Big Bang Seeing the First Sign of Realization with the Public Fund Infusion," February 2, 1998, pp. 10–13.

"Big Firms Going Under in Alarming Numbers," Nikkei Weekly (Japan), Nov. 5, 2001

"BIS Ratio of Owned Capital," Shukan Toh-yo Keizai, February 2, 1998, p. 43.

Choy, J. Nationalization of Nippon Credit Bank Fails to Quell Bad-Loan Fears, Japan Econ. Inst. Rep., Jan. 8, 1999, available at http://www.jei.org/Archive/JEIR98/9847w1.html.

Corporate Income Tax Law (Law No. 34 of 1965, Japan).

"Curtailment of Financial Institutions — Last Decision (Disappearing Banks, Remaining Banks)," Shukan Toh-yo Keizai, April 17, 1999, pp. 30–33.

---

[60] Yoshihiro Fujii, Banks, Parent Firms Need Clear Lending Rules. Softbank Group Takeover of Nippon Credit Raises Questions of Probity, Nikkei Weekly (Japan), Mar. 13, 2000, at 7; NCB's Debts, *Supra* note 57 at 10; Makoto Sato, Naysayers Doubt Success of Nippon Credit Rebirth, Nikkei Weekly (Japan), Aug. 28, 2000.

Economic Planning Agency Cabinet Office, available at http://www.cao.go.jp/index-e.html.

Financial Services Agency Online, Risk Management Loans of All Japanese Banks as of the End of March 2000 (2001), available at http://www.fsa.go.jp/news/newse/e20000728-1b.html (last visited Nov. 9, 2004).

Financial Services Agency, Pamphlet 2, available at http://www.fsa.go.jp./info/infoe/pamphlet_e.pdf (last visited Nov. 28, 2004).

FSA, http://www.fsa.go.jp.

Fujii, T. President's introduction to Nippon Credit Bank, Ltd., 1999 Annual Report (July 1999), available at http://www.aozorabank.co.jp/en/company/ir/library/annual/download/annual1999/1999_1.pdf (last visited Nov. 28, 2004).

Fujii, Y. Banks, Parent Firms Need Clear Lending Rules. Softbank Group Takeover of Nippon Credit Raises Questions of Probity, Nikkei Weekly (Japan), Mar. 13, 2000, at 7.

Hajime Matsuura, "Foreign Brokers Upset at Stricter Inspections," Nikkei Weekly (Japan), Sept. 25, 2001.

"Ineffective Public Fund Infusion," Shukan Toh-yo Keizai, January 1, 1998, pp.10–14.

International Monetary Fund, 1996 Annual Report of the Executive Board 28 N.4, 30 (1997) (Citing Int'l Monetary Fund, International Capital Markets: Developments, Prospects, And Policy Issues (Aug. 1995)).

Ishibashi, A. Another Bank Nationalization Looms: Government Deems Nippon Credit Bank Insolvent, Moves To Put Institution Under Temporary State Control, Nikkei Weekly (Japan) Dec. 14, 1998, at 1.

Japanese Bankers Association, Statistical Data, available at http://www.zenginkyo.or.jp/stat/kessan/stat0503.html (Japanese) (last visited Dec. 27, 2004).

"Japanese Big Bang," Shukan Toh-yo Keizai, July 25, 1998, p. 43.

"Japanese Disclosures Not Showing Real Pictures," Nikkei Weekly (Japan), Jan. 25, 1995.

Law Concerning Emergency Measures for the Reconstruction of the Functions of the Financial System, No. 132 (1998), available at http://www.dpj.or.jp/seisaku/zaisei/BOX2192.html (Japanese) (last visited Dec. 27, 2004).

"Loss on Disposal of Bad Loans of All Japanese Banks (1998)," Financial Services Agency Online, available at http://www.fsa.go.jp/p_fsa/news/newse/ne_002b. html (last visited Nov. 9, 2004).

Minjisaisei-ho [Civil Rehabilitation Act], Law No. 225 (1999) (Japan).

Misawa, M. "Bad Loans of Japanese Banks — Directors' Civil and Criminal Liabilities," Fall edition, Temple International and Comparative Law Journal, December 2004, Volume 18, Number 2, pp. 101–127.

Misawa, M. "Lenders' Liability in the Japanese Financial Market — A Case of Jusen, the Largest Problem Loan in Japan," Management Japan, Volume 30, Number 2, Autumn 1997, pp.18–28 and Volume 31, Number 1, Spring 1998, pp.19–28.

Misawa, M. "Revitalization of Japanese Banks: Japan's Big Bang Reform", in: Risk Management, 2nd Revised and Enlarged Edition, Edited by Michael Frenkel, Ulrich Hommel, and Markus Rudolf, Springer 2005, pp. 801–820.

Misawa, M. Daiwa Bank Scandal in New York: Its Causes, Significance and Lessons in the International Society, 29 Vand. J. Transnat'l L. 1023 (1996).

Misawa, M., Lenders' Liability in the Japanese Financial Market — A Case of Jusen, the Largest Problem Loan in Japan, 31 Management Japan 19, 19–28 (1998).

Mycal Corporation, Company Profile, available at http://www.mycal.co.jp (Japanese) (last visited Dec. 27, 2004).

"Mycal Goes Belly-Up After Banks Refuse to Extend Further Support," Nikkei Weekly (Japan), Sept. 17, 2001.

"NCB and LTCB Financial Figures," Nikkei Weekly (Japan), http://www.nikkei. com (Japanese), June 26, 1998 (LTCB's seventy-fourth term) and June 27, 1998 (NCB's sixty-fifth term).

"NCB's Debts Exceed Assets by 3.04 Trillion Yen," Nikkei Weekly (Japan), June 21, 1999, at 10 [hereinafter NCB's Debts].

Nihon Keizai Shimbun, August 20, 1999, pp. 1–2.

Nihon Keizai Shimbun, August 29, 1999, p. 13.

Nippon Credit Bank, Ltd., 2000 Annual Report 1 (Oct. 2000), available at http://www.aozorabank.co.jp/en/company/ir/library/annual/download/annual2000/2000_1. pdf (last visited Nov. 28, 2004).

Orix Corp., Corporate Outline, available at http://www.orix.co.jp/grp/co_e/index.htm (providing corporate and other general information) (last visited Dec. 27, 2004).

"Pay-off," Shukan Toh-yo Keizai, February 2, 1998, p. 40.

Reaction to the New Development of Financial Intermediary Function, May 26, 1995.

"Reality of Banks' Bad Debts," Shukan Toh-yo Keizai, April 4, 1998, pp. 38–40.

"Reluctance to Lend phenomenon," Shukan Toh-yo Keizai, February 2, 1998, p. 49.

Sato, M. Nationalization Threatens Convoy System: Supervisory Agency Faces Test in Closure of Nippon Credit Bank, Nikkei Weekly (Japan), Dec. 21, 1998, Finance, at 12.

Sato, M. Naysayers Doubt Success of Nippon Credit Rebirth, Nikkei Weekly (Japan), Aug. 28, 2000.

"Severity of the Crisis as Indicated in Key Words," Shukan Toh-yo Keizai, Feb. 2, 1998, p. 46.

Shinsei Bank, 1999 Annual Report 1 (Sept. 1999), available at http://www.shinseibank.com/investors/en/ir/report/report_1998/pdf/ar99eng.pdf (last visited Nov. 28, 2004).

Shinsei Bank, 2000 Annual Report 6 (Aug. 2000), available at http://www.shinsei-style.com/investors/en/ir/report/report_1999/pdf/ar00eng.pdf (last visited Nov. 9, 2004) [hereinafter Shinsei Bank 2000].

Shinsei Bank, Ltd., Company Profile, available at http://www.shinsei-style.com/investors/en/about/ company/profile.html (citing information as of Mar. 31, 2004) (last visited Nov. 28, 2004).

Softbank Corporation, Corporate Profile, available at http://www.softbank.co.jp/english/index.html (providing corporate information) (last visited Dec. 27, 2004).

"Why Banks Made Big Mistakes?" Shukan Toh-yo Keizai, March 28, 1998, pp. 30–34.

World Bank Group, Total GNI 2003, Atlas Method (Sept. 2004), available at http://www.worldbank.org/data/databytopic/GNI.pdf.

World Bank, Change in Terminology, available at http://www.worldbank.org/data/changinterm.html (last visited Nov. 27, 2004).

Chapter 4

Banks and Bad Loans in Japan

Part One

Bad Loans: A Comparative Study of US and Japanese Regulations Concerning Loan Loss Reserves[a]

In this article, the author investigates the methods of processing bad loans and disclosures practiced by Japanese banks. The author also compares the differing United States and Japanese legal regulations and business practices, concluding that the various rules and regulations concerning loan loss reserves in Japan are very much behind those of the United States.

In August 1995, annual report of the International Monetary Fund ("IMF"),[1] Japan's banking policy administration was criticized, accused of failing to take effective measures against the deterioration of its

---

[a] This chapter is based on the author's previously published articles.
1. Mitsuru Misawa, "Bad Loans: A Comparative Study of US and Japanese Regulations Concerning Loan Loss Reserves," The Banking Law Journal, November/December 2004, Volume 121, Number 10, pp. 918–946.
2. Mitsuru Misawa, "Laws and Regulations on Problem Loans in Japan — Is Application of International Accounting Standards Possible?" Columbia Journal of Asian Law, Vol. 18, No. 1, Fall 2004, pp. 1–45.

[1] IMF, Annual Report, 1996, "International Market," p. 29.

banking system. The report further pointed out that "waiting would not recover the loss, but rather increase it," and asked Japan to take speedy action to correct problematic banks. The report also stated that market mechanisms that were supposed to help depositors and investors in selecting banks were not working because of insufficient disclosures of the operating information of the banks, and it was necessary to establish a clear-cut rule specifying how the necessary funds for cleaning bad debts of the problematic banks, including public funds, were to be borne by the stakeholders.[2]

The Economic Planning Agency ("EPA")[3] strongly asserted that the major cause of the current deep downturn of the Japanese economy was the delay in the disposal of bad loans of financial institutions. This is primarily caused by the private sector and the government, which as a result aggravated the aftereffects of the burst of the "bubble" economy. It is said that reasons for delaying the disposal of bad loans were:

1. optimism that merchandise and land prices would eventually go up again;
2. as a result of their traditional conservatism, waiting to see what others would do, the banks failed to take necessary action and;
3. the financial institutions failed to sufficiently disclose information.[4]

Simultaneous with the EPA's announcement, the FSA published the results of the thorough inspection conducted on major banks.   The result of the inspections conducted over the major 19 banks (including LTCB and NCB) during the period of July through September 1998 indicated that even inspections of bad loans conducted by major banks were

---

[2] An article titled, "Japanese disclosures not showing real pictures," appeared on the January 25, 1995 issue of Nihon Keizai Shinbun (Japan Economic Journal, hereafter "Nikkei"), and discussed a way to solve the bad debts, referring also to the IMF's report.

[3] In 1997, the Economic Planning Agency ("EPA") was absorbed into the Cabinet Office of the government due to the restructuring of Japanese government agencies. Most of the information about the EPA can be found in the web site of the Cabinet Office at http://www.cao.go.jp/index-e.html.

[4] Economic Planning Agency, "Retrospect and Tasks of Japanese Economy," December 27, 1998.

generally loose, revealing a total shortage of loan loss reserves of ¥5.40 trillion.[5]

In an article that appeared in April 2001, the Nikkei stated that, according to an FSA estimate, a sum of approximately ¥150 trillion was loaned to questionable borrowers. In essence, it revealed that in addition to a sum of ¥81 trillion in questionable loans as previously identified by the FSA, ¥70 trillion continued to be lent out to questionable borrowers.

In September 2001, Japan retailer Mycal Corporation,[6] a failed business from all practical standpoints with a debt of ¥1.74 trillion that applied for court-mandated protection under the Civil Rehabilitation Law,[7] was reported to have been classified by its main banks as a borrower needing cautions as its provision rate of loan loss reserve was believed to be no more than three to five percent.[8] This provision rate was obviously too low. Although the financial institutions claimed that this provision rate was estimated based upon the past records of businesses going down together, it was a questionable undertaking in light of the following facts: that past records had little significance when facing an incredibly large amount of bad loans, which it had never previously experienced, and that the uncollectible amount was basically an estimate of the future amount, and should have been evaluated on a case by case basis. As can be seen from this example, all parties involved (the FSA, financial institutions, and auditors) in the issue of reserves for bad debts were governed by old corporate accounting principles.

A closer look at NCB showed an asset deficiency of ¥94.4 billion as of the March 1998 year-end and the net asset deficiency including the unrealized loss of negotiable securities at ¥274.7 billion, as well as its net worth ratio at zero, according to the FSA's inspection result released in

---

[5] Nikkei, April 8, 2001, p. 3.
[6] At the time of the application, Mycal Corporation was located in Osaka, Japan with capital of ¥74 million and with 20,178 employees. For details, see http://www.mycal.co.jp/.
[7] Law No. 225 of 1999, as amended as Law No. 128 in 2000. For details, see http://www.ron.gr.jp/law/law/minji_sa.htm.
[8] Nikkei, September 15, 2001, p. 1.

December 1998.[9] Since the bank announced in the closing public statement for the March 1998 fiscal year-end that its net worth ratio was eight percent, it was clear that there was a significant difference between its own publicized value and the net value based on the inspection.

More importantly, it was reported that NCB, which was under special state control (temporary nationalization), had approximately ¥3 trillion of asset deficiency as of December 1998 (the point the bank was placed under the state special control).[10] This ¥3 trillion of asset deficiency was indeed ten times larger than the publicized ¥274.7 billion (Table 2) asset deficiency of the FY3/98 year-end. This indicated a large discrepancy between the publicized data and the actual data.

Realizing this ¥3 trillion asset deficiency, the Japanese government decided to infuse a sum of approximately ¥3.5 trillion of public funds and to transfer NCB to domestic financial institutions including SOFTBANK Corporation[11] and ORIX Corporation.[12,13]

Japanese Corporate Accounting Principles

Why were such loose loan loss reserve practices allowed in Japan? One of the reasons can be found in the "Corporate Accounting Principles"[14] established in 1949 based on the Commercial Code of Japan.[15] More specifically, the "Corporate Accounting Principles" were generated as an interim report by the Corporate Accounting Rule Investigative

---

[9] Nikkei, December 14, 1998, p. 1.

[10] Nikkei, June 13, 1999, p. 4.

[11] Holding company, started out as wholesaler of PC software and publisher of PC magazine. Head office located at 24-1, Nihonbashi-Hakozakicho, Chuo-ku, Tokyo 103-8501, Japan. Sales as of March 2003 were 440,000 million yen.

[12] Largest general leasing company. Diversifying into life insurance, securities, and trust banking. Head office located at 3-22-8, Shiba, Minatoku, Tokyo 105-8683, Japan. Sales as of March 2003 were 600,000 million yen.

[13] Nikkei, March 7, 2000, p. (7).

[14] July 9, 1949, as amended in July 14, 1954, November 5, 1961, August 30, 1972 and April 20, 1980 (hereinafter cited "Corporate Accounting Principles"). For details, see wysiwyg://18/http://www.ron.gr.jp/law/etc_txt/kigyokai.htm.

[15] Law No. 48, enacted on March 9, 1899, amended 18 times (hereafter cited as the "Commercial Code"). For details see wysiwyg://6/http://www.ron.gr.jp/law/law/syouhou1.htm.

Committee of the Economic Stabilization Agency[16] in 1949 and the "Annotations to Corporate Accounting Principles" as an interim report by the Corporate Accounting Council of the Ministry of Finance[17] in 1950.

According to its preamble, it states that "The Corporate Accounting Principles consist of the summary of practices recognized as generally fair and reasonable among those practices evolved within actual corporate accounting works and they represent the rules to be abided by all corporations in processing their accountings without really having to be regulated by the laws and regulations."

In the "Corporate Accounting Principles," there is a description entitled "On Reserves," which states, "When there is a specific expense or loss that may result from a phenomenon occurred prior to the current term, whose probability of occurrence is high, and whose amount can be logically estimated, the amount that belongs to the burden of the current term is accounted for as the current term's expense or loss in the reserve, and the balance of said reserve is written on the debt side or the asset side of the balance sheet."[18] It also shows 11 items including loan loss reserves as examples. It also states that "no reserve can be accounted for expenses or losses concerning a contingent phenomenon of a low probability of occurrence." That is all that this accounting standard has and no specific rulings can be found.

Consequently, in Japanese accounting, it is customary to honor traditional accounting practices as the practical rule to follow. This has bred a tendency for companies to look around and follow whatever others do. This did not present any shortcoming when the economy was all but rosy in the years after World War II, but the same practice is now causing a problem as it inevitably creates loose reserve formats everywhere generating an enormous amount of bad loans, which no one

---

[16] It was established in the government as a control organ to restore the Japanese economy after World War II in 1946 and was abolished in 1952 since it finished the functions. See the details at http://www.nira.go.jp/pubj/seiken/v08n07.html.

[17] The Ministry of Finance was reorganized on January 6, 2001. The name was changed from Okurasho to Zaimucho in Japanese, but the English name still remains the same. For the more information about the reorganization, see http://www.mof.go.jp.

[18] Corporate Accounting Principle, Art. 18.

has ever previously experienced. The reality of accounting scenes includes a backward calculation of "amortization source assets" such as unrealized stock profits. In other words, the total amount of funds that can be allocated for reserves is first determined, and then bad loans are assessed while adjusting the reserves so that they can fit into the range. Therefore, there can be no bad loan processing that exceeds the amortization source assets.[19]

The "Corporate Accounting Principles" have the dominating power in Japan. For example, an auditor has to issue a favorable opinion as long as accounting is done in accordance to "Corporate Accounting Principles." Therefore, we can safely assume that the root cause of the delay in determining the amounts of bad loans lies in the basic philosophy of the "Corporate Accounting Principles." A loan balance after deducting reserves must be indicated in a "net realizable value" if the US accounting standard is applied. In this case, the particular Japanese accounting procedure can be considered a fraudulent act under the US standard. This will be discussed below.

An accounting standard, from the international standpoint, is a generally accepted rule, resulting from research and development geared for proper representation of accounting practices. It is not something that evolved through mere practices, but rather something that has developed theoretically and is meant to be applied to the practices in order to provide proper information disclosure. The accounting standards used in the US and Europe are researched and upgraded constantly by permanently established organizations in order to keep up with economic changes. The Japanese "Corporate Accounting Principles" that were developed more than half a century ago are extremely different from today's international standards and are no longer fit for today's economy.[20]

---

[19] Refer to "BOJ and FSA, Which is Wrong?" by Tsuyoshi Kimura, pp. 118-125. Bungei Shunju, October 2001 issue.   According to the author, a strange phenomenon is that the total amount of reserve is decreasing while the remaining balance of the bad loans is increasing, exemplifying the abovementioned condition occurring in the actual process. He also criticizes the Japanese banks for unduly delaying the clean up process of bad loans.

[20] The term "accounting principles" is not a term recognized internationally.   It is called "Financial Accounting Standards" in the United States, and will be called "International

The problem is that even the FSA of Japan is still honoring the existing "Corporate Accounting Principles." The FSA also provides administrative services for the Corporate Accounting Rule Council,[21] which had prepared the accounting principles. In addition, it also has the Banking Supervisory Agency[22] under its wing. It is in a position to improve the accounting principles if any problems with the principles are identified. The biggest problem lies in the fact that the administrative offices of the Japanese government are not realizing the importance of the accounting standard.[23]

Japanese Legal Regulations on Bad Loans

Since an enterprise operates based on the profit ratio of capital, it must regularly identify the change in its assets and the profit/loss results. For a joint-stock corporation in which a plurality of stockholders participate with a common object of sharing the earned profit of the corporation, the only collateral for creditors is the asset of the corporation. The corporate accounting, which is the technique of recording the performance of the corporation objectively and accurately, is not only necessary for rational management for the corporation but also indispensable for the protection of stockholders and creditors. Thus, the corporate accounting, in which a great many people have interest, incorporates regulations established

---

Financial Reporting Standards ("IFRS")" by the International Accounting Standard Board (30 Cannon St. London EC4M 6XH, U.K. hereafter, "IASB") in its new standard to be published. For the details of IASB, see http://www.iasc.org.uk/cmt/0001.asp.

[21] See *supra* note 24.

[22] See *supra* note 8.

[23] Prime Minister Koizumi frequently conferred with Minister of the FSA, Yanagisawa, in order to press forward on the fundamental clean up of the bad loan problems as his pet project of the reform he is pushing. The FSA resisted the change claiming that they "cannot issue policies that contradict with the traditional financial administration policies and accounting principles," which clearly shows FSA's poor understanding of the bad loan problems. For detail, see Nikkei, September 21, 2002 issue, p. 3.

along the purposes of the Commercial Code,[24] the Security Exchange Law,[25] and the Corporate Tax Law.[26]

Commercial Code

The part of the corporate accounting regulations related to the Commercial Code are used to place its evaluation basis for the corporation asset on liquidation and conversion into money from the standpoint of protecting corporate creditors. In other words, its basic philosophy is centered around the asset purpose, wherein a balance sheet is prepared by the inventory method based on a list of assets prepared in accordance with the current value principle. This position of asset calculation is definitely unreasonable. The investment attitude of a stockholder is usually determined by the profit and loss of the corporation as an on-going concern in an operating year, its causes, and its contents, rather than by the quantity of the assets the corporation holds. The profit and loss calculation method by means of distributing costs and profits over periods based on the assumption of the corporation being a going concern is more agreeable with the corporation's creditors as well, if not neglecting the assets held by the corporation totally. Thus, the current Commercial Code upholds the period profit and loss calculation method, and its balance sheet is prepared directly from accounting books by means of the derivative method.[27]

---

[24] *See supra* note 17.

[25] Law No. 25, enacted on April 13, 1948, amended 27 times, (hereinafter cited "Securities Exchange Law"). For details, see http://www.houko.com/00/01/S23/025.htm.

[26] Law No. 34, enacted on March 31, 1965, amended many times, (hereinafter cited the "Corporate Tax Law"). For the details, see http://www.houko.com/00/01/S40/034.htm.

[27] Commercial Code, Article 33 provides,
1. The following matters shall systematically and clearly be stated in the accounting books:
   (1) Business properties and values thereof at the commencement of business and once in each year at a fixed time, as for a company, business properties and values thereof at the time of incorporation and at each settlement of accounts;
   (2) Transactions, and other matters which give influence to business properties.

Although a detailed regulation concerning the accounting of a joint-stock corporation can be found in the Commercial Code,[28] the rules of the Commercial Code's General Regulations Concerning Commercial Books[29] are applied to items that are not specifically defined there. It is also requested that "fair accounting practices should be considered" in interpreting the existing rules.[30] While the accounting of a joint-stock corporation is interpreted as being intended for adjusting personal interests between individuals, especially for regulating the dividends, there are overlapping areas between the aforementioned "Corporate Accounting Principles" and the Commercial Code in terms of rules for representation. The Commercial Code seems to have a higher weight on the "fairness" portion in the "fair and reasonable" practices that the "Corporate Accounting Principles" is asking for.

The rules of the Commercial Code regarding bad loans specify that if concerns exist about being unable to collect the money claims written

---

2. A balance sheet shall be prepared based on accounting books at the time of commencement of business and once in each year at a fixed time; and a company shall prepare it based thereon at the time of incorporation and at each settlement of accounts.

3. A balance sheet shall be compiled and bound together, or shall be entered in a book specially kept for that purpose.

4. A balance sheet shall contain the signature of the person who prepared it.

[28] Commercial Code, Article 281 provides;

1. The Directors shall prepare the following documents and the annexed specifications thereof every period for settlement of accounts:
   (1) A balance sheet;
   (2) A profit and loss account;
   (3) A business report;
   (4) Proposals relating to the reserve fund and the distribution of profits or interest.

2. The documents under the preceding paragraph need be audited by the auditors.

[29] Commercial Code, Articles 32-36. Commercial Code, Article 32 provides:

1. Every trader shall prepare accounting books and balance sheets for making clear the conditions of business properties and profit and loss.

2. In construing the provisions concerning preparation of the books of account, authentic accounting practices shall be taken into consideration.

[30] Commercial Code, Article 285-4 provides:

1. The monetary claims shall be valued at the nominal amount thereof; provided that, if they were purchased at the proceeds lower than the nominal amount or there is any reasonable ground, they shall be valued with reasonable decrease.

2. If there is a fear of being impossible to collect the monetary claims, the estimated amount of being impossible to collect shall be deducted in valuation.

in the liquid asset category, it should be written in such a manner as to deduct the estimated uncollectible amount (bad loan reserve) for each item that each money claim belonged to, or showing only the balance after deducting the estimated uncollectible amount indicating the estimated uncollectible amount as a footnote.[31] It is also stipulated that if a reserve is to be accounted for, with respect to an amount that is expected to be uncollectible, the said reserve is not necessarily a liability in the legal sense. It is a reserve prepared for a specific expense in the future or an estimate of a cost so that it is allowed to be written in a section of reserves provided in the liabilities area, wherein that reserve needs to be entered with a specific label indicting the purpose of its entering.[32]

That is as far as the Commercial Code goes, and there are no specific rules that advise how bad loans are to be handled. This also leaves a corporation to openly maneuver for bad loans as it wishes.

Securities Exchange Law

The Securities Exchange Law[33] stipulates the terms, formats and methods in the preparation of a balance sheet, a profit and loss statement, and other documents related to financial calculations. Items that are submitted in accordance with the law have to also be prepared in accordance with the rules generally recognized as fair and reasonable using the terms, formats and method of preparation specified in the Ministry of Finance ("MOF")[34] Ordinance.[35]

---

[31] Commercial Code, Article 287-2 provides:
1. When the preparation money is accounted on the debit side of the balance sheet for preparing against a specified defrayal or loss, the purpose thereof shall be made clear in the balance sheet.
2. If the preparation money under the preceding paragraph is used for the purpose other than its proper purpose, the reason shall be stated in the profit and loss account.

[32] Article 287, Section 2.

[33] *See supra* note 33. For the development of Tokyo Stock Market, see Misturu Misawa, "Tokyo as an International Capital Market — Its Economics and Legal Aspects," 8 Vanderbilt Journal of Transnational Law 1-38 (1974).

[34] *See supra* note 17.

[35] Article 193.

The essence of this ordinance is, first, from a formatting perspective, to define the method of preparing the documents and others based on an assumption that issuing companies are obligated to submit financial calculation documents. [36] Next, from a more practical standpoint, financial calculation documents provide extremely important information as they are related to the evaluations of the subject negotiable securities among the variety of information provided concerning the issuing company at the time of share placement or public offering of stocks. Based on this, the ordinance favors regulating representations in such a way that they be prepared based on a non-interruptive, uniform standard so that period and position comparisons can be easily performed. Therefore, this ordinance supports making administrative investigations smoother and faster, and increasing the fairness of transactions by providing more accurate representations while allowing them to be handled in a smoother fashion through a rational format that facilitates faster analyses.

The orders of the MOF, created in line with the rules of this ordinance are known as the Rules on Financial Statements, [37] the Rules of Consolidated Financial Statements, [38] and the Rules of Intermediate Financial Statements. [39] In these ministerial orders and related notices, the items that are not specified are supposed to follow the "corporate accounting practices generally accepted as fair and reasonable." For example, the Rules on Financial Statements explain, "The items that are not defined in these rules shall follow the corporate accounting practices generally accepted as fair and reason-able." [40] In other words, the Rules on Financial Statements is a ministerial order consigned by the Securities Exchange Law to add rules on representation in order to accomplish the object of the law. We must pay attention to the fact that the basic

---

[36] Article 24 stipulates that the issuer of securities must submit a Securities Report ("Yukashoken Hokokusho").

[37] The MOF Ordinance No. 36, issued on November 27, 1963. For details see http://www.mof.go.jp/hourei.htm.

[38] The MOF Ordinance No. 28, issued on October 30, 1976. For details, see http://www.mof.go.jp/hourei.htm.

[39] The MOF Ordinance No. 24, issued on March 30, 1999. For details, see http://www.mof.go.jp/hourei.htm.

[40] Article 1-1.

philosophy of the rules promotes healthy, democratic development of the national economy, which is the purpose of the "Corporate Accounting Principles" under the Commercial Code. The concept of the "corporate accounting practices generally accepted as fair and reasonable" mentioned here matches the concept of the "Corporate Accounting Principles," which has a ruling capability as a custom.

A concept of the modern accounting philosophy was clearly shown in the "Corporate Accounting Principles" under the Commercial Code as it placed importance on the profit and loss calculation for a particular period, assuming that the particular corporation is of on-going concern. However, the "Corporate Accounting Principles" does not have any enforcing power so its ability to perform as a legal code depends on how it is defined and interpreted in the Commercial Code and the Securities Exchange Law.

The corporate accounting principles also based on the Securities Exchange Law define the standards for processing bad loans as shown above, but it is also notable that they do not require them to be disclosed by footnotes. The Securities Exchange Law was introduced after World War II copying the same laws established in 1933 and 1934 in the United States.[41,42] When it comes to the corporate accounting principles and other rules that are required for the full implementation of the laws, it has yet to be developed to reach the international level. This is why one wonders whether the Japanese accounting standard can be trusted.

It is worth noting that some of the financial statements are required to include a legend as requested by the US[43] According to the current rule, it is necessary for financial statements of some Japanese corporations written in English to have notations (legends) such as "This

---

[41] They are the United States Securities Act of 1933 and of the Securities Exchange Act of 1934. *See* 15 U.S.C. §§ 77a-77mm (1934), as amended, 15 U.S.C. §§ 77a-77mm (1970) and 15 U.S.C. §§ 78a-78jj (1934), as amended, 15 U.S.C. §§ 78a-78hh (1) (1970).

[42] Refer to Mitsuru Misawa, Securities Regulation in Japan, 6 *Vanderbilt Journal of Transnational Law* 447–510 (1973), on the history of how the Japanese Security Exchange Law was established.

[43] This inclusion of the legend was requested by the Big 5 accounting firms of the US For the details of the backgrounds of the requests, see http://glovia.fujitsu.com/jp/cybersmr/e4-1.html.

is prepared in accordance with the Japanese Securities Exchange Law and accounting standard, and not under the accounting standards of any other countries."[44] This means that the Japanese accounting process is no longer trusted internationally because of Japan's closed-mindedness and its insensitivity to what is happening internationally.[45] The problem does not lie with the corporations that are forced to write such statements but rather the problem is derivative of the accounting system of Japan. The parties who are negatively affected as a result of these immature accounting standards are the corporations who fail to be trusted and investors (users of the financial statements) who cannot obtain accurate information.

---

[44] The following is an example of a legend. "Summary of Significant Accounting Policies. Basis of presentation, Nissan Motor Co., Ltd. (the "Company") and its· domestic subsidiaries maintain their books of account in conformity with the financial accounting standards of Japan, and its foreign subsidiaries maintain their books of account in conformity with those of the countries of their domicile. The accompanying consolidated financial statements have been prepared in accordance with accounting principles and practices generally accepted in Japan and are compiled from the consolidated financial statements filed with the Minister of Finance as required by the Securities Exchange Law of Japan. Accordingly, the accompanying consolidated financial statements are not intended to present the consolidated financial position, results of operations and cash flows in accordance with accounting principles and practices generally accepted in countries and jurisdictions other than Japan." For detail, please obtain a pdf file of Nissan's Annual Report from the Nissan's home page on the Internet. The legends of cautionary statements can only be found in the English version of financial statements based on the Japanese Securities Exchange Law, not in any financial statements of SEC registered companies prepared based on the US Accounting Standards. See, for example, Nissan Motor's Annual Report, 2002, p. 57. (http://www.infinitinews.com/nav.html).

[45] Nippon Keidanren (Japan Business Federation, equivalent to the Business Round-table in the US), in which its mission is to achieve a private sector-led, vital and affluent economy and society in Japan, for which it is demonstrating its leadership in setting the path for the country, is officially against the inclusion of the legend, and advocates the necessity of internationalizing Japanese accounting standards. For Nippon Keidanren's announcement of the issue, *see* http://www.keidan-ren.or.jp/japanese/policy/2001/013/honbun.html. For the Keidanren, see http://www.keidanren.or.jp/english/profile/pro001.html.

Corporate Tax Laws

There is a specific and detailed rule in Japanese tax law outlining the limit that can be reserved for bad debts. The corporate tax law[46] stipulates the following four kinds of limits of the loan loss reserves:
1. a method of reserving at a fixed rate for each business type;
2. a reserving method based on the rate of lending loss in the past;
3. reserving 50 percent of the outstanding loans as the fixed outstanding loan depreciation special account when the debtor is banned from bill clearing transactions, applies for the protection under the corporate reorganization law[47] or the bankruptcy law,[48] or declares the account clearance; and
4. a method of appropriating the reserve amount approved by the director of the governing tax office as a loss when the debtor is incapable of repayment and an asset deficient condition is continuing for a substantial period.[49]

Since the tax law includes such specific and detailed rules, a consensus and custom have developed to show that it is safe to follow the abovementioned first method, i.e., "a method of reserving at a fixed rate" as specified in the tax law. It seems that corporations conveniently relied on the tax law as the accounting standard lacks detailed regulations. In other words, we cannot deny the fact that the tax law played the role of the general accounting standard.

Thus, the rules of the corporate tax law played a major role in the accounting practices for loan loss reserves until the calculation of limits for loan loss reserves was fundamentally changed in 1998.[50] Thus, the difference between the corporate accounting and the tax accounting was not recognized until the rule of statutory reserve rate as mentioned above in the first method, i.e., appropriating a fixed rate of loan loss reserves, was cancelled by the tax law revision in 1998 to be gradually

---

[46] Law No. 34 enacted on March 31, 1965, amended 46 times thereafter. *See* details at http://www.houko.com/00/01/S40/034.htm.
[47] Law No. 172 enacted on June 7, 1952, amended on December 13, 2002 (Law No. 154). For details, see wysiwyg://8/http://www.ron.gr.jp/law/law/kaishak1.htm.
[48] Law No. 71 enacted on April 25, 1922, amended 11 times thereafter. For details, see http://www.houko.com/00/01/T11/071.htm.
[49] Article 52.
[50] Revised on April 1, 1998.

implemented by 2002. The tax law and the corporate accounting principle are essentially two different things as the tax law is determined by the Diet in order to pursue various policies from time to time, while the corporate accounting is for showing the performance of a corporation. As the rule of the abovementioned tax law indicates, the rule of the tax law is a calculation method that cannot be an evaluation standard for securities on the closing date. The loan loss reserves in corporate accounting are used for estimating the loan loss reserves on the closing date, so that the credits, less the loan loss reserves, should show the "collectible amount," but the tax law does not use it as the basis of the calculation.

Legal Precedents

There has been no legal case concerning the amount of loan loss reserves fought on any civil court in Japan. However, there have been several cases wherein the responsibilities of bank managements are challenged, accused of having failed to appropriate sufficient amounts of reserves while realizing that they are dealing with bad loans and thus camouflaging the existences of the bad loans.

Consider the situation of LTCB as the leading case.[51] This is a case in which the court denied any claim of responsibility of the managers.

Outline of the Case

This was a case wherein the plaintiff (bankruptcy administrator) sued the defendants (the bank president and other directors at the time of the incident); the defendants' bank, which was known as the Japan Long Term Credit Bank of Japan, Ltd. ("LTCB") at the time of the incident, lent ¥6 billion to E.I.E. International[52] ("Non-Litigant Company") on April 27, 1990 ("Loan") and further extended the repayment term of the

---

[51] Claim for damage, Tokyo District Court, Heisei 11 (Wa) No. 28167, Judgment delivered on July 18, 2002.

[52] The company, a resort development company, filed a bankruptcy claim on June 21, 2000 with the debt of ¥ 609 billion. For details, see http://www.tv-tokyo.co.jp/wbs/2000/06/21/news_day/f3.html.

Loan on July 26, 1990 ("Extension"). The plaintiff, still unable to collect a portion of the loan because the Non-Litigant Company subsequently bankrupted, asked the defendant directors for payment of a portion of the uncollectible money and the delay damages thereof based on the right to seek damages on the reason of breach of fiduciary duty on the director's part approving the Loan and the Extension.

Issues

The plaintiff claimed as follows citing that there was a breach of fiduciary duty on the part of the defendants:

> Bank directors should manage their banks with a priority focus on maintaining health and safety, limiting the directors' judgment power in situations of loaning needs. As a person authorized to decide the lending, the director has to make an appropriate judgment on the probability of loan collection only after thoroughly investigating the borrower's financial and operating conditions, manager's capability, assets, credit information of the past, the loan amount and purpose, repayment capability, method of acquiring funds for repayment and probability (including other outstanding loans and repayment statuses), collaterals that can be offered and the values thereof, etc., as well as the present and future economic trend (business trend and asset price trend including the expansion or decline). Also, if borrowers whose financial status is deteriorating as a result of deteriorating profit and fund liquidity request additional loans, the director must make proper judgment on whether such an additional loan should be executed based on aggressive investigations of the borrower company's management status and future outlook, as well as comparison of the portions of the total loan estimated to be collectible in cases the additional loan is made and also based on the reason for the borrower's request for the additional loan and collateral.

In reality, the Loan lacked a decent collectibility outlook and needs, so that the execution should have been stopped.

Court's Judgment

The Loan was approved on a judgment based on the related departments' analyses and evaluations of information collected and accumulated systematically by the bank through its historical transactions with the Non-Litigant Company, under a constraint of time limitation, coming to a conclusion that there was a need for the Loan and that there was no concern about loan collection in consideration of the measures taken for securing debt collection. One has to see that there is no evidence that there was any error beyond the scope of the judgment requirements either on the fact recognition, which is the basis of the judgment, or in the contents of the judgment under the circumstance.

Therefore, it seems that there was no breach of fiduciary duty by the defendants as the loan approval decision makers in the decision made on the Loan.

Comment

The problem with the decision of this case is that the court only decided that there was no fiduciary duty on the part of the directors concerning the point that the problem of insufficient collateral for the Loan was temporarily camouflaged by executing an additional loan. However, the suit was not fought on the point if there was a sufficient loan loss reserve against the possibility of the borrower becoming unable to pay back, and the court did not either make any judgment on that point or seek potential negligence of the defendants. As seen later it looks as if it is possible to make a claim of breach of fiduciary duty on the part of the defendants on said point for cases in the US In essence, it seems that it is difficult to seek legal responsibility for such negligence in Japan because there is no solid legal requirement for loan loss reserves, as seen above.

Regulations on Bad Loans in the US

SEC Laws

The SEC relies on an independent, private sector standards-setting process that is thorough, open, and deliberate. While the SEC has the statutory authority to set accounting principles, it has looked to the private sector for leadership in establishing and improving accounting standards.[53] Therefore, the quality of US accounting standards may be attributed in large part to the private sector standards-setting process, as overseen by the SEC.

The primary private sector standards-setter is the Financial Accounting Standards Board (the "FASB"), which was established in 1972. The FASB's standards are designated as the primary level of "generally accepted accounting principles," which is the framework for accounting. The FASB's standards set forth recognition, measurement, and disclosure principles to be used in preparing financial statements.

The accounting principles are contained in Statement of Financial Accounting Standards ("FAS") No. 5, "Accounting for Contingencies"[54] and FAS No. 15, "Accounting for Debtors and Creditors for Troubled Debt Restructurings,"[55] issued by the FASB. These standards determine

---

[53] Accounting Series Release (ASR) No. 4 (April 1938) and ASR No. 150 (December 1972). Also see SEC Codification of Financial Reporting Policies § 101; Garrett, The Accounting Profession and Accounting Principles (address before Second Annual Robert M. Trueblood Memorial Conference, Ill. C.P.A. Foundation, Chicago, Oct. 3, 1975).

[54] FAS, Statement No. 5, "Accounting for Contingencies," March 1975, is summarized as follows:

> "This Statement establishes standards of financial accounting and reporting for loss contingencies. It requires accrual by a charge to income (and disclosure) for an estimated loss from a loss contingency if two conditions are met: (a) information available prior to issuance of the financial statements indicates that it is probable that an asset had been impaired or a liability had been incurred at the date of the financial statements, and (b) the amount of loss can be reasonably estimated."

For the details, see wysiwyg://28/http://www.fasb.org/st/summary/stsum5.

[55] FAS, statement No. 15, "Accounting for Debtors and Creditors for Troubled Debt Restructurings (Issued 6/77)," is summarized as follows:

> "This Statement establishes standards of financial accounting and reporting by the debtor and by the creditor for a troubled debt restructuring. This Statement requires adjustments in payment terms from a troubled debt restructuring generally to be considered adjustments of the yield (effective interest rate) of the loan. So long as the aggregate payments (both principal and interest) to be received by the creditor are not less than the creditor's carrying amount of the loan, the creditor recognizes no loss, only a lower yield over the term of the restructured debt. Similarly, the debtor recognizes no gain unless the aggregate future payments (including amounts contingently payable) are less than the debtor's recorded liability."

For the details, see wysiwyg://28/http://www.fasb.org/st/summary/stsum15.

the timing and adequacy of specific provisions. Specifically, an estimated loss should be accrued by a charge to income (provision) if it is probable that an asset has been impaired or a liability has been incurred and if the amount of the loss can be reasonably estimated. There are further standards as to impaired assets and loans. It requires that impaired loans be measured based upon the present realizable cash value.[56] The present realizable cash value is the present value of expected cash flows discounted at the loan's effective interest rate.[57]

---

[56] See, Accounting Research Bulletin No. 43, "Restatement and Revision of Accounting Research Bulletins," June 1953 (replaced ARB's issued September 1939January 1953), Chapter 3A-9. It stipulates:

"The amounts at which various current assets are carried do not always represent their present realizable cash values. Accounts receivable net of allowances for uncollectible accounts, and for unearned discounts where unearned discounts are considered, are effectively stated at the amount of cash estimated as realizable."

[57] FAS, Statement No. 114, "Accounting by Creditors for Impairment of a Loan — an amendment of FASB Statements No. 5 and 15 (Issued 5/93)" says:

"It requires that impaired loans that are within the scope of this Statement be measured based on the present value of expected future cash flows discounted at the loan's effective interest rate or, as a practical expedient, at the loan's observable market price or the fair value of the collateral dependent.

"This Statement amends FASB Statement No. 5, Accounting for Contingencies, to clarify that a creditor should evaluate the collectbility of both contractual interests and contractual principle of all receivables when assessing the need for a loss accrual. This Statement also amends FASB Statement No. 15, Accounting by Debtors and Creditors for Trouble Debt Restructurings, to require a creditor to measure all loans that are restructured in a troubled debt restructuring involving a modification of terms in accordance with this Statement."

Further, FAS, Statement No. 118, "Accounting by Creditors for Impairment of a Loan-Income Recognition and Disclosures — an amendment of FASB Statement No. 114 (Issued 10/94)" says:

"This Statement does not change the provisions in Statement 114 that require a creditor to measure impairment. This Statement amends the disclosure requirements in Statement 114 to require information about the recorded investment in certain impaired loans and about how a creditor recognizes interest income related to those impaired loans."

Tax Laws

Under the law, a portion of the bank's current earnings may be sheltered from taxes to help prepare for bad loans. The annual loan-loss provision is deducted from current revenues before taxes are applied to earnings. Prior to passage of the Tax Reform Act of 1986,[58] all US banks could figure their loan-loss deductions using either:

1. the *experience method* (in which the amount of deductible loan-loss expense would be the product of the average ratio of net loan charge-offs to total loans in the most recent six years times the current total of outstanding loans), or

2. the *reserve method* (which allowed banks to automatically deduct, without being taxed, up to 0.6 percent of their eligible loans at year-end).

Among the two methods, US banks could choose the particular loan-loss expensing method that resulted in the greatest tax savings.

The Tax Reform Act required large US banks and bank holdings companies to use

3. the s*pecific charge-off method,* which allows them to add to loan-loss reserves out of pretax income each year no more than the amount of those loans actually written off as uncollectible. The expensing of a worthless loan usually must occur in the year that loan becomes worthless. However, small banks and banking companies (under $500 million in assets) could continue to use the experience method or switch to the specific charge-off method.

Legal Precedents: Case 1

This is a case that the court held that the defendant kept a loan loss reserve artificially low.

For the financial statements of ASB Bank,[59] the court said:
"Like other banks, ASB had a loan loss reserve to cover all losses in its loan portfolios as well as other potential losses. If the loan loss reserve was understated for any given period,

---

[58] *See* Tax Reform Act of 1986, Pub. L. No. 99-514, 100 Stat. 2085 (1986).

[59] United States of America v. Ralph H. Whitmore, Jr., 35 Fed. Appx. 307; 2002 US App. Lexis 2364.

ASB's income would be overstated as it would not accurately reflect the bank's true assets. At ASB, Whitmore (the defendant) had the sole responsibility for determining the loan loss reserve and had no formal method of making this determination.

"In 1987, Whitmore kept the loan loss reserve artificially low in ASB's reports so as to mask the financial difficulties the bank was facing. Despite opposition from ASB officers who refused to sign such falsified financial forms, Whitmore's loan loss reserve calculations for 1987 misstated the true financial status of ASB."

Legal Precedents: Case 2

In this case,[60] the court concluded that the plaintiff adequately set forth the necessary *prima facie* case for negligent misrepresentation, based on the allegations set forth in the complaint. The complaint alleged that, "the individual defendants knew, based upon their business sophistication, experience, and knowledge of accounting, that Boston Chicken's (the lender's) financial statements were false and misleading. It alleged that a loan loss reserve was required, but was not taken against the substantial loans made to the FADs (the borrower) because the loans were impaired; the Boston Chicken's reported revenues, being largely the result of loans made the FAD's and recycled bank to Boston Chicken, were fictitious. The complaint also alleged that the individual defendants knew the financial statements audited by Arthur Andersen were false and misleading. Apparently, these false and misleading financial statements enabled Boston Chicken to raise hundreds of millions of dollars of debt and equity capital from the investing public."

There are many cases regarding loan loss reserves in the US such as those holding that statements characterizing a loan loss reserve as "soundly underwritten" are actionable.[61]

---

[60] *Gerald K. Smith v. Arthur Anderson L.L.P.,* 175 F. Supp. 2d 1180; 2001 US Dist. Lexis 20377.

[61] For example, the Third Circuit in *Shapiro v. UJB Financial Corp.,* 964 F.2d 272 (3rd Cir.), *cert. denied,* 121 L. Ed. 2d 278, 113 S. Ct. 365 (1992), held that statements

Official Views of the Japanese Government on Bad Loans

In October 2002, FSA revealed its policy to tackle with bad loan problems of banks by issuing a paper titled, "Financial Revitalization Program — Economic revitalization through solutions to bad loan problems of major banks."[62] In other words, it made clear that the agency will review the standard for the asset evaluation in order to tighten further on asset evaluation of financial institutions.

According to the paper, the agency says that it will seek consistencies in the asset evaluation standard with the market value. With reference to loan loss reserves, the agency says it will apply the American style DCF (discount cash flow) technique.[63] It will use the individual reserve method based on the DCF technique concerning large borrowers on the warning lists of major banks.

What FSA is intending to do is to introduce DDF, an American style quantitative measurement technique, addressing the point that there has been chronic insufficiency in reserves for problematic borrowers, in order to force the banks to do more accurate market value evaluations and to make them appropriate more reserves to fill the gaps between book values and market values. This is a very aggressive banking policy unheard of from the Japanese government up until this time.

In implementing the DCF method, FSA revised its financial inspection manual and asked major lenders to use it starting with the FY2003. However, little is known as to its specificity of its contents and techniques involved.

DCF essentially predicts future cash flow and seeks its present value, and the biggest hurdle in applying the DCF method is how to select an appropriate discount rate reflecting the risk premium. In case of a bad

---

characterizing loan loss reserve as "adequate," describing the loan portfolio as "well collateralized" and of high "quality," and praising internal controls as properly centralized, supervised, and managed, could state a claim. Also, the Sixth Circuit in *Mayer v. Mylod*, 988 F.2d 635 (6th Cir. 1993), held that statements characterizing the loan portfolio as "soundly underwritten" were actionable along with allegations of misrepresentation concerning non-performing assets and inadequate loan loss reserves.

[62] FSA, October 30, 2002, Memorandum.

[63] For DCF see Ross, Westerfield and Jaffe, "Corporate Finance," 6th edition. The McGraw-Hill Companies, Inc. pp. 67–95.

loan with a risk of default, it is necessary to consider the risk (credit risk). In such a case, it is not enough to calculate just the estimated default probability. It is necessary to use a discount rate obtained by applying the risk premium on top of the market interest rate. In dealing with a corporation with an especially high borrowing rate, it may be necessary to use a higher risk premium. If a contracted interest rate is used as a discount rate, it may result in evaluating the value of a loan extremely large. Although the DCF method is a correct method, the result can be misleading if a wrong discount ratio is used. Although it is difficult yet to judge how the DCF method will be used in Japan and if it meets the expectation of FSA, it is no doubt that a new system has begun.

Conclusion

In order to restore the Japanese financial system and the financial administration to trustworthiness, and to rebuild a financial market that can be respected by the world, it is mandatory first to solve the bad loan problems of the major banks. It is not only the expectation of IMF as mentioned above, but it is also the whole-hearted expectation of various countries including the United States that believe that the economic recovery of Japan will lead to the economic recovery of the world. It is necessary to aim for building a more solid financial system that can lower the bad loan ratios of major banks, fix various related problems, and support the overall restructuring of socio-economic systems, which mandates major banks more stringent evaluations of their assets, enrichment of their own capitals, and strengthening of their governances.

There are a few noteworthy cases in this area in Japan. In one civil case, directors of the bank were asked for payments of a portion of uncollectible money and the delayed damages due to alleged breach of fiduciary duty. The court judged that there was no breach of fiduciary duty. However, the problem was that the court did not either make any judgment on the point of whether there was a sufficient loan loss reserve against the possibility of the borrower becoming unable to pay back to seek potential negligence of the directors.

For the criminal case concerning a criminal responsibility related to an accounting procedure for bad loans, the defendants were indicted on account of a violation of the Commercial Code. However the judgment is questionable since it created a criminal based upon unclear accounting standards.

It is clear now that the problems of the judgments in both cases were caused by the fact that there is no express law in Japan concerning the "fair accounting practice."

Above all, it is necessary for them to appropriate necessary minimum reserves against loan losses through more stringent evaluation of bad loan risks. Japanese banks must improve their shortcomings in this area to regain their international credibility. This article pointed out that various rules and regulations concerning loan loss reserves in Japan are so much behind those in the United States.

Bad loans are not limited to banks, but can occur accidentally in any business operations. Therefore, there is a need to have a clear-cut standard for loan loss reserves. Although there should be a range from the lowest to the highest in the estimation of a bad loan loss, there should be an accounting standard for an accidental phenomenon. However, there is no clear-cut accounting standard on that in Japan.

Cases where banks that were making profits and distributing dividends go under in just six months leaving huge asset deficiencies in the corrected balance sheets are actually happening in Japan as in the cases of Nippon Credit Bank and Long Term Credit Bank of Japan, reviewed above in this article. This is a phenomenon that cannot happen under the accounting standard of the United States. This is because, in the United States, an accounting auditor expresses its opinion that a financial statement is properly prepared according to the generally accepted accounting standards. Since the accounting auditor is supposed to express its opinion whether a financial statement is prepared according to an accounting standards, the accountant's opinion becomes unclear if said accounting standards do not clarify the standard for accounting procedures and the standard for disclosure. The reason accounting auditors can function in the US is partially because they have clear-cut accounting standards they can rely on.

The question of how to identify the real status of bad loans and how to deal with them can be essentially reduced to the question of accounting standards. The entire accounting standards, not just on loan loss reserves, should be reviewed and revamped in Japan, so that the Japanese market can regain the world's trust. Japan should deeply recognize the need that Japan should try on its own to improve the world's trust on Japan in order to achieve the recovery of the Japanese market and economy, which is essential for the world economy.

Part Two　　　　　　　　　　．

Bank Director's Decisions on Bad Loans: A Comparative Study of US and Japanese Standards of Required Care[a]

As a result of the extensive failures of financial institutions that have occurred since 1995 in Japan, legal actions against previous bank directors is expected to increase in the future. The question is, what should be the duty of care for a bank director, and in particular, what should be the court standard for determining if the duty of care has been breached by the director. This article examines the laws related to bank directors' responsibilities and discusses some Japanese court cases. The differences in legal systems and the court rulings in Japan and the United States also are compared.

The fact that so many questionable loans were made by Japanese banks suggests that the Japanese standard for violations of bankers' duty of care is too lenient as compared to that of the United States, which has overcome its own bad loan problem. The following analysis is based on the hypothesis that these lenient standards are the biggest cause of the large number of bad loans made in Japan.

---

[a] This chapter is based on the author's previously published article.
Mitsuru Misawa, "Bank Directors' Decisions on Bad Loans: A Comparative Study of US and Japanese Standards of Required Care," The Banking Law Journal, May 2005, Volume 122, Number 5, pp. 429–466.

This analysis is significant because the GDP of Japan is the second largest in the world and Japanese banks are receiving large sums of money from around the world to operate funds internationally. How the directors of these Japanese banks are operating and whether they are paying full attention to their duty of care should be a matter of grave concern to the international banking world.

In order to build and maintain a Japanese financial market that can be respected by the rest of the world, it is first necessary to solve the basic problems underlining the legal system, such as the accounting standards. For Tokyo to be a real world capital market, it is necessary to build a more efficient legal environment and support the overall restructuring of its socio-economic systems. The strengthening of bank directors' responsibilities is an essential part of this. Such a refurbishment of the system will enable the users of Japanese financial services around the world to select combinations of risks and returns more securely.

Introduction

During the second half of the 20th century, the banking business in Japan was under the so-called Convoy System[1] by the Ministry of Finance (MOF).[2] During that time not a single bank failed, which created the

---

[1] The treatment of Japanese banks by the Ministry of Finance (MOF) is best understood by an analogy to a convoy forming a large group consisting of warships, cruisers, and destroyers to ride out rough seas and opposition. The "convoy system" is a concept to approve the government backup system.

[2] The MOF was reorganized on January 6, 2001. The name was changed from Okurasho to Zaimucho in Japanese, but the English name still remains the same. For more information about the reorganization, see *http://www.mof.go.jp*. The Financial Services Agency (FSA) was created as of July 1, 1997, with the integration of the Banking Supervisory Agency and the Financial System Planning Bureau of the Ministry of Finance. The new FSA has integral responsibility over planning of the financial system and supervision and inspection of financial institutions. In view of the rapid changes in the environment surrounding the economy and financial markets, the planning of the financial system focused on building a stable and vigorous financial system, and securing the efficiency and fairness in the financial markets. In the supervision and inspection of financial institutions, further efforts to maintain and improve the soundness of financial institutions were made. Coordination with foreign financial authorities was strengthened

myth that "financial institutions never go under." Japan's financial institutions have gone through drastic changes as a result of the fundamental changes in the financial market including the financial relaxation after the "Japanese Financial Big Bang" and the deflation after the "Bubble" burst. In today's environment financial institutions are expected to be managed with tighter controls based on the directors' own responsibilities.

Due to the rampant failures of financial institutions that occurred since 1995 when the Bubble Economy collapsed, the Resolution and Collection Corporation (RCC)[3] was created by the Deposit Insurance Corporation of Japan, a government organization, as the major shareholder in order to expedite the cleanup of defaulted loans. The RCC's responsibilities include:

1. Receiving the defaulted financial institutions' assets and collecting them;
2. Reestablishing bankrupt corporations; and
3. Pursuing the directors involved in the defaulted financial institutions for violating their duties of care.

So far the RCC has received the assets of 172 defaulted financial institutions and has taken 122 legal actions against 86 defaulted financial institutions seeking damages for violations of the duty of care.[4] The issue in each of these legal actions is whether the loan execution judgments of the previous management team constituted violations of the duty of care for directors under the Commercial Code.[5]

Actions against the previous directors are expected to increase in the future. The question is: What is the duty of care for a director of a bank

---

in order to cope adequately with the globalization of finance. For details of the FSA, see *http://www.fsa.go.jp*.

[3] The Resolution and Collection Corporation (RCC) was established on April 1, 1999 with a capital of ¥212 billion. Its major shareholder is the Deposit Insurance Corporation of Japan (DICJ), which was established under the Deposit Insurance Law (Law No. 34, April 1, 1971) as a joint effort of the Government of Japan, the Bank of Japan, and private financial institutions for the purpose of the protection of depositors and the maintenance of orderly credit conditions. For the details of RCC, see *http://www.kaishukikou.co.jp/intro/refer_004.html*. For the details of DICJ, see *http://www.dic.go.jp/soshiki/soahiki.html*.

[4] See the RCC's website; *http://www.kaishukikou.co.jp/intro/refer_001.html*.

[5] Law No. 48 of 1899.

and, in particular, what should be the criterion for a court in determining whether or not a director of a financial institution has violated that duty. This article discusses the direction Japan should take in the future by examining the Japanese laws related to bank directors' responsibilities and some actual cases in Japan, referencing the bank directors' responsibilities in the United States as well.

The fact that so many questionable loans were made by Japanese banks suggests a strong possibility that the Japanese standard for violations of bankers' duty of care is far too lenient as compared to that of the United States, which has overcome its own bad loan problem. The following analysis is based on the hypothesis that the lenient duty of care standard is the main cause of the large number of bad loans in Japan. Thus the comparison of the legal systems and the court judgments of Japan and the United States is appropriate.

Also, this analysis is significant because the GDP of Japan is the second largest in the world and Japanese banks are receiving large sums of money from around the world to operate funds internationally. How the directors of these Japanese banks are operating and whether they are paying full attention to their duty of care should be a matter of grave concern to the international banking world.

The total amount of overseas funds Japanese banks have taken in (liabilities) as $523 billion, while the total amount of funds they have discharged (claimable assets) is $564 billion as of June 2004. The reason that such large amounts of funds are flowing into Japanese banks is because foreign lenders trust Japanese banks. However, it is doubtful if those same lenders would continue to trust Japanese banks if they knew that the standard of duty of care required of Japanese Bank Directors is much lower than those required of bank directors in the United States.

Duty of Care Required from Directors in Japan

Bona Fide Director's Duty of Care

Rules of entrustment are applied to the legal relation between a company and its directors.[6] Therefore, if a director is to conduct his or her job as a member of the board of directors, or as a representative director, he or she is under the duty of care as a bona fide manager under the Civil Code,[7,8] and is obligated to perform his or her duty with proper care as a bona fide manager. An entrusting contract is a contract based on the relationship between the parties involved, the bona fide manager's duty of care is judged based on the differences in the knowledge, talent, and skills of the parties involved as well as the degree of trust between the parties.

The duty of care comes from the nature of an entrusting contract. Therefore, it doesn't make a difference whether monetary compensation is provided or not. On the other hand, there is a theory that the duty is reduced commensurate with the compensation. Therefore, it should be understood that a high degree of expectation for the duty of care does not exist if the compensation is low.

In addition to the bona fide manager's duty of care, the Commercial Code defines "the duty for faithfully performing its job for the benefits of the company honóring laws and regulations, articles of incorporation, and resolutions of shareholders' meetings,"[9] which is collectively called the director's "duty of loyalty." The "bona fide manager's duty of care" is the director's duty to give necessary care to company matters in accordance with the director's job, while the "duty of loyalty" obligates a director not to engage in any activities for his or her own benefit or the benefit of a third party at the expense of the company's benefit. The third fundamental duty of a director is the "duty of monitoring and supervising the execution of other directors' jobs,"[10] or "duty of monitoring."

Whether a person is a representative director or a plain director, directors are supposed to fully understand the company's business, participate in the proper execution of the company's business as members of the board of directors, and monitor/supervise the execution of other directors' jobs based on the "bona fide manager's duty of care,"

---

[6] Commercial Code, art. 254(3).
[7] Law No. 89 of 1902.
[8] Civil Code, art. 644.
[9] Commercial Code, art. 254-3.
[10] Commercial Code, art. 260(1).

"duty of loyalty," and "duty of monitoring." This article focuses on the "bona fide manager's duty of care."

Principle of Management Judgment

One type of misconduct considered a violation of the bona fide manager's duty of care is "management judgment error." This is an action by a manager, based on the manager's judgment that causes substantial damage to the company, although it is not a violation of any law. For example, a company invests in a new business that results in a series of losses and eventually the company has to pull out of the venture unable to collect the invested funds. Another typical case of management misjudgment is a loan to an affiliated company, but the affiliated company's management falters and the company ends up being unable to salvage the loan.

When a director's duty is at issue in litigation for the company's loss, the verdict will invariably be that the director's managerial misjudgment is the cause of the loss so that the director is responsible for damages. However, if a director, as an individual, is to be judged liable for the violation of the bona fide manager's duty of care in such a case, the job of a director becomes too precarious and may result in no one accepting the position of director.

Of course, if a large loan is made without due diligence, without any collateral, and looks too risky for a reasonable person there is no question that such a management decision will be judged as unreasonable conduct and as showing lack of care. However, if the management decision was based on a certain level of investigation and a reasonable analysis, it is unreasonable and undue to judge that the management decision was wrong.

Management of a corporation includes a certain amount of risks and adventures as well as uncertainties. If management of a corporation were governed by a rule that no new investments could be made without a 100 percent profit return guaranteed or no loans could be made to any company that has some credit risks, it would be impossible to successfully run the corporation or to secure able directors. The shareholders have entrusted the responsibility of management to the directors based on the directors' capabilities, accepting some uncertainties.

Therefore, the acceptable theory is that "a director shall not be accused of a mismanagement judgment unless it is obviously irrational from the standpoint of an ordinary managerial capability." In Japan, this is called "the principle of management judgment" or "the judgment principle concerning the rationality of management." This theory developed through case law in the United States is known as the "business judgment rule."[11] It has become a well-accepted theory in Japan as a concept prevailing in case and theoretical studies.

Japanese Case Law

The following sections examine how the rules of the Commercial Code and the Civil Code concerning the director's duty are applied in specific cases.

Director's Duty of Care as an Ordinary Corporate Person (Chukyo Bank Case)

Facts

In the Chukyo Bank Case[12] the representative director and 12 common directors of Chukyo Bank were sued for damages of ¥640 million. This is considered the leading case in Japan for many other cases that followed, in which bank directors were charged for violations of the bona fide manager's duty of care.

None of the directors were found guilty of violating the bona fide manager's duty of care and thus were not liable for damages. What was fought for was the directors' collective action concerning the loans made by the bank.

---

[11] See note 47 infra.

[12] Chukyo Bank was established on Feb. 10, 1943. Its headquarters are located at 3-3, Naka-ku, Nagoya, Japan. Its current capital is 32 billion yen and they have 1289 employees. For details, see *http://www.chukyo-bank.co.jp/toshika/menu_01.html*. Judgment of January 20, 1997 at Nagoya District Court. For details, refer to *http://www.eiko.gr.jp/4kigyou/kigou_01.htm*.

Chukyo Bank loaned a total of ¥2.7 billion to Company A in three installments during a period from 1988 through the summer of 1990, but Company A went bankrupt in July 1991 and the bank ended up with uncollectible loans of ¥640 million in total. The plaintiffs claimed:

> The loan decision by the directors of Chukyo Bank included the violation of the bona fide manager's duty of care in that a building in the United States they accepted as the collateral for the first loan would be difficult to sell and was managed poorly, so the loan decision was inappropriate. For the second loan, they accepted a government bond whose interest coupon was detached as collateral, which was also an inappropriate decision. For the third loan, they accepted another government bond whose interest coupon was detached as collateral when they knew that the management condition of Company A was already in trouble.

> These loans were decided by the Board of Managing Directors, so all directors who attended the meeting were responsible for approving the loans without checking the situations sufficiently. Directors who were not on the Board of Managing Directors were liable for negligence in not developing a system to check the decisions of the Board of Managing Directors and for failing to question the decision of the Board of Managing Directors. The representative director is liable for neglecting to take any action for debt collection despite the fact he knew the deteriorating condition of Company A and for failing to properly supervise the employees concerning loan business.[13]

Court Decision

Whether a director violated the bona fide manager's duty of care is based on whether the director made any inexcusable mistake or failure as an

---

[13] Translated by the author.

Ordinary Corporate Person[14] in the carrying out of his or her job, in particular, in the process of recognizing facts, which formed the basis of the decision, or in the decisionmaking process itself, so that the particular management decision violated the scope of the discretionary power entrusted to the director.

Even if a loan becomes uncollectible or difficult to collect, the decision to make said loan should not automatically be determined to violate the bona fide manager's duty of care, but rather it should be considered a violation if the director made any inexcusable mistake or failure as an Ordinary Corporate Person[15] from the loan condition, contents, repayment plan, presence or lack of and contents of collateral, the borrower's asset and management condition, and various other situations.

Concerning the case in question, the collateral for the first loan was not inappropriate. As to the second and third loans, the bank provided loans even though the collaterals were lower than the loan amounts to be collateralized. However, the situation of Company A is such that, despite the fact its debt was increasing and its profit rate was declining, it was because the company's business was expanding. Such a phenomenon is not necessarily unusual for a company making a lot of anticipatory investment. The direct cause of Company A's bankruptcy was the tightening of the money supply by the government in the second half of 1990, which could not be foreseen by banks. Although it is unusual to accept government bonds whose interest coupons are detached, it was not that they had recourse to such an unusual action after Company A's management condition got deteriorated.

Despite its knowledge of the insufficient collateral, the Board of Managing Directors made its decision considering such things as Company A's business performance, past transaction records, future growth potential, and Company A's cooperation during the bank's transactions on government bonds. It is impossible to see any inexcusable errors or mistakes as Ordinary Corporate Persons[16] in the

---

[14] Emphasis added by the author.
[15] Emphasis added by the author.
[16] *Id.*

decision making process. Therefore, it is impossible to find any violations of the bona fide manager's duty of care on the part of the directors who attended the Board Meeting of Managing Directors.

It is also difficult to accuse the directors who were not members of the Board of Managing Directors for allowing the board to make the loans, because it is reasonable for a financial institution to allow the Board of Managing Directors, which is more maneuverable than the Board of Directors, to make loans that are part of ordinary business activities. It is always possible for the Board of Directors, if they suspect any illegality or inappropriateness in the actions of the Board of Managing Directors to demand corrections. When it was learned that the Company A's managing condition deteriorated, the bank requested Company A to increase the collateral, but Company A was no longer able to respond to the request at that point, so that it cannot be judged that there was an error in the bank's loan management.[17]

Comment

As the case mentioned, even if a loan becomes uncollectible or difficult to collect, the decision made by directors for said loan should not automatically be considered a violation of the bona fide manager's duty of care. This is quite understandable because directors' liability is not absolute liability or liability without fault. Therefore, a director can be accused of the violation of bona fide manager's duty of care only when the director is proven to be negligent, in other words, failed to take necessary care, or failed to investigate the situation when it could have been easily ascertained that the loan should not have been offered.

However, in reality, a judgment on whether to offer a loan or discontinue a loan is not so simple. The banking business is not always so clear cut. A company may not be able to provide sufficient collateral but may be running a financially sound business. A bank may offer a loan based on the borrower company's future growth potential.

---

[17] Translated by the author.

Moreover, even if a borrower company's performance is deteriorating, a bank may choose not to reject a loan request. A bank may see a potential for recovery for the borrower with the additional lending or a bank may offer a loan because it sees potential for increasing the recovery amount by cooperating with the borrower to prolong its operation rather than letting the borrower bankrupt immediately.

Possibly it is a situation in which a bank expects other merits (*e.g.*, to use the relationship as a beachhead for the bank's overseas operation plan) by sustaining the relationship with the borrower company in addition to the profit making expectation of the loan itself. The flipside of this is that the bank's severance from the particular borrower company may cause the company to bankrupt immediately, sending many of its employees to the unemployment line and causing a series of bankruptcies among companies doing business with the borrower.

Therefore, the current prevailing opinion among courts and academic theories in Japan is business decisions such as those described above, which require a lot of consideration should not be judged mechanically by a court of law but rather should be left to the directors' discretion to a certain degree.

The Chukyo Bank case provides a standard for the scope of discretionary power entrusted to the director by stating that (whether there was any violation) "should be judged based on whether the director made any inexcusable mistake or failure as an *Ordinary Corporate Person*[18] in the decision concerning the director's job execution, in particular, in the process of recognizing facts, which formed the basis of the decision, or in the decisionmaking process itself." In other words, a director shall not be held liable for negligence other than in situations as just mentioned. This means that a director is given a broad scope of discretion and the exposure to liability is lessened.

---

[18] Emphasis added by the author.

Management Decision (Nomura Securities Case)

Facts

Before loss compensation procedures became illegal by the Revision of the Securities and Exchange Law in 1991,[19] Nomura Securities[20] compensated such losses.[21]

Court Decision

In a representative action seeking damages against the directors, the Tokyo High Court supported the decision of the first trial by the Tokyo District Court, which held the directors not liable and rejected the claim by the plaintiff.[22] While the court found that loss compensation is an unfair trading method in violation of the Antimonopoly Law,[23] it also decided that the Antimonopoly Law does not fit with the rules concerning the application of the Commercial Code with regard to damage caused by a violation of the directors.[24] The reason for this is that the party that receives the loss is not the company, but the competitor. The decision also stated that the loss compensation was within the normal boundaries of the *Management Decision*,[25] and neither a violation of the duty of due care nor a violation of the duty of loyalty to the company was found.[26] Thus, the directors were not liable.

The Court further stated: (1) the management decision of a corporation is a comprehensive one requiring a professional, predictive, policy-making judgment capability for analyzing unpredictable, fluid,

---

[19] Law No. 25 of 1948.

[20] A securities broker listed at Tokyo Stock Exchange. Address: 1-9-1 Chuo-ku, Tokyo. The company was established on Dec. 25, 1925. Its current capital is 10 billion yen. For the details, see *http://www.nomura.co.jp/introduc/company/index.html.*

[21] For loss compensation, see Mitsuru Misawa, "Loss Compensation in the Japanese Securities Market: Causes, Significance, and Search for a Remedy," *Vanderbilt J of Transnational Law,* Vol. 25, No. 1. 1992.

[22] Ikenaga v. Tabuchi. Tokyo High Court. September 26, 1995. 16th Civil Dept. 1993 (ne) No. 3778.

[23] Law No. 54 or 1947. Art. 19.

[24] Law No. 48 of 1899. Kaisha ni Taisuru Sekinin (Responsibilities to Company). Art. 266-1-5.

[25] Emphasis added.

[26] Tokyo District Court. December 22, 1994. Civil Sec. No. 8. 1993 (wa) No. 18447.

and complex factors, so that it tends to be broad and complex; and (2) a court should examine the actual management judgment of the directors itself from the standpoint of whether there were any careless mistakes in examining the facts that were used as premises, and whether the decision-making process based on the facts was not illogical.[27]

Comment

It seems that the court is deferring to the management decisions of directors as much as possible. The court, however, considered that directors might be subject to liability in certain situations. First, even if an act may be viewed as an act indispensable for business reasons, the director who committed the act may still be punished if it is an illegal act for which a person can be sent to jail. For example, bribery is a criminal offense punishable by up to three years of imprisonment under the Criminal Code,[28] and acquisition of one's own company stock is a criminal offense punishable by up to five years of imprisonment under the Commercial Code.[29] On the other hand, loss compensation conducted before 1991 is not a criminal offense punishable by imprisonment, and no penalty rules are applicable to violations of the Antimonopoly Law.

Second, assuming that an act is not a criminal offense, directors will not be punished simply because they caused a loss to the company, if other directors in the same industry could have made the same mistake.

Third, a director who performs a certain prohibited act or fails to supervise another such director; a director or auditor who attended the board of directors meeting at which the execution plan for such an act was adopted; or an auditor who attended the auditors meeting which examined such a plan, may be liable.

---

[27] *Id.*

[28] Law No. 45 of 1907. Zouwai, Assen Zouwai (Bribery, Mediating Bribery). Art. 198.

[29] Commercial Code, *supra* note 4. Kaisha Zaisan wo Ayauku suru Tsumi (Crime to Risk Company's Assets). Art. 489.

Reliance Rule (Long Tem Credit Bank Case)

In a case claiming damages by the former Long Term Credit Bank of Japan (currently Shinsei Bank),[30] the Tokyo District Court ordered the bank's former executive vice president to pay approximately ¥100 million ($1 million) for the alleged violation of duty of care concerning an additional loan to a resort development project.[31]

Facts

This case is an action for damages wherein the plaintiff Shinsei Bank sued its former executive vice president seeking repayment of a portion of an uncollectible loan alleging that the defendant violated the bona fide manager's duty of care as a director responsible for providing an additional loan related to a loan originally provided by the bank's forerunner, Long Term Credit Bank of Japan, to a project for developing and managing large scale resort facilities in Hatsushima, Shizuoka prefecture. The project failed and the loan became uncollectible. After filing the legal action, the plaintiff Shinsei Bank transferred its right to seek damages to the RCC,[32] so the RCC is currently seeking the damages.

---

[30] "Following the selection of the preferred acquirer of the Long Term Credit Bank of Japan, Ltd. [LTCB] on March 1, 2000, all common shares of the LTCB were transferred to Partners [New LTCB Partners C.V., an investment group comprised of leading US and European financial institutions and other investors], and as a result the temporary nationalization came to an end." SHINSEI BANK, 2000 ANNUAL REPORT 6 (Aug. 2000), *available at* http://www.shinsei-style.com/investors/en/ir/report/report_1999/pdf/ar00eng.pdf. On June 5, 2000, the LTCB changed its name to Shinsei Bank, Limited. With the name change, a new beginning was forged. To emphasize this, the bank selected the name "Shinsei," because in Japanese it means "new birth." It began operations anew as a private bank under new management. Shinsei Bank, Limited is now located at 1–8 Uchisaiwaicho 2-chome, Chiyoda-ku, Tokyo, Japan with ¥451.2 billion of capital and with 2,122 employees. Shinsei Bank, Ltd., Company Profile *at http://www.shinsei-style.com/investors/en/about/company/profile.html* (citing information as of Mar. 31, 2004).

[31] Tokyo District Court, Civil Case No. 8 Dept., April 25, 2002, Shojihome, No. 1629, May 25, 2002, pp. 58–59.

[32] See note 3.

The plaintiff claims that the defendant failed to gather sufficient information and analyze the information carefully, failed to specifically examine the advantages and disadvantages of providing the additional loan, and actually extended a large loan that had no possibility of collection, thus causing the plaintiff a loss of at least ¥1.6 billion. The plaintiff further claimed that the defendant:

1. Should have reinvestigated the estimate of future sales of memberships, but failed to do so and nonchalantly determined that the loan could be collected;

2. Failed to gather sufficient information and analysis of whether the plaintiff would experience any credibility and/or social liability problems if the plaintiff did not provide the additional loan and how probable those occurrences might be (there was no indication of a high probability of loss to the plaintiff if the plaintiff did not provide the additional loan); and

3. Is liable for negligence because, although the defendant claims that a director of a large corporation is allowed to make decisions based on the reports and analyses provided by the subordinates (Right of Reliance), a director should not rely on the reports and analyses provided by other directors or subordinates when "circumstances that raise warnings" or "abnormal facts" exist. A director cannot be excused for not conducting sufficient information gathering and careful investigation.

Judgment

The court acknowledged that the plaintiff incurred approximately ¥6.1 billion loss as a result of the loan, and ordered the defendant to pay approximately ¥100 million to the RCC. The final judgment of the court in this case stated:

The defendant who executed the additional loan of this case failed to perform collection and analysis of information believed to be reasonable under the circumstances, evaluated the risk of being unable to collect the additionally loaned fund excessively small relative to the possible loss for not providing any further loan, making an inequitable misjudgment there, and actually executed a large amount of additional loan to the project of the case which had a poor chance of collection, which constitutes a violation of the bona fide manager's duty of care exceeding the limit of discretion entrusted to a director.

Comment

Through this case, the Japanese court showed its conservative position concerning "Right of Reliance," which is approved as an acceptable notion in the United States,[33] and established a principle that a director is not allowed to rely on the reports and analyses provided by other directors and subordinates if "abnormal facts" exist.

Standard of Duty of Care Required in the United States

Corporate Law in General

Section 142 of the Delaware General Corporation Law[34] does not specify the duties of directors. However, Delaware corporate common law recognizes that directors owe fiduciary duties to the corporation and its shareholders consisting of the duties of care, loyalty, and good faith.[35]

The duty of care requires directors to act on an informed basis and the duty of loyalty requires directors to serve the corporation and its shareholders to the exclusion of all other interests. The duty of good faith is an overarching duty incorporating principles underlying the duties of care and loyalty.

Under Delaware law, directors must exhibit "honesty, good faith and loyal conduct" in their positions of "trust and confidence." "While technically not trustees, they stand in a fiduciary relation to the

---

[33] See note 35.
[34] For Delaware Corporate Law, see *http://www.delcode.state.de.us/title8/c001 /index.htm#TopOfPage*.
[35] Dennis J. Block, Nancy E. Barton & Stephen A. Radin, *The Business Judgment Rule: Fiduciary Duties of Corporate Directors* (5th Ed. 1998). See Chapter 2, Fiduciary Duties of Corporate Directors.

corporations and its stockholders."[36] Delaware law further provides that director decisions are presumed under the business judgment rule to be made in a manner consistent with their fiduciary duties and accordingly a plaintiff challenging director action bears the evidentiary burden to plead and prove facts that the directors failed to act with the requisite care or in good faith. If the plaintiff succeeds in meeting this burden, the business judgment rule presumption will not apply.[37]

Under Delaware law, the business judgment rule is the offspring of the fundamental principle, codified in Section 141(a), that the business and affairs of a Delaware corporation are managed by or under its board of directors.[38] The controlling principle is that the substance of a business decision made by a corporation's board of directors will not be reviewed or scrutinized by a court so long as "the acts of the directors objected to were performed in good faith, in the exercise of their best judgment, and for what they believed to be the advantage of the corporation an all its stockholders.[39]

Therefore, directors actions are outside of the protection of the business judgment rule on finding "fraud, actual or constructive, such as improper motive or personal gain or arbitrary action or conscious disregard of the interests of the corporation and the right of its stockholders,"[40] or "fraud or gross abuse of discretion,"[41] or "bad faith in the transaction,"[42] or if the transaction is "so manifestly unfair as to indicate fraud,"[43] or "if there is a showing of gross and palpable overreaching."[44]

---

[36] Guth v. Loft, Inc., 23 Del. Ch. 255, 270, 5 A.2d 503, 510 (Sup. Ct. 1939).

[37] Edward P. Welch and Andrew J. Tarezyn, "Folk on the Delaware General Corporation Law", Little, Brown and Company, 1993, p. 99–100.

[38] Polk v. Good, 507 A.2d 531, 536 (Del. 1986).

[39] Bodell v. General Gas & Elec. Corp., 15 Del. Ch. 420, 429–430, 140 A. 264, 268 (Sup. Ct. 1927).

[40] Davis v. Louisville Gas & Elec. Co., 16 Del. Ch. 157, 169, 142 A. 654, 659 (Ch. 1928).

[41] Moskowitz v. Bantrell, 41 Del. Ch. 177, 179, 189 A. 2d 749, 750 (Sup. Ct. 1963).

[42] Allied Chem. & Dye Corp. v. Steel & Tube Co. of America, 14 Del. Ch. 64, 73, 122 A. 142, 146 (Ch. 1923).

[43] Robinson v. Pittsburgh Oil Ref. Corp., 14 Del. Ch. 193, 199–200, 126 A. 46, 50 (Ch. 1924).

[44] Meyerson v. El Paso Nat. Gas Co., 246 A. 2d 789, 794 (Del. Ch. 1967).

US Case Law

As to suggested standards, directors of ordinary business corporations, and of banks, are liable only for gross negligence.[45] The New York courts purport to hold directors, at least of banks, to that degree of care which an ordinarily prudent man would exercise in the management of his own business or affairs.[46] The more usual rule requires that degree of care which an ordinarily prudent director would exercise in a similar position under similar circumstances.[47]

The following cases discuss bank director's duty under various circumstances.

Specific Duty of Care

The question is whether a more specific duty of care should be owed by the officers and directors of banks than by those of a general corporation. The court first had given a general instruction that the standard of care was that which "ordinarily prudent persons in a like position would use under similar circumstances."[48] In 1991 in the challenged portion, the court made the instruction somewhat more *specific*[49] by focusing on the circumstance applicable to officers and directors of savings and loans--investing the savings of others.[50]

---

[45] Swentzel v. Penn Bank, 147 Pa. 140, 23 Atl. 405, 15 L. R. A. 305, 30 Am. St. Rep 718 (1892); Hathaway v. Huntley, 284 Mass. 587, 188 N. E. 616, 619 (1933); Speigel v. Beacon Participations, Inc., 297 Mass. 398, 8 N.E.2d 895, 904 (1937), "If directors, acting in good faith, nevertheless act imprudently, they cannot ordinarily be held to be personally responsible unless there is a 'clear and gross negligence' in their conduct."

[46] Hun v. Cary, 82 N.Y. 65 (1880); People v. Mancuso, 255 N.Y. 463, 175 N.E. 177, 76 A.L.R. 514 (1931).

[47] Lippitt v. Ashley, 89 Conn. 451, 94 Atl. 995 (1915); Atherton v. Anderson, 99 F.2d 883 (6th Cir. 1938).

[48] See *First Nat'l Bank of La Marque v. Smith*, 436 F. Supp. 824, 831 (D.C.S.D.Tex.1977), *modified on other grounds*, 610 F.2d 1258 (1980); *Gadd v. Pearson*, 351 F.Supp. 895, 903 (D.C.M.D.Fla.1972); *Litwin v. Allen*, 25.

[49] Emphases added by the author.

[50] Tom J. Billman, *et al.* v. State of Maryland Deposit Insurance Fund Corporation, *et al.*, 88 Md. App. 79; 593 A.2d 684; 1991 Md. App. Lexis 156.

The instruction was supported by a number of judicial decisions. In an old action in 1938[51] by the receiver of a national bank against its directors, the court said:

> The directors are required...to use ordinary diligence; and by ordinary diligence is meant, that degree of care demanded by the circumstances....They must keep in mind that a national bank is not a private corporation in which stockholders alone are interested.... One of its principal purposes among others is to hold and safe keep the money of its depositors.[52]

Higher Standards

In 1934 at the time of the great depression, the Supreme Court of New York ruled that banking directors are held to a higher standard of diligence as compared to that of other corporations. The reason is that the directors are charged with the trust responsibility to see that the depositors' funds are safely and providently invested.[53] In this case, a director of a bank is required under the Banking Law[54] to diligently and honestly administer the affairs of the bank and that the director will not knowingly violate, or willingly permit to be violated, any of the provisions of law applicable to the bank. Directors, who knowingly made loans in excess of 10 percent of the capital and surplus of their bank[55] in

---

[51] Atherton, *et al.* v. Anderson, No. 7298, 99 F.2d 883; 1938 US App. Lexis 3015.

[52] *Id.*

[53] Joseph A. Broderick, as Superintendent of Banks of the State of New York, Plaintiff, v. Bernard K. Marcus and Others, Defendants, 152 Misc. 413; 272 N.Y.S. 455; 1934 N.Y. Misc. Lexis 1377.

[54] Section 124 of the Banking Law provides that "Each director, when appointed or elected, shall take an oath that he will, so far as the duty devolves on him, diligently and honestly administer the affairs of the bank, and will not knowingly violate, or willingly permit to be violated, any of the provisions of law applicable to such bank."

[55] *Id.* , section 108, subdivisions 1 and 7, for the violation of both of which it is sought to hold the directors liable, reads as follows:

"A bank subject to the provisions of this article

1. Shall not directly or indirectly lend to any individual, partnership, unincorporated association, corporation or body politic, by means of letters of credit or by acceptance of drafts for, or the discount or purchase of the notes, bills of exchange or other obligations of, such individual, partnership, unincorporated association, corporation or body politic, will exceed one-tenth part of the capital stock and surplus of such bank: . . .

violation of the Banking Law as well as those who acquiesced in such loans or failed to inquire into the character of the same, are liable to the extent of the loss of the excess. Likewise, losses on loans which were made by the directors without security for the purpose of enabling the borrowers to pay for or hold shares of stock of the bank in violation of the Banking Law[56] are chargeable to the directors.

While directors are entitled under the law to commit the banking business to the duly authorized officers, it does not absolve them from the duty of reasonable supervision, nor ought they to be permitted to be shielded from liability because of want of knowledge of wrongdoing, if that ignorance is a result of gross inattention.

The court judged as follows:

The reason for the higher[57] standard of diligence required of banking directors as compared with that of other corporations is obvious. While legalistically the relation between the bank and its depositors is that of debtor and creditor, practically the directors are charged with the trust responsibility to see that depositors' funds are safely and providently invested. The bulk of the funds of a bank are usually spread out in the form of loans to the business community to help the wheels of industry revolve, and the main responsibility of the director is for the safe and legal application of the bank funds in the form of loans and investments. It is not for him to wait until the facts are thrust in his face. He must at all times take the initiative in

---

(d) In computing the total liabilities of any individual to a bank there shall be included all liabilities to the bank of any partnership or unincorporated association of which he is a member, and any loans made for his benefit or for the benefit of such partnership or association; of any partnership or incorporated association to a bank there shall be included all liabilities of its individual members and all loans made for the benefit of such partnership or unincorporated association or *any member thereof*; and of any corporation to a bank there shall be included all loans made for the benefit of the corporation . . .

7. Shall not knowingly lend, directly or indirectly, any money or property for the purpose of enabling any person to pay for or hold shares of its stock, unless the loan is made upon security having an ascertained or market value of at least fifteen per centum more than the amount of the loan. Any bank violating the provisions of this subdivision shall forfeit to the people of the state twice the amount of the loan."

[56] See note 54 *supra*.

[57] Emphasis added by the author.

examining the loan portfolios. It is no defense, therefore, as one or two of the directors have attempted to assert, that certain loans were not called to their attention or that they were absent at a certain meeting when a particular loan was approved. A sufficient period elapsed since the making of the loan to enable them to inquire into its propriety, and, since they took no steps in protest, they must be deemed to have ratified it.

The disregard of all sound banking principles in the making of the speculative, unsecured and improvident loans resulted in huge losses, for which not only those who actively directed the making of such loans are responsible, but also those who as directors supinely acquiesced in them or failed to inquire into the character of the loans. Ever vestige of possible defense based upon an honest mistake of judgment is destroyed by the fact that the loans which resulted in the losses were made in violation of the banking laws."[58]

Principle of Trusting Right

There are a few cases arguing trusting right or reliance.

In 1938, the US Court of Appeals judged that the business at a bank may be entrusted to its officers on the assumption that they are honest and faithful but they are not to be regarded as infallible. It further judged that if defendants had maintained any reasonable method of supervision over the account, these large and wasteful overdrafts would certainly have been discovered.

It is not unusual for banks to meet disaster through the malfeasance of trusted officials. This is one of the dangers to be apprehended and guarded against. For this reason the law requires and depositors have a right to expect that directors should retain and maintain a reasonable control and supervision over the affairs of the Bank, especially its larger

---

[58] See note 53 *supra*.

and more important ones, to the end that they may keep themselves informed of its condition. In the discharge of this duty the directors are required not only in the observance of their official oath but by common law to use ordinary diligence; and by ordinary diligence is meant, that degree of care demanded by the circumstances. They have their own responsibilities which they may not put aside. They must keep in mind hat a national bank is not a private corporation in which stockholders alone are interested. It is a quasi governmental agency and one of its principal purposes among others is to hold and safe keep the money of its depositors. We think it may be fairly assumed, that if appellants had maintained any reasonable method of supervision over the Wagon Company account or over the general affairs of the Bank, these large and wasteful overdrafts occurring almost daily over a period of six years and periodically renewed, would certainly have been discovered.[59]

In 1993,[60] the court judged that a director may not rely on the judgment of others, especially when there is notice of mismanagement and that when an investment poses an obvious risk, a director cannot rely blindly on the judgment of others. The court specifically recognized a need for heightened responsibility among those directors who have an inkling of trouble brewing, and they cited:[61]

If nothing has come to the knowledge to awaken suspicion that something is going wrong, ordinary attention to the affairs of the institution is sufficient. If, upon the other hand, directors know, or by the exercise of ordinary care should have known, any facts which would awaken suspicion and put a prudent man on his guard, then a degree of care commensurate with the evil to be avoided is required, and a want of that care makes them responsible. Directors cannot, in justice to those

---

[59] See note 51 *supra.*
[60] See note 63 *infra.*
[61] 149 F. at 1013. In Rankin the directors relied entirely on the bank president to conduct the business of the bank. However, rumors began to circulate that the president was mismanaging.

who deal with the bank, shut their eyes to what is going on around them.[62]

With respect to the appropriate standard of care, the court held that the degree of care to which the bank directors were bound is that which ordinarily prudent and diligent persons would exercise under similar circumstances. Under this standard, the directors had a duty to ascertain the condition of the bank and exercise reasonable control and supervision over it. This duty requires that the directors devote a sufficient amount of time and energy to overseeing the bank's affairs, to attending meetings, and to reading the reports of federal and state bank examiners. These duties were not delegable and could not be discharged *solely by reliance on others.*[63,64]

Standard of Care as the Specialists

The court elaborated, as the basic principles, on the duties of bank directors in 1993:[65]

(1) Directors are charged with the duty of reasonable supervision over the affairs of the bank. It is their duty to use ordinary diligence in ascertaining the condition of its business, and to exercise reasonable control and supervision over its affairs. (2) They are not insurers or guarantors of the fidelity and proper conduct of the executive officers of the bank, and they are not responsible for losses resulting from their wrongful acts or omissions provided they have exercised ordinary care in the discharge of their duties as directors. (3) Ordinary care, in this matter as in other departments of the law, means that degree of care which ordinarily prudent and

---

[62] Reliance arguments are especially weak when regulators have told directors to take action. See, *e.g.*, FDIC v. Brickner, 747 F.2d 1198, 1202 (8th Cir. 1984) (directors could not ignore bank examiner warnings).

[63] Federal Deposit Insurance Corporation, in its corporate capacity, Plaintiff-Appellee, v. Gilbert Bierman, V. Edgar Stanley, Robert Marcuccilli, Judith Stanley, Dan Stanley, and John Boley, Defendants-Appellants, 2 F.3d 1424; 1993 US App. Lexis 20459; 127 A.L.R. Fed. 703.

[64] Emphasis added by the author.

[65] See note 63 *supra*.

diligent men would exercise under similar circumstances. (4) The degree of care required further depends upon the subject to which it is to be applied, and each case is to be determined in view of all circumstances.

The court further judged that the bankers are specialists and the duties of care required should include something more than ordinary care.

Directors must exercise ordinary care and prudence in the administration of the affairs of a bank, and this includes something more than officiating as figure-heads.[66] They are entitled under the law to commit the banking business, as defined, to their duly-authorized officers, but this does not absolve them from the duty of reasonable supervision, nor ought they to be permitted to be shielded from liability because of want of wrongdoing, if that ignorance is the result of gross inattention.

The Business Judgment Rule

The business judgment rule originated in Cates v. Sparkman,[67] when the Texas Supreme Court held:

[The] negligence of a director, no matter how unwise or imprudent, does not constitute a breach of duty if the acts of the director were "within the exercise of their discretion and judgment in the development or prosecution of the enterprise in which their interests are involved."

The court reviewed the relationship between the fiduciary duties owed by officers and directors and the business judgment rule.[68]

Officers and directors have three fiduciary duties: the duty of obedience, the duty of loyalty, and the duty of care. The duty of obedience forbids ultra vires acts, that is, acts outside the

---

[66] Emphasis added by the author.

[67] Cates v. Sparkman, 73 Tex. 619, 11 S.W. 846, 849 (1889).

[68] Resolution Trust Corporation, in its corporate capacity, Plaintiff v. Charles D. Acton, David Clayton, William F. Courtney, Richard L. Davidson, and John R. Rittenberry, Defendants, 844 F. Supp. 307; 1994 US Dist. Lexis 1750.

scope of corporate power. The duty of loyalty requires that officers and directors act in good faith; this duty forbids them from engaging in 'interested' transactions. The duty of care requires officers and directors to manage the corporation's affairs with diligence and prudence.

These definitions illustrate an inherent tension between the duty of care and the protection of the business judgment rule. When directors of the bank provided 100 percent financing for the borrowers even though the financial statements showed them to be insolvent, the court judged that the business judgment rule was not a defense to the allegations.[69] The court also said that the business judgment rule is not a defense to allegations of fraud, nor self-dealing.

Comparison of Japan vs. the United States

Let's first consider the United States. In the Broderick v. Marcus case,[70] the court judged that "bank directors are liable for more careful judgments than directors of other businesses" because "(bank directors) are responsible for monitoring depositors' funds to see if they are securely and carefully managed." Although directors claimed that they "did their best in providing reasonable monitoring of a certain business of the bank" in the Atherton v. Anderson case,[71] the court held that they "could have detected said fraudulent action if they read the materials distributed in the board of directors' meeting." This case cited the special nature of the banking business, and held that bank directors shall not only bear the duty of care but also be liable to depositors. In the FDIC v. Bierman, Stanley case[72] in relation to the director's duty of monitoring, the court held that "bank directors shall bear fiduciary duty of providing reasonable monitoring relative to bank operations" and the directors shall "properly monitor lending functions" as bankers. The same opinion further stated that bank directors shall be liable for "ascertaining the

---

[69] *Id.*
[70] See note 53 *supra.*
[71] See note 51 *supra.*
[72] See note 63 *supra.*

situations of the bank, and monitoring them exercising their monitoring right in reasonable manners." As can be seen from these examples, bank directors in the United States are considered different from general directors; they have duties to ascertain bank operations thoroughly and monitor the operations with prudence and diligence. The underlying concept of the courts' judgments in these cases is the notion of the fiduciary duty of care in Anglo-American law.[73] In other words, the basic concept of the fiduciary duty is that a specialist has a professional capability clearly different from an ordinary person, and is liable as a professional for protecting, prioritizing, performing the entrusted job fully, and fulfilling the rigorous duty of care.

On the other hand in Japan, in the Chukyo Bank case, the court stated that "because some inexcusable impropriety and omission as an Ordinary Corporate Person were found in the facts-recognition and decisionmaking processes, the judgment whether they were beyond the limit of the discretion entrusted in a director" should be the basis for determining the violation of the duty of care, and the bank director's standard as a professional was not questioned. Therefore, the director's decision to use the government bond missing the interest coupon having a value of only 40 percent of the collateralized debt didn't constitute a violation of the duty of care as a "bank director's decision." Japanese courts do not believe that a bank director has a duty to ascertain the risk of a particular transaction and establish the managing system accordingly as a professional of financial transactions.

The concept of fiduciary duty of care prevailing in the United States should be introduced into Japan, because Japanese banks are operating internationally. A bank director should perform his or her duty as a Banking professional in such a manner that a violation of duty as a professional constitutes a violation of a bona fide manager's duty of care. The large number of failures of financial institutions in recent years in Japan can be considered a result of the lack of a fiduciary duty standard. If the Anglo-American fiduciary duty is applied, not just as an ethical rule, but as a practical rule to all managers of corporations as well as to

---

[73] See note 35 *supra*.

various other professionals involved in financial matters, reckless and irresponsible actions can be prevented.

The reason why Japanese laws are behind US laws in this respect is due to historical developments. The Commercial Code in Japan was introduced by Germany in 1899 as part of the general acceptance of Western law during the Meiji era. During the period of occupation, SCAP[74] reformed the Commercial Code, with intentions to adopt the Anglo-American approach to corporate law. However, the specific part of the Commercial Code that defines the duty of care for directors has been untouched without introducing American legal theories.

Bank directors are professionals dealing primarily with loan transactions. Because of Japan's life-time employment practice, most of these professionals have climbed the corporate ladder from the bottom; as a result they normally have more than 30 years of experience in the banking business. This makes it reasonable to expect a higher and more rigorous level of knowledge and duty of care from bank directors as professionals than from an ordinary company offering a loan.

Although the Japanese courts cite the "Business Judgment Rule" and "Reliance Rule" established in the United States and use them as the means for proving exemption from liability, they do so assuming ordinary corporations and have not yet applied the "Business Judgment Rule" and "Reliance Rule" on professional business judgments made by bank directors. In the Nomura Securities case,[75] it was shown that "it should be judged from the standpoint of whether there were any careless mistakes made in the process of recognition of facts and whether the decisionmaking process based on said facts was extremely unreasonable as an Ordinary Corporate Person," arguing that that is how a violation of a director's duty of care and the Business Judgment Rule should be recognized. However, this author believes that this rule should be applied more rigorously to a bank director, although the same violation of duty care may be exempted from liability if it is a business judgment made by an Ordinary Corporate Person.

---

[74] The official name of the occupation authorities is the General Headquarters for the Supreme Commander for Allied Powers (commonly termed SCAP).
[75] See note 22 *supra*.

Conclusion

One of the reasons that so many problematic lending cases occurred in Japan is that the level of duty of care required of bank directors in Japan is not as rigorous and sophisticated as in the United States. The rule stipulated in the Commercial Code of Japan that the Japanese courts apply to violations of duty of care by bank directors is based on the premise of ordinary corporate persons. The Banking Law of Japan does not identify any specific duty of care for bank directors either. None of the cases heard so far by the Japanese courts requested any professional and higher level duty of care standard for bank directors.

It is natural then that Japanese bank directors have never been held to the same level of duty care as US bank directors either in terms of applicable laws or in application of laws in the courts. Although the macro reasons, such as the occurrence of the economic bubble and its abrupt demise were undeniable, the lax legal standard discussed herein was a cause of so many bad debts. It seems that this loose standard tolerated the freer judgments of managers in operating banks. The economic bubble and its abrupt demise was the result of an indiscriminate pumping of huge amounts of funds into the market by banks, and it is essentially wrong for bank directors to try to avoid their responsibilities as if it was the result of a macro phenomenon that they had nothing to do with.

Japan is no different from other countries in that all the banks are operated under government licenses, different from all other businesses, and each bank carries a public responsibility that can affect the credit system profoundly if it fails. Moreover, banking jobs require extremely high professionalism and a high level of knowledge. Therefore, determining if there has been a violation of the duty of care should be based on whether the particular decision made was a "decision that would have been made by a bank director in a similar position having an ordinary corporate sense" as practiced in the United States. The legal theory concerning the fiduciary duty is not established in Japan as a private law theory and it has not become popular yet as a code of conduct for bank directors. An aggressive move is needed in Japan in order to establish a theory of *fiduciary duty*[76] specifically and clearly as an industry-wide code of conduct for bank directors in Japan.

Japanese banks are currently taking in a lot of funds from US and European markets. The international movement of funds has sharply risen since the 1980s due to the globalization of the financial market. For example, the international capital movement on gross base in terms of the GDP ratio among G7 countries was stable from the 1970s through the middle of 1980 at 2 to 3 percent, but rose sharply thereafter to reach the current level exceeding 10 percent.[77] If we include international transfer of risks using derivative transactions, it is safe to say that the scale of international capital, funds and risks is increasing phenomenally. It is obvious that the level of duty of care required of Japanese bank directors who operate huge sums of international funds can't be uniquely lower than the international standard. The improvement is acutely needed for further international development of the Japanese banking industry. It is a necessary courtesy to the current market as well.

While a reformation of the financial system is under way in Japan at the present time, it is essential to promote "new financial flow" and to normalize the risk distribution as well as to improve efficiency in the economic society as a whole in order to seek further development. As a premise to this, a renewal of financial services to support such a reform is indispensable. The strengthening of bank directors' responsibilities is an essential part of the reform. Such a refurbishment of the system will enable the users of Japanese financial services around the world to select combinations of risks and returns more securely.

---

[76] Emphasis added by the author.

[77] Bank of Japan, BIS statistics. See *http://www.boj.or.jp/intl//99/bis9904b.htm*.

Part Three

Case Study of the Long Term Credit Bank of Japan[a,b]

The Long Term Credit Bank of Japan (LTCB) was one of the most aggressive banks in loaning to real estate developers during the 1990s. Their financing activities covered projects all over the Pan Pacific areas including Australia, Vietnam, Saipan, and Hawaii, as well as parts of the continental United States. Australia is particularly noteworthy for LTCB, because it is the loan made by LTCB that caused Bond University in Queensland, Australia's first private university, to go under.

LTCB, once one of Japan's three top ranked long-term credit banks, was placed under state control in October, 1998, and collapsed under the weight of bad-loan losses in 2000. Were bank director's civil and criminal liabilities sufficiently pursued in the LTCB cases? The three cases of LTCB--two for civil liability and one for criminal liability--are discussed.

Bank Directors were held accountable for violating the duty of care in their decisions on making the various loans that ultimately failed. The problem, however, is that directors, as individuals, have limited resources for paying

---

[a] For this chapter, permission is granted to reprint by the University of Melbourne Law School, The Australian Journal of Law, Mitsuru Misawa, "Case Note, The Long Term Credit Litigation" from The Australian Journal of Asian Law, Vol. 8, No. 1, August 2006, pp. 104–119.

[b] For the specific issue of this Journal on International Accounting Standards, other authors as below are highly distinguished observers. This issue covers an international symposium on the U.S., Europe and Japan. I wrote the article on Japan.

* David Ruder, Professor at Northwestern Law School, former chairman of the US Securities and Exchange Commission
* Sir David Tweedie, Chairman, International Accounting Standards Board
* Alexander Schaub, Director-General, Inter Market and Services, European Commission
* Robert Heinz, Chairman, Financial Accounting Standards Board
* Donald Nicolaisen, Chief Accountant, the US Securities and Exchange Commission
* Mary Tokar, Partner, KPMG International and Member, International Financial Reporting Interpretations Committee

151

enormous damages awarded by the courts. The real issue is whether the banks can be held responsible (lender liability) in Japan.
The lawsuit by E.I.E. International (EIE) against LTCB settled in 2004. This could have been a leading case for establishing lender liability in Japan.

Introduction

During the years following the signing of the Plaza Accord[1] of 1985, a money glut existed in Japan. Banks were busily collecting funds from the general public and lending them to big corporations for capital investment. Then the government implemented the deregulation of financial activities (deregulation of deposit interest rates), sending all Japanese banks scurrying to raise their deposit interest rates in order to sustain, if not increase, their share of the lending business. This in turn made it difficult for the banks to find entities to loan the funds they collected. It was not only because industries began to decrease capital investments due to the change in the industrial structure, but also because corporations learned to finance capital investment directly by issuing bonds and new stocks rather than by borrowing money. Thus the banks searched for new and more lucrative lending opportunities. They loaned money to businesses investing in stocks and real estate, which inevitably caused real estate and stock prices to rise beyond their economic real values, therefore, the emergence of the bubble boom.

The bankruptcies of financial institutions and the resolution of bad loans became serious problems in 1995. A huge amount of credit (¥40 trillion) based on real estate became uncollectible and put enormous pressure on financial institutions to keep up their profit levels. In 1999, ¥7 trillion in tax money was used to save the faltering financial institutions.[2]

---

[1] This was an agreement signed on September 22, 1985 by the then G-5 nations (France, Germany, Japan, the United States, and the United Kingdom). The G-5 agreed to devalue the US dollar against the Japanese yen and German Deutsche Mark by intervening in currency markets. For the details, see *http://en.wikipedia.org/wiki/Plaza_Accord*.

[2] For a discussion of the tax money infusion, *see* Mitsuru Misawa, "The Japanese Big Bank: Will it be Successful?," *Risk Management*, (Edited by Professor Michael Frenkel Wrish Hommel and Markus Rudolf, WHU-Otto-Beisheim University), October 2004, pp. 801–820.

The Long Term Credit Bank of Japan (LTCB)[3] was one of the banks that were most aggressive in loaning to real estate developers during the bubble era. Their financing activities covered projects all over the Pan Pacific including: Australia, Vietnam, Saipan, and Hawaii as well as parts of the continental United States. LTCB was heavily relying on loans to construction and real estate related industries (19.5%) as can be seen from Table 1. Most of these loans turned out to be unrecoverable, and LTCB, which was once rated as AAA by Standard & Poor, bankrupted in 1998.[4]

Resolution and Reconstruction Corporation (RCC)

RCC[5] claimed in three separate cases that the LTCB's management team was liable for lending to E.I.E. International (EIE).[6] Table 2 illustrates

---

[3] LTCB was placed under state control in October 1998, when it collapsed under the weight of bad-loan losses. Following the selection of the preferred acquirer of LTCB on March 1, 2000, all common shares of the LTCB were transferred to Partners [New LTCB Partners C.V., an investment group comprised of leading US and European financial institutions and other investors], and as a result the temporary nationalization came to an end." SHINSEI BANK, 2000 ANNUAL REPORT 6(Aug. 2000), available at *http://www.shinsei-style.com/investors/en/ir/report/report_1999/pdf/ar00eng.pdf.* On June 5, 2000, the LTCB changed its name to Shinsei Bank, Limited. With the name change, came a new beginning. To emphasize this, the bank selected the name "Shinsei," meaning "new birth" in Japanese. It began operations anew as a private bank under new management. Shinsei Bank, Limited is now located at 1-8 Uchisaiwaicho 2-chome, Chiyoda-ku, Tokyo, Japan with ¥451.2 billion of capital and with 2,122 employees. Shinsei Bank, Ltd., Company Profile at *http://www.shinsei-style.com/investors/en/about/company/profile.html.*

[4] For the details of the bankruptcy development, *see http://www.findai.com/vogo/0023.htm.*

[5] The Resolution and Collection Corporation (RCC) was established on April 1, 1999, with capital of ¥212 billion. Its major shareholder is the Deposit Insurance Corporation of Japan (DICJ), which was established under the Deposit Insurance Law (Law No. 34, April 1, 1971) on April 1, 1971 as a joint effort of the Government of Japan, the Bank of Japan, and private financial institutions for the purpose of the protection of depositors and the maintenance of orderly credit conditions. For the details of the RCC, see *http://www.kaishukikou.co.jp/intro/refer_004.html.* For the details of DICJ, see *http://www.dic.go.jp/soshiki/soahiki.html.*

[6] EIE is known to have made speculative investments in real estate overseas. It was headed by Harunori Takahashi, former managing director of the now defunct Tokyo Kyowa Credit Association, which is at the center of a larger speculative loan scandal involving LTCB. As the owner of said company, Takahashi, was once called the King of

how heavily LTCB was lending to this company. EIE was LTCB's fifth largest borrower.

RCC claimed as follows:

"LTCB started lending in 1986 to EIE (non-party of the case) and thereafter accelerated its lending to the non-party company, which was busy investing in numerous golf clubs and other overseas real estate. These loans were executed under the heading "project finance" claiming that the bank would check the profit and loss balance project-by-project only, without checking the management and financial status of the non-party company and its affiliates as a whole. By February 1990, LTCB finally got concerned about the bulging amount of lending and announced that it changed its policy from a by-project credit judgment to a credit judgment based on the financial status of the non-party company as a whole. It turned out that the credit amount as of the end of March immediately after the policy change was ¥24.9 billion plus $60.4 million and the total loan balance of the LTCB's affiliated non-bank institutions to the affiliated companies of the non-party company amounted to ¥89.7 billion.

Despite the policy change in the credit judgment standard, LTCB provided a loan (the first loan) of ¥6 billion in April 1990 without the confirmation of the financial condition of the non-party's group as a whole, which was followed by an additional loan of ¥83 billion (the second loan) between December of 1990 and March 1991 and yet another loan (the third loan) of ¥107.5 billion between April 1991 and July 1992 to keep said non-party company afloat, although there was no real hope of recovery. As a result, approximately ¥160 billion

---

Resorts by investing more than ¥1 billion in overseas projects in Australia and Hawaii. Although his company was a C class company in the credit rating, he was able to borrow a sum of ¥380 billion from LTCB. He invested heavily, particularly in Vietnam, including developments of an oil field and a six story floating hotel, both of which turned out to be failures. Takahashi had several on-going projects in Australia at one point and used to fly Japanese politicians and MOF (Japanese Government) officials in his own airplane to Australia to show off his projects. See *http://www.kaisyukikou.co.jp/announce/announce_315.html.*

of funds became uncollectible from the total of ¥196.5 billion thus weakening LTCB's financial soundness; paving the way to LTCB's eventual bankruptcy. The loans were executed by LTCB without asking for any substantial collateral, even though it didn't have any clear understanding of the management and financial situations or of the potential shortage of funds of the non-party company and its affiliates. Also the non-party company's explanation of the potential fund shortage was barely understandable. The duty of care exists for lending funds without acquiring any collateral with little hope of recovery. Extending a due date without making any collection and taking no collateral on the due date is also a problem."[7]

LTCB became a Special Publicly Managed Bank. It transferred all its rights to damages and other claims to RCC on February 28, 2000, based on Section 1, Article 53 of the Financial Reconstruction Law.[8] Although the damages for the first loan were claimed by LTCB prior to this transfer, RCC decided to bring charges against the former directors of LTCB, because the RCC determined they could not be lenient in regard to the directors' liabilities for allowing the second and third loans which were collectively of such a size that they clearly lead to LTCB's eventual bankruptcy.

Civil Liability (1)

In *RCC v. Onogi*, the court found against any claim of manager responsibility.[9] For the first loans (6 billion yen) by LTCB to EIE,[10] the Tokyo District Court rejected a demand from the RCC in 2002 that four

---

[7] Announcement at a press interview by Akio Onioi, representative director of RCC on March 7, 2002. For details see *http://www.kaisyukikou.co.jp/announce/announce_315.html*. Translated by the author.

[8] Law No. 132 of 1998. For the details, see http://www.hokkokubank.co.jp/ir/disclosure/pdf/p65_67.pdf.

[9] RCC v. Onogi, Tokyo District Court, Heisei 11 (Wa) No. 28167, judgment delivered, July 18, 2002.

[10] See *supra* note 6.

former executives of the LTCB pay the state damages (300 million yen) for "illicit decisions" to extend loans in 1990 to the now-defunct real-estate developer EIE.

The presiding judge said,

"There is no evidence to prove they made errors that were tantamount to overstepping the boundaries of their jurisdiction in making a decision to extend bank loans. The loan decisions were logical considering the specific conditions in those days, as the managers concluded that it would not be difficult for the bank to recover the loans in light of its position as the main bank (for EIE International) and in view of the fact that the loans would be short-term."[11]

The ruling marked the first defeat to the RCC, the government-backed dept-collection entity, in a lawsuit in which it asked the managers of an insolvent financial institution to take responsibility for lending decisions that led to its own failure.[12]

Outline of the Case

In *Onogi* the bankruptcy administrator sued the bank president and other directors of defendants' bank, at the time known as the Japan LTCB, because they lent ¥6 billion to EIE[13] (Non-Litigant Company) on April 27, 1990, and further extended the repayment term of the loan on July 26, 1990. The plaintiff remained unable to collect a portion of the loan because the Non-Litigant Company subsequently went bankrupt. The plaintiff asked the defendant directors to repay a portion of the uncollectible money, as well as the delay damages, based on the directors' breach of the duty of care for approving the loan and the extension.

---

[11] Translated by the author.

[12] In April 2002, the same judge ordered former LTCB Executive Vice President Keiji Omi to pay damages in connection with his decisions on a loan to EIE International related to a resort-development project. See *infra* note 20.

[13] The resort development company filed a bankruptcy claim on June 21, 2000 with a debt of ¥609 billion. TV-Tokyo, Declaration of Bankruptcy Received, at *http://www.tv-tokyo.com*. See *supra* note 6.

Issues

The plaintiff claimed the following, citing that there was a breach of fiduciary duty on the part of the defendants:

"Bank directors should manage their banks with a priority on maintaining health and safety, limiting the directors' power in deciding loans. As a person authorized to make loan decisions, the director has to determine the probability of loan collection only after thoroughly investigating the borrower's financial and operating conditions, manager's capability, assets, past credit information, the loan amount and purpose, repayment capability, method of acquiring funds for repayment and probability (including other outstanding loans and repayment statuses), collateral that can be offered and the value thereof, etc., as well as the present and future economic trends (business trends and asset price trends including expansion or decline). Also, if borrowers with a deteriorating financial status as a result of decreasing profits and fund liquidity request additional loans (or an extension), the director's decision of whether such an additional loan should be made should be based on aggressive investigation of the borrower company's management status and future outlook, as well as a comparison of the portion of the total loan estimated to be collectible in case the additional loan is made, and also based on the reason for the borrower's request for the additional loan and collateral."[14,15]

In reality, the loan lacked a decent outlook and chance of collection, thus the execution of the loan should have been stopped.

Court's Judgment

The loan was approved based on the related departments' analyses and evaluations of information collected and systematically accumulated by the bank through its historical transactions with the Non-Litigant

---

[14] Court Judgment, Tokyo District Court, Heisei 11 (Wa) No. 28167.
[15] Translated by the author.

Company. It was concluded that there was a need for the loan, that there was no concern about loan collection, and, therefore, no measures taken for securing debt collection.[16] There is no evidence of error beyond the scope of the judgment either on the recognition of facts, which was the basis of the judgment, or in the contents of the judgment under such circumstances.[17]

There seems to be no breach of duty of care by the defendants (as the loan approvers) relating to the loan decisions.[18]

Comments

The problem with the court's judgment in this case is that it dismissed any duty of care for the directors, particularly at the point when the problem of insufficient collateral for the loan was temporarily camouflaged by executing an additional loan. In addition, the court did not take any steps to determine potential negligence by the defendants.

Civil Liability (2)

In a case claiming damages by the LTCB (currently Shinsei Bank),[19] the Tokyo District Court ordered the bank's former executive vice president to pay approximately ¥100 million ($1 million) for the alleged violation of duty of care concerning an additional loan to a resort development project.[20]

Facts

This case is an action for damages wherein the plaintiff Shinsei Bank sued its former executive vice president seeking repayment of a portion of an uncollectible loan alleging that the defendant violated the bona fide

---

[16] See *supra* note14.
[17] *Id.*
[18] *Id.*
[19] See note 3.
[20] Tokyo District Court, Civil Case No. 8 Dept., April 25, 2002, Shojihome, No. 1629, May 25, 2002, pp. 58–59.

manager's duty of care as a director responsible for providing an additional loan related to a loan originally provided by the bank's forerunner, LTCB, to a project for developing and managing large scale resort facilities in Hatsushima, Shizuoka prefecture, Japan. The project failed and the loan became uncollectible. After filing the legal action, the plaintiff Shinsei Bank transferred its right to seek damages to the RCC,[21] so the RCC is currently seeking the damages.

The plaintiff claims that the defendant failed to gather sufficient information and analyze the information carefully, failed to specific examine the advantages and disadvantages of providing the additional loan, and actually extended a large loan that had no possibility of collection, thus causing the plaintiff a loss of at least ¥1.6 billion. The plaintiff further claimed that the defendant:

1. Should have reinvestigated the estimate of future sales of memberships, but failed to do so and nonchalantly determined that the loan could be collected;

2. Failed to gather sufficient information and analysis of whether the plaintiff would experience any credibility and/or social liability problems if the plaintiff did not provide the additional loan and how probable those occurrences might be (there was no indication of a high probability of loss to the plaintiff if the plaintiff did not provide the additional loan); and

3. Is liable for negligence because, although the defendant claims that a director of a large corporation is allowed to make decisions based on the reports and analyses provided by the subordinates (Right of Reliance), a director should not rely on the reports and analyses provided by other directors or subordinates when "circumstances that raise warnings" or "abnormal facts" exist. A director cannot be excused for not conducting sufficient information gathering and careful investigation.

---

[21] See note 5.

Court's Judgment

The court acknowledged that the plaintiff incurred approximately ¥6.1 billion loss as a result of the loan, and ordered the defendant to pay approximately ¥100 million to the RCC. The final judgment of the court in this case stated:

> "[T]he defendant who executed the additional loan of this case failed to perform collection and analysis of information believed to be reasonable under the circumstances, evaluated the risk of being unable to collect the additionally loaned fund excessively small relative to the possible loss for not providing any further loan, making an inequitable misjudgment there, and actually executed a large amount of additional loan to the project of the case which had a poor chance of collection, which constitutes a violation of the bona fide manager's duty of care exceeding the limit of discretion entrusted to a director."[22]

Comments

Through this case, the Japanese court showed its conservative position concerning "Right of Reliance," which is approved as an acceptable notion in the United States,[23] and established a principle that a director is not allowed to rely on the reports and analyses provided by other directors and subordinates if "abnormal facts" exist.

Criminal Liability

Legal action has been taken concerning criminal responsibility related to an accounting procedure for bad debts.[24]   A criminal conviction was

---

[22] Translated by the author.

[23] Dennis J. Block, Nancy E. Barton & Stephen A. Radin, *The Business Judgment Rule: Fiduciary Duties of Corporate Directors* (5th Ed. 1998). See Chapter 2, Fiduciary Duties of Corporate Directors.

[24] RCC v. Onogi, Tokyo District Court, Heisei 11, (special Wa), No. 2139 (2002) [hereinafter Criminal Judgment].

made against the former directors of LTCB.[25]   Convicted by the Tokyo District Court on September 10, 2002, the suit accused three directors, including the bank's former president, of violating the Securities Exchange Law and the Commercial Code.[26]   The judgment of the court recognized the criminal responsibilities of the defendants, pointing out a violation of the notice of the MOF.[27]   The case is currently being appealed.[28]

Facts

In June 1998, the defendants submitted to the Director-General of the Securities Bureau in charge of the Kanto area of the Ministry of Finance LTBC's financial statements for fiscal year 1997, April 1997-March 1998 (FY '97), including a balance sheet, a profit and loss statement, and an appropriation statement indicating an undisposed loss of ¥271.6 billion, which was substantially less than the actual loss of ¥584.684 billion.[29]   They excluded write-offs and reserves for loans totaling ¥313.1 billion that were expected to be uncollectible.[30]   The act of submitting financial statements with false information on such an important item was determined to be a violation of Article 197-1 of the Securities Exchange Law.[31]   Moreover, on June 25, 1998, the defendants issued a closing statement at the normal shareholders meeting for its approval,

---

[25] *Id.*
[26] *Id.*
[27] *Id.*
[28] See Nikkei Weekly, Sept. 12, 2002.   In Japan, information about an appealed criminal case is not disclosed until the court judgment is given in order to protect the defendant's privacy.
[29] Criminal Judgment, Tokyo District Court, Heisei 11, (special Wa), No. 2139.
[30] *Id.*
[31] The Securities exchange law (Law No.25 of 1948) provides:
Any person falling under any of the following respective items shall be punished by penal servitude for not more than three years, or by fine of not more than three hundred thousand yen:
(1) Who has, for invitation of subscription or offering-sale, purchase or sale or other transactions of securities, or with the purpose to fluctuate quotations of securities, circulated false rumors, used deceptive schemes, or employed methods of assault and battery of intimidation. . . .).
Securities Exchange Law, Law No. 25 of 1948 (am. 18 times), art. 197.

proposing a profit dividend payout of ¥3 per share, or a total sum of ¥7,178,647,455, out of the unappropriated reserve based on the undisposed loss of ¥271.6 billion mentioned earlier.[32]   In fact, there was an undisposed loss of ¥584.7 billion, no surplus was found at the closing of the fiscal year, and the bank paid out an amount of ¥7,166,002,360 to the shareholders, thus violating the law.[33]   This act allegedly violated Article 489 of the Commercial Code[34] because it was a distribution against Article 290 of the Commercial Code.[35]   Consequently the defendants were indicted for violating both the Securities Exchange Law and the Commercial Code.

Points of Issue

The act of falsifying securities transaction reports is a crime in violation of Article 197-1 of the Securities Exchange Law, which stipulates that "submitting a securities transaction report containing a false statement on a substantial matter" constitutes a crime, wherein the central issue is the existence of a false statement."[36] The method of preparing a securities

---

[32] Criminal Judgment, Tokyo District Court, Heisei 11, (special Wa), No. 2139.

[33] *Id.*

[34] *Id.* The Commercial Code (Law No. 48 of 1899) states:
The persons mentioned in Article 486 paragraph 1 and inspectors shall be liable to imprisonment with forced labor for a term not exceeding five years or to a fine not exceeding two million yen in any of the following cases:
(1) If they have made an untrue statement to or have concealed facts from the Court or the general meeting in respect of the taking up of or payment on all the shares to be issued or of delivery of the property forming the subject-matter of the contribution of property other than money at the time of the incorporation of a company or of any of the particulars mentioned in Article 168 paragraph 1 or Article 280-2 paragraph 1 item (3);
(2) If, for the account of the company, they have wrongfully acquired the shares of the company or have so received them in pledge, irrespective of the name they have used in so acting;
(3) If they have distributed profits or interest, or distributed money under Article 293-5 paragraph 1 in contravention of the provisions of any law or ordinance or of the articles of incorporation;
(4) If, outside the scope of the company's business, they have disposed of the company's property in speculative transactions.
Commercial Code, Law No. 48 of 1899 as amended, art. 489.

[35] *Id.* art. 290.

[36] Securities Exchange Law, Law No. 25 of 1948 (am. 18 times), art. 197-1.

transaction report is defined in the Ministerial Ordinance Balance Sheet, and Profit and Loss Statement, indicating that a balance sheet, a profit and loss statement, and an appropriation statement (or a loss disposition statement) must be shown as the "accounting status" of the corporation in the securities transaction report.[37] These documents must be written in accordance with the Rules of Financial Statements based on Article 193 of the Securities Exchange Law.[38] According to Article 1-1 of the Rules of Financial Statements, etc., the terms, format, and method of constituting the financial statement should be based on these rules, or the "standards of corporation accounting which are generally considered as fair and appropriate" for matters that are not stipulated in the rules.[39]

Meanwhile, the Rules of Financial Statements, etc., which are based on the Securities Exchange Law, show only the superficial contents of the disclosure, so that the essential standards for the accounting procedure for financial statements are based on the Commercial Code.[40] Therefore, the problem of bad loans, the issue of the present case, relates to whether Article 285-4, subsection one and two of the Commercial Code can be applied.[41] The contention here is whether "an amount estimated to be un-collectable has been deducted" with reference to a loan that is "likely to be un-collectable."[42]

---

[37] Ministry of Justice Ordinance, No. 31 of 1963.
[38] The Securities Exchange Law states:
Balance sheets, profit and loss statements, and other documents relating to financial statements to be filed in accordance with the provisions of this Law shall be prepared using such words, manner and method of drawing as prescribed by Ministry of Finance Ordinance according to such standards as generally deemed fair and appropriate by the Minister of Finance.
Securities Exchange Law, Law No. 25 of 1948 (am. 18 times), art. 193; see [Rules on financial statements], Min. Fin. Ord. No. 36 of 1963.
[39] [Rules on financial statements], Min. Fin. Ord. No. 36 of 1963, art. 1-1.
[40] Commercial Code, Law No. 48 of 1899 as amended, art. 489; Criminal Judgment, *supra* note 24.
[41] The Commercial Code states:
The monetary claims shall be valued at the nominal amount thereof; provided that, if they were purchased at the proceeds lower than the nominal amount or there is any reasonable ground, they shall be valued with reasonable decrease. If there is fear of being impossible to collect the monetary claims, the estimated amount of being impossible to collect shall be deducted in valuation.
Commercial Code, Law No. 48 of 1899 as amended, art. 285-4
[42] See *Id.* art. 285-4; Criminal Judgment, *supra* note 24.

However, because the Commercial Code is not specific as to whether a loan is likely to be uncollectible or whether an amount estimated to be uncollectible has been deducted, we have to "rely on the fair accounting practices" as stipulated in Article 32-2 of the Commercial Code.[43]

Next, the unlawful distribution among crimes that threaten the assets of a corporation is defined according to Article 489-3 of the Commercial Code as distributing profits or interests in violation of law or the by-laws of corporation by the directors and others defined in Article 486-1.[44] Here the "law" means Article 290-1 of the Commercial Code, which pertains to the distribution of profits and stipulates that the "distribution of profits" is allowed up to an amount left after deducting a certain amount of money "from the amount of net assets on the balance sheet."[45]

---

[43] "Every trader shall prepare accounting books and balance sheets for making clear the conditions of business properties and profit and loss.   In construing the provisions concerning preparation of the books of account, fair accounting practices shall be taken into consideration."   Commercial Code, Law No. 48 of 1899 as amended, art. 32-2.

[44] The Commercial Code states:

If promoters, directors, auditors, acting directors or auditors under Article 188 paragraph 3, Article 258 paragraph 2, or Article 280 paragraph 1, manager or any other employees commissioned to undertake certain kinds of matters or specified matters relating to the business, have inflicted damage of a proprietary nature on the company in breach of their duties with a view to benefiting themselves or any third person or to damaging the company, they shall be liable to imprisonment with forced labor for a term not exceeding seven years or to a fine not exceeding three million yen.

Id. art. 486.

[45] Article 290 of the Commercial Code states:

The distribution of profits may be made to the extent of the amount computed by deducting the following amounts from the amount of net assets on the balance sheet:

(1) The amount of stated capital;

(2) The total sum of the capital surplus reserve and the earned surplus reserve;

(3) The amount of the earned surplus reserve necessary to be accumulated in the period for the settlement of accounts;

(4) If the total sum of the amounts accounted on the assets side of the balance sheet in accordance with the provisions of Article 286-2 and 286-3 exceeds the total sum of surplus reserves under the preceding two items, such excess.

(5) The total of the amounts entered on the assets side of a balance sheet regarding the shares acquired and held in the case mentioned in item (5) of Article 210, or in accordance with the provision of Article 210-2 paragraph 1 or Article 210-3 of paragraph 1. (If profits have been distributed in contravention of the provisions of the preceding paragraph, any creditor of the company may demand that such profits be refunded.).

Id. art. 290.

As the net asset amount on the balance sheet is evaluated according to the rules of Article 284-2 and other sections of the Commercial Code, LTCB's loans are to be evaluated according to Article 285-4 of the Commercial Code.[46]   Thus, the crime of unlawful distribution according to Article 489-3 of the Commercial Code is essentially a violation of Article 290 of the Commercial Code, and its applicability to the present case depends on whether the evaluation of the LTCB's loans violate Article 285-4 of the Commercial Code.

As can be seen from above, the crime of falsifying a securities transaction report and the crime of unlawful distribution are applicable to the present case depending on whether the defendants failed to "deduct an amount estimated to be un-collectable" with reference to a loan that is "likely to be un-collectable."[47]   Article 285-4, subsection two of the Commercial Code defines the basic principles of the evaluation of the money claim concerning the loans in LTCB's FY '98 closing statement.[48]   In essence, as to the two crimes in question, the issue is how to define "an amount estimated to be un-collectable when it is likely to be un-collectable."[49]

Court's Judgment

The court found the charges were substantiated and the defendants were declared guilty of the crime of falsifying a securities transaction report according to the Securities Exchange Law and the crime of unlawful distribution according to the Commercial Code.[50]

The judgment made clear that determining the standards for judging "an amount likely to be un-collectable" and "an amount estimated to be un-collectable" required "rely[ing] on the fair accounting practices" as

---

[46]   Commercial Code, Law No. 48 of 1899 as amended, arts. 284-2, 285 (stipulating on valuations).

[47]   Criminal Judgment, *supra* note 24.

[48]   Commercial Code, Law No. 48 of 1899 as amended, art. 285-4(2) (stating "[i]f there is fear of being impossible to collect the monetary claims, the estimated amount of being impossible to collect shall be deducted in valuations").

[49]   See Criminal Judgment, *supra* note 24.

[50]   Commercial Code, Law No. 48 of 1899 as amended, art. 290; see also Criminal Judgment, *supra* note 24.

stipulated in Article 32-2 of the Commercial Code.[51]   In other words, according to the judgment, "[o]n the Fund Assessment in a Financial Inspection after the Early Correction System is Implemented (Asset Investigation Notice)," notice issued by the Minister of Finance is a "fair accounting practice" according to Article 32-2 of the Commercial Code and is the only accounting process standard for financial institutions.[52] Therefore, a violation of the notice violates Article 285-4 of the Commercial Code, which concerns the evaluation of credits. [53] Consequently, the accounting process violating said Asset Investigation Notice constitutes a "false representation" under the Securities Exchange Law as well as an illegal distribution in violation of Article 290 of the Commercial Code.[54]

Comments

The point of contention in this case is whether the accounting of the bad debts violates the Commercial Code.[55]   The court passed judgment that the notice issued by the MOF was covered by the Commercial Code, specifically Article 32-2. [56]   However, the author questions this judgment based on the following facts.   First, a minister (higher authority) has jurisdiction to order or instruct an organization under its control (lower authority), but does not have the power to provide rules directly to citizens about their rights or obligations.[57]   However, an administrative notice has power through Article 32-2 of the Commercial Code stating "fair accounting practices."[58]   It is incorrect to assume that

---

[51] Criminal Judgment, *supra* note 24 (paraphrasing Commercial Code, Law No. 48 of 1899 as amended, art. 32-2).
[52] *Id.*
[53] Commercial Code, Law No. 48 of 1899 as amended, art. 285-4.
[54] *Id.* art. 290; see Securities Exchange Law, Law No. 25 of 1948 (am. 18 times).
[55] See Criminal Judgment, *supra* note 24.
[56] Commercial Code, Law No. 48 of 1899 as amended, art. 32-2; Criminal Judgment, *supra* note 24.
[57] See generally The National Administrative Office of Japan, Prime Minister of Japan and His Cabinet, at http://www.kantei.go.jp/foreign/constitution_and_government_of_japan/national_adm_e.html (detailing the responsibility of ministers of finance) (last visited Nov. 22, 2004).
[58] Commercial Code, Law No. 48 of 1899 as amended, art. 32-2.

a notice issued by an authority for the purpose of controlling a specific industry (banking) is acting as law (Commercial Code) for controlling miscellaneous corporations.

Second, the Asset Investigation Notice issued by the MOF, who has the supervisory authority over banks, should provide guidance for "the calculation of the net worth ratios of financial institutions," and is not intended for "clarifying the managerial responsibility of directors by means of disclosing the financial status or operational performances of a corporation from the standpoint of protecting the benefits of the corporation's creditors or shareholders."[59]   It seems reasonable to think that the legal power against an act that violates such a notice is available only for the purpose of exercising the relevant administrative authority. More specifically, it should be understood that the Notice can only be used as the basis for the MOF to take action based on the Banking Law against a bank for violations of the Notice.   There is a problem in viewing an act violating a notice issued by the MOF as a violation of the Commercial Code via Article 32-2.

Finally, there are many problems surrounding the legality of treating a violation of a notice or an administrative guidance order as criminally punishable.   The demand for rigorousness in evaluating assets is necessary for the sound financial administration of the banking business. In order to make it criminally punishable, there should be an accounting standard established as law in express terms.   The creation of a crime based on an unclear accounting standard rather than law should be avoided.

With respect to such a consideration, the recent LTCB case, in which the criminal punishment decision was made against the defendants for the violations of the Securities Exchange Law and the Commercial Code (which is essentially based on the violation of a ministerial notice), presents various problems.   It is clear that the problems were caused by the absence of an express law in Japan regarding "fair accounting practice."

---

[59] Criminal Judgment, *supra* note 24.

Litigation by EIE against LTCB

The bankruptcy administrator of EIE, a resort developer, whose main bank was LTCB, sued LTCB for selling the bad debts below their market values for collection purposes and made a claim against the Shinsei Bank[60] for damages in the order of a few hundred billion yen.

The assets of Mr. Harunori Takahashi,[61] the president of EIE, who was once called the "Pan Pacific King of Resorts" and then later called the "real culprit of the bankruptcy of LTCB," were sold at below market prices by LTCB's directors. Once they found their own management was in trouble, the LTCB's directors made an about-face and started to ask for repayments of their loans with the strategy of "starving Takahashi to death" or "planning a quiet funeral" choking Takahashi little by little. In this secret operation, the bond center Takahashi owned in Hong Kong was sold at a giveaway price of ¥5 billion. It was a shame that the same bond center in Hong Kong was resold at ¥23 billion after only a few months. The Regent Hotel (The Four Seasons) in New York City was also sold at a giveaway price. Mr. Takahashi must have thought that his risks were low as his investments were well diversified throughout Hong Kong, Australia, and other countries. Mr. Takahashi sued the Shinsei Bank, the successor of LTCB, claiming that "he incurred damages because his assets were sold unduly cheap by LTCB." The claim for damages against Shinsei Bank related to the Hyatt Regency Saipan Hotel, the EIE's assets related to its Regency business, and all other assets of EIE throughout the world.[62]

Because the Shinsei Bank wanted to settle quickly on the issue of the LTCB's management and did not want to have a prolonged court battle involving multiple jurisdictions that would require substantial personal and material resources, the case reached a settlement in June 2004 for ¥21.8 billion.[63]

---

[60] See *supra* note 3.

[61] See *supra* note 6.

[62] Refer to the following article of Nikkan Kogyo Shimbun on the background of this suit: *http://www.jij.co.jp/news/market/art-20040217210401-OICMHWLEML.nwc.*

[63] Refer to the Shinsei Bank's homepage dated March 9, March 23, and May 24, 2004 as well as its press release dated May 24, 2004. For further details, see *http://www.shinseibank.com/.*

Conclusion

It seems that a number of civil and criminal charges have been made against bank directors concerning bad loans since the LTCB case, and the number should keep increasing depending on how RCC views director responsibility. However, the problem is that directors as individuals have limited capabilities of paying, regardless of how enormous the damages granted by the courts. Therefore, the next issue will be whether the banks can be held responsible and pursued for damages. This concept of lender liability has been recognized in the United States in the leading case, *Conner v. Great Western Savings & Loan Association.*[64]

Lender liability is the obligation of the person who conducts the business of lending money. A financial institution has various responsibilities to borrowers imposed under public and private laws in various situations.[65]

The action EIE filed against LTCB (Shinsei Bank) seeking damages for the bank's bad loan decisions was a typical example of a lender liability lawsuit and had the potential for becoming the leading case for other cases to follow, but Shinsei Bank chose to settle instead.[66]

At the peak of the financial heyday, LTCB was always looking for borrowers. In fact, it even devised projects and recommended them to corporations. LTCB would evaluate the borrowers' real estate assets to the maximum limit on the assumption that the value of real estate would continue to rise. In some situations, it offered loans even considering the interest payments for the existing loans, exceeding its own lending limits. In other words, LTCB was more eager than the borrowers in agreeing on loans. Everything was rationalized on the assumption that the value of real estate would keep rising. When it all collapsed and the price of real

---

[64] Conner v. Great Western Savings & Loan Association, 69 Cal. 2d 850, 447 P. 2d 609, 73 Cal. Rptr. 369 (1968). *See also* United States v. Fleet Factors Corp., 901 F. 2d 1550 (11th Cir. 1990) in which the court admitted lender liability for environment corruption.

[65] For the first case recognizing lender liability in Japan, see Y Bank vs. A developer, Nagoya district court, (Sept. 26, 1994), Hanji No. 1523, P. 114.

[66] See *supra* note 63.

estate dropped to one fourth of its peak price,[67] most borrowers were unable to pay back their loans. Under pressure to clean up its bad loans, LTCB demanded the borrowers pay back the loans by selling off their collateral real estate. Many companies ended up billions of yen in debt even after selling off their long term real estate assets.

In any lending situation, both the lender and the borrower examine the probability of repayment. No loan is made if they know that repayment is impossible. However, if the repayment scheme is loose, the likelihood of default is high. Some of LTCB's loans did not fail necessarily because of the collapse of the real estate market, as their repayment plans were found to be quite shaky. Both the bank and the borrower assumed that the price of real estate would continue to rise. However, the assumption that the price of land would keep rising at the rate of 20 to 30 percent was utterly incredible. The bank thought that the credit was secure as long as it took real estate as collateral. But it forgot that the client's repaying capability depended on the profit from its business and apparently didn't make the connection that the disposal of the collateral real estate would mean the end of the borrower's business activities.

The LTCB's transactions are characterized by the fact that the financing bank provided loans intentionally distorting the borrower's contract judgment, failing to provide sufficient and reliable information critical to the borrower's judgment, and allowing the borrower to have insufficient understanding and recognition of what it was liable for.

Consequently, it is reasonable that the borrower who incurred damages would want to make a claim against the financing bank for failing to fulfill its legal responsibilities. However, in Japan, the thought has been why should the lender be liable when the lender was only kindly providing money to the borrower in response to the borrower's request, with no recognition of the legal responsibilities of the bank. The "lender liability" concept that originated in the United States is now

---

[67] See the 9th ASIACONSTRUCT Conference report in Australia in Dec. 2003 prepared by the Research Institute of Construction and Economy (RICE), p.8. It indicates that the price index of the commercial land in the major cities in Japan dropped from 350 in 1990 to 90 in 2003. For the details, see Rice, *http://www.rice.or.jp*. For the report, see *http://www.rice.or.jp/j-home/asiaconstruct/9thhihonhoukoku(new).pdf*.

fostering the idea in Japan that the bank (the party that provided the funds) can be pursued for damages in its loan operation.[68] Further development in this area is expected.

Bibliography

Accounting Series Release No. 150, Accounting Series Release (ASR), No. 4 (April 1938) (December 1972).

Allied Chem. & Dye Corp. v. Steel & Tube Co. of America, 14 Del. Ch. 64, 73, 122 A. 142, 146 (Ch. 1923).

Aozora Bank, Ltd., http://www.aozorabank.co.jp/.

Atherton et. al. v. Anderson, No. 7298, 99 F.2d 883; 1938 U.S. App. Lexis 3015.

Bank of Japan, BIS statistics, http://www.boj.or.jp/intl//99/bis9904b.htm.

Banking Law, Section 124.

Bankruptcy Development, see http://www.findai.com/vogo/0023.htm.

Bankruptcy Law, Law No. 71 enacted on April 25, 1922, amended 11 times thereafter, http://www.houko.com/00/01/T11/071.htm.

Bodell v. General Gas & Elec. Corp., 15 Del. Ch. 420, 429–430, 140 A. 264, 268 (Sup. Ct. 1927).

Cabinet Office, EPA, http://www.cao.go.jp/index-e.html.

Cates v. Sparkman, 73 Tex. 619, 11 S.W. 846, 849 (1889).

Chukyo Bank, http://www.chukyo-bank.co.jp/toshika/menu_01.html.

Civil Code, art. 644.

Civil Rehabilitation Law, Law No. 225 of 1999, as amended as Law No. 128 in 2000, http://www.ron.gr.jp/law/law/minji_sa.htm.

Commercial Code, Law No. 48, enacted on March 9, 1899, amended 18 times, wysiwyg://6/http://www.ron.gr.jp/law/law/ syouhou1.htm.

Commercial Code, Law No. 48 of 1899. Kaisha ni Taisuru Sekinin (Responsibilities to Company). Article 266-1-5.

Commercial Code, Article 281.

Commercial Code, Article 285-4.

Commercial Code, Article 287-2.

Commercial Code, Article 33.

Commercial Code, Articles 32-36.

Commercial Code, Article 489.

Commercial Code, Articles 284-2, 285.

Commercial Code, Article 254(3).

Commercial Code, Article 254-3.

---

[68] Recently, there have been a few cases in which the court recognized lender liability in tort. See, *e.g.*, Y Bank v. B Construction Company, Tokyo District Court, Feb. 23, 1995, Hanrei Times, No. 891, p. 208; Y Bank v. A Company, Nagoya District Court, Sept. 26, 1994, Kinpou, No. 1403, p.30.

Commercial Code, Article 260(1).

Commercial Code, Article 290.

Conner v. Great Western Savings & Loan Association, 69 Cal. 2d 850, 447 P. 2d 609, 73 Cal. Rptr. 369 (1968). See also United States v. Fleet Factors Corp., 901 F. 2d 1550 (11th Cir. 1990).

Corporate Accounting Principles, July 9, 1949, as amended in July 14, 1954, November 5, 1961, August 30, 1972 and April 20, 1980, Article 18, wysiwyg://18/http://www.ron.gr.jp/law/etc_txt/kigyokai.htm.

Corporate Rehabilitation Law, Law No. 172 enacted on June 7, 1952, amended on December 13, 2002 (Law No. 154), wysiwyg://8/http://www.ron.gr.jp/law/law/kaishak1.htm.

Corporate Tax Law, Law No. 34, enacted on March 31, 1965, amended many times, http://www.houko.com/00/01/S40/034.htm.

Court Judgment, Tokyo District Court, Heisei 11 (Wa) No. 28167.

Criminal Judgment, Tokyo District Court, Heisei 11, (special Wa), No. 2139.

Criminal Law, Law No. 45 of 1907. Zouwai, Assen Zouwai (Bribery, Mediating Bribery). Art. 198DICJ, see http://www.dic.go.jp/soshiki/soahiki.html.

Davis v. Louisville Gas & Elec. Co., 16 Del. Ch. 157, 169, 142 A. 654, 659 (Ch. 1928).

Delaware Corporate Law, http://www.delcode.state.de.us/title8/c001/index.htm#TopOfPage.

Dennis J. Block, Nancy E. Barton & Stephen A. Radin, *The Business Judgment Rule: Fiduciary Duties of Corporate Directors* (5th Ed. 1998). See Chapter 2, <u>Fiduciary Duties of Corporate Directors</u>.

Deposit Insurance Law, Law No. 34 enacted on March 31, 1965, amended 46 times thereafter, http://www.houko.com/00/01/S40/034.htm.

Edward P. Welch and Andrew J. Tarezyn, "Folk on the Delaware General Corporation Law", Little, Brown and Company, 1993, p. 99–100.

FAS, Statement No. 114, "Accounting by Creditors for Impairment of a Loan — an amendment of FASB Statements No. 5 and 15 (Issued 5/93)".

FAS, Statement No. 118, "Accounting by Creditors for Impairment of a Loan-Income Recognition and Disclosures — an amendment of FASB Statement No. 114 (Issued 10/94)".

FAS, Statement No. 5, "Accounting for Contingencies," March 1975, wysiwyg://28/http://www.fasb.org/st/summary/stsum5.

FAS, statement No. 15, "Accounting for Debtors and Creditors for Troubled Debt Restructurings (Issued 6/77), wysiwyg://28/http://www.fasb.org/st/summary/stsum15.

FDIC v. Brickner, 747 F.2d 1198, 1202 (8th Cir. 1984) (directors could not ignore bank examiner warnings).

FSA, October 30, 2002, Memorandum.

FSA, see http://www.fsa.go.jp.

Fair Trade Act, Law No. 54 of 1947. art. 19.

Federal Deposit Insurance Corporation, in its corporate capacity, Plaintiff-Appellee, v. Gilbert Bierman, V. Edgar Stanley, Robert Marcuccilli, Judith Stanley, Dan

Stanley, and John Boley, Defendants-Appellants, 2 F.3d 1424; 1993 U.S. App. Lexis 20459; 127 A.L.R. Fed. 703.

Financial Services Agency, http://www.fsa.go.jp.

First Nat'l Bank of La Marque v. Smith, 436 F. Supp. 824, 831 (D.C.S.D.Tex.1977), *modified on other grounds*, 610 F.2d 1258 (1980); *Gadd v. Pearson*, 351 F.Supp. 895, 903 (D.C.M.D.Fla.1972); *Litwin v. Allen*, 25.

Gerald K. Smith v. *Arthur Anderson L.L.P.,* 175 F. Supp. 2d 1180; 2001 U.S. Dist. Lexis 20377.

Guth v. Loft, Inc., 23 Del. Ch. 255, 270, 5 A.2d 503, 510 (Sup. Ct. 1939).

Hun v. Cary, 82 N.Y. 65 (1880); People v. Mancuso, 255 N.Y. 463, 175 N.E. 177, 76 A.L.R. 514 (1931).

IMF, Annual Report, 1996, "International Market," p. 29.

Ikenaga v. Tabuchi. Tokyo High Court. September 26, 1995. 16th Civil Dept. 1993 (ne) No. 3778.

International Accounting Standards Board, http://www.iasc.org.uk/cmt/0001.asp.

Japan Economic Journal Weekly, Sept. 12, 2002.

Japan Economic Journal, Apr. 8, 2001, p. 3.

Japan Economic Journal, Dec. 14, 1998, p. 1.

Japan Economic Journal, June 13, 1999, p. 4.

Japan Economic Journal, Mar. 7, 2000, p. (7).

Japan Economic Journal, Sept. 15, 2001, p. 1.

Japan Economic Journal, Sept. 21, 2002 issue, p. 3.

Japan Economic Journal, "Japanese disclosures not showing real pictures," Jan. 25, 1995.

Joseph A. Broderick, as Superintendent of Banks of the State of New York, Plaintiff, v. Bernard K. Marcus and Others, Defendants, 152 Misc. 413; 272 N.Y.S. 455; 1934 N.Y. Misc. Lexis 1377.

Kimura, T. "BOJ and FSA, Which is Wrong?" Bungei Shunju, October 2001 issue, pp.

LTCB's Annual Report, 2000.

LTCB's Annual Report, "Partners," 1999.

Law Concerning Emergency Measures for the Reconstruction of the Functions of the Financial System, Law No. 132, 1998, http://www.dpj.or.jp/seisaku/zaisei/BOX2192.html.

Lippitt v. Ashley, 89 Conn. 451, 94 Atl. 995 (1915); Atherton v. Anderson, 99 F.2d 883 (6th Cir. 1938).

MOF Ordinance No. 24, issued on March 30, 1999, http://www.mof.go.jp/hourei.htm.

MOF Ordinance No. 28, issued on October 30, 1976, http://www.mof.go.jp/hourei.htm.

MOF Ordinance No. 36, issued on November 27, 1963, http://www.mof.go.jp/hourei.htm.

MOF, http://www.mof.go.jp.

Meyerson v. El Paso Nat. Gas Co., 246 A. 2d 789, 794 (Del. Ch. 1967).

Ministry of Finance, http://www.mof.go.jp.

Ministry of Justice Ordinance, No. 31 of 1963.

Misawa, M. Securities Regulation in Japan, 6 Vanderbilt Journal of Transnational Law 447–510 (1973).

Misawa, M. "Bad Loans: A Comparative Study of U.S. and Japanese Regulations Concerning Loan Loss Reserves," The Banking Law Journal, November/December 2004, Volume 121, Number 10, pp. 918–946.

Misawa, M. "Bank Directors' Decisions on Bad Loans: A Comparative Study of U.S. and Japanese Standards of Required Care," The Banking Law Journal, May 2005, Volume 122, Number 5, pp. 429–466.

Misawa, M. "Daiwa Bank Scandal in New York — Its Causes, Significance and Lessons in the International Society," Vanderbilt Journal of Transnational Law, Vol. 29, No. 5, 1996.

Misawa, M. "Laws and Regulations on Problem Loans in Japan — Is Application of International Accounting Standards Possible?" Columbia Journal of Asian Law, Vol. 18, No. 1, Fall 2004, pp. 1–45.

Misawa, M. "Loss Compensation in the Japanese Securities Market: Causes, Significance, and Search for a Remedy," Vanderbilt Journal of Transnational Law, Vol. 25,   No. 1. 1992.

Misawa, M. "The Japanese Big Bank: Will it be Successful?" Risk Management, (Edited by Professor Michael Frenkel Wrish Hommel and Markus Rudolf, WHU-Otto-Beisheim University), October 2004, pp. 801–820.

Misawa, M. "Tokyo as an International Capital Market — Its Economics and Legal Aspects," 8 Vanderbilt Journal of Transnational Law 1–38 (1974).

Moskowitz v. Bantrell, 41 Del. Ch. 177, 179, 189 A. 2d 749, 750 (Sup. Ct. 1963).

Mycal Corporation, http://www.mycal.co.jp/.

Nagoya District Court, Judgment of January 20, 1997, http://www.eiko.gr.jp/4kigyou/kigou_01.htm.

Nikkan Kogyo Shimbun, http://www.jij.co.jp/news/market/art-20040217210401-OICMHWLEML.nwc.

Nippon Keidanren Announcement, http://www.keidan-ren.or.jp/japanese/policy/2001/013/honbun.html.

Nippon Keidanren, http://www.keidanren.or.jp/english/profile/pro001.html.

Nissan Motor's Annual Report, 2002, p. 57. (http://www.infinitinews.com/nav.html).

Nomura Securities, http://www.nomura.co.jp/introduc/company/index.html.

Onioi, A. Representative director of RCC, Announcement at a press interview, on March 7, 2002, http://www.kaisyukikou.co.jp/announce/announce_315.html.

Plaza Accord, http://en.wikipedia.org/wiki/Plaza_Accord.

Polk v. Good, 507 A.2d 531, 536 (Del. 1986).

RCC v. Onogi, Tokyo District Court, Heisei 11 (Wa) No. 28167, judgment delivered, July 18, 2002.

RCC v. Onogi, Tokyo District Court, Heisei 11, (special Wa), No. 2139 (2002)

Research Institute of Construction and Economy (RICE), 9th ASIACONSTRUCT Conference report in Australia in Dec. 2003, p. 8, http://www.rice.or.jp and http://www.rice.or.jp/j-home/asiaconstruct/9thhihonhoukoku(new).pdf.

Resolution Trust Corporation, in its corporate capacity, Plaintiff v. Charles D. Acton, David Clayton, William F. Courtney, Richard L. Davidson, and John R. Rittenberry, Defendants, 844 F. Supp. 307; 1994 U.S. Dist. Lexis 1750.

Resolution and Collection Corporation (RCC) website; http://www.kaishukikou.co.jp/intro/refer_001.html.

Resolution and Collection Corporation (RCC), see http://www.kaishukikou.co.jp/intro/refer_004.html.

"Restatement and Revision of Accounting Research Bulletins," Accounting Research Bulletin No. 43, June 1953 (replaced ARB's issued September 1939 January 1953), Chapter 3A-9.

"Retrospect and Tasks of Japanese Economy," Economic Planning Agency, December 27, 1998.

Robinson v. Pittsburgh Oil Ref. Corp., 14 Del. Ch. 193, 199–200, 126 A. 46, 50 (Ch. 1924).

Ross, Westerfield and Jaffe, "Corporate Finance," 6th edition. The McGraw-Hill Companies, Inc. pp. 67–95.

Rules on financial statements, Min. Fin. Ord. No. 36 of 1963, art. 1-1.

SEC Codification of Financial Reporting Policies § 101; Garrett, The Accounting Profession and Accounting Principles (address before Second Annual Robert M. Trueblood Memorial Conference, Ill. C.P.A. Foundation, Chicago, Oct. 3, 1975).

Securities Exchange Law, Law No. 25, enacted on April 13, 1948, amended 27 times, http://www.houko.com/00/01/S23/ 025.htm.

Securities Exchange Law, Law No. 25 of 1948 (am. 18 times), art. 197.

Securities Exchange Law, Law No. 25 of 1948 (am. 18 times), art. 197-1.

Securities Exchange Law, Law No. 25 of 1948 (am. 18 times), art. 193.

Shinsei Bank, Annual Report 2000, http://www.shinsei-style.com/investors/en/ir/report/report_1999/pdf/ar00eng.pdf.

Shinsei Bank, Ltd., Company Profile *at* http://www.shinsei-style.com/investors/en/about/company/profile.html (citing information as of Mar. 31, 2004).

Shinsei Bank, http://www.shin-seibank.co.jp.

Shinsei Bank's homepage dated March 9, March 23, and May 24, 2004, and press release dated May 24, 2004, http://www.shinseibank.com/.

Sixth Circuit in *Mayer* v. *Mylod,* 988 F.2d 635 (6th Cir. 1993).

Swentzel v. Penn Bank, 147 Pa. 140, 23 Atl. 405, 15 L. R. A. 305, 30 Am. St. Rep 718 (1892); Hathaway v. Huntley, 284 Mass. 587, 188 N. E. 616, 619 (1933); Speigel v. Beacon Participations, Inc., 297 Mass. 398, 8 N.E.2d 895, 904 (1937).

Tax Reform Act of 1986, Pub. L. No. 99-514, 100 Stat. 2085 (1986).

The Law Concerning Emergency Measures for the Reconstruction of the Functions of the Financial System, Law No. 132, 1998, http://www.fsa.go.jp/frc/hourei.html.

The National Administrative Office of Japan, Prime Minister of Japan and His Cabinet, http://www.kantei.go.jp/foreign/constitution_and_government_of_japan/national_adm_e.html (detailing the responsibility of ministers of finance) (last visited Nov. 22, 2004).

Third Circuit in *Shapiro* v. *UJB Financial Corp.,* 964 F.2d 272 (3rd Cir.), *cert. denied,* 121 L. Ed. 2d 278, 113 S. Ct. 365 (1992).

Tokyo District Court, Civil Case No. 8 Dept., April 25, 2002, Shojihome, No. 1629, May 25, 2002, pp. 58–59.

Tokyo District Court, Civil Case No. 8 Dept., April 25, 2002, Shojihome, No. 1629, May 25, 2002, pp. 58–59.

Tokyo District Court, Claim for damage, Heisei 11 (Wa) No. 28167, Judgment delivered on July 18, 2002.

Tokyo District Court. December 22, 1994. Civil Sec. No. 8. 1993 (wa) No. 18447.

Tom J. Billman, et. al. v. State of Maryland Deposit Insurance Fund Corporation, et. al., 88 Md. App. 79; 593 A.2d 684; 1991 Md. App. Lexis 156.

United States Securities Act of 1933 and of the Securities Exchange Act of 1934.   See 15 U.S.C. §§ 77a-77mm (1934), as amended, 15 U.S.C. §§ 77a 77mm (1970) and 15 U.S.C. §§ 78a-78jj (1934), as amended, 15 U.S.C. §§ 78a-78hh(1) (1970).

United States of America v. Ralph H. Whitmore, Jr., 35 Fed. Appx. 307; 2002 U.S. App. Lexis 2364.

Y Bank v. B Construction Company, Tokyo District Court, Feb. 23, 1995, Hanrei Times, No. 891, p. 208; Y Bank v. A Company, Nagoya District Court, Sept. 26, 1994, Kinpou, No. 1403, p.30.

Y Bank vs. A developer, Nagoya district court, (Sept. 26, 1994), Hanji No. 1523, P. 114.

Chapter 5

Disclosure Principle in Japan

Part One

A Comparative Study of US and Japanese Bank Directors' Duty of Disclosure[a]

As a publicly-held company, a bank is required to make timely and appropriate disclosures of corporate information to the public, including investors. In this article, the author studies what a Japanese bank is required to disclose in regard to its important management information including bad debts in terms of its timing and contents under the Japanese Commercial Law, Securities Exchange Law, Banking Law, and Financial Revitalization Law. After explaining comparable obligations under United States law, the author suggests changes to the Japanese policies.

It is important to better understand how Japanese banks operate and their required disclosure, if US banks are to compete with their Japanese counterparts, the second largest GDP country in the world. This advance knowledge is critical not only for US investors in Japanese banks but also for US institutional investors involved in transactions with Japanese

---

[a] This chapter is based on the author's previously published article:
Mitsuru Misawa, "A Comparative Study of US and Japanese Bank Directors' Duty of Disclosure," The Banking Law Journal, January 2006, Volume 123, Number 1, pp. 39–79.

banks. The code of ethics of the Japanese Banking Association[1] defines the importance of disclosure by its member banks as follows:

A bank, in consideration of its social responsibility and public mission, is required to obtain broad understanding and trust from the society, in particular, from its shareholders and investors.

Fair disclosure of management information for being selected and judged by the market and users should contribute to not only the promotion of the society's understanding of and trust on the bank but also to its own self-cleaning capability in order to achieve healthier management.

Such management information disclosures should be geared toward timely and appropriate provisions of various types of information required for rational judgments by shareholders, investor, and users.[2]

Generally speaking, it is not a desirable thing for a bank to disclose all corporate information. It is analogous to individuals disclosing their bookkeeping information, the amount of money they carry in their wallets or the amount of their pay check. However, if we consider that a bank is constantly involved in financial activities on a large scale, we can easily understand why those who are on the opposite side of those deals want such disclosures. It is also not difficult to understand that a bank wants to disclose positive information but negative information as well, because the latter will probably benefit the bank in the long run.

Persons on the other side of a bank transaction who want information about the bank include:

1. the "government agency" who is to control the bank's operation;
2. the "auditor"[3] of a company who is to monitor the bank's operation;

---

[1] *See* http://www.zenginkyo.or.jp/en/index.html (last visited July 8, 2005).

[2] Federation of Bankers Association, http://www009.upp.so-net.ne.jp/juka/zenginkyo_code.htm (last visited July 8, 2005).

[3] Refer to Commercial Law, Article 273 ff.

3.   the shareholder [4] (Incidentally, the shareholder wants such information not necessarily for its desire to participate in the management of the bank but rather for judging the optimum timing for trading the bank's shares.); and
4.   the bank's "transaction partner."

The transaction partner wants information in order to decide whether to participate in a deal with the bank or what to do with a deal already in existence. Such information is important for the bank's creditors and the bank's customers (depositors).

However, it is not unusual for a bank to be unwilling to disclose information voluntarily or to want to disclose only beneficial information. Various laws and regulations are set up to prevent banks from controlling information disclosure to their advantage, and those laws and regulations specify the types of information to be disclosed and who should receive them.

Statutory Regulation for Disclosure in Japan

Securities Exchange Law

The Securities Exchange Law[5] defines a disclosure system concerning securities exchange reports in order to provide investment judgment information to investors concerning the issuing market and the secondary market that constitute the securities market for the purpose of proper management of national economy and protection of investors.[6]

Disclosure of corporate information that can result in insider trading is particularly important.   Information disclosure becomes a critical issue particularly in a takeover bid ("TOB")[7] and when a large amount of stocks is held by a shareholder.[8] There are "TOBs by persons other

---

[4]   *Id.*, Article 230-10 ff.
[5]   The Securities Exchange Law of Japan, Law No. 25 of 1948, art. 127, no. 4 [hereinafter Securities Exchange Law], *available at* http://www.japanlaw.info/f_statements/ PARENT/DX.htm (last visited July 8, 2005).
[6]   Securities Exchange Law, Article 1.
[7]   *Id.*, Article 27-2 ff.
[8]   *Id.*, Article 27-23.

than the issuer"[9] and "TOBs for listed stocks by the issuing company."[10] In the former instance, disclosed information becomes the basis of judgment for shareholders who are general investors if they deal in the particular stocks, i.e., whether they should sell the stocks in response to a TOB. Concerning TOBs, the Securities Exchange Law of Japan demands very strict accounting information disclosure for foreign companies as well, the same as in its source law, the US Securities Exchange Law.

The Commercial Law

The Commercial Law[11] obligates corporations to submit various statements (operating statement, balance sheet, profit & loss statement, profit disposal plan, and schedules of financial statements) for reconciliation of interests among shareholders and creditors.[12]

The Commercial Law, which governs all companies involved in commercial activities, also sets forth rules concerning information disclosure. It defines specifically the rules concerning: publication of items related to corporate registration,[13] efficacies of registrations and publications,[14] submission of financial statements and schedules for financial statements to auditors,[15] maintaining and publicly reporting financial statements, etc.,[16] and reporting, approving, and publicly reporting financial statements.[17]

The corporate information disclosure system under the Commercial Law differs from the disclosure system under the Securities Exchange Law in the following ways:

---

[9] *Id.*, Article 27-2 to 27-22.
[10] *Id.*, Article 27-22-2 to 27-22-4.
[11] The Commercial Law of Japan, Law No. 48 (Mar. 9, 1899) (amended 18 times) [hereinafter Commercial Law], for details, *see* http://www.ron.gr.jp/law/law/syouhou1.htm (last visited July 8, 2005).
[12] Commercial Law, Articles 11 and 188.
[13] Commercial Law, Article 12.
[14] Commercial Law, Article 12.
[15] Commercial Law Article 281-2,
[16] Commercial Law, Article 282.
[17] Commercial Law, Article 283.

1. A disclosure under the Commercial Law is aimed primarily at shareholders and creditors, but a disclosure under the Securities Exchange Law is aimed at the general public including those who are not the shareholders of the particular company.
2. A disclosure under the Commercial Law is aimed at primarily reporting dividend generating profits and the collateral capability of a corporation, while a disclosure under the Securities Exchange Law is aimed at providing information for making investment judgments, thus the disclosures are more detailed and cover a wider scope.
3. The protection of shareholders and creditors under the Commercial Law falls in the category of protection of private interests so that it is relying on an autonomous control under the private law, while the protection of investors under the Securities Law is based on a national objective aimed at proper management of the national economy through fair issuing and trading of securities.

Banking Law

Far more important to a bank, than the general regulations of the Commercial Law and the Securities Exchange Law, is the disclosure duty defined in the Banking Law.[18] For a bank, which is engaged in a special business of handling another person's asset, the contents of information to be disclosed and the method of disclosure are more specifically defined in this special law.

According to the Banking Law, a bank is obligated to generate an interim business report and a business report for each fiscal year and to submit them to the Financial Revitalization Committee.[19] It mandates that balance sheets and profit & loss statements must be publicly disclosed.[20] It also obligates a bank to prepare explanatory documents concerning business and asset status for each fiscal year and display

---

[18] The Banking Law of Japan, Law No. 59 of 1981[hereinafter Banking Law], *available at* http://law.e-gov.go.jp/cgi-bin/idxsearch.cg (last visited July 8, 2005).
[19] Banking Law, Article 19. For the homepage of FRC, *see* http://www.fsa.go.jp/frc/ (last visited July 8, 2005).
[20] *Id.*, Article 20.

them in each branch office for inspection by the public.[21] In addition, there is a rule that obligates a bank to submit reports and reference data to the Financial Revitalization Committee as required.

Financial Revitalization Law

According to the Financial Revitalization Law, a bank is obligated to strive to prevent occurrences of bad debts as well as to eliminate them actively through providing a sufficient amount of bad debt reserve, liquidating bad debts, and actively disclosing bad debts once they are generated.[22]

As to the disclosure of bad debts, a bank must disclose risk-management loans, i.e., loans to bankrupt debtors, loans in default for three months or more, and loans with relaxed loan conditions. These loans are to be delineated by failure to make interest payments or a relaxing of loan conditions; this disclosure is required under the Banking Law.[23]

The Financial Revitalization Law also requires a financial institution to disclose loans it owns classifying them according to the financial status and business record of each debtor, i.e., bankruptcy/rehabilitation loans and equivalent loans, dangerous loans, management-requiring loans, and normal loans.[24] The definition of loan in this situation covers the entire scope of credits including not just loaned money but also debt guaranty.[25]

---

[21]   *Id.*, Article 21.

[22]   The Finance Revitalization Law, Law No. of 1998 [hereinafter Finance Revitalization Law], *available at* http://law.e-gov.go.jp/cgi-bin/idxsearch.cgi (last visited July 8, 2005).

[23]   Enforcement Regulation of Banking Law, Article 19-2, For the Banking Law Ordinance (March 31,1982, MOF No.10), *see* http://law.e-gov.go.jp/cgi-bin/idxsearch.cgi (last visited July 8, 2005).

[24]   Enforcement Regulation of Financial Revitalization Law, Article 5, For the Finance Revitalization Law Ordinance (December 15, 1998, Finance Revitalization Committee No.2), *see* http://law.e-gov.go.jp/cgi-bin/idxsearch.cgi (last visited July 8, 2005).

[25]   *Id.*, Article 4.

Duty of Disclosure in the United States

Statutory Laws

Federal and state laws impose a duty on the officers and directors of corporations to disclose to current and potential investor all facts that are "material" to the corporation's present and future financial health. The scope of "material" information is broad, and is generally regarded to be any information that a reasonable investor would consider important. Disclosure failures can lead to corporate liability, as well as the personal liability of officers and directors. Regarding public companies, the primary laws are the Securities Act of 1933 and the Securities Exchange Act of 1934.[26] These laws require the disclosure of material information in connection with the registration, offering, and sale of securities, and the solicitation of proxies. They also require the reporting of financial conditions in annual 10-K,[27] quarterly 10-Q,[28] and other reports. This can include the reporting of not only past and current financial conditions, but also information that could have an effect on future financial conditions.

Unfortunately, the Securities Exchange Commission ("SEC") has not yet offered specific advice regarding the scope of necessary disclosures for business entities such as banks whose activities are highly regulated by particular government agencies. These agencies have promulgated rules or guidelines. As an example, pursuant to notices issue by the

---

[26] 15 U.S.C. § § 77a–77mm (1934), as amended, 15 U.S.C. § § 77a–77mm (1970), and 15 U.S.C. § § 78a–78jj (1934), as amended, 15 U.S.C. § § 78a–78hh (1). The Act of 1933 was intended to achieve "truth in securities" related to the public offerings in the issuing market, while the Act of 1934 intends mainly to control activities of brokers and dealers as well as the securities market where they operate; at the same time, it established a disclosure system (Securities Report System) that obligates them to disclose pertinent information continuously.

[27] F must be filed within 90 days after the close of the registrant's fiscal year by registrants who do not meet the definition of an accelerated filer. For the details, *see* SEC home page, http://www.sec.gov/(last visited July 8, 2005).

[28] Form 10-Q shall be used for quarterly reports under Section 13 or 15(d) of the Securities Exchange Act of 1934. For the details, *see* SEC home page, http://www.sec.gov/ (last visited July 8, 2005).

Federal Financial Institutions Examination Council ("FFIEC"),[29] banks may be subject to closer scrutiny if disclosure sufficiency questions arise. Other disclosure obligations to investors may arise owing to reporting duties imposed on accountants, auditors, and other professionals, or from contractual obligations to creditors or other parties.

The Sarbanes-Oxley Act[30] was passed in 2002 after the run of corporate scandals. The intent was to bolster the governance of boards of directors at public companies and regulate the activities of the accounting profession. The act tightens auditing and accounting rules, primarily by requiring CEO and CFO certification of financial statements and the setup of independent audit committees. Although banks met many of Sarbanes-Oxley's requirements through the Federal Deposit Insurance Improvement Act, the scrutiny is now greater. A ramping up of the disclosure effort is now required in order for banks to comply with the new rules that have come into play.

Delaware's Duty of Disclosure (Common Law)

In general, Delaware recognizes that directors owe fiduciary duties to the corporation and its shareholders consisting of the duties of care, loyalty, and good faith.[31] The duty of care requires directors to act on an informed basis and the duty of loyalty requires directors to serve the corporation and its shareholders to the exclusion of all other interests. The duty of good faith is an overarching duty incorporating principles underlying the duties of care and loyalty.

---

[29] The Council is a formal interagency body empowered to prescribe uniform principles, standards, and report forms for the federal examination of financial institutions by the Board of Governors of the Federal Reserve System and to make recommendations to promote uniformity in the supervision of financial institutions. For the details of the Council, *see* http://www.ffiec.gov/ (last visited July 8, 2005).

[30] It is said that the Sarbanes-Oxley Act, passed in response to major corporate accounting scandals such as Enron and Tyco, is the most sweeping regulatory reform of publicly traded markets since the 1930s. For details, *see* The Sarbanes-Oxley Act Community Forum, http://www.sarbanes-oxley-forum.com/.

[31] *See generally* Dennis J. Block, Nancy E. Barton & Stephen A. Radin, *The Business Judgment Rule: Fiduciary Duties of Corporate Directors* (5th ed. 1998).

Delaware law also recognizes that directors are subject to a fiduciary duty to disclose fully and fairly all material information within the directors' control when it seeks shareholder action, such as in proxy solicitations or self-tender offers.[32] In such cases, litigants need not establish reliance, causation, or actual monetary damages.[33] Thus, in a traditional duty of disclosure case, Delaware courts focus on whether the allegedly misrepresented or omitted information is material to the shareholder action requested and whether it was communicated in a balanced and truthful manner.[34] In this regard, Delaware courts have adopted the materiality standard articulated by the US Supreme Court with respect to the federal securities laws.[35] "There must be a substantial likelihood that the disclosure of the omitted fact would have been viewed by the reasonable investor as having significantly altered the 'total mix' of information made available."[36]

In one decision, the Delaware Supreme Court appeared to expand claims based on disclosure allegations beyond those permitted under the traditional duty of disclosure, although under very narrow circumstances. In the leading case, *Malone v. Brincat*,[37] shareholders of Mercury Finance Company brought a class action alleging that Mercury's directors made false and misleading public disclosures and filed reports with the SEC over a four-year period that grossly overstated the company's earnings, financial performance, and shareholders' equity. The complaint further alleged that Mercury's announcement in late 1996 that the company would have to restate its earning for the prior three years caused an almost total depreciation of the company' $2 billion market value.

On appeal, the Delaware Supreme Court sitting *en banc* held that the complaint should have been dismissed without prejudice because the plaintiffs alleged that defendants damaged the corporation but failed to assert a proper derivative claim. The Court recognized that the traditional

---

[32] *Stroud v. Grace,* 606 A.2d 75, 84, (Del. 1992).

[33] *Cinerama, Inc. v. Technicolor, Inc.,* 663 A.2d 1156, 1163 (Del. 1995).

[34] *See Arnold v. Society for Savings Bancorp, Inc.,* 650 A.2d 1270, 1277 (Del. 1994).

[35] *Rosenblatt v. Getty Oil Co.,* 493 A.2d 929, 944 (Del. 1985).

[36] *TSC Industries, Inc. v. Northway, Inc.,* 426 US 438, 449 (1976).

[37] *Malone v. Brincat,* 722 A.2d 5 (Del. 1998).

duty to disclose was not implicated because the directors were not seeking shareholder action. The Court explained that the disclosure duty is a "specific application" of the more general fiduciary duties of care, loyalty, and good faith that is implicated only when directors seek such action.[38] In such cases, the Court noted directors are required to disclose all material information within the directors' control regarding the requested action. Therefore, litigants need not establish reliance, causation, or actual monetary damage to recover under the duty of disclosure. Rather, the central issue is whether the disputed information is material to the shareholder action requested and whether it is communicated in a balanced and truthful manner. In that regard, the Court, quoting *Zirn*,[39] confirmed that "a good faith erroneous judgment as to the proper scope or context of required disclosure implicates the duty of care rather than duty of loyalty.[40]

International Standard Applicable to the United States and Japan

Non-Financial Disclosure

In 1998, The International Organization of Securities Commissions ("IOSCO")[41] endorsed the International Disclosure Standards for

---

[38] *See Lynch v. Vickers Energy Corp.*, 383 A.2d 278 (Del. 1978); *see also* Lawrence A. Hamermesh, "Calling off the Lynch Mob: the Corporate Director's Fiduciary Disclosure Duty," 49 *Vand. L. Rev.* 1089 (1996).

[39] *Zirn v. VLI Corp.*, 621 A.2d 773 (Del. 1993).

[40] *See Lynch v. Vickers Energy Corp.*, 383 A.2d 278 (Del. 1978); *see also* Lawrence A. Hamermesh, "Calling off the Lynch Mob: the Corporate Director's Fiduciary Disclosure Duty," 49 *Vand. L. Rev.* 1089 (1996).

[41] The International Organization of Securities Commissions (IOSCO) was born in 1983 from the transformation of its ancestor inter-American regional association (created in 1974) into a truly international cooperative body. Now IOSCO's membership stands at 181 members and it is still growing rapidly. The SEC of the United States and the MOF of Japan are also the active members. The Organization's members regulate more than 90 percent of the world's securities markets and IOSCO is today the world's most important international cooperative forum for securities regulatory agencies. Among the recent key achievements of IOSCO is the adoption in 1998 of a comprehensive set of Objectives and Principles of Securities Regulation (IOSCO Principles) recognized today by the world financial community as international benchmarks for all markets. For the details of IOSCO, http://www.iosco.org/about/see.

Cross-Border Offerings and Initial Listings by Foreign Issuers for equity securities ("IDS98"), [42] which set forth non-financial statement disclosure standards for offerings and listings of equity securities. These standards are very significant for Japanese banks in regard to what disclosures are needed.

IOSCO recognizes that:

Reliable, timely and readily accessible information is fundamental for investors. Information should be disclosed on a timely basis, whether in connection with an initial public offering or listing, continuously, currently or periodically, and in a form or manner either prescribed by accounting standards, regulations, listing rules or law, together with the information that is provided by the management under the principles of fair presentation. [43]

IOSCO supports international accounting standards [44] and does not have an accounting standard of its own. As an agency responsible for controlling the securities business and markets, the SEC in the United States has never had its own accounting standard either. [45] The SEC explicitly states that it relies on the Financial Accounting Standard Board ("FASB") as to the accounting standard. On the contrary, the Finance Ministry of Japan [46] has jurisdictions over both the "establishment of the accounting standard" and the "control of the securities business and market." It is a common practice in developed countries to have an

---

[42] For the details of IDS98, see http://www.iosco.org/pubdocs/pdf/IOSCOPD132.pdf.

[43] *Id.*, p.2.

[44] This is a collective name for accounting standards established by the International Accounting Standards Board (IASB) with the purpose of being approved and observed internationally. International Accounting Standards (IAS) were issued by the International Accounting Standards Committee (IASC) from 1973 to 2000. The IASB replaced the IASC in 2001. Since then, the IASB has amended some IAS, has proposed to amend other IAS, has proposed to replace some IAS with new International Financial Reporting Standards (IFRS), and has adopted or proposed certain new IFRS on topics for which there were no previous IAS. See generally the Web site of the IASB at http://www.iasb.org (last visited July 8, 2005).

[45] *See* SEC Concept Release: International Accounting Standards, http://www.sec.gov/.

[46] The Ministry of Finance was reorganized on January 6, 2001. The name was changed from "Okurasho" to "Zaimucho" in Japanese, but the English name still remains the same. For more information about the reorganization, *see* the Ministry's Web site at http://www.mof.go.jp (last visited July 8, 2005).

independent institution for setting the "accounting standard" so that the standard is free from any political interventions.   Japan is the only developed country in which the office responsible for controlling the securities business and markets is also responsible for establishing the accounting standard.

On May 17, 2000, IOSCO approved 40 items of core standards that the International Accounting Standards Committee ("IASC") had requested IOSCO to approve concerning cross boarder financial reporting.   IOSCO made clear that it would approve the International Accounting Standard as the accounting standard when a company acquires funds overseas.   Once this is approved in each country, every company of every country will be able to acquire funds in all other countries using financial statements based on the International Accounting Standard.

IOSCO is developing a comparable set of international disclosure standards for cross-border offerings and initial listings of debt securities by foreign issuers that would be based on IDS98. The adoption of both sets of non-financial statement disclosure standards by jurisdictions would facilitate cross-border offerings because a foreign issuer could use one disclosure document that would be accepted in multiple jurisdictions. At the same time, adequate investor protection would be assured through the use of the high quality disclosure standards of the IDS98.[47]

Because most investors participate in the market through secondary trading rather than initial public offerings, providing high quality information to the markets on a periodic basis is crucial, even if a company only infrequently makes public offerings.[48] Most retail investors also participate in the securities markets through secondary trading rather than through initial offerings of securities. Material information should be updated and provided on an ongoing basis to the public, so those who participate through secondary trading, and who are most in need of regulatory protection, can benefit from this same type of disclosure on an ongoing basis.[49]

IOSCO claims that:

---

[47] *Id.*
[48] *Id.*
[49] *Id.*

The fundamental principle of full and fair disclosure is that the listed entity should provide all information that would be material to an investor's investment decision. Such information also includes management's discussion and analysis ("MD &A"), where required, which could be disclosed in a separate report or included as part of a periodic report.[50]

IOSCO also recognizes that competent authorities in different jurisdictions have used two basic approaches, as well as a combination of the two, in order to ensure appropriate disclosure of information by listed entities in view of the interest of investors: (1) a "general obligation" approach and (2) a "prescription approach."[51] IOSCO further states that in spite of the different approaches used, most jurisdictions agree that listed entities should have an ongoing obligation to disclose information that would be material to an investor's investment decision and that is necessary for full and fair disclo-sure.[52]

According to IOSCO, regulators in the European Union employ the general obligation approach and require listed entities to disclose information under a general obligation of materiality comprising price sensitive information, without specifically describing the types of events that would be deemed material. Such information, if determined price sensitive or material, would have to be disclosed immediately by issuers without any further qualification.[53] This approach includes information that is typically assessed against (1) the likely effect of the information on the price or value of the relevant equities, (2) the information expectations of a reasonable investor in the market, and (3) the information to be disclosed has not been made available to the public. Some jurisdictions have indicated events that typically can be considered material.[54]

The United States and Japan, according to IOSCO, employ the pre-scription approach. In this approach a set of rules specify the disclosures that issuers must provide to investors and the public, and that are

---

[50] *Id.*
[51] *Id.* at p.3.
[52] *Id.*
[53] *Id.*
[54] *Id.*

presumptively material. The US SEC requires all public domestic companies to file annual and quarterly periodic reports that address certain specified disclosure items. In addition, all public domestic companies must file current reports on Form 8-K in the intervening period between periodic reports to disclose a specific, comprehensive list of events that are presumptively material. Such disclosure must be made within a few business days after occurrence of the corporate event that must be disclosed. It has been proposed to substantially increase the list of events that are presumptively material.[55]

The US exchanges require disclosure of price sensitive information. The definition of materiality that is used by the SEC has been developed by the courts and is not delimited by the notion of the effect on the price of an issuer's securities. Thus, while the listed entity is required by the United States, the SEC's rules require the disclosure of specific information or events in a prescribed manner. If investors feel that the disclosure is inadequate or misleading they can take legal action against the issuer and the courts will determine the materiality of the disclosure or non-disclosure.[56]

Also Japan provides a list of corporate events that are presumed to be material and require compulsory disclosure.[57] It is noteworthy that consolidated financial statements were not required in the past in Japan but are now required in addition to individual financial statements for corporations who own subsidiaries.[58] In the Ministry of Justice Ordinance, a "subsidiary company" is defined as one in which 50 per cent or more if its stock is held by the parent company.[59] The Securities Exchange Law of Japan requires that the financial statements of an "important subsidiary company" be included in the securities report of the parent company.[60] The Ministry of Finance Ordinance definition of a "subsidiary company" is the same as that in the Ministry of Justice

---

[55] *Id.* at p.7.
[56] *Id.*
[57] *Id.* at p.10.
[58] Ministry of Justice Ordinance, no.22, (May 29, 2002).   For the details, *see* http://www.moj.go.jp/PUBLIC/MINJI29/refer01.html.
[59] Ministry of Justice Ordinance of note 55, Art. 9.
[60] Securities Exchange Law, Arts. 23, 24.   See Ministry of Finance Regulation of June 1, 1972, Concerning Registration of Offers and Sales of Securities No. 32, Art. 15.

Ordinance, but an "important subsidiary" is defined as one whose assets or sales are large enough to have a great effect on the financial situation of the parent company.[61] Because different information concerning a subsidiary is required by the two ministries, what information is to be disclosed will depend on which ordinance is followed.

Financial Disclosure

Although the business activities of corporations are becoming more international every year, the accounting systems of individual countries seem to remain very local, differing from country to country. Recently, a cry was heard for the need for an international standardization of the accounting system so that investors can understand and properly compare the performance of corporations of other countries when they seek financing overseas. As a result of these concerns, international accounting standards are gradually taking shape.

The Norwalk Agreement was the result of a joint meeting between the US Financial Accounting Standards Boards ("FASB")[62] and the International Accounting Standards Board ("IASB")[63] in September 2002. The agreement sought convergence between the International Financial Reporting Standards ("IFRS")[64] and US standards, and laid the

---

[61] Ministry of Finance Ordinance, No. 32, (June 1, 1971), Art 15.

[62] "The mission of the Financial Accounting Standards Board is to establish and improve standards of financial accounting and reporting for the guidance and education of the public, including issuers, auditors, and users of financial information." Financial Accounting Standards Board, Mission Statement, *available at* http://www.fasb.org/ (last visited Feb. 24, 2005).

[63] In June 1973, the International Accounting Standards Committee was established through the joint efforts of 10 countries, including the United States, Japan, England, France, and Germany. This committee was reorganized as the IASB in April 2001.

[64] This is a collective name for accounting standards established by the International Accounting Standards Board ("IASB") with the purpose of being approved and observed internationally. International Accounting Standards ("IAS") were issued by the International Accounting Standards Committee ("IASC") from 1973 to 2000. The IASB replaced the IASC in 2001. Since then, the IASB has amended some IAS, has proposed to amend other IAS, has proposed to replace some IAS with new International Financial Reporting Standards (IFRS), and has adopted or proposed certain new IFRS on topics for which there was no previous IAS. *See generally* the IASB Web site at http://www.iasb.org (last visited July 8, 2005).

foundation for further convergence of various international accounting standards.[65] It was decided that the IFRS is to be adopted officially in 2005 as the financial reporting standard for corporations in the European Union whose stocks are traded in markets.

The European Union has asked non-EU entities operating in the European Union to disclose information based on the "IFRS or an equivalent standard" starting in 2005. As of now, more than 250 Japanese corporations and Japanese local governments have issued stocks and bonds in the European Union. Most of these Japanese corporations disclosed financial information using Japanese accounting standards.[66]

During the years that followed the mid 1990s, many Japanese companies whose operations appeared healthy on financial statements started to fail one after the other, causing a general distrust in the Japanese accounting system. Facing such a situation, the Japanese corporate accounting system made an about-face starting to rehabilitate its standard, and is currently on its way to matching the International Accounting Standard. The recent revamping of the accounting rules in Japan is trying to eliminate the gap with the US accounting standard and the International Accounting Standard from the standpoint of providing an accounting standard that provides information useful for investors and creditors in decisionmaking, which is the basic principle of the global standard. The US accounting standard and the International Accounting Standard are considered the embodiments of the global standard in Japan and it is now regarded as an urgent and extremely important issue to make the corporate accounting system match the global standard.

---

[65] In October 2002, SEC Chairman Harvey C. Pitt applauded the decisions by the FASB and the IASB to work together toward greater convergence between US Generally Accepted Accounting Principles and international accounting standards. He said, "This is a positive step for investors in the United States and around the world. It means that reducing the differences in two widely used sets of accounting standards will receive consideration by both boards, as they work to improve accounting principles and address issues in financial reporting." *See* US Securities and Exchange Commission, Press Release, Actions by FASB, IASB Praised (Oct. 29 2002) *at* http://www.sec.gov/news/press/2002-154.htm (last visited July 8, 2005).

[66] Kazuo Hiramatsu and Shigeo Naruse, Kaikei Kijun — Nichi Ou Sougo Shounin WoNikkei [Accounting Standards — Hoping for Mutual Acceptance between Europe and Japan], Nikkei, July 27, 2004, at 27.

Japan is now negotiating diligently with the European Union and is asking for its approval of the Japanese accounting standard as an equivalent to the IFRS. If the Japanese accounting standard fails to be recognized as an equivalent of the IFRS, disclosure by Japanese companies based on the Japanese accounting standard currently in the European Union would not be allowed, severely affecting the financing activities of Japanese companies seeking to raise funds in the European Union. Japanese corporations also are concerned about the possibility that Japanese accounting standards could be branded as inferior to the European or US Accounting Standards, thus causing a general mistrust among investors in Japanese capital markets.[67]

There have been divergent opinions from the government and private sectors about the adoption of the IFRS in Japan and no consensus has yet been reached.

Selective Disclosure of Corporate Information in the United States

Background

In October 2001, the SEC implemented Regulation FD concerning selective disclosure.[68] The rule was intended to prohibit US companies' directors from selectively disclosing unpublished important information to analysts and institutional investors. In other words, if a company

---

[67] Japanese Ministry of Economy, Trade and Industry, Report on the Internationalization of Business Accounting in Japan (July 21, 2004), *available at* http://www.iasplus.com/resource/0406ifrsjapangaap.pdf (last visited July 8, 2005).

[68] The US SEC made the following statement as a reason for establishing Regulation FD: "SEC had had a concern over the rising number of cases where important corporate information is disclosed only selectively. In various cases reported, companies chose to provide important information such as future profit estimates to be disclosed the to selected securities analyst and/or institutional investors in private meetings and conference calls shutting out the general public and mass media people. Those who received the selectively disclosed information will be in unfairly advantageous positions compared to those who will receive the information when the securities issuers make official announcements.... Selective disclosure damages the investors' trusts on our market and can cause serious conflict of interest among securities analysts." SEC Proposed Rule: Selective Disclosure and Insider Trading (57-31-99) dated December 15, 1999. *See* http://www.sec.gov/rules/proposed/34-42259.htm (last visited July 8, 2005).

wishes to disclose unpublished information, the company cannot disclose it to selected people, but rather must disclose it broadly to the general public. If it has selectively disclosed unpublished important information by mistake, it must disclose the same information immediately to the general public. If a company fails to follow Regulation FD, the SEC is entitled to issue an elimination order or to file a civil suit seeking an injunction and payment of a fine.[69]

The SEC feels that corporate information is the lifeline of the market and fairness and equity must be maintained in providing information. Selective disclosure of information that can affect share prices results in profit gaining opportunities for certain people only. Such disclosure can damage investors' trust in the market, and thus must be prohibited. On the other hand, there are concerns that restriction of information disclosure by legal punishment may force corporations to be too cautious about information disclosure and may result in a reduction of information available to the public,[70] thus increasing volatility of stock prices.[71]

Regulation FD has not been introduced in Japan. However, Regulation FD does seem to be the right direction for further development of the market and it is hoped that there will be serious discussions among those involved and that improvements will be made in advancing fair and just information disclosures. Regulation FD in the United States is not applicable to offshore companies, but some of the Japanese companies, especially those that are listed on the US markets,

---

[69] *Id.*

[70] The Securities Industry Association (SIA) stated in its letter to the SEC dated June 13, 2000 that, while it agrees that company officers' ill-intended selective disclosure of information to specific analysts and investors must be avoided by all means, the proposed rule will not be proper for achieving its goal but rather may prevent the flow of information to the market on the contrary. Although it admits that there is a need for some rule concerning selective disclosure, the letter suggests that there could have been a better approach if a review for further refining the means of preventing fraudulent acts had been made based on the past court cases of fraudulent acts. See the letter of Stuart J. Kaswell, SVP, SIA to Arthur Levitt, Chairman, SEC, on June 13, 2000, http://www.sia.com/2000_comment_letters/.

[71] Henry M. Paulson, the chairman of board of Goldman Sachs, made a negative evaluation of the rule that "FD's motive was good but, but it ended up increasing the market's volatility in the actuality." *See* Alan McNee, ERisk, "End of the Line for Fair Disclosure?," on Tuesday, April 17, 2001, http://www.erisk.com/ResourceCenter/Regulation/EndoftheLineforFairDisclo.asp.

are already reviewing their information disclosure practices as a result of the implementation of Regulation FD.

Although Regulation FD gives some examples as to what is "important information," there is no exact definition of important information. Its scope may cover a much wider range than the important information defined in the Japanese Securities Exchange Law. [72] Consequently, those Japanese companies are reviewing their disclosure practices on the assumption that information that falls into a gray zone between the assumed scope of Regulation FD and the important information defined in the Japanese Securities Exchange Law may be treated on the same basis.

Difference between US and Japanese Insider Trading Regulations

In adopting a regulation in Japan similar to Regulation FD in the United States, the differences between the US and Japanese regulations concerning insider trading must be kept in mind. Even though it is punishable under the Japanese regulation if some people gain profits as a result of selective disclosure of information,[73] it may be difficult to do so under US law.

In contrast to Japan, there is no statutory law that supports the insider trading regulation in the United States. Regulations and remedial actions have been accomplished under the common law developed under Section 10 of the Securities Exchange Law of 1934, which was originally intended to control market manipulations; this is on what SEC Rule 10b-5 is based. This US common law followed the concept that insiders of a company who trade securities using internal information are punishable under the Securities Exchange Law, if their acts constitute breach of their duties to the shareholders of the company that issued the securities.[74] Although the scope of cases to which the violation of the Securities Exchange Law is applicable was expanded later to include cases in which the violators breached their fiduciary duties to those who

---

[72] Securities Exchange Law, Art 166-2.
[73] Security Exchange Law, Arts 166-1, 166-2, 166-3.
[74] *Chianella v. United States,* 445 US 222 (1980).

are outside the company that issued the securities,[75] violations that are punishable as insider trading are nonetheless still limited to cases in which the use of undisclosed information constitutes a breach of duty to certain people.

It has been considered that a person who trades securities based on information received from an insider can be accused of insider trading only when the insider's information constitutes a breach of the insider's fiduciary duty and the person receiving the information knew or was in a position to know about it.[76] In such a situation, it was also considered that the judgment as to whether the insider was breaching the fiduciary duty should be based on an implied datum whether the insider gained any personal profits directly or indirectly.[77]

Under such a common law, it was difficult to prove wrongdoing of a company in a situation when the company selectively discloses its performance information to analysts and the like in order to avoid erratic fluctuations of its stock price, resultantly allowing some people to obtain personal gains using such information. Thus it was difficult to regulate such a situation within the framework of the insider trading rule.

In Japan, however, detailed regulations exist concerning insider trading. The Securities Exchange Law, as well as related ordinances, formally define insider trading. Breach of fiduciary duty is not listed as a requirement for insider trading in Japan.   Therefore, the insider trading regulation is applicable in Japan if a company provides guidance to certain analysts, as in the United States, this guidance corresponds to unpublished important information defined in Section 166-1 of the Securities Exchange Law, and the analyst or the corporation the analyst belongs to tried to trade the particular company's stocks.

Moreover, unlike the US common law, the Japanese Securities Exchange Law and related ordinances (some have umbrella clauses) provide detailed definitions, including numerical standards as to what constitutes important information in each category of determined facts,[78]

---

[75] *United States v. Newman*, 664 F.2d 12 (2d Cir. 1981), *aff'd after remand*, 722 F.2d 729 (2d Cir. 1983), *cert. denied*, 464 US 863 (1983).

[76] *Dirks v. SEC*, 463 US 646 (1983).

[77] *SEC v. Adler*, 137 F.2d 1325 (1998).

[78] Securities Exchange Law, Art. 166-2.

occurred facts, and closing or estimated value concerning profits. This helps companies decide whether a piece of information is an important fact or not, and whether or not to disclose the information to certain people only, or to disclose it to the public.

Consequently, the problems associated with selective disclosures that have been noted in the United States can be avoided in Japan simply by following the disclosure laws and the insider trading regulations already in existence. This has delayed the introduction of Regulation FD in Japan, because it has not been seen as necessary.

Conclusion

After World War II, Japan enacted the Securities Exchange Law (based on two American statutes: (1) the Securities Act of 1933 and (2) the Securities Exchange Act of 1934), which called for detailed disclosure to insure the protection of investors. However, the disclosure requirements in Japan have a few material defects when compared to its American counterparts. For instance, the Japanese law does not require the preparation of quarterly consolidated financial statements; something very customary in the United States. This difference is vital because a consistent internationally-oriented government policy toward investment and securities regulation is an indispensable prerequisite to the internationalization of the Tokyo market.

Every corporation, including banks, listed on the securities exchange must disclose its business contents accurately. It is a basic requirement if corporations and stock markets are to be trusted. Generally Japanese companies and banks have not felt a need to immediately disclose important information, until now. It is important for Japanese companies and banks to observe the disclosure principle more stringently and to disclose pertinent operating information to stakeholders, such as stockholders and corporate customers, earlier, more quickly, more frequently, and more thoroughly, rather than reporting it privately to authorities such as the Ministry of Finance. The more thoroughly Japanese companies and banks conduct disclosure, the higher their market evaluations will be. By assuming full and strict responsibility of management and supervision, they will be able to regain the trust of the international securities market.

To maintain a trustworthy Japanese disclosure system, and to build a financial market that can be respected by the rest of the world, it is first mandatory to solve the basic problems underlying the system, such as the accounting standards. The economic recovery of Japan will foster the economic recovery of the world. For Tokyo to be a real world market, it is necessary to build a more efficient disclosure system and support the overall restructuring of socio-economic systems in Japan.

While a reformation of the financial system is currently under way in Japan, it is essential to promote a "new financial flow" and to normalize the risk of distribution as well as to improve efficiency in the economic society as a whole in order to seek further development. As a premise to this, a renewal of financial services to support such a reform is indispensable. The strengthening of the disclosure system, especially the accounting standards, is most essential. Such a refurbishment of the system will enable users of Japanese financial services around the world to select combinations of risks and returns with more peace of mind.

A series of actions taken in the United States, triggered by the Enron incident, starting with the "Sarbanes-Oxley Act" of July 2002, strongly suggested to the world that enhancement of accounting, disclosure, and auditing as well as corporate governance are keys to the vitalization of the economic society. Efforts by governments of various countries, the IOSCO, and others toward "standardization" are accelerating. With Japan's economic activities becoming more international and versatile, its standard environment cannot be isolated from the "international trend." The government must get more involved in reshaping and improving the system from the standpoint of "international harmonization."

As each country has its own history, value system, and political system, so each country's corporate accounting is uniquely its own. However, due to economic globalization, business environments are starting to homogenize across borders. Therefore, it is important to adapt the corporate accounting system in Japan to the global economy, not only for financial and capital market reform, but also for supporting international activities of Japanese companies and banks. The more global the company's activities are, the more important it will be for the company to compete under the same international rules. If Japan as a nation fails to follow the global standard, it will be more difficult for Japanese companies and banks to finance overseas and the Japanese economy will eventually lose its vitality.

Part Two

Case of Seibu Group — Recent Problems on Japanese Corporate Disclosure System

Introduction

The Securities Exchange Law was introduced after World War II, and at that time, aimed to copy the same laws established in 1933 and 1934 in the United States. It is now appropriate to evaluate the efficacy of the transplanted systems. The question is to the congeniality of the environment into which the American system was transplanted.

First of all, the difference in perspective between the two countries, US and Japan, made substantially different development of the disclosure systems. It includes an essential problem that cannot be brushed away as a difference of culture. A wide discrepancy exists between the two countries in the way the laws regarding the disclosure system of corporate information are applied. It is mandatory for US corporate management to "disclose important information in the *earliest possible* chance." However, it is quite different in Japan. It is generally thought that a disclosure should be made at a carefully selected, proper timing. Even the Ministry of Finance considers matters in this way. This misconception between the two countries is really the largest factor that created the difference in the current disclosure systems.

Disclosure is a good subject for US and Japanese readers, since the Seibu Scandal was revealed recently in Japan, which gave the investors of the world to Japanese companies some doubts as to the Japanese disclosure system. As you may know, Seibu is one of the leading Japanese listed companies and disclosed wrong information as to the share holdings by affiliated companies for some 40 years. It is considered to be the Japanese "Enron" Case, as the scandal caused large shocks to the Japanese business community and international investors to Japan. We also study the Daiwa Bank case to see the differences in disclosure requirements and practices existing in the US and Japan.

Japanese corporate behavior and practice raises a number of issues for international lawyers in the US   Japan's economy is the second largest in the world but there are many things that American lawyers find difficult to understand.   Their interest in the current Japanese market and economy is significant and increasingly prominent.

Efficacy of Japanese Disclosure System and the Seibu Case

Yoshiaki Tsutsumi, the former chairman of the board of Kokudo Corp.,[1] who used to lead the Seibu Group[2] as the owner of the group in a practical sense, was arrested by the Tokyo District Public Prosecutors Office on March 3, 2005 and subsequently indicted by the same on March 24, 2005 on a charge of violations of the Security Exchange Law[3] concerning the stocks of Seibu Railway Co., Ltd. (hereinafter called "Seibu") owned by Kokudo Corp.

The alleged charge was divided into two accounts. One of them is that while in fact Kokudo owned approximately 64% of the outstanding shares of Seibu, it hid a portion of it and reported the Ministry of Finance (MOF)[4] a false ratio of stock holding 43% on the financial statements. (See Fig. 1 for the total picture of the Seibu Group with Kokudo sitting at the top.) Another account is that of an insider trading in selling a portion

---

[1] Hereinafter called "Kokudo".
[2] For the details, see the home page of the Seibu Group, http://www.seibu-group.co.jp
[3] Nikkei, March 24, 2005, p. 1.
[4] The Ministry of Finance (MOF) was reorganized on January 6, 2001. The name was changed from Okurasho to Zaimucho in Japanese, but the English name still remains the same. For more information about the reorganization, see http://www.mof.go.jp. The Financial Services Agency ("FSA") was created as of July 1, 1997, with the integration of the Banking Supervisory Agency and the Financial System Planning Bureau of the Ministry of Finance. See MOF website at http://www.fsa.go.jp/news/newsj/15/ singi/f-20040624-1/01.pdf.

of the Seibu stocks without disclosing the fact that such falsified numbers had been submitted year after year, "an important fact concerning the business," which he was well aware of.

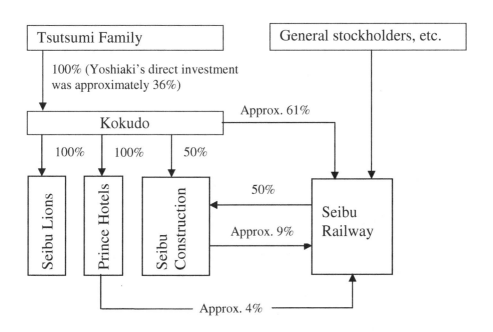

Fig. 1. Stockholdings in the Seibu Group.

Fearing that the fact that the total of the shares owned by the current ten largest shareholders of Seibu is in excess of 80% of the total outstanding shares, which is the threshold for the eligibility of listing on the Tokyo Stock Exchange, may become a public knowledge, Kokudo sold 70 million Seibu shares to 72 corporations including those that do business with Kokudo at a total price of ¥65 billion during a period of August through October 2004 in order to maintain Seibu's eligibility to be listed on the Tokyo Stock Exchange.[5] Of the alleged illegal transactions, the prosecutors claimed that Mr. Tsutsumi was deeply involved in the sale of at least 18 million shares to 10 corporations, for example, by personally negotiating the transactions.[6] Furthermore, the Tokyo District Public Prosecutors Office applied the rule of penalty against employer and employee of the Security Exchange Law,[7] and

---

[5] Learning that it would be certain that the Commercial Code would be changed to legalize electronic trading of stocks in lieu of paper stock certificates as of the latter half of 2003, the management members of Seibu and Kokudo confer how to deal with the extra amount of Seibu shares Kokudo owns by means of disguising ownerships using personal names. This is because they realized that the process of confirming ownerships under personal names associated with the change of law might reveal their wrongdoing. See Nikkei, February 25, 2005, p. 1. For the Commercial Code, Law No. 48, enacted on March 9, 1899, amended 18 times (hereinafter cited as the Commercial Code). For details of the law, see http://www.ron.gr.jp/law/law/syouhou1.htm.

Commercial Code was modeled after German laws, while the Securities and Exchange Law was copied from the US laws after WWII. Germany is a civil law country, while the United States is a country of the common law. Any confusion in the concepts of disclosure in Japan may be attributed to the slight difference in the disclosure rules of the two source countries. For an examination of the development of the Japanese securities market, see Mitsuru Misawa. *Securities Regulation in Japan*. 6 Vand. J. Transnational L. 447 (1973). Further, as to the internationalization of the Tokyo Stock Market, see Mitsuru Misawa. *Tokyo as an International Capital Market – It's Economic and Legal Aspects*. 8 Vand. J. Transnational L. 1 (1974). It is safe to say that when the loyalty of employees to the company is compared to their loyalty to their stockholders, the latter is given priority. The loyalty to the company not to disclose prematurely is a part of the traditional social system in Japan and the lifetime employment system goes hand in hand with this loyalty. This loyalty given by directors and employees to the company is one of the basic principles of the Commercial Code of Japan.

[6] Nikkei, March 4, 2005, p. 1.

[7] The penalty against employer and employee means not just punishment of directors and employees but also the company they belong to are to be punished for the same wrongdoing. It is applicable to crimes related to the Securities Exchange Law, the Banking Law and the Antitrust Law. The company will not be punished if it can be proven that it is faultless since it provided proper cautionary instructions for prevention of illegal acts.

For the Securiteis Exchange Law, see Law No. 25 of Apr. 13, 1948 (Japan). Subsequent amendments to the law reflected United States developments. Most recently the law was amended on Mar. 3, 1971. Law No. 4 of 1971 [hereinafter cited as Securities Exchange Law]. For details, see http://www.houko.com/00/01/S23/025.HTM.

For the Banking Law, Law No. 59 of June 1, 1981 (Japan), see http://law.e-gov.go.jp/cgi-bin/idxsearch.cgi

For the Antitrust Law, Law No. 54 of April 14, 1947 (Japan), see http://law.e-gov.go.jp/cgi-bin/idxsearch.cgi

indicted both Seibu and Kokudo holding criminally responsible on two accounts of misstatement and insider trading.[8]

The Seibu Group currently consists of 135 companies where a total of approximately 30,000 people work. The business model of Seibu was consistent through the high-growth period after the WW II. It was to buy lands, construct buildings (or facilities), carry people or goods, and provide lodgings and entertainments. Purchase of lands was primarily done by Kokudo. Business chances associated with purchased lands were carried out monopolistically by the group companies.

During the latter half of 1980s through the early part of 1990s, Kokudo was making ¥5–14 billion of operating profits annually. On the other end, it was paying ¥6–17 billion of interests on loans annually, so that the end profits were compressed to ¥0.1–0.2 billion annually. Heavy interest burdens helped to reduce the income. In addition, the suppression of earning power resulted in reduction of the corporate value of Kokudo, which was in line with the intention of the Tsutsumi family to reduce the inheritance tax of each successor of the family.

Questioned in the present case are the falsification of the financial statements and the violation of the Securities Exchange Law including the inside trading. From the Commercial Code standpoint, there are also questions about the company's liabilities concerning the act of obtaining shares under third parties' names or transfer of shares on this basis on the list of shareholders. The author wishes here to examine the possibilities of legal responsibilities of those involved from the standpoints of both civil and criminal offenses examining "who did what." Furthermore, the author intends to discuss a fundamental problem of how we can recover the trusts of world's investors to the securities market in Japan.

There are some US companies which are interested in buying Seibu, so that there seems to be a keen interest in how the abovementioned criminal and civil cases evolve. For example, a US investment bank, Goldman Sacks, is offering a purchase plan of buying the Seibu Group at a total price of approximately ¥9.0 billion.[9] If this materialize, it will be the largest ever M&A involving a Japanese corporation as a target.

---

[8] Yomiuri, March 19, 2005, p. 1 and Nikkei, March 4, 2005, p. 3.
[9] Nikkei, March 25, 2005, p. 1.

The intention of Goldman Sacks is to obtain the land lots the Seibu Group has under its umbrella, which is said to total approximately 15,000 hectare of land in Japan, and pick and choose the assets of 169 major facilities including domestic and overseas hotels and golf courses to reorganize the business foundation. Although Seibu Group is trying to restructure itself to create a new Seibu Group, the scenario involving a foreign investor is a very likely one if the self-help effort fails.[10]

Falsification of Financial Statements

On February 1, 2005, an action for damages of ¥350 million was brought up by a group of 213 shareholders of Seibu, which is now removed from the listing of the Tokyo Stock Exchange, claiming falsifications of financial statements against Seibu, Kokudo and Yoshiaki Tsutsumi.[11] The shareholders are claiming that they incurred losses due to the drops of stock prices in the market and asking the directors for damages under the Commercial Code, Article 266-3, Paragraph 2. In this case, the shareholders are asking the damages against the directors claiming that the loss they incurred due to the removal from the listing of the Tokyo Stock Exchange as the direct loss due to the directors' failure to meet their fiduciary responsibilities in accordance with the Paragraph 1 of the aforementioned article. The damages correspond to the difference between ¥1,081, the share price as of October 2004, when Seibu announced the falsification, and ¥268, the price on November 16, 2004, when the Tokyo Stock Exchange decided to oust Seibu from its listing.

However, there is a difficulty in pursuing the violation of the information disclosure responsibility under this civil case. It seems that there are two hurdles for the investors who don't have sufficient information collecting capabilities. Firstly, it is the legal side. Unless there is a criminal record, it takes a lot of work to prove the illegality. Internal documents to prove accounting frauds and false statements are difficult to be disclosed in the court. Secondly, it is the practical side. Different from the United States, the claimants cannot ask the authority

---

[10] Nikkei, March 25, 2005, p. 1.
[11] Nikkei, February 26, 2005, p. 16.

such as the Securities and Exchange Surveillance Committee to ask to provide evidences in Japan.

There are regulations on the Securities Exchange Law concerning civil and criminal responsibilities when disclosed documents contain falsifications.[12] These are divided into the responsibilities in the issuing market and the responsibilities in the secondary market. While those who are responsible in case of the issuing market are issuing companies, their directors, auditors, brokerage firms, etc., the same in case of the secondary market are only directors and auditors; issuing companies are not responsible. The reason for this is that a company can issue shares based on falsified documents to collect money in case of the issuing market, so that the law requires the company to return the money the company falsely collected. On the other hand, falsified documents do not bring money to the company in the secondary market. Moreover, in the latter case, those who lose money are not just the people who responded to the issuing, but also all other people who traded the stocks based on the disclosed documents. In this case, if the company pay damages to the investors who lost money, the company's asset reduces that much so that its stock value drops. This means those investors who received payments for damages end up recovering the loss on the sacrifices of those investors who did not receive payments for damages due to its stock value drops. That was the reason why only directors and auditors were held responsible for disclosing falsified documents and the issuing company was not held liable in the secondary market.

However, the revision of the law in 2004 made it possible for a person can ask for damages against the issuing company, if the person has acquired securities during a period when financial statements, security registration statements, mid-term reports, extraordinary reports, etc., with falsified statements are placed for public viewing.[13] The intention was to make the civil responsibility system, which has been little used, easier to use. The revision includes an estimation rule for the amount of damage and causal relationship. More specifically, a person, who acquired securities within one year prior to the day it is announced

---

[12] Securities Exchange Law, Articles 16-22, Article 24-4 and 5, and Articles 197-227.
[13] Revised Security Exchange Law (Law No. 97 of December 1,2004), Article 21-2.

that the related document is falsified, is eligible for asking the amount calculated by subtracting the average value of the market prices during a month before the announcement from the average value of the market prices during a month after the announcement as the damage amount. If the issuing company is to claim that the price drop occurred due to other reasons, the company has the responsibility to prove it.

Moreover, as to the issuing company's responsibility to a person who responded to an issue of securities when there was a falsified statement in a security registration statement, the statute of limitation of a relatively short period of one year from the day a false statement was discovered or five years after the registration becomes effective was extended to three and five years respectively in the amended rule.[14]

While Seibu reported in the financial statement published for a fiscal year ended in March 2004 that the combined share holding ratio of the leading shareholder Kokudo and its subsidiary Prince Hotel was approximately 44%, Seibu later corrected it to be approximately 70% as both of those companies owned in reality a substantial amount of shares under personal names.[15]   Since this Seibu case occurred prior to December 1 2004, the day the Revised Security Exchange Law was implemented, so that the revised law does not apply to it. If the revised law existed at the time of the incident, the case could have been proven rather easily as a civil suit.

So far, all cases that have been indicted against criminal and civil responsibilities concerning falsified financial statements[16] have been the cases involving fraudulent accounts or illegal dividends.

1.   A case where three defendants claimed to have prepared and submitted a financial statement including a balance sheet and a profit & loss statement showing fraudulently increased sales revenues based on fictitious revenues in conspiracy with accomplices, and were sentenced to two years in prison with suspension.[17]

---

[14]   *Id.*, Article 20.

[15]   Nikkei, October 15, 2004, p. 2.

[16]   It will be sentence to a maximum sentence of five years in prison or a maximum penalty of ¥5 million or both under Securities Exchange Law, Article 197-1, Para. 1.

[17]   Hanreishu (Collection of Precedents), Osaka District Court, October 8, 2002, un-registered.

2. Two representative directors of a brokerage firm conspiring with two other representative directors submitted to the MOF a financial statement comprising a balance sheet, a profit & loss statement and profit disposal statement showing fraudulently compressed current term loss based on off-the-book disposals of securities containing latent loss. The president and the chairman of the board were found guilty of falsification of financial statements and sentenced to two years six month of imprisonment and two years six month of imprisonment with five years of suspension respectively.[18]

3. In this case, the defendant director twice paid illegal dividends by falsifying financial statements while there was no profit for making dividend possible, publicized fraudulent financial statements, and submitted the same to the MOF. As a consequence, he was sentenced to three years in prison with five years of suspension on charges of violations of the Commercial Code and the Securities Exchange Law based on the judgment that the defendant's criminal responsibility was quite heavy because of its vicious nature of crime as can be judged from the process leading up to the criminal act and the extent, mode and result of fraudulence, and that the crime was performed in complete negligence of a heavy public responsibility expected to be born by a noted corporation and its manager, thus giving a strong shock to the society in general and damaged people's trust on various social systems including the Commercial Code.[19]

4. In this case at an appellant court, the former president, a managing director in charge of accounting, and an auditing company of a bank were sought for damages comparable to the purchase price of shares under a claim that there were fraudulent statements in the bank's financial statements for, concerning the situation where the shares became valueless when the bank was placed under a special government control, in that the bad debt reserve accounted for was too small and the evaluation loss related to option transaction of shares the bank owned was not accounted for. The appellant claimed that the defendants should

---

[18] Hanreijihou (Precedents Report), Tokyo District Court, March 28, 2000, No. 1730, p. 162.
[19] Shiryouban Shoujihoumu (Reference Commercial Code Report), Shizuoka Prefectural Court, March 31, 1999, No. 187, p. 216.

have marked the shares in question and put options to market in accordance with the hedge accounting principle, but the court dismissed the appellation based on the judgment that it was impossible to mark them to market, since the hedge accounting principle was not yet adopted as a generally accepted accounting principle at that time.[20]

Let us now examine how the civil and criminal responsibilities of the company can be judged for falsified financial statements from the standpoint of the Securities Exchange Law in a case like this Seibu Case where no fraudulent accounts or illegal dividends are involved. Domestic companies are required by law to report in their financial statements about "major shareholders," specifying name, address, number of shares it owns, and ratio of shares it owns relative to the total outstanding shares. Approximately 10 major shareholders are required to be reported in the order of the higher number of shares, and the number of shares owned by each shareholder should include those it owns under other persons' (including tentative persons) names.[21] Seibu reported false information on major shareholders to MOF. The question is where the major shareholders information can be called "important" information sufficient for seeking civil and criminal responsibilities of the company. There has been no precedence on this matter and future judgments by courts will be closely studied.

Insider Trading

The Securities Exchange Law of Japan is trying to make the regulations concerning insider trading to cover every facet of the matter by listing all the specific constituent insider information elements and providing a basket clause in order to accommodate the requirements of the legality principle.[22] In the Seibu case, Seibu stocks were eventually removed from the list, but the question is whether there was any insider trading. Many companies bought Seibu's shares upon requests from Seibu, but they asked Kokudo to buy back the shares as the share price dropped

---

[20] Hanreijihou (Precedents Report), Osaka High Court, May 25, 2004, No. 1863, p. 115.
[21] "Cabinet's Order Concerning Disclosure of Corporate Contents" Third Format
[22] Securities Exchange Law, Article 167-2, Para. 1-4.

upon the discovery of the wrongdoing. The issue is whether the trading of these Seibu shares should be considered as insider trading.

The delisting of Seibu shares this time is not based on Seibu's initiative, but is a punishment of the Tokyo Stock Exchange.[23] It is true that the delisting is important information that "seriously affect the investor's investment decision" as specified in the Securities Exchange Law. However, there was no evidence that makes one suspect that Kokudo knew about the delisting when the seller, i.e., Kokudo sold the Seibu stocks. It seems that Kokudo, at the most, might have suspected of a possibility that Seibu could become delisted if the truth became known to the Tokyo Stock Exchange. The fact is that the delisting was essentially a punishment by the Tokyo Stock Exchange initiated after it had become aware of the incident, not that Kokudo traded the shares "with the knowledge of the important information." It is questionable whether the insider trading rule can be applied in this case also because the selling of the shares was intended for avoiding the violation of the threshold of the delisting standard, not for profit making or avoiding any loss.

Moreover, although the Special Investigation Department judged that the defendant Tsutsumi's off-the-market disposal of a large amount of Seibu shared held by Kokudo amounts on to insider trading, the insider trading rule's application to an off-the-market private negotiation transaction has no precedence in Japan. Also, whether Kokudo is legally liable for buying back the Seibu shares it has sold as many of the companies which bought them are requesting, depends on the understanding whether the right of rescission of the trading exists under the Civil Code.[24]

---

[23] This was a decision made by the executing organization based on "Request Concerning Termination of the Listing of Stocks on the Stock Exchange" specified in the Securities Exchange Law Enforcement Regulations, Article 28-5, which is based on Securities Exchange Law, Article 167-2, Para. 1-Yo.

[24] Commercial Code, Article 204-12.

Owning Shares Under Other Names

The Commercial Law adopts a concept that the collective legal relation of a company and its shareholders requires a uniform treatment based on the acknowledgment that stocks are freely transferable and it is impossible for the company to identify each individual true shareholder.[25]

Therefore, if there was a share transfer and some shares were transferred to a party Y, it is necessary for the new shareholder Y to have the shares officially transferred on the shareholder list in order to exercise its right.[26]   Even if the party Y effectively received the shares from a party X, the party Y cannot claim against the company that it is a true shareholder until the shares are officially transferred on the shareholder list. It suffices for the company to treat the party X as the true owner of the shares until the transfer is officially executed on the shareholder list.

Unless the transfer request is not received, the company should still treat the shareholder on the list as a shareholder even if the company is aware of the transfer. Otherwise, the company could be accused of a willful decision, because such an act could lead to a danger of treating the party Y as a shareholder if Y is a convenient party and not treating Y as a shareholder if Y is not a convenient party, which is against the equality principle of shareholders.

However, a court precedent states that "The definitive power of the shareholder list is for providing a system for the convenience of the company to treat the collective legal relation uniformly, so that the company is allowed on its own risk to treat a party who owns shares as of the reference date even if the transfer is not yet officially executed on the list and approve the particular party to execute its right."[27]

Next, there is a question whether the party Y is eligible to execute its shareholder's right either when it didn't use its true personal name or trade name in the official transfer on the list, or when it used a

---

[25] *Ibid.*
[26] Commercial Code, Article 206-1.
[27] Supreme Court Precedents, October 20, 1955, Civil Cases, Vol. 9, No. 11, p. 1657.

non-existent personal name or a personal name without obtaining the person's approval.

Let us now review the precedents.

Facts

A party A acquired the shares of a company X three times under the names of fictitious parties B and C on the first and third times, and under the name of a real person D, but without obtaining the person's approval on the second time, acquiring official transfers on the list on all of them using the party A's own address as each of their addresses, and owning each person's registered stamp by A. (See Fig. 2)

Judgment at the District Court[28]

The court made a decision that "Since ① the intention of requiring the names and addresses of persons who acquired shares on the shareholder list is to identify who are the shareholders, ② preparation of the shareholder list is required for allowing and prompting numerous, constantly changing shareholders to execute their rights as the shareholders, and ③ shareholders and the company's creditors are allowed to view or make copies of the list, it is obvious that 'name' and 'address' should be such that allow the share holder be identified with them. Therefore, the 'name' should be construed as the name on the family registry (birth certificate) with the exception that a vernacular name can be used as a name here, if said name has been used by a shareholder as his/her own name for a long time so that it is well known as the particular shareholder's name. This means that a person who used a name other than his/her name of the family registry on the shareholder list cannot contest the company as a shareholder.

---

[28] Tokyo District Court, January 28, 1988, Hanreijiho, No. 1269, p.144.

Judgment at the Appellant Court

An opposite judgment[29] was given for the same case by an appellant court. It indicated that "even though the party A was not listed as a shareholder on the company X's shareholder list, it can acknowledge the party A as the shareholder before the transfer in reality or in a litigation, approve its excise the right, and clarify that the person is a shareholder." In other words, the appellant court's position is that the company X shall approve the party A to exercise its right while maintaining the name on the shareholder's list as is if the party A can prove that the name on the list truly means himself/herself.

Comment

In case of a publicly-traded company, the company has no way of intervening the process of a share transfer in the form of approving the share transfer. Therefore, even if the party A uses a fictitious name, the company X does not have the ground for checking it. Moreover, considering the fact that transfers using the names of the person's family members are popular in Japan, it is reasonable to understood that it is impossible to deny the exercise of right by a person who used a name other than the person's real name on the family registry or vernacular name in the process of acquiring shares, so that the appellant court's decision is correct.

However, it does not mean that the company has a legal obligation to find the identity of a person requesting the transfer. In this regard, in case of the publicly-traded company, it is necessary for a shareholder to submit a report to the company if the real ratio of the owned share is in excess of 5% on account of the Large Quantity Ownership Report System,[30] the submission being required by the Security Exchange Law.[31] Comparison of the shareholder list and the Large Quantity Ownership Report can clarify the names of real shareholders and the

---

[29] Tokyo High Court, June 28, 1988, Kinyu Houmu Jijo (Financial Legal Matters), No. 1206, p. 32.
[30] Security Exchange Law, Article 27-23.
[31] Security Exchange Law, Article 27-27.

numbers of shares they own. However, that doesn't mean those that are not the shareholders on the list can be treated as shareholders based on the Large Quantity Ownership Report.[32] Who can be treated as shareholders by the company under the Commercial Code is determined by who are listed on the list, which is based on the shareholders' requests.

Order	→	1	→	2	→	3
Name		B		D		C
		(Fictitious person)		(Actual person without approval)		(Fictitious person)
Address		A's address		Ditto		Ditto
Registered		B's		D's		C's
stamp		(Held by A)		(Ditto)		(Ditto)

Fig. 2. Transfer of X company share by party A.

Let us apply this precedent to the case of Seibu.

It is a tentative conclusion of the case at the appellant court that the mere fact that the company (Seibu) allowed the material shareholder (Kokudo), i.e., shareholder in a practical sense, to exercise its right as a shareholder cannot be considered illegal, since this is a case where the material shareholder (Kokudo) is listed on the shareholder list under the names of other individuals (such as Kokudo's employees), so long as it

---

[32] The submission of the Large Quantity Ownership Report was made mandatory by the Security Exchange Law in 1990 as a countermeasure against rampant large quantity share collecting activities that occurred during 1980s. Those shareholders who own more than 5% shares of a company are obliged to submit a report to the MOF within five days when more than 1% of change occurs in its ownership. The purpose is to prompt major shareholders to disclose their ownerships in timely manner and it is called "5% rule." The problem is that there is an exception for the period of submission. While the basic period of submission is five days, longer periods are approved for financial institutions, investment consulting firms and other institutional investors. Since these investors may trade frequently, they are normally allowed to report once in three months. A more essential problem is that the penalty does not act as a preventive measure against violations of submission obligation. The Security Exchange Law gives a maximum penalty of "three years of imprisonment or ¥3 million," but offenders are very rarely caught, while many late reports are being submitted nonchalantly. For details, see Nikkei, March 11, 2005, p. 21.

can be proven that the material shareholder used those other person's names for the purpose of showing itself on the list. However, the fact that this case is essentially different from the precedent is the existence of Kokudo's malicious intention of having hidden for so many years the fact that the real number of shares it held is the total sum of the number of shares including those under the names of other people such as its employees in order to circumvent the violation limit of 80% of the Delisting Standard.[33] In order to hide the number of shares held by the major shareholder, the details of the shareholder list have been practically neglected. Kokudo has been practically using and appreciating the voting right and the profit dividend request right.

The shareholder list is open for shareholders and the company's creditors for viewing and copying.[34] The information concerning who are the shareholders and how much shares each person owns is important to know who controls the company. The fact that important corporate information concerning this major shareholder had been intentionally distorted is more important from the standpoint of protecting shareholders than the fact that the company allowed said shareholder to execute its voting right or dividend request right. We will be watching how this point will eventually be handled by the court.

Conclusion

Every corporation listed on the securities exchange must disclose its business contents accurately. It is the minimum rule for corporations and stock market to be trusted. For the disclosure, there was a marked difference between the United States and Japan regarding strictness in the pursuit of disclosure duties of corporations. It was safe to say that an average Japanese company had not felt a need to immediately disclose important information, until now.

This lack of sternness in the law enforcement system has created sloppy risk managements and concealing attitudes among Japanese companies, which resulted in the Daiwa Bank case when one of such

---

[33] Tokyo Stock Exchange's Share Delisting Standard, Article 2-1, Para. 2-a (a).
[34] Commercial Code, Article 263.

Japanese companies operated in the US with the same loose attitudes. In order to prevent this kind of case, more rigorous attitudes are necessary to make sure that directors be more responsible for their duties of disclosures.

The Seibu Group intentionally hid the information of a major shareholder's information. This crime shows that the chairman Tsutsumi did not fully understand the meaning of disclosure.

Mr. Tsutsumi had something to defend by even taking a risk of an illegal act. It was the parent company Kokudo's right to control the Seibu. In order to control a listed company Seibu, he maintained Kokudo's capital extremely small and the majority of shares under third parties' names.

Although the Kokudo shares under Mr. Tsutsumi's name was only 36%, the intention of his father, late Mr. Yasujiro Tsutsumi, was to maintain his family's control over the entire Seibu Group by controlling approximately 90% of their listed shares using those under the fictitious third parties' names. The scheme of strange control over the corporations and inheritance countermeasures by means of an enormous asset by the dictator finally failed.

In order to restore the Japanese disclosure system to be trusted again, and to rebuild a financial market that can be respected by the world, it is mandatory first to solve the basic problems of underlining the system. It is not only the expectation of IMF as mentioned before, but it is also the whole-hearted expectation of various countries that believe that the economic recovery of Japan will lead to the economic recover of the world. It is necessary to aim for building a more efficient disclosure system and support the overall restructuring of socio-economic systems.

Bibliography

15 U.S.C. § § 77a–77mm (1934), as amended, 15 U.S.C. § § 77a–77mm (1970), and 15 U.S.C. § § 78a–78jj (1934), as amended, 15 U.S.C. § § 78a–78hh (1).

Aktiengesellschaft, Bayer. Report of Foreign Issuer, available at http://www.sec.gov/cgi-bin/browse-edgar?company=&CIK=0001144145&filenum=&State=&SIC=&owner=include&action=getcompany (last visited Feb. 27, 2005).

Antitrust Law, Law No. 54 of April 14, 1947 (Japan), See http://law.e-gov.go.jp/
cgi-bin/idxsearch.cgi

Arnold v. Society for Savings Bancorp, Inc., 650 A.2d 1270, 1277 (Del. 1994).

Banking Law of Japan, Law No. 59 of 1981[hereinafter Banking Law], available at
http://law.e-gov.go.jp/cgi-bin/idxsearch.cg (last visited July 8, 2005).

Banking Law, Article 19. For the homepage of FRC, see http://www.fsa.go.jp/frc/ (last
visited July 8, 2005).

Chianella v. United States, 445 US 222 (1980).

Cinerama, Inc. v. Technicolor, Inc., 663 A.2d 1156, 1163 (Del. 1995).

Commercial Law of Japan, Law No. 48 (Mar. 9, 1899) (amended 18 times) [hereinafter
Commercial Law], for details, see http://www.ron.gr.jp/law/law/syouhou1.htm
(last visited July 8, 2005).

Commercial Code, Article 204-12.

Commercial Code, Article 206-1.

Commercial Code, Article 263.

Commercial Code Article 281-2,

Commercial Code, Article 12.

Commercial Code, Article 12.

Commercial Code, Article 230-10 ff.

Commercial Code, Article 273 ff.

Commercial Code, Article 282.

Commercial Code, Article 283.

Commercial Code, Articles 11 and 188.

Dennis J. Block, Nancy E. Barton & Stephen A. Radin, *The Business Judgment Rule:
Fiduciary Duties of Corporate Directors* (5th ed. 1998).

Designated Structural Reform District Promotion Office, Prime Minister's Office, Record
on International Accounting Standards, available at http://www.kantei.go.jp/jp/
singi/kouzou/kouhyou/021022/kaitou03.pdf (last visited July 8, 2005).

Dirks v. SEC, 463 US 646 (1983).

Enforcement Regulation of Banking Law, Article 19-2, For the Banking Law Ordinance
(March 31,1982, MOF No. 10), see http://law.e-gov.go.jp/cgi-bin/idxsearch.cgi
(last visited July 8, 2005).

Enforcement Regulation of Financial Revitalization Law, Article 5, For the Finance
Revitalization Law Ordinance (December 15, 1998, Finance Revitalization
Committee No. 2), see http://law.e-gov.go.jp/cgi-bin/idxsearch.cgi (last visited July
8, 2005).

Federation of Bankers Association, http://www009.upp.so-net.ne.jp/juka/
zenginkyo_code.htm (last visited July 8, 2005).

Finance Revitalization Law, Law No. of 1998 [hereinafter Finance Revitalization Law],
available at http://law.e-gov.go.jp/cgi-bin/idxsearch.cgi (last visited July 8, 2005).

Financial Accounting Standards Board, Mission Statement, available at
http://www.fasb.org/ (last visited Feb. 24, 2005).

Hanreijihou (Precedents Report), Osaka High Court, May 25, 2004, No. 1863, p. 115.

Hanreijihou (Precedents Report), Tokyo District Court, March 28, 2000, No. 1730,
p. 162.

Hanreishu (Collection of Precedents), Osaka District Court, October 8, 2002, un-registered.

Hiramatsu, Kazuo and Naruse, Shigeo. Kaikei Kijun — Nichi Ou Sougo Shounin WoNikkei [Accounting Standards — Hoping for Mutual Acceptance between Europe and Japan], Nikkei, July 27, 2004, at 27.

IASB, http://www.iasb.org (last visited July 8, 2005).

IDS98, http://www.iosco.org/pubdocs/pdf/IOSCOPD132.pdf.

IOSCO, http://www.iosco.org/about/see.

Japan Federation of Economic Organizations, Announcement, available at http://www.keidanren.or.jp/japanese/policy/2004/032.html (Apr. 20, 2004) (last visited July 8, 2005).

Japan Federation of Economic Organizations, Economic Release No. 25, available at http://www.keidanren.or.jp/japanese/journal/CLIP/2003/0722/ index.html (July 22, 2003) (last visited July 8, 2005) (translated by author).

Japanese Ministry of Economy, Trade and Industry, Report on the Internationalization of Business Accounting in Japan (July 21, 2004), available at http://www.iasplus.com/resource/0406ifrsjapangaap.pdf (last visited July 8, 2005).

Kimco Realty Corporation, Reconciling Non-GAAP Financial Measures, available at http://www.kimcorealty.com/file/Fin_SupplementalReports/ 2ndQuarterSupplementalPackage_7-29-2003_8-37-32AM.pdf (last visited July 8, 2005).

Letter of Stuart J. Kaswell, SVP, SIA to Arthur Levitt, Chairman, SEC, on June 13, 2000, http://www.sia.com/2000_comment_letters/.

Lynch v. *Vickers Energy Corp.*, 383 A.2d 278 (Del. 1978); see also Lawrence A. Hamermesh, "Calling off the Lynch Mob: the Corporate Director's Fiduciary Disclosure Duty," 49 *Vand. L. Rev.* 1089 (1996).

Malone v. *Brincat*, 722 A.2d 5 (Del. 1998).

McNee, Alan. ERisk, "End of the Line for Fair Disclosure?," on Tuesday, April 17, 2001, http://www.erisk.com/ResourceCenter/Regulation/EndoftheLineforFairDisclo.asp.

Ministry of Finance Ordinance, No. 32, (June 1, 1971), Art. 15.

Ministry of Finance, http://www.mof.go.jp (last visited July 8, 2005).

Ministry of Justice Ordinance, no.22, (May 29, 2002), http://www.moj.go.jp/PUBLIC/ MINJI29/refer01.html.

Ministry of Justice Ordinance, Art. 9.

Misawa, Mitsuru. "A Comparative Study of US and Japanese Bank Directors' Duty of Disclosure," The Banking Law Journal, January 2006, Volume 123, Number 1, pp. 39–79.

Misawa, Mitsuru. *Securities Regulation in Japan*. 6 Vand. J. Transnational L. 447 (1973). Further, as to the internationalization of the Tokyo Stock Market, see Mitsuru Misawa. *Tokyo as an International Capital Market — It's Economic and Legal Aspects*. 8 (1974).

MOF website, http://www.fsa.go.jp/news/newsj/15/singi/f-20040624-1/01.pdf.

Nikkei, February 26, 2005, p. 16.

Nikkei, March 4, 2005, p. 1.

Nikkei, March 11, 2005, p. 21.

Nikkei, March 24, 2005, p. 1.

Nikkei, March 25, 2005, p. 1.

Nikkei, October 15, 2004, p. 2.

PetroChina, Annual Report, *available at* http://www.petrochina.com.cn/english/ tzzgx/ndbg.htm (last visited July 8, 2005).

Revised Security Exchange Law (Law No. 97 of December 1,2004), Article 21-2.

Rosenblatt v. *Getty Oil Co.,* 493 A.2d 929, 944 (Del. 1985).

Rostelecom, SEC Reports, *available at* http://www.rt.ru/en/icenter/reports/ sec/ (last visited July 8, 2005).

SEC Concept Release: International Accounting Standards, http://www.sec.gov/.

SEC home page, http://www.sec.gov/(last visited July 8, 2005).

SEC Proposed Rule: Selective Disclosure and Insider Trading (57-31-99) dated December 15, 1999. *See* http://www.sec.gov/rules/proposed/34-42259.htm (last visited July 8, 2005).

SEC v. *Adler,* 137 F.2d 1325 (1998).

Securities Exchange Law, see Law No. 25 of Apr. 13, 1948 (Japan). Subsequent amendments to the law reflected United States developments. Most recently the law was amended on Mar. 3, 1971. Law No. 4 of 1971 [hereinafter cited as Securities Exchange Law]. For details, see http://www.houko.com/00/01/ S23/025.HTM.

Securities Exchange Law Enforcement Regulations, Article 28-5, which is based on Securities Exchange Law, Article 167-2, Para. 1-Yo.

Securities Exchange Law of Japan, Law No. 25 of 1948, art. 127, no. 4

Securities Exchange Law, Article 166-2.

Securities Exchange Law, Article 166-2.

Securities Exchange Law, Article 1.

Securities Exchange Law, Article 167-2, Para. 1-4.

Securities Exchange Law, Article 197-1, Para. 1.

Securities Exchange Law, Article 27-2 ff.

Securities Exchange Law, Article 27-2 to 27-22.

Securities Exchange Law, Article 27-22-2 to 27-22-4.

Securities Exchange Law, Article 27-23.

Securities Exchange Law, Articles 16-22, Article 24-4 and 5, and Articles 197-227.

Securities Exchange Law, Articles. 23, 24. See Ministry of Finance Regulation of June 1, 1972, Concerning Registration of Offers and Sales of Securities No. 32, Art. 15.

Security Exchange Law, Article 27-23.

Security Exchange Law, Article 27-27.

Security Exchange Law, Articles 166-1, 166-2, 166-3.

Seibu Group, http://www.seibu-group.co.jp

Shiryouban Shoujihoumu (Reference Commercial Code Report), Shizuoka Prefectural Court, March 31, 1999, No. 187, p. 216.

Stroud v. *Grace,* 606 A.2d 75, 84, (Del. 1992).

Supreme Court Precedents, October 20, 1955, Civil Cases, Vol. 9, No. 11, p. 1657.

The Japanese Federation of Economic Organizations, http://www.keidanren.or.jp/ Japanese/profile/pro001.htm (last visited July 8, 2005).

The Sarbanes-Oxley Act Community Forum, http://www.sarbanes-oxley-forum.com/.

Tokyo District Court, January 28, 1988, Hanreijiho, No. 1269, p.144.

Tokyo High Court, June 28, 1988, Kinyu Houmu Jijo (Financial Legal Matters), No. 1206, p. 32.

Tokyo Stock Exchange's Share Delisting Standard, Article 2-1, Para. 2-a (a).

TSC Industries, Inc. v. *Northway, Inc.*, 426 US 438, 449 (1976).

US Securities and Exchange Commission, Press Release, Actions by FASB, IASB Praised (Oct. 29 2002) available at http://www.sec.gov/news/press/2002-154.htm (last visited July 8, 2005).

US Securities and Exchange Commission, Press Release, SEC Adopts New Disclosure Requirements for Foreign Companies, available at http://www.sec.gov/news/ press/pressarchive/ 1999/99-125.txt (Sep. 29, 1999) [hereinafter SEC Press Release].

United States v. *Newman*, 664 F.2d 12 (2d Cir. 1981), *aff'd after remand*, 722 F.2d 729 (2d Cir. 1983), *cert. denied*, 464 US 863 (1983).

Yomiuri, March 19, 2005, p. 1 and Nikkei, March 4, 2005, p. 3.

Zirn v. *VLI Corp.*, 621 A.2d 773 (Del. 1993).

Chapter 6

Sales Recognition in Japan and the US — Possibility of Adopting International Accounting Standard in Japan

Introduction

Trading companies are unique institutions found only in Japan; nonetheless their importance is widely recognized, even internationally. However, marked changes have been noted recently in their amounts of sales. The changes appeared in the list of top 500 corporations of the world in the July 2003 issue of "Fortune," a leading US financial magazine. In the ranking based on the sales amount of corporations, the rankings of Japanese trading companies made nose dives from the high ranking positions they used to hold every year. For example, Mitsubishi, which held 10th place a year ago, plummeted to 389th and Mitsui from 11th a year ago to the 171st position.

The five major trading companies had been using the US accounting standard except for the sales amount, for which they used the Japanese standard for disclosure. This is due to the fact that their positions in the industry were used to be judged based on the sales amount. However, when they saw the US accounting standard had come to adopt a stricter definition, they started to use the US standard for the sales amount. The problem with the accounting system of Japanese companies is that such an important change is made haphazardly with no prudence. The definition of the sales amount according to the Japanese accounting standard is not clear and is left to each industry's custom.

Japanese corporate behavior and practice raises a number of issues for international businessmen, accountants, and lawyers. Japan's economy is the second largest in the world, next to the U.S., and its financial markets are one of the major ones in the world, but there are many things that they find difficult to understand. Their interest in the current Japanese market and economy is even more significant and increasingly prominent now. One of the fundamental questions of the world on Japan now is their accounting systems.

It is worth noting that some of the Japanese financial statements are required to include a legend as requested by the US. This inclusion of the legend was requested by the Big 5 accounting firms of the US. According to the current rule, it is necessary for financial statements of some Japanese corporations written in English to have notations (legends) such as "This is prepared in accordance with the Japanese Securities Exchange Law and accounting standard, and not under accounting standards of any other countries." This means that the Japanese accounting process is not trusted internationally. The problem does not lie with the corporations that are forced to write such statements but rather the problem is derivative of the accounting system of Japan. The parties who are negatively affected as a result of these different accounting standards are the Japanese corporations who fail to be trusted and also more importantly investors of the world (users of the Japanese financial statements) who cannot obtain accurate information on Japanese corporations.

While the business activities of corporations are becoming more international every year, the accounting system of each country seems to remain nationalistic, differing from one country to another. It has been a while since a cry was heard for the need of an international standardization of the accounting system so that investors can understand and properly compare the performances of corporations fairly and equitably. In response to such a cry, international accounting standards are gradually taking shape.

As a result of a joint meeting between the US Financial Accounting Standards Boards ("FASB") and the International Accounting Standards Board ("IASB") held in September 2002, an agreement called the Norfolk Agreement was reached among them in order to seek a convergence between the International Financial Reporting Standards ("IFRS") and the US standards, which laid the foundation for further convergence of various international accounting standards. It has been decided that the IFRS is to be adopted officially as of 2005 as the financial reporting standards for corporations in EU whose stocks are traded in markets and there is a possibility that it will be approved in Japan as well to prepare financial statements according to IFRS.

However, there have been quite a few different opinions from both government and private sectors about the adoption of the IFRS in Japan and no consensus has been reached yet. The author concludes that a quick adoption of the International Standard in Japan is less likely to occur; it will most likely occur rather slowly. The author also concludes that it is a problem to be considered and solved in the overall process of total internationalization of the system of the Japanese economy, although it is a correct direction to change the Japanese accounting standards to international standards. The Japanese accounting standards were not built overnight but are rather backed by a long history and are deeply entangled with other regulations. Currently dual accounting regulations exist in Japan; the Securities Exchange Law and the Commercial Code. In order to adopt the International Accounting Standards in Japan, reviews of other related laws such as the Commercial Law, the Securities Exchange Law and the Tax Law would become necessary. Also, there are other factors such as differences of culture and sense of values existing behind the different accounting systems.

Although Japanese efforts of international convergence of Japanese accounting standards is essential on the long term basis, Japan will have to take a position on the short term basis that each country should adopt "mutual approval" policy as long as the accounting standards of the respective countries are equivalent. This will be a realistic measure for Japan for the time being.

Sales Recognition for Japanese Corporations

One of the important financial indices concerning corporate performances, "Sales Amount," is now becoming an issue in Japan in terms of its definition and timing of accounting it. Sales is the largest single item in financial statements, and issues involving sale recognition are among the most important and difficult that standards setters and accountants face in Japan. A step ahead of Japan is the United States, where the accounting rule concerning the sales amount has recently been upgraded with a more rigorous definition, which in turn has given a serious impact on Japanese corporations using US accounting standards, making it another source of international criticism on the blurry state of the Japanese accounting standard. In this article, we will first review the recent trend among Japanese corporations in terms of the "Sales Amount."

Trading Companies

Trading Companies are unique institutions only found in Japan; nonetheless their importance is widely recognized, even internationally. However, marked changes have been noted in their amounts of sales. The changes appeared in the list of top 500 corporations of the world in the July 2003 issue of "Fortune," a leading US financial magazine. In the ranking based on the sales amount of corporations, the rankings of Japanese trading companies made nose dives from the high ranking positions they used to hold every year. For example, Mitsubishi,[1] which held 10th place a year ago, plummeted to 389th and Mitsui[2], 11th a year ago to 171st position.

The reason for the downgrading was that the amounts of sales for the five leading trading companies were accounted for using the figures

---

[1] Mitsubishi is the largest trading house and on of the core firms of the Mitsubishi group. They are strong in the field of energies including LNG. They have many excellent subsidiaries in the food-related area, and boast strong resources development capability. Their dividend income is hefty, and they are listed on London and Paris stock exchanges. Mitsubishi is moving into satellite communications thru JV. Their sales in 2002 amount to 13500 billion yen. Established in April of 1950, their principal office is located at 2-6-3, Marunouchi, Chiyoda-ku, Tokyo 100-8086. For the details, see Toyo Keizai, Inc., Japan Company Handbook, Summer 2001, p. 1115.

[2] Mitsui & Co. is a general trading company vying with Mitsubishi Corp. for top position. They rank 2nd next to Mitsubishi Corp. in foodstuffs trade but 1st in chemicals and steel. Mitsui is strengthening partnership strategies with US Douglas, Unisys and other big companies, and stress is placed on LNG business. Sales in 2002 totaled 13400 billion. Established in July of 1947, their principal office is located at 1-2-1, Ohtemachi, Chiyoda-ku, Tokyo 100-0004. For details, see *Ibid.*, p. 1099.

calculated according to the US accounting standards instead of the figures based on the Japanese accounting standard for the first time that year. For example, the consolidated sales amount for Mitsubishi for its fiscal year which ended March exceeded ¥15 trillion according to the Japanese standard, but shrank to 1/10 of it according to the US standard. As a combined sales amount of the five companies, a little over ¥40 trillion disappeared.

In accounting the brokerage business, which trading companies are most good at, the sales amount is the gross amount of the merchandise the trading company brokered under the Japanese standard. However, in the US standard, only the profit margin shall be accounted for as the sales amount. Although the profit does not change in either standard, the sales amount makes a big difference depending on which standard is used.

The five major trading companies had been using the US standard except for the sales amount, for which they used the Japanese standard for disclosure. This is due to the fact that their positions in the industry were used to be judged based on the sales amount. However, when they saw the US standard have come to adopt a stricter definition, they started to use the US standard for the sales amount.

Chart 1. Difference in Japanese vs US Sales Amount (Trading Company).

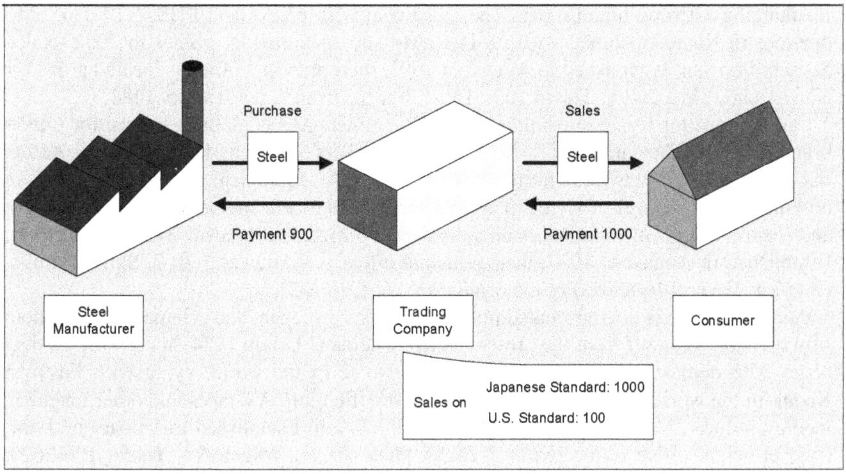

The problem with the accounting system of Japanese companies is that such an important change is made haphazardly with no prudence. The sales amount represents the size of a company, and the size is interpreted as credit power. Japanese trading companies were able to expand their businesses worldwide because of their names associated with large amounts of sales. It is a problem that they change the sales amount just because profit figure does not change.

Manufacturing Industry

For the same reason, more than ¥500 billion of sales amount evaporated from the fiscal report of NTT DoCoMo[3] for the year ending in March 2003. This was caused by the fact that they switched from filing the sales fees for portable terminals paid to the sales agents as expenses to the method of deducting from the sales amount. This is done so based on the thought that actual status can be more accurately represented by deducting the amount that corresponds to a discount from the sales amount.

Similar accounting procedures affected the sales figures of Cannon,[4] Fuji Film[5] and other companies which followed the US standard and

---

[3] NTT DoCoMo is the elite telecommunications company of NTT group, which spun off from NTT in 1981. They enjoy overwhelming market share in mobile phones, maintaining a strong brand name. They also deal with pagers and PHS. NTT DoCoMo operates in Kanto-Koshinetsu with 8 DoCoMo subs nationwide. Sales in 2002 totaled 5000 billion yen. Established in August of 1991, their principal office is located at 2-11-1, Nagata-cho, Chiyoda-ku, Tokyo 100-6150. For the details, see *Ibid.*, p. 1484.

[4] Canon is the top ranked manufacturer of PC printers and is globally known for Canon brand cameras. They are one of 3 largest copier makers, including Ricoh and Fuji Xerox, but have also diversified from copiers into OA equipment. Canon is now an all-embracing producer of visual image, LCDs and solar cells and information equipment, and leads others in multinationalization. Sales in 2002 totaled 3450 billion yen. Established in August of 1937, their principal office is located at 3-30-2, Shimomaruko, Ohta-ku, Tokyo 146-8501. For the details, see *Ibid.*, p. 1021.

[5] Fuji Photo Film is the top-ranked photo film maker in Japan, and originally was a photo film division, spun off from the present Daicel Chemical Ind. in 1934. In color films, they boast 70% domestic market share and ranks No. 2 in the world, vying with Eastman Kodak in the world market. They have also diversified into AV tapes and other magnetic media products. Sales in 2002 totaled 2470 billion yen. Established in January of 1934, their principal office is located at 2-26-30, Nishi-Azabu, Minato-ku, Tokyo 106-8620. For details, see *Ibid.*, p. 490.

resulted in a reduction in the order of several ten billion yen in each case, despite the fact that the profit figure did not change. Nissan Motors[6] also lost an amount of close to ¥100 billion in the consolidated sales amount because its US subsidiary switched to a similar accounting procedure.

Tokyo Electron[7] which markets semiconductor manufacturing devices changed its estimate of the consolidated profit for the fiscal year ending March 2005 from ¥85 billion to ¥60 billion in September 2004. This downward shift was due to switching of the sales posting from the time of shipment to the time of completion of the installation. This didn't change the profit figure either. Tokyo Electron described the reason of change as: "There was a general tendency of the period between shipment and acceptance getting longer, some of the domestic customers taking as much as several months, so that a substantial gap developed between the time of posting sales and the actual acceptance by the customer."[8]

A company normally posts the sale when it sells the merchandize. The question is when the sale is completed. In Japan, as in the U.S., there are two major thoughts: (1) when the merchandise is shipped; or (2) when the customer accepts the merchandise. The choice makes a difference in the timing of sales posting, but a problem is that the decision has been left to the particular industry's custom in Japan.

---

[6] Nissan Motor is one of the largest automakers in Japan, vying with Honda for the 2nd position. They are ahead of Toyota in overseas production, producing cars in US, UK, and elsewhere. Nissan Motor forms a capital tie-up with Renault (France). They are regaining strength thru 3-year restructuring programs under aegis of Renault. They sold their space/defense business. Sales in 2002 totaled 6050 billion yen. Established in December of 1933, their principal office is located at 6-17-1, Ginza, Chuo-ku, Tokyo 104-8023. For details, see *Ibid.*, p. 926.

[7] Tokyo Electron is a specialized electronics trading company and is a pioneer in import of IC production and test equipment to Japan. They boast high technical ability and are the world's class maker of in-house produced semiconductor and LCD manufacturing systems. Tokyo Electron is shifting emphasis to domestic production thru subs and on exports from mainline imports/sales. Sales in 2002 totaled 578 billion. Established in November of 1963, their principal office is located at 5-3-6, Akasaka, Minato-ku, Tokyo 107-8481. For the details, see *Ibid.*, p. 1101.

[8] Nikkei, December 9, 2004, p. 17.

In May 2003, Itochu Techno Science Corporation (CTC)[9] corrected the closing statement for its fiscal year ended in March 2003, which was already published, lowering its sales amount and net profit. This unusual correction caused a correction of the closing statement of this parent company, ITOCHU Corporation.[10] The incident was related to CTC's previous practice concerning the posting the amounts of sales concerning umbrella contracts for system product delivery, in which they used to post the sales amount at the end of the term even though it had not been delivered on the premise that it would be shipped within three months. However, it was revealed by an external auditor that some of the deliveries failed to be shipped within three months. Thus, they decided to eliminate the sales amount of all those that failed to be delivered by the end of the current term.

Construction Industry

An accounting practice prevailing in the construction industry in Japan allows a construction company to choose from the "In-progress Reporting Standard," in which the sales amount is reported for the portion of a construction project already completed, and the "On-completion Reporting Standard," in which the sales amount is reported only after the entire construction project is completed.

---

[9] Itochu Techno-Science Corporation (CTC) uses leading edge computers, networks, and applications to create total solutions in system consultation, integration, administration, maintenance/support, training, and outsourcing. Sales in 2003 totaled 266.1 billion yen. Established in April of 1972, their principal office is located at The Kasumigaseki Building, 2-5, Kasumigaseki 3 chome, Chiyoda-ku, Tokyo 100-6080. For details, see http://www.ctc-g.co.jp/

[10] Itochu is one of the Big 5 general trading firms, boasting the strongest arm of textiles, and they belong to Mizuho group. They are moving aggressively into new fields, which include satellite communications to bolster their position in new multimedia field. Itochu leads other trading houses in data communications and China business. Sales in 2002 totaled 11500 billion yen. Established in December of 1949, their principal office is located at 4-1-3, Kyutaro-machi, Chuo-ku, Osaka 541-8577. For details, see note 1 *supra*, p. 1077.

Taisei Corporation[11] expanded the range of projects to be covered by the In-progress Reporting Standard starting from March 2005. The reason for the change is that the In-progress Reporting Standard allows it to post sales and costs simultaneously so that it enables the company to avoid seasonal changes, thus reporting the performance of its operation more appropriately.

Chart 2. Difference Between On-completion Reporting Standard and In-progress Reporting Standard (Construction Industry).

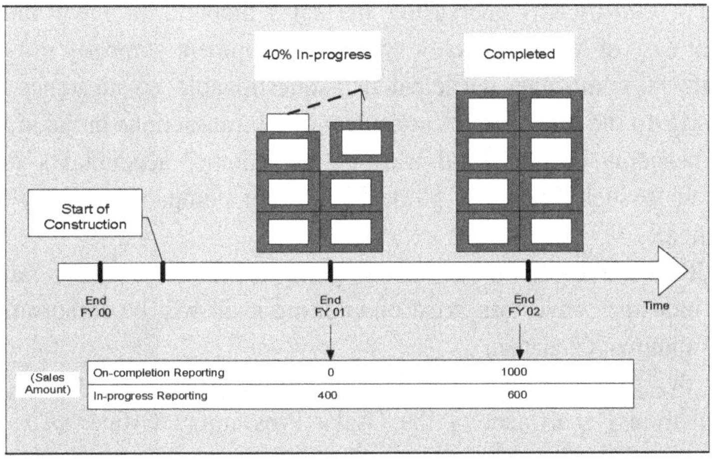

However, the method has a problem that it tends to allow corporations to make their own judgments. Kumagai Gumi[12] adopted the

---

[11] Taisei is a major general contractor of Fuyo group. They form the largest-class corporate group in the industry with subs in lines of housing, real estate, and road construction, sports facilities, as well as overseas operations. Taisei is downsizing real estate development operations including hotel business. The company is managed by non-family members. Sales in 2002 totaled 1680 billion yen. Established in December of 1917, their principal office is located at 1-25-1, Nishi-Shinjuku, Shinjuku-ku, Tokyo 163-0606. For the details, see *Ibid.*, p. 90.

[12] Kumagai Gumi is a general contractor with its primary strength in large-scale civil engineering shield-processing projects, including dams and tunnels. They are also well-established in general construction. They are aiming to clear domestic and overseas nonperforming assets in one sweep, and are restructuring with backing from Sumitomo Bank. Sales in 2002 totaled 630 billion yen. Established in January of 1938, their principal office is located at 2-1, Tsukudo-cho, Shinjuku-ku, Tokyo 162-8557. For details, see *Ibid.*, p. 130.

In-progress Reporting Standard for its closing statement for the fiscal year ended in March 2002. It was barely able to report a final profit of ¥2.5 billion by the profit jack-up effect amounting to ¥3.1 billion using said accounting method.

Information Technology (IT) Industry

The Japanese Institute of Certified Public Accountants (JICPA) is launching an investigation whether the information technology (IT) industry is artificially increasing the sales amount. In the fraudulent account case of Media Links, a system development company in Osaka, multiple IT companies participated in questionable no-substance deals just to rig up the sales. JICPA considers those transactions in the industry as a menacing problem and warning its member accountants to pay attention to such deals and guide their client companies to stay away from them.

JICPA believes that if such padding of sales figures has been rampant in the industry, "investors' trust on auditing itself will be compromised" (Aki Fujinuma, Chairman).

In the Media Links case, which was exposed by the Special Investigation Department of the Osaka Prosecutors Office, sales were fraudulently filed as if packages of information system consisting of equipment and software were sold to other companies in the same industry. After the products had passed on through multiple companies, they are bought back by Media Links, thus causing to increase the sales figures of those companies.

It is believed that similar tricks have been routinely used among companies in the IT industry, although not as bad as the Media Links case. This is intended to deceive potential investors in the IT industry, who are closely monitoring sales figures trying to make highly selective choices.

Media Links is assumed to have been artificially jacking up the sales figures in order to maintain its listing on the market, even at a cost of losing money. Those companies involved in this scheme are assumed to have made approximately 1% of the product price as the handling charge. Their fictitious sales were bulging.

Those companies involved that all the deals were legitimate with purchase orders and actual money moving from one hand to another. However, whether actual products exchanged hands are not proven yet, so that there is a possibility that everything was only on paper plus accounting processes.

Many people have been pointing out that transactions with no substance have become daily matters in the IT industry. There is a strong possibility that this type of fraudulent business transactions became rampant in the industry as a result of increasing pressure for price reductions from users, while the companies are under pressures for achieving their sales goals.

Accounting Standards on Sales in Japan

In an income statement, income is calculated by subtracting "cost" from "sales amount." There are two issues in the corporate accounting procedure, one being the definition of the sales amount and the other being the timing of recognition. The definition of the sales amount according to the Japanese accounting standard is not clear and is left to each industry's accounting custom as indicated below.

The "Accounting Principles for Business Enterprises"[13] based on the Japanese Commercial Code[14] and Securities Exchange Law[15] says:

"The sales amount is limited to those that are realized according to the sales of merchandises or offering of services

---

[13] The "Accounting Principles for Business Enterprises," an interim report of the Business Enterprise Accounting System Study Commission of the Economic Stabilization Agency, represents a summary of practical business enterprise accounting guidelines historically formed in the industry, which should be followed by all corporations although it is not enforced by law. For the details of this memorandum, see http://www.kai-kei.ceo-jp.com/ks/kg-m.htm.

[14] Shoho (Commercial Code). Law No. 48 of 1899 was modeled after German laws, while the Securities and Exchange Law was copied from the L.S. laws after WWII. Germany is a civil law country, while the United States is a country of the common law.

[15] Shoken Torihiki Ho (Securities and Exchange Law). Law No. 25 of 1948, translated in 3 Int'l Sec. Reg. Japan Booklet 2. at. 14 (1992) (hereinafter Securities and Exchange Law). Subsequent amendments to this law reflected developments in the United States. For details of the law, see http://www.houko.com/00/01/S23/025.HTM.

according to the principle of realization. However an unfinished construction project which runs for a long period is allowed to make a reasonable estimate of profits and report it in the profit/loss statement of the current period."

The principle of realization mentioned here refers to the concept of recognizing the profit at the time of realization. The time of realization means the transfer of goods or services and the acquisition of cash or its equivalent. If we are to determine the performance of a business enterprise in a most accurate way, it is necessary to recognize the enterprise's effort in the whole process of forming added values from the purchase of merchandises or manufacturing materials to the sales of merchandises or products, not just to recognize the revenue when the merchandise is sold. In other words, it is appropriate to recognize the revenue at the occurrence stage (pure occurrence principle). On the contrary, reporting a sales amount based on the fact of selling merchandise (realization principle) is denying the enterprise's effort in the added value forming process from the manufacture of merchandises or products to sales.

The reason that the "realization principle" is adopted in the current accounting systems in Japan including "Accounting Principles for Business Enterprises" despite this shortcoming is that the realization principle is an excellent revenue recognition principle in the following points.

Recognizing the revenue based on the enterprise's effort in the added value forming process in the sales process of a merchandise, i.e., trying to post revenue according to the occurrence principle, is to report an insecure revenue, which may not realize. As oppose to it, if revenue is reported based on the principle of realization, only the revenue that is securely recognized will be reported as it is based on the fact that the merchandise was sold to a third party.

Trying to recognize the revenue in an added value forming process, i.e., revenue generating process, results in reporting a sales amount that has no backing of currency-based asset, such as cash and account receivables, which is the consideration for the sale, and any profit calculated based on such a revenue shall of course have no backing of currency-based asset, so that there is a problem from the standpoint of profit disposability. On the contrary, the recognition of profit based on the realization principle is reporting a sales amount backed by currency-based asset, such as cash or cash-equivalents, so that the profit calculated based on it has a backing of currency-based asset.

The "Accounting Principles for Business Enterprises" specifies that the standard of realizing sales revenues for special sales agreements such as consignment sales, sales on approval, subscription sales, and installment sales, shall be as follows:

Consignment Sales

"In case of consignment sales, the day the consignee completes the sale of the consigned goods is considered the day the sales revenue was realized. Therefore, if the fact that a sale was made by the closing date becomes evident by receiving an invoice statement (account sales) during the closing process, said sales amount shall be included in the statement of the current period. However, if the invoice statement is issued for each sale, it is allowed to consider the day the particular invoice statement is received as the day the sales revenue is realized."

Consignment Sales

"Since the consignment sale is realized when the client displays the intention of purchase, the posting of its sale should be made only at that point."

Subscription Sales

"In case of subscription sales, only the amounts, for which merchandises have been delivered or services have been provided by the closing date among the amounts received for subscriptions, shall be reported as the sales amount for the current period, and the balance shall be listed as a liability on the balance sheet to be carried over to the next period."

Installment Sales

> "In case of installment sales, the day merchandise is handed over shall be considered the day the sales revenue is realized. However, since it takes a long time to collect the payment, which is paid in installments and the risk of collection is higher in case of installment sales compared to regular sales, it needs a special consideration for reserves for bad debts, collection fees, after service costs, and others, the calculation of which accompanies some uncertainties and complications. Therefore, it is also allowed to use the installment collection deadline date or the day the payment is received as the day of sales revenue realization."[16]

As to the construction revenue, the "Accounting Principles for Business Enterprises" specifies as follows:

> "As to posting the revenue concerning a contract construction that takes a long time to complete, either the In-progress Reporting Standard or the On-completion Reporting Standard is allowed to be selected.

In-progress Reporting Standard

> "At the end of the fiscal year, estimate the progress of the construction and report a portion of the construction revenue based on a proper construction revenue ratio to the profit/loss of the current term."

(b)　On-completion Reporting Standard

> "When the construction is completed and delivered to the client, report the construction revenue."[17]

These are the only legal definitions concerning the sales amount in Japan. The Japanese accounting standard is not up to the complex status of trades and it lacks the overall rule for when each sales account to be reported. It is too simple so that it is causing various problems concerning the timing of sales amount reporting in addition to the

---

[16] See note 8 *supra.*
[17] See note 13 *supra.*

definition of sales amount. One of the problems is that transactions between companies have become so complex making it difficult to see if sales have actually occurred. While sales in the manufacturing industry can be identified by the delivery of goods, judgment is more difficult in industries where information and services are provided. By that, the profit may often vary from year to year

Accounting Standards on Sales in the US

Let us study accounting standards on sales in the US. As shown below, they are not perfect at all but are much better and comprehensive than those of Japan. Because no comprehensive standard on sale recognition exists, there is a significant gap between the broad conceptual guidance in the Concepts Statements by Financial Accounting Standard Boards of the US (hereinafter referred to as FASB), and the detailed guidance in the authoritative literature.[18] The Securities Exchange Commission (SEC) sought to fill the gap in the accounting literature with SAB No. 101, *Revenue Recognition in Financial Statements*, which was issued in December 1999 and the companion document, *Revenue Recognition in Financial Statements – Frequently Asked Questions and Answers*, which was issued in October 2000.[19] SAB 101 was superseded by SAB 104, *Revenue Recognition*, in December 2003.[20] SAB 104 states that if a

---

[18] Most of the authoritative literature provides industry or transaction-specific implementation guidance, and it has been developed largely on an ad hoc basis and issued in numerous pronouncements with differing degrees of authority. Those pronouncements include Accounting Principles Board (APB) Opinions, FASB Statements, American Institute of Certified Public Accountants (AICPA) Audit and Accounting Guides, AICPA Statements of Position (SOPs), FASB Interpretations, Emerging Issues Task Force (EITF) Issues, Securities and Exchange Commission (SEC) Staff Accounting Bulletins (SAB), and the like. Each focuses on a specific practice problem and has a narrow scope, and the guidance is not always consistent across pronouncements.

[19] SEC Staff Accounting Bulletin: No. 101 — Revenue Recognition in Financial Statements, 17 CFR Part 211, Release No. SAB 101, Staff Accounting Bulletin No. 101. For details, see http://www.sec.gov/interps/account/sab101.htm.

[20] Sec Staff Accounting Bulletin: No. 104 — Revenue Recognition in Financial Statements, 17 CFR Part 211, Release No. SAB 104, Staff Accounting Bulletin No. 104. For details, see http://www.sec.gov/interps/account/sab104.pdf.

transaction falls within the scope of specific authoritative literature on revenue recognition, that guidance should be followed; in the absence of such guidance, the revenue recognition criteria in Concepts Statements 5 by FASB (namely, that revenue should not be recognized until it is (a) *realized or realizable* and (b) *earned*), should be followed.   However, SAB 104 is more specific, stating additional requirements for meeting those criteria, and reflects the SEC staff's view that the four basic criteria for revenue recognition in AICPA SOP 97-2, *Software Revenue Recognition*,[21] should be a foundation for all basic revenue recognition principles.   Those criteria are:

(a) Persuasive evidence of an arrangement exists when:

Delivery has occurred

The vendor's fee is fixed or determinable

Collectibility is probable

Revenue Recognition pointed out by the SEC in late 1999 has attracted a lot of attention from Wall Street.   Much of that attention has been fueled by recent controversies involving Enron Corp.'s special-purpose entities, as well as some energy companies' use of "round-trip" trades to inflate sales.

In an effort to provide better and more comprehensive guidance as to when companies should record revenues, FASB has recently added a project on revenue recognition to its agenda.[22]

As part of its project on revenue recognition, the FASB will seek to eliminate inconsistencies in the existing accounting literature and accepted practices, fill voids in the guidance that have recently emerged and provide further guidance for addressing issues that arise in the future.[23]

---

[21] For the details, see http://www.aicpa.org/members/div/acctstd/general/tpa5.htm.

[22] "Revenue usually is the largest item in financial statements, and revenue recognition issues top the list of reasons for financial reporting restatements.   The FASB's proposed project would address such matters by developing one accounting standard that would apply to a broad range of industries," commented L. Todd Johnson, FASB Senior Project Manager.   For details, see http://executivecaliber.ws/sys-tmpl/revenuerecognition

[23] For details of the FASB project, see FASB's Revenue Recognition, http://www.fasb.org/project/revenue_recognition.shtml.

The Board decided that, in the interim while the standard is being developed, the Emerging Issues Task Force should continue to provide guidance on issues of revenue recognition based on the existing authoritative literature.

In developing the revenue recognition standard, the Board has decided to reconsider, as necessary, the guidance pertinent to revenue recognition in its Concepts Statements, particularly that in FASB Concepts Statement No. 5, Recognition and Measurement in Financial Statements of Business Enterprises.[24]

Until the new revenue recognition standard is developed by the FASB, the current FASB Concepts Statement No. 5 (Revenue Recognition) is still valid.

FASB defines that:[25]

> Further guidance for recognition of revenues is intended to provide an acceptable level of assurance of the existence and amounts of revenues before they are recognized. Revenues of an enterprise during a period are generally measured by the exchange values of the assets (goods or services) or liabilities involved, and recognition involves consideration of two factors (a) being realized or realizable and (b) being earned, with sometimes one and sometimes the other being the more important consideration.
>
> (a) Realized or realizable. Revenues generally are not recognized until realized of realizable.[26] Revenues are realized when products (goods or services), merchandise, or other assets are exchanged for cash or claims to cash.

---

[24] FASB, Statement of Financial Accounting Concepts, No.5, Recognition and Measurement in Financial Statements of Business Enterprises, Con 5 Status Page, December 1984. For details, see http://www.fasb.org/pdf/con5.pdf

[25] *Ibid.*, article 83 and 84.

[26] CON5, Footnote 50 by FASB — The terms realized and realizable are used in the Board's conceptual framework in precise senses, focusing on conversion or convertibility of noncash assets into cash or claims to cash (Concepts Statement 3, par.83). Realized has sometimes been used in a different, broader sense: for example, some have used that term to include realizable or to include certain conversions of noncash assets into other assets that are also not cash claims to cash. APB Statement 4, paragraphs 148-153, used the term realization even more broadly as a synonym for recognition.

Revenues are realizable when related assets received or held are readily convertible to known amounts of cash or claims to cash. Readily convertible assets have (i) interchangeable (fungible) units and (ii) quoted prices available in an active market that can rapidly absorb the quantity held by the entity without significantly affecting the price.

(b) Earned. Revenues are not recognized until earned. An entity's revenue-earning activities involve delivering or producing goods, rendering services, or other activities that constitute its ongoing major or central operations,[27] and revenues are considered to have been earned when the entity has substantially accomplished what it must do to be entitled to the benefits represented by the revenues.

In recognizing revenues:

(a) The two conditions (being realized or realizable and being earned) are usually met by the time product or merchandise is delivered or services are rendered to customers and revenues from manufacturing and selling activities.[28]

(b) If sale or cash receipt (or both) precedes production and delivery (for example, magazine subscriptions), revenues may be recognized as earned by production and delivery.

(c) If product is contracted for before production, revenues may be recognized by percentage-of-completion method as earned — as production takes place — provided reasonable

---

[27] CON5, Footnote 51 by FASB — "Most types of revenue are the joint result of many profit-directed activities of an enterprise and revenue is often described as being 'earned' gradually and continuously by the whole of enterprise activities. Earning in this sense is a technical term that refers to the activities that give rise to the revenue — purchasing, manufacturing, selling, rendering service, delivering goods, allowing other entities to use enterprise assets, the occurrence of an event specified in a contract, and so forth. All of the profit-directed activities of an enterprise that comprise the process by which revenue is earned may be called the earning process" (APB Statement 4, par. 149). Concepts Statement 3, paragraph 64, footnote 31, contains the same concept.

[28] CON5, Footnote 52 by FASB — The requirement that revenue be earned before it is recorded "usually or units of constant purchasing power" (Concepts Statement 1, par.2, footnote 2).

estimates of results at completion and reliable measures of progress are available.[29]

(d) If services are rendered or rights to use assets extend continuously over time (for example, interest or rent), reliable measures based on contractual prices established in advance are commonly available, and revenues may be recognized as earned as time passes.

(e) If products or other assets are readily realizable because they are salable at reliably determinable prices without significant effort (for example, certain agricultural products, precious metals, and marketable securities), revenues may be recognized at completion of production or when prices of the assets change. Paragraph 83(a) describes readily realizable (convertible) assets.

(f) If product, services, or other assets are exchanged for nonmonetary assets that are not readily convertible into cash, revenues may be recognized on the basis that they have been earned and the transaction is completed. Recognition depends on the provision that the fair values involved can be determined within reasonable limits.

(g) If collectibility of assets received for product, services, or other assets is doubtful, revenues may be recognized based on cash received.

Based upon what we have found for revenue recognitions under Japanese and US standards together with International standards, we can summarize them in Table 1. It is found that Japanese standards are much less comprehensive and are relying on practices and customs.

---

[29] CON5, Footnote 53 by FASB — If production is long in relation to reporting periods, such as for long-term, construction-type contracts, recognizing revenues as earned has often been deemed to result in information that is significantly more relevant and representationally faithful than information based on waiting for delivery, although at the sacrifice of some verifiability. (Concepts Statement 2, paragraph 42-45, describes trade-offs of that kind.)

Table 1 — Revenue Recognitions under Japanese, US and International Standards.

Item	Japanese Standards	US Standards	International Accounting Standards
Revenue recognition	The realization principle is adopted. The criteria of realization are : (i) Goods or services are offered. (ii) Cash equivalents are received.	The following two requirements are considered: (1) Revenue is realized or realizable, and (2) Revenue is earned. Requirements of Income Recognition (SAB 104) (a) Persuasive evidence of an arrangement exists (b) Deliver has occurred (c) The vendor's fee is fixed or determinable (d) Collectibility is probable	Revenue is recognized in the income statement when future economic benefits relating to an increase in assets or a decrease in liabilities are generated and they can be measured reliably. This is believed to be consistent with the asset liability approach.
Sale of goods	In practice, revenue is recognized when it is acknowledged to have taken place, based on the delivery standards, shipping standards or commercial practice.	Seven examples are presented as cases of revenue and income recognition.	Revenue is recognized when all five conditions, including the transfer of material risks and economic value to the buyer, are met. In many cases, this occurs simultaneously with the transfer of legal title and possession to the buyer.
Income recognition — services offered	When services are offered only once, revenue is recognized when the services are complete. When services are offered continuously in accordance with an agreement, revenue recognition is based on the passage of time.	It is interpreted that income is recognized in accordance with the offer of services.	As a general rule, the stage of completion method is used.

Table 1. *continuous*

Item	Japanese Standards	US Standards	International Accounting Standards
Recognition of construction contract income .	Either the percentage-of-completion or the completed-contract method is selected for long-term construction contracts.	Generally, with long-term construction contracts, (1) The percentage-of-completion method is preferred if the cost estimate and the degree of progress until completion can be estimated rationally. (2) The completed-contract method is preferred in the absence of a reliable estimate, and when forecast figures. are doubtful, due to inherent obstacles.	(1) If the outcome of the construction contract can be estimated reliably, the percentage-of-completion method is used and recognition is made in accordance with the progress. (2) If the outcome cannot be estimated reliably, of the actually incurred cost, recognition is made up to the amount that is projected to be recoverable. (3) Use of the completed-contract method is not approved.

Source: Japanese MITI, "Report Concerning Internationalization of Japan's Business Accounting", p. 14, http://www.meti.go.jp/english/report/downloadfiles/IBAreporte.pdf

Adoption of International Accounting Standard in Japan

Investors may make wrong judgments if an inflated "sales amount" is shown by the proprietor's decision. The tightening of the US standard in this regard has influenced Japan and caused the Japanese Institute of Certified Public Accountants[30] to announce that "there is a necessity for specific rules" concerning the reporting of the sales amount. The

---

[30] Information concerning the Institute available at http://www.jicpa.or.jp/

Committee for Business Enterprises Accounting Standard[31] is also saying that it will be examined as a long range task. For investors, accurate financial statements are indispensable. In order to improve the reliability of the capital market, Japan has come to a point of reviewing the posting standard for sales figures.

However, the problem of "sales amount" is only the tip of the iceberg; indicating the problems lying in the Japanese accounting standard. The basic problem is that the Japanese accounting system is so different from the international accounting standard in various aspects. Therefore, it has been drawing criticisms from overseas that the Japanese accounting system is not reflecting the actual states of business enterprises. Even as a domestic issue, the problem is that a corporation needs to disclose its performance from two viewpoints, i.e., the Commercial Code and Security Exchange Law, and their integration is strongly desired. Against such a backdrop, whether International accounting standard should be adopted has become an urgent issue.

While the business activities of corporations are becoming more international every year, the accounting system of each country seems to remain nationalistic, differing from one country to another. It has been a while since a cry was heard for the need of an international standardization of the accounting system so that investors can understand and properly compare the performances of corporations of other countries when they seek financing overseas. In response to such a cry, international accounting standards are gradually taking shape.

As a result of a joint meeting between the US Financial Accounting Standards Boards ("FASB")[32] and the International Accounting Standards Board ("IASB")[33] held in September 2002, an agreement called the Norfolk Agreement was reached among them in order to seek a convergence between the International Financial Reporting Standards

---

[31] See *supra* note 13.

[32] The mission of the Financial Accounting Standards Board is to establish and improve standards of financial accounting and reporting for the guidance and education of the public, including issuers, auditors, and users of financial information. For the details, see http://www.fasb.org/.

[33] In June 1973, International Accounting Standards Committee was established by joint efforts of 10 countries, including USA, Japan, England, France, and Germany. This committee was reorganized as IASB in April 2001.

("IFRS")[34] and the US standards, which laid the foundation for further convergence of various international accounting standards.[35] It has been decided that the IFRS is to be adopted officially as of 2005 as the financial reporting standards for corporations in EU whose stocks are traded in markets and it seems likely that it will be approved in Japan as well to prepare financial statements according to the IFRS.

However, there have been quite a few opinions from both government and private sectors about the adoption of the IFRS in Japan and no consensus has been reached yet.   In the midst of this, on June 24, 2004, the Business Accounting Council [36] of the Japanese Government Ministry of Finance, hereafter "MOF"[37], published a memorandum titled

---

[34] It is a collective name for accounting standards established by the International Accounting Standards Board ("IASB") with a purpose of being approved and observed internationally, a part of which is the International Accounting standards ("IAS").

[35] In October 2002, SEC Chairman, Harvey C. Pitt applauded the decisions by the FASB and the IASB to work together toward greater convergence between US Generally Accepted Accounting Principles and international accounting standards.
He said, "This is a positive step for investors in the US and around the world. It means that reducing the differences in two widely used sets of accounting standards will receive consideration by both boards, as they work to improve accounting principles and address issues in financial reporting."   For details, see http://www.sec.gov/news/press/2002-154.htm.

[36] Its role is defined in Article 24 of the Organizational   Ordinance, MOF, that "the Business Accounting Council shall investigate and examine the processes of the establishment of business accounting and auditing standards, the standardization of cost calculation and refurbishments or improvements of corporate accounting systems as well as to report the results of such investigations and examinations to the Prime Minister, the Commissioner of Financial Services Agency, and related organizations and consult with them."

[37] The Ministry of Finance was reorganized on January 6, 2001. The name was changed from Okurasho to Zaimucho in Japanese, but the English name still remains the same. For more information about the reorganization, see http://www.mof.go.jp.
The Financial Services Agency (FSA) was created as of July 1, 1997, with the integration of the Banking Supervisory Agency and the Financial System Planning Bureau of the Ministry of Finance (MOF). The new FSA has integral responsibility over planning of the financial system and supervision and inspection of financial institutions. In view of the rapid changes in the environment surrounding the economy and financial markets, the planning of the financial system focused on building a stable and vigorous financial system, and securing the efficiency and fairness in the financial markets. In the supervision and inspection of financial institutions, further efforts to maintain and improve the soundness of financial institutions were made. Coordination with foreign financial authorities was strengthened in order to cope adequately with the globalization of finance. For details of the FSA, see http://www.fsa.go.jp.

"Adoption of International Accounting Standards in Japan"[38] ("MOF Memorandum"). Its purpose was to canvass and compile various arguments about what should be done in Japan from the official standpoint as to the international accounting standards coinciding with its adoption by EU in 2005.

The Business Accounting Council took up this issue from the standpoint of refurbishing the business accounting system in realization of its major obligation of setting up the business accounting system and auditing standard. In the MOF Memorandum, as a first step, it made a general observation of the international trends surrounding the IFRS, summarized the arguments and comments about the IFRS from judicial system standpoints, and provided the council's comment about future tasks. It also provided a summary on the thoughts about the application of the IFRS on foreign as well as domestic corporations.[39]

Bibliography

Business Enterprise Accounting System Study Commission of the Economic Stabilization Agency, Accounting Principles for Business Enterprises, http://www.kai-kei.ceo-jp.com/ks/kg-m.htm.

CON5, Footnote 50 by FASB — The terms realized and realizable are used in the Board's conceptual framework in precise senses, focusing on conversion or convertibility of noncash assets into cash or claims to cash (Concepts Statement 3, par.83). Realized has sometimes been used in a different, broader sense: for example, some have used that term to include realizable or to include certain conversions of noncash assets into other assets that are also not cash claims to cash. APB Statement 4, paragraphs 148–153, used the term realization even more broadly as a synonym for recognition.

CON5, Footnote 51 by FASB — "Most types of revenue are the joint result of many profit-directed activities of an enterprise and revenue is often described as being 'earned' gradually and continuously by the whole of enterprise activities. Earning in this sense is a technical term that refers to the activities that give rise to the revenue — purchasing, manufacturing, selling, rendering service, delivering goods, allowing other entities to use enterprise assets, the occurrence of an event specified in a contract, and so forth. All of the profit-directed activities of an

---

[38]   See MOF website "http://www.fsa.go.jp/news/newsj/15/singi/f-20040624-1/01.pdf

[39]   The MOF Memorandum consists of chapters such as 1. History; 2. International Trend; 3. Treatment of Foreign Companies in Accordance with IFRS; 4. Treatment of Domestic Companies in Accordance with IFRS; and 5. Future Tasks.

enterprise that comprise the process by which revenue is earned may be called the earning process" (APB Statement 4, par. 149). Concepts Statement 3, paragraph 64, footnote 31, contains the same concept.

CON5, Footnote 52 by FASB — The requirement that revenue be earned before it is recorded "usually or units of constant purchasing power" (Concepts Statement 1, par.2, footnote 2).

CON5, Footnote 53 by FASB — If production is long in relation to reporting periods, such as for long-term, construction-type contracts, recognizing revenues as earned has often been deemed to result in information that is significantly more relevant and representationally faithful than information based on waiting for delivery, although at the sacrifice of some verifiability. (Concepts Statement 2, paragraph 42-45, describes trade-offs of that kind.)

FASB, Statement of Financial Accounting Concepts, No.5, Recognition and Measurement in Financial Statements of Business Enterprises, Con 5 Status Page, December 1984, http://www.fasb.org/pdf/con5.pdf

FASB, Revenue Recognition, http://www.fasb.org/project/revenue_recognition.shtml.

Financial Accounting Standards Board, http://www.fasb.org/.

Itochu Techno-Science Corporation (CTC), http://www.ctc-g.co.jp/

Japanese Institute of Certified Public Accountants, http://www.jicpa.or.jp/

Johnson, Todd L. FASB Senior Project Manager, May 20, 2002, http://executivecaliber.ws/ sys-tmpl/revenuerecognition

Ministry of Finance, see http://www.mof.go.jp.

MOF website, http://www.fsa.go.jp/news/newsj/15/singi/f-20040624-1/01.pdf.

Nikkei, December 9, 2004, p. 17.

SEC, Actions by FASB, IASB Praised, October 29, 2002, http://www.sec.gov/news/ press/2002-154.htm.

SEC Staff Accounting Bulletin: No. 101 — Revenue Recognition in Financial Statements, 17 CFR Part 211, Release No. SAB 101, Staff Accounting Bulletin No. 101, http://www.sec.gov/interps/account/sab101.htm.

SEC Staff Accounting Bulletin: No. 104 — Revenue Recognition in Financial Statements, 17 CFR Part 211, Release No. SAB 104, Staff Accounting Bulletin No. 104, http://www.sec.gov/interps/account/sab104.pdf.

Shoho (Commercial Code). Law No. 48 of 1899.

Shoken Torihiki Ho (Securities and Exchange Law), Law No. 25 of 1948, translated in 3 Int'l Sec. Reg. Japan Booklet 2. at. 14 (1992). Subsequent amendments to this law reflected developments in the United States. For details of the law, see http://www.houko.com/00/01/S23/025.HTM.

SOP 97-2, Software Revenue Recognition Questions and Answers, American Institute of Certified Public Accountants, 2006, http://www.aicpa.org/members/div/acctstd/ general/tpa5.htm.

The Financial Services Agency (FSA), http://www.fsa.go.jp.

Toyo Keizai, Inc., Japan Company Handbook, Summer 2001, pp. 90, 130, 490, 926, 1021, 1077, 1099, 1101, 1115, 1484.

Chapter 7

The Japanese Issues and Perspective on the Convergence of International Accounting Standards[a]

Introduction

While the business activities of corporations are becoming more international every year, the accounting systems of individual countries seem to remain very local, differing from country to country. Recently, a cry was heard for the need for an international standardization of the accounting system so that investors can understand and properly compare the performance of corporations of other countries when they seek financing overseas. As a result of these concerns, international accounting standards are gradually taking shape.

The Norwalk Agreement was the result of a joint meeting between the US Financial Accounting Standards Boards (FASB)[1] and the

---

[a] For this chapter, permission is granted to reprint by Northwestern University School of Law, Northwestern Journal of International Law and Business, Mitsuru Misawa, *"Japanese Issues and Perspective on the Convergence of International Accounting Standards"* from <u>Northwestern Journal of International Law and Business</u>, Vol. 25, No.3 , Spring 2005 Symposium Issue, April 2005, pp. 711–745.

[1] "The mission of the Financial Accounting Standards Board is to establish and improve standards of financial accounting and reporting for the guidance and education of the public, including issuers, auditors, and users of financial information." Financial Accounting Standards Board, Mission Statement, *available at* http://www.fasb.org/ (last visited Feb. 24, 2005).

International Accounting Standards Board (IASB)[2] in September 2002. The agreement sought convergence between the International Financial Reporting Standards (IFRS)[3] and US standards, and laid the foundation for further convergence of various international accounting standards.[4] It was decided that the IFRS is to be adopted officially in 2005 as the financial reporting standard for corporations in the European Union whose stocks are traded in markets.

The European Union has asked non-E.U. entities operating in the European Union to disclose information based on the "IFRSs or an equivalent standard" starting in 2005. As of now, more than 250 Japanese corporations and Japanese local governments have issued stocks and bonds in the European Union. Most of these Japanese corporations disclosed financial information using Japanese accounting standards.[5]

Japanese efforts may be successful because Japan is negotiating diligently with the European Union and is asking for its approval of the Japanese accounting standard as an equivalent to the IFRSs. If the

---

[2] In June 1973, the International Accounting Standards Committee was established by the joint efforts of ten countries, including the United States, Japan, England, France, and Germany. This committee was reorganized as the IASB in April 2001.

[3] This is a collective name for accounting standards established by the International Accounting Standards Board (IASB) with the purpose of being approved and observed internationally. International Accounting Standards (IASs) were issued by the International Accounting Standards Committee (IASC) from 1973 to 2000. The IASB replaced the IASC in 2001. Since then, the IASB has amended some IASs, has proposed to amend other IASs, has proposed to replace some IASs with new International Financial Reporting Standards (IFRSs), and has adopted or proposed certain new IFRSs on topics for which there were no previous IASs. *See generally* the website of the IASB at http://www.iasb.org (last visited Mar. 28, 2005).

[4] In October 2002, SEC Chairman Harvey C. Pitt applauded the decisions by the FASB and the IASB to work together toward greater convergence between US Generally Accepted Accounting Principles (US GAAP) and international accounting standards. He said, "This is a positive step for investors in the US and around the world. It means that reducing the differences in two widely used sets of accounting standards will receive consideration by both boards, as they work to improve accounting principles and address issues in financial reporting." Press Release, US Securities and Exchange Commission, Actions by FASB, IASB Praised (Oct. 29, 2002), *available at* http://www.sec.gov/news/press/2002-154.htm.

[5] Kazuo Hiramatsu and Shigeo Naruse, Kaikei Kijun — Nichi Ou Sougo Shounin WoNikkei [Accounting Standards — Hoping for Mutual Acceptance between Europe and Japan], NIKKEI, July 27, 2004, at 27.

Japanese accounting standard fails to be recognized as an equivalent of the IFRSs, disclosure by Japanese companies based on the Japanese accounting standard currently in the European Union would not be allowed. This would severely affect the financing activities of Japanese companies seeking to raise funds in the European Union. Japanese corporations are also concerned about the possibility that Japanese accounting standards could be branded as inferior to the European or US Accounting Standards, thus causing a general mistrust among investors in Japanese capital markets.[6]

There have been divergent opinions from both government and private sectors about the adoption of the IFRSs in Japan and no consensus has yet been reached. In the midst of this, on June 24, 2004, the Corporate Accounting Rule Council[7] of the Japanese Government Ministry of Finance (MOF),[8] published a memorandum entitled "Adoption of International Accounting Standards in Japan" (MOF

---

[6]Japanese Ministry of Economy, Trade and Industry, Report on the Internationalization of Business Accounting in Japan, *available at* http://www.iasplus.com/resource/0406ifrsjapangaap.pdf. (July 21, 2004).

[7] The mandate of the Corporate Accounting Rule Council is defined as: "the Corporate Accounting Rule Council shall investigate and examine the processes of the establishment of business accounting and auditing standards, the standardization of cost calculation and refurbishments or improvements of corporate accounting systems as well as to report the results of such investigations and examinations to the Prime Minister, the Commissioner of Financial Services Agency, and related organizations and consult with them." *See* Japanese Government Ministry of Finance, Organizational Ordinance, Article 24, No. 392 (1998), *available at* http://www.soumu.go.jp/s-news/2002/pdf/021017_3_06.pdf (last visited Feb. 27, 2005) [hereinafter Organizational Ordinance].

[8] The Ministry of Finance was reorganized on January 6, 2001. The name was changed from "Okurasho" to "Zaimucho" in Japanese, but the English name still remains the same. For more information, see the Ministry's website at http://www.mof.go.jp (last visited Mar. 28, 2005) [hereinafter MOF website]. The Financial Services Agency (FSA) was created on July 1, 1997, with the integration of the Banking Supervisory Agency and the Financial System Planning Bureau of the Ministry of Finance. The new FSA has integral responsibility over planning of the financial system, and supervision and inspection of financial institutions. In view of the rapid changes in the environment surrounding the economy and financial markets, the planning of the financial system focused on building a stable and vigorous financial system, and securing the efficiency and fairness in the financial markets. In the supervision and inspection of financial institutions, further efforts to maintain and improve the soundness of financial institutions were made. Coordination with foreign financial authorities was strengthened in order to cope adequately with the globalization of finance. Details on the FSA, *available at* http://www.fsa.go.jp (last visited Mar. 28, 2005) [hereinafter FSA website].

Memorandum).[9] The purpose of the MOF Memorandum was to canvass and compile various arguments about what should be done in Japan, from an official standpoint, regarding adopting international accounting standards to coincide with the European Union's adoption of the IFRS in 2005.

The Japanese Corporate Accounting Rule Council (the Council) received the responsibility of setting up the business accounting system and auditing standard.[10]   In the MOF Memorandum, as a first step, the Council made a general observation of the international trends surrounding the IFRSs, summarized the arguments and comments about the IFRSs from a legal standpoint, and provided the Council's comment about future tasks.   The Council also provided its opinions regarding the application of the IFRSs to foreign as well as domestic corporations.[11]

This article summarizes various arguments existing in Japan on the current issue of standardization as well as the official position of the Japanese government expressed in the MOF Memorandum.   The Japanese government's position as expressed in the MOF Memorandum is extremely important to investors in foreign countries.   The author analyzes the government's positions and makes comments on the problems and issues indicated in the MOF Memorandum.

Various Arguments about the IFRS in Japan

Opinions of the government

Japanese corporations typically generate two sets of financial statements in accordance with two laws: the Commercial Code and the Securities Exchange Law.   Corporations would be freed once and for all from the burden of preparing two financial statements if the IASs were adopted.

---

[9] Memorandum from the Ministry of Finance on the Adoption of International Accounting Standards in Japan (June 24, 2004), *available at* http://www.fsa.go.jp/news/newsj/15/singi/f-20040624-1/01.pdf [hereinafter MOF Memorandum].

[10] Organizational Ordinance, *supra* note 7, at art. 24.

[11] The council decided on Feb. 20, 2002 to take up the issue of IFRS and discuss the issue in the light of accounting and auditing standards.

However, both the Ministry of Justice, which has jurisdiction over the Commercial Code, and the Financial Services Agency (FSA)[12], which has jurisdiction over the Securities Exchange Law, are objecting to the adoption of the IASs. The major differences between the Japanese commercial law and the IASs are shown in Appendix I, *infra*.[13]

International standards are generally more comprehensive concerning the extent of the required disclosures, but this is not always the case. For example:

1. Japan's Commercial Code does not require disclosures of a shareholder's share variation statement and cash flow statement, which are required under international standards.

2. A profit appropriation plan and supplemental statement (as to securities held, fixed assets, capital account, and reserve account) are required under the Japanese Commercial Code but are not required under international standards.

3. Under the Commercial Code, only large corporations are required to disclose consolidated statements, whereas international standards require disclosure of consolidated statements regardless of the size of the companies.

4. The Commercial Code requires disclosure of single year financial statements, but international standards require disclosure of comparative multi year financial statements.

5. Annotation is limited under the Commercial Code but it is an important part of disclosure under international standards.

One of the reasons for opposing the imposition of international standards, the FSA states, is that "it is not accepted as a practice even in the United States to apply the International Accounting Standards to both domestic and foreign corporations as fair and appropriate accounting standards."[14] However, the position of the FSA is inaccurate, since the

---

[12] FSA website, *supra* note 8.

[13] Appendix I, infra.

[14] Designated Structural Reform District Promotion Office, Prime Minister's Office, Record on International Accounting Standards, available at http://www.kantei.go.jp/jp/singi/kouzou/kouhyou/021022/kaitou03.pdf (last visited Mar. 31, 2005).

US Securities and Exchange Commission (SEC) allows the use of foreign accounting standards, including the International Accounting Standards on the condition of reconciling these figures with US Generally Accepted Accounting Practice (US GAAP).[15] For example, Bayer AG,[16] a German pharmaceutical company, filed its financial statements prepared in accordance with the International Accounting Standards (Form 20-F) with the SEC in order to be listed on the New York Stock Exchange in January 2002.[17] The same rule has also been applied to Russian and Chinese corporations. Rostelecom (a Russian company) was listed on the New York Stock Exchange on February 17, 1998.[18] The American Depositary Shares of PetroChina (a Chinese company) were listed on the New York Stock Exchange on April 6, 2000.[19] Both filed their financial statements in accordance with Form 20-F. The New York Stock Exchange welcomes foreign corporations for trade and approves the use of the International Accounting Standards. The flexible position of the New York Stock Exchange corresponds to the change of the SEC's position on September 29, 1999 for new disclosure requirements for foreign companies that were allowed to use international accounting standards.[20]

---

[15] Kimco Realty Corporation, Reconciling Non-GAAP Financial Measures, *available at* http://www.kimcorealty.com/file/Fin_SupplementalReports/2ndQuarterSupplementalPac kage_7-29-2003_8-37-32AM.pdf (last visited Feb. 27, 2005).

[16] Bayer Aktiengesellschaft, Report of Foreign Issuer, *available at* http://www.sec.gov/ edgar/searchedgar/companysearch.html (last visited Apr. 4, 2005).

[17] Press Release, US Securities and Exchange Commission, SEC Adopts New Disclosure Requirements for Foreign Companies, (Sept. 29, 1999), *available at* http://www.sec.gov/ news/press/pressarchive/1999/99-125.txt [hereinafter SEC Press Release]. The SEC adopted new disclosure requirements for foreign companies in 1999. The changes brought SEC disclosure requirements for foreign companies closer to the international standards endorsed in 1998 by the International Organization of Securities Commissions, the global association of securities regulators. This reduced the barriers foreign companies face when raising capital or listing their securities in more than one country. The rule changes incorporated these standards into Form 20-F, the basic disclosure form for foreign private issuers. The new requirements became effective September 30, 2000.

[18] Rostelecom, SEC Reports, *available at* http://www.rt.ru/en/icenter/reports/sec/ (last visited Feb. 26, 2005).

[19] PetroChina, Annual Report, *available at* http://www.petrochina.com.cn/english/ tzzgx/ndbg.htm (last visited Feb. 26, 2005).

[20] SEC Press Release, *supra* note 17.

Also, the Counselor for the FSA stated his opinion in a speech he made at the General Assembly of the Corporate Accounting Rule Council on December 6, 2002 concerning his recognition of the IASB:

> In a sense, I myself have a certain level of awareness that it is probably necessary to have 'restraint' against 'excessive inclination' toward IASB. I also think it is very important to grasp the situation accurately, to make sure that their discussions are based on balanced thoughts, and what kind of measures are available to guarantee such a balance. Of course I understand that IASB has no enforcing power. I think we would most likely adjust our thoughts to theirs as to what degree and in what areas based on the standpoint of cost vs. benefit. In other words, I think it is like putting the cart before the horse if the actual state of economy or industry is interpreted differently depending on which accounting principle is to be used. Therefore, I believe it is necessary to approach the issue from the standpoints of what kind of 'check' is needed on the IASB discussions or how we should lead the discussions reflecting the actual economic states of our country or how to achieve a more appropriate unbiased system.[21]

On March 3, 2003, Mark Norbom (president & CEO of GE Japan Ltd.), who sat on the 25th Japan Investment Council's meeting held under the auspices of the government of Japan to collect the wisdom of economic circles, expressed his opinion concerning the introduction of the International Accounting Standards. Norbom stated that the "introduction of the International Accounting Standards should be accelerated." The Japanese FSA responded, stating that "as to the disclosures of financial statements based on the ISA, we will judge them case by case and treat them based on the agreement at the IOSCO.[22] We

---

[21] Shizuki Saito, Statement at the Meeting of the Corporate Accounting Rule Council, *available at* http://www.fsa.go.jp/singi/singi_kigyou/ top.html (Dec. 6, 2002) (Mr. Saito was Chairman of Section 1 of the Council).

[22] The International Organization of Securities Commissions (IOSCO) was established in 1988 under the auspices of authorities who controlled securities markets of various countries such as the Ministry of Finance of Japan and the US Securities and Exchange Commission. This coincided with the expansion of corporations seeking funding in overseas markets. The IOSCO established principles concerning securities administration for authorities in charge of securities in order to achieve three objectives: (1) protect investors, (2) increase the transparency of markets for fair and efficient transactions, and (3) minimize system risks. IOSCO is a member of the International Accounting Standards Committee (IASC) and does not have its own accounting standards.

will also be watching closely the discussions made on the Financial Accounting Standards Committee of Japan [(FASCJ)]."[23]

Opinions of private sectors

The Japanese Federation of Economic Organizations (known as Keidanren in Japanese)[24] is also taking a negative position with regard to standardization.[25] On July 24, 2003, the IASB Chairman Sir David Tweedie visited the Keidanren and stated that:

> The purpose of IASB is to establish a uniform high quality accounting standard that can be used in all markets of the world. On account of the fact that people lost trust in accounting practices in various countries of the world through the experiences of unfortunate incidents exemplified by the Enron incident in the US and the financial crises of Asian countries, it is strongly desired to establish an international uniform accounting standard. We dearly wish Japan's cooperation in this regard.[26]

The Keidanren responded to this plea by saying:

Information concerning the IOSCO available at http://www.iosco.org/ (last visited Feb. 26, 2005).

[23] The FASCJ was established on July 26, 2001 by ten organizations including the Japan Federation of Economic Organizations, Japanese Institute of Public Accountants, National Securities Exchange Conference, Japan Securities Dealers Association, Japanese Bankers Association, Life Insurance Association of Japan, General Insurance Association of Japan, and Japan Chamber of Commerce and Industry for the establishment of accounting standards using the US FASB as a model. It is notable that the Japanese government did not participate in it.

[24] The Japanese Federation of Economic Organizations is a general economic organization consisting of 1,623 companies and other organizations, which include 91 companies with foreign capital affiliations and 1,306 major representative Japanese companies. It is the strongest interest group in Japan that applies pressure on the government as well as overseas organizations by collecting opinions from business communities on many important issues for business communities ranging from economic and industrial issues to labor issues urging speedy solutions. See the Federation's website at http://www.keidanren.or.jp/Japanese/profile/pro001.htm (last visited Mar. 28, 2005).

[25] Japan Federation of Economic Organizations, Announcement, *available at* http://www.keidanren.or.jp/japanese/policy/2004/032.html (Apr. 20, 2004).

[26] Japan Federation of Economic Organizations, Economic Release No. 25, *available at* http://www.keidanren.or.jp/japanese/journal/CLIP/2003/0722/index.html (July 22, 2003) (translation by author).

> We have yet to see the evidence that any evaluation has been made of the opinion we submitted to the IASB concerning the draft of the accounting standards and any reasons why our opinion was not adopted. Thus, we would like to see an improvement on the evaluation procedure. We believe that the IASB's thought is too biased and we wish the IASB to conduct discussion with more considerations on the realities of practical business matters.[27]

The Keidanren's comments are purposefully vague and unclear. This is a typical way in which the Japanese show hesitation in accepting another's position. The Keidanren's position is a "wait and see" position, and since the Keidanren's opinion is a collection of all companies who are members (1623 companies), this "wait and see" position is the consensus of most Japanese companies today.

Opinions of journalists

The Nihon Keizai Shimbun (Japan Economic Journal) discussed this issue in an editorial article entitled "Haphazard Accounting Reforms,"[28] claiming that corporate accountants have lost their confidence and Japan should switch to the International Accounting Standards since "Japanese closing statements are not reliable."[29] A pertinent portion of the article reads:

> The entire Japanese accounting system is scrutinized with eyes of doubts. One viable alternative is to switch entirely to the international accounting standards rather than waiting for the national reform of the accounting system. At this moment, twenty-eight companies have turned self-defensive by switching to the US accounting standards and eight companies (one duplicated) are adopting the International Accounting Standards to distance themselves from the suspicions of the Japanese accounting system.[30]

---

[27] *Id.*
[28] Editorial, Haphazard Accounting Reforms, NIKKEI, Nov. 12, 1999, at 2 (Translation by author).
[29] *Id.*
[30] *Id.*

The 2005 Problem

The MOF Memorandum describes the problems expected to occur in Japan when the European Union adopts the new standards in 2005. The MOF Memorandum summarizes the expected movements in Europe as follows:

> The European Union ("E.U.") decided a policy in July 2002 to make it mandatory for companies that are to make any public offerings or are traded on the markets within the E.U. to adopt the International Financial Reporting Standards ("IFRS") as the standards for preparing their consolidated financial statements as of January 2005. In accordance with this, the E.U. has decided to adopt the Prospectus Directive for controlling disclosures related to issues in July 2003, and the Transparency Directive for controlling continuation disclosures (periodical disclosures) later, requiring "the IFRS or accounting standards comparable to the IFRS" to be used as the standards for preparing consolidated financial statements in both directives.[31]

The Prospectus Directive issued by the European Union in April 2004 sets out the initial disclosure obligations for issuers of securities that are offered to the public or admitted to trading on a regulated market in the European Union. It is a single passport for issuers that enables them to raise capital across the European Union on the basis of a single prospectus.[32] The directive only concerns initial disclosure requirements. Conditions for admissions listing remain subject to existing European and national requirements. The Transparency Directive aims to enhance transparency in E.U. capital markets by establishing rules for the disclosure of periodic financial reports and of major shareholdings for whom securities are admitted to trading on a regulated market in the European Union.[33]

---

[31] MOF website, *supra* note 8.

[32] Commission Regulation 809/2004 of 29 April 2004 Implementing Directive 2003/71/EC of the European Parliament and of the Council as Regards Information Contained in Prospectuses, 2004 O.J. (L 149) 1 [hereinafter Prospectus Directive].

[33] Council Directive 2004/109 of 31 December 2004 on Harmonization of Transparency Requirements, 2004 O.J. (L 309) 38 [hereinafter Transparency Directive].

Last year, members of both the public and private sectors in Japan started to see warning signs in Japan that it would be difficult for Japanese corporations and securities issuers to raise funds in the European Union unless the European Union would recognize Japanese accounting standards as equivalent to the IFRSs. This eventually became known as the "2005 Problem."[34]

In coordination with the FSA, various organizations in Japan, including the Accounting Standards Board of Japan (ASBJ), [35] the Keidanren, the Japanese Institute of Public Accountants, and the Tokyo Stock Exchange contracted with the European Commission (EC) and various organizations of E.U. countries, asking them to accept the Japanese accounting standards as equivalents to the IFRS.[36]

The FSA prepared data (in English, French and German) comparing the IFRS and the US and Japanese accounting standards to standards of various European organizations, especially those of the European Union. It then tried to explain, on various occasions, the differences and similarities in standards directly to the officials of the related organizations and systems, in order to convince them that Japanese standards are of the same caliber as US and European accounting standards.[37]

As a result of such efforts, it was decided that the European Union would make a further specific examination into whether the Japanese financial standards are "accounting standards that are equivalent to IFRS."[38] The Committee of European Securities Regulations (CESR) will make a specific examination into the financial standards and the

---

[34] For instance, Keidanren issued a paper stating that the accounting standards of Japan, the United States, and Europe have to be accepted mutually as the first step of convergence of accounting standards, and that the MOF in particular must negotiate with the authorities of member countries to accept the Japanese accounting standards. *See* Economic Release No. 25, *supra* note 26.

[35] The ASBJ was established in April 2004 as a subordinate organization of the FASCJ.

[36] MOF Memorandum, *supra* note 9, at 2.

[37] This assertion is by the Japanese government. Ministry of Economy, Trade and Industry, Report on the Internationalization of Business Accounting in Japan 13 (July 21, 2004), *available at* http://www.meti.go.jp/english/report/downloadfiles/IBAreporte.pdf.

[38] MOF Memorandum, *supra* note 9, at 2, 6.

European Union will make the final decision. The examination by the CESR is scheduled to be completed by June, 2005.[39]

The European Union also determined that the use of "home country standards" is acceptable for companies of the countries outside the European Union until the end of 2006 for both the Prospectus Directive and the Transparency Directive.[40] With this time extension, the Japanese companies are now allowed to use Japanese standards until the end of 2006.[41]

Current Disclosure Requirements in Japanese Markets Based upon Different Accounting Standards

Because of the uniqueness of Japanese accounting standards and the emergence of IFRSs, three different types of disclosures have been created in the Japanese market: (1) those based on the Japanese accounting standards; (2) those based on accounting standards of foreign countries; and (3) those based on the IFRSs. As a result, a difficult problem has surfaced: how should Japanese authorities handle disclosures? Should all three standards be accepted as legitimate? What are the conditions of acceptance?[42]

The Securities Exchange Law of Japan originally assumed a scenario in which Japanese companies would disclose information based on the Japanese Accounting Standard. However, the Japanese market has since become internationalized and foreign companies have come to seek financing in Japan. This presented the MOF with the problem of how to handle foreign companies that disclose their information based on their countries' or a third countries' accounting standards. The Japanese Securities Exchange Law deals with this, as explained below. As more and more Japanese companies finance overseas, some of them are now disclosing their reports in Japan based on foreign accounting standards. How the Japanese Securities Exchange Law is dealing with those cases is

---

[39] *Id.* at 6.

[40] Prospectus Directive, *supra* note 32; Transparency Directive, *supra* note 33.

[41] MOF Memorandum, *supra* note 9, at 2.

[42] *Id.* at 10-11.

also described below. It is now up to the MOF to decide whether to accept the disclosures in Japan by Japanese and/or foreign companies based on the IFRSs. The Japanese law has not yet addressed these disclosure's, so one can certainly anticipate a MOF response to this issue. The MOF Memorandum reveals the official viewpoint about the IFRS for the first time, specifically whether and how disclosures made by Japanese and non-Japanese companies in accordance with the IFRS should be accepted.

This article analyzes the MOF's viewpoint on the following six potential problems presented by the convergence of Japanese and international accounting standards. These six potential cases are set out in Table 1.

Table 1 — Disclosures under Various Standards in the Japanese Market

	Foreign Company	Japanese Company
Japanese Accounting Std.	Case 1	Case 4
Foreign Accounting Std.	Case 2	Case 5
IFRS	Case 3	Case 6

Cases of foreign companies

Treatment by foreign companies of the Japanese standards under the existing law in Japan (Case 1)

As long as foreign companies submit financial documents prepared according to Japanese accounting standards, these documents are regarded as not compromising the protection of public interests or investors (Case 1). This disclosure is treated the same as disclosures by Japanese companies who submitted financial documents prepared according to Japanese accounting standards. The disclosure is subject to the Japanese Securities Exchange Law.[43]

---

[43] Shoken Torihiki Ho [Securities Exchange Law], Law No. 25 of 1948, art. 127, no. 4 , *available at* http://www.japanlaw.info/f_statements/PARENT/DX.htm (last visited Feb. 28, 2005) [hereinafter Securities Exchange Law].

Treatment by foreign companies of the "home country standards" or the "third country standards" under the existing law in Japan (Case 2)

The Rules for Financial Statements under the Japanese Securities Exchange Law [44] define the basic treatment of foreign companies concerning their financial papers:

> Under the current system, it is allowed for a foreign company to submit documents concerning financial calculations that are disclosed in its 'home country' or in a country outside of Japan and different from its home country ('third country') and are prepared according to the 'home country standards' or 'third country standards' as long as the Commissioner of Financial Services Agency of Japan agrees that [the documents] are regarded as not compromising the protection of public interests or investors. [45]

Based on the above rule, a judgment is made for each financial document concerning whether it can be accepted or not and, as a result, 150 filing documents and twenty foreign financial statements have been received from July 2002 to June 2003. They were prepared according to "home country standards" or "third country standards." The accounting standards of various countries including the United States, Canada, Mexico, the United Kingdom, Germany, France, Spain, the Netherlands, Switzerland, Luxemburg, Ireland, Finland, Australia, Republic of Korea, Malaysia, Singapore, Taiwan, and Hong Kong are currently accepted and the number of accepted country standards is increasing. [46]

---

[44] *Id.* at art. 127. The Securities Exchange Law was enacted on April 13, 1948, and has been amended 27 times. Amendments are available at http://www.houko.com/00/01/S23/025.HTM (last visited Feb. 27, 2005).

[45] Securities Exchange Law, *supra* note 43, at art. 193; Regulations Concerning Terminology, Forms and Methods of Preparation of Financial Statements, MOF Ordinance No. 36, art. 127, §§ 1, 2, *available at* http://www.mof.go.jp/hourei.htm (Nov. 27, 1963) [hereinafter Ministry of Finance Ordinance]. *See also* Consolidated Financial Statement Rules, MOF Ordinance No. 28, *available at* http://www.mof.go.jp/ hourei.htm (Oct. 30, 1976) [hereinafter Consolidated Financial Statement Rules]; Rules of Intermediate Financial Statements, MOF Ordinance No. 24, *available at* http://www.mof.go.jp/hourei.htm (Mar. 30, 1999).

[46] Discussion Memorandum from the Japanese Corporate Accounting Rule Council, at 9–10 (June 17, 2003), *available at* http://www.fsa.go.jp/singi/singi_kigyou/gijiroku/ kikaku/f-20040617_k-giji.pdf [hereinafter Discussion Memorandum].

The Securities Exchange Law stipulates that the financial documents to be submitted, regardless of their origins, must be prepared "in generally fair and appropriate manners in accordance with the terminologies, formats and methods of preparation stipulated in the Cabinet Office regulations."[47] Acceptance of these financial documents and this treatment of foreign countries indicate that the authorities regard reports prepared under the foreign accounting standards as "generally fair and appropriate."

Japan has not published specific rules or guidelines regarding the way in which certain documents are determined to be "not compromising the protection of public interests or investors." The Rules for Financial Statements, however, state that this judgment is made "from the standpoint of whether the document generally has a disclosure level which is internationally acceptable." [48] This judgment has to be made by Japanese authorities, but they have been quite flexible and liberal in accepting foreign standards in this regard.[49]

The MOF Memorandum reveals an understanding that Japan's current system has functioned well based on a principle of broadly accepting foreign financial documents, relying on the authorities making individual judgments of "[those that] are regarded as not compromising the protection of public interests or investors." [50] Further, the MOF Memorandum describes the reason why financial documents (Case 2) based on "home country standards" or "third country standards" rather than on the Japanese accounting standards (Case 1) are allowed to be disclosed as follows:

> (a) the Japanese authorities had hopes for contributing to the internationalization of the domestic market with such a move and meeting foreign companies' specific demands about wanting to be able to conduct public offerings and to have their stocks traded in the market;

---

[47] Securities Exchange Law, *supra* note 43, at art. 193.

[48] Yoshitoshi Asaike, Zaimushohyou tou Kisoku Chikujokai [Providing a Detailed Article-by-Article Analysis of the Rules on Financial Statements] 523 (Chuou Keizai, ed., 3rd ed. 1997).

[49] MOF Memorandum, *supra* note 9, at 2-6. *See also* Discussion Memorandum, *supra* note 46, at 10.

[50] MOF Memorandum, *supra* note 9, at 2.

(b) evaluations of foreign companies and formations of their securities' prices based on their financial statements already existed in their home countries and third countries. It is expected that the "judgment" function of the international market concerning such evaluations and formations of their securities' prices is expected to work so that the authorities thought it is possible to prevent the biased existence of information for investors in the domestic market with such a move; and

(c) the authorities thought it would not cause any problem from the standpoint of "the protection of public interests or investors" in Japan so long as the financial documents of companies which are already published in the markets of their home countries or third countries where proper legal systems and accounting systems exist are to be published in Japanese in accordance with the Japanese disclosure formats. [51]

Furthermore, the MOF Memorandum implicitly assumes that the current system is based on "secondary" disclosures (i.e., financial documents that have been appropriately disclosed for a specific period of time in the home or third country before being disclosed in Japan). [52] However, in reality, there are a few cases of "primary" disclosures (financial statements that have not been appropriately disclosed for a specific period in the home or third country that are then disclosed in Japan) of foreign companies that are subjected to the Japanese Security Exchange Law and submit their disclosure documents under the Japanese standards. [53] In these cases, the disclosures are examined by Japanese certified public accountants or accounting firms.

Arguments about foreign companies who use IFRS (Case 3)

The IFRSs does not meet the definition of either "home country standards" or "third country standards." Therefore, the MOF is not yet sure of how to accept the financial documents prepared by foreign companies based upon IFRSs. This is especially true for foreign companies' "primary" disclosures based upon IFRSs. The MOF

---

[51] *Id.*
[52] *Id.*
[53] Securities Exchange Law, *supra* note 43, at art. 127, no. 4.

Memorandum raises the following two questions concerning foreign companies: (1) should "secondary" cases, where financial documents of foreign companies are based on the IFRSs, be treated as falling under "home country standards" or "third country standards?" and (2) how should financial documents based on the IFRSs be treated when they are submitted as "primary" cases?

The MOF Memorandum proposes to maintain basically the current system for "secondary" cases. It asserts that it is unproblematic, from the standpoint of "the protection of public interests or investors" in Japan, for a foreign company to make "secondary" disclosures in Japan of financial documents based on the IFRSs as the "home country standard" or "third country standard" that have already been disclosed in that company's home country or a third country. Although market evaluations on these documents have not been conducted in Japan, it is permissible because those companies' securities have been valued and market studies have been conducted in their home country or in third countries. This treatment is similar to the acceptance Japan currently gives to documents that are prepared according to foreign accounting standards.

Additionally, the MOF Memorandum points out that it might be appropriate to conduct an "equivalency evaluation" of foreign companies' accounting, auditing, and disclosure standards against Japanese standards as a basis for judging the quality of "the protection of public interests or investors."[54] If such an idea is adopted, there is a possibility that some currently accepted foreign accounting standards may be rejected on the ground that they lack equivalency.

The MOF's suggestion to conduct an "equivalency evaluation" of the IFRSs, which is used by foreign companies against those of Japan, is very appropriate since the European Union is currently examining whether the Japanese financial standards are equivalent to the IFRSs. The MOF's attitude is considered to be reciprocal to the position of the European Union and is widely supported in Japan.[55]

---

[54] MOF Memorandum, *supra* note 9, at 12.

[55] For example, the Security Analysts Association of Japan (SAAJ) expressed its support of the MOF's position. *See* Press Release, Security Analysts Association of Japan, The

The MOF Memorandum then discusses cases where disclosures are made on a "primary" basis. It claims that the Japanese Government should subject all disclosures to the Japanese accounting standards in accordance with the "market-based principle," which seeks the observance of the nation's standards from the standpoint of the protection of public interest and investors.[56] This position is opposed to the MOF's current official position, which says that "if it is regarded appropriate for the protection of investors in Japan as well, to disclose the financial statements that the particular company is disclosing in accordance with rules and customs of its home country for the purpose of protection of investors in said country, said financial statements can be used for said purpose."[57] The MOF adopted the home country doctrine in 1973, when it made an announcement stating that "the standards of the accounting process to be used in preparing the financial statements shall be the standards used in the home country of said company."[58] Therefore, the MOF Memorandum suggests a change in the MOF's position from home country doctrine to market-based principles for disclosures on a primary basis.

The MOF's current position in support of market-based principles for primary issues is more appropriate since primary issues have higher risks in Japanese markets. Contrary to secondary issues, which are tested for risks in their home countries or third countries, primary issues are not tested in any markets.[59]

The MOF memorandum indicates, however, that a foreign company can use foreign accounting standards in Japan, including IFRS, even when documents are disclosed as "primary" disclosures. To do so, a company must meet the following conditions:

SAAJ's Opinion on the MOF's Memorandum of the International Accounting Standards (Aug. 31, 2004), *available at* http://www.saa.or.jp [hereinafter SAAJ Press Release].

[56] MOF Memorandum, supra note 9, at 11.

[57] Announcement, Japanese Ministry of Finance, On Financial Documents of Foreign Companies in Accordance with the Business Performance Disclosure System of Japan (Sept. 4, 1973), *available at* http://www.fsa.go.jp/news/newsj/15/singi/f-20040311-1/02-02.pdf.

[58] *Id.*

[59] *See* SAAJ Press Release, *supra* note 55.

(a) As an exception, financial documents based on the IFRS or the "home country standards" can be allowed to be disclosed in Japan if the Commissioner of Financial Services Agency examines them individually and "recognizes that they do not compromise the protection of public interests or investors," even when said financial documents have not been disclosed in the home country or a third country. In this case, however, the documents have to obey the basic rule that the documents need to be audited based on the Japanese auditing principles and the documents are written in Japanese and disclosed in accordance with the Japanese disclosure standards.

(b) As an exception, financial documents based on the "home country standards" can be allowed to be disclosed in Japan if the Commissioner of Financial Services Agency conducts the "equivalency evaluation" of the accounting, auditing, and disclosure standards of the home countries against those of Japan and "recognizes that they do not compromise the protection of public interests or investors in Japan," even when said financial documents have not been disclosed in the home country or a third country. In following such a thought, the IFRS can be approved by conducting the "equivalency evaluation" in the accounting standards in Japan. The "equivalency evaluation" can be based on a comparison between the accounting, auditing, and disclosure standards of the home countries and those of Japan, or a comparison between international standards (e.g., the SEC standards in the U.S.) that are generally considered matching the Japanese standards.[60]

These two concepts are exceptions to the market-based principle. The real difference between these two concepts, (a) and (b), is that in (b) an "equivalency evaluation" is conducted as a premise for recognizing that the standards do not compromise the protection of public interests or investors. Concept (b) is better in light of securing transparency and avoiding arbitrariness.[61] The "equivalency evaluation" in terms of accounting, auditing, and disclosure standards could be a task associated with substantial difficulty. Considering it has been predicted that the European Union would take more than one year to evaluate the Japanese

---

[60] MOF Memorandum, *supra* note 9, at 11-12.
[61] SAAJ Press Release, *supra* note 55.

accounting standards, it is necessary to assume that Japan's "equivalency evaluation" would require the same level of accuracy and time.[62]

The MOF Memorandum states that in order to secure reliability and objectivity when judging each standard under an "equivalency evaluation," it is necessary to examine both proper and improper applications.[63] This means that it is necessary to examine if the application is done properly under each standard, in addition to only a comparative examination of the standards' text, regardless of the secondary or primary disclosure. The equivalency evaluation of the applications of standards is going to be more difficult than simply comparing the text of the standards.

Cases of Japanese companies

The current system requires Japanese companies to prepare their documents in accordance with the Japanese accounting, auditing and disclosure standards from the standpoint of "the protection of public interests or investors" and does not allow Japanese companies to disclose consolidated financial statements based on accounting standards of foreign countries (Case 4).[64] As an exception (Case 5), the treatment of "U.S.-style consolidated financial statements" of Japanese companies is allowed and defined in the rules for terminology, form and preparation method of consolidated financial statements (Consolidated Financial Statement Rules or CFSR).[65]

According to the CFSR, a company registered with the SEC in the United States can submit US-style consolidated financial statements in accordance with the rules of the Security Exchange Law of Japan if the Commissioner of Financial Services Agency "recognizes that they do not compromise the protection of public interests or investors."[66] This rule no longer applies if that company ceases to be registered with the SEC in

---

[62] Shizuki Saito, Press Release, "Equivalency Evaluation" in Accounting, NIKKEI (Dec. 4, 2004), at 15.

[63] MOF Memorandum, *supra* note 9, at 13.

[64] *Id.*

[65] Ministry of Finance Ordinance, *supra* note 45, at arts. 87-88.

[66] *Id.*

the United States.[67] Japanese companies which submit US-style consolidated financial statements in Japan must provide annotations describing how they were prepared and filed with the SEC, compared to the case of preparing documents based on the Consolidated Financial Statement Rules in Japan.[68]

The MOF Memorandum explains that the current system was a special measure taken when Japanese companies issued American Depository Receipts to obtain funds based on consolidated financial statements in accordance with SEC standards in the United States.[69] This measure was approved on the premise that consolidated financial statements approved in the United States are based on SEC standards.[70] Due to the SEC's restrictive conditions, Japanese companies can submit U.S.-style consolidated financial statements in Japan.

The MOF Memorandum raises two questions pertaining to Case (6): (1) should Japanese companies be allowed to disclose consolidated financial statements prepared in conformance to the IFRSs?; and (2) if so, what kind of relations have to be maintained with the auditing and disclosure standards?[71] The basic thought here is that in addition to accounting standards, the international convergence of auditing and disclosure standards will be necessary.[72]

---

[67] Consolidated Financial Statement Rules, *supra* note 45, at arts. 87-88.

[68] *Id*. at art. 90.

[69] An American Depository Receipt (ADR) is a certificate of ownership issued by a US bank, representing a claim on underlying foreign securities. ADRs may be traded in the United States in lieu of trading in the actual underlying shares in Japan. ADRs can be listed on the NYSE, AMEX, or NASDAQ. Currently thirty-one Japanese companies are issuing ADRs in US markets. *See* Takoz, ADR, *at* http://takoz.page.ne.jp/stock/adr (last visited Feb. 27, 2005) (providing a list of these 31 companies); Investopedia, ADRs, *at* http://www.investopedia.com/terms/a/adr.asp (last visited Feb. 20, 2005) (providing further details on ADRs).

[70] Before the SEC's standards took effect in 1981, the United States allowed the use of disclosure documents that were not based on US standards. Also, foreign companies are only allowed to use accounting standards different from those in the United States on the condition that they use the adjusting disclosure method. Under this method, a foreign company submitting documents according to non-US accounting standards is required to explain the differences between the foreign and US accounting standards to the SEC. However, no Japanese company has yet used the adjusting disclosure method. *See* HIROKO AWOKI, INTERNATIONAL SECURITIES TRANSACTIONS AND DISCLOSURE 202 (2000).

[71] MOF Memorandum, *supra* note 9, at 14.

[72] SAAJ is proposing further convergence. *See* SAAJ Press Release, *supra* note 55.

The MOF Memorandum offered the following two positions:

(a) While the current system requires the submitted financial documents to be prepared according to generally fair and appropriate standards, it does not say specifically whether the accounting standards they are conforming to have to be the Japanese accounting standards.

However, if we take the position of the "market principle," meaning that the documents submitted in Japan need to be prepared conforming to the Japanese standards from the standpoint of "the protection of public interests or investors," it may be reasonable to require Japanese companies to prepare their documents according to the Japanese accounting standards when they are disclosing their financial documents as a "primary" disclosure in Japan. (Case 4)

(b) As to the foreign accounting standards (Case 5), it may be reasonable to accept them under the premise of a certain qualification such as "equivalency evaluation," while seeking the clarification of the difference between the standards to conform to and the Japanese standards, as it is expected that it will not cause any particular problem from the standpoint of "the protection of public interests or investors" in Japan if the documents are disclosed in Japanese conforming to the formats of the Japanese disclosure standards.

While the MOF Memorandum indicated the two thoughts as shown above, it does not give any clear answer to the question of which standard is better. The MOF Memorandum also showed that the MOF believes it is appropriate to make judgments focusing more on the directions that Japanese companies take, while wanting to maintain its position of honoring Japanese accounting standards not only in Japan but also in other markets as well (including the European Union).[73]

In other words, the MOF takes the position that it should move cautiously in making a decision on the standards, considering the fact that the European Union will be making an "equivalency evaluation" as to the Japanese standards by June of 2006. The MOF chose not to provide clear guidance at this point, thinking that it is better to wait for the European Union's decision regarding the treatment of Japanese standards. The MOF Memorandum also states that it is necessary to

---

[73] MOF Memorandum, *supra* note 9, at 15-16.

consider providing annotations on the differences in the principles, procedures and display methods of the accounting processes if the disclosures of consolidated financial statements conforming to the IFRSs are to be allowed for Japanese companies (Case 6).[74]

The MOF Memorandum recognizes that there have only been a limited number of financial document disclosures based on the IFRSs in the world capital market, and the rules for actual applications of the IFRSs, such as practical guides and interpretation guides, are not available for Japanese companies.[75] Consequently, in order for Japanese companies to use the IFRSs (Case 6), the Memorandum says that it would be necessary to gather the input of the concerned organizations to study how to implement them. This study would take into consideration the status of the IFRSs after its introduction in the European Union as well as the guidelines to be provided by the International Financial Reporting Interpretations Committee (IFRIC).[76] The Memorandum also points out that there is concern about whether Japanese companies can really prepare consolidated financial statements based on the IFRS and/or conduct auditing with the currently available, and surely insufficient, interpretations and guidelines.[77]

Dual Accounting Regulations in Japan

Dual accounting regulations have always caused problems for corporations in Japan because of the time and expense involved in duplicating work. This is one of the reasons why some Japanese companies are advocating the application of International Accounting Standards. The Securities Exchange Law in Japan was enacted as a condition imposed by the occupation authorities for the reopening of the

---

[74] *Id.* at 16.

[75] *Id.*

[76] The IFRIC is a standards interpretation organization of the IASB. In June 1973, the International Accounting Standards Committee was established by joint efforts of 10 countries, including the United States, Japan, England, France, and Germany. This committee was reorganized as the IASB in April 2001.

[77] MOF Memorandum, *supra* note 9, at 16.

securities exchanges.[78] The Japanese law borrowed elements of the US Securities Act of 1933[79] and Securities Exchange Act of 1934,[80] and its disclosure and regulation provisions are quite similar to those found in the United States. The Japanese Commercial Code[81] also contains disclosure and regulatory provisions different from those in the United States. The Japanese Commercial Code was derived in 1899 from the German Commercial Code as part of a general trend of acceptance and usage of Western law during the Meiji era.[82] Later, during the occupation, the Commercial Code was once again reformed to be more like Anglo-American systems of company law.[83] There were three different types of amendments made to the Commercial Code in 1950: "(1) the rearrangement of corporate powers among shareholders, the board of directors and the corporate auditors; (2) the adoption of new ways of attracting capital into the markets; and (3) the increasing of the rights of individual shareholders."[84] Of these three, the second factor was the most important, concerning the development of the securities markets. American practice provided the concepts of authorized capital stock[85] and no-par value stock.[86] Other introductions were redeemable stock,[87] stock dividends,[88] stock split-ups[89] and transfers from reserves to stated capital.[90]

---

[78] *See* Mitsuru Misawa, *Securities Regulations in Japan*, 6 VAND. J. TRANSNAT'L L. 449 (1973) (discussing the history of Japanese markets).
[79] Securities Act of 1933, 15 U.S.C. §§ 77a-77mm (1934), *as amended* 15 U.S.C. §§ 77a-77m (1970).
[80] Securities Exchange Act of 1934, 15 U.S.C. §§ 78a-78jj (1934), *as amended* 15 U.S.C. §§ 78a-78hh(1) (1970).
[81] Commercial Code of Japan, Law No. 48 (Mar. 9, 1899) (amended 18 times), *available at* http://www.ron.gr.jp/law/law/syouhou1.htm [hereinafter Commercial Code].
[82] Subsequent amendments to the Commercial Code in 1899, 1911, and 1938 in the field of corporation law mainly reflected German developments. See Kotaro Shida, Nihon Shohoten No Hensan To Sono Kaisei [Codification of Japanese Commercial Code and its Amendments] (1934).
[83] *See* Misawa, *supra* note 78, at 450-54.
[84] *Id.* at 450.
[85] Commercial Code, *supra* note 81, at art. 166
[86] *Id.* at arts. 166, 199.
[87] *Id.* at art. 22.
[88] *Id.* at art. 293(2).
[89] *Id.* at art. 293(4).
[90] *Id.* at art. 293(3).

The duality of accounting regulations is due in large part to historical developments. The Commercial Code regulates corporate accounting procedures [91] for the primary purpose of accurately determining the amount of capital available for dividends so that the position of creditors would not be jeopardized because of an impairment of corporate properties from excessive dividend distributions. In 1950, pursuant to the Securities Exchange Law, the MOF promulgated "Regulations Concerning Terminology, Forms and Method of Preparation of Financial Statements." [92]   Subsequently, in 1963, a separate set of regulations, "Regulations Concerning Balance Sheet and Income Statements of Corporations" (Ministry of Justice Ordinance), [93] was issued to complement the accounting regulations specified in the Commercial Code. The Ministry of Justice Ordinance is applicable to all companies in Japan, although the Ministry of Finance Ordinance is applicable to only companies issuing or listed. These accounting regulations were probably more sophisticated than in any other country including, in some respects, the United States. Unfortunately, serious problems arose in Japan because of discrepancies between the dual accounting regulations.

The Commercial Code upheld the period profit and loss calculation method and its balance sheet template was prepared directly from accounting books by means of the derivative method. [94]   Although a detailed regulation concerning corporate accounting could be found in

---

[91] Commercial Code, *supra* note 81, at arts. 281-295.

[92] Securities Exchange Law, *supra* note 43.

[93] Japanese Government Ministry of Finance, Ministry of Justice Ordinance No. 31 (1963), available at http://www.normanet.ne.jp/~hourei/sh031R/s380330sh031.htm (last visited Mar. 31, 2005) [hereinafter Ministry of Justice Ordinance].

[94] Commercial Code, *supra* note 81, at art. 33 provides:

   1. The following matters shall systematically and clearly be stated in the accounting books:
      (1) Business properties and values thereof at the commencement of business and once in each year at a fixed time, as for a company, business properties and values thereof at the time of incorporation and at each settlement of accounts;
      (2) Transactions and other matters which give influence to business properties.
   2. A balance sheet shall be prepared based on accounting books at the time commencement of business and once in each year at a fixed time; and a company shall prepare it based thereon at the time of incorporation and at each settlement of accounts.
   3. A balance sheet shall be compiled and bound together, or shall be entered in a book specially kept for that purpose.
   4. A balance sheet shall contain the signature of the person who prepared it.

the Commercial Code,[95] the rule of the Commercial Code's General Regulations Concerning Commercial Books,[96] and other Ministry of Justice Ordinances were applied to items that were not specifically defined there.[97] It was requested that fair accounting practices (GAAP) be considered in interpreting the existing rules.[98]

The Securities Exchange Law stipulated the terms, formats and methods to be used in the preparation of a balance sheet, a profit and loss statement, and other documents related to financial calculations. Items that were submitted in accordance with the law had to be prepared in accordance with the rules generally recognized as fair and reasonable using the terms, formats and method of preparation specified in the MOF Ordinance.[99]

The initial essence of this ordinance was, from a formatting perspective, to define the method of preparing these documents and others based on an assumption that issuing companies were obligated to submit financial calculation documents. From a more practical standpoint, financial calculation documents provide important information related to evaluations of negotiable securities and the issuing company at the time of share placement or public offering of stocks. Therefore, the ordinance favored regulating representations in such a way that they be prepared based on a non-interruptive, uniform standard so that period and position comparisons could be easily performed. This

---

[95] Commercial Code, *supra* note 81 at art. 281 provides:
  1. The Directors shall prepare the following documents and the annexed specifications thereof every period for settlement of accounts:
    (1) A balance sheet; (2) A profit and loss account; (3) A business report; (4) Proposals relating to the reserve fund and the distribution of profits or interest.
  2. The documents under the preceding paragraph need be audited by the auditors.
[96] Commercial Code, *supra* note 81, at art. 32 provides:
  1. Every trader shall prepare accounting books and balance sheets for making clear the conditions of business properties and profit and loss.
  2. In construing the provisions concerning preparation of the books of account, authentic accounting practices shall be taken into consideration."
[97] Ministry of Justice Ordinance No. 31, *supra* note 93.
[98] Commercial Code, *supra* note 81, at arts. 285-4 provides:
  1. The monetary claims shall be valued at the nominal amount thereof; provided that, of they were purchased at the proceeds lower than the nominal amount or there is any reasonable ground, they shall be valued with reasonable decrease.
  2. If there is a fear of being impossible to collect the monetary claims, the estimated amount of being impossible to collect shall be deducted in valuation.
[99] *Id.* at art. 193.

ordinance supported making administrative investigations smoother and faster. The ordinance increased the fairness of transactions by providing more accurate representations while allowing them to be handled in a smoother fashion through a rational format that facilitated faster analyses. Here, a higher priority was placed on "consistency."

MOF ordinances (known as the Rules on Financial Statements, the Rules of Consolidated Financial Statements, and the Rules of Intermediate Financial Statements)[100] stipulated that the items that are not specified were supposed to follow the "corporate accounting practices" generally accepted as fair and reasonable (GAAP). For example, the Rules on Financial Statements explained, "the items that are not defined in these rules shall follow the corporate accounting practices generally accepted as fair and reasonable."[101] In other words, the Rules on Financial Statements, a ministerial order promulgated under the Securities Exchange Law to add rules and accomplish the objective of the law encompassed the basic philosophy of promoting healthy, democratic development of the national economy. This was also the purpose of the Commercial Code. The concept of the "corporate accounting practices generally accepted as fair and reasonable" mentioned here matched the concept of the GAAP under the Commercial Code.

The Securities Exchange Law was introduced after World War II and aimed to copy the same laws established in 1933 and 1934 in the United States.[102] The basic assumption of occupation authorities in suggesting the new corporate and securities legislation appears to have been that what worked well in the United States would also work in Japan. No question was raised as to the congeniality of the environment into which the new legislation was being transplanted. If Japanese procedures did not adapt well to the corporate practices of Anglo-American origin, then

---

[100] Ministry of Finance Ordinance, *supra* note 45; Consolidated Financial Statement Rules, *supra* note 45; Rules of Intermediate Financial Statements, *supra* note 45.

[101] Ministry of Finance Ordinance, *supra* note 45, at art. 1-1.

[102] *See* Misawa, *supra* note 78 (history of how the Japanese Security Exchange Law was established). For the development of the Tokyo Stock Market, *see* Mitsuru Misawa, *Tokyo as an International Capital Market — Its Economics and Legal Aspects,* 8 Vand. J. Transnat'l L. 1 (1974–75).

Japanese markets could not perform as efficiently as desired. Almost sixty years have passed since the general securities legislation was adopted and the amendments to the Commercial Code were made. It is now appropriate to evaluate the efficacy and functioning of the transplanted practices. It is apparent now that this is one of the big shortfalls in the corporate accounting principles and other rules that were required for the full implementation of the laws.

"Legend" Issue

Noteworthy for the adoption of International Accounting Standards in Japan is that some of the financial statements were required to include a legend as requested by the United States.[103] According to the current rule, it was necessary for financial statements of Japanese corporations written in English to have notations (legends) such as "[t]his is prepared in accordance with the Japanese Securities Exchange Law and accounting standard, and not under the accounting standards of any other countries."[104] This meant that the Japanese accounting process was not

---

[103] This inclusion of the legend was requested by the Big Five accounting firms in the United States. For the details on the backgrounds of the requestors, *see* Fujitsu, Legends, *at* http://glovia.fujitsu.com/jp/cybersmr/e4-1.html (last visited Feb. 21, 2005).

[104] The following is an example of a legend:
Summary of Significant Accounting Policies. Basis of presentation, Nissan Motor Co., Ltd. (the "Company") and its domestic subsidiaries maintain their books of account in conformity with the financial accounting standards of Japan, and its foreign subsidiaries maintain their books of account in conformity with those of the countries of their domicile. The accompanying consolidated financial statements have been prepared in accordance with accounting principles and practices generally accepted in Japan and are compiled from the consolidated financial statements filed with the Minister of Finance as required by the Securities Exchange Law of Japan. Accordingly, the accompanying consolidated financial statements are not intended to present the consolidated financial position, results of operations and cash flows in accordance with accounting principles and practices generally accepted in countries and jurisdictions other than Japan.
Nissan, 2003 Annual Report, *available at* http://www.infinitinews.com/corporate/corpover/ NissanAR2004_en.pdf (Mar. 31, 2004). The legends of cautionary statements can only be found in the English version of financial statements based on the Japanese Securities Exchange Law, not in any financial statements of SEC registered companies prepared based on the US Accounting Standards. *See, e.g.*, Nissan, 2002 Annual Report at 57, *available at* http://www.infinitinews.com/corporate/corpover/ NissanAR2002_en.pdf (Mar. 31, 2003).

fully trusted internationally.[105]   The problem did not lie with the corporations that were forced to write such statements, but rather was derivative of the antiquated accounting system of Japan. The parties who were injured as a result of these unique accounting standards were the corporations who were not trusted and the investors (users of the financial statements) who were unable to obtain accurate financial information.

One can point to another problem with Japanese accounting practices. In the August 1995 annual report of the International Monetary Fund (IMF),[106] Japan's banking policy administration was accused of failing to take effective measures to revive the deteriorating banking system. It was further pointed out that "waiting would not recover the loss, but rather increase it," and the IMF asked Japan to take speedy action to correct these problem banks. The report also stated that: (1) market mechanisms that were supposed to help depositors and investors in selecting banks were not working because of insufficient disclosures of the operating information of the banks; and (2) it was necessary for stakeholders to demand establishment of a more clear-cut rule specifying how the necessary funds be secured for cleaning bad debts of the problematic banks, including public funds.[107]

Another problem in this area concerns Japanese GAAP. As seen so far, the Commercial Code and the Securities Exchange Law were reliant on a comprehensive GAAP for proper implementation. The Japanese

---

[105] Nippon Keidanren is officially against the inclusion of the legend and advocates the necessity of internationalizing Japanese accounting standards. *See* Press Release, Nippon Keidanren, The Proposition Regarding the Enterprise Accounting System (Mar. 27, 2001), *at* http://www.keidanren.or.jp/japanese/policy/2001/013/honbun.html. *See also* "What's Nippon's Keidanren?" *available at* http://www.keidanren.or.jp/english/profile/pro001.html (last visited Feb. 21, 2005).

[106] International Monetary Fund, IMF Annual Report (1996) at 29, *available at* http://www.imf.org/external/pubs/ft/ar/96/pdf/part04.pdf (last visited Feb. 21, 2005) [hereinafter IMF Annual Report].

[107] Editorial, *Nihon Keizai Shinbun* [*Japanese Disclosures not Showing Real Pictures*], Nikkei, Jan. 25. 1995 (discussing a way to solve the bad debts, referring also to the IMF's report).

GAAP was incorporated in the Corporate Accounting Principles,[108] established in 1949 and based on the Commercial Code of Japan.[109] More specifically, the Corporate Accounting Principles were generated as an interim report by the Corporate Accounting Rule Investigative Committee of the Economic Stabilization Agency in 1949,[110] and the "Annotations to Corporate Accounting Principles" were generated as an interim report by the Corporate Accounting Rule Council[111] of the Ministry of Finance in 1950. The concept of the accounting philosophy as shown in the Corporate Accounting Principles placed importance on the profit and loss calculation for a particular period, assuming that the particular period and the particular corporation was of on-going concern.

According to its preamble:

> The Corporate Accounting Principles consist of the summary of practices recognized as generally fair and reasonable among those practices evolved within actual corporate accounting works and they represent the rules to be abided by corporations in processing their accountings without really having to be regulated by the laws and regulations.[112]

Consequently, in Japanese accounting, it is customary to honor traditional accounting practices as the practical rule to follow. This has resulted in a tendency for companies to mimic and follow whatever others are doing. This did not present any shortcomings when the

---

[108] These principles were established on July 9, 1949, and amended on July 14, 1954, November 5, 1961, August 30, 1972, and April 20, 1980. *See* Commercial Code, *supra* note 81.

[109] Commercial Code, *supra* note 81.

[110] The Economic Stabilization Agency was established in the government as a control organ to restore the Japanese economy after World War II in 1946 and was abolished in 1952 after it had completed its functions. *See* National Institute for Research Advancement, The Economic Stabilization Agency, *available at* http://www.nira.go.jp/pubj/seiken/ v08n07.html (last visited Feb. 21, 2005).

[111] The principle role of the Corporate Accounting Rule Council was to refurbish the financial accounting standards of Japan. This function has now been delegated to the ASBJ.

[112] Commercial Code, *supra* note 81.

economy was rosy in the years after World War II, but the same practice has caused problems in more recent years.[113]

The GAAP has strong enforcement power in Japan. For example, an auditor has to issue a favorable opinion as long as accounting is done in accordance with the GAAP. Therefore, it can be safely assumed, for the issue pointed out by the IMF,[114] that the root cause of the delay in determining the amounts of bad loans lies in the basic, overly generalized philosophy contained within the Corporate Accounting Principles. If the US accounting standard was applied, a loan balance, after deducting reserves, must be specified in a "net realizable value."[115]

An accounting standard, from the international standpoint, resulted from thorough research and development, was generally accepted internationally, and was aimed at properly representing legal and fair accounting practices. It was not something that evolved through mere practices, but rather something that had developed theoretically and that was applied to the practices in order to provide proper information disclosure. The accounting standards used in the United States and Europe were researched and upgraded constantly by permanently established organizations to keep up with economic changes and trends. The Japanese GAAP, developed more than half a century before, was

---

[113] For example, Keidanren acknowledged that the Japanese accounting system needs to be changed. *See* Keidanren, Discussion Memo of May 25, 2000 General Meeting, *available at* http://www.keidanren.or.jp/japanese/profile/soukai/063/01-houkoku/kaigo.html.

[114] IMF Annual Report, *supra* note 106.

[115] "Net Realizable Value" is a method of determining the present value of a troubled asset to its present owner based on the assumption that the asset will be held for a period of time and sold at some future date. The present value includes future earnings that the asset is expected to generate, less the cost of owning, holding, developing and operating the asset. To compensate for these costs, the asset's projected future net cash flows are discounted using a formula that incorporates the cost of capital (the cost of paying dividends and interest). Net realizable value, therefore, is based on a formula incorporating what the asset must earn in order to pay for its share of the costs of running the business. Net realizable value is one accounting method used to calculate the present value of an asset (a loan) at some point after the loan has become past due and a book value is no longer valid. The synonym is "fair value." For the discussion of "fair value" measurements by FASB, *see* Financial Accounting Standards Board, Project Updates: Revenue Recognition, *available at* http://www.fasb.org/project/revenue_recognition.shtml (Jan. 25, 2005).

somewhat different from current international standards and was no longer deemed fit for today's economy.[116]

The problem was that even the FSA of Japan was still honoring the existing GAAP. The FSA also provided administrative services for the Corporate Accounting Rule Council, which had prepared the accounting principles. It was in a position to improve the accounting principles once problems with the principles were identified. The biggest problem resulted from the fact that the administrative offices of the Japanese government did not necessarily realize the importance of a revised accounting standard.[117]

Differences between Japanese Accounting Standard and IFRSs

It is important to see how the Japanese Accounting Standard is different from IFRSs. Since 1998, Japan has been aggressively working on renovating its accounting standard, i.e., the so-called "Accounting Big Bang," including reviewing the scope of consolidation, tax effect accounting, accounting for retirement benefits, financial instruments accounting, asset-impairment accounting and others, mainly to provide international alignment in consideration of the IFRSs and the US Accounting Standard.

The Accounting Big Bang placed big burdens on the balance sheets of companies through market price evaluations of financial products and

---

[116] The term "accounting principles" is not a term recognized internationally. It is called "Financial Accounting Standards" in the United States and will be called "International Financial Reporting Standards" by the International Accounting Standard Board. The Japanese GAAP is essentially maintained as a kind of conceptual framework for Japanese Accounting Standards. More specific and practical rules and guidance are provided by the Japan Institute of Certified Public Accountants (JICPA) in order to keep up with economic changes. Especially after the Japanese "accounting big bang" in the recent few years, efforts to resolve the major differences in accounting standards between the Japanese GAAP and the US GAAP have been made in order to fit today's economy.

[117] Prime Minister Koizumi frequently conferred with the Minister of the FSA, Yanagisawa, in order to press forward on the fundamental clean up of the bad loan problem as his pet project of the reform he was pushing. The FSA resisted the change, claiming that they "cannot issue policies that contradict with the traditional financial administration policies and accounting principles," which clearly shows FSA's poor understanding of the bad loan problems.

estimations of pension liabilities. For example, while the special losses of 400 major Japanese companies used to be at most several trillion yen, the same came to exceed ten trillion yen since 1999.[118] On the other hand, the Accounting Big Bang contributed to promoting corporate realignment and making corporate balance sheets healthier, thus contributing to a structural renovation of the Japanese economy.

In late March 2004, when the major elements of the IFRSs were made clear, the Ministry of Economy, Trade and Industry (METI)[119] of Japan declared that the Japanese Accounting Standard is equivalent to the IFRSs based on its comparison of the Japanese Accounting Standard against the IFRSs and the US Accounting Standard, in particular, twenty-three major items including expressions of financial reports, accounting for retirement benefits, financial instruments accounting, and asset-impairment accounting.[120] It says:

> With respect to the standards for recognizing impairment losses of fixed assets, Japanese accounting standards, which will be enforced in Japan from the end of March 2006, as well as US accounting standards, use undiscounted cash flows as the basis whereas the IFRS uses the recoverable amount as the basis. Regarding the standards for the measurement of impairment losses, however, both Japanese accounting standards and the IFRS use the recoverable amount. Therefore, no significant difference exists between the two. With respect to the treatment when the recoverable amount bounces back, the IFRS permits reversing, whereas neither the Japanese accounting standards nor the US accounting standards permit a reversal. Thus, Japanese accounting standards can thus be said to be more conservative.[121]

---

[118] Editorial, NIKKEI, July 27, 2004, at 27.

[119] *See* Ministry of Economy, Trade, and Industry, *at* http://www.meti.go.jp (last visited Mar. 29, 2005). METI is in charge of international trade and industry in the Japanese Government.

[120] Japanese METI, Report Concerning Internationalization of Japan's Business Accounting, at 14, *available at* http://www.meti.go.jp/english/report/downloadfiles/IBAreporte.pdf (last visited Mar. 29, 2005).

[121] *Id.* at 12.

Based on such an analysis, METI concluded that, despite minor technical differences, the Japanese standard is on an equal or better level than the IFRS.[122]

Challenging Tasks for Japan

In consideration of such issues as dual accounting regulations and legends, it is advisable for Japan to change its current accounting standards to international standards. However, the MOF Memorandum lists the following five items as challenging tasks for Japan:

1. As to the "equivalency evaluation" of the Japanese accounting standards to be conducted in the European Union, it is important that the representatives of the government and private sectors jointly push E.U. representatives to approve the Japanese standards in the European Union as the "accounting standards comparable to the IFRSs" after 2007.

2. The ASBJ should actively make efforts to be involved in refurbishing and improving the Japanese accounting standards, so that its legal position can be clearly defined and the operating basis of the "FASCJ" more fully expanded.

3. Only a few financial documents based on the IFRSs have been disclosed at this time and there are not sufficient indices that can be used for judging them from the standpoint of "the protection of public interests or investors" in Japan. Therefore, it is important to closely watch the problems and tasks that arise from actual implementations of IFRS from this point on.

4. In order to allow Japanese companies to disclose their financial documents based on the IFRSs, the MOF Memorandum states that further evaluations and clarifications are needed on various issues including, but not limited to, those listed below:
   a) Relations between consolidated financial statements and individual financial statements;

---

[122] *Id.* at 13.

b) Retrospective corrections of consolidated financial statements of previous years when there have been changes in accounting policies; and

c) Problems of insufficiency such as missing items and missing disclosure items such as annotations due to the differences in the preparation standards.

5. The so-called "legends" are said to be "epigrams" to alleviate overseas users' risks of misunderstanding the consolidated financial statements prepared according to the Japanese accounting standards as if they were prepared according to the SEC standards or the IFRSs.[123]

The MOF Memorandum takes the stand that certain entities, such as the Japanese Institute of Public Accountants, need to actively work to improve the international notions about Japanese documents. Such attitudes persist despite the fact that the Japanese standards themselves are essentially on a level comparable to international standards. While such notions are caused by the "legends," the wording of these legends contained within Japanese documents has improved greatly since then.

Under the situation, the countermeasures Japan can take may include a short term goal and a long term goal.

Short term goal

In the midst of the current trend of more active global corporations, international commonality is becoming mandatory and thus a global standard of corporate accounting is being developed based on the IFRSs. However, corporate accounting has been nurtured for many years in each country based on the capital market of the country. In Japan specifically, the development of corporate accounting has served a certain purpose and function in the Security Exchange Law, Commercial Law and Corporate Tax Law.

In order to avoid problems in the global activities of corporations, such as corporate financing, considering the specific situation of each

---

[123] MOF Memorandum, *supra* note 9 (Translation by author).

country's accounting standard, each country should adopt a "mutual approval" policy, as long as the accounting standards of the respective countries are equivalent.

Whether they are "equivalent" can be evaluated by considering the opinions of market participants such as investors and corporations. More specifically, if the reference items required by investors are clearly defined in an explainable format and they are on the same level from a standpoint of usefulness and comparability, those standards should be considered equivalent.

In other words, even if there are some differences among the accounting standards, this should not present problems to investors as long as there are rational reasons for the differences and the effects of the differences are disclosed to a certain degree. Moreover, it would make more sense to simply use the standard prevailing in the country where the company's main place of business is located.

The FSA announced that it will negotiate with the European Union, with the help of Nippon Keidanren and the Japanese Institute of Certified Public Accountants, and attempt to reach an agreement to allow Japanese corporations operating in the European Union to use the Japanese Accounting Standard. The FSA wishes to counter the European Union's announcement, making the use of the International Accounting Standard mandatory to all corporations operating in the European Union, claiming that the Japanese Accounting Standard is indeed "equivalent".

Long term goal

In the long term, the effort to converge various accounting standards to an international uniform standard is essential. The international convergence of corporate accounting is a long term goal with mutual approval as an intermediate step. It is preferable that equivalent accounting standards of various countries eventually converge into a single accounting standard of a higher quality through international cooperation. It is necessary for the IASB to take notice of the accounting standards of the important markets of the world, i.e., Japan, Europe and the United States. It should also take into account the opinions of market participants such as investors and companies and should reach a uniform integrated standard through international cooperation.

Conclusion

Various problems exist in Japan for both domestic and international companies because the Japanese accounting system is different from international standards. Even in "sales," Japanese accounting standards are not clear and the process of defining specific terms is left to each industry's custom. In the midst of the expansion of the capital market across national boundaries, the isolation of the Japanese market from the rest of the world due to the accounting standards problem will continue to be disadvantageous to all investors and corporations of the world, as it robs worldwide investors of valuable choices and narrows the fund-raising choices for corporations.

Benefits and disadvantages to Japanese companies of adopting international accounting standards

Domestically, Japanese companies are burdened with the need to prepare two kinds of financial statements due to the legal requirements to conform to both the Commercial Code and the Securities Exchange Law. The adoption of international standards will free them from this burden.

Moreover, when Japanese companies try to issue bonds and stocks, the government requires them to add a note to their financial statements such as, "This is prepared based on the Japanese accounting standards, not on international standards." This so-called "legend" problem can be eliminated once international standards are adopted.

However, since the Japanese accounting method is so unique, Japanese companies trying to receive international financing are requested to disclose information concerning their performance based on the foreign country's standards, or to disclose their methodology for adjusting differences with these standards. It will be a major handicap for those Japanese companies as they will have difficulty in efficiently raising funds in the overseas markets.

In addition, the financial statements of overseas subsidiary companies, prepared according to the foreign countries' standards, will have to be consolidated with the financial statements of Japanese parent companies which are prepared according to the Japanese standards. This phenomenon certainly goes against the international goal of uniform accounting standards and will need to be addressed.

Benefits for foreign companies that intend to raise funds in Japan

Foreign companies are allowed to submit financial statements which are prepared according to "home country standards" or "third country standards" to the MOF. However, the FSA evaluates these statements to see if the documents run the risk of compromising the protection of domestic Japanese investors. This process, of course, places heavy burdens on the foreign corporations. As a result, foreign companies may try to raise funds elsewhere in markets other than Japan. The use of international accounting standards could alleviate this problem and should be further explored with this goal in mind.

Benefits for foreign companies that conduct business in Japan

The financial statements that need to be submitted to the MOF by foreign companies doing business in Japan currently need to be prepared according to the Japanese accounting principles. This places a heavy burden on foreign corporations. Those companies also have to prepare financial documents according to the standards for reporting to their headquarters in foreign countries, causing a needless duplication of efforts.

In consideration of these problems, changing Japanese accounting standards to international standards would be an ideal solution. However, Japanese accounting standards were not built overnight, but rather are backed by a long history and are deeply entangled with other regulations. There are other factors, such as differences of culture and sense of values, that can prevent any conversion from proceeding efficiently. In order to adopt the International Accounting Standards, review of other related laws, such as the Commercial Law, the Securities Exchange Law and the Tax Law, would be necessary.

Consequently, a quick adoption of the International Accounting Standards is less likely to occur; chances are that change will occur slowly. It is also a problem to be considered and solved in the overall process of total internationalization of the Japanese economy.

Appendix I — Major Differences between Financial Documents/Consolidated Financial Documents of the Japanese Commercial Code and International Accounting Standards[124]

Commercial Code	International Standards	Major differences
(1) System - Balance sheet - Earning statement - Profit appropriation plan -Supplemental statement	(1) System - Balance sheet - Earning statement - Shareholder's share variation statement - Cash flow statement - Descriptive annotation	The Commercial Code lacks basic financial tables, such as shareholder's share variation statement and cash flow statement. Also, annotation is poor. A profit appropriation plan is not required by international standards. A "supplemental statement" defined in Art. 281, Sec. 1 of the Commercial Code is not a required disclosure document and thus shareholders do not see it. The concept of a "supplementary statement" does not exist in international standards.
(2) Disclosed documents (of large corp-orations) - Individual statements - Consolidated statement	(2) Disclosed documents - Consolidated statement only if subsidiaries exist - Individual statement only if no subsidiary exists	Under international standards, only one financial statement is disclosed; in other words, a consolidated statement is only disclosed if subsidiaries exist.
(3) Single year statements only	(3) Comparative multiyear financial statements	International standards require disclosure of financial statements to be compared with previous year's statements. Single year statements are not required by international standards.
(4) Annotation is limited.	(4) Annotation is an important part of financial statements.	Annotations in international standards disclose rich contents.

---

[124] See Japanese MITI, Report Concerning Internationalization of Japan's Business Accounting, at 2-3, *available at* http://www.meti.go.jp/english/report/downloadfiles/IBAreporte.pdf (last visited Feb. 26, 2005); Akira Yokoyama, International Accounting Standards and Japanese Accounting, *available at* http://www.hi-ho.ne.jp/yokoyama-a/ias&jgaap.htm (last visited Feb. 26, 2005).

Appendix II — Accounting for Impairment under Japanese, US, and
International Standards[125]

Item	Japanese Standards	US Standards	International Accounting Standards
Criteria for recognition of impairment	Impairment loss is recognized when the sum of undiscounted future cash flows is less than the book value.	Impairment loss is recognized when the sum of undiscounted future cash flows is less than the book value.	Impairment loss is immediately recognized when the recoverable amount is less than the book value.
Criteria for measurement of impairment	The recoverable amount is used as the basis for the measurement of impairment loss. The difference between the book value and the recoverable amount is recognized as impairment loss.	The fair value is used as the basis for the measurement of impairment loss. The difference between the book value and the fair value is recognized as impairment loss.	The recoverable amount is used as the basis for the measurement of impairment loss. The difference between the book value and the recoverable amount is recognized as impairment loss.
Impairment loss of goodwill	(1) When there is an indication of impairment, testing for impairment loss is performed on a unit that is large enough to include both a group of assets that are associated with the operation to which the good will is attributed, and good will. Any increase in the amount of impairment loss that is computed by adding good will is allocated to good will as a general rule. (2) When it is possible to allocate the book value of goodwill to groups of assets that are	Testing for the recognition of impairment loss relating to goodwill is performed in two steps, as follows: Step 1: The fair value and the book value of the reporting unit are compared. If the fair value of the reporting unit is less than its book value, Step 2 is performed. Step 2: The fair value of goodwill is computed by deducting from the fair value of the reporting unit the fair value of all recognized and unrecognized assets and liabilities. The excess of the carrying amount of goodwill over this amount is recognized as impairment loss.	(1) Good will is allocated to a cash-generating unit at the time it is acquired as the result of business combinations. When it cannot be allocated, a comparison is made between the book value excluding good will and the recoverable amount of the cash-generating unit being examined. (2) When the book value of good will can be allocated to a cash-generating unit, it is allocated to the cash-generating unit being examined. A comparison is made between the book value after goodwill

---

[125] Japanese METI, Report Concerning Internationalization of Japan's Business Accounting, at 8, *available at* http://www.meti.go.jp/english/report/downloadfiles/ IBAreporte.pdf, Table of Contents (last visited Mar. 29, 2005).

	associated with the attributed operation on a reasonable basis, the book value of good will is allocated to individual asset groups first, and then the recognition of impairment loss is tested. Recognized impairment loss is allocated to good will first, and the remainder is allocated over individual component assets using a rational method, such as allocation that is proportionate with book values.	Only when a group of assets is a reporting unit or includes a reporting unit, goodwill is included in the group of assets for testing of impairment loss recognition.	allocation and the recoverable amount, either annually or whenever there is an indication. In connection with (1) and (2) mentioned above, if the recoverable amount is less than the book value, impairment loss is recognized at the level of the smallest unit to which good will can be allocated. The impairment loss thus recognized is allocated to goodwill first, and the remainder is allocated over individual component assets using a rational method, such as allocation proportionate with book values.

Bibliography

Bayer Aktiengesellschaft, Report of Foreign Issuer, available at http://www.sec.gov/edgar/searchedgar/companysearch.html (last visited Apr. 4, 2005).

Commercial Code of Japan, Law No. 48 (Mar. 9, 1899) (amended 18 times), available at http://www.ron.gr.jp/law/law/syouhou1.htm.

Commission Regulation 809/2004 of 29 April 2004 Implementing Directive 2003/71/EC of the European Parliament and of the Council as Regards Information Contained in Prospectuses, 2004 O.J. (L 149) 1.

Council Directive 2004/109 of 31 December 2004, Harmonization of Transparency Requirements, 2004 O.J. (L 309) 38.

Corporate Accounting Rule Council, Discussion Memorandum, at 9–10 (June 17, 2003), available at http://www.fsa.go.jp/singi/singi_kigyou/gijiroku/kikaku/f-20040617_k-giji.pdf.

Editorial, "Haphazard Accounting Reforms," Nikkei, Nov. 12, 1999, at 2 (Translation by the author).

Editorial, "Japanese Disclosures not Showing Real Pictures," Nikkei, Jan. 25. 1995 (discussing a way to solve the bad debts, referring also to the IMF's report).

Editorial, Nikkei, July 27, 2004, at 27.

Financial Accounting Standards Board, Mission Statement, available at http://www.fasb.org/ (last visited Feb. 24, 2005).

Financial Accounting Standards Board, Project Updates: Revenue Recognition, http://www.fasb.org/project/revenue_recognition.shtml (Jan. 25, 2005).

FSA, available at http://www.fsa.go.jp (last visited Mar. 28, 2005).

Fujitsu, Legends, http://glovia.fujitsu.com/jp/cybersmr/e4-1.html (last visited Feb. 21, 2005).

Hiramatsu, Kazuo and Naruse, Shigeo, "Kaikei Kijun — Nichi Ou Sougo Shounin Wo Nikkei" [Accounting Standards – Hoping for Mutual Acceptance between Europe and Japan], Nikkei, July 27, 2004, at 27.

Hiroko Awoki, International Securities Transactions and Disclosure, 202 (2000).

IASB, http://www.iasb.org (last visited Mar. 28, 2005).

International Monetary Fund, IMF Annual Report (1996) at 29, available at http://www.imf.org/external/pubs/ft/ar/96/pdf/part04.pdf (last visited Feb. 21, 2005).

Investopedia, ADRs, at http://www.investopedia.com/terms/a/adr.asp (last visited Feb. 20, 2005).

IOSCO, http://www.iosco.org/ (last visited Feb. 26, 2005).

Japan Federation of Economic Organizations, Announcement, http://www.keidanren.or.jp/japanese/policy/2004/032.html (Apr. 20, 2004).

Japan Federation of Economic Organizations, Economic Release No. 25, http://www.keidanren.or.jp/japanese/journal/CLIP/2003/0722/index.html (July 22, 2003) (translation by author).

Japanese Government METI, Report Concerning Internationalization of Japan's Business Accounting, at 14, available at http://www.meti.go.jp/english/report/downloadfiles/IBAreporte.pdf (last visited Mar. 29, 2005).

Japanese Government METI, Report Concerning Internationalization of Japan's Business Accounting, at 8, available at http://www.meti.go.jp/english/report/downloadfiles/IBAreporte.pdf, Table of Contents (last visited Mar. 29, 2005).

Japanese Government Ministry of Economy, Trade, and Industry, available at http://www.meti.go.jp (last visited Mar. 29, 2005).

Japanese Government Ministry of Economy, Trade and Industry, Report on the Internationalization of Business Accounting in Japan, http://www.iasplus.com/resource/0406ifrsjapangaap.pdf. (July 21, 2004).

Japanese Government Ministry of Economy, Trade and Industry, Report on the Internationalization of Business Accounting in Japan 13 (July 21, 2004), available at http://www.meti.go.jp/english/report/downloadfiles/IBAreporte.pdf.

Japanese Government Ministry of Finance, http://www.mof.go.jp (last visited Mar. 28, 2005).

Japanese Government Ministry of Finance, Adoption of International Accounting Standards in Japan (June 24, 2004), http://www.fsa.go.jp/ news/newsj/15/singi/f-20040624-1/01.pdf.

Japanese Government   Ministry of Finance, On Financial Documents of Foreign Companies in Accordance with the Business Performance Disclosure System of Japan (Sept. 4, 1973), http://www.fsa.go.jp/news/newsj/15/singi/f-20040311-1/02-02.pdf.

Japanese Government Ministry of Finance, Organizational Ordinance, Article 24, No. 392 (1998), http://www.soumu.go.jp/s-news/2002/pdf/021017_3_06.pdf (last visited Feb. 27, 2005)[hereinafter Organizational Ordinance].

Japanese Government Ministry of Finance, Rules of Intermediate Financial Statements, MOF Ordinance No. 24, http://www.mof.go.jp/hourei.htm (Mar. 30, 1999).

Japanese Government Ministry of Finance, Securities Exchange Law, Regulations Concerning Terminology, Forms and Methods of Preparation of Financial Statements, MOF Ordinance No. 36, art. 127, §§ 1, 2, available at http://www.mof.go.jp/hourei.htm (Nov. 27, 1963).

Japanese Government Ministry of Ordinance, Ministry of Justice Ordinance No. 31 (1963), available at http://www.normanet.ne.jp/~hourei/sh031R/s380330sh031.htm (last visited Mar. 31, 2005).

Japanese MITI, Report Concerning Internationalization of Japan's Business Accounting, at 2–3, available at http://www.meti.go.jp/english/report/downloadfiles/IBAreporte.pdf (last visited Feb. 26, 2005).

Keidanren, Discussion Memo of May 25, 2000 General Meeting, http://www.keidanren.or.jp/japanese/profile/soukai/063/01-houkoku/kaigo.html.

Keidanren, "What's Nippon's Keidanren?" http://www.keidanren.or.jp/english/profile/pro001.html (last visited Feb. 21, 2005).

Kimco Realty Corporation, Reconciling Non-GAAP Financial Measures, available at http://www.kimcorealty.com/file/Fin_SupplementalReports/2ndQuarterSupplementalPackage_7-29-2003_8-37-32AM.pdf (last visited Feb. 27, 2005).

Kotaro Shida, Nihon Shohoten No Hensan To Sono Kaisei [Codification of Japanese Commercial Code and its Amendments] (1934).

Misawa, Mitsuru. *"Japanese Issues and Perspective on the Convergence of International Accounting Standards"* from Northwestern Journal of International Law and Business, Vol. 25, No.3 , Spring 2005 Symposium Issue, April 2005, pp. 711–745.

Misawa, Mitsuru. Securities Regulations in Japan, 6 VAND. J. TRANSNAT'L L. 449 (1973).

Misawa, Mitsuru. *Tokyo as an International Capital Market — Its Economics and Legal Aspects,* 8 VAND. J. TRANSNAT'L L. 1 (1974–75).

MOF Ordinance No. 28, Consolidated Financial Statement Rules, http://www.mof.go.jp/hourei.htm (Oct. 30, 1976).

National Institute for Research Advancement, Japanese, Government, The Economic Stabilization Agency, http://www.nira.go.jp/pubj/seiken/ v08n07.html (last visited Feb. 21, 2005).

Nippon Keidanren, Press Release, The Proposition Regarding the Enterprise Accounting System (Mar. 27, 2001), available at http://www.keidanren.or.jp/japanese/policy/2001/013/honbun.html.

Nissan, 2002 Annual Report at 57, http://www.infinitinews.com/corporate/corpover/NissanAR2002_en.pdf (Mar. 31, 2003).

Nissan, 2003 Annual Report, http://www.infinitinews.com/corporate/corpover/ NissanAR2004_en.pdf (Mar. 31, 2004).

PetroChina, Annual Report, available at http://www.petrochina.com.cn/english/ tzzgx/ndbg.htm (last visited Feb. 26, 2005).

Prime Minister's Office, Designated Structural Reform District Promotion Office, Record on International Accounting Standards, available at http://www.kantei.go.jp/jp/ singi/kouzou/kouhyou/021022/kaitou03.pdf (last visited Mar. 31, 2005).

Rostelecom, SEC Reports, available at http://www.rt.ru/en/icenter/reports/sec/ (last visited Feb. 26, 2005).

Saito Shizuki, Press Release, "'Equivalency Evaluation' in Accounting," Nikkei (Dec. 4, 2004), at 15.

Saito, Shizuki, Statement at the Meeting of the Corporate Accounting Rule Council, available at http://www.fsa.go.jp/singi/singi_kigyou/ top.html (Dec. 6, 2002) (Mr. Saito was Chairman of Section 1 of the Council).

Securities Act of 1933, 15 U.S.C. §§ 77a-77mm (1934), *as amended* 15 U.S.C. §§ 77a-77m (1970).

Securities Exchange Act of 1934, 15 U.S.C. §§ 78a-78jj (1934), *as amended* 15 U.S.C. §§ 78a-78hh(1) (1970).

Security Analysts Association of Japan, Press Release, The SAAJ's Opinion on the MOF's Memorandum of the International Accounting Standards (Aug. 31, 2004), available at http://www.saa.or.jp [hereinafter SAAJ Press Release].

Shoken Torihiki Ho [Securities Exchange Law], Law No. 25 of 1948, art. 127, no. 4 , available at http://www.japanlaw.info/f_statements/PARENT/DX.htm (last visited Feb. 28, 2005).

Takoz, ADR, available at http://takoz.page.ne.jp/stock/adr (last visited Feb. 27, 2005) (providing a list of these 31 companies).

The Japanese Federation of Economic Organizations, http://www.keidanren.or.jp/ Japanese/profile/pro001.htm (last visited Mar. 28, 2005).

US Securities and Exchange Commission, Press Release, Actions by FASB, IASB Praised (Oct. 29, 2002), http://www.sec.gov/news/ press/2002-154.htm.

US Securities and Exchange Commission, Press Release, SEC Adopts New Disclosure Requirements for Foreign Companies, (Sept. 29, 1999), available at http://www.sec.gov/news/press/pressarchive/1999/99-125.txt.

Yokoyama, Akira. International Accounting Standards and Japanese Accounting, available at http://www.hi-ho.ne.jp/yokoyama-a/ias&jgaap.htm (last visited Feb. 26, 2005).

Yoshitoshi Asaike, Zaimushohyou tou Kisoku Chikujokai [Providing a Detailed Article-by-Article Analysis of the Rules on Financial Statements] 523 (Chuou Keizai, ed., 3rd ed. 1997).

Chapter 8

Shareholders' Action and Director's Responsibility in Japan[a]

The New York Daiwa Bank scandal in 1995, which involved Daiwa Bank's concealment of the $1.1 billion in losses from the illegal funding of US Treasury bonds, resulted in the most severe economic penalties ever imposed by the United States on Japan. These penalties included the termination of Daiwa Bank's US operations and a substantiated international distrust of Japanese financial institutions, including their closely aligned governmental regulators, the Ministry of Finance.

In September 2000, a Japanese court handed down a decision in this shareholders' representative action that ordered the defendants, twelve directors of Daiwa Bank, to pay bank damages totaling $775 million (approximately 82.9 billion yen). These damages ranged from $530 million (approximately 56.7 billion yen) to $70 million (approximately 7.5 billion yen) per person, and shocked the international society because of the costly size of the penalties. The award raised many basic legal and economic issues regarding the shareholders' representative action system in Japan, which was first introduced to Japan by the US in 1950. Due to the importance of the Japanese economy in a global sense, the system's behavior is expected to have a tremendous effect on the international economic society. International communities are watching closely whether the administrative, legal, and legislative arms of the Japanese

[a] This chapter is based on the author's previously published article:
Mitsuru Misawa, "Shareholders' Derivative Action and Directors' Responsibility in Japan," Penn State International Law Review (The Dickinson School of Law), Volume 24, Summer 2005, No.1, pp.1–57.

government as well as the private sectors can respond to the enrichment and improvement of the shareholders' action system enforcing responsibilities of directors.

The recent court decision regarding the shareholders' action was quite meaningful in examining the duties assumed by the directors of a financial institution, which require them to establish an internal control system for controlling risks and adhering to laws and regulations, differences in the duties of care among the directors, and the objects of the responsibilities, as well as the scope of damages.

Also, the court decision sounded a very important alarm about how Japanese corporations are managed. The background that allowed Japanese companies to be run loosely seemed to be the fact that the supervising authorities and the legal system failed to rigorously pursue the lack of risk management and the concealment of responsibilities.

The present case served to reveal the fact that it is extremely dangerous for Japanese financial institutions to try to operate overseas without mending their looseness in risk management and their sloppiness in legal compliance Japanese financial supervising authorities must accept this new mind set. Another such an incident could invite international mistrust in the Japanese society itself. The current status of the legal and organizational systems of the Japanese financial supervising authorities is not up to the level of handling international financial businesses.

This lack of sternness in the law enforcement system has created sloppy risk management and concealing attitudes among Japanese companies, which resulted in the current case when one such Japanese company operated in the US with the same loose attitude. In order to prevent this kind of case, more rigorous attitudes are necessary to ensure that directors are more responsible for their duties. That should give the proper incentive to Japanese companies to establish effective risk management and law-abidance systems. It is notable that shareholders' representative actions have finally started to function as an effective means of law enforcement in Japan.

In this article, the author compares the differing United States and Japanese reactions to the New York Daiwa Bank scandal on legal, economic, and sociological levels. Based on his analysis, the author concludes that cultural differences between the United States and Japan lie at the heart of the scandalous proportions of the Daiwa Bank incident in New York. Furthermore, the author believes that the Daiwa Bank case offers an important lesson for the US and Japanese companies with international operations: "When in Rome, do as the Romans do."

Introduction

An incredible incident was disclosed in 1995 at Daiwa Bank's New York Branch: one of its employees had been illegally trading US Treasury bonds for over eleven years without detection, causing the bank an accumulated loss of $1.1 billion. Since then, this incident mushroomed into an international scandal, resulting in civil, criminal, and administrative liabilities in both the United States and Japan. There had never been an economic incident with such a tremendous international impact between Japan and the United States.

The concerns about the incident expressed by the supervising authorities of both countries, as well as by stakeholders, such as corresponding foreign banks and the Bank's stockholders, resulted in specific actions taken to manage the situation in its aftermath.[1] Those

---

[1] It was August 8, 1995 when the president, an executive vice president in charge of international operations and a managing director of Daiwa Bank met with the Director General of the Banking Bureau of MOF at the bank's club to report an illegal incident. In response, the Director General of the Banking Bureau told the representatives of the bank that "it [was] bad timing[.]" as disclosure might trigger instability in financial circles, and kept the secret in his pocket. It waited more than 40 days until September 18, 1995 when the MOF finally notified the US authorities. *MOF's Confusion at its Peak: Distrust of Japan's Financial Administration Heightens Regarding Daiwa Bank Scandal: Disbanding of MOF is Suggested*, SHUKAN TOYO KEIZAI, Dec 2, 1995, at 16. As an example, a Wall Street Journal article stated:

[The real rogue in Japan's [MOF]. In the Daiwa affair and in its handling of Japan's banking crisis, the [MOF] has shown its remarkable overconfidence and its willingness to bamboozle US bank regulators, the Japanese public and even itself... So maybe it wasn't surprising that the [MOF] thought it could flout US banking regulations this summer by failing to report — for six weeks — what it had learned about Daiwa's illegal trades in the US The trades cost Daiwa $1.1 billion. But they cost the [MOF] its reputation.

John Bussey, *Japan's Bungling Ministry of Finance*, WALL ST. J., Nov. 10, 1995, at A14.

actions, in return, caused further questions on both sides of the Pacific. It seems that all these opinions, actions, and questions stem from the differences in Japanese and American social systems and thought patterns.[2]

Daiwa Bank (hereinafter Daiwa or the Bank) and the Ministry of Finance (hereinafter MOF), the authority within the Japanese government that supervises the Daiwa Bank, did not acknowledge any fault in the matter despite the fact that the incident drew severe criticism internationally and caused Japan to lose credibility in the finance industry.[3] Why? Is there really a difference in the legal systems of the two countries that makes an act illegal in the United States and legal in Japan? Are there any conceptual differences between the systems of the two countries as to a corporation's responsibility for the disclosure of important information regarding its performance?

Another example that is causing criticisms against the MOF from this perspective is the "Jusen" problem. Although MOF claims that the interest-free preferential credits of Japanese banks against Specialized Housing Finance Companies (Jusen) is ¥40 trillion, the actual figure is rumored to be ¥70 trillion. The US authorities are irritated that MOF is not disclosing information in a straightforward manner and have the impression that MOF is engaged in a cover up, as in the Daiwa Bank case. *See Nippon Island of Bad Debts*. SHUKAN TOYO KEIZAI. Feb. 24, 1996, at 12-17. For "Jusen," see Mitsuru Misawa, *Lenders' Liability in the Japanese Financial Market; A case of 'Jusen,' the largest problem loan in Japan, Part I*. 30 MGMT. JAPAN No. 2. 18-28 (Autumn 1997); and Mitsuru Misawa, *Lenders' Liability in the Japanese Financial Market; A case of 'Jusen,' the largest problem loan in Japan, Part II*. 31 MNGT. JAPAN No. 1, 18–28 (Spring 1998).

[2]   The MOF has tried rebutting this criticism regarding the delayed report on various occasions. While the MOF is trying to convince the world by saying "there is nothing to be concerned about in the financial system," it has taken actions which indicate that it is deeply concerned by the loss of its credibility. For example, after the announcement of the affair, MOF showed keen interests in how it was perceived by overseas observers as exemplified by the Deputy Vice-Minister holding an explanatory meeting in Washington D.C., and the special press conference held by General Directors of Banking Business and International Finance Bureau with foreign correspondents in Tokyo. *See Outlandishness of Japanese Financial System Revealed: MOF Agonizes as its Rebuttals are Ignored*. NIHON KEIZAI SHIMBUN. Oct 18, 1995, at. 3.

[3]   SHUKAN TOYO KEIZAI, *supra* note 1.

In addition, the people of Japan had long accepted the mutually supportive relationship between the Japanese government and Japanese industry — often called the "convoy" system.[4] The rest of the world, however, had become more suspicious of this relationship.[5] Accordingly, the Daiwa incident caused the MOF to lose its credibility as a competent authority in the eyes of international observers.[6] Is such a relationship unacceptable in international society? Does MOF need an overhaul?

Furthermore, Japan disapproved of retaliatory steps taken by the United States.[7] For instance, the US Federal Reserve Board (hereinafter FRB) ordered Daiwa Bank to cease its operations in the United States.[8] Some in Japan considered this action to be too severe.[9] What caused this decision by the FRB? What were the legal grounds for it?

---

[4] The treatment of Japanese banks by MOF is best understood by an analogy to a convoy forming a large group consisting of warships, cruisers, and destroyers to ride out rough seas and opposition.

[5] In the Senate Banking Committee's hearing on the Daiwa Bank incident, Mr. Alan Greenspan, Chairman of the Federal Reserve Board (FRB) said about MOF's delay in reporting to the US Authorities that "it is regretful that MOF made this error," while Chairman of the Banking Committee, Senator D'Amato criticized MOF saying, "MOF, which prevented the speedy report to the US authorities in a collusion with Daiwa, severely damaged the trust between the two governments." *MOF's Failures are Regrettable*, Nihon Keizai Simbun, Nov. 29, 1995, at 2.

[6] After Japan acknowledged that it had failed to notify American banking authorities for six weeks after it learned of a $1.1 billion scandal at the Daiwa Bank in New York. Treasury Secretary Robert E. Rubin and his Japanese counterpart, Masayoshi Takemura, talked on October 11, 1995 to air their differences. Rubin's aides said that officials of Japan's MOF characterized the conversation as an apology, but Japanese officials said in Tokyo on October 12 that no apology had been offered. *See Cloistered Japanese Banks*, N.Y Times, Oct. 13, 1995, at A1.

[7] The MOF has tried rebutting this criticisms regarding the delayed report on various occasions. While MOF is trying to convince the world by saying "there is nothing to be concerned about in the financial system," it has taken actions which indicate that it is deeply concerned by the loss of its credibility. For example, after the announcement of the affair, MOF showed keen interests in how it was perceived by overseas observers as exemplified by the Deputy Vice-Minister holding an explanatory meeting in Washington D.C., and the special press conference held by General Directors of Banking Business and International Finance Bureau with foreign correspondents in Tokyo). *See Outlandishness of Japanese Financial System Revealed: MOF Agonizes as its Rebuttals are Ignored*, Nihon Keizai Shimbun, Oct. 18, 1995, at 3.

[8] *Court Decision,* note 11 *infra*, at 7.

[9] *US Intensifies Criticism Against MOF: MOF Should Not Discuss Its Role*, Shukan Toyo Keizai, Dec. 2, 1995, at 22 [hereinafter *US Intensifies Criticism*].

In 1995, Daiwa's stockholders brought a representative action against the Bank regarding this incident.[10] A Japanese court made a decision in this shareholder's representative action in September 2000.[11] It ordered the defendants, twelve directors of Daiwa Bank, to pay to the bank damages totaling $775 million (approximately 82.9 billion yen), which ranged from $530 million (approximately 56.7 billion yen) to $70 million (approximately 7.5 billion yen) per person; the amount of the damages shocked international society.[12] The case raised many basic issues regarding the shareholder's representative action system in Japan.[13] Due to the importance of the Japanese economy to the overall world economy, the Japanese legal system's behavior is expected to have a tremendous effect on the international economic society, with international communities watching closely to see whether the administrative, legal and legislative arms of the Japanese government can respond to the enrichment and improvement of the system.[14]

The shareholder's derivative action system originally was introduced under the influence of the US system as a part of the revision of the Commercial Code[15] in 1950 but it took a long time to implement because its characteristics were rather exotic to the Japanese culture. The future of the shareholder's derivative action system, including the adequacy of the recent court decision on the Daiwa Bank, also was being discussed thoroughly by the international community.[16]

---

[10] Kaisha ni Taisuru Sekinin (Responsibilities to Company), Commercial Code Law No. 48 of 1899, art 266-1-5, [hereinafter Kaisha ni Taisuru Senkini].

[11] Osaka District Court, Sept. 20, 2000, Shoji Homu, No. 1573, at 4-51. [hereinafter Court Decision.] (All the parts of the court judgment cited in this article are translated to English by the author.)

[12] *See generally* Mitsuo Kondo and Toshiaki Hasegawa, et a., *Various Issues of Shareholder's Suit in Japan* (in Japanese) YOBOU JIHYO, 26-35, Summer 2001, *at* http://home.kobe-u.com/tokyo/topics/topics011.html.

[13] *Id.*

[14] *Id.* at 35.

[15] Commerical Code Law No. 48 of 1899.

[16] Hiroshi Okuda, Chairman of Japan Business Federation, is reported to have commented concerning this court decision that "I believe it is better if people refrain from filing shareholder's representative actions" NIHON KEIZAI SHIMBUN, Sept. 21, 2000, at 3. Reporting the court decision, newspapers generally pointed out the problem of secretive atmosphere of the Japanese financial communities and their lack of responsibilities through their editorials and objected the modification of the law claiming that the

The case involved a locally hired employee of the New York branch of a Japanese bank, a Japanese American, and attracted a lot of international media attention, due to its international nature.[17]   More specifically, the related shareholder's representative action was drawing the attention of US corporations (more particularly US banks) operating in Japan, as the case was indicative of a potential risk.[18]   It was assumed that there were many US international lawyers who were sought out for advice concerning the responsibilities of directors in Japan.[19]   The intention of this article is to clarify for these attorneys and the rest of the legal community the problems that are caused by the differences between Japan and the US.

The recent court decision was meaningful in examining the duties assumed by directors of financial institutions which required them to establish an internal control system for controlling risks and abiding by laws and regulations, deciphering the differences in the duties of care among the directors, interpreting the meaning of the "laws" in Section 1-5, Article 266 of the Commercial Code, and the objects of the responsibilities in said section as well as the scope of its damages.[20]

There is still room for doubt in this court decision as to whether sufficient examination has been made as to the judgment on identifying specific negligence. The instant case presents legislative questions such as whether it is reasonable to order a director to pay the full amount of damages when the damages amount to an enormous sum, or possible to set an upper limit to damages, or even to pardon the responsibility of the defendant. In Part I, the article will outline the case, examine these various issues, and study the meaning of the present case, simultaneously examining the goals for which the shareholder's representative action system should aim. In order to do so, the article will also study various cases of shareholder's representative action in Japan, which preceded the

---

revision is intended to make the law ineffectual using this court decision as a reason. *Asahi Shimbun,* Sept. 21, 2000, at 2.

[17] *See infra* notes 5, 6, 246, and 257.

[18] *See* Kondo and Hasegawa, *supra* note 12.

[19] *Id.* In this discussion, one of the American lawyers practicing in Japan pointed this out.

[20] *See,* Kimura Toshio, *Management Responsibility in the Daiwa Bank Case* (in Japanese), JAPAN BUSINESS NEWS, *at* http://www.japan-bus.pwc.com/ins-sol/business/bushot_pre2001.html.

present case to clarify the importance of the present case. The article will also discuss the basic issues between the financial institutions and the financial administration of the government concerning international financial business, issues which became evident by the instant case.

This case contains a broad range of complex issues, encompassing the government and business circles of Japan and the US Therefore, the method of analysis for these issues requires an extensive multi-disciplinary approach based on jurisprudential, economical, sociological, and international comparative studies. This article seeks to provide such a multi-disciplinary analysis.

In Part II, this article discusses past suits and the subsequent standards of directors' liability and applies this standard to the Daiwa Bank suit. Part III of this article reviews the factual background of the Daiwa Bank case. Part IV, reviews the court decision of the recent Daiwa Bank shareholder's suit. Part V, examines the legal actions taken against the Daiwa Bank by the United States and suggests that such actions fall within the general trend of increased supervision by US authorities over foreign banks. Part VI explains and reviews the meanings and issues of derivative action against Daiwa Bank. Part VII compares and contrasts the duty of disclosure under United States and Japanese law. It also discusses the reporting responsibilities of the MOF. Part VIII of this article points out the other effects of the court decision on the shareholder's derivative action.

Finally, the article concludes that both autonomous responsibility principles and free market doctrine are necessary to further Japanese banking in the international market and that further improvement of the relations between the Unites States and Japan requires a consensus regarding international business. This article further concludes that the Daiwa Bank court decision on the shareholder's derivative action should be considered an alarm, warning against the way Japanese corporations are managed. The case points out the background that allowed Japanese companies to be run loosely seems to be in the fact that the supervising authorities and the legal system failed to rigorously pursue the looseness of risk management and concealing of responsibilities.[21]

Stockholder's Derivative Suits in Japan

The stockholders' representative action is a rather new form of litigation introduced in the United States in 1950, which has not functioned properly in Japan.[22] While the number of stockholders' representative actions is increasing and several judgments have been made in cases where the directors' responsibilities were at issue, it is too early to say that the system operating such actions has been well established. The Daiwa Bank case drew much attention from international business circles due to the size of the claim, and will be a leading case in the future. However, examination of a few other typical cases is proper and appears below.

Case A: Mitsui Mining Co., Ltd.

In a stockholders' representative action, the directors of Mitsui Mining Co., Ltd.[23] were sued for damages caused by having to coerce its wholly owned subsidiary into purchasing its stock at a high price and then selling the stock to the Mitsui Group at a lower price. The suit alleges that this action violated the rule prohibiting the acquisition of a company's own stock. The Supreme Court, finding that the acquisition of the stock of their own company was a violation of the Commercial Code,[24] rendered a guilty verdict against the directors.[25] Although this

---

[21] This article is a continuation of an older article, Mitsuru Misawa, *Daiwa Bank Scandal in New York – It's Causes, Significance, and Lessons in the International Society*, 29 VAND J. TRANSNAT'L L. No. 5 (1996). For the various development of this case since its disclosure in September 1995 to November 1996, please read that article.

[22] In order to make this system function properly, a revision of the Commercial Code was enacted in October 1993 containing: (1) a reduction of the petition fee and (2) allowing plaintiff stockholders to petition for recovery of litigation expenses from the company if the plaintiffs win. *Amendments to the Commercial Code*, June 14, 1993, No. 62.

[23] A mining concern listed on the Tokyo Stock Exchange.

[24] According to the Commercial Code at that time, a company was prohibited from acquiring its own stocks. Jiko Kabushiki no Shutoko [Acquisition of Own Stock] art. 210.

representative action requested the payment of ¥100 billion (approximately $1 billion), the Supreme Court supported the judgment of the Second Tokyo High Court that found ¥3.5 billion (approximately $350 million) in damages.[26]

Case B: Hazama Gumi Ltd.

In a representative action requesting damages from a director of Hazama-gumi Ltd.,[27] for a bribe paid to the mayor of Sanwamachi, Ibaragi-ken by the company, the Tokyo District Court rendered a guilty verdict in December 1994.[28] The verdict against the directors ordered them to pay ¥14 million (approximately $140,000) in damages, a sum equal to the amount of the bribery.[29] In delivering the verdict, the Tokyo District Court ruled that: (1) using as a means of business a crime of a highly unsocial nature, such as bribery, should not be tolerated; and (2) bribery cannot be justified as a means of business simply because it brings a profit to the company, it is difficult to get an order without it (as competitors do the same), or it is customary in the industry.[30]   The defendants did not appeal the case.

Also, a subsidiary is prohibited from acquiring the stocks of its parent company. The rule recognizes the oneness of the parent company and a subsidiary and applies the rule to the transaction between the two. Jiko Kabushiki no Shutoku [Acquisition of Own Stock] art. 211-2. However, a company is allowed to acquire its own stocks by the revision of the Treasury Shares portion of the Commercial Code in 2001.

[25] Ariyoshi v. Mitsui Mining Co., 1400, Ist Small Court. 1989, (Sup. Ct., Sept. 9, 1993).

[26] Tokyo District Court, May 29, 1986, Harei Jihyo, No. 1194 at 33; Shoji Homu, No. 1078 at 43; and Tokyo High Court, July 3, 1988, Shoji Homu, No. 1188 at 36.

[27] A general construction company listed at Tokyo Stock Exchange.

[28] Matsumaru v. Otsu, Tokyo District Court, Dec. 22, 1994, Civil Sec. No. 8, 1993 (wa) No. 18447.

[29] No. 153 Diet Record (Justice Committee, No. 13), Nov. 27, 2001 (in Japanese), at http://www.shugiin.go.jp/itdb_kaigiroku.nsf/html/kaigiroku/000415320011127013.htm.

[30] *Id.*

Case C: Nomura Securities

Before loss compensation procedures became illegal by the Revision of 1991 of the Securities and Exchange Law,[31] Nomura Securities [32] compensated such losses.[33] In a representative action seeking damages against the directors, the Tokyo High Court supported the decision of the first trial by the Tokyo District Court, which did not hold the directors liable and rejected the claim by the plaintiff.[34] While it found that loss compensation is an unfair trading method in violation of the Antimonopoly Law,[35] the court also decided that the Antimonopoly Law may conflict with the rules that apply in the Commercial Code with regard to damage caused by a violation of the directors.[36] The reason for this is that the party that receives the loss under the Antimonopoly law is not the company, but the competitor.[37] The decision also stated that the loss compensation was within the normal boundaries of the management's judgment, and neither the violation of the duty of due care nor the violation of the duty of loyalty to the company was found.[38] Thus, the directors were not liable.

Standard of Directors' Liability

The facts of these three example representative actions are completely different. By comparing these three decisions, however, one can deduce the following standard of directors' liability.

First, as the decision of the Tokyo District Court stated in Nomura Securities: (1) the management judgment of a corporation is a comprehensive one requiring a professional, predictive, policy-making

---

[31] The Securities and Exchange Law, Law No. 25 of 1948.

[32] A securities broker listed at Tokyo Stock Exchange.

[33] *See* Mitsuru Misawa, *Loss Compensation in the Japanese Securities Market: Causes, Significance, and Search for a Remedy*, 25 VAND J. TRANSNAT'L L., 37-58 (1992) (discussing loss compensation).

[34] Ikenaga v. Tabuchi. Tokyo High Court, Sept. 26, 1995, 16th Civil Dept., 1993 (ne) No. 3778 [hereinafter Ikenaga].

[35] Antimonopoly Law, Law No. 54 of 1947, art. 19.

[36] Kaisha ni Taisuru, *supra* note 10, at art. 266-1-5.

[37] *See* Misawa, *supra* note 33.

[38] Tokyo District Court, Dec. 22, 1994, Civil Sec. No. 8., 1993 (wa) No. 18447.

judgment capability for analyzing unpredictable, fluid, and complex factors, so that it tends to be broad and complex; and (2) a court should examine the actual management judgment of the directors itself from the standpoint of whether there were any careless mistakes in examining the facts that were used as premises, and whether the decision-making process based on the facts was not illogical.[39] In essence, it seems that the court is trying to honor the business judgment of directors as much as possible.

The court, however, considered that directors might be subject to liability in certain situations. First, even if an act may be viewed as indispensable for business reasons, the director who committed the act may still be punished if it is an illegal act for which a person can be sent to jail.[40] In the above three cases, bribery can be a criminal offense punishable by up to three years of imprisonment under a Criminal Code,[41] and acquisition of one's own company stock can be a criminal

---

[39] *Id.*

For the business judgment rule in the US, it originated in Cates v. Sparkman (Cates v. Sparkman, 73 Tex. 619, 11 S.W. 846, 849, 1889) when the Texas Supreme Court held:

"[The] negligence of a director, no matter how unwise or imprudent, does not constitute a breach of duty if the acts of the director were 'within the exercise of their discretion and judgment in the development or prosecution of the enterprise in which their interests are involved'."

The court reviewed the relationship between the fiduciary duties owed by officers and directors and the business judgment rule. (Resolution Trust Corporation, in its corporate capacity, Plaintiff v. Charles D. Acton, David Clayton, William F. Courtney, Richard L. Davidson, and John R. Rittenberry, Defendants, 844 F. Supp. 307; 1994 US Dist. Lexis 1750.)

"Officers and directors have three fiduciary duties: the duty of obedience, the duty of loyalty, and the duty of care. The duty of obedience forbids ultra vires acts, that is, acts outside the scope of corporate power. The duty of loyalty requires that officers and directors act in good faith; this duty forbids them from engaging in 'interested' transactions. The duty of care requires officers and directors to manage the corporation's affairs with diligence and prudence."

These definitions illustrate an inherent tension between the duty of care and the protection of the business judgment rule. For the case that directors of the bank provided 100% financing for the borrowers when the financial statements showed them to be insolvent, the court judged that the business judgment rule is not a defense to the allegations. The court also said that the business judgment rule is not a defense to allegations of fraud, nor self-dealing.

[40] *Id.*

[41] Zouwai, Assen Zouwai (Bribery, Mediating Bribery), Criminal Code Law No. 45 of 1907, art. 198.

offense punishable by up to five years of imprisonment under the Commercial Code.[42] On the other hand, loss compensation conducted before 1991 is not a criminal offense punishable by imprisonment, and no penalty rules are applicable to violations of the Antimonopoly Law.[43]

Second, assuming that an act is not a criminal offense, directors will not be punished simply because they caused a loss to the company, if other directors in the same industry could have made the same mistake.[44]

Third, a director who performs a certain prohibited act or fails to supervise another such a director, a director or auditor who attended the board of directors meeting where the execution plan for such an act was adopted, or an auditor who attended the auditors meeting which examined such a plan, may be liable.[45]

Application of old standards to the Daiwa Bank case

These principles should be applied when reviewing the Daiwa Bank case. In light of the first principle, if the court in New York decides that the action of the directors stationed at the New York Branch at the time of the incident is a criminal offense punishable by imprisonment then the same directors will be held liable in the representative action in Japan as well. According to the third principle, not only the directors who actually performed the actions, but also the directors who failed to monitor the directors who performed the actions, as well as the directors and auditors who attended the board meeting at which the action was approved, face liability.

If such action is not a criminal offense punishable by imprisonment, it should then be examined through the second principle.[46] In other words, if the action of the director that caused a loss to the company is the type of action that would have been performed by many directors in the same

---

[42] Kaisha Zaisan wo Ayauku suru Tsumi (Crime to Risk Company's Assets), Commercial Code Law No. 54 of 1947, art. 489-2.
[43] *See* Misawa, *supra* note 33 (discussing the illegality of loss compensation).
[44] Tokyo District Court, *supra* note 38.
[45] Misawa *supra* note 33.
[46] Kondo and Hasegawa, *supra,* note 12.

industry, the director is not liable.[47] The question is whether the action performed by the directors stationed at the New York Branch can be considered to be the kind of action that would have been performed by many directors in the same industry. The answer to that question is no; the present case is a very unusual case in view of the common sense of the particular industry. Therefore, it is likely that the directors will be held liable, even if the action does not constitute a criminal offense punishable by imprisonment.

In addition, in the Daiwa Bank case, responsibilities of the directors will be evaluated from new perspectives. For example, is it reasonable to impose supervisory liability on the directors, who resided in Japan at the time, when the incident occurred in New York? The general sentiment of Japanese managers is that "directors who reside in Japan cannot be held responsible for an incident that happened at a place so far away."[48] Even though it happened on foreign soil, it may still be reasonable for the stockholders to hold the directors who resided in Japan responsible for a breach of supervisory duty because of the extensive length of time — eleven years — that they remained unaware of what was happening.

The Japanese should welcome the opportunity brought by the judgment in the present case to think about the responsibilities of directors in the expanding international environment and to clarify these standards of responsibilities.

Factual Background of the Daiwa Bank Case in New York

Daiwa Bank[49] disclosed on September 26, 1995, that a Bank Vice-President Toshihide Iguchi,[50] who was in charge of securities trading and

---

[47] *Id.*

[48] *Id.*

[49] Daiwa Bank was the 17th largest bank in 1995 in the world with about $318 billion in assets and more than 9,000 employees. The corporation stock was listed in the Tokyo Stock Exchange. Established in 1918 its main office was located at 2-1 Bingo-Machi, 2-Chome, Chuo-ku, Osaka-shi, Osaka Japan. Tokyo Keizai Japan Company Handbook, 1100 (1996).

[50] On September 26, 1995, the Federal Bureau of Investigations (FBI) arrested Toshihide Iguchi (age 44), a former employee of Daiwa Bank's New York Branch. *See Daiwa*

control at its New York Branch, had been selling securities that the Bank had in its custody to cover up the loss created by his own unauthorized, unlisted trading of US Treasury bonds.[51] His trading caused Gush's bank to lose a total of approximately $1.1 billion (approximately ¥110 billion).[52] Iguchi's cover up consisted of the concealment of transaction certificates.[53] The amount of Daiwa's loss is among the highest in the history of similar known cases.[54]

Although the loss in this case was caused by the criminal conduct of an individual, the multiple review of transaction, one of the basic rules for all financial institutions did not work in this case. It is astonishing that this illegal trading remained undetected for eleven years.[55] Thus, it is important to see how it was concealed.[56]

When a bank trades US Treasury Bonds, securities companies – the bank's counterpart in the transactions — normally send transaction confirmation statements to the transaction control section of the bank.[57] Iguchi, however, instructed the securities companies to send those statements directly to him.[58] He also hid the true securities balance statements sent from custodial banks, which held the traded Treasury bonds and delivered forged statements to the custodial control section of the Bank.[59]

How could this happen? First, Iguchi was in charge of both securities trading and securities control. Second, he held these positions in the section that traded Treasury bonds for eleven years. It is quite unusual,

---

Bank's Huge Loss, 30,000 Unauthorized Transactions: FBI Announces Arrest of Daiwa Bank's Former Employee, NIHON KEIZAI SHIMBUN, Sept. 27, 1995, at 1.

[51] Court Decision, *supra* note 11, at 5.

[52] *Id.*

[53] *See* Yoshiyuki Watanabe, *Daiwa Bank Conceals Wrongdoings*, BUNGEI SHUNJU, Dec. 1995, at 94-104 (outlining details of the concealment by Daiwa Bank).

[54] *See* Mitsuru Misawa, *Daiwa Bank Scandal in New York — It's Causes, Significance, and Lessons in the International Society*, 29 VAND J. TRANSNAT'L L. 1023 (1996).

[55] The incident became known to the management of the bank through Iguchi's confession letter dated July 24, 1995 and addressed to the president. For details of the confession letter, see *Exclusive Publication of Defendant Toshihide Iguchi's Confession*, BUNGEI SHUNJU, Jan. 1996, 112-31.

[56] *Id.*

[57] Court Decision, *supra* note 11, at 5.

[58] *Id.*

[59] *Id.*

even among Japanese banks, for an employee to remain essentially in one position for such a long period. Third, although it is customary for bank employees in the United States and Europe to take a long vacation once a year while another employee handles his or her job.[60] Iguchi never took any long vacations during the eleven-year period. Finally, with regard to market risk management, it is customary for Japanese banks to set up a trading limit for each trader.[61] In this case, however, the Bank failed to detect the loss, which substantially exceeded the capacity of its New York Branch.[62] While it is granted that the loss was covered up by unlisted or out-of-books transactions, the management's responsibility for the lack of more effective and stringent control is indisputable.

In 1995, certain stockholders[63] brought suit in the District Court of Osaka claiming $1.1 billion (¥110 billion) in damages, caused by the loss at the New York Branch of Daiwa Bank, against 49 defendants, including the former chairman of the board, former officers, and the current president and officers of the Bank.[64] The Bank's stockholders originally requested that Daiwa Bank's auditor initiate an action against the management of the Bank within thirty days, but the auditor refused to do so.[65] As a result, those stockholders decided to sue the Bank's directors themselves in accordance with the Commercial Code.[66]

In this shareholder's representative action, plaintiffs P_1 and P_2 as well as a participant S claimed the defendants D_1 through D_{16}, D_{28} through D_{30}, and D_{32} through D_{49}, all of whom were directors or auditors of Daiwa Bank, should pay damages in a sum of $1.1 billion, claiming that those defendants caused a loss of $1.1 billion to Daiwa Bank, wherein the representative directors and the directors who served as the New York branch managers during the period relevant to the case for failing to perform their duties of care and loyalty as good managers by failing to

---

[60] Tokyo District Court, *supra* note 26.
[61] Court Decision, *supra* note 11, at 8.
[62] *Id.*
[63] Two individual stockholders and one corporation stockholder.
[64] *Stockholders Representative Action to be Filed Tomorrow Asking 1.1 Billion Dollars in Damages*, NIHON KEIZAI SHIMBUN, Nov. 26, 1995, at 30.
[65] Court Decision, *supra* note 11, at 8.
[66] Kaisha ni Taisuru Senkini, *supra* note 10, arts. 267, 275-74.

establish a control system for preventing misconducts of employees and minimizing damages that can be caused by such misconducts ("internal control system").[67] In addition, the other directors and auditors failed to perform their duties of care and loyalty for checking to see if said representative directors, and said directors who served as the New York branch managers established the internal control system, and thus failed to prevent the present case.[68] This is "case A." The court granted only a portion of the damages for D_2 for case A.[69]

After the case was disclosed to the public, Daiwa Bank became the target of a criminal prosecution,[70] primarily on the grounds that it failed to report to the Federal Government the incurred loss of approximately $1.1 billion related to the case.[71] They ended up admitting guilt for 16 counts and paid the penalty of $340 million.[72] In a shareholder's representative action, P_1, P_2, and S claimed that the defendants D_1 through D_{32} violated their duty of care and loyalty as directors or auditors of the bank, causing a loss of $340 million in penalties plus a lawyer's fee of $10 million, for a total of $350 million and that D_1 through D_{32} should pay the damages.[73] This is "case B."

The plaintiffs claimed that, of the counts to which the defendants admitted guilt, counts 14 through 20 directly were related to the fact that the representative directors and the directors who served as the New York branch managers during the concerned period failed to fulfill their duty of care and loyalty for establishing an internal control system, while other directors and auditors failed to check if the internal control system was established by the representative directors and the directors who served as the New York branch managers.[74] Thus, all of them prevented the non-party Iguchi from making false statements in various documents that constituted those counts.[75] Counts 1 through 7, 23 and 24 were

---

[67] Court Decision, *supra* note 11, at 8.
[68] *Id.* at 5.
[69] *Id.* at 47.
[70] *Id.* at 6.
[71] *Id.* at 5.
[72] *Id.* at 8.
[73] *Id.*
[74] *Id.* at 10.
[75] *Id.*

related to the performance of the directors, who served as the New York branch managers during the concerned period, and who performed in breach of the US law and violated of their duties of care and loyalty as a good manager.[76] These counts also related to the fact that other directors' and auditors' failure to check if the representative directors and the directors who served as the New York branch managers were observing the pertinent US laws. This was the violation of their duties of care and loyalty. The failure eventually led to the parties being unable to prevent the accused wrong-doing.[77] The court provided a decision allowing only a part of the claims against the defendants D_1 through D_4, D_6 through D_{10}, and D_{27} as to case B.[78]

The Court Decision for the Daiwa Bank Shareholders' Suit in 2002

First, looking into the facts of the case admitted into the court for the decision, it is noted that on July 18, 1995, Iguchi sent a letter confessing his unauthorized dealings to a defendant D_1, the president of Daiwa Bank, and D_1 received it on July 24.[79] Upon receiving it, D_1 immediately disclosed the letter to a defendant D_2 (vice president)[80], a defendant D_3 (vice president),[81] a defendant D_4 (the chairman of the board and a former president),[82] a defendant D_5 (director in charge of general affairs and human resources),[83] a defendant D_6 (director and the international department manager as well as a former New York branch manager),[84] and a defendant D_7 (director in charge of planning, accounting and securities departments).[85] Incidentally, Daiwa Bank issued 50 million

---

[76] *Id.* at 15.
[77] *Id.* at 8.
[78] *Id.*
[79] *Id.* at 30.
[80] *Id.*
[81] *Id.*
[82] *Id.* at 8.
[83] *Id.*
[84] *Id.*
[85] *Id.*

shares of preferred stocks on July 27, 1995 without publicly disclosing the incident.[86]

Meanwhile, D_1 instructed D_2, D_6, and D_3, who was the New York branch manager at that time, to investigate the incident secretly.[87] While they came to realize the facts of the matter, D_1 instructed those investigators to keep it secret.[88] Accordingly, on July 31, a defendant D_8 filed a false call report to the US Treasury Department, reporting that the Treasury bills (T-bills) sold without authorization existed as a property of the New York branch of the Bank.[89] D_6 either instructed or knew about this report, and both D_1 and D_2 acknowledged it, at least after the fact.[90]

On August 8, 1995, D_1, D_2, D_6, D_9, and D_{10} met with the Director-General of the Banking Bureau and the Director of the Commercial Banks Division of the Ministry of Finance to report the outline of the case and their plan on how to handle the matter, asking the Ministry's opinions on how the case should be disclosed to the public.[91] The Director-General of the Banking Bureau stated that the coming September would be the worst time to disclose it considering the financial situation of Japan and requested that bank representatives hold the information in tight security to prevent any leakage.[92]

In late August 1995, in consideration of an opinion from the department in charge of the US operation that there were strict regulations in the US,[93] D_1 instructed D_6 to consult with a US lawyer about the specific regulations of related US laws.[94] In accordance with the instruction, D_6 reported to D_1, D_2, D_7, D_9, and D_{10} that Daiwa Bank legally was obligated to report the case to the Federal Reserve Board (FRB) and the State of New York Banking Department.[95] Upon receiving this report, D_1 decided to report the matter to the FRB in mid-

---

[86] *Id.*
[87] *Id.* at 8.
[88] *Id.*
[89] *Id.*
[90] *Id.*
[91] *Id.* at 31.
[92] *Id.*
[93] *Id.* at 32.
[94] *Id.*
[95] *Id.* at 33-34.

September and reported that decision to the Director of the Commercial Banks Division of the Ministry of Finance.[96]   On September 18, D₂ reported the case to the Vice Chairman of the FRB and the Superintendent of Banks of the New York Banking Department.[97]

D₁ disclosed the matter at the board meeting held on September 25 1995, at which time all 13 defendants, D₁₄ through D₂₆ (directors), came to know about the case for the first time.[98]   Three defendants D₁₁ through D₁₃ (representative directors) learned about the case in a management meeting held on September 7.[99]   On September 26, a disclosure of the case was made also to three defendants D₂₈ through D₃₀ (standing auditors) as well as to two defendants D₃₁ and D₃₂ (non-standing auditors or outside auditors), whereupon D₁ attended a news conference to disclose the matter, essentially making a public announcement of the case on the same day.[100]

Based upon these facts, the claims were partially granted by the court and the results were as follows:

Issue 1: whether nonfeasance existed regarding duties of establishing an internal control system

According to the Commercial Code,[101] decisions are made by the board of directors, and these decisions are required for these directors to perform important business of a corporation.[102]   The outline of the internal control system [103] that touches on the basics of corporate management,[104] needs to be determined by the board of directors and representative directors, as well as the director who was in charge of a

---

[96] *Id.*
[97] *Id.*
[98] *Id.* at 8.
[99] *Id.*
[100] *Id.*
[101] Commercial Code Law No. 54 of 1947, art. 260-2.
[102] Court Decision, *supra* note 11, at 36-41.
[103] *Id.*
[104] *Id.*

concerned business unit and had the duty to lay out a risk management system based on the provided outline.[105]

The abovementioned constitutes the contents of the duties of care and loyalty for directors as good managers. Auditors, on the other hand, have a duty to monitor, to check whether the directors were operating conscientiously and refurbishing the risk management system as needed.[106]

However, the contents of the risk management system to be installed became enriched as knowledge was gained from various cases and accidents and research on risk management advanced.[107] Therefore, it was not appropriate to use the current level of the risk management system required at this point as the judgment standard for the present case.[108] Moreover, it was a matter of judgment by management to decide what kind of risk management system refurbishing should be made so that there was wide latitude of decision making ability provided to directors who were essentially corporation management specialists.[109]

Directors have duties to establish a law abiding system in order to prevent employees from engaging in illegal conduct while doing their jobs, which also constitutes their duties of care and loyalty as directors.[110] Refurbishment of a system for controlling operation risks also means refurbishing of a law-abiding system.[111]

The procedures for checking the storage balance of T-bills adopted by the headquarters of Daiwa Bank (inspection department),[112] the New York Branch, and the accounting auditor employed by the bank were extremely inadequate.[113] To check the balance, it was mandatory to use a method appropriate for the nature of securities in storage; in other words, it was necessary to check actual securities.[114]

---

[105] *Id.*
[106] *Id.*
[107] *Id.* at 36-41.
[108] *Id.*
[109] *Id.*
[110] *Id.*
[111] *Id.*
[112] *Id.* at 36-41.
[113] *Id.*
[114] *Id.*

An in-shop inspection was conducted using the inspection department's standards, which were based on the inspection rule prepared by the inspection department and approved by the director in charge of the inspection department.[115] Since the on-site inspection was executed strictly in accordance with the abovementioned inspection rule, the director in charge of the inspection department was then responsible for negligence in performing his job as an employee/director because the method of checking the storage balance of T-bills was still deemed inadequate.[116] Moreover, since the in-shop inspection and the audit performed by the person in charge of internal auditing were conducted under the supervision of the New York branch manager, the director who happened to be the branch manager at that period was also negligent in his job performance.[117] Consequently, the three defendants D_2, D_6, and D_8 who served as New York mangers at different, but inclusive points in time pertinent to the case, were also negligent.[118]

In a large, dynamic corporation such as Daiwa Bank, the president or vice presidents were allowed to delegate some of their jobs to directors.[119] In doing so, the presidents and vice presidents were generally relieved of supervisory responsibilities, with the exception of special circumstances.[120] There were no claims made in the action as to such special circumstances.[121]

Directors who were not involved in the chain of command within the inspection department or the New York branch (including the representative directors) have the responsibility of monitoring whether the risk management system was properly established. However, it was unreasonable to claim that the risk management system was not outlined properly, nor was its specific structure clear, which made it difficult to blame those directors for being negligent in their monitoring of proper inspection methods.

---

[115] *Id.*
[116] *Id.*
[117] *Id.* at 36-41.
[118] *Id.*
[119] *Id.*
[120] *Id.*
[121] *Id.*

The auditors, irrespective of whether they were standing or non-standing, internal or external, except those auditors who actually attended the check by the accounting auditors, are assumed to have been unaware of any problems associated with the method of checking the balance, clearing them of any liability.

The defendant D_{33}, who visited the New York branch for inspection in September 1993, should have found that the method used by the accounting auditors to confirm the storage balance of T-bills was inappropriate, yet failed to acknowledge and correct it. This failure to act made the defendant liable.[122]

Issue 2: whether nonfeasance existed regarding duties concerning the violations of US laws

The Commercial Code obligates directors of corporations, as a basis of corporation management, to abide by applicable laws, laws not only of Japan but also of foreign countries, if a corporation operates overseas.[123] Abiding by laws of foreign countries is indeed within the jurisdiction of a director's duty as a good manager.

The FRB required New York branches of foreign banks to report to the United States Secret Service when they had any doubts about potential criminal activities of their employees and if the suspect matters required immediate action.[124] Such reports of suspect matters could be done via emergency telephone calls, followed by written reports submitted within 30 days of the initial report.[125] In violation of this obligation, D_1, who was the representative director of Daiwa Bank, caused others to call the FRB to report the fraudulent contents and entries on the books and records of its New York branch,[126] while concealing the facts from the US authorities and failing to file the criminal report within the period required by the law.[127]

---

[122] *Id.*
[123] Commercial Code Law No. 54 of 1947, art. 266-1-5.
[124] Court Decision, *supra* note 11, at 41–47.
[125] 12 C.F.R. § 208.20 (1996).
[126] Court Decision, *supra* note 11, at 41–47.
[127] *Id.*

It was quite unconceivable that the defendants of the case B were unaware of the unlawfulness of intentionally calling to report fraudulent contents to the FRB. It was not difficult to assume that they at least knew the generalities of the US laws and regulations concerning those reports and filings. It also was quite reasonable to conclude that they intended deceitfully represent themselves to the FRB.

The act of D_6 (New York branch manager) was a violation of the United States Code and was considered to be a violation of the director's duty of care as a good manager.[128]

D_2 (general manager of the American operations department at the main office) did not commit the acts in question, but he could have prevented then from being executed.[129] Therefore, he was considered to have violated the director's duties of care and loyalty as a good manager.[130]

D_4, upon hearing about the report from D_1, should have urged the representative directors to file the report to the US authorities. He also could have prevented the call to report the fraudulent contents. Therefore, he also was considered to have violated the director's duties of care and loyalty as a good manager.

D_1 (representative director & president), D_2 (representative director & vice president in charge of international operations), and D_3 (representative director & general manager of the international department) failed to report to the US authorities while knowing about the unauthorized transactions.[131] As to the filing of the call report of the fraudulent contents, it can only be assumed that they either gave explicit instructions or approved for the fraudulent call, but it is surely known that they failed to prevent it, thus constituting violations of supervising duties as the superiors in the chain of command. This kind of conduct clearly was a violation of the United States Code[132] and is considered a violation of the director's duties of care and loyalty as a good manager.

---

[128] *Id.*
[129] *Id.*
[130] *Id.*
[131] *Id.*
[132] *Id.*

D_3 (representative director & vice president), D_9 (representative director), D_5 (representative director), and D_7 (representative director) failed to report to the US authorities while they were aware of the unauthorized transactions.[133] They could have prevented such an act.[134] Therefore, they were considered to have violated the directors' duties of care and loyalty as good managers.[135]

D_{10} and D_{27} were aware of the unauthorized trading of this case, and they should have urged the representative directors to report to the US authorities.[136] Therefore, they were considered to have violated the directors' duties of care and loyalty as good managers.[137]

D_8 (New York branch manager) failed to report to the US authorities despite having full knowledge of the unauthorized trading of this case.[138] He also committed the crimes of filing a call report of fraudulent contents to the FBI and made false entries into the books and records of the New York branch, both of which were violations of the United States Code.[139] He was then considered to have violated the director's duties of care and loyalty as a good manager.[140]

The three defendants, D_{11} through $D_{13,}$ came to know about the unauthorized dealings after the fact and circumstances have not proven that they could have previously known the facts of the crime.[141] Therefore, they could not be accused of any violations of the directors' duties of care and loyalty as good managers.[142]

The thirteen director defendants, D_{14} through $D_{26,}$ came to know about the unauthorized dealings after the fact — on the day before the case was made public — and the five auditors–defendants, D_{28} through $D_{32,}$ received the report about the case on the day everything was made

---

[133] *Id.*
[134] *Id.*
[135] *Id.*
[136] *Id.*
[137] *Id.*
[138] *Id.*
[139] *Id.*
[140] *Id.*
[141] *Id.*
[142] *Id.*

public.[143] All those defendants who were informed of the case after the fact could not be held liable for any violations of the directors' duties of care and loyalty as good managers.[144]

A director generally was given a wide range of discretionary power in executing his/her job.[145] Therefore, in order to bring up a charge against a director challenging past business decisions as being made in violation of his/her duties of care and loyalty, the challenger must bring proof of a material and negligent error as the basis of the director's decision.[146] However, the discretionary power of a director did not go beyond the boundary of applicable laws and a director was not given the authority to judge whether or not his/her business decisions violated laws, in particular, laws of foreign countries.[147]

The defendants of the case B claimed that there were no expectation probabilities for reporting unauthorized dealings with the US authorities against the wish or suggestion of the Ministry of Finance (MOF).[148] However, no evidence was filed with the court to prove that the MOF instructed or ordered D₁, et al. not to report the matter to the US authorities.[149]

The defendants of case B claim that they were not aware of the rules and regulations of the United States involving banks, but the claim could not be justified.[150] If it is assumed that they were not fully aware of the details of the relevant rules and regulations of the United States, they should have immediately investigated and studied the appropriate rules and regulations of the United States no matter how rare and unusual the case. As managers of a corporation conducting business in the United States, this was critical. Instead, they failed to take any action until such time that they received a suggestion from the department in charge of the particular operation.[151] The investigation was obviously too late and

---

[143] *Id.*
[144] *Id.*
[145] *Id.*
[146] *Id.*
[147] *Id.*
[148] *Id.*
[149] *Id.*
[150] *Id.*
[151] *Id.*

inexcusable; an inevitable circumstance that stems from ignorance of the rules and regulations.

As can be seen from the above, D_1, et al. made an extremely unreasonable and inappropriate business decision as the business managers, overlooking the severe condition Daiwa Bank was facing. It then is reasonable to say that they violated the directors' duties of care and loyalty as good managers.

Issue 3: existence and scope of damage

1.   Case A
      (1) D_2

            The defendant was not responsible for the damages that were already incurred when he arrived in New York as the branch manager.[152] Therefore, he is liable for repaying the damages, which are conservatively estimated to be approximately $570 million of the total damages of approximately $1.1 billion.[153]

      (2) D_6, D_7

            It was unclear if the damages occurred after either of them assumed the position of the branch manager, and no evidence had been filed to the court to prove that the damages were incurred because either of them neglected their duties.

      (3) D_{23}

            It was unclear if the damages occurred after he conducted a survey of the branch, and no evidence had been filed to the court to prove that the damages occurred because he neglected his duties.

2.   Case B
      The defendants of the case B claimed that the plaintiffs' claimed that the defendants of the case B were negligent in the establishment of a risk

---

[152] *Id.*
[153] *Id.*

management system had no causal relation with the result that Daiwa Bank, a corporation, paid a penalty.[154]

However, if the New York branch had adopted an appropriate inspection method,[155] Iguchi's act that corresponded to the counts 14 through 20 could have been prevented,[156] and resultantly Daiwa Bank could not have been punished with the penalty, so that it was reasonable to assume a legal causal relation.[157]

(1) D_4, D_1, D_8, D_7

Since the guilty pleas of this case, which were the causes of the penalty that consisted of sixteen counts (and the defendants D_4 et al. were liable only for seven of them),[158] it was not reasonable to ask D_4 et al. to be responsible for repaying the damages equivalent to the sum of the penalty and the legal fee.[159] It was more reasonable to make a proportionate distribution of causal relation based on their individual contribution to the case.[160]

It was reasonable to have each of the defendants bear the payment responsibility up to the limitation of $105 million, which was the most conservative estimate, i.e., 30% of said sum of the penalty and the lawyer's fee, $350 million.[161]

(2) D_2, D_6

Based on the same reasoning, these defendants were liable to pay up to the limitation of $204 million, which was the most conservative estimate, i.e., seventy percent f $350 million.[162]

---

[154] *Id.*
[155] *Id.*
[156] *Id.*
[157] *Id.*
[158] *Id.*
[159] *Id.*
[160] *Id.*
[161] *Id.*
[162] *Id.*

(3) D$_9$, D$_{10}$, D$_{27}$

> Based on the same reasoning, these defendants were liable to pay up to the limitation of $70 million, which was the most conservative estimate, i.e., twenty percent of $350 million.[163]

(4) D$_8$

> Based on the same reasoning, the defendant was liable to pay up to the limitation of $157.5 million, which was the most conservative estimate, i.e., fourty-five percent of $350 million.[164]

US Administrative Legal Actions against Daiwa Bank in 1995

To understand the background of the court decision for this shareholders' derivative suit, it is necessary to review how the US administrative legal actions were made against Daiwa Bank that took place before this court decision.[165]   On November 2, 1995, the FRB ordered Daiwa Bank to close its branches and terminate all operations in the United States within ninety days.[166]   Moreover, for the next three years, Daiwa Bank was obligated to submit a petition in writing if either the Bank or its affiliates wished to reopen operations in the United States.[167]   This petition was then subject to the discretionary control of US authorities.[168]   In practical terms, this meant that Daiwa Bank had been completely banished from the United States.[169]   This action by US authorities was viewed as an "abnormally" severe punishment in Japan.[170]   This article next examines whether this Japanese claim had any merit by reviewing the legal grounds of the FRB's action and the judgment that resulted from it.

---

[163] *Id.*

[164] *Id.*

[165] *Id.* at 7.

[166] Senjin Kishi, *Fault of MOF Which Betrayed World and Japan: Japan Financial Administration. Far Apart From Anglo-Saxon Logic*, ECONOMIST (Japan), Dec. 5, 1995, at 40–42.

[167] Court Decision, *supra* note 11, at 7.

[168] Kishi, *supra* note 166.

[169] *US Intensifies Criticism*, *supra* note 9, at 22.

[170] *Id.*

According to the International Banking Act (IBA),[171] there were two grounds on which FRB could base its decision of the deportation of Daiwa Bank. First, Daiwa Bank did not obey the supervision of regulation of the MOF.[172] Since Daiwa Bank had been consulting with the MOF, it was unlikely that this was the reason for the FRB's decision. It is better to assume that the FRB's action was based on the second reason: Daiwa Bank's operations included those that could be considered unsafe and unsound banking practices.[173]

First, Daiwa Bank violated the law that imposes certain reporting obligations. Daiwa Bank failed to file a criminal referral report within thirty days after the date of detection, the period defined in Regulation H.[174] [175] It seems inconceivable, however, that the FRB decided to expel

---

[171] 12 USC. § 611 (1994).

[172] *See* §§ 7(e) and 10(b) of the International Banking Act, added in 1991 as amendments.

The Board may order a foreign bank to terminate the activities of such branch, agency, or subsidiary, if the Board finds that –
the foreign bank is not subject to comprehensive supervision or regulation on a consolidated basis by the appropriate authorities in its home country; or
(B)(1) there is reasonable cause to believe that such a foreign bank or any affiliate of such foreign bank, has committed a violation of law or engaged in an unsafe or unsound banking practice in the United States; and as a result of such violation or practice, the continued operation of the foreign bank's branch, agency, or commercial lending company subsidiary in the United States would not be consistent with the public interest or with the purposes of this Act, the Bank Holding Company Act of 1956 or the Federal Deposit Insurance Act. *Id.*

[hereinafter IBA §§ 7(e) and 10(b)].

See also 12 U.S.C. § 3107(b) (1994).

And in case of termination of a Federal branch of agency:
The Board may transmit to the Comptroller of the Currency a recommendation that the license of any Federal branch or Federal agency of a foreign bank be terminated in accordance with section 4(1)[12 U.S.C. § 3102(I)] if the Board has reasonable cause to believe that such foreign bank or any affiliate of such foreign bank has engaged in conduct for which the activities of any State branch or agency may be terminated. 12 U.S.C. § 2105(e)(5) (1994).

[173] *Id.*
[174] 12 C.F.R. § 208.20 (1996).
[175] *Id.*

Daiwa Bank permanently from the US solely on the grounds that the Bank violated this reporting rule. The punishment for a violation of the reporting duty alone should entail, at most, a fine imposed on the Bank or a criminal penalty against the individual(s) involved.[176]

In addition to the reporting rule violation mentioned above, Daiwa Bank committed two additional violations.[177] The Bank had been making false reports to the authorities for the past eleven years in order

---

A state member bank shall file a criminal referral report... in every situation where the State member bank suspects one of its directors, officers, employees, agents, or other institution-affiliated parties of having committed or aided in the commission of a crime... A state member bank shall file the report... no later than 30 calendar days after the date of detection of the loss or the known or suspected criminal violation or activity. If no suspect has been identified within 30 calendar days after the date of detection of the loss, or the known, attempted, or suspected criminal violation or activity, reporting may be delayed an additional 30 calendar days or until a suspect has been identified; but in no case shall reporting of known or suspected crimes be delayed more than 60 calendar days after the date of detection of the loss or known, attempted, or suspected criminal violation or activity. When a report requirement is triggered by the identification of a suspect or group of suspects, the reporting period commences with the identification of each suspect or group of suspects.

[176] *Id.*

Any foreign bank or any office or subsidiary of a foreign bank, that –
fails to make, submit, or publish such reports or information as may be required under this Act or under regulations prescribed by the Board or the Comptroller of the Currency pursuant to this Act, within the time period specified by such agency; or
submits or publishes any false or misleading report or information... shall be subject to a penalty of not more than $20,000 for each day during which such failure continues or such false or misleading information is not corrected.

See also 12 U.S.C. § 3110(c) (1994)

Whoever, with the intent to deceive, to gain financially, or to cause financial gain or loss to any person, knowingly violates any provision of this Act or any regulation or order issued by the appropriate Federal banking agency under this Act shall be imprisoned not more than 5 years or fined not more than $1,000,000 for each day during which a violation continues, or both.

[177] Per the complaint of the US prosecution authorities. *See Former N.Y. Branch Manager Claimed Not Guilty: Defendants Lawyers of Daiwa Bank Case Claim Main Case Itself is Illegitimate as Well*, NIHON KEIZAI SHIMBUN, Nov. 22, 1995, at 4 [hereinafter *Former N.Y. Branch Manager*].

to conceal the unlawful trading.[178] In addition, it continued to conceal these facts of this situation after management received Iguchi's confession.[179] The Bank conducted a systematic concealment operation regarding the loss generated by Daiwa Bank Trust, the subsidiary of the Daiwa Bank.[180] It is assumed that when the FRB discovered these two violations, in addition to the reporting rule violation, it concluded that the Bank had been conducting an "unsafe and unsound banking practice."[181]

As the backdrop of the FRB's decision is the Bank of Credit and Commerce International (BCCI) case.[182] BCCI was notorious for its underground activities, such as drug money laundering, and was called "the world's dirtiest bank."[183] In 1991, British authorities ordered BCCI to stop its operations, which practically forced BCCI into bankruptcy.[184] In the United States, authorities found that BCCI was illegally lending to one if the nation's largest banks, Washington, D.C.- based First American Bank.[185] As a result, the United States fined BCCI $200

---

[178] Court Decision, *supra* note 11, at 7.

[179] *Former N.Y. Branch Manager, supra* note 177.

[180] Court Decision, *supra* note 11, at 7.

[181] *Former N.Y. Branch Manager, supra* note 177.

[182] The BCCI (Bank of Credit and Commerce International) group is a multinational group of financial institutions having 365 offices in sixty-nine countries around the world and was one of the largest Arabian financial institutions. A Pakistani businessman established the BCCI GROUP in 1972 and the largest group stockholders consist of the Emirate of Abu Dhabi and the people related to its government. BCCI Holding, the holding company of the BCCI group, has a token head office in Luxembourg for the purpose of registration and the actual head office in London. *See generally BCCI Case's Full Picture: Other Countries Responses and Developments in Japan*, KINYU HOHMU JIJYOU [Financial and Legal Affairs], Nov. 25, 1991 at 4-12 [hereinafter *BCCI Case's Full Picture*].

The BCCI group had been suspected of drug money laundering for some time. *Id.* When its performance deteriorated due to failures of loans without collateral as well as dealing failures, it covered up its settlements with window dressing. *Id.*

On July 5, 1991, having been convicted of BCCI's long term window dressing settlement practices, Bank of England, in coordination with the financial authorities of the United States (where First American Bank, its subsidiary in a practical sense, exists), ordered BCCI to halt its operation and froze its assets in each country in order to prevent its customers' run on the bank and the insiders from hiding its assets. *Id.*

[183] Court Decision, *supra* note 11, at 7.

[184] *Id.*

[185] *Id.*

million and permanently expelled nine people involved in the case from banking in the US.[186]

In contrast to the Daiwa Bank case, however, US authorities did no take expulsion actions were taken against BCCI itself by US authorities. BCCI, however, stopped its operations on its own initiative and retreated from the United States.[187] From the FRB's standpoint, the most serious violation by BCCI was the false report it made to US authorities when it purchased First American Bank.[188] As a result of this incident, a revision of the IBA was introduced in 1991 to enhance the FRB's authority substantially, giving it powers such as canceling licenses and examining all foreign bank branches in the United States.[189]

The FRB's order, directed at Daiwa Bank to terminate operations, was the first action of its kind taken by the FRB since the revision of the IBA in 1991.[190] While some people thought that this action was too severe, it was neither unusual nor unduly harsh, if one understood the trend toward increased supervision by US authorities over foreign banks.[191]

Meanings and Issues of Derivative Action against Daiwa Bank in 2002

Responsibilities of directors concerning violations of US laws

Meaning of "laws" in Article 266, Section 1–5 of Commercial Code[192]

---

[186] See BCCI Case's Full Picture, *supra* note 182.

[187] Court Decision, *supra* note 11, at 7.

[188] *Id.*

[189] See IBA §§ 7(e) and 10(b), *supra* note 172.

[190] Kishi, *supra* note 166; US Intensifies Criticism, *supra* note 169.

[191] *Id.*

[192] Article 266 of the Commercial Code provides:
  1. In the following cases, directors who have done any one of the acts mentioned there shall be jointly and severely liable in effecting performance or in damages to the company, in the case of item (1) for the amount which has been distributed or divided legally, in the case of item (2) for the amount of loans not yet repaid, or in the cases of items (3) to (5) inclusive for the amount of any damage caused to the company:

The court's decision to hold Daiwa Bank liable for damages totaling $350 million, including the penalty and the lawyers' fees, demonstrates that the defendants D_1 et al. were responsible as directors of a corporation operating overseas by setting up branches and liaison offices. As such, the defendants had a have duties of care as good managers to obey the laws of the country where they were operating.[193] As a consequence, this case created a precedent, which now includes foreign "laws" that are applicable to overseas branches within Article 266, Section 1–5 of the Commercial Law.[194]

The understanding of the "laws" has a plurality of theories in Japan. The first is a recent decision made by the Supreme Court on a case of the shareholder's representative action regarding Nomura Securities' loss compensation, which indicated that the "laws" include all regulations of the Commercial Law and other laws that are to be obeyed by a company

---

    (1) Where they have submitted to a general meeting the proposal for the distribution of profits in contravention of the provision of Article 290 paragraph 1, or they have distributed money in contravention of the provision of Article 293-5 paragraph 3;

    (2) Where they have loaned money to another director;

    (3) Where they have effected any transaction in contravention of the provision of the Article 264 paragraph 1;

    (4) Where they have effected any transaction mentioned in the preceding Article;

    (5) Where they have done any act, which violates any law or ordinance or the articles of incorporation.

2. In cases where any act mentioned in the preceding paragraph has been done in accordance with the resolution of the board of directors, the directors who have assented to such resolution shall be deemed to have done such act.

3. The directors who have participated in the resolution mentioned in the preceding paragraph and who have not expressed their dissent in the minutes shall be presumed to have assented to such resolution.

4. The liability if directors mentioned in paragraph 1 cannot be released except by the unanimous consent of all the shareholders.

5. The liability of directors in respect of the transaction mentioned in item (4) of paragraph 1 may be released by majority of two-thirds or more of the votes of the total number of the issued shares, notwithstanding the provisions of the preceding paragraph. In this case, the directors shall show all material facts as to such transaction at a general meeting of shareholders.

[193] The present decision by the court indicated 12 U.S.C. §208.20 as a specific law violated by D_1 et al.

[194] Court Decision, *supra* note 11, at 15.

in conducting its business using the company as the addressee.[195] Japan considers this decision by the Supreme Court as the majority theory in Japan for the moment. This indicates that the understanding of the "laws" is based on the idea that companies have law-abiding obligations and the directors' adherence to these laws that specify the company as the addressee in the course of their job executions, belong to their job-related duties for the company.[196]

The second theory only includes within the "laws" the regulations of the Commercial Law (essentially a substantive corporate law) and regulations that cover public policies for corporate directors. Consideration for all other laws suffices if those laws are considered from the standpoint of whether a decision causes any violation of the director's duty of care.[197]

The third theory defines "laws" as those laws that directly or indirectly try to maintain the soundness of the asset of a company.[198] Violations of any other laws matter only from the standpoint of liabilities to damages.[199]

Despite the differences between these three theories, they do share a common ground. All three require companies operating overseas, through establishing branches, to abide by the local laws.

Principle of respondent superior

The question about the present court decision has been questioned because it presumes that the law concerning the defendants' responsibilities is Article 266, Section 1–5 of the Commercial Code. It is questioned because a common theory in Japan in regard to a shareholder's representative action is that the entire liability of a director to the company, not just the responsibility according to Article 266 of the

---

[195] Supreme Court decision, July 7, 2000; KINYU/SHOJI HANREI [FINANCIAL/COMMERCIAL PRECEDENCE], 1096, at 3 (2000).
[196] Court Decision, *supra* note 11, at 15.
[197] Mitsuo Kondo, *Torishimariyaku no Keieijo no Kashitsu to Kaisha nitaisuru Sekinin* [*Directors' Errors in Management and Their Responsibilities for Company*] KINYU FOMU JIJO [Financial Legal Situations], 1372, at 10.
[198] SHIGERU MORIMOTO, KAISHAHO [CORPORATE LAW] 253 (2nd edition, YEAR?).
[199] *Id.*

Commercial Code, can be the target of a shareholders' action. In case of (employee/director who happened to be the New York branch manager), for example, there can be a view that his responsibility as an employer being the New York branch manager was prosecuted.

In November 1995, D3, the former New York Branch general manager of Daiwa Bank was arrested and indicted in Federal District Court of the Southern District of New York as being guilty of misprision of felony.[200] Also the allegations were made against the Bank as a corporation of misprision of felony and obstruction of the examination of the financial institution by the authorities.[201]

While the prosecutor alleged that Daiwa Bank was liable under *respondeat superior* for the damages its customers and the US financial authorities suffered due to illegal transactions, Daiwa Bank alleged that the case was a personal wrongdoing committed by defendant Iguchi, and that "the bank was a victim and was not responsible for the misconduct."[202]

The disparity between Japanese and US laws regarding *respondeat superior*, caused a difference of opinion between US authorities and Daiwa Bank in this case. According to common law principle operating in the United States, an employer was held liable for the conduct of its employee that results in damages to third parties during the course of his or her employment, regardless of whether or not the employer was at fault.[203] According to Japanese law, an employer was liable only when the employer was negligent in the selection and supervision of the employee.[204] However, Japanese law placed more responsibility on the employer in its interpretation of an employee's course of employment.[205]

Daiwa Bank agreed in 1996 to plea bargain with the prosecutor to settle the case by admitting some wrongdoing and paying a penalty.[206] It

---

[200] Court Decision, *supra* note 11, at 6.

[201] *Former N.Y. Branch Manager*, *supra* note 177, at 4.

[202] *See Daiwa Bank Has Employer's Responsibility: Federal Prosecutor's Rebuttal Stresses Legitimacy of Accusation*, NIHON KEIZAI SHIMBUN, Feb. 13, 1996, at 3.

[203] Court Decision, *supra* note 11, at 6.

[204] *Id.*

[205] Civil Code, Law No. 89 of 1898, art. 715.

[206] See generally Daiwa Bank Seeks Judicial Settlement, Admits Huge Loss and Conspiracy: Federal Prosecutor Charges $35.6 Billion Penalty for 16 Accounts Including

admitted wrongdoings as to sixteen of the allegations. Most notably were the intentional concealment and conspiracy regarding a loss, which were regarded as the center of the accusations.[207] Daiwa Bank paid $350 million in penalties.[208] However, since plea-bargaining does not exist under Japanese law there had been some strong criticism in Japanese economic circles of this mode of settlement by Daiwa Bank, arguing that the bank should have fought to the end to clarify its role in the matter.[209]

Negligence concerning recognition of illegality

D_1 et al. claimed that they were unaware of the contents of the laws and regulations about banks in the US.[210] A previous Japanese Supreme Court's decision on a case of the shareholder's representative action regarding Nomura Securities' loss compensation indicated that it was necessary to prove that it was an intentional or negligent act of the defendants violating laws in order to seek their liabilities for the damages from the standpoint of violations of laws based on Article 266, Section 1–5 of the Commercial Code.[211] Therefore, the issue regarding D_1 et al. became whether they were aware of the applicable US laws and regulations and whether there was a negligent act if they were unaware of them.

Ultimately, the court decision rendered it unthinkable that the defendants were unaware of the fact that it is illegal to file a report of fraudulent contents to the FRB.[212] However, doubt remained about whether each defendant was award of the specific law or regulation of the US that prohibited the act. It was possible to assume that the defendants were not so knowledgeable because things they received US

Delayed Report: Affected by MOF's Intention, Nihon Keizai Shimbun, Feb. 29, 1996, at 1 (giving the details of the plea bargain agreement) [hereinafter Daiwa Bank Seeks Judicial Settlement].

[207] Court Decision, *supra* note 11, at 6-7.
[208] *Id.*
[209] *Id.*
[210] *Id.* at 42.
[211] Supreme Court decision, July 7, 2000 of *supra* note 195. For the decision of the Tokyo High Court for the same case, see *supra* note 34.
[212] Court Decision, *supra* note 11, at 42.

legal consultation only after they heard from the department in charge of the US operation. The reality was that many of Japanese financial institutions were unaware of the US laws and the fact that their law-abiding systems were inadequate.[213] Similarly, some American bankers were only vaguely aware of the banking law requirements, along with their punishments.[214] Thus, it was likely that D, et al. were not well aware of the applicable laws and regulations in the US[215]

The question then was whether we could conclude that the defendants were aware of the possible violation, or at least they were negligent, if they had some notion that they could be pursued for violation of some laws. If we were to assume a position that the defendants could not be judged as having been negligent unless they were cognizant of violation of specific laws,[216] it would be necessary to make a more finite fact recognition of whether they were required to take immediate action (i.e. such as contacting a local US law office even under the circumstance they were facing, or comparing their case with those of American bank managers). It was a case where recognition that their action could be illegal, or at least negligent, was a possibility.

In November 1995, in Federal District Court of the Southern District of New York, Daiwa Bank itself and D3, the former director and general manager of the New York Branch admitted their guilt regarding a number of the charges and agreed to a plea bargain with the US prosecutor.[217] The plaintiffs in the stockholders' representative action

---

[213] *See* Brian P. Volkman, *The Global Convergence of Bank Regulations and Standards for Compliance*, 115 BANKING L. J. 550, 554 (1998).

[214] Steven A. Miller, *How Daiwa Self-Destructed* 113 BANKING L. J. 560, 565 (1996).

[215] If Daiwa Bank concealed a fact of unauthorized dealings from the Japanese authorities in charge of overseeing banking activities, the penalties such as $350 million, or approximately ¥37 billion, which was charged in the US is inconceivable in Japan. If a bank files a fraudulent report to the Financial Reestablishment Commission, the penalty is less than ¥3 million in Japan. Banking Law of Japan, art. 63, § 1.

[216] Tokyo High Court Decision, February 23, 1999; *see also* SHOUJI HOUMU (COMMERCIAL LAW) 192, at 164-168 (2000) (explaining that it is necessary to prove the recognition or possibility of recognition of specific illegality in order for a director's liability for damages to be established).

[217] Court Decision, *supra* note 11, at 6.

used this plea bargain as indisputable evidence showing that they had knowledge that their actions constituted a wrongful action.[218]

Claim of "management decision"

Rather than debate the existence or lack of a malfeasance, the defendants claimed that the "management decision" was correct at the time of the incident.[219] In other words, the defendants argued whether the response of the directors to the incidents was "extremely unreasonable."

For this point, the present court decision stated a general theory that a director's responsibility was pursuable only when either a material or negligent error existed in the recognition of a fact which became the premise of the director's judgment at the time of taking the particular business measure, or the decision-making processes or its contents were particularly unreasonable or inappropriate, considering the fact that a director was given a wide range of discretionary power in making a management decision.[220] If this was compared to the leading case of the management decision principle, the general theory of the management decision principle in the verdict of the first hearing in the case of the shareholder's representative action regarding Nomura Securities' loss compensation,[221] the decision was notable in that it said it was possible to seek the directors' responsibilities not only on the decision-making processes, but also on the contents if they were unreasonable or inappropriate. However, the court found D₁ et al. responsible without applying this principle, noting that the discretionary power given to a director was limited to a range that does not violate any laws,[222] and in particular, that the director was not given any discretionary power to judge if a decision abides by a foreign law or not.[223]

It was true that a sufficient amount of precedence existed to support the ruling that the management decision principle was not applicable to

---

[218] *Id.* at 17
[219] *Id.* at 45.
[220] *Id.*
[221] Ikenaga, *supra* note 34.
[222] Court Decision, *supra* note 11, at 45.
[223] *Id.*

illegal actions out of malice even in the United States where the management decision principle was born.[224] Additionally, there was no argument about it in Japan.[225] It went without saying that a director could not evade responsibility if the director engaged in an action that was knowingly illegal, judging from the notion that the "laws" of Article 266, Section 1–5 included any laws that were applicable to the company.[226] Therefore, it would be difficult to apply the management decision principle if there was at least some recognition that the action could be illegal.

However, if D_1 et al. had no notion of illegality, and there was only a possibility of negligence, the management decision principle could be an issue. In that case, a close examination would be required to determine if there were any material and negligent error existed in the recognition of the fact which was the preamble of the judgment by D_1 et al., or if there was any mismatch in the decision making processes and contents. There was a high probability that D_1 et al. at least were cognizant that their action could be illegal.[227]

Intervention of MOF (expectation probability)

D_1 et al. also claimed that there was no expectation probability for reporting to the US authorities against the MOF's request or suggestion.[228] In fact, Daiwa Bank seemed to have thought that it was adequate to report the incident to the MOF and simply to obey the guidance of the MOF.[229] The MOF, however, did not tell Daiwa Bank what to do in this case.[230] Thus, Daiwa Bank inadvertently broke the

---

[224] Miller v. A.T. & T. Co., 507 F.2d 759 (3rd Cir. 1974); *see also* A.LI., PRINCIPLES OF CORPORATE GOVERNANCE, Comment d to § 4.01(a).

[225] Setsu Takita, HANSETSU SHOUJI HOUMU (COMMERCIAL LAW) 145, at 28–31 (1997).

[226] Court Decision, *supra* note 11, at 46.

[227] *See Daiwa Bank Seeks Judicial Settlement, supra* note 207 (explaining recognition of illegality.

[228] Court Decision, *supra* note 11, at 31.

[229] *Id.*

[230] *Id.*

IBA's reporting rule that an incident has to be reported within thirty days after it was discovered.[231]

A detailed analysis of the above is provided below, since it contains extremely important factors in understanding the background of the present case such as special relations between the government and civilian sectors and the difference of cultures between Japan and US.[232]

Aside from focusing on the attempts by Daiwa Bank to hide losses, US criticism had also targeted the closed-room administrative practices of the MOF.[233] Such criticism arose from the MOF's failure to notify US financial authorities for six weeks after the MOF received its report from Daiwa Bank.[234] These numerous criticisms suggested that the MOF was really at fault in the matter rather than Daiwa Bank since it failed to follow necessary procedures after receiving the report from the Bank.[235]

As mentioned above, Daiwa Bank was "obligated to report to the FRB within 30 days after the criminal case was suspected," according to Regulation H.[236] While the MOF's reporting duty does not stem directly from this law, it should have advised Daiwa Bank to report to the FRB.[237] The MOF is accused of being morally responsible for this nonfeasance.[238] Moreover, even though there was no legal regulation to abide by, the MOF should have inferred from the purpose of the law that they had a responsibility to report this kind of information quickly to the FRB.

As for this implicit responsibility for the nonfeasance of the MOF,[239] there was a strong view among the informed sources in the Japanese

---

[231] *Id.*
[232] *See supra* text accompanying note 7.
[233] *See supra* note 5 and accompanying text.
[234] *See supra* note 1.
[235] *Id.*
[236] *See supra* note 174.
[237] *Suggestion for Disbanding of MOF Surfaced Abruptly with Daiwa Bank Sandal,* SHUKAN TOYO KEIZAI, Dec. 2, 1995, at 12.
[238] *Id.*
[239] The attitude taken by MOF in this case is a violation of the agreement among the banking supervisory agencies of various national governments established to control international banking transactions. Basle Committee on Banking Supervision, *Minimum Standards for the Supervision of International Banking Groups and Their Cross-Border Establishments* (July, 1992) at http://www.bis.org/publ/bcbsc314.pdf.

financial world that the MOF did not know about this thirty-day disclosure duty under the US IBA.[240] However, the FRB and US prosecutors did not think that this was true.[241] This reporting requirement was created based on the experience of the BCCI affair, which shook the world.[242] It was difficult for them to believe that the MOF and Daiwa Bank, which had been operating in the United States for many years, did not have knowledge of the thirty-day disclosure duty. Even if the MOF and the Bank did not have knowledge of the law, it is well-established in both Japan and the United States, that lack of knowledge of the law does not disprove the existence of intent or *mens rea*.[243] Since the FRB's opinion was that the "MOF neither disclosed important information nor honored the reporting duty between the bank supervising authorities of the two countries" and that "[t]his was a breach of faith,"[244] the expulsion of Daiwa Bank should be understood as an indirect warning on the part of the FRB to the MOF.

The characteristics of the response of the MOF to the Daiwa Bank incidents can best be described as obfuscation and delay, which is the traditional technique of the MOF based on their governing principle: "Never let them know; let them rely on us."[245] "Obfuscation" and "delay" as well as "secrecy" are the key words often used these days in

---

When BBCI went bankrupt, the Japanese financial institutions experienced a severe blow due to the delay of UK's supervisory authorities. Compared to the US where legal systems such as the International Banking Act of 1978 and the Foreign Bank Supervision Enhancement Act of 1991 are established, Japan is extremely retarded in dealing with foreign banks activities in the nation. *See* Japanese Banking Act, art. 47.

[240] *See* Court Decision, *supra* note 11, at 10.

[241] *Id.*

[242] *Id.*

[243] "Ignorance of the law excuses no one (Ignorantia legis neminem excusat)" is one of the basic principles of the common law in the United States. In other word, everyone must know the ordinary laws of the country in which one lives, and ignorance therefore does not excuse oneself from being charged with either civil or criminal liability. The same principle applies to the citizens of Japan. *See* Criminal Code, Law No. 45 of 1906, art.38-3.

[244] *MOF's Failures are Regrettable*, Nihon Keizai Simbun, Nov. 29, 1995, at 2.

[245] Diet Record No. 153 (Justice Committee), Nov. 28, 2001, at http://www.shugiin.go.jp/itdb_kaigiroku.nsf/html/ kaigiroku/000415320011128014.htm.

criticizing the Japanese financial system. [246]   They are analogous to "equivocation" and are taken as a kind of cover-up. All of these words suggest not an attitude of clarifying the problem and solving it, but of an attempt to make the status and magnitude of the problem fuzzier, which is a typical form of "responsibility evasion." [247]

This secrecy-prone administrative technique by the MOF had severely damaged the international credibility of Japan. [248] Nevertheless, the MOF insisted that this problem was created by the "difference of culture between Japan and the [United States]," [249] and did not accept its fault, which was really the crux of the problem. [250]   Such denial was similar to the fact that the management of Daiwa Bank did not realize its duty to disclose the important information at the earliest opportunity.

However, a "difference of culture" cannot be used to rationalize negligence with regard to rules and violations. International business is conducted under a certain set of rules and develops when mutual trust deepens as agreements and contracts are exchanged and honored. It became quite clear that there is a marked difference between Japan and the United States in the understanding of this principle. The violation of the reporting duty is a clear violation of a rule. The MOF clearly showed how selfish the Japanese financial system was and how difficult it was

---

[246] Shigeo Nakao, *Globalization to be Reconsidered*, at http://koho.osaka-cu.ac.jp/vuniv2002/nakao2002/nakao2002-10.html.

[247] Another example that is causing criticisms against the MOF from this perspective is the "Jusen" problem. Although MOF claims that the interest-free preferential credits of - Japanese banks against Specialized Housing Finance Companies (Jusen) is ¥40 trillion, the actual figure is rumored to be ¥70 trillion. The US authorities are irritated that MOF is not disclosing information in a straightforward manner and have the impression that MOF is engaged in a cover up, as in the Daiwa Bank case. *See Nippon Island of Bad Debts*, SHUKAN TOYO KEIZAI, Feb. 24, 1996, at 12–17. For "Jusen," *see* Mitsuru Misawa, *Lenders' Liability in the Japanese Financial Market; A case of 'Jusen,' the largest problem loan in Japan, Part I*, MANAGEMENT JAPAN, Autumn 1997, 18–28; Mitsuru Misawa, *Lenders' Liability in the Japanese Financial Market; A case of 'Jusen,' the largest problem loan in Japan, Part II*, MANAGEMENT JAPAN, Spring 1998, 18–28.

[248] *See supra* note 6.

[249] At a press conference held on September 18, 1995 for foreign correspondents in Japan, MOF explained that "the problem resided in the difference of culture." *See Suggestions of Splitting MOF Surfaced Abruptly with Daiwa Bank Scandal; MOF Campaign of Bureaucracy, Shows Sign of Fatigue*, SHUKAN TOYO KEZAI, Dec. 2, 1995, at 16 [hereinafter *Suggestions of Splitting MOF Surfaced Abruptly*].

[250] *See supra* note 7.

for the system to be accepted internationally. In that sense, the "Daiwa Bank problem" was a "Japanese" problem as well.

Of course, it goes without saying that it is essential to have open communication and tight cooperation among countries in order to maintain an international financial system. In an age of progressively globalized finances, where money can be transferred within a split second, mistrust between financial supervisory authorities may lead to a financial crisis. We have to conclude that the MOF's understanding of this point was too naïve.

The root of this case was the collaboration between the MOF and the Japanese Banking industry regarding the so-called "administrative guidance," which was indistinct and secretive.[251] Such an administrative method delayed healing and worsened the damage. When it became impossible to hold back the information any more, and the truth was finally made public, a huge irrevocable international and domestic loss of trust resulted. Why then did the Japanese financial industry depend on the "administrative guidance" of the secret room? Why did it not want to act and take responsibility for its own acts?

The first reason is that, since the end of World War II, there have not been clear rules established for the financial world in Japan under which it could act on its own operating principles and take responsibility for its own activities.[252] Rather, it had to adhere to the murky rules of "administrative guidance," whereby it was required to ask the intentions of the MOF.[253] In this case, for example, there was no explicit rule stating that the Bank had to report within a specific number of days after it learned about such an incident. There was simply a guiding principle that it had to be reported as soon as possible.

Secondly, the reason that such a secretive collaboration between the administration and the industry, and its lack of disclosure, lasted so long were the existence of the so-called "convoy system"[254] — a concept to approve the government backup system as a desirable matter — and the

---

[251] Shigeo Nakao, "What is Japanese Finance?", http://koho.osaka-cu.ac.jp/vuniv2002/ nakao2002/nakao2002-4.pdf .

[252] *Id.*

[253] *Id.*

[254] *See supra* note 4.

increase in real-estate and stock prices that continued to rise for years and years due to the continuous expansion of the Japanese economy.[255] Under such conditions, it was easier for industry to obey administration policy, as the profit would automatically flow in with the expansion of the Japanese economy.[256] Even if industry officials made a mistake in managing the Bank, the damage would be healed automatically by the rise of the real-estate and stock market prices if they "kept their mouths shut" and acted in collaboration with the administration.[257]

Thirdly, from the international viewpoint, the Japanese financial institutions, despite their limited international experience, had quickly become giants in size during the last ten years, mainly because of a sharp yen appreciation against the US dollar.[258] Their holding increased twofold in terms of the dollar, and the amount of funds they controlled increased sharply.[259] Thus, the Japanese financial institutions, big in size, but rather primitive in international etiquette, felt that they had to depend on the administration's guidance in order to compete amongst the more sophisticated institutions of the world,[260] which, in comparison, have survived years of tough competition and merger battles while being responsible for their own acts.[261] The MOF's shallow understanding of what the international financial system should be was the true cause of the joint failure of the MOF, on whom Daiwa Bank relied for guidance, and Daiwa Bank to comply with US law.[262]

Nonetheless, the court's decision declared that there was no evidence to prove that the MOF instructed or ordered D_1 et al. not to report to the US authorities and that it was inexcusable that they chose not to make

---

[255] Then Prime Minister Hashimoto's Report on MOF's misadministration to the diet on Feb. 5, 1998, at
http://www.kantei.go.jp/jp/hasimotosouri/speech/1998/0209soriokura.html.
[256] *Id.*
[257] *Id.*
[258] *See MOF's Confusion at its Peak: Distrust of Japan's Financial Administration Heightens Regarding Daiwa Bank Scandal: Disbanding of MOF is Suggested.* SHUKAN TOYO KEIZAI. Dec 2, 1995, at 16. [hereinafter *MOF's Confusion at its Peak*].
[259] *Id.*
[260] *Id.*
[261] *See* John Bussey, *Japan's Bungling Ministry of Finance,* WALL ST. J., Nov. 10, 1995, at A14.
[262] *Id.*

any decision on their own, relying solely on the MOF's judgment or support.[263]

Judging from the contents of their meeting with the Director-General of the Banking Bureau of the MOF, it was unclear whether MOF requested D_1 et al. to delay not only the disclosure timing, but also the report to the US authorities. [264]   Therefore, in order to deny their responsibilities, it was necessary to prove the specific request of the MOF officers.[265]   Moreover, even if the MOF's request was made clear, it alone could not deny their responsibilities.   Even if they received such a request, their illegal action in view of the US laws would not be tolerated unless they were forced to do so under a certain law.[266]   If ever their responsibilities had to be removed, it had to be proven that a very unusual situation existed where they had no choice but to obey MOF's instruction.

Responsibility for establishing internal control system

Responsibility of establishment

The court stated that directors of a corporation were generally responsible for establishing a risk control system and a law-abiding system, an internal control system,[267] and decided that the directors of the case were responsible under Article 266, Section 1-5 because the system was inadequate. [268]   The court also decided that the auditors were responsible because they failed to monitor the system properly.[269]   The decision established precedence, as there had been no prior decision that had made such an explicit statement.

---

[263] Court Decision, *supra* note 11, at 31.
[264] *Id.*
[265] *Id.* at 45.
[266] *Id.*
[267] *Id.* at 34–35.
[268] *Id.* at 31.
[269] *Id.*

No one could deny that risk management and law-abiding operations were extremely important in present day corporations, particularly financial institutions. In addition, it was no secret that directors were responsible for supervising those operations. However, as the court pointed out, it was impossible for directors to guide and supervise all employees directly in large organizations. Consequently, the directors' responsibilities of care were to establish risk management and law abiding systems for employees and monitor them.[270] Theories have recognized such responsibilities for many years.[271] Establishment of the system was a fundamental part of the company management,[272] so that its outline needed to be formalized in the board room.[273] Representative directors and directors in charge of operations were responsible for establishing such a system, while other directors were responsible for monitoring the system.[274]

For a financial institution such as Daiwa Bank, establishment of such an internal control system was particularly important and constituted a part of the basic responsibilities of a director. It was written clearly in the financial inspection manual of the Financial Services Agency [275] formulated in 1999 and it was self-evident that whether an internal control system concerning risk management and a compliance system was established, was the main objective of the financial inspection by the Financial Services Agency.[276]

---

[270] *Id.*
[271] *See* KENICHI YOSHIMOTO, SHOUJI HOUMU [COMMERCIAL LAW] 1562, 40–42 (2000).
[272] Court Decision, *supra* note 11, at 11.
[273] *Id.*
[274] *Id.*
[275] The Financial Reconstruction Committee (FRC) was merged into the Financial Services Agency on January 6, 2001. The FRC had been working to restore stability and vitality in the financial system through the quick resolution of failed financial institutions under the Financial Revitalization Law and capital injection into viable institutions using public funds under the Financial Function Early Strengthening Law. Law No. 143 (1998). With these efforts, the environment surrounding financial institutions had on the whole regained stability. For details, *see* http://www.fsa.go.jp.
[276] *Check List for Inspection of Law Abidance System* and *Check List for Inspection of Risk Management System*, KINYU KENSAI MANYUARU [FINANCIAL INSPECTION MANUAL], July 1999, see http://www.fsa.go.jp/p_fsa/news/news-j.html.

However, it also must be realized that since such an internal control system had been introduced recently, it was not appropriate to judge the responsibilities of a director required at the time when the incident occurred with the level of internal control system currently required. One also should have considered the discretionary power given to a director as a management judgment issue. Nonetheless, even though it was not clearly recognized as an issue of establishing an internal control system, a risk management system or a law-abidance system per se,[277] it was fair to say that some of their concepts were part of a director's responsibility of care, especially as a part of the monitoring responsibility. Although the issue was related to the discretionary power of a director, limits existed with such power, as can be seen from the status of a compliance system that was a target of a financial inspection. Part of the order for filing an improvement plan or a business stop order was issued according to the Japanese Banking Law[278] if the status was poor. This rule also applied to any corporation other than financial institutions, although the degree of severity might have varied by industry.

Responsibility of care

If it is assumed that all agree on the notion that directors were responsible for establishing an internal control system, the next question is whether it was reasonable to seek the defendants' violations of specific duties related to the care in this regard as the court did.

The plaintiffs claimed the lack of separation between the securities trading department and the fund settlement/administration department, as well as an inadequate forced holiday system, as the problems with the risk management system of Daiwa Bank's New York office.[279] These points claimed by the plaintiffs are certainly the check items for risk management found in the financial inspection manual.[280] However, the court rejected all of these claims, except the claim pointing to the

---

[277] Court Decision, *supra* note 11, at 34.
[278] Japanese Banking Law, Law No. 21 of 1927, art. 26.
[279] Court Decision, *supra* note 11, at 8.
[280] *Supra* note 276.

inadequacy of the routine to check the storage balance of actual T-bills.[281]

It was true that Iguchi's unauthorized transactions could have been exposed much earlier if such a check on actual T-bills was implemented. However, a more careful examination should have been made as to the legal evaluation whether the lack of confirmations of actual T-bills was extremely inadequate or not.

The defendants rebutted that the inspection method for checking the securities in storage by means of storage balance statements normally used by other banks and auditing firms,[282] while the method of checking the storage balance by usually viewing actual T-bills at the secondary storage site was not necessarily used, even at that time.[283] It was true that the fact that the same method that was used by other financial institutions could not be used as a basis for arguing that the particular inspection method was not inadequate, if the method was grossly deficient.[284] However, one cannot deny the fact that the actual method practiced by other Japanese bank branches and US banks in New York could be used as a reference in judging whether the particular inspection method was grossly deficient or not. In that sense, the fact that, while the particular New York branch had been audited by an auditing company, inspected by both the Japanese and US banking supervisory authorities, and had been subjected to internal auditing by the bank's internal American auditor, it was never demonstrated that there was any deficiency in the method of storage balance confirmation. This means that there was a possibility that all the US and Japanese financial inspectors did not consider it a deficient method. One could not adopt today's level of risk management system as the basis for assessing the case. In addition, the level of risk management involved is a factor of management judgment, so that there would be room for a manager's discretionary power. Although the fact that there was no physical confirmation of actual T-bills, it may be considered a material deficiency of the risk control system at that time. Once the public knew what had transpired, it left a

---

[281] Court Decision, *supra* note 11, at 34.
[282] *Id.* at 10–13.
[283] *Id.* at 39–40.
[284] *Id.*

question in everyone's mind as to whether it was indeed such a severe deficiency at the time of the incident.

Principle of trusting right

The persons who were accused of job-related negligence concerning the establishment of the risk control system in the case A were the three directors D_2, D_6 and D_8, all of whom had served as New York branch managers,[285] and who were accused of inadequacies in the method of confirming the storage balance of T-bills[286] and the auditor, D_{33}, who visited New York branch in September 1993 for auditing, but failed to correct the method of confirming the storage balance of T-bills, although he could have found that it was inadequate.[287] As to D_1, who was the president, and D_3, who was the vice president, they were not accused of negligence of supervisory responsibilities on the ground that they were allowed to delegate their responsibilities to directors in charge of the inspection department, which was responsible for inspecting the storage balance of T-bills, and the directors in charge of the New York branch.[288] The corporate organization was structured in such a way that the president and the vice president were found not to have supervisory responsibilities, unless there were special circumstances that raised doubts about the job performance of those directors who had the frontline responsibilities.[289] For the same reasons, other directors were also discharged of their supervisory responsibilities unless there were special circumstances that created doubts of adequate job performance.[290]

Such a thought in the court decision at that time was assumed to have its ground in the principle of "trusting right," whereby directors and auditors could delegate portions of their jobs to other directors and auditors, or employees, and the directors were allowed to assume that there were no problems in the delegated jobs unless there were special

---

[285] *Id.* at 39–41.
[286] *Id.*
[287] *Id.*
[288] *Id.*
[289] *Id.*
[290] *Id.*

circumstances that created doubt about adequate job performance.[291] Such a theory also could be found among Japanese academic circles.[292]

There was no question that directors could not do everything on their own in such a large company and that they had to delegate some of the work load to other directors in charge of special areas or employees. That was the reason why various internal organizations existed.[293] It also was difficult for a director to monitor the details of the work performed by the people to whom the director had delegated his/her work.[294] This idea has been wildly accepted in the United States and is called "Trusting Right."[295] Such a protection in the US was given to a director, however, only when the trust was reasonable and the individual worthy. In other words, the director could trustingly accept reports from a person whom he/she has delegated work without feeling the need to investigate them, except under special circumstances.[296]

The question then becomes, what kind of a circumstance would be considered a special case, and was a system established to enable the director to trust the person in charge. It was unrealistic to expect a director, who did not have the frontline responsibilities to perform such a detailed task, to check the storage balance report by visually checking the actual T-bills.[297] The author considers that the court decision to accept "trusting rights" therefore was appropriate.

Responsibility of Information Disclosure

Despite the fact that Daiwa Bank learned of a huge loss due to Iguchi's unauthorized dealings, it issued 50 million shares of preferred stocks on July 27, 1995.[298] If this is considered to be an act of deceiving shareholders, its directors could be indicted for criminal and civil

---

[291] Court Decision, *supra* note 11, at 39–41.
[292] KATSUO KANZAKI, HANHYO SHOUJI HOUMU [COMMERCIAL LAW], 1492, 76–78 (1998).
[293] Court Decision, *supra* note 11, at 39–47.
[294] *Id.*
[295] A.L.I., *Principles of Corporate Governance: Analysis and Recommendations*, § 4.02.
[296] Court Decision, *supra* note 11, at 41.
[297] *Id.*
[298] *Id.* at 30.

responsibilities under the Japanese Securities Exchange Law.[299] This point is not a count of this suit and there were no claims in this shareholders' derivative action as to this point.[300] However, this should not be overlooked.

Although they knew about the huge loss described above, the management of Daiwa Bank delayed disclosure of that information to the FRB for a substantial period.[301] The FRB thought that this delay was a serious violation of the reporting rule under the IBA.[302] In addition, Daiwa Bank may have been required to disclose this important information, which logically is expected to influence the securities market for stockholders as well as to the public, which includes other stakeholders.[303] While this is not the direct concern of the FRB, if the management of Daiwa Bank felt it had responsibility to the stockholders to disclose, it should have reported such information to the United States and Japanese authorities at the appropriate time. From this standpoint, whether the bank and its directors were obligated to disclose such information to the stockholders is deeply related to the reporting duty to the FRB. Furthermore, the Bank and its directors may have been responsible for the disclosure of important information under the

---

[299] The Securities and Exchange Law of Japan also prohibits fraudulent operations with Article 58 against illegal trading which corresponds to Article 17(a) of US Securities Act of 1933 and against manipulation of the stock market with Article 125 which corresponds to Article 9 of US Securities Exchange Act of 1934. The difference between Article 58 and Article 125 is that Article 58 is a comprehensive prohibition rule to prohibit all fraudulent actions in general while Article 125 is intended to secure a free and open market. Due to the nature of these two rules, it often happens that a case violates Article 125 and Article 58 at the same time.

[300] Court Decision, *supra* note 11, at 4–8.

[301] A wide range of international observers desires the necessity for disclosure by Japanese banks. For example, Kevin Mellyrin, a consultant, and Arthur M. Mitchell, a lawyer, claimed that "[I]f Japan wants to develop world-class financial institutions that are necessary to secure its position in the world economy, it is necessary for Japan to ask for a more thorough and consistent disclosure practice from its bank." *Self-Renovation of Japanese Banks Desired Urgently*, NIHON KEIZAI SHIMBUN, Dec. 4, 1995, at 23.

[302] Court Decision, *supra* note 11, at 43.

[303] Note 349, infra.

Securities and Exchange Law of Japan, as Daiwa Bank's stock was traded on Japan's stock market.[304]

What is notable here is that Daiwa Bank asked a third party to purchase its stock without disclosing the losses, thus causing damage to this third party. Daiwa Bank issued 50 million shares of preferred stock on July 27, 1995.[305] Asahi Mutual Life Insurance Co. (Asahi Seimei), a major life insurance company in Japan,[306] bought a large sum of Daiwa Banks common stocks shortly before the incident was disclosed.[307] Asahi Seimei commented later that "the stock purchase was made on the request of Daiwa and it was regretful that the loss disclosure was not made.[308]

The facts of this case reveal that a "director of Daiwa Bank urged Asahi Seimei to buy Daiwa Bank's stock from the open market without disclosing an important piece of information regarding Daiwa Bank that might affect the market negatively."[309] Asahi Seimei already owned 2.7 million shares of Daiwa Bank stock at that point.[310] Asahi Seimei decided, however, that additional shares would be helpful to enhance its business in the Kansai District, where Daiwa Bank had its head office, and thus, bought a total of five million shares in six installments between late August and late September 1995, immediately before the disclosure

---

[304] If Daiwa Banks stocks were traded on the US market, or if Daiwa Bank had been issuing its securities in the United States, so that there were stockholders in the United States, then the US Securities Acts would have been applied. However, this was not the case.

[305] Court Decision, *supra* note 11, at 30.

[306] At that time, the fifth largest life insurance company in Japan.

[307] *Daiwa Bank's Huge Loss Case, Disclosure Tardiness Undeniable: Finding of Preferred Stock Issuance After Former Bank Employee's Confession Causes Distrust in Domestic and Overseas Markets*, NIHON KEIZAI SHIMBUN, Nov. 29, 1995, at 3 [hereinafter *Daiwa Bank's Huge Loss Case*] .

[308] *Id.* Although a company is now allowed to own its own stocks in the form of Treasury Stocks in Japan as it is so in the U.S., it was forbidden to do so in Japan. Commercial Code, Law No. 48 of 1899, art. 210. Therefore, when a company wanted to ask the third party to obtain the company's stock or increase the number of stocks the third party owns, it was a common practice in Japan to ask the third party to purchase the company's stocks through the stock market. *Id.*

[309] *Daiwa Bank's Huge Loss Case, supra* note 307.

[310] *Id.*

of this incident.[311] During this period, Daiwa Bank shares traded at slightly over 800 yen per share. The price subsequently dropped to about 600 yen per share, causing the insurance company to incur an unrealized loss of ¥650 million (about $6.5 million).[312]

The next question to be examined is whether Daiwa Bank had a duty to disclose this important information to stockholders, including Asahi Seimei, according to the Securities and Exchange Law of Japan. When a director discloses an important piece of information about a company, he or she may either disclose it or make the company disclose it. In either case, the director must always choose between the following duties: (1) the duty owed to stockholders to disclose the information as soon as possible;[313] and (2) the duty owed to the company not to disclose any information without first investigating thoroughly the accuracy of the information.[314] In some cases, this choice can be extremely difficult. While the director did not sell the stock he owned to Asahi Seimei, Seimei would not have purchased Daiwa Bank stock if it had known of the negative information.[315] Therefore, as far as the director's duty of disclosure is concerned, it is reasonable to assume that the case is similar to the director's selling of his own stock to another stockholder without disclosing the negative information. The *Asahi Seimei* case illustrates the difference in director's duties under United States and Japanese law.

The disclosure duty under the common law in United States is as follows: For liability to occur: (1) a party involved in a business transaction must intentionally prevent another party from obtaining an important piece of information by concealment or otherwise;[316] or (2) a party must owe to another party a duty "to exercise reasonable care to disclose matters known to him that the other party is entitled to know because of a fiduciary or other similar relation of trust and confidence

---

[311] *Id.*

[312] *Id.*

[313] *See* Oliver v. Oliver, 118 Ga. 362, 368, 45 S. E. 232, 234 (1903); Cady, Robers & Co., SEC 907, 911 (1961); Rogen v. Ilikon Corp., 361 F. 2d 260, 268 (1st Cir. 1966) (discussing US common law); *see* Court Decision, *supra* note 11, at 15 and 31 (discussing this case).

[314] Court Decision, *supra* note 11, at 15 and 31.

[315] *Id.* at 30.

[316] RESTATEMENT (SECOND) OF TORTS § 550 (1976).

between them."[317] Otherwise, a party cannot be sued for fraud based on its failure to disclose information. As for the fiduciary, however, the party not only has an "affirmative duty of utmost good faith, and full and fair disclosure of all material facts," but also has an affirmative duty to "employ reasonable care to avoid misleading his clients."[318]

Under US case law, it has been discussed extensively whether a fiduciary relationship exists between a director and a stockholder.[319] It is clear that such a fiduciary relationship does exist between a director and a stockholder when a director buys the company's stock from a stockholder and takes advantage of knowledge of internal information of the company.[320] Similarly, there exists the question of whether or not Daiwa Bank had a disclosure duty with regard to Asahi Seimei, a stockholder, in urging Asahi Seimei to buy shares from the market.

The "majority" rule is that, "officers and directors do not have active liabilities for disclosure responsibilities unless misstatement, unclear representation, or intentional concealment were made either verbally or by actions.[321] However, since they have fiduciary obligations to the company and the stockholders with regard to trading with the company and for the company, they have the disclosure duties."[322] According to this rule, it is fair to conclude that the directors of Daiwa Bank had a disclosure duty in the Asahi Seimei case.

The "minority" rule states that "the insider (officers, directors, and majority shareholders owning more than 10% of the stocks) of a company is construed to have a fiduciary relation with a stockholder in a stock trading so that the former has to make a complete disclosure on all

---

[317] *Id at* § 551(2)(a).

[318] SEC v. Capital Gains Research Bureau, Inc., 375 US 180, 194 (1963). In equity law, fraud includes all actions, omissions, and concealment that cause damages to other people, with violations of duties, trusts, or confidence duly placed under the common law or the equity law, or all actions, omissions or concealment to deprive other people inappropriately and unconscientiously of opportunities to make profits.

[319] Speed v. Transamerica Corp. (I), 71 F. Supp. 457 (D. Del. 1947).

[320] *Id.*

[321] The leading case for this view is Carpenter v. Danforth, 52 Barb. 581 (N.Y. Sup. Ct. 1868).

[322] *Id.*

important matters."[323]   Based on this standpoint, there is no question that a disclosure duty exists for those Daiwa Bank directors in the Asahi Seimei case.[324]

Against this backdrop of US common law, the securities laws[325] contain several prohibitive rules against fraudulent activities.[326]   In particular, they deem illegal an "insider's" use of insider information in trading securities.[327]   Specifically, Section 10(b) of the Securities Exchange Act of 1934 obligates certain insiders, namely officers, directors, and major stockholders, to pay the company any profit they earned due to insider information within the past six months.[328]   Whether such an action is to be construed as "insider trading" is judged according to Rule 10b-5, a derivative rule of Section 10(b).[329]

It is difficult to believe that the insiders of Daiwa Bank did not trade Daiwa Bank's stock at all while important information was being withheld.   If there were any such trading, Rule 10b-5 should be applied

---

[323] Oliver v. Oliver. 45 S.E. 232, 234-35 (1903); Stewart v. Harris. 77 P. 277, 279 (1904); Jacobson v. Yaschik, 155 S.E.2d 601, 605-06 (1967).

[324] A third theory on this matter is an intermediate position in that it states that an insider owes a responsibility for non-disclosure in special circumstances. Even from this standpoint, the disclosure duty of Daiwa Bank is undeniable. *See* Strong v. Repide, 213 US 419, 431 (1909) (discussing a third theory). The court held that the purchase of stocks from minor stockholders by a dominant stockholder and administrative general without disclosing the pending sale of a company asset, constituted an unlawful fraud. Its decision was based on its finding that it was the defendants' duties to act honestly and disclose the facts prior to the purchase, *given the defendants' positions as insiders and the special knowledge they had. Id.*

[325] Unites States Securities Act of 1933, 15 U.S.C. §§ 77a-78mm (1934) and the Securities Exchange Act of 1934, 15 U.S.C. §§ 77a – 78jj (1934). The Act of 1933 was intended to achieve "truth in securities" related to the public offerings in the issuing market, while the Act of 1934 intends mainly to control offerings in the issuing markets, while the Act of 1934 intends mainly to control activities of brokers and dealers a well as the securities market where they operate; at the same time, it established a disclosure system (Securities Report System) that obligates them to disclose pertinent information continuously.

[326] The most important ones are Section 17(a) of Securities Act of 1933 and Sections 9(a)(4) an d10(b) of Securities Exchange Act of 1934. These rules determine that "the use of market maneuvering or fraudulent device or contrivance related to the issuing, buying, or selling securities is illegal."

[327] LOUIS LOSS, SECURITIES REGULATION, 1445–1473 (1961).

[328] *Id.*

[329] *Id.*

in the US. The directors of Daiwa Bank must have had the choice "either to disclose the important information or to abstain from trading."[330] It must have been the same in the case of asking Asahi Seimei to buy Daiwa Bank's stock from the market. The particular director of Daiwa Bank must have had the choice "either to disclose or not to ask for such a trade."[331]

In the United States, the disclosure duty, according to Rule 10b-5, is not limited to the case of a direct deal between an insider and a stockholder,[332] but rather it imposes a wider duty on insiders to urge the company to disclose fully any important information that might influence the evaluation of the stock of the company on the stock market.[333] It seems that, although the responsibility of disclosure by the company is stressed, the company's response is generally slow and limited by its pursuit of its own interests. Thus, the responsibility of disclosing to the general public seems to fall on the insiders themselves.

There is no question that insiders will be charged with violations of 10b-5 for distributing false information through reports, newspaper releases, comments by directors, or any other methods, even if they were not involved in any trading.[334] The question, however, is whether or not they will be convicted of violating Rule 10b-5 when they fail to announce an important piece of information that most likely would have

---

[330] *Id.*

[331] *Id.*

[332] *Daiwa Bank's Huge Loss Case, supra* note 307.

[333] *Id.*

[334] In the Texas Gulf Sulpher case, where the focus of the lawsuit was a misleading newspaper report describing a large mineral deposit found in Canada as uncompromising, the Second Circuit Court stated in its final judgment that it seems that it is not unfair to hold the management of a company to be responsible to confirm the accuracy of any announcements the company makes to stockholders or the general public. SEC v. Texas Gulf Sulpher Co (I), 401 F.2d 833, 861-6 (2d Cir. 1968), cert. denied sub nom. Coates v. SEC and Kline v. SEC. 394 US 976 (1969). In other words, the court delivered a judgment that rule 10b-5 is always considered to be violated in a case such as follows: when an announcement was made in a rationally calculated method in order to influence the investing public, e.g. by media reporting financial status, and said announcement was fraudulent or likely to cause misunderstanding or, so imperfect as to cause misunderstanding irrespective of whether the announcement was motivated by secret purpose of the officers of the company or not.

affected the market price.[335] There is no Supreme Court case that deals with this particular issue. Both the SEC[336] and the US courts[337] consider it appropriate to temporarily withhold an important piece of information from the market if there is a sufficient business reason to do so. During this period, when the information is withheld, neither the issuer nor the insiders may conduct trading. If this concept is applied to the Asahi Seimei case, Daiwa Bank's (or its directors') request that the third party purchase the Bank's stock is equivalent to doing the trading by itself, and thus, a court is likely to find that it is not possible to conduct such trading legally while withholding such information for a substantial period of time.

Accordingly, leading stock exchanges in the United States request listed companies to "quickly disclose any news or information that is reasonably expected to provide a serious effect on the securities market," and to "take actions to deny quickly any groundless rumors that otherwise might cause abnormal market reactions or price fluctuations."[338]

Taking these rules and regulations in the United States as the premise, the *Asahi Seimei* case, in which a director of Daiwa Bank asked, and actually made, the third party buy the Bank's shares, though acquired in the stock market, can be considered a violation of the law because of its similarity to the case where an insider would be involved in the transaction itself. In this case, the insider was obligated to disclose the important information known to him because of his position, but unknown to the other party, which would have affected the other party's investment judgment.[339] In such a case, a clash is inevitable between the Rule 10b-5 duty of a director to disclose important information as soon as possible and the duty of a director under the common law not to disclose information prematurely.[340] If disclosure prior to the buying or

---

[335] Loss, *supra* note 327.
[336] Investors Management Co., Inc., 44 S.E.C. 633, 646 (1971).
[337] Dolgow v. Anderson, 438 F.2d 825, 829 (2d Cir. 1971).
[338] NEW YORK STOCK EXCHANGE LISTED COMPANY MANUAL, 202.05 Timely Disclosure of Material News Developments (Last modified in 2004). For the details, see http://www.nyse.com/Frameset.html?displayPage=/listed/1022221393251.html.
[339] Loss, *supra* note 327.
[340] *Id.*

selling is inappropriate or unrealistic, then the only choice left is to give up trading. Moreover, if it is proven that the director not only failed to disclose such important information, but also intentionally concealed it, there is a possibility that he would be accused of violating both the general fraud prohibition provision, Section 9(a)(4), which prohibits market manipulation, and Rule 10b-5.[341]

The present case, however, appears entirely different under Japanese law. It is difficult under Japanese law to establish a complaint against Daiwa Bank and its directors as to the non-disclosure of the important information. Although disclosing fraudulent information is an offense under Japanese law as well, failure to disclose information that would affect the stock price is not an offense.

Based on the US Securities Act of 1933 and the Securities Exchange Act of 1934, the Securities and Exchange Law[342] of Japan contains a detailed rule on disclosures by corporations. The Securities Exchange Law of Japan is intended to protect past and future investors in corporations by focusing on the disclosure system.[343] While rules of investor protection existed in the Commercial Code, they did not sufficiently cover the disclosure of corporate accounting.[344] Therefore,

---

[341] *Id.*

[342] Securities and Exchange Law, Law No. 25 of 1948, [translated in 3 INT'L SEC. REG. JAPAN BOOKLET 2, at 14 (1992) [hereinafter Securities and Exchange Law]. Subsequent amendments to this law reflected developments in the Untied States. The occupation authorities enacted the Securities and Exchange Law at the end of the Second World War as a condition of the reopening of the securities exchange market in Japan.

[343] ICHIRO KAWAMOTO AND KASUNAMI OHTAKE, SHOKEN TORIHIKIHO [THE SECURITIES EXCHANGE LAW], 34–35 (1996).

[344] The Commercial Code Law No. 48 of 1899 was modeled after German laws, while the Securities and Exchange Law was copied from the US laws after World War II. Germany is a civil law country, while the United States is a country of the common law. Any confusion in the concept of disclosure in Japan may be attributed to the slight difference in the disclosure rules of the two source countries. For an examination of the development of the Japanese securities market, *see* Mitsuru Misawa, *Securities Regulation in Japan*. 6 VAND. J. TRANSNAT'L L. 447 (1973). Further, as to the internationalization of the Tokyo Stock Market, *see* Mitsuru Misawa, *Tokyo as an International Capital Market — It's Economic and Legal Aspects,* 8 VAND. J. TRANSNAT'L L. 1 (1974). It is safe to say that when the loyalty of employees to the company is compared to their loyalty to their stockholders, the latter is given priority. The loyalty to the company not to disclose prematurely is a part of the traditional social system in Japan and the lifetime employment system goes hand in hand with this loyalty.

the Securities and Exchange Law was introduced as a supplement to secure smooth and fair-trading of securities, as well as to protect investors.[345]

Like Rule 10b-5 of the US Securities Act of 1934, Japanese law also prohibits insider trading.[346] However, if an insider owns the stock of his own company under the name of a third party or a fictitious person, voluntary reporting will probably be meaningless.[347] In addition to the fact that it is practically impossible to detect the violation, the stipulation that the director who benefited from the insider trading must return the resulting profit to the company, makes it difficult to expect any significant effects, given the social custom of Japan, unless there is an internal power struggle within management.[348] Consequently, it is less seldom that this Japanese insider-trading rule is activated.

As a result, the question of whether or not a director of a company has a duty to inform the other party about inside information when trading his or her own company stocks has been met generally with a negative answer. In fact, except in a clear case of fraud, the contract will not be negated. A director will not be obligated to indemnify the other party just because the director failed to disclose a piece of inside information about the company that the director came to know in the course of his or her work, unless the other party asked the director to disclose such information. Moreover, a director will not be held legally accountable for his or her company's nonfeasance in failing to disclose important information, even if it was information that could be reasonably expected to have a substantial influence on the securities market according to this rule.[349] Therefore, it is impossible to label the

---

This loyalty given by directors and employees to the company is one of the basic principles of the Commercial Code of Japan.
[345] *Id.*
[346] Securities and Exchange Law, *supra* note 342, at 189.
[347] KAWAMOTO, *supra* note 343.
[348] *Id.*
[349] The disclosure of important information based on the request of the stock exchange also is not uncommon in Japan as a follow-up procedure of information already announced. After the incident was disclosed, the possibility of merger between Daiwa Bank and Sumitoma Bank was rumored. In response to this, the Tokyo Stock Exchange requested both banks to disclose information in writing, but both banks responded by saying that "there is no specific merger plan." *Chairman of Tokyo Stock Exchange Asks*

responsibility of any particular director for non-disclosure of the information in the Asahi Seimei case as a violation of Section 189 of the Securities and Exchange Law of Japan, which corresponds to Rule 10b-5 of the US Securities Exchange Act of 1934.[350]

Even in Japan, however, the situation would be different if a person is actively involved in concealing information, in addition to delaying its disclosure.[351] Although it is difficult to seek punishment based on violation of the Insider Trading Prohibition, Article 189 of the Securities and Exchange Law of Japan, as those cases in the United States[352] are not established in Japan, such action can probably be prosecuted as an illegal transaction that violates the general fraud rule.[353]

In essence, one must conclude that it is difficult to hold a director in Japan legally accountable in these cases, unless the failure to disclose important information is accompanied with some fraudulent action, such as concealment. While numerous investors, in addition to Asahi Seimei, must have brought Daiwa Bank's stock prior to the disclosure of the incident and incurred damage due to the price drop of the stocks,[354] there is no legal remedy based on the Securities and Exchange Law of Japan.[355] The only way to obtain a remedy was to bring a derivative suit

---

for *Disclosure if any Changes Exist in Sumitoma Bank and Daiwa Bank Merger*, NIHON KEIZAI SHIMBUN, Nov. 22, 1995, at 4. The Tokyo Stock Exchange further asked both banks to "disclose information as quickly as possible if any changes occur, since the merger was expected to affect the stock prices." *Id.*

[350] *See MOF's Confusion at its Peak , supra* note 258.

[351] *See surpa* text accompanying note 299.

[352] Investors Management Co., Inc., 44 S.E.C. 633, 646 (1971); Dolgow v. Anderson, 438 F.2d 825, 829 (2d Cir. 1971).

[353] See *supra* note 299 and accompanying text.

[354] *No Procedural Fault in Issuing Preferred Stocks After Confession for Former Employees, MOF's Vice Minister Asserts*, NIHON KEIZAI SHIMBUN, Oct. 6, 1995, at 7.

[355] As the result of the experience, Daiwa Bank installed an internal proposal organization to promote the disclosure of the management information by the end of 1995. This was received as a progressive effort. In order to prevent any recurrence of such an incident and to improve the transparency of the management, an organization called "Action Direction Committee," a permanent proposition organization consisting of outsiders was started. The committee members included owner/operators of other companies, scholars, and professionals, journalists, and general saving customers, totaling about ten people. The committee discussed and proposed ideas relating to the issues of how to retain customers and corporate customers and how to provide more informative communications to the stockholders. *Mechanisms for Management Information*

under the Commercial Code,[356] charging a violation of the duty of loyalty of the directors to the company.

Although MOF did not comment on the case of Asahi Seimei's purchase of the stocks, it commented on the issuance of preferred stocks in Japan by Daiwa Bank immediately before the incident was disclosed, saying, "there is no specific procedural problem in regard to the Securities and Exchange Law.[357]

Effect of Court's Decision in 2002

This decision profoundly effected directors' responsibilities in Japanese companies and how the shareholder's representative action system should be. It resulted in an amendment[358] of the Commercial Code in December 2001 concerning corporate governance.[359]

Abatement of shareholder's responsibility to corporation; rationalization of shareholder's representative action

Abatements of responsibilities of directors and others to corporation

Although it had been ruled that the responsibility of a director to its corporation cannot be removed without consent of the entire shareholders, the new rule states that any portion that exceeds four times the particular director's annual compensation could be pardoned with a special voting decision of the shareholder's meeting or a voting decision of the board of director's meeting based on the rules of the article of association unless the director failed to perform its duty conscientiously and there was a material mistake on the director's part.[360] However, the

---

Disclosure Suggestions to be Installed in Daiwa Bank by Year End, NIHON KEIZAI SHIMBUN, Oct. 13, 1995, at 7.

[356] *See supra* note 344 and accompanying text.

[357] *See MOF's Confusion at its Peak* , *supra* note 1.

[358] Enacted on December 5, 2001. Implemented on May 1, 2002.

[359] *See* Japan Auditor's Association, *Amendments of the Commercial Code*, June 13, 2002, at arts. 4–5, 11–25, *at* http://www.kansa.or.jp/PDF/el03_kh14613.pdf. [hereinafter *Amended Commercial Code*].

[360] *Amended Commercial Code*, *supra* note 358, at arts. 266-7 – 266-11, 266-17 – 266-18.

ceiling amount is six years for a director with a representative director and two years for an outside director or an auditor.[361]

Abatement of outside director's responsibility

It is permissible to have an agreement to limit the responsibilities of an outside director in advance.[362] However, it is required, as a prerequisite condition, to establish a rule in the article of association that a limited responsibility agreement could be established.[363]

Rationalization of shareholder's representative action

Extension of consideration period

The revised law extends the consideration period for a company to decide whether to take legal action, when the shareholders demand that the company take an action against its directors' seeking their responsibilities, from the previous period of thirty days to sixty days.[364] The intention behind the revision was to provide a sufficient length of time for the auditors to investigate whether such an action was needed.[365]

Revision concerning public announcement and notice to shareholders

The revised law requires a company to make a public announcement and notify its shareholders without delay when it takes a legal action against its directors seeking their responsibilities or when the company received a notice of a shareholder's representative action from the shareholders.[366]

---

[361] *Id.*
[362] *Id.* at arts. 266-19 – 266-23.
[363] *Id.*
[364] *Id.* at arts. 267-1 – 267-3.
[365] *Amended Commercial Code, supra* note 358.
[366] *Id.* at arts. 268-4.

Improvement on rules concerning amicable settlement on action

The revised law allows a company to make an amicable settlement with its defendant directors without consent from the entire shareholders when it takes legal action against its directors seeking their responsibilities.[367]

Company's assistance for defendant directors in shareholder's representative action

The revised law explicitly allows a company to participate in a shareholder's representative action and assist defendant directors, on the condition that an agreement from its entire auditors is available, except in case of a small corporation specified in the Special Case Law of the Commercial Code.[368]

In September 2000, at the same time as the amendment to the Commercial Code was passed,[369] and the Osaka District Court issued a decision for a shareholder's representative action concerning a huge loss of Daiwa Bank New York branch and ordering eleven directors to pay damages in the total amount of ¥83 billion ($775 million), the defendants gave up the right of appeal and sought a settlement for a joint payment of ¥250 million ($2.3 million).[370]

It was originally predicted that the case would go all the way up to the Supreme Court, but it was said the parties involved agreed in an early settlement.[371] However, the value of this first trial as the leading case of shareholder's representative actions in Japan was not tarnished by the early settlement.[372]

---

[367] *Id.* at arts. 268-5 – 268-7.
[368] *Id.* at arts. 268-8.
[369] *Supra* note 358.
[370] Asahi Shimbun, Dec. 12, 2001, at 11.
[371] *Id.*
[372] *Id.*

Conclusion

In all of the cases preceding the present case, directors' responsibilities were recognized almost exclusively in cases where directors were involved in malicious illegal acts themselves, while cases of being charged with responsibilities of negligence were almost non-existent, partially because the management decision principle was admitted. None of those cases ended up with such a huge amount of damages as in the *Daiwa Bank* case. Most cases ended up with rejections or withdrawals for reasons of disobeying the pledge offering orders, or dismissal of claims. In almost no circumstance could directors be charged for responsibilities if they had conscientiously conducted their jobs as long as the facts were studied carefully and the legal principles were applied correctly. Thus, the present case, in which the defendants were asked to pay a phenomenal amount of damages totaling several tens of billions yen, just as a loss recovery, was an extremely unusual case.

Although the case attracted the attention of many people, it is an unusual case among precedents, so that it is not appropriate to discuss the entire precedence of shareholders' representative actions and criticize the shareholder's representative action system, based on this action alone.

However, the decision sounded a very important alarm about how Japanese corporations are managed. The background that allowed Japanese companies to be run loosely seems to be the fact that the supervising authorities and the legal system failed to pursue the lack of risk management and concealment of responsibilities rigorously. In this case, Iguchi succeeded in hiding the location of the custody operation from the MOF's inspection, thereby deceiving the inspector, but, to this point it is unknown if the ministry has tried to punish MOF severely for the oversight. Additionally, it is unknown if any severe punishment was made, or responsibility was sought after, based on the Securities Exchange Law in the case of the bank issuing preferred stocks, concealing the unauthorized dealings. In Japan, lack of stern punishment by the authorities, strictly according to the law, invites a lack of loose risk management, negligent adherence to laws, and concealments of illegal acts.[373]

As for the disclosure, there was a marked difference between the United States and Japan regarding strictness in the pursuit of disclosure duties of corporations. It was safe to say that an average Japanese company did not feel a need to immediately disclose important information until now. One lesson from the *Daiwa Bank* case is it is important for Japanese banks to observe the disclosure principle more stringently and to disclose pertinent operating information to stakeholders, such as stockholders and corporate customers, earlier, more quickly, more frequently, and more thoroughly, rather than reporting it privately to authorities, such as the MOF. The more thoroughly Japanese banks conduct disclosure, the higher their market valuations will be. By assuming full and strict responsibility of management and supervision, they will be able to regain the trust of the international securities market.

This lack of sternness in the law enforcement system has created sloppy risk managements and concealing attitudes among Japanese companies, which resulted in the current case when one of such Japanese companies operated in the US with the same loose attitudes. In order to prevent this kind of case, more rigorous attitudes are necessary to ensure that directors are more responsible for their duties. That should provide incentives to Japanese companies to establish effective risk management and law-abidance systems. It is notable that shareholder's representative actions finally have started to function as an effective means of law enforcement in Japan.

The present case served to reveal the fact that it is extremely dangerous for Japanese financial institutions to try to operate overseas without mending their lack of risk managements and their sloppiness in legal compliance. Japanese financial supervising authorities must also accept this new mindset. Such an incident could invite international mistrust in the Japanese society itself. The current status of the legal and organizational systems of the Japanese financial supervising authorities is not up to the level necessary to handle international financial businesses.

---

[373] MOF's Confusion at its Peak , *supra* note 1.

Economic relations between Japan and the United States have been turbulent in recent years due to the trade imbalance problem. Various disagreements in thinking were exposed between the two countries in the *Daiwa Bank* case. This incident provided a new and serious impact on relations between the two countries. The central issue of this incident is not that an employee of Daiwa Bank engaged in illegal operations, nor is it the huge loss that those operations caused. Those things often occur in both countries, and such a thing should not cause such a profound impact. The real problems are that Daiwa Bank failed to report to US authorities, and that the Bank covered up its losses for an extended period of time.

Moreover, the MOF failed to notify the US authorities quickly after it was contacted by the Bank. The fact that the Director-General of the Banking Bureau, and other officials of the MOF, failed to report the unauthorized transactions to the US Financial Supervisory Authority, was a material violation of the international agreement between banking supervisory authorities of member countries. This surely triggered a great mistrust of the Japanese officials in the minds of the officers the US Financial Supervisory Authority.

These delays are the reason why the United States is calling the Japanese activities "a serious betrayal of the trust between the United States and Japan."[374] A further problem is that the Japanese, including the MOF, seem to lack any awareness that they may be at fault. "There was no mishandling of the matter," said the MOF. "The reason the Americans are upset stems from the cultural difference between the two countries."[375]

This difference in perspective between the two countries makes this case more complex and multifaceted. It includes an essential problem that cannot be brushed away as a difference of culture. A wide discrepancy exists between the two countries in the way in which the laws regarding the disclosure system of corporate information are applied. It is mandatory for US corporate management to "disclose important information in the *earliest possible* chance."[376] However, it is

---

[374] *See supra* note 244 and accompanying text.
[375] *See Suggestions of Splitting MOF Surfaced Abruptly, supra* note 249.
[376] *See* New York Stock Exchange Listed Company Manual, *supra* note 338.

quite different in Japan. It generally is thought that a disclosure should be made at a carefully selected point. Even the MOF agrees with this concept. This misconception between the two countries was the largest factor causing this case and created the difference in the perceptions of the seriousness of the matter. As a result of that misconception, the handling of the matter by the Japanese was criticized extensively.

Japanese industries should understand clearly that their legal interpretations, as well as people's conceptions and manners of dealing with various matters, while acceptable in Japan, may not necessarily be correct in the United States. It is common sense that, as long as one wishes to conduct business in the United States, one should obey the rules of the Untied States. In Japan, we have our own version of the saying, "When in Rome, do as the Romans do." This important realization was missing from Daiwa Bank and the MOF.

Japanese companies operating overseas today are all confronted with a question: to what extent should the Japanese way of thinking, i.e. Japanese management style, be implanted into their overseas subsidiaries.[377] The backdrop to that dilemma is hat, although the Japanese management style was thought of highly at one time, more criticisms of it are arising, especially in foreign countries, with the demise of the Japanese economic boom.[378]

The present case clearly shows how far it is possible to press the Japanese way of thinking and way of handling matters overseas. It is a great lesson, which teaches Japanese companies that there is a limit in applying their management styles on foreign soils. This is especially true of Japanese companies, which are undergoing internationalization. It has been nearly twenty years since the full-scale internationalization of Japanese industries commenced. As international corporations, they have done from being "infant industries," to now entering the age of maturity. The present case is arguably something Japanese companies were

---

[377] For the difference of the management styles, *see* Mitsuru Misawa, *New Japanese-Style Management in a Changing Era*, Colum J. World Bus., Winter 1987, at 9.
[378] For a recent criticism of Japanese management styles, *see* Mitsuru Misawa, *Portrait of the International Entrepreneurs* [Interview with Japanese Business Leaders in the United States], Sekai Shuho, Jan. 31, 1995, at 44-45. 1995).

destined to experience as they mature into full-fledged multinational corporations.

Because of this incident, Japanese banks are paying a hefty intangible penalty, namely the loss of trust in the international market. This penalty against Japanese banks will eventually be born by all Japanese industries. It is necessary for Japanese industries to have a positive attitude and accept these legal, economical, and social penalties, and not try to resist them. Instead, these industries must learn the lessons necessary for them to grow further and make a fresh start. It also is necessary for Japan to rethink the relationship between the government and industries, which has been taken for granted until now, and to make necessary changes in its thinking. Restructuring the excessively large government may be necessary.

The Japanese people must have the modesty to analyze this case thoroughly through multiple approaches and learn whatever there is to be learned. On the other hand, the American people should not repel Japan simply by labeling them "different," but rather, understand better the viewpoint of the Japanese people, and industries that are in the midst of a process of internationalization. Americans should study how the Japanese thought and reacted in this case and should try to understand the Japanese legal, economical and sociological situations. The further improvement of relations between these two countries will create a consensus regarding international business between them through mutual understanding. In that way, some consolation can be found in this extremely regretful case. As is said in Japan, it is not impossible to turn bad luck into good luck.

Bibliography

12 C.F.R. § 208.20 (1996).

12 C.F.R. § 208.20 (1996).

12 U.S.C. § 2105(e)(5) (1994).

12 U.S.C. § 3110(c) (1994)

12 U.S.C. § 611 (1994).

A.L.I., Principles of Corporate Governance: Analysis and Recommendations, § 4.02.

A.L.I., Principles of Corporate Governance, Comment d to § 4.01(a).

Amendments to the Commercial Code, June 14, 1993, No. 62.

Antimonopoly Law, Law No. 54 of 1947, art. 19.

Ariyoshi v. Mitsui Mining Co., 1400, Ist Small Court. 1989, (Sup. Ct., Sept. 9, 1993).

Asahi Shimbun, Dec. 12, 2001, at 11.

Asahi Shimbun, Sept. 21, 2000, at 2.

Banking Law of Japan, art. 63, § 1.

Basle Committee on Banking Supervision, Minimum Standards for the Supervision of International Banking Groups and Their Cross-Border Establishments (July, 1992) available at http://www.bis.org/publ/bcbsc314.pdf.

BCCI Case's Full Picture: Other Countries Responses and Developments in Japan, Kinyu Hohmu Jijyou [Financial and Legal Affairs], Nov. 25, 1991 at 4-12.

Bussey, John. *Japan's Bungling Ministry of Finance,* Wall St. J., Nov. 10, 1995, at A14.

Carpenter v. Danforth, 52 Barb. 581 (N.Y. Sup. Ct. 1868).

Check List for Inspection of Law Abidance System and *Check List for Inspection of Risk Management System,* Kinyu Kensai Manyuaru [Financial Inspection Manual], July 1999, see http://www.fsa.go.jp/p_fsa/news/news-j.html.

Civil Code, Law No. 89 of 1898, art. 715.

Commercial Code Law No. 48 of 1899.

Commercial Code, Law No. 48 of 1898, art. 266.

Commercial Code Law No. 48 of 1899, art 266-1-5.

Commercial Code Law No. 54 of 1947, art. 489-2.

Commercial Code Law No. 54 of 1947, art. 260-2.

Commercial Code Law No. 54 of 1947, art. 266-1-5.

Criminal Code, Law No. 45 of 1906, art.38-3.

Criminal Code Law No. 45 of 1907, art. 198.

Daiwa Bank Seeks Judicial Settlement, Admits Huge Loss and Conspiracy: Federal Prosecutor Charges $35.6 Billion Penalty for 16 Accounts Including Delayed Report: Affected by MOF's Intention, Nihon Keizai Shimbun, Feb. 29, 1996, at 1 (giving the details of the plea bargain agreement).

Diet Record No. 153 (Justice Committee), Nov. 28, 2001, at http://www.shugiin.go.jp/ itdb_kaigiroku.nsf/html/ and kaigiroku/000415320011128014.htm.

Dolgow v. Anderson, 438 F.2d 825, 829 (2d Cir. 1971).

Exclusive Publication of Defendant Toshihide Iguchi's Confession, Bungei Shunju, Jan. 1996, 112–31.

Hansetsu Shouji Houmu (Commercial Law) 145. Takita, Setsu. at 28-31 (1997).

Ikenaga v. Tabuchi. Tokyo High Court, Sept. 26, 1995, 16th Civil Dept., 1993 (ne) No. 3778.

International Banking Act, added in 1991 as amendments, §§ 7(e) and 10(b).

Investors Management Co., Inc., 44 S.E.C. 633, 646 (1971).

Investors Management Co., Inc., 44 S.E.C. 633, 646 (1971); Dolgow v. Anderson, 438 F.2d 825, 829 (2d Cir. 1971).

Japan Auditor's Association, *Amendments of the Commercial Code,* June 13, 2002, at arts. 4–5, 11–25, available at http://www.kansa.or.jp/PDF/el03_kh14613.pdf.

Jiko Kabushiki no Shutoku [Acquisition of Own Stock] art. 211-2.

John Bussey, *Japan's Bungling Ministry of Finance,* Wall St. J., Nov. 10, 1995, at A14.

Kanzaki, Katsuo. Hanhyo Shouji Houmu [Commercial Law], 1492, 76–78 (1998).

Kawamoto, Ichiro and Ohtake, Kasunami. Shoken Torihikiho [The Securities Exchange Law], 34–35 (1996).

Kinyu/Shoji Hanrei [Financial/Commercial Precedence], Supreme Court decision, July 7, 2000; 1096, at 3 (2000).

Kishi, Senjin. *Fault of MOF Which Betrayed World and Japan: Japan Financial Administration.* Far Apart From Anglo-Saxon Logic, Economist (Japan), Dec. 5, 1995, at 40–42.

Kondo, Mitsuo and Hasegawa, Toshiaki, et al., *Various Issues of Shareholder's Suit in Japan* (in Japanese) Yobou jihyo, 26–35, Summer 2001, available at http://home.kobe-u.com/tokyo/topics/topics011.html.

Kondo, Mitsuo. *Torishimariyaku no Keieijo no Kashitsu to Kaisha nitaisuru Sekinin [Directors' Errors in Management and Their Responsibilities for Company]* Kinyu Fomu Jijo [Financial Legal Situations], 1372, at 10.

Louis Loss, Securities Regulation, 1445–1473 (1961).

Matsumaru v. Otsu, Tokyo District Court, Dec. 22, 1994, Civil Sec. No. 8, 1993 (wa) No. 18447.

Miller v. A.T. & T. Co., 507 F.2d 759 (3rd Cir. 1974).

Miller, Steven A., *How Daiwa Self-Destructed* 113 Banking L. J. 560, 565 (1996).

Misawa, Mitsuru. "Shareholders' Derivative Action and Directors' Responsibility in Japan," Penn State International Law Review (The Dickinson School of Law), Vol. 24, Summer 2005, No.1, pp. 1–57.

Misawa, Mitsuru. *Daiwa Bank Scandal in New York — It's Causes, Significance, and Lessons in the International Society*, 29 VAND J. TRANSNAT'L L. No. 5 (1996).

Misawa, Mitsuru. *Lenders' Liability in the Japanese Financial Market; A case of 'Jusen,' the largest problem loan in Japan, Part I.* 30 MGMT. JAPAN No. 2. 18–28 (Autumn 1997)

Misawa, Mitsuru. *Lenders' Liability in the Japanese Financial Market; A case of 'Jusen,' the largest problem loan in Japan, Part II.* 31 MNGT. JAPAN No. 1, 18–28 (Spring 1998).

Misawa, Mitsuru. *Lenders' Liability in the Japanese Financial Market; A case of 'Jusen,' the largest problem loan in Japan, Part I*, Management Japan, Autumn 1997, 18–28.

Misawa, Mitsuru. *Lenders' Liability in the Japanese Financial Market; A case of 'Jusen,' the largest problem loan in Japan, Part II*, Management Japan, Spring 1998, 18–28.

Misawa, Mitsuru. *Loss Compensation in the Japanese Securities Market: Causes, Significance, and Search for a Remedy*, 25 VAND J. TRANSNAT'L L., 37–58 (1992) (discussing loss compensation).

Misawa, Mitsuru. *New Japanese-Style Management in a Changing Era*, Colum J. World Bus., Winter 1987, at 9.

Misawa, Mitsuru. *Portrait of the International Entrepreneurs* [Interview with Japanese Business Leaders in the United States], Sekai Shuho, Jan. 31, 1995, at 44–45. 1995).

Misawa, Mitsuru. *Daiwa Bank Scandal in New York — It's Causes, Significance, and Lessons in the International Society*, 29 Vand J. Transnat'l L. 1023 (1996).

Morimoto, Shigeru, Kaishaho [Corporate Law] 253 (2nd Edition, 1995).

Nakao, Shigeo, *Globalization to be Reconsidered*, available at http://koho.osaka-cu.ac.jp/ vuniv2002/nakao2002/nakao2002-10.html.

Nakao, Shigeo. "What is Japanese Finance?", http://koho.osaka-cu.ac.jp/ vuniv2002/nakao2002/nakao2002-4.pdf .

New York Stock Exchange Listed Company Manual, 202.05 Timely Disclosure of Material News Developments (Last modified in 2004), http://www.nyse.com/ Frameset.html?displayPage=/listed/1022221393251.html.

Nihon Keizai Shimbun, *Chairman of Tokyo Stock Exchange Asks for Disclosure if any Changes Exist in Sumitoma Bank and Daiwa Bank Merger*, Nov. 22, 1995, at 4.

Nihon Keizai Shimbun, *Daiwa Bank Has Employer's Responsibility: Federal Prosecutor's Rebuttal Stresses Legitimacy of Accusation*, Feb. 13, 1996, at 3.

Nihon Keizai Shimbun, *Daiwa Bank's Huge Loss Case, Disclosure Tardiness Undeniable: Finding of Preferred Stock Issuance After Former Bank Employee's Confession Causes Distrust in Domestic and Overseas Markets*, Nov. 29, 1995, at 3.

Nihon Keizai Shimbun, *Daiwa Bank's Huge Loss, 30,000 Unauthorized Transactions: FBI Announces Arrest of Daiwa Bank's Former Employee*, Sept. 27, 1995, at 1.

Nihon Keizai Shimbun, *Former N.Y. Branch Manager Claimed Not Guilty: Defendants Lawyers of Daiwa Bank Case Claim Main Case Itself is Illegitimate as Well*, Nov. 22, 1995, at 4.

Nihon Keizai Shimbun, *Mechanisms for Management Information Disclosure Suggestions to be Installed in Daiwa Bank by Year End*, Oct. 13, 1995, at 7.

Nihon Keizai Shimbun, *MOF's Failures are Regrettable*, Nov. 29, 1995, at 2.

Nihon Keizai Shimbun, *No Procedural Fault in Issuing Preferred Stocks After Confession for Former Employees, MOF's Vice Minister Asserts*, Oct. 6, 1995, at 7.

Nihon Keizai Shimbun, *Outlandishness of Japanese Financial System Revealed: MOF Agonizes as its Rebuttals are Ignored*. Oct 18, 1995, at. 3.

Nihon Keizai Shimbun, *Self-Renovation of Japanese Banks Desired Urgently*, Dec. 4, 1995, at 23.

Nihon Keizai Shimbun, Sept. 21, 2000, at 3.

Nihon Keizai Shimbun, *Stockholders Representative Action to be Filed Tomorrow Asking 1.1 Billion Dollars in Damages*, Nov. 26, 1995, at 30.

No. 153 Diet Record (Justice Committee, No. 13), Nov. 27, 2001 (in Japanese), available at http://www.shugiin.go.jp/itdb_kaigiroku.nsf/html/kaigiroku/0004153200111270 13.htm.

N.Y Times, *Cloistered Japanese Banks*, Oct. 13, 1995, at A1.

Oliver v. Oliver, 118 Ga. 362, 368, 45 S. E. 232, 234 (1903); Cady, Robers & Co., SEC 907, 911 (1961); Rogen v. Ilikon Corp., 361 F. 2d 260, 268 (1st Cir. 1966) (discussing U.S. common law).

Oliver v. Oliver. 45 S.E. 232, 234-35 (1903); Stewart v. Harris. 77 P. 277, 279 (1904); Jacobson v. Yaschik, 155 S.E.2d 601, 605-06 (1967).

Resolution Trust Corporation, in its corporate capacity, Plaintiff v. Charles D. Acton, David Clayton, William F. Courtney, Richard L. Davidson, and John R. Rittenberry, Defendants, 844 F. Supp. 307; 1994 U.S. Dist. Lexis 1750.

Restatement (Second) of Torts) § 550 (1976).
SEC v. Capital Gains Research Bureau, Inc., 375 U.S. 180, 194 (1963).
SEC v. Texas Gulf Sulpher Co (I), 401 F.2d 833, 861-6 (2d Cir. 1968), cert. denied sub
    nom. Coates v. SEC and Kline v. SEC. 394 U.S. 976 (1969).
Securities and Exchange Law, Law No. 25 of 1948, [translated in 3] Int'l Sec. Reg. Japan
    Booklet 2, at 14 (1992).
Securities and Exchange Law, Law No. 25 of 1948.
Shoji Houmu (Commercial Law) 192, at 164-168 (2000).
Shoji Homu, Osaka District Court, Sept. 20, 2000, No. 1573, at 4-51.
Shoji Homu, Tokyo High Court, July 3, 1988, No. 1188 at 36.
Shukan Toyo Keizai, *MOF's Confusion at its Peak: Distrust of Japan's Financial
    Administration Heightens Regarding Daiwa Bank Scandal: Disbanding of MOF is
    Suggested*, Dec 2, 1995, at 16.
Shukan Toyo Keizai, *Nippon Island of Bad Debts*, Feb. 24, 1996, at 12–17. Speed v.
    Transamerica Corp. (I), 71 F. Supp. 457 (D. Del. 1947).
Shukan Toyo Keizai, *Suggestion for Disbanding of MOF Surfaced Abruptly with Daiwa
    Bank Sandal*, Dec. 2, 1995, at 12.
Shukan Toyo Keizai, *Suggestions of Splitting MOF Surfaced Abruptly with Daiwa Bank
    Scandal; MOF Campaign of Bureaucracy, Shows Sign of Fatigue*, Dec. 2, 1995, at
    16.
Shukan Toyo Keizai, *U.S. Intensifies Criticism Against MOF: MOF Should Not Discuss
    Its Role*, Dec. 2, 1995, at 22.
Strong v. Repide, 213 U.S. 419, 431 (1909) (discussing a third theory).
Then Prime Minister Hashimoto's Report on MOF's misadministration to the diet on Feb.
    5, 1998, at http://www.kantei.go.jp/jp/hasimotosouri/speech/1998/0209soriokura.
    html.
Tokyo District Court, Dec. 22, 1994, Civil Sec. No. 8., 1993 (wa) No. 18447.
Tokyo District Court, May 29, 1986, Harei Jihyo, No. 1194 at 33; Shoji Homu, No. 1078
    at 43.
Tokyo High Court Decision, February 23, 1999.
Tokyo Keizai Japan Company Handbook, 1100 (1996).
Toshio, Kimura. *Management Responsibility in the Daiwa Bank Case* (in Japanese),
    Japan Business News, available at http://www.japan-bus.pwc.com/ins-sol/
    business/bushot_pre2001.html.
United States Securities Act of 1933, 15 U.S.C. §§ 77a-78mm (1934) and the Securities
    Exchange Act of 1934, 15 U.S.C. §§ 77a – 78jj (1934).
Volkman, Brian P., *The Global Convergence of Bank Regulations and Standards for
    Compliance*, 115 Banking L. J. 550, 554 (1998).
Watanabe, Yoshiyuki. *Daiwa Bank Conceals Wrongdoings*, Bungei Shunju, Dec. 1995,
    at 94–104 (outlining details of the concealment by Daiwa Bank).
Yoshimoto, Kenichi. Shouji Houmo [Commercial Law] 1562, 40–42 (2000).

Chapter 9

A New Trend in Japan's Security Regulations — Efficiency Test of US Laws in the Different Markets

Introduction

The Commercial Code[1] was transplanted from Germany to Japan in 1899 as a part of the general acceptance of Western law in the Meiji period. The post-war methods of corporate disclosures in Japan were modeled after those adopted by the United States in 1933 and 1934.[2] The Securities Exchange Law of Japan enacted in 1948[3] was imposed by the occupation authorities as a condition for the reopening of the securities exchanges. This Japanese law contained disclosure provisions substantially similar to the requirements of the American law.

---

[1] Shoho (Commercial Code). Law No. 48 of 1899 was modeled after German laws, while the Securities and Exchange Law was copied from the U.S. laws after WWII. Germany is a civil law country, while the United States is a country of the common law. Any confusion in the concepts of disclosure in Japan may be attributed to the slight difference in the disclosure rules of the two source countries. For an examination of the development of the Japanese securities market, see Mitsuru Misawa. *Securities Regulation in Japan.* 6 Vand. J. Transnational L. 447 (1973). Further, as to the internationalization of the Tokyo Stock Market, see Mitsuru Misawa. *Tokyo as an International Capital Market — It's Economic and Legal Aspects.* 8 Vand. J. Transnational L. 1 (1974).

[2] See notes 15 and 16 infra.

[3] Shoken Torihiki Ho (Securities and Exchange Law). Law No. 25 of 1948, translated in 3 Int'l Sec. Reg. Japan Booklet 2. at. 14 (1992) (hereinafter Securities and Exchange Law).

The basic assumption of occupation authorities in suggesting the new corporate and securities legislation appears to have been that what worked well in the United States would also work in Japan. No question was raised as to the congeniality of the environment into which the new legislation was being transplanted. If transplanted control methods and corporate practices of Anglo-American origin should not be well adapted to Japanese procedures, then Japanese markets would be prevented from performing their functions as efficiently as desires.

On this basis a material revision of the Securities Exchange Law of Japan[4] was made in 2004. The Law[5] has gone through scores of changes, but the recent change was a major in order to improve and enhance the financial system focusing on its market functions, such as enhancement of market monitoring function and enrichment of marketing venues for securities, in response to the changes occurring in domestic and foreign economic and financial trends.[6]

More specifically, it modified the basic stance taken in the original issue in the sense that it approved banks' participation in securities business among other things. The changes were also made to accommodate new trends occurring in the markets such as the Takeover Bids (TOB) system,[7] the Proprietary Trading System (PTS),[8] the Green Sheet Market[9] and the Best Execution Policy[10] of the securities companies. Enhancement of market monitoring[11] through the Securities Exchange Surveillance Committee[12] was another major change in the securities regulation.

---

[4] Subsequent amendments to this law after it was enacted in 1948 reflected developments in the United States. For details of the law, see horei (http://law.e-gov.go.jp/cgi-bin/idxsearch.cgi).

[5] For the history of Japanese securities regulations, see Mitsuru Misawa, note 1.

[6] The revision bill was sent by the government on March 5, 2004 to the 159th Regular Session of the Diet, approved, made a law, and was published on June 9 (Law No. 97, 2004; hereinafter called "Revised Law").

[7] It is stipulated in articles 27 ff of the Securities Exchange Law.

[8] See note 63 infra.

[9] See note 64 infra.

[10] See note 78 infra.

[11] See note 112 infra.

[12] *Ibid.*

To see the reasons of the resent revision, it is necessary to understand the historical development of Japanese securities regulations.[13] The Japanese economy was almost at standstill for a certain period after Japan was defeated on August 15, 1945 in the Second World War. The security exchange did not exist. It is understandable that no one thought of securities investment when Japan was under severe inflation and average people were managing barely enough to eat.

In 1948, the government decided to establish a law to reopen the securities exchange. While the government thought that it would be enough to add a slight modification to the former Securities Exchange Law of Japan,[14] GHQ did not approve it so that it ended up rewriting the law using the Securities Act of 1933[15] and the Securities Exchange Act of 1934[16, 17] as the models and issued the Japanese Securities Exchange Law[18] as a result. However, although GHQ approved it once, it changed its mind and caused the government to scrap it. The new Securities Exchange Law of Japan was rewritten this time based on the US laws (the Securities Act of 1933 and the Securities Exchange Act of 1934) and finally made public on April 13, 1947 and enacted on May 6 of the same year, which is still the law today.[19] What should be noted here is that items which later caused very large effects on securities, financial and corporate businesses were included in the law based on a strong request from GHQ. They are: separation of securities business, particularly underwriting business, from financial institutions such as banks and trust companies,[20] preparation of financial

---

[13] See note 1 *supra*.

[14] For the former Securities Exchange Laws before the World War II, see, "History of the Ministry of Finance", http://www.mof.go.jp/zaimu/50nenn/main/000200.htm.

[15] 15 U.S.C. §§77a-77mm (1934), as amended, 15 U.S.C.§§77a-77mm (1970).

[16] 2 15 U.S.C. §§78a-78jj (1934), as amended, 15 U.S.C.§§78a-78hh (1).

[17] GHQ means General Headquarters. For the period of 1945–51, General Douglas MacArthur was Supreme Commander for the Allied Powers, or SCAP. For the details, see MacArthur and the Japanese Occupation (1945–1951), http://wgordon.web.wesleyan.edu/ papers/alliedoc.htm.

[18] Law No. 22, 1947.

[19] See, note 3.

[20] The financial institutions which are prohibited from conducting securities business are banks, trust companies, insurance companies, mutual loan companies, and money market

statements[21] and regulation of the soliciting method for proxy voting of listed stocks,[22] all of which later became the targets of discussions. With this historical background, it is now appropriate to evaluate the efficacy of the Japanese securities regulations which are basically the transplanted practice and systems of the US origin to Japan with Japanese modifications tailored to the needs of the markets since then. Almost fifty-five years have passed since the general securities legislation was adopted from the US. It is now appropriate to evaluate the efficacy and functioning of the total regulations in light of the current Japanese markets needs which are very internationalized. In the Japanese stock market, the number of shares held by non-Japanese investors is about 20% and the sales volume by them is about 50%.[23]

Rationalization of Disclosure

While the importance of proper disclosures in the securities exchange market is always expected to increase more, it is also necessary to restrain the scope of information within a sufficient and necessary range in accordance with the needs of investors in order to prevent thinning of information.

Two revisions were made in the Revised Law: revision of the prospectus system and revision of Takeover Bids ("TOB").

Revision of prospectus system

The new law defines prospectus as "a document describing the business and other matters of the issuer who issues negotiable securities for offering or solicitations of sales, which will be provided to interested parties or when such a document is requested by interested parties,"[24]

---

dealers. See Article 65, Section 1 of the Securities Exchange Law and Article 1–9 of its Enforcement Regulations.

[21] *Id.*

[22] *Id.*

[23] For the details of data, see Nomura Securities, http://www.nomura.co.jp/terms/japan/ka/gai_tousika.html.

[24] The Revised Law, Article 2, Section 10.

and defines all other representations through documents other than prospectuses, drawings, verbal exchanges, the Internet, etc., used for the purpose of public offering of securities as "reference materials". [25] Consequently, items such as a "summary prospectus" that summarizes the contents of a regular prospectus and a "tombstone prospectus" that informs only the place where a prospectus is delivered are included in the "reference materials," thus allowing to eliminate the regulations concerning summary and tombstone prospectuses from the previous law. [26]

The contents of a prospectus are items that need to be included in the Securities Registration Statement[27] (including Corrected Prospectus) and special notations[28] same as in the previous law. However, in order to better serve the needs of all types of investors, prospectuses are divided into two categories, i.e., those that are obligated to be delivered automatically to all investors (Delivered Prospectus),[29] and those that are to be delivered immediately when requested by investors (Requested Prospectus).[30] The contents of each category of prospectuses (Delivered Prospectus, Requested Prospectus and Corrected Prospectus) are defined separately in accordance with their respective purposes. [31] More specifically, the contents of the Securities Registration Statement are divided into:

1) Information that can materially affect the investor's investment judgment;

2) Information that can seriously affect the investor's investment judgment; and

3) Information laid open to the public.

---

[25] *Id.*, Article 13, Section 5.

[26] Article 13, Sections 3 and 5 of the previous law.

[27] See *supra* note 3.

[28] According to Article 14 of the Cabinet Order concerning disclosures of corporations' businesses. (MOF Ordinance, No.5,1973). For the details of this MOF Ordinance, see http://www.fsa.go.jp/news/newsj/16/syouken/f-20050308-1.html.

[29] Revised Law, Article 15, Section 2.

[30] Revised Law, Article 15, Section 3.

[31] Revised Law, Article 15, Section 3.

It also says that the Delivered Prospectus is to contain the information 1), while the Requested Prospectus is to contain the information 2).[32]

Moreover, in addition to the rule of the previous law that the obligation of delivering prospectuses is pardoned in case when securities are offered or obtained by qualified institutional investors, the Revised Law provides that the obligation of delivering prospectuses is also pardoned in the following cases as well:[33]

1) When investors who own the same brand of securities agree mutually that they do not desire to receive the prospectus for the particular securities; and

2) When a housemate of an investor has already received the prospectus for the particular securities, the particular investor is certain of receiving it, and further agrees not to receive it.

However, if the agreed investors in the abovementioned cases request the delivery of the prospectus prior to obtaining the particular securities through offerings or solicitations of sales, the prospectuses have to be delivered regardless.[34]

The Revised Law also pardons the securities issuer's obligation of delivering prospectuses in a special case when the Corrected Prospectus is issued without fixing the price in an offering or a solicitation of sales based on the book-building method[35] and such but clearly indicating a

---

[32] *Id.*

[33] Revised Law, Article 15, Section 2, Paragraphs 1 and 2.

[34] *Id.*

[35] There are two kinds of selling and underwriting procedure;

(i) Book Building — in which the underwriters do road shows and take non-binding orders from investors before setting the issue price.

(ii) Auctions — in which the company sets a price range to be used as a non-restrictive guideline for investors, than accepts bids, each specifying a number of shares and a price the investor is willing to pay for them, finally, the market-clearing price set by the investors approximates the real price the shares will command in the market.

In 1997, Japan introduced book building method, an alternative to an auction method of IPO pricing that had been required since 1989. Shortly after its authorization, all IPOs in Japan were priced by book building. The shift occurred despite economic arguments and evidence suggesting that the auction method reduced underpricing.

For details of this shift in Japan, see Kenji Kutsuna and Richard L. Smith, "Issue Cost and Method of IPO Underwriting: Japan's Change from Auction Method Pricing to Book Building", http://ideas.repec.org/p/clm/clmeco/2000-35.html.

specific method of announcing the price at the time when the price is fixed in the future.[36,37] In such a case, the issuer is nonetheless obligated to issue a Corrected Prospectus concerning the particular price, etc.[38]

Revision of TOB system

Reviews and revisions of the Takeover Bids (TOB) system were made this time concerning the range of securities which are the targets of a TOB by parties other than the issuer and the method of announcement in a TOB.

A review was made on the range of the issuers of securities which are to be covered by the TOB system, and a definition was introduced specifying those specific companies as "issuers who are obliged to file financial statements concerning their stocks, etc." among all those companies obligated to file financial reports.[39] This is based on the thought that it is not necessary to extend the TOB regulation to those companies which are obligated to make disclosures continually simply because they issued company bonds. More specifically, the stocks and such of a company whose stocks and such correspond to one of those listed below are the target of the regulation:

1. Stocks listed on the securities exchange.
2. Stocks listed for over-the-counter trading and such.
3. Stocks for which Securities Registration Statements were filed in connection with offerings and solicitations.
4. Stocks and such that are issued by a company that corresponds to a standard: more than 500 shareholders existed at the end of at least one of the most recent five years.

Since the nature of investment trusts and investment securities issued by an investment corporation based on the law concerning investment

---

[36] A cabinet order is expected to be issued specifying a particular method such as "in addition to an announcement to be carried by a major daily newspaper, additional announcements must be made on the issuer's and underwriter's websites" or something to that effect. See Revised Law, Article 15, Sections 4 and 5.

[37] Revised Law, Article 15, Section 2, Paragraphs 1 and 2.

[38] The revised rule concerning prospectuses went into effect on December 1, 2004.

[39] Revised Law, Article 27-2, Section 1.

funds is considered equal to that of stocks, so that it was decided to include them in securities that are the target of the TOB system considering the purpose of the TOB system. More specifically, investment trusts and securities are added to the list of securities that are covered by the TOB system under the Implementation Order of the Securities Exchange Law. [40] As a consequence, the expression "company" in the regulation of the Securities Exchange Law is changed to "issuer." [41]

The publication method in the TOB was also reviewed this time. From the standpoint of improving the agility of the procedure for announcing the start of a TOB in order to reduce the cost of publication while maintaining a high capability of informing shareholders and investors, it was decided to expand the method. [42] A preparation was made for enhancing the regulation which will later be made official through a legislative decree. [43] As a means of enhancement of the regulation, the government is expected to implement "electronic publication methods using the Internet" in addition to "announcements to be carried by major daily newspapers." The electronic publication shall be implemented through the electronic publication system in Japan: EDINET (Electronic Disclosure for Investors' NETwork). [44,45]

Legalization of Securities Brokerage Business by Banks

Article 65 of the previous Securities Exchange Law was the fortress defending the securities industry. In other words, the article prevented banks, trust banks, insurance companies, mutual loan companies and credit unions from entering into securities business. [46] The reason was

---

[40] Law No. 321, September 30, 1965 (hereinafter Implementation Order).

[41] Revised Law, Article 2-2, Paragraph 1.

[42] *Id.* Article 27-3, Section 1.

[43] *Id.*

[44] For the details of EDINET, see http://info.edinet.go.jp/EdiHtml/main.htm.

[45] Among these revised regulations due to the review of the TOB, the revision of the range of issuers of securities covered by the TOB system and the revision of the range of securities to be targeted were implemented on December 1, 2004, and the revision of the publication method according to the TOB system was implemented on April 1, 2005.

[46] Securities Exchange Law, Article 65, Section 1, Implementation Order, Article 1-2.

that while there was no separation between financial business and securities business prior to the end of WWII, it was considered necessary to avoid concentrations of economic power such as financial institutions' operating the two businesses, and to let securities companies to stand on their own feet by encouraging and supporting them. There was also a secondary reason that preventing banks from entering into securities business, which is a speculative business, helps them to be more secure in protecting depositors' money which is their most important responsibility.

However, as a result of an amendment of the Securities Exchange Law in 2003,[47] the Securities Brokerage System was enacted from the standpoint of enriching the sales venues and implemented as of April 1, 2004. As a result, any individual or company can operate a securities brokerage business on consignment of securities companies, so long as they are licensed by the Prime Minister,[48] but financial institutions such as banks (hereinafter called "banks") [49] were excluded from the abovementioned rule as they were basically prohibited from operating securities by Article 65 from the standpoint of conflict of interests between banking and securities industries as well as eliminating the possibility of excessive influence on corporations in general.

There have been concerns on banks handling stocks in consideration of possible uses of their powerful influences on others and classic cases of conflicts of interests such as collecting funds by forcing borrower companies to issue securities to collect funds. However, it was thought meaningful for banks to operate securities brokerage business in enhancing the clients' benefits, enlarging the investor population, and improving the accessibility in regions where securities companies' branches are limited in number, so that the aforementioned restriction was finally lifted at this time implementing sufficient means for preventing the harmful effects at the same time.

---

[47] Law No. 54, May 30, 2003.
[48] Securities Exchange Law, Article 2, Section 11.
[49] The financial institutions which are prohibited from conducting securities business are banks, trust companies, insurance companies, mutual loan companies, and money market dealers See, Article 65, Section 1 of the Securities Exchange Law and Article 1-9 of Enforcement Regulations.

Banks had been able to handle government and municipal bonds, fluidizing merchandises such as CP (commercial papers) and SPC,[50] mutual funds, etc. under license of the Prime Minister,[51] but the lifting of bans on securities brokerage business of the Revised Law has now enabled them to handle all kinds of securities[52] including stocks, company bonds, foreign government bonds (hereinafter called "stocks and such") within the range of brokerage of buying and selling and soliciting activities. It does not require banks to acquire additional licenses as securities brokers[53] in addition to the existing license as financial institutions. However, they are bound by the condition that they can handle stocks and such only under commissions from securities companies.[54]

While banks had been basically prohibited from operating securities business under Article 65, Section 1, they had been allowed to operate certain securities business as exceptions according to Article 65, Section 2 (hereinafter called "licensed securities business") so that the newly released securities brokerage business have similar accommodations under Article 65, Section 2, Paragraph 3 and Paragraph 4.Different from securities brokerage firms, banks are in such a business as handling of savings under Banking Law[55] for the businesses that are controlled by financial regulations, so that they are not controlled by such regulations that cover securities brokerage firms prohibiting them from providing cash and securities depositary services[56] or clarify the employers'

---

[50] Commercial papers issued by special purpose companies. For the details, see http://www.azsa.or.jp/b_info/letter/16/01.html.

[51] Revised Law, Article 65-2, Section 1.

[52] The securities that are allowed to be handled by banks by the Revised Law include stocks, preferred investment securities, subscription certificates, covered warrants, depositary receipts, corporate bond certificates, special corporation bonds, foreign government bonds, and foreign municipal bonds. See, Revised Law, Article 65-2, Section 1.

[53] Revised Law, Article 66-2.

[54] *Id.*

[55] The Banking Law of Japan, Law No. 59 of 1981[hereinafter Banking Law], *available at* http://law.e-gov.go.jp/cgi-bin/idxsearch.cg.

[56] *Id.* Article 66-12.

responsibilities for securities companies and such that consign the sales of securities.[57]

As to the points of personnel and organizational isolations between lending and securities brokerage departments, prohibition of sending and receiving classified information, and disclosure obligation of fund usages, it is expected to be defined by a future cabinet order. As to the handling of personal information, banks are obligated to operate properly under Personal Information Protection Law of 2003.[58] As to securing the effectiveness of these problem countermeasures, the Committee for Monitoring Securities Trading[59] has found some illegal activities so far and the committee is expected to make sure in securing the effectiveness through enhancement of its market monitoring function and system.

Banks can enter securities business through their subsidiaries as well[60] and banks are also now eligible for brokering the trading and handle offering of stocks and such by the recent revision of the law. However, banks are still prohibited from underwriting stocks and such by themselves.[61] As to this point, it is believed that it is still premature to make any fundamental revisions on the range of business for banks as (1) the conflict of interest and the possibility of abuse by banks of their overwhelmingly powerful positions that were the basis of consideration for Article 65 are still critical subjects of discussions and (2) the first order of business for the banks is now to regain citizens' trusts on banks by solving the bad debt issue.

The present revision is based on the viewpoint that a bank will provide a broad range of financial products as a one-stop-provider in the future, although it many not be as a direct provider, but at least indirectly as a financial service agency, for the convenience of clients, while advancing differentiation and specialization of the functions as a financial brokerage institution in terms of operations and supplies of

---

[57] *Id.* Article 66-22.
[58] Law No. 57, May 30, 2003. The law was implemented in April 2005. For the details, see http://www5.cao.go.jp/seikatsu/kojin/houritsu/index.html.
[59] This committee belongs to Ministry of Finance. For the details, MOF web: http://www.mof.go.jp/search/hpsearch.php.
[60] Financial System Reform Law (Law No. 87, June 26, 1992) (http://www.fsa.go.jp/p_fsa/guide/guidej/yokin/y008.html).
[61] Securities Exchange Law, Article 65.

funds on the other hand. However, the present revision is not to deviate substantially from the basic concept of Article 65 that basically prohibits banks from performing securities businesses.

Since the securities businesses are allowed for banks in the present revision based on the government's proper inspections of each bank whether it has a proper internal control system on the points of personnel and organizational isolations between lending and securities brokerage departments, the legalization is considered to be dependent on the government's authorization of each application for the permit. Irrespective of whether the checking is done before or after the authorization, any harmful effect under the permit ruling shall be clearly defined by law and any improper conducts shall be punished accordingly by the governing agency.

Securities brokerage businesses by banks are legalized as of December 1, 2004. Any financial institutions which have been conducting securities businesses such as sales of mutual funds are to start securities brokerage businesses by registering changes in the Business and Service Documents with Ministry of Finance.[62]

Enrichment of Institutional Framework for Competition Among Stock Exchanges

Reform of financial system

Securities are traded on 220 exchanges around the world. In the fast-moving global markets, investors and broker/dealers need to monitor real-time prices and keep abreast of market news to make informed decisions. They also require reliable electronic trading systems which provide liquidity in their markets. Institutional investors aim to achieve best price and execution on their orders. They need trading systems which give them insight into trading patterns and access to a large pool of brokers. They also want trading systems that are quick and easy to use

---

[62] For the changes in Business and Service Documents prepared by each banks, see MOF Securities Division Ordinance dated March 31, 1983 (http://www.mof.go.jp/zaimu/40nenn/main/020302.htm).

and which allow them to direct orders to multiple brokers in the market from a single platform.

They want trading systems integrated within their information services to let them review stock market data and order indications on one screen. To keep track of progress, they look for systems which enable them to check order status and the value of executed trades in real time and to generate electronic reports.

Japan is not an exception to that needs. In order to provide different platforms for fund acquisition for a company in accordance with its different growth steps and a variety of attractive funds operating targets for an individual in Japan, several measures were taken including (1) stock exchange concentration is abolished and the proprietary transaction system (PTS)[63] was introduced as a platform for extra-stock-exchange transactions, (2) over-the-counter stock exchange was positioned as an equivalent venue as the stock exchange, and (3) a green sheets market[64] was established in July 1997 by the Japan Securities Dealers Association (JSDA)[65] as an exchange platform for unlisted stocks.

This was planned in the present reform of the financial system in order to make the Tokyo Stock Exchange[66] comparable with the New York Stock Exchange[67] and London Stock Exchange[68] as an international stock exchange, and in the considerations that the growth of the

---

[63] End-to-end electronic trade processing has become a vital factor in the drive to increase efficiency and risk control. Trading systems must integrate seamlessly with other in-house and third-party systems if financial institutions are to manage their risk and automate trade settlement effectively. For the details of Japanese PTS, see the web. of PTS(http://www.pts-info.jp/).

[64] The green sheets market in Japan is equivalent to the pink sheets market in the US for trading unlisted securities. For the details of Japanese green sheets market, see Japanese financial words dictionary, http://www.findai.com/yogo/0008.htm. For the details of the US pink sheet s market, see http://www.pinksheets.com/.

[65] JSDA is an association of securities companies and dealers active in Japan. The mission is to promote the further development of the Japanese securities market and the enhancement of investors' confidence. For the details, see the web: http://www.jsda.or.jp/html/eigo/index.html.

For the legal basis of the establishment of the green sheets market in Japan, see Securities Exchange Law, art. 2-8-7.

[66] For the details, see the web: http://www.tse.or.jp/.

[67] For the details, see the web: http://www.nyse.com/.

[68] For the details, see the web: http://www.londonstockexchange.com/.

Proprietary Trading System (PTS)[69] contributed in the competition among the stock exchanges in the US, the NASDAQ[70] market became as active as the NYSE, and wide range of unlisted stocks are exchanged on the pinks sheet in the US.[71]

As to the abolishment of the obligation of stock exchange concentration, it was decided that a transaction shall be executed in the stock exchange unless the client specifies an out-of-stock-exchange transaction (basic rule of the stock exchange) because, different from the US, there is no system in Japan for automatically transferring an order to a market which provides the optimum condition for the client, and the price determining method in the PTS[72] was restricted by law in order to differentiate it from the stock exchange. This institutional restriction on PTS had been pointed out as the cause of inactiveness in the PTS, so that it was decided to advance the institutional reform one step further as the expansion of out-of-stock-exchange transactions is considered effective in improving the incentive toward the more efficient operation of the stock exchange itself and bringing about more effective competitions among stock exchanges. It is decided to secure the equal footing in the competition between the stock exchange and the PTS, introduce the best execution obligation for securities companies revising the basic rule of the stock exchange, and allow the PTS to use the same price determining method as the stock exchange, i.e., price determination through auctioning. It was decided also for the green sheet market[73] to raise its recognition among people by defining its rules in the Securities Exchange Law similar to what is done for the over-the-counter exchange

---

[69] For the development of PTS in the U.S. see, for example, Reuters, http://about.reuters. com/pressoffice/history/technology.asp.

[70] See the web. http://www.nasdaq.com/.

[71] A company whose shares are traded on the so-called "pink sheets" in the U.S .is commonly one that does not meet the minimal criteria for capitalization and number of shareholders that are required by the NASDAQ and OTC and most exchanges to be listed there. The "pink sheet" designation is a holdover from the days when the quotes for these stocks were printed on pink paper. For the details, see http://www.pinksheets.com/.

[72] For Japanese PTS, see the press release of Tokyo Stock Exchange of April 30, 2002 (http://www.jsda.or.jp/html/kisoku/pdf/c015.pdf).

[73] Currently 90 issues are listed in the green sheets market in Japan. See the details, the web. of the Green Sheet in Japan: http://www.jsda.or.jp/html/greensheet/.

in the reforming of the financial system so that it can be operated with a higher reliability under the unfair transaction controlling rule.

The securing of transparency in the stock exchange is considered most important for operating a fair and efficient exchange market both in the US and Japan.[74] Similar to what is being done in the US, the obligations of reporting, notifying and publicizing prices and such by the stock exchange and the Japan Securities Dealers Association (JSDA)[75] will be expanded in conjunction with the introduction of the best execution responsibility of securities companies and clarification of the position of the green sheet in the Securities Exchange Law.[76,77]

Best execution obligation

The best execution policy defines the policy and method with which a securities company is to execute a transaction for a client at the most suitable condition for the client in accordance with the revised Securities Exchange Law.[78] When a securities company is contracted to trade securities, the company has an obligation to trade the securities with a goodwill manager's care under the will of the trust.[79] The goodwill manager's obligation is construed to include the fiduciary duty of the securities company to take rational cares in executing a trade to maximize the client's benefit.[80] The best execution obligation is considered as a part of the fiduciary duty of loyalty on the common law

---

[74] See, Transparency and Market Fragmentation, IOSCO, November 2001. (http://www.iosco.org/ library/pubdocs/pdf/IOSCOPD124.pdf).

[75] See the fair market rules on PTS established by the Tokyo Stock Exchange and JSDA dated on March 15,2005(http://www.pts-info.jp/).

[76] Revised Law, Articles 79-2, 79-3, 79-4, 116, and 117. By the revision, the green sheets market is now regulated by the Securities Exchange Law from April 1, 2005. For the details, see the web. of Green Sheet (http://www.jsda.or.jp/html/greensheet/info.html).

[77] All these rulings were implemented as of April 1, 2005.

[78] Article 43-2, Section 1.

[79] Article 644, Civil Law of Japan, Law No. 89, April 27, 1896. For the details, see http://www.houko.com/00/01/M29/089.HTM.

[80] KANZAKI, Takuro. "Securing Best Execution of Investor's Orders" Investment Vol. 50, No. 4 (1997) p. 6. For specifics, see the website of Nihon Shoken Daikousha.

in the US, and it is clearly stated that securities companies are obligated to conduct under NYSE regulation and NASDA regulation.[81]

Concerning the best execution obligation, it is considered appropriate in Japan that due to the fact that it is most suitable for the investors' benefits to have the trading of stocks to be executed in stock exchanges, the obligation of a securities company is to execute the trading of stocks considering not only prices but also various other factors such as cost, speed and capability of execution, decide on its own and present a specific execution method to its client, and provide reports and announcements whether the transaction is done accordingly.[82]

Although the price is the most meaningful factor in the execution of the best execution obligation, the speed and sureness of the execution are also considered important. How does a securities company act specifically is unpredictable as it depends on the securities market condition and the particular client's preference. It is also being pointed out in the US that the concept of the best execution obligation is getting blur and the problem is becoming more complicated due to increased varieties of venues of transactions and trading practices such as the introductions of PTS,[83] payment for order flow,[84] preferencing,[85]

---

[81] NYSE regulation 123A and NASDA regulation 2320. For the details, see OHSAKI, Sadakazu. "What is Best Execution Duty?" Capital Market Quarterly, Vol. 1, No. 1 (1998), p. 83. The description of the best execution in the US below this line owes greatly to this article.

[82] For the example, see the case of The Shinko Security Company (http://www.shinko-sec.co.jp/shikkou.htmlof Japan).

[83] See the note 63 *supra*.

[84] As a way to attract orders from brokers, some exchanges or market-makers pay broker's firm for routing the order to them, perhaps a penny or more per share. This is called "payment for order flow." Payment for order flow is one of the ways your broker's firm can make money from executing the trade. For the details, see The SEC release, March 17, 2000 (http://www.sec.gov/answers/payordf.htm).

[85] The term "preferencing" is defined in Section 510(c)(3) of the National Securities Markets Improvement Act of 1996 ("NSMIA"), [Pub. L. No. 104-290, 110 Stat. 3416 (1996).] as "the practice of a broker acting as a dealer on a national securities exchange, directing the orders of customers to buy or sell securities to itself for execution under rules that permit the broker to take priority in execution over same-priced orders or quotations entered prior in time." For the details, see SEC release, April 15,1997 (http://www.sec.gov/news/studies/prefrep.htm).

internalization.[86,87]

According to the recent revision of the law, securities companies have decided to determine a policy and a method for executing trading of stocks under optimum transaction conditions (hereinafter called "policy"),[88] make an announcement of such a policy, and operate accordingly, concerning clients' orders of securities trading, including forward dealings on foreign markets securities, and over-the-counter derivatives trading. In particular, it was decided that, upon receiving an order from a client for trading securities listed on the securities exchange board or securities traded over the counter, a securities company is to provide a document describing the policy concerning the particular transaction, and a document describing how the particular order is executed in accordance with the best execution policy and such after the order is executed. These documents are allowed to be done electronically.[89]

Moreover, it was decided that (1) pre-trade disclosure is not required if a qualified institutional investor agrees since a qualified investor is normally capable of verifying the policy and such of its own transaction[90] and (2) rulings prohibiting counter bucket trading and bucket

---

[86] When an order is placed to buy or sell a stock, the broker has choices on where to execute the order. Instead of routing the order to a market or market-makers for execution, the broker may fill the order from the firm's own inventory. This is called "internalization." In this way, the broker's firm may make money on the "spread" which is the difference between the purchase price and the sale price. For the details, see SEC release, March 20,2000 (http://www.sec.gov/answers/payordf.htm).

[87] OHSAKI, Sadakazu. "On Regulation NMS (National Market System) — Trends in Review of Stock Market Regulation in US" Capital Market Quarterly, Vol. 7, No. 4 (2004), p. 18. The SEC of the U.S. proposed on February 26, 2004, Regulation NMS, which is intended to modernize the regulations governing the US equity markets to better address current market conditions. The national market system (NMS) was created in the 1970s under § 11A of the Securities Exchange Act of 1934, which grants the SEC rulemaking authority to assure equal regulation of all markets for NMS securities. For the details, see SEC Release, October 24,2005 (http://www.sec.gov/spotlight/regnms.htm).

[88] See the announcement by JSDA dated on March 15, 2005 as to "The introduction of best execution obligation," (http://www.jsda.or.jp/html/oshirase/public/050209041.pdf).

[89] Revised Law, Article 43-2.

[90] Deletion of the previous Article 38.

trading[91,92] since there is little chance that a client's benefit is affected due to bucket trading as long as securities are traded based on the policy. If we understand the contents of the best execution obligation as described in the above, we would not be able to claim that the result of a trading is against this article because it turned out to be less than the best achievable by simply focusing on the price. On the other hand, as it was argued in the Newton v. Merrill Lynch case[93] in the US, it is a questionable act to determine an execution method to enjoy a spread without taking any risk by indicating the best quotation on the NASDAQ market, which is less profitable than a price technically achievable by using PTS, playing the role of a trading partner itself, and canceling it out with a better price using PTS on its own position; it is considered a violation of this article in Japan.

Improvement of price forming function of transaction system by PTS

On December 1, 1998, "Law Concerning Improvement of Laws Related to Financial System Reform" (hereinafter called "Financial System Reform Law") was introduced materializing the so-called "Japanese-style Big Ban," which carried a banner reading a "Free, Fair, and Global" system in the form of a law, and the Security Exchange Law went through a substantial revision simultaneously.[94]

---

[91] Deletion of the previous Articles 39 and 129.

[92] Bucket tradings are sometimes called the boiler room trading in the US. The US has laws restricting bucket trading practices by limiting the ability of brokerage houses to create and trade certain types of over-the-counter securities. Bucket shops would do trades all day long, throwing the ticket into a bucket. At the end of the day they would decide which accounts to award the winning and losing trades. For the details, see Investopedia (http://www.investopedia.com/terms/b/bucketshop.asp).

In the counter bucket trading, the security company represents both sides for the same transaction. For the details, see Cabinet Order of March 27, 2001 (http://www.soumu.go.jp/s-news/2005/pdf/050603_2_03.pdf).

[93] United States court of appeals for the third circuit (no. 96-5045) Kenneth E. Newton; MLPF&S Cust. Bruce Zakheim Ira FBO Bruce Zakheim v. Merrill, Lynch, Pierce, Fenner & Smith, inc.; Painewebber inc.; Dean Witter Reynolds (d.c. no. 94-cv-05343) (opinion filed January 30, 1998). See http://lw.bna.com/lw/19980210/965045.htm.

[94] Law No. 107, October 13, 1998. For the detail. see Diet Release (No. 143) (http://www.shugiin.go.jp/itdb_housei.nsf/html/housei/kaiji143_l.htm).

Consequently, the obligation which had been imposed on all transactions concerning stocks listed on the stock exchange to be centrically conducted at the stock exchange was removed, thus allowing transactions of stocks listed on the stock exchange to be conducted outside of the stock exchange. At the same time, a regulation concerning the Proprietary Trading System ("PTS") was added to the Security Exchange Law [95] in order to improve the convenience of investors through competitions among different markets. In other words, PTS was officially recognized as a part of the securities industry. [96]

According to the Revised Securities Exchange, the Proprietary Trading System is defined as "trading of securities, or mediation, brokerage, or representation thereof, conducted using electronic information processing institutions with a plurality of parties acting as a party or individual parties of the transaction performed in accordance with the price determining method shown below or a method similar to it." [97] As securities companies were introducing PTS as a part of the securities industry, there was an anticipation of a new securities transaction system having a highly advanced collective and systematic contract formation capability, i.e., a phenomenal jump from the traditional method relying on telephone or face-to-face contracts.

PTS is also called ATS (Alternative Trading System) [98] or ECN (Electronic Communications Network) [99] and it is actively operating and collecting a substantial amount of orders in the U.S. Under the

---

[95] Article 2, Section 8.
[96] For PTS, see webpage of the Japan Securities Dealers Association (JSDA) (http://www.pts-info.jo/html/pts001.html).
[97] Article 2, Section 8, Paragraph 7.
[98] On December 8, 1998, the SEC of the U.S. adopted new rules and rule amendments to allow alternative trading systems to choose whether to register as national securities exchanges, or to register as broker-dealers and comply with additional requirements under Regulation ATS, depending on their activities and trading volume. For the details, see Securities Exchange Act Release No. 40760 (Dec. 8, 1998), 63 FR 70844 (December 22, 1998) ("Adopting Release") (http://www.sec.gov/rules/final/34-43651.htm).
[99] Electronic Communications Networks(ECNs), as defined in Rule 600(b)(23) of Regulation NMS in the U.S., are electronic trading systems that automatically match buy and sell orders at specified prices. ECNs register with the SEC as broker-dealers and are subject to Regulation Alternative trading System. For the details, see the SEC's release of November 4, 2005 (http://www.sec.gov/divisions/marketreg/mrecn.shtml).

circumstance, in introducing PTS, an unknown territory, into Japan, it was decided to have at least a minimum amount of restrictions, i.e., an authorization process, in order to protect investors. PTS is now allowed to use the same price determining method as the stock exchange, i.e., price determination through auctioning. Thus, it was decided to differentiate PTS from the stock exchange based on the transaction volume instead of the price forming function which was the case in the past, now requiring PTS to apply for authorization as an exchange when the amount of transaction exceeds a certain limit.[100]

Green sheet market

Green Sheet Market was established in July 1997 in Japan and operated by the Japan Securities Dealers Association (JSDA) as a securities market in which the shares of unlisted companies can be traded.[101] In August 2002, the Financial Service Agency's program to energize the securities market called for market expansion. In response, in April 2003 the JSDA revised its regulations and set up a market system intended to function alongside the over-the-counter (OTC) market.

The issues are classified as emerging (venture companies and companies aiming for growth), phoenix (companies whose shares have been delisted for trading), regional (other companies) and investment trusts and special purpose companies (SPC).[102] As of June 30, 2004, 83 issues were listed in the Green Sheet Market, and of these 59 were emerging issues. About 50 issues in the emerging issues category were registered as new issues over two years, and currently two to three new issues are registered every month. In July 2003 JSDA's system was approved as a personal trading system (PTS) by the FSA and the Green Sheet trading system began operating. JSDA implemented a number of improvements to the market system to enhance its functionality as an essentially OTC market.

---

[100] Revised Law, Article 2-8-7-(i).

[101] For the characteristics of the Green Sheet Market in Japan, see Japanese FSA's public release of September 30, 2005 (http://www.fsa.go.jp/en/newsletter/2005/11d.html).

[102] For the SPC, see Nomura dictionary (http://www.nomura.co.jp/terms/english/s/spc.html).

Investors of "green sheet" stocks[103] are generally known to be those who are responding to new stock offerings within family circles, are not generally familiar with stocks, and tend to own stocks for long periods, so that they have a potential of providing a new group of personal investors of a wide range once the green sheet is used widely among small to medium sized corporations. As a result, it was decided to regulate green sheet stocks under the securities exchange law similar to the over-the-counter market order to make it a more reliable system.

More specifically, "those securities that are not prohibited of solicitations of trading and other transactions according to the rulings of the JSDA[104] among stocks, corporate bonds with new share warrant right, and other securities defined by the cabinet order (except securities listed on the stock exchange and over-the-counter securities)" are defined as "handled securities," which require the handling parties to issue documents describing the outlines of transactions before the contracts are finalized,[105] and file reports to the JSDA,[106] and which will also be covered under the Insider Trading Control Regulations.[107]

As to "handled securities" in the over-the-counter securities, the plan of bring them under the control of the regulations concerning market manipulations[108] was shelved, but they are controlled by general regulations prohibiting illegal transactions[109] and prohibiting spreading rumors,[110] so that spreading rumors with an intention of changing the market prices of these securities, for example, will be punishable as a violation of article of prohibiting spreading rumors (by a jail term of five years or less or a fine of less than five million yen).[111]

---

[103] See note 64 *supra*.
[104] See the web. of JSDA (Green Sheet) (http://www.jsda.or.jp/html/greensheet/index.html).
[105] The Revised Law, Article 40, Section 1, Paragraph 1.
[106] The Revised Law, Article 79, Section 2, Paragraphs 1 and 3, Article 160.
[107] The Revised Law, Article 163–167.
[108] The Securities Exchange Law, Article 159.
[109] *Ibid.*, Article 157.
[110] *Ibid.*, Article 158.
[111] *Ibid.*, Article 197, Section 1, Paragraph 7.

Enhancement of Market Monitoring Function and System

Introduction of surcharge system

The market's reliability is expected to improve as the Securities Exchange Surveillance Committee [112] applies various new tools in correspondence with the severity of illegal actions and varieties of styles. As the securities market in Japan becomes more internationalized, it is desirable that the rules that warrant a fair market in Japan match their international counterparts as closely as possible.

On the other hand, the reasons that cause hesitations among the general public in getting involved in the market is not only their insufficient knowledge of securities investments but also their concerns if they will be treated fairly by the market. While there is a wide range of severities in illegality among actual illegal actions, there is a need to apply punishments selectively and in a controlled manner as the punishments affect the violators severely, thus resulting in many illegal actions of lighter nature being unpunished. Noting this reality, a surcharge system was introduced to apply monetary burden on the violators of a certain rules of the Securities Exchange Law as an administrative measure to achieve an administrative goal of upholding the securities exchange laws and regulations effective by making the violators realize that illegal actions do not pay.

The level of the surcharge is set to be equivalent to the economical gain obtained by the illegal act as the necessary minimum level to guarantee the effectiveness of the regulation as this is the first time the regulation is introduced. The following acts are the targets of the surcharge:

---

[112] In the autumn of 1991, an Advisory Committee to the Prime Minister recommended the establishment of an inspections & surveillance commission which is independent from the supervisory function of the Ministry of Finance. Based on the recommendation, the Securities & Exchange Surveillance Commission (SESC) was formally launched on 20th July 1992 within the ambit of the Ministry of Finance. For the details, see the web. of SESC (http://www.fsa.go.jp/sesc/english/aboutsesc/aboutsesc.htm).

1. False descriptions on Securities Registration Statements, i.e., so-called violations of issuance disclosure duty.[113]
2. Violations of rules prohibiting spread of rumors and trickery.[114]
3. Violations of rules prohibiting market manipulation acts.[115]
4. Violations of rules prohibiting insider trading.[116]

The level of the surcharge is set specifically for each type of act in order to avoid the discretion of each administrative agency as much as possible, [117] and no room for discretion is provided for each administrative agency as to whether to order the surcharge payment or not.

These illegal acts have been the targets of criminal punishments, but they are now met by additionally by forfeiture/penalty collection of all assets obtained by the criminal acts, in other words, they will be the targets of necessary forfeiture regulation.[118] An adjustment rule was also provided to deduct the forfeiture/penalty collection amount from the surcharge amount on a political standpoint that it is not necessary to apply surcharge on the entire amount of the economical gain in cases where the assets generated by illegal acts have already been forfeited/collected by the particular rules of the Securities Exchange Law.[119]

Although a surcharge payment order is issued under the name of the Prime Minister officially, judges located at the Financial Services Agency [120] (normally consisting of three judges) are to conduct an examination, open to the public, issue a definitive plan prepared in the course of the examination, and finalize the surcharge payment order.[121]

---

[113] The Securities Exchange Law, Articles 5, 23-3, 23-8.
[114] *Ibid.*, Article 158.
[115] *Ibid.*, Article 159, Section 2, Paragraph 1.
[116] *Ibid.*, Articles 166 and 167.
[117] The Revised Law, Articles 172 through 175.
[118] *Ibid.*, Article 198-2.
[119] *Ibid.* Articles 185-7, 185-8.
[120] *Ibid.*, Article 178 through Article 185-17.
[121] The surcharge system was implemented as of April 1, 2005.

Review of civil responsibility regulation

Although an investor can ask for payment of damages caused by illegal acts of a violator when an investor incurs losses due to violations of the Securities Exchange Law by the violator such as a securities company[122], it is not easy for the investor to prove whether it was caused by an intentional act or negligence of the violator and prove how much of the market price drop is due to the criminal act as the price of securities varies with various factors of the market, thus making it difficult to help the victim.

Therefore, the revised Securities Exchange Law obligates a person who issued a disclosure document with a false statement to compensate for no-fault damages to a person who obtained the related securities without the knowledge of said false statement in the trading market[123] in addition to the existing rule that such a violator is liable to a person who obtained such securities responding to solicitation or offering in the issuing market if such a violator can't proof the no- fault.[124] Also the expiring date of the damage request right is revised from 1 to 3 years.[125]

In order to make easier to prove the damages of investors, it was also made possible to assume the amount calculated by subtracting the average market price during one month after the announcement of a document with a false statement from the average market price during one month prior to the announcement as the loss and damage due to false statement.[126]

However, this assumption is applicable to those who obtained the particular securities within one year prior to the announcement of the false information and still owned the particular securities on the day of the announcement.[127] This is because the rationality of assumption will be lost if the purchase occurred more than one year prior to the announcement of the false information, as the price of the securities can vary with reasons other than the false information, and also those who

---

[122] The Securities Exchange Law, Article 160.
[123] Revised Law, Articles 21-2, Section 1 and 21-3.
[124] The Securities Exchange Law, Articles 18 or 20.
[125] See note 122 *supra.*
[126] The Revised Law, Article 21-2, Section 2 ff.
[127] *Ibid.*

sold the securities before the announcement can not be considered to have incurred any damages due to the false information.

Since this is an assuming rule, neither the victimizer nor the victim is prevented from proving an actual loss different from the assumed amount. If it is difficult to prove, a court can verify such a loss on its judgment.[128, 129]

Expansion of inspection authority of securities exchange surveillance committee

Since the Securities Exchange Surveillance Committee130 (hereinafter SESC) was established coincidentally with certain illegal securities activities, its target is considered to be illegal transactions of domestic as well as foreign securities companies while the Inspection Bureau of the Financial Services Agency [131] is responsible for the monitoring of financial and internal control systems of securities companies, mutual fund trust companies, and investment consulting firms. In its review report by an Advisory Committee to the Prime Minister,[132] the policy was set that the inspection authority shall be expanded and the organization of the SESC shall be enhanced as a part of the overall market monitoring system.

Based on this report, it was decided that the Commissioner of the Financial Services Agency shall be able to commission to the SESC its inspection authority over (1) inspection of the financial and internal control system of securities companies and (2) inspection of mutual fund trust companies and investment consultant companies.[133]

It was stipulated that the SESC should report expeditiously upon a commissioned matter to the Commissioner of the Financial Services Agency. In coordination with the expansion of the inspection range, the

---

[128] *Ibid.*
[129] These rulings were implemented as of December 1, 2004.
[130] See note 112 *supra.*
[131] *Ibid.*
[132] *Ibid.*
[133] The Revised Law, Article 194-6.

range of the SESC's proposal and suggestion was also expanded as well.[134,135]

Conclusion

While the center of economy is a company in today's capitalistic society, the issuance of stocks and bonds is what is characteristic in the method of financing in a company as it is observed from the viewpoint of the legal system. What is instrumental in enabling a company to finance through stocks and bonds is the stock exchange that offers a venue for freely exchanging stocks and bonds, i.e., securities, for money. The importance of securities market and securities exchange conducted there can be easily understood from the fact that each and every capitalistic country has its securities market without exception.

The Securities Exchange Act of 1934,[136] for example, states that the Congress confirms that "The securities markets are an important national asset which must be preserved and strengthened". [137] These words beautifully express the capital market, or securities market is indispensably important in the continuation and expansion of the capitalistic economic system, or more aptly called, free corporate economic system.

However, the securities market, which is an indispensable element of a capitalistic country, cannot achieve its objective if the market is not properly and smoothly operated. It must provide a basis for investors to invest safely. The Securities Exchange Law of Japan[138] is the tool for guaranteeing the needs. When Japan became the world's second largest economic power, internationalization of Japan advanced with a

---

[134] Articles 20 and 21 of the Law on the Establishment of Financial Services Agency. The law was enacted on October 16,1998 as Law No.130. For the details, see http://www.ron.gr.jp/law/law/kinyucho.htm.

[135] The regulation concerning the expansion of these inspection ranges was implemented on July 1, 2005.

[136] See note 16 *supra*.

[137] Article 11-A, Section (a), Paragraph (1) (A).

[138] See note 3 *supra*.

tremendous momentum. When such a fast movement occurs in economy, laws often tend to be unable to catch up with the motion.

This tendency was found in the change that occurred in the Securities Exchange Law of Japan as well. The original Securities Exchange Law[139] was established under guidance of GHQ after WWII and the securities system operated under the tight guard of the United States. For example, the securities business of securities companies were protected and nurtured by the Securities Exchange Law. However, the guard provided by the United States was removed in accordance with the Peace Treaty of 1951 between Japan and the United States,[140] and subsequent economic developments started in the latter half of 1950s. Arrival of freer financial and securities activities, which took off in the latter half of 1960s, introduced various problems which had never been thought of and which cannot be dealt with the existing Securities Exchange Law. Arrival of foreign securities dealers in Japan was one of those problems, which was eventually addressed to by the enactment of "Law Concerning Foreign Securities Dealers," a special law of the Securities Exchange Law.[141]

In so far as domestic problems are concerned, an inter-industrial problem developed related to over-the-counter sales of government bonds at banks, which could not be handled by the Securities Exchange Law, and which led to the revision of the Banking Law.[142] Stock price index future trading, which is unrelated to securities, was introduced in 1988, which was then followed by option trading introduced in 1989, the latter being useful economically but more problematic as it is difficult to be dealt with legally. In 1992, banking operations and securities operations came to be entered mutually through subsidiaries as a reform of the entire financial system across the boarder of the Securities Exchange Law.[143]

This is essentially what had been considered necessary for the securities regulations in Japan since it caused one by one gap between their contents of what happened and the Securities Exchange Law. It is

---

[139] See note 14 *supra.*
[140] For the peace treaty, see http://www.tabiken.com/history/doc/H/H191L200.HTM.
[141] The Law No. of 5, March 3, 1971.
[142] The Law No. of 59, June 1, 1980.
[143] See note 3 *supra.*

unquestionable that the Securities Exchange Law has to be able to deal with these changes, but what is important to be questioned there is the purpose of the Securities Exchange Law. The objective of the current Securities Exchange Law is defined in Article 1, which reads: "The purpose of this law is to make issuance and trading of securities and such to be conducted fairly and distribution of securities to be conducted smoothly in order to contribute to proper operation of national economy and protection of investors." In other words, the ultimate goal of the Securities Exchange Law is the protection of investors. The protection of investors consists of two sides, namely (1) prevention of damages caused by insufficient information and (2) prevention of damages caused by unfair trading. There is no question that the Securities Exchange Law has to grow further to deal with new changes to come in the future. Whatever the future revisions of the Securities Exchange Law bring, they have to be checked against the abovementioned principles of protection of investors, (1) and (2).Whether the present revision functions properly in the market relative to the viewpoints of (1) and (2) has yet to be monitored by the government, industry and investors.

Bibliography

15 U.S.C. §§77a-77mm (1934), as amended, 15 U.S.C.§§77a-77mm (1970).
2 15 U.S.C. §§78a-78jj (1934), as amended, 15 U.S.C.§§78a-78hh (1).
Article 11-A, Section (a), Paragraph (1) (A).
Article 2, Section 8, Paragraph 7.
Article 2, Section 8.
Article 43-2, Section 1.
Banking Law of Japan, Law No. 59 of 1981, http://law.e-gov.go.jp/cgi-bin/idxsearch.cg.
Banking Law, Article 66-12.
Banking Law, Article 66-22.
Cabinet Order, March 27, 2001, http://www.soumu.go.jp/s-news/2005/pdf/050603_2_03.pdf.
Civil Law of Japan, Law No.89, April 27, 1896, Article 644.
Commercial papers issued by special purpose companies. For the details, see http://www.azsa.or.jp/b_info/letter/16/01.html.
Diet Release (No.143), Law No. 107, October 13, 1998, http://www.shugiin.go.jp/itdb_housei.nsf/html/housei/kaiji143_1.htm.
EDINET, see http://info.edinet.go.jp/EdiHtml/main.htm.
Enforcement Regulations, Article 1-9.

Fair Market Rules on PTS established by the Tokyo Stock Exchange and JSDA, March 15, 2005, http://www.pts-info.jp/.

Financial System Reform Law (Law No. 87, June 26, 1992) (http://www.fsa.go.jp/ p_fsa/guide/guidej/yokin/y008.html).

Green Sheet in Japan, http://www.jsda.or.jp/html/greensheet/.

History of the Ministry of Finance, http://www.mof.go.jp/zaimu/50nenn/main/ 000200.htm.

Horei, http://law.e-gov.go.jp/cgi-bin/idxsearch.cgi.

IOSCO, Transparency and Market Fragmentation, November, 2001, http://www.iosco. org/library/pubdocs/pdf/IOSCOPD124.pdf.

Implementation Order, Law No. 321, September 30, 1965.

Implementation Order, Article 1-2.

Investopedia, Bucketshop, http://www.investopedia.com/terms/b/bucketshop.asp.

Japan Securities Dealers Association (JSDA), PTS, http://www.pts-info.jo/html/ pts001.html.

Japanese Financial Words Dictionary, Japanese green sheets market, http://www.findai. com/yogo/0008.htm.

Japanese FSA, Public Release of September 30, 2005, http://www.fsa.go.jp/en/ newsletter/2005/11d.html.

Japanese PTS, see the website of PTS, http://www.pts-info.jp/.

JSDA (Green Sheet), http://www.jsda.or.jp/html/greensheet/index.html.

JSDA website, http://www.jsda.or.jp/html/eigo/index.html.

JSDA, "The introduction of best execution obligation," March 15, 2005, http://www.jsda. or.jp/html/oshirase/public/050209041.pdf.

Kanzaki, Takuro. "Securing Best Execution of Investor's Orders" Investment Vol. 50, No. 4 (1997) p. 6.

Kutsuna, Kenji and Smith, Richard L., "Issue Cost and Method of IPO Underwriting: Japan's Change from Auction Method Pricing to Book Building", http://ideas.repec.org/p/clm/clmeco/2000-35.html.

Law No. 57, May 30, 2003. The law was implemented in April 2005, http://www5.cao.go.jp/seikatsu/kojin/houritsu/index.html.

Law on the Establishment of Financial Services Agency, Articles 20 and 21.Law enacted on October 16, 1998 as Law No. 130, http://www.ron.gr.jp/law/law/kinyucho.htm.

London Stock Exchange, http://www.londonstockexchange.com/.

MacArthur and the Japanese Occupation (1945–1951), http://wgordon.web.wesleyan. edu/papers/alliedoc.htm.

Misawa, Mitsuru. *Securities Regulation in Japan*. 6 Vand. J. Transnational L. 447 (1973).

Misawa, Mitsuru. *Tokyo as an International Capital Market — It's Economic and Legal Aspects*. 8 Vand. J. Transnational L. 1 (1974).

MOF Ordinance, Article 14, see http://www.fsa.go.jp/news/newsj/16/syouken/f-20050308-1.html.

MOF Securities Division Ordinance, dated March 31, 1983 http://www.mof.go.jp/zaimu/ 40nenn/main/020302.htm.

MOF website, http://www.mof.go.jp/search/hpsearch.php.

Nasdaq, http://www.nasdaq.com/.

New York Stock Exchange, http://www.nyse.com/.

Newton, Kenneth E., United States court of appeals for the third circuit (no. 96-5045); MLPF&S Cust. Bruce Zakheim Ira FBO Bruce Zakheim v. Merrill, Lynch, Pierce, Fenner & Smith, inc.; Painewebber inc.; Dean Witter Reynolds (d.c. no. 94-cv-05343) (opinion filed January 30, 1998), http://lw.bna.com/lw/19980210/965045.htm.

Nomura Dictionary, SPC, http://www.nomura.co.jp/terms/english/s/spc.html.

Nomura Securities, http://www.nomura.co.jp/terms/japan/ka/gai_tousika.html.

Ohsaki, Sadakazu. "On Regulation NMS(National Market System) — Trends in Review of Stock Market Regulation in US" Capital Market Quarterly, Vol. 7, No. 4 (2004), p. 18.

Ohsaki, Sadakazu. "What is Best Execution Duty?" Capital Market Quarterly, Vol. 1, No. 1 (1998), p. 83.

Peace Treaty, http://www.tabiken.com/history/doc/H/H191L200.HTM.

Reuters, http://about.reuters.com/pressoffice/history/technology.asp.

SEC release, April 15, 1997, http://www.sec.gov/news/studies/prefrep.htm.

SEC release, March 17, 2000, http://www.sec.gov/answers/payordf.htm.

SEC release, March 20, 2000, http://www.sec.gov/answers/payordf.htm.

SEC release, November 4, 2005, http://www.sec.gov/divisions/marketreg/mrecn.shtml.

SEC release, October 24, 2005, http://www.sec.gov/spotlight/regnms.htm.

Securities and Exchange Law, Law No. 25 of 1948, translated in 3 Int'l Sec. Reg. Japan Booklet 2. at. 14 (1992).

Securities Exchange Act Release No. 40760 (Dec. 8, 1998), 63 FR 70844 (December 22, 1998) ("Adopting Release"), http://www.sec.gov/rules/final/34-43651.htm.

Securities Exchange Law, Article 2-8-7.

Securities Exchange Law, Article 65, Section 1.

Securities Exchange Law, Article 157.

Securities Exchange Law, Article 158.

Securities Exchange Law, Article 158.

Securities Exchange Law, Article 159, Section 2, Paragraph 1.

Securities Exchange Law, Article 159.

Securities Exchange Law, Article 197, Section 1, Paragraph 7.

Securities Exchange Law, Article 2, Section 11.

Securities Exchange Law, Article 65, Section 1.

Securities Exchange Law, Article 65, Section 1.

Securities Exchange Law, Article 65.

Securities Exchange Law, Articles 166 and 167.

Securities Exchange Law, Articles 27 ff.

Securities Exchange Law, Articles 5, 23-3, 23-8.

SESC, http://www.fsa.go.jp/sesc/english/aboutsesc/aboutsesc.htm.

The Law No. of 5, March 3, 1971.

The Law No. of 59, June 1, 1980.

The Revised Securities Exchange (hereinafter The Revised Law), Article 13, Sections 3 and 5.

The Revised Law, Article 15, Section 2, Paragraphs 1 and 2.

The Revised Law, Article 15, Section 2.
The Revised Law, Article 15, Section 3.
The Revised Law, Article 15, Sections 4 and 5.
The Revised Law, Article 163-167.
The Revised Law, Article 178 through Article 185-17.
The Revised Law, Article 194-6.
The Revised Law, Article 198-2.
The Revised Law, Article 2, Section 10.
The Revised Law, Article 21-2, Section 2 ff.
The Revised Law, Article 2-2, Paragraph 1.
The Revised Law, Article 27-2, Section 1.
The Revised Law, Article 27-3, Section 1.
The Revised Law, Article 2-8-7-(i).
The Revised Law, Article 40, Section 1, Paragraph 1.
The Revised Law, Article 43-2.
The Revised Law, Article 65-2, Section 1.
The Revised Law, Article 65-2, Section 1.
The Revised Law, Article 66-2.
The Revised Law, Article 79, Section 2, Paragraphs 1 and 3, Article 160.
The Revised Law, Articles 172 through 175.
The Revised Law, Articles 21-2, Section 1 and 21-3.
The Revised Law, Articles 79-2, 79-3, 79-4, 116, and 117, http://www.jsda.or.jp/html/greensheet/info.html.
The Revised Law, Law No. 97, 2004.
The Revised Law, Articles 185-7, 185-8.
The Securities Exchange Law, Article 160.
The Securities Exchange Law, Articles 18 or 20.
The Shinko Security Company, http://www.shinko-sec.co.jp/shikkou.htmlof Japan.
Tokyo Stock Exchange, April 30,2002, http://www.jsda.or.jp/html/kisoku/pdf/c015.pdf.
Tokyo Stock Exchange, http://www.tse.or.jp/.
US pink sheets market, http://www.pinksheets.com/.

Chapter 10

M&A for Foreign Investments in Japan

Japanese companies have been solidly guarded against mergers and acquisitions (M&A) under the Japanese Commercial Law. However, it will be easier in the future for offshore companies to acquire Japanese companies under the new evolving Commercial Law. The coming of takeovers to Japan has been anticipated for a long time and now, at last, they would emerge.

Recently, a small IT-related company, Livedoor, succeeded in buying out a leading radio broadcasting company, Nippon Broadcasting System, Inc., owned by Fuji TV Sankei Group, a leading media conglomerate of Japan. Livedoor employed a US style hostile takeover technique. This is the first large scale hostile takeover which materialized in Japan. All eyes in Japan were fixed as the breathtaking drama was unfolded. There has been an outcry by Japanese industries that "foreign companies are coming, coming to invade us! We need defensive tactics." The absence of takeovers in the past resulted in little clamor for defensive tactics but with a threat on the horizon, demand for protection developed especially against anticipated foreign hostile takeovers.

Totally unprepared for such an event, the government, politicians, financial circles, and securities exchange markets are now scurrying to come up with new takeover countermeasures as well as revisions of related laws and regulations suitable for the new M&A age. This change will be a step forward for the Japanese capital market, which will be welcomed by investors of the world.

Statistical Observation of M&A in Japan

A large amount of friendly M&A activity has actually occurred in Japan. The total number of M&A cases in Japan in 2004 was 2,133 (an increase of 1.1 percent from the previous year) still maintaining a high level.[1] (*See* Exhibit 1.) From a viewpoint of M&A styles, the number of stock

Exhibit 1 — M&A in Japan

(Number, %)

Year	Between Japanese Companies		Japanese Companies → Foreign Companies		Foreign Companies → Japanese Companies		Total	
	Number	% increase	Number	% increase	Number	% increase	Number	% increase
1986	68	-	146	-	5	-	219	-
1987	98	44.1	199	36.3	1	-80.0	298	36.1
1988	161	64.3	270	35.7	7	600.0	438	47.0
1989	172	6.8	408	51.1	10	42.9	590	34.7
1990	341	98.3	450	10.3	9	-10.0	800	35.6
1991	385	12.9	246	-45.3	12	20.0	64	-19.7
1992	417	8.3	174	-29.3	33	175.0	624	-3.0
1993	486	16.5	112	-35.6	36	9.1	634	1.6
1994	421	-13.4	159	42.0	38	5.6	618	-2.5
1995	381	-9.5	179	12.6	42	10.5	602	-2.6
1996	433	13.6	203	13.4	38	-9.5	674	12.0
1997	567	30.9	182	-10.3	60	57.9	809	20.0
1998	703	24.0	192	5.5	97	61.7	992	22.6
1999	1,057	50.4	194	1.0	115	18.6	1,366	37.7
2000	1,436	35.9	298	53.6	146	27.0	1,880	37.6
2001	1,545	7.6	239	-19.8	125	-14.4	1,909	1.5
2002	1,993	29.0	260	8.8	121	-3.2	2,374	24.4
2003	1,799	-9.7	209	-19.6	102	-15.7	2,110	-11.1
2004	1,752	-2.6	286	36.8	95	-6.9	2,133	1.1

Source: Nomura Securities Co., "Trend of Japanese M&A", p.4.
http://www.nomuraholdings.com/jp/press/securities/050111/050111_a.pdf.

---

[1] For details, see Nomura Securities, http://www.nomura.co.jp/terms/japan/ki/m_and_a.html.

buyouts (an increase of 13.0 percent from the previous year) recorded in 2004 was 590 cases, the highest in history. In particular, there were 99 cases of stock exchange, which was an increase of 45.6 percent from the previous year. The number of stock acquisition cases, primarily consisting of cases involving new share issues and cases in which the buyers are buyout funds, increased 9.8 percent as well. Cases in which business units were the targets of acquisition, a parent company typically converting its business units into separate entities and selling off the shares of thus created spun-off companies, also contributed to the record increase of stock buyouts.

The number of mergers in 2004 was 350 (a 9.8 percent drop from the previous year).In addition to mergers among financial companies and pharmaceutical companies, mergers among subsidiaries due to reorganization of a group were also notable. There were 337 cases of capital participations (a 6.3 percent increase from the previous year). An increase of cases involving capital increase particularly in information/telecommunication and fund businesses was observed. The following is an analysis of these trends classifying them as whether the participants are Japanese or foreign companies. (*See also* Exhibit 2.)

Exhibit 2 — Trend of M&A of Japanese Companies by Foreign Companies

(Unit: Number)

Year	Area				Methods				Total	
	North America	Asia Oceania	Europe	Others	Conso-lidation	Stock Purchase	Asset Purchase	Capital Participation		% increase
1993	23	6	7	0	1	18	4	13	36	-
1994	22	4	12	0	1	21	4	12	38	5.6
1995	19	11	12	0	1	20	7	14	42	10.5
1996	15	11	11	1	0	20	7	11	38	-9.5
1997	35	14	11	0	0	28	12	20	60	57.9
1998	54	16	22	5	4	52	22	19	97	61.7
1999	60	11	41	3	2	52	24	37	115	18.6
2000	81	24	40	1	3	58	35	50	146	27.0
2001	54	22	49	0	2	53	30	40	125	-14.4
2002	59	25	35	2	2	45	40	34	121	-3.2
2003	39	27	30	6	3	39	32	28	102	-15.7
2004	47	29	19	0	2	35	34	24	95	-6.9

Source: Nomura Securities Co., "Trend of Japanese M&A", p.4.
http://www.nomuraholdings.com/jp/press/securities/050111/050111_a.pdf.

1. **IN–IN** (M&A between Japanese companies) amounted to 1,752 cases (2.6 percent drop from the previous year) with a marked trend for large scale M&A for enhancement of existing businesses and aggressive business expansion plans.

2. **IN–OUT** (M&A of offshore companies by Japanese companies) amounted to 286 cases (36.8 percent from the previous year) and it was close to the peak of 298 cases reached in 2000. In terms of geographical areas, 126 cases of M&A were recorded for the Asia-Oceania region, in particular, China. Cases involving operations located in North America increased substantially to 91 cases (35.8 percent from the previous year), and the same in Europe also increased to 64 cases (12.3 percent from the previous year). In terms of types of business, there is no specific field more frequently represented, although there is an increasing trend in such fields as electrical machinery, chemical, financial, and pharmaceutical industries in Asian countries, in particular, China, as well as in US corporations' participations in buyouts and capital participations.

3. **OUT–IN** (M&A of Japanese companies by offshore companies) amounted to only 95 cases. (Exhibit 2.) M&A by US companies reached 47 cases (20.5 percent increase from the previous year) and the increase was mainly due to acquisitions of Japanese companies by buyout funds, particularly acquisitions of fixed assets such as golf courses. In most other areas, the tendency was down with 29 cases by Asia-Oceania based companies (a 2 case drop from the previous year), 19 M&A cases by European companies (an 11 case drop from the previous year), and zero cases by companies based in other areas (a 6 case drop from the previous year). In terms of styles, asset acquisition only increased to 34 cases (a 2 case increase from the previous year), while stock purchase fell to 35 cases (a 4 case drop from the previous year) and capital participation fell to 24 cases (a 4 case drop from the previous year).

Livedoor vs. Fuji TV

Amidst these M&A trends, an eye-catching large scale hostile event occurred recently in Japan. Because the event was about the potential buyouts of two leading media companies, Nippon Broadcasting System

Inc.[2] (hereinafter Nippon Broadcasting) and Fuji Television Network, Inc.[3] (hereinafter Fuji TV), the event was widely reported on all media, and what was once a relatively unfamiliar subject to the average citizen of Japan, hostile M&A became the topic of conversation for months in living rooms all over the country; this will undoubtedly be one of the top 10 events of 2005.

Some of the eye-catching factors of this case are:

1. In the contest between Fuji TV vs. Livedoor Co. 4 (hereinafter Livedoor) the little fish tried to swallow the big fish.
2. Fuji TV is a member of Keidanren,5 i.e., a corporation representing the establishment of Japan, while Livedoor is a startup IT company.
3. The consensus of the market was that Livedoor was backed by US capital, so it was regarded as a fierce battle between offshore capital and Japanese capital.

In the end, Livedoor succeeded in essentially keeping control of the capital of Nippon Broadcasting System, a successful founder of Fuji TV. This success story about M&A involving Japanese companies, which had been considered difficult to accomplish, will not fade away for some time to come.

Certainly hostile takeovers of Japanese companies will be more popular as a result of this event. For a long time it has been a desire of US companies to expand their activities into the country with the world's second largest GDP. Therefore, analyzing Livedoor vs. Fuji TV, studying the countermeasures being taken by Japanese companies as a

---

[2] For the company profile, see http://www.jolf.co.jp/company/IR1242/index.html.
[3] For the company profile, see http://www.fujitv.co.jp/jp/.
[4] For the company profile, see http://corp.livedoor.com/company/outline.html.
[5] The Japanese Federation of Economic Organizations is a general economic organization consisting of 1,623 companies and other organizations, which include 91 companies with foreign capital affiliations and 1,306 major representative Japanese companies. It is the strongest interest group in Japan that applies pressure on the government as well as overseas organizations by collecting opinions from business communities on many important issues for business communities ranging from economic and industrial issues to labor issues urging speedy solutions. See the Federation's Web site at http://www.keidanren.or.jp/Japanese/profile/pro001.htm (last visited July 11, 2005).

defense against such attempts, and the defensive moves of Japanese companies and the government as a whole against foreign capitals, including suggestions for modifying the Commercial Law[6] and the Securities Exchange Law[7] will be most beneficial for US companies who are attempting to take over Japanese companies.

The battle between Livedoor and Fuji TV trying to capture Nippon Broadcasting System's stock used tactics bordering on illegal and many forbidden techniques (*see* Exhibit 3). It was kicked off with Livedoor's

Exhibit 3 — Buyout Battle Involving Nippon Broadcasting System

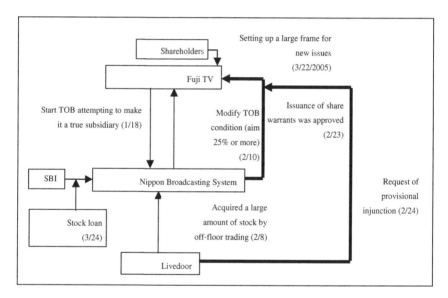

acquisition of a large amount of Nippon Broadcasting shares via the off-floor trading of the Tokyo Stock Exchange (TSE). The Securities Exchange Law prohibits the trading of a large amount of shares that can affect the management right of a company through off-floor transactions

---

[6] The Commercial Law of Japan, Law No. 48 (Mar. 9, 1899) (amended 18 times) [hereinafter Commercial Law]. For details, *see http://www.ron.gr.jp/law/law/syouhou1.htm* (last visited July 8, 2005).

[7] The Securities Exchange Law of Japan, Law No. 25 of 1948, art. 127, no. 4 [hereinafter Securities Exchange Law], *available at http://www.japanlaw.info/f_statements/PARENT/DX.htm* (last visited July 8, 2005).

other than for a take over bid (TOB).[8] Off-floor trading is a quasi rule-breaking technique based on a perfunctory understanding of in-market trading, but off-floor trading is essentially an off-market trading in that it is a negotiated transaction. It is contrary to the intent of the law — to provide information to all investors so that they can trade fairly. Facing this situation, in spite of the fact that it had been in the process of a TOB against Nippon Broadcasting System, Fuji TV countered Livedoor's attempt by temporarily freezing the voting rights of its own shares Nippon Broadcasting System owned as a defensive measure. This was probably because Fuji TV lost some confidence about obtaining the majority shares. But the modification of a TOB condition by lowering the number of buyout shares is against the Securities Exchange Law.[9] Such an act may confuse investors and affect the stock price.

Moving Strike Convertible Bonds (MSCB)[10] used by Livedoor for funding their take over attempt can be regarded as a beneficial (to subscribers) issuance that might affect the benefits of the existing shareholders, which is prohibited by the Commercial Law.[11] MSCBs can certainly be advantageous to subscribers when combined with loaned stocks.

Another question is the legality of the issuance of new share warrants Nippon Broadcasting System decided to issue to Fuji TV as an exclusive subscriber.[12] If Nippon Broadcasting could increase the number of outstanding shares up to 2.4 times by allocating new issues to Fuji TV,

---

[8] Securities Exchange Law, Art.27-2.

[9] Securities Exchange Law Ordinance, Law No.321, September 30, 1964, Art.13-1.

[10] This is the bond with share warrant. Due to the amendment of the commercial law in 2002, the bonds are defined as: (1) common bonds and (2) bonds with share warrants. For the details, *see* Nomura Securities, *http://www.nomura.co.jp/terms/japan/te/ sinkabuyoyakus.html.*

[11] MSCB, which Livedoor used to obtain ¥80 billion from Lehman Brothers, Tokyo to finance the purchase of Nippon Broadcasting System's shares, was criticized as "very likely a betrayal of shareholders' trust," because "it is obvious that Horie, Livedoor's president, had lent his shares, which were put to short sell, resulting in stock price drops, thus hurting shareholders" (*Economist* [Japanese Economic Journal] 4/11/2005, p. 9).

[12] For details, see press releases by Nippon Broadcasting "Notice Regarding Issuance of Stock Acquisition Rights Through Third-Party Allocation," on February 23, 2005 and "Approval of Issuance of Stock Acquisition Rights," on February 24, 2005, *http://www.jolf.co.jp/company/IR1242/index.html.*

Fuji TV would be able make Nippon Broadcasting its subsidiary regardless of the outcome of the TOB. In that scenario, existing shareholders would have no choice but to accept the TOB because the drop in share price is inevitable as a result of large scale dilution.

Increasing capital on a large scale by means of directors arbitrarily selecting shareholders is against the basic principle of a corporation that the shareholders are entitled to select directors. The legality of this issuance by Nippon Broadcasting was fought in a court battle in which Livedoor requested a temporary injunction against the issuance.[13] The specific issue was whether the Nippon Broadcasting System's claim that "becoming a subsidiary of Fuji TV increases the corporate value" could be allowed at the expense of the existing shareholders.[14] Furthermore, Fuji TV tried to pour cold water on Livedoor's enthusiasm with "Crown Jewel" tactics. In the meanwhile, Nippon Broadcasting took a new defensive measure by "loaning stocks." On top of that, Fuji TV set up a large "frame for new issues" to prevent Livedoor from taking it over. These series of actions have not been well settled nor their legalities determined.

Off-floor trading (TOSNET-1)

Two kinds of stock trading are recognized at the moment in Tokyo: (1) "on-market trading" in which stocks are traded within a stock exchange, and (2) "off-market trading" in which stocks are traded between a seller and a buyer outside of a stock market. The on-market trading can be further divided into the normal trading that is used by general investors during the sessions and the "off-floor trading," which is executed in time zones when normal trading is done.[15] Off-market trading and off-floor

---

[13] *Id.*

[14] *Economist* (Japan), April 1, 2005, p. 9.

[15] The tradings are executed from 8:20 am to 9:00 am, from 11 am to 12.30 pm and from 3:00 pm to 4:30 pm through ToSTNet at the Tokyo Stock Exchange. For the details, *see* Tokyo Stock Exchange, *http://www.tse.or.jp/glossary/gloss_t/tachiaigai.html* (last visited July 11, 2005).

trading are typically used by institutional investors for trading a large volume of stocks.

A large amount of Nippon Broadcasting's shares was acquired by Livedoor in an off-floor trade. A stock purchase that may cause a change in the management right of a company is required by the Securities Exchange Law to be executed either (1) on market or (2) TOB, if it is to be executed off-market.[16] Although off-floor trading is technically "on-market trading," it is no different from "off-market trading" in that general investors have difficulty in accessing information and have a problem in terms of information disclosure. TOB is the way Livedoor should have gone.

Consequently, the Financial Services Agency is currently reviewing the trading rule to modify the Securities Exchange Law in such a way as to regard the off-floor trading a TOB when one third of the shares are to be acquired.

Share warrant

One preventive measure against hostile takeover is to issue share warrants to third parties (not restricted to existing shareholders)[17] in advance, when the other side is expected to use such tactics as "Green Mailer,"[18] forcing the company to buy back its own shares at higher prices. There are no restrictions, such as targeted subscribers or a subscription right exercising period; the price is set in advance. This technique has been recognized as a means of friendly takeover in Japan, since the US company, Wal-Mart,[19] for all practical purposes, placed Seiyu[20] under its umbrella in 2002 by obtaining its share warrants.[21]

---

[16] Securities Exchange Law, Art.27-2.

[17] Commercial Law, Art.280-2.

[18] In Japan it is consider a hostile takeover to buy the shares in the market and ask the company to buy them at the higher prices. For details, *see http://learning.xrea.jp/ %A5%B0%A5%EA%A1%BC%A5%F3%A5%E1%A1%BC%A5%E9%A1%BC.html* (last visited July 13, 2005).

[19] *See* Wal-Mart homepage, *http://www.walmart.com/* (last visited July 13, 2005).

[20] *See* Seiyu homepage, *http://www.seiyu.co.jp/* (last visited July 13, 2005).

[21] For details of the friendly takeover of Seiyu by Wal-Mart, *see http://www.cool-knowledge.com/020411wal-mart-toiu-vision.htm* (last visited July 13, 2005).

In the present case, Nippon Broadcasting's announcement that it intended to use this technique as a defensive measure against the hostile takeover attracted a lot of attention. Its scheme was basically to lower the ratio of voting rights of the party who was attempting the hostile takeover, by providing share warrants to its existing shareholders in advance and then make them exercise their rights when the hostile takeover becomes a reality, thus increasing the number of outstanding shares. A corporate law amendment expected to be introduced in 2006 will enable the use of share warrants as a "poison pill" by coercing shareholders to exercise warrants when needed for a company having modified the articles of incorporation in advance.[22]

Corporate value

"What is corporate value" became a big question people discussed during the TOB against Nippon Broadcasting, because increasing the corporate value was thought to be the most effective tactic in preventing a hostile takeover. In the United States, corporate value is considered as the "net present value (NPV) (of the cash flow the particular corporation generates in the future discounted by the opportunity cost."[23] Because cash flow is difficult to calculate, corporate value is normally regarded in Japan as the "value obtained by subtracting the current cash and deposit from the sum of the aggregate market value of its stocks plus the interest generating liabilities." [24] Because the aggregate market value is the amount the shareholders can collect in the market, it is "shareholders' value." Therefore, when corporate managers say "increasing the corporate value is the most efficient countermeasure against a hostile takeover attempt," they normally mean raising the value of the company in the market in order to make the buyout more difficult.

---

[22] *Economist* (Japan), April 11, 2005, p.18.
[23] For the definition, *see http://www.investopedia.com/terms/n/npv.asp* (last visited July 13, 2005).
[24] For the Japanese definition, see http://vic-si-e-financial.g.hatena.ne.jp/keyword/%E4%BC%81%E6%A5%AD%E4%BE%A1%E5%80%A4?kid=1345 (last visited July 13, 2005).

In Japan, corporate value also includes providing employment opportunities, contribution to the local society, and relations with stakeholders.[25] Although these factors look unrelated to the shareholders' value, they don't contradict the shareholders' value in the long run. For example, assume a company reduces the number of employees and R&D costs artificially in order to jack up the profit temporarily. The stock price may go up because of the increase of profit. However, loss of workforce and delay in development of new products weaken the company's competitive capability, resulting in a reduced cash flow, and causing its stock price to go down, thus reducing the shareholders' value. Japanese managers think that it is indispensable to achieve the stakeholders' favorable evaluation on a long-term basis, not just for the short-term pursuit of profit, in order to increase the shareholders' value on a long-term basis.[26]

Crown jewels

If we are to analogize a target company in a takeover bid to a king's crown, the company's important assets and major businesses are jewels on the crown. Without jewels, a crown is just a cap. Similarly, if valuable assets of the company are transferred to the third party, the company becomes less attractive to the party who is trying to take it over. Transfer of crown jewels is a scorched earth defense.[27]

The "crown jewels" of Nippon Broadcasting are the Fuji TV stock it owns, worth approximately ¥140 billion. The stock Nippon Broadcasting owned was approximately 70 percent of the total market value of Nippon Broadcasting. Even if Livedoor bought out more than half of the stocks of Nippon Broadcasting, it still is less than that. Another jewel is the Pony Canyon stock[28] (Nippon Broadcasting owns more than 56 percent

---

[25] *Id.*

[26] *Id.*

[27] According to the *Japan Times*, March 26, 2005, a firm that sells off its valuable and desired assets, called "crown jewels," is undertaking a scorched earth policy. For details, *see http://search.japantimes.co.jp/print/business/nb03-2005/nb20050326a3.htm* (last visited July 13, 2005).

[28] For the homepage, *see http://music.ponycanyon.co.jp/* (last visited July 13, 2005).

of the outstanding shares of Pony Canyon) that is earning more than half of the consolidated sales amount. However, a logical explanation to shareholders is necessary in order to sell the important assets.

Stock loan as a countermeasure against hostile takeover

On March 24, 2005, Fuji TV announced that Softbank Investment (SBI), which is a venture capital company of the Softbank Group,[29] became the leading shareholder having 14.6 percent of Fuji TV's voting rights.[30] If Nippon Broadcasting lends its Fuji TV's shares to SBI, it is no longer a shareholder of Fuji TV. Nippon Broadcasting's intention is to prevent Livedoor, who captured the managing right of Nippon Broadcasting, from controlling Fuji TV. This defensive measure relies on the use of the voting right of Fuji TV, which is the prime asset of Nippon Broadcasting — it is a "scorched earth defense operation." On the other hand, SBI is also a "white knight," in that it becomes a new major shareholder who is an ally to Fuji TV, which eliminates the indirect influence of Livedoor.

A loaned stock is a stock that is loaned for a certain period of time by a contract called a "stock loan agreement,"[31] in which the loan period can be arbitrarily established and the ownership is transferred to the borrower for that period. The borrower returns the stocks to the lender after the period and pays the rent. In the present case, Nippon Broadcasting is the lender, SBI is the borrower, and Fuji TV's stocks are the loaned stocks. If a right ascertaining day occurs during the period, the borrower's name, not the name of the real owner, will be recorded on the shareholder's list. It is also the borrower who has the right to exercise the voting rights and receive dividends. In other words, the borrower gets all the benefits without buying the stock.

Conspicuous borrowers these days in Japan are hedge fund operators from overseas. They borrow stocks they think are too highly appreciated

---

[29] For the homepage, *see http://www.softbank.co.jp/* (last visited July 13, 2005).

[30] For details, see press release by Nippon Broadcasting on February 23, 2005 "Notice of Lending of Fuji Television's Shares," *http://www.jolf.co.jp/company/IR1242/index.html* (lat visited July 13, 2005).

[31] *Id.*

and earn on margins by selling them short. A recent trend is to use them in combination with convertible bonds with share warrants. A securities company that accepts convertible bonds issued by a company sells loaned stocks at a market price set in advance, and obtains a margin by changing the convertible bonds into stocks when the stock price drops and selling them when the stock price comes back. Because the period is negotiated, it can be set arbitrarily based on the agreement between the lender and borrower. If it is used in a margin trading, it is usually set for six months because of the normal settlement date arrangement.

As for the stocks loaned by Nippon Broadcasting to SBI, the period was as long as five years. Therefore, there is the possibility that it will be recognized as essentially a selling transaction if the case gets to court. In addition to that, if it is recognized as "an important part of the operation," it may require a special decision by a stockholder's meeting.[32] Livedoor may claim damages in tort, but this requires a number of legal processes to prove, so realistically it is not doable for Livedoor.[33]

New issue frame

A new issue frame is a mechanism to predetermine the amount of the total sum to be issued for a company which is issuing stocks. By reporting the issuing frame to the Ministry of Finance[34] in advance, a company is allowed to issue new shares at any time within a predetermined period of time within the predetermined frame without reporting to the Ministry of Finance each time. While it takes normally about a month or so, the issuing process can be simplified by establishing the issuing frame in advance, and the whole process can be shortened to approximately two weeks.

---

[32] Commercial Law, Art. 245.

[33] Civil Law, Law No. 899 (April 27, 1896), Art. 709. For the law, *see http://law.e-gov.go.jp/cgi-bin/idxsearch.cgi.*

[34] The Ministry of Finance was reorganized on January 6, 2001. The name was changed from "Okurasho" to "Zaimusho" in Japanese, but the English name still remains the same. For more information about the reorganization, *see* the Ministry's Web site *at http://www.mof.go.jp* (last visited July 13, 2005).

On March 22, 2005, Fuji TV established the new issue frame of approximately ¥50 billion. The move was to fend off the attack of Livedoor, which then seemed to be focusing on Fuji TV as its target. The idea was that even if Livedoor tried to execute a TOB aiming to capture as much as 50 percent (1.27 million shares) of Fuji TV's outstanding shares, Fuji TV could increase the number of shares up to six million by using its newly established issue frame before the TOB period ended. In other words, even if Livedoor succeeded in the TOB, its shareholding ratio would be a mere 21 percent, so that Livedoor would not be able to control Fuji TV.

Court Judgment

The battle fought between Fuji TV and Livedoor reached a settlement on April 18, 2005, [35] both parties agreeing on capital and business cooperation, etc. In addition to making Nippon Broadcasting its true subsidiary by buying the Nippon Broadcasting shares owned by Livedoor, Fuji TV agreed to invest in Livedoor up to 12.75 percent by accepting its allocation of new shares to a third party. Fuji TV was to pay Livedoor a sum of ¥147.3 billion. The hostile takeover battle that shook Japan found reconciliation in a monetary exchange. (*See* Exhibits 4 and 5.)

Although Fuji TV finally succeeded in making Nippon Broadcasting its true subsidiary,[36] it is going to cost approximately ¥90 billion more than its original estimate. Livedoor turned out to be the winner earning about ¥44 billion as a result. Livedoor had better create a truly meaningful cooperation with Fuji TV if it doesn't want to be known as a "green mailer."

As to the case, noteworthy court judgments were made. Livedoor requested a temporary injunction on the share warrants to be issued to

---

[35] For details, see press release by Nippon Broadcasting on April 18, 2005 on "Notification of Basic Agreement Making Nippon Broadcasting System a Wholly Owned Subsidiary," *http://www.jolf.co.jp/company/IR1242/index.html*.
[36] *Id.*

Exhibit 4 — Timeline of the Battle among Fuji TV, Nippon Broadcasting, and Livedoor

1/17/2005	Fuji TV announces its plan of a TOB against Nippon.
2/8	Livedoor acquires more than one third of Nippon Broadcasting's outstanding shares in off-floor trading, etc.
2/23	Nippon Broadcasting decides to issue new share warrants.
2/24	Livedoor requests Tokyo District Court to issue an injunction order against the issue of share warrants.
3/8	Fuji TV announces that it has acquired approximately 37 percent of Nippon Broadcasting's shares.
3/11	Tokyo District Court issues an injunction order against the issue of share warrants by Nippon Broadcasting.
3/12	Livedoor warns Nippon Broadcasting's directors that removal of crown jewels is illegal.
3/15	Fuji TV announces that it will increase annual dividends net five fold.
3/16	Livedoor announces that it has acquired more than 50 percent of Nippon Broadcasting's shares on the voting right base.
	Tokyo District Court rejects Nippon Broadcasting's appeal.
3/22	Fuji TV establishes a new issue frame of ¥50 billion.
3/23	Tokyo High Court also decides against new share warrants. It decides that a discussion on corporate value is not proper for the court.
3/24	Nippon Broadcasting decides to loan Fuji TV shares it owns to SBI, which suddenly appears as a white knight.
3/31	Three outside board members of Nippon Broadcasting quit.
4/18	Fuji TV and Livedoor reach settlement.

Exhibit 5 — Structure of Settlement between Fuji TV and Livedoor

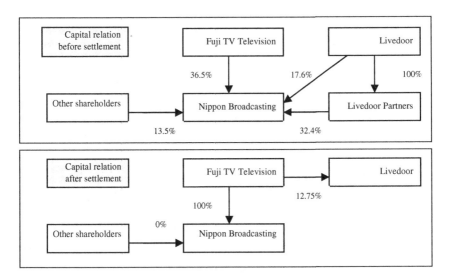

Fuji TV Television which Nippon Broadcasting tried as a countermeasure against Livedoor's hostile takeover attempt, [37] the legality of the allocation of new shares to a third party was fought over, and the Tokyo High Court rejected Nippon Broadcasting's appeal for a preservative disposition.[38]

The Tokyo High Court ruled that, when a conflict exists between the managing right of a company and an attempt to maintain and secure the managing right of the existing manager or a specific shareholder, an issue of share warrants with which to reduce the shareholding ratio of a party, who is attempting a hostile takeover, is considered to be an "extremely unfair method" in accordance with Article 280, Section 39-4 and Article 280, Section 10 of the Commercial Law.[39]

The court decision provided examples of improper acquisitions of shares:

1. Green mailer — when the buyer is merely interested in selling shares by artificially raising stock price without any sincere intention of participating in the company's management.

2. Scorched earth operation — If the buyer's intention is a so-called scorched earth operation in which the buyer transfers the company's intellectual property, know-how, confidential information, clients, etc. to itself or its affiliate companies.

3. Company's assets are used for wrong purposes, such as in a leveraged buyout — when the buyer intends to use the company's assets as collateral to raise funds to pay off the buyer's or its affiliate company's debts or obligations.

---

[37] For the decision of the Tokyo Lower Court, see press releases by Nippon Broadcasting "Notice of Regarding Ruling on Request for Court Injunction Blocking Issuance of Stock Acquisition Rights and Appeal Against the Ruling," on March 11, 2005 and "Notification Regarding Rejection of Objection to Temporary Court Injunction Blocking Issuance of Stock Acquisition Rights and of Appeal Against the Ruling," on March 16, 2005. For both, *see http://www.jolf.co.jp/company/IR1242/index.html.*

[38] Tokyo High Court, The 16th Civil Section, March 23, 2005. For details, see press release by Nippon Broadcasting "Notification Regarding Dismissal of Appeal Against Lower Court of Temporary Injunction to Block Issuance of Stock Acquisition Rights," on March 23, 2005, *http://www.jolf.co.jp/company/IR1242/index.html* (last visited July 13, 2005).

[39] *See Id.* Also, for details of the court decision, *see Nikkei*, March 24, 2005, p. 12.

4. High dividend payments or selling shares at high prices is intended — when the buyer intends to dispose of the company's large assets such as real estate and negotiable instruments to make it possible to offer high dividends temporarily or to sell the shares when the stock price rises sharply.

The court stated that a person or entity waging such a hostile takeover does not deserve protection as a shareholder, and that the board of directors is justified in issuing share warrants with the principal objective of maintaining and securing management rights as a countermeasure. However, the management is responsible for proving that such an extraordinary circumstance exists.

The court judged that the issuance of share warrants in the present case was expected to reduce the share ratio of Livedoor, support the incumbent management, and apply influence on the matter. The court also judged that, because the issuance of share warrants was intended for securing the managing right of Nippon Broadcasting by Fuji TV, it was extremely unfair as it was against the shareholders' benefit. The court further stated:

1. There is no concrete evidence that Livedoor is attempting a hostile takeover primarily as a money game;
2. the judgment on whether Livedoor's control of the company may damage the corporate value of the company is a management determination that should be made based on the judgments and evaluations of the shareholders and securities markets and it is not proper for the court to make; and
3. Because ToSNet trading is trading on the securities exchange market owned and operated by the TSE under the Securities Exchange Law, it does not violate the Securities Exchange Law[40] and the use of this system by Livedoor does not constitute any particular circumstance that justifies the issue warrants by Nippon Broadcasting System of the present case.

---

[40] Securities Exchange Law, Art. 27-2.

Based on this, the Tokyo High Court ruled that the issuance of share warrants in such a large amount in this case constituted a misuse of rights provided to the board of directors of Nippon Broadcasting. Upon hearing this decision, Nippon Broadcasting withdrew the issuance of share warrants as of the day of said court judgment.

What is notable is that the Tokyo High Court clearly indicated the examples of a justifiable issuance of share warrants. In other words, although it judged that the Nippon Broadcasting's countermeasure using share warrants was an excessive defense in this situation, it did indicate that defenses against certain takeover acts are lawful. One can say that an "infrastructure," *i.e.*, a standard, is now in place for facing the great M&A age to come. This court decision is viewed as a "monumental decision to be remembered in the M&A history of Japanese companies."[41] Although the concept of share warrants was introduced in the last amended Commercial Law,[42] it was never used as a defensive measure against a hostile takeover, because it was thought that "the outcome is unpredictable as there is no court's judgment standard" to take the battle around the validity of the defensive measure to a court.

The court decision indicated four situations in which defensive measures using share warrants are approved as countermeasures to hostile takeovers that are opposed by incumbent management teams. Possible situations included a leveraged buyout (LBO), in which funds are borrowed using existing assets as collateral, and a takeover seeking high dividends and selling shares at the highest price.

Issuing share warrants will not be approved as a defensive measure in the United States simply because it is an LBO type takeover, in which the buyer is expected to acquire funds using the target company's assets as collateral.[43] Compared with US Court decisions, the decision in this

---

[41] *Nikkei* (Japan Financial Times), March 24, 2005, p.11.
[42] Amendment of Commercial Law in April 1, 2002. For details, *see* *http://members.at.infoseek.co.jp/barexam/note/history_sh.htm* (last visited July 17, 2005).
[43] When triggered, this poison pill allows shareholders to acquire additional shares below market price, thereby increasing the number of shares outstanding and making the takeover prohibitively expensive. Such plans are the subject of some controversy in the United States, a corporate provision to combat hostile takeover. The vast majority of pills were instituted after November 1985, when the Delaware Supreme Court upheld a company's right to adopt a poison pill without shareholder approval in *Moran v.*

case is favorable to the management of the target company. It is not necessarily a bad thing for a hostile buyer to try and use the poorly managed assets and know-how of a company more efficiently. While the present decision can be appreciated because it clarifies the rule for defensive measures, it is too far reaching;[44] it makes it easier for a company, which is the target of a hostile takeover, to introduce defensive poison pills, as long as they can show that the buyer is motivated by one of these four types of improper acquisition of shares. Poison pills generally have been criticized in Japan by shareholders as tools for securing managers' jobs or a response to the risk of a share price drop, therefore, Japanese companies thinking about introducing poison pills are happy about this court decision.[45]

Responses from Japanese Government and Stock Exchange to M&A Countermeasures

To what extent are countermeasures against hostile takeovers allowed? The battle over Nippon Broadcasting between Fuji TV and Livedoor not only ushered in the great M&A age but also presented a challenge to politicians, government, the private sector, as well as the capital market. It demanded a new rule suitable for the new age.

Ministry of Justice — revision of Corporate Law

The Corporate Law is scheduled to be revised in April 2006. The revised Corporate Law is expected to allow for poison pills that will forcefully bring down the voting right ratios of those attempting a takeover and allow for golden shares that give veto powers to friendly shareholders.[46] Defensive measures that substantially have the same effect as poison pills can be used under the present Commercial Law. These measures, however, are rather complicated requiring the use of special purpose

---

Household International, Inc., Del.Ch., 490 A.2d 1059 (1985). For the case, *see* *http://www.law.unlv.edu/faculty/rlawless/mergers/moran.htm* (last visited July 13, 2005).
[44] See *supra* n. 41.
[45] *Id.*
[46] *See supra* n. 14, p. 18.

companies; only a limited number of types of these companies have been available.[47]

The share warrant method considered under the new Corporate Law, gives existing shareholders share warrants in advance with which they can acquire common shares. When a hostile buyer appears and buys shares up to a predetermined number, the warrants are exercised automatically to issue common shares.[48] A method of forcefully converting the shares of a party who is recognized as a hostile buyer into shares without voting rights will also be made possible.[49] The objective is to nullify the voting rights of the takeover buyer.

The task of recognizing "hostile" activity will be given to management and the conditions for taking action will be defined in the articles of incorporation. If a company is armed with these measures, the company is less likely to be the target of a hostile takeover. Thus, these types of defensive measures are "warning" type measures. Preferred and subordinate shares that provide special rights to shareholders become easier to use with the revision of the law.[50] "Golden shares" that provide vetoes to shareholders are also a defensive measure. Under the revised Corporate Law, a company listed on the stock market can have transfer limitation only for golden shares.[51] It provides an almighty veto power to friendly shareholders, while preventing double-crossing.[52]

However, the TSE has been asking listed companies to refrain from using share warrants and golden shares because they change the equality of the shareholders rights. The TSE intends to make it an official rule by the end of 2005 and will de-list those companies who fail to obey the rule. There is a good chance that such a defensive measure as eliminating the voting right of the hostile buyer will not be allowed either. It is thought that share warrants that forcefully convert the shares of the hostile buyer to shares without voting rights will be rejected by overseas investors. Keep in mind that many of these defensive measures require a

---

[47] *Id.* at p. 35.
[48] *Id.* at p. 18.
[49] *Id.*
[50] *Id.*
[51] *Id.*
[52] *Id.*

2/3 vote of the shareholders present at a shareholders' meeting to be ratified.

The view of Ministry of Economy, Trade and Industry on defensive measures against hostile takeover

In May 2005, the Ministry, together with the Ministry of Justice jointly announced an instruction for companies using a defensive measure against a hostile takeover. The instruction requests companies to disclose the content of a defensive measure prior to its implementation in order to honor shareholders' wishes, placing a hedge against managers' wanton use of the defensive measure in the interest of their own job security. The instruction also requests that the introduction of a poison pill for lowering the buyer's voting right ratio require approval at the shareholders' meeting.[53] This instruction is a guideline for whether a defensive measure is legal or reasonable from the market's point of view. It does not have any legal enforceability, but prompts companies to obey the rules when introducing defensive measures.

Further, the instruction suggests that companies hold shareholder meetings before introducing poison pills. The intent is to stop excessively defensive plans that might interfere with proper takeovers that will help raise the value of the corporation. Even though the defensive measure should be voted on at the shareholders meeting, a rule should be established beforehand that a defensive measure will be cancelled if the purchase proposal benefits all of the shareholders. It further states that, even after an issuance of share warrants, shareholder meetings should be held periodically to revisit whether the defensive measure should be sustained.

Because it is difficult to hold shareholders meeting on short notice, defensive measures can be taken based on a decision by the directors. In that case certain conditions need to be met, such as "objective conditions for canceling the defensive measure are determined in advance" or that "checks by outside members such as outside board members are mandated." The objective is to make sure that the board of directors does

---

[53] *Nikkei*, May 28, 2005, pp. 2–5.

not make a decision that is purely self motivated. It is also a means of establishing a procedure for the shareholders to cancel a defensive measure taken by board of directors if they so desire.

The instruction lists instances in which a defensive measure is appropriate: (1) a "green mail," situation, *i.e.*, the buyer's intention is to ask the company to buy back shares at peak price; (2) "scorched earth tactics," *i.e.*, the buyer's intention is to sell off the assets of the company; (3) an "oppressive two-step buyout," *i.e.*, the buyer essentially forces the shareholders to sell shares, etc. The instruction requests that companies be careful not to reject proper purchase offers, and to be mindful of shareholders' interests.

The instruction warns against "golden shares" in particular, as they "treat shareholders discriminately." It generally indicates a negative opinion about golden shares by stating "a listed company should be cautious about issuing golden shares without having a mechanism to cancel them."

Financial Services Agency

The takeover battle for Nippon Broadcasting exposed various loop holes in the government's policy concerning the financial market, such as acquisition of shares through a niche in the TOB system and the deficiencies of the "Large Ownership Report"[54] system, which obligates those shareholders who own more than 5 percent of the outstanding shares of a listed company to report this fact. The limitation of the existing administrative control was made obvious as well.

Investment funds that trade shares daily are not required by the Large Ownership Report to report the changes in their share ownership ratios. This special treatment is for the convenience of institutional investors who trade shares in large quantities. However, such a lopsided treatment is sure to cause trouble in the future. In the United States, the SEC vigilantly monitors the market for any problems and establishes rules

---

[54] Japanese companies are required to report 10 major shareholders annually to the Ministry of Finance. For details of the requirements, *see http://www.smrj.go.jp/isif/ series/okabunushi_y24.html* (last visited July 14, 2007).

almost monthly based on court precedents.[55] In Japan, the issuing of a rule normally requires a change of law, thus problems have been dealt with on a case by case basis by the Financial Services Agency responding to questions concerning interpretations of the law.

As mergers and acquisitions become more versatile as the result of new venture businesses and foreign capital, keeping the "gray zone" of the rule will increase the risk of confusion. At the same time, narrowing the rule will stifle transactions. Whether transparency can be achieved without excessive control will depend on how the government handles this situation.

Tokyo Stock Exchange

The TSE is concerned that "a substantial number of companies may try to adopt defensive measures neglecting general investors as a result" in the aftermath of the takeover battle for Nippon Broadcasting System. It prepared a directive asking companies to voluntarily restrain from using excessively defensive measures that violate investors' rights, such as golden shares, and issued a notice requesting compliance dated April 21, 2005.[56] It is said that the TSE intends to make an official policy by the fall of 2005 and to apply severe punishments to non-complying companies.

Use of golden shares and share warrants will be easier and legal under the new corporate law to be introduced in 2006.[57] However, the TSE feels that any defensive measures that violate the equal rights of investors or result in unexpected damages to investors are improper, even if they are allowed by law. The intention is therefore obvious that the TSE seeks a higher standard.[58]

While the New York Stock Exchange (NYSE) prohibits an issuance of golden shares once the particular company becomes a listed

---

[55] The US SEC proposes to update and simplify the rules and regulations constantly. See SEC homepage *http://www.sec.gov/* (last visited July 15, 2005).

[56] *Nikkei* (Japanese Financial Times), June 30, 2005, p. 3.

[57] *Id.*

[58] *Id.*

company,[59] the TSE will not allow an issuance of golden shares even before a company becomes a listed company. Even when a listed holding company is to provide golden shares to a non-listed subsidiary, the TSE advises against providing golden shares to a subsidiary that can dictate the value of the corporation as a whole. The TSE is also asking for voluntary restraint against issuing shares with multiple voting rights, *e.g.*, one share with 100 voting rights. As for poison pills that weaken the buyer's control using share warrants, the TSE is requesting they not be provided only to the shareholders at the time of introduction, but rather be provided to all shareholders when a buyer appears.

The TSE seeks the enhancement of disclosure of information to shareholders that clearly indicates the purpose of defensive countermeasures and the possible effects on shareholders. It also obligates companies to disclose the procedures and standards of implementation of the countermeasures. If the articles of incorporation are to be modified with future introduction of countermeasures in mind, the intention should be disclosed.

Japanese courts — recent precedents on share warrant

When Nireco Corporation, an industrial control equipment manufacturer, introduced a poison pill issuing share warrants[60] as a countermeasure against a hostile takeover, a shareholder, which was an investment fund,[61] requested a temporary injunction of the issuance of the share warrants. In response to this, the Tokyo District Court granted an injunction against the issuance on June 1, 2005, on the ground that "it

---

[59] The NYSE allows US companies to list dual-class voting shares. Once shares are listed, however, companies cannot reduce the voting rights of the existing shares or issue a new class of superior voting shares. For details, see Golden Share, *http://www.investopedia.com/terms/g/goldenshare.asp* (last visited July 16, 2005).

[60] Nireco introduced a poison pill providing two share warrants, free of charge, to each shareholder as of the end of March, 2005, with which each shareholder is eligible to acquire a new share at the price of one yen per share on June 16, 2005.

[61] A US investment fund located in the Caymans Islands that holds approximately 6.8 percent of Nireco shares requested an injunction against the issuance on May 9, 2005.

corresponds to an extremely unfair issuance that the Commercial Law prohibits."[62]

As a reason for the decision, the court pointed out that an issuance of share warrants for the purpose of defense against a hostile takeover requires "basically a decision at a shareholders meeting." However, it can be replaced with a decision of the board if: (1) there is a mechanism to reflect the opinion of the shareholders; (2) a willful activation of the defensive measure by the board can be prevented; and (3) it does not cause any unexpected damage to shareholders.

In addition, the court judged that Nireco had not set up a device to check the opinion of the shareholders at the shareholders meeting to be held in June, 2005, and that there was room for the board of directors to not obey the recommendation of the special committee concerning the exercise of the share warrants. Thus, the court concluded that it "lacks the justifiability as a premeditated countermeasure against the hostile takeover based on the board of directors' decision" considering the fact that "there is a risk of existing shareholders incurring unexpected damages because of dilution of stocks."

The *Nireco* case, in which the Tokyo District Court issued an injunction against the issuance of share warrants, was a special scheme in which share warrants were issued to shareholders as of a specific day prior to the start of the takeover. The court questioned two points that were determinative of the board members' positions: (1) Were highly independent outside members judging the justifiability of the defensive measure; and (2) Under what circumstance would the defensive measure be activated.

In the *Livedoor* case, the Tokyo High Court gave examples of situations in which the issuance of share warrants was considered appropriate, such as when the buyer asks the company to buy back shares at high prices or disposes of the company's assets in order to obtain temporary profits.[63] Nireco claimed that a defensive measure is justifiable when the takeover is contrary to the benefit of the stakeholders, *e.g.*, employees, customers and suppliers, in addition to the

---

[62] *Nikkei*, June 2, 2005, p. 1.
[63] See *supra* n. 38.

conditions Tokyo High Court indicated in the *Livedoor* case. In response, the Tokyo District Court ruled that "such a judgment standard is too broad and lacks clarity to be used as a means of preventing willful judgments of the board of directors." If the justification conditions are the same as those of emergency situations, a preplanned defensive measure may become meaningless.

Countermeasures Taken by Japanese Companies

According to the "Survey of 100 Presidents," conducted by Nikkei in April 2005, more than 40 percent of these managers had started to study defensive countermeasures, which they became familiar with during the battle between Fuji TV and Livedoor.[64] Among those responding to the survey, 41.5 percent were "considering introduction" of countermeasures against hostile takeovers, and a total of 61.5 percent of those who have already "introduced" and those who "are not yet studying but feel a need for" answered positively to the need for defensive countermeasures. Only 12.3 percent felt "there is no need for that."

The managers' specific plans include:

1. Maintaining stability — Raise stock price to increase aggregate market price, enrich returns to shareholder, e.g., increase of dividends, etc.
2. Revising articles of incorporation — Change the articles of incorporation in order to "expand stock issuing frame," "predetermine upper limit of number of directors," "enable board of directors to change reference date for execution of voting right," etc.
3. Cross-shareholding — Cross-shareholding is unique to Japan, and is regaining popularity. As to its benefits, 3.1 percent said "it is a useful defensive measure and will be preserved;" 6.9 percent said "enhancement as an emergency measure should be allowed;" and 61.5 percent said "cross-shareholding is necessary for business cooperation." Approximately 70 percent of those surveyed approved or conditionally approved it.

---

[64] Nikkei, April 23, 2005, p. 11.

4. Use of US type techniques — "Poison pill" is the most popular (58.5 percent); followed by "white knight," wishing for a friendly buyer (17.4 percent); "crown jewel," disposing of important assets (7.3 percent); "scorched earth operation," selling off everything to create a hollow company, etc. The Packman defense[65] (4 percent) and golden parachute[66] and others (9.8 percent) are also being studied.

While the survey by Nikkei portrays what the managers of Japanese companies have in mind, the following are the typical defensive measures Japanese companies are already considering.

Not lowering the hurdles for dismissing directors

A dismissal of a director currently requires a special resolution approved by 2/3 of the entire votes at the shareholders' meeting.[67] The revised Corporate Law will relax it to an approval by a majority of the votes.[68] However, if the articles of incorporation are modified to require a special resolution, the same condition can be continued.[69]

While it is not uncommon for the articles of incorporation to simply state that the number of directors be more than three, it is risky from the point of view of preventing a takeover. In a takeover, Company A acquired the majority of shares of Company B, sent in 15 new directors in addition to existing 14 directors, and succeeded in replacing the representative director. An effective way to prevent such a takeover is to state a maximum number of directors, *e.g.*, "no more than 15," by a resolution of the shareholders and always keep the frame filled. If the

---

[65] The acquiree may take an offensive, proactive stand, for details, *see* http://media.wiley.com/product_data/excerpt/51/04713277/0471327751.pdf (last visited July 15, 2005).
[66]This maneuver results in significant compensation to the acquiree's top executives if a change in control of the acquiree occurs and the executive is terminated from the position currently held. For details, *see id.*
[67] Corporate Law, Art. 257.
[68] For details, see http://www.meinan.net/h17zeiseikaisei/10syouho1.htm (last visited July 15, 2005).
[69] *Id.*

frame is only half filled, the buyer will be able to control the board of directors so long as the buyer acquires the majority of the voting rights.

This tactic does not work for a company if the term of the director is one year. It is useful for controlling the company until the next election if the term is at least two years and the takeover buyer has not bought out more than two thirds of the entire shares.[70]

Make friendly trading partners a part of the defense plan

This is an agreement with a major trading partner that states "the trading partner can cancel the agreement unilaterally if a change occurs to the controlling shareholder." While its basic objective is to maintain a stable relation with a trading partner on the premise of certain management policies, it can be used as a defense mechanism against a hostile takeover by hinting to the other side the possibility of losing a major trading partner. Nippon Broadcasting, which was targeted by Livedoor, decided to issue share warrants to Fuji TV recognizing the necessity for defending itself. It also added a cancellation clause to its agreement with a trading partner, a professional baseball team. The Tokyo High Court noted that this was an action "intended to benefit their battle," and did not approve these issues. A different court decision could have been made if such an agreement existed prior to the battle.[71]

Always have a business plan ready

While issuing new shares to a third party, in particular, to a friendly company, in order to reduce the hostile buyer's voting right ratio, is a viable alternative defense in an emergency, authorized capital should not be forgotten. A company is entitled to issue new shares so long as the total number of shares is within the frame authorized by the shareholders' meeting.[72] If there is no room left within the frame, it may be necessary to have it expanded beforehand by the shareholders'

---

[70] Nikkei, June 30, 2005, p. 3.
[71] Kinyu Zaisei Homu Jijyo (Banking and Financial Legal Issues), Kinyu Zaisei Jijyo Kenkyuukai, No. 1733, March 15, 2005, pp. 10–17.
[72] Commercial Law Art. 166.

meeting. If the main objective relates to a change in the shareholders' composition, it will not be allowed. In order for the elimination of the hostile buyer not to be considered the main objective, a bona fide business plan must be prepared in advance.

The Tokyo District Court approved an injunction against the issuance of share warrants by Nippon Broadcasting.[73] The Tokyo High Court, in support of the lower court's decision, judged that the main objective of the share warrants was to maintain the existing control of the company, stating that the purpose of the funds to be raised by the issuance of the share warrants was "difficult to believe as it [the purpose] was more likely devised as an excuse after the conflict occurred."[74]

Other defensive measures

The followings are tactics employed by some Japanese companies:

1. A merger partner — Prepare a plan to merger with an affiliated company with a stable shareholder ratio so that the merger plan can be readily resolved by the shareholders meeting.
2. Reduce the directors' responsibility — If duly part of the articles of incorporation, the board of directors can reduce the upper limit of a director's damages to an amount equivalent to two years' compensation. With it, the company can fight out the battle with the outside directors only.[75]
3. Capable auditor — An auditor is eligible to request a court injunction against illegal actions by directors. It is possible to fight against a corporate raider with such a capable auditor with a term as long as four years.[76]
4. Predetermine the directors' retirement pay — Determining the directors' retirement pay at the shareholders meeting in advance removes any worries the directors may have concerning their

---

[73] See *supra* n. 37.
[74] See *supra* n. 38.
[75] *Nikkei*, June 30, 2005, p. 3.
[76] *Id.*

income after their retirement, thus allowing them to concentrate on defending against the hostile takeover.[77]

Possibility of M&A of Japanese Companies by Overseas Sources

Tactics

Various styles of M&A that can be used in Japan are as shown. (*See also* Exhibit 6.)

Exhibit 6 — Various Styles of M&A in Japan

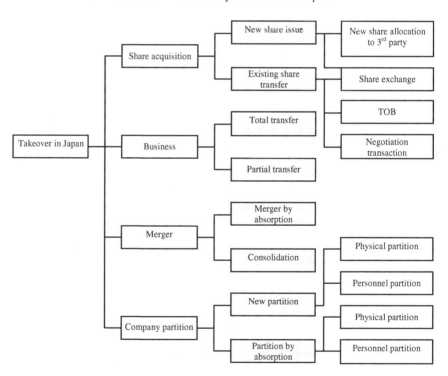

---

[77] *Id.*

1. Share acquisition.[78]
    a. Acquisition of existing shares — Possible styles in this method include market buying or takeover buying, but are limited to negotiation transactions for unlisted shares. Negotiation transactions are a simpler process so it is the most frequently used in M&A.
    b. Shares issued to a third party — The buyer subscribes to shares issued by the company, in which existing shares and new shares issued to the third party can be mixed.
    c. Share exchange — This is a method by which the buyer buys the shares not with cash but in exchange for new shares issued by the buyer or its treasury stock. This is desirable for making the target company a 100 percent subsidiary and is convenient for a listed company.

2. Business transfer.[79] Business transfer is a transfer of all or a portion of the business in which the seller company is involved. The transfer applies not only to tangible business assets, such as land, building, equipment, and machines but also intangible assets, such as employees and trading partners. Because the buyer can pick and choose whatever he needs, there is no risk of inadvertently acquiring any hidden liability.

3. Merger.[80] A merger is uniting two or more companies under a contract. While a merger can be a "merger by absorption" in which one of the companies becomes a surviving company and other company or companies are dissolved, or a "consolidation" in which all companies are dissolved to form a new company. Most mergers are by "merger by absorption" because it is the simplest.

4. Partition of company.[81] Partition of a company is when "a company allows all or a portion of its business to be succeeded wholly by another company." It looks similar to a business transfer but it is quite different in that it allows its business to be succeeded wholly. The partition can be either a "new partition" in which the business

---

[78] Securities Exchange Law, Art. 27-2.
[79] Commercial Law, Arts. 25–29.
[80] Commercial Law, Art. 56.
[81] Commercial Law, Art. 373.

of the company being split is succeeded by a newly created company, or "partition by absorption" in which the business is succeeded by an existing company. Its unique feature is that in either situation the price of the partition is paid for by shares, so that M&A is made possible without the need of cash.

Percentage of shares that need to be bought

To what degree a company can be controlled by a hostile buyer depends on the proportion of the shares acquired. The voting power and influence on management achievable in Japan by acquisition of shares is illustrated in Exhibit 7.

Exhibit 7 — Voting Power and Influence on Management Depending on the Ratio of Shares

Voting Power	Ratio of Shares Needed
Eligible to decide merger, business transfer, change in articles of incorporation, etc.	Over Two Thirds
Select directors	Majority
Eligible to reject decide merger, business transfer, change of article of incorporation, etc.	Over one third
Eligible to call shareholders meeting and request dismissal of directors	Over 3 percent (*)
Eligible to propose a topic of discussion	More than 1 percent or 300 shares (*)
Cast a vote for a bill in shareholders meeting	More than one share

*Eligibility if it is held more than six months.

It should be noted that the voting right will be lost if shares are cross-owned between a parent company and its subsidiary according to the Japanese Commercial Law. When Company A owns over 25 percent of Company B's shares, Company B loses its voting rights of Company A's shares. When Company A and its subsidiary A^1 together hold or A^1 subsidiary alone holds more than 25 percent of the voting rights of Company C, Company C does not have any voting rights of Company A's shares.[82]

---

[82] Commercial Law, Art. 211-2.

Merger using offshore shares

The Ministry of Justice of Japan has made new conditions concerning mergers using offshore shares, which are difficult to trade domestically in Japan.[83] Because there is concern about hostile takeovers of Japanese companies by offshore capital, the ministry feels a need to set up certain limitations. The plan the ministry is considering is expected to be tough on merger conditions when using offshore shares not traded domestically to pay for the acquisition. While the Ministry of Justice's intention is to protect domestic investors who are to be provided with offshore shares in mergers, it is moving cautiously as such a move may bring criticism as a means of "fending off offshore capital."

Using offshore shares as counter values in merger deals is a new technique to be employed by offshore companies in acquiring Japanese companies and is called "triangular merger." (*See* Exhibit 8.) When an offshore company arranges to merge its subsidiary established in Japan

Exhibit 8 — Triangular Scheme of Using Offshore Shares for Payment

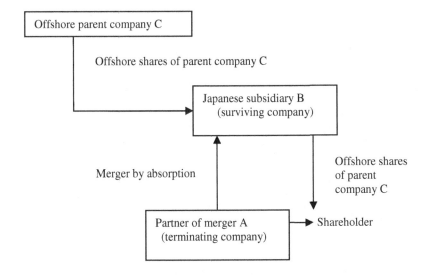

---

[83] *See* n. 14 at p. 11.

with a Japanese company in order to prompt reorganization, it is allowed to assign the shares of the offshore parent company to shareholders of the Japanese company. The new rule gives the offshore company having a large market value the advantage of executing M&A in Japan using its own shares to pay for the transactions. The new rule, however, has raised a chorus of criticism in Japan that "it will simply promote hostile takeover of Japanese industries by foreign companies." Therefore, the ministry has to adjust the range of offshore shares that can be applied.

The Ministry of Justice plans to clarify, by means of a ministerial ordinance after the bill has been adopted, the scope and condition of offshore shares that can be used. Specifically, the ministry intends to require a "special resolution" rather than a normal resolution to approve the merger of a Japanese company to be bought out in a triangular merger using non-listed offshore shares to pay for the deal in the Japanese market. A special resolution requires approval by two thirds of the attendees of a shareholders' meeting, represented by a majority of shareholders in terms of voting rights. This will make it very difficult for a company with a large number of individual shareholders to satisfy the requirements.

The shares to be provided may not be shares of European and US companies where the securities markets are advanced. Considering the ease of cashability and the ease of obtaining information in Japanese, it is not unreasonable to set some differences in the requirements for merger resolutions. In particular, there may be a situation in which shares are bought beforehand to "coerce" a triangular merger, which is supposed to be a friendly corporate reorganization. The ministry should consider the possibility of a malicious corporate raider and make its first ruling fairly conservative.

One anticipated objection is that "it does not give a sufficient way of selecting offshore companies, which are not listed on the Tokyo Stock Exchange." However, if the buyer really wants to buy a company in Japan, he can use cash. It is not infrequent to use cash for an international corporate reorganization. If the hurdle of "to be listed on the exchange board" is too high, use the condition "to disclose business contents in Japan continuously." However, a Japanese company can be either "one being bought" or "one buying." A transparent and fair rule not only improves the managing standard of Japanese companies but is indispensable for survival in international competition. At first the government was planning to execute this new policy in April 2006, but decided to delay the implementation one year allowing for comments from businesses in Japan, which requested a more cautious approach.[84]

Shares of Japanese companies are relatively inexpensive — opportune time to buy

In the latter half of 1980, the trading market grew rapidly. It was triggered by the Plaza Accord (September 1985), which paved the way for the depreciation of the US dollar through international coordination. In order to deal with the sharp advance of the yen appreciation as a result of the Plaza Accord, a low interest, volumetric relaxation policy was introduced to suppress excessive yen appreciation and to stimulate domestic business activities.

In the midst of this, expectations that Japan would become "a trade surplus super power, credit super power nation" increased, leading to a sharp rise in credit creating activities through bank lending, a huge influx of funds into the stock and real estate markets, and asset inflation. All of this was happening toward the end of the 1980s, which later was tagged as the "bubble economy." "Equity finance" became popular with large corporations, and stock prices grew sharply keeping in pace with the substantial increase of trading volume in the stock market. Future/option trading of bond and stock price indices was introduced in the latter half of 1980s, making the securities market in Japan the world's largest international securities market in terms of size and organization.

Because of the increase in the central bank's lending rate, which was increased six times from May 1989 through August 1990, as well as the introduction of the total volume control of real estate-related loans in March 1990, the bubble economy headed down the road to collapse in the beginning of the 1990s. The progress of asset deflation accompanying price reduction of stocks and real estate began to compress the actual economy and the myth of uninterruptible economic

---

[84] *Id.*

growth began to crumble. The failure of Hyogo Bank, the first bank failure since the end of WWII, was a blow to the belief that banks never fail and financial uncertainty began to surface. In the stock market, a huge loss cover-up of a major client assisted by a major securities company was uncovered (1991), causing a substantial loss of trust by investors, a sharp drop in stock prices, and a major decrease in trading volume, which brought a downward trend in the trading market. The share issuing market sank in a big way due to the doldrums of the trading market.

In the spring of 2000, the stock prices in the United States, which had been increasing for some time thanks to the "information technology revolution," finally turned downward after reaching its peak in January through March 2000. The Japanese stock market, which had been recovering to a degree, headed downward again. Moreover, financial instability increased under the pressure applied by the government to accelerate bad-debt cleanups of banks. The Nikkei average hit bottom at ¥7,067.88 in April 2003. (*See* Exhibit 9.) It was a drop of 63.5 percent from a peak (¥20,833.21) recorded in April 2000, and a whopping 80.5

Exhibit 9 — Trends of Stock Price After WWII

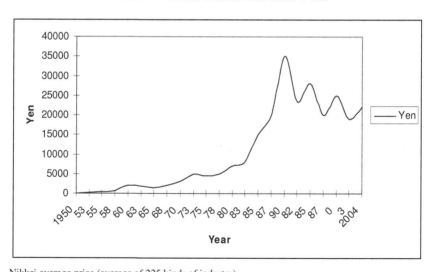

Nikkei average price (average of 225 kinds of industry)
Source: Annual average price, Nihon Keizai Shimbun, Inc., Tokyo Stock Exchange

percent drop compared to the historical peak (¥38,915.87) recorded at the end of 1989. This drop is close to the drop recorded during the stock market collapse in the United States, which started the Great Depression of the 1930s. The Dow Jones Industrial Average fell 89.2 percent from a peak ($381.17) in September 1929 to the bottom ($41.22) in July 1932.

In the course of this historic fall of stock prices in Japan, the "cross-shareholding system" cultivated during the years after WWII, crumbled and a dramatic change occurred in share composition. Various reforms and market adjustment policies were implemented in order to enhance the functions of and revitalize the securities market, in particular, the stock market, aimed toward renewal of the financial systems under the financial administrative guidance of the government. Consequently, banks, which played the central role in the "cross-shareholding system" as the core of the financial system, began compressing the volume of shares they held at a remarkable pace. For example, the total amount of shares held by domestic banks was approximately ¥46 trillion or approximately 160 percent of the total of their owned capital at the end of 1996. In contrast, the same amount at the end of November 2004 dropped to approximately ¥23 trillion, or just about one half of its peak. Life insurance companies, which were also an important supporter of the "cross-shareholding system" as major stable shareholding investors, compressed their holdings more than banks did, lowering the ratio of stock holdings compared to the total assets from 18.6 percent at the end of 1994 to 8.8 percent at the end of November 2004.

The dramatic reduction of shareholding by banks and life insurance companies, as well as a decreasing shareholding ratio of industrial companies, are accelerating the collapse of the "cross-shareholding system" and the major reasons for the stock price doldrums in Japan. The average stock price in Japan is ¥11,063 (May 19, 2005), which is 28.4 percent of the peak reached in 1989. At the moment Japanese stock prices are at an historical low. This presents an opportune time for US companies to buy Japanese companies.

Conclusion

Livedoor's "hostile takeover" of Nippon Broadcasting is the first domestic case of a hostile takeover by a business seeking a synergistic effect. The incident will no doubt serve as a trigger for more hostile takeovers of Japanese companies by offshore companies, particularly US firms. The new Corporate Law, which will be introduced in 2006, is designed to provide defensive measures against hostile takeovers and to make it easier for offshore shares to be traded domestically in Japan by "triangular merger" in which offshore companies buy Japanese companies using share exchange through Japanese subsidiaries. The fear that Japanese companies will be swallowed up by foreign investors has prompted the postponement of the triangular merger rules for one year. However, Livedoor's takeover indicates that it is not difficult to attempt a hostile takeover under the current rule, so postponing the triangular merger rules doesn't seem that meaningful.

The new Japanese value concept that "any company that produces no profit is worth nothing to society" is well understood by companies that are fiercely competing in the world market. Hostile takeovers may wake up sleeping managers. From now on, Japanese companies must view their managing policies from a global standpoint, cognizant that they may be the target of a hostile takeover at any moment. But allowing for defensive tactics that are too strong could make it difficult to conduct M&A to improve companies through the dismissal of ineffective managers.

Although there are many Japanese companies warning about the threat of hostile takeovers by offshore companies, so far most of the direct investments by offshore capital have been friendly. Of course, there will be hostile ones. It is important to promote investment in Japan in the world market and yet be careful to defend against hostile takeovers.

With these enhancements of the corporate defenses, Japanese companies are expected to change in the right direction. The respect for shareholders will be accelerated and the functions of outside directors and outside auditors will be better appreciated. Outside directors will have a larger role as they are given greater authority and more responsibility. Institutional investors are expected to recognize their responsibilities as shareholders more acutely and will do more to help companies increase their corporate values. Japanese companies will then be recognized as more attractive targets of buyouts and the true internationalization of Japanese industry will be realized.

Bibliography

Amendment of Commercial Law in April 1, 2002, last visited July 17, 2005, http://members.at.infoseek.co.jp/barexam/note/history_sh.htm.
Civil Law, Law No. 899 (April 27, 1896), Art. 709, http://law.e-gov.go.jp/cgi-bin/idxsearch.cgi.
Commercial Law of Japan, Law No. 48 (Mar. 9, 1899) (amended 18 times) [hereinafter Commercial Law], last visited July 8, 2005, http://www.ron.gr.jp/law/law/syouhou1.htm.
Commercial Law, Art. 166.
Commercial Law, Art. 211-2.
Commercial Law, Art. 245.
Commercial Law, Art. 373.
Commercial Law, Art. 56.
Commercial Law, Art.280-2.
Commercial Law, Arts. 25–29.
Corporate Law, Art. 257.
Economist (Japan), April 1, 2005, p. 9.
Economist (Japan), April 11, 2005, p. 18.
Economist (Japan), MSCB, April 11, 2005, p. 9.
Friendly Takeover of Seiyu by Wal-Mart, last visited July 13, 2005, http://www.cool-knowledge.com/020411wal-mart-toiu-vision.htm.
Fuji Television Network, http://www.fujitv.co.jp/jp/.
Introduction to Business Combinations, last visited July 15, 2005, http://media.wiley.com/product_data/excerpt/51/04713277/0471327751.pdf.
Investopedia, Golden Share, last visited July 16, 2005, http://www.investopedia.com/terms/g/goldenshare.asp.
Investopedia, NPV, last visited July 13, 2005, http://www.investopedia.com/terms/n/npv.asp.
Japan Times, Crown Jewels, last visited July 13, 2005, http://search.japantimes.co.jp/print/business/nb03-2005/nb20050326a3.htm.
Japanese Definition, http://vic-si-e-financial.g.hatena.ne.jp/keyword/%E4%BC%81%E6%A5%AD%E4%BE%A1%E5%80%A4?kid=1345 (last visited July 13, 2005).
Japanese Federation of Economic Organizations, last visited July 11, 2005, http://www.keidanren.or.jp/Japanese/profile/pro001.htm.
Kinyu Zaisei Jijyo Kenkyuukai, Kinyu Zaisei Homu Jijyo (Banking and Financial Legal Issues),_No.1733, March 15, 2005, pp.10–17.
Livedoor Co., http://corp.livedoor.com/company/outline.html.

Ministry of Finance Website, last visited July 13, 2005, http://www.mof.go.jp.

Moran v. *Household International, Inc.,* Del.Ch., 490 A.2d 1059 (1985), last visited July 13, 2005, http://www.law.unlv.edu/faculty/rlawless/mergers/moran.htm.

Nikkei, April 23, 2005, p. 11.

Nikkei, June 2, 2005, p. 1.

Nikkei, June 30, 2005, p. 3.

Nikkei, June 30, 2005, p. 3.

Nikkei, June 30, 2005, p. 3.

Nikkei, March 24, 2005, p. 11.

Nikkei, March 24, 2005, p. 12.

Nikkei, May 28, 2005, pp. 2–5.

Nippon Broadcasting System, Inc., http://www.jolf.co.jp/company/IR1242/index.html.

Nippon Broadcasting, "Approval of Issuance of Stock Acquisition Rights," February 24, 2005, http://www.jolf.co.jp/company/IR1242/index.html.

Nippon Broadcasting, "Notice of Regarding Ruling on Request for Court Injunction Blocking Issuance of Stock Acquisition Rights and Appeal Against the Ruling," March 11, 2005, http://www.jolf.co.jp/company/IR1242/index.html.

Nippon Broadcasting, "Notice Regarding Issuance of Stock Acquisition Rights Through Third-Party Allocation," February 23, 2005, http://www.jolf.co.jp/company/ IR1242/index.html.

Nippon Broadcasting, "Notification of Basic Agreement Making Nippon Broadcasting System a Wholly Owned Subsidiary," April 18, 2005, http://www.jolf.co.jp/ company/IR1242/index.html.

Nippon Broadcasting, "Notification Regarding Rejection of Objection to Temporary Court Injunction Blocking Issuance of Stock Acquisition Rights and of Appeal Against the Ruling," March 16, 2005, http://www.jolf.co.jp/company/IR1242/ index.html.

Nippon Broadcasting, "Notice of Lending of Fuji Television's Shares," February 23, 2005, last visited July 13, 2005, http://www.jolf.co.jp/company/IR1242/ index.html.

Nippon Broadcasting, Tokyo High Court, The 16th Civil Section, March 23, 2005, "Notification Regarding Dismissal of Appeal Against Lower Court of Temporary Injunction to Block Issuance of Stock Acquisition Rights," on March 23, 2005, http://www.jolf.co.jp/company/IR1242/index.html.

Nomura Securities, http://www.nomura.co.jp/terms/japan/ki/m_and_a.html.

Nomura Securities, http://www.nomura.co.jp/terms/japan/te/sinkabuyoyakus.html.

Pony Canyon, last visited July 13, 2005, http://music.ponycanyon.co.jp/.

Requirements, last visited July 14, 2007, http://www.smrj.go.jp/isif/series/ okabunushi_y24.html.

SEC homepage, last visited July 15, 2005, http://www.sec.gov/.

Securities Exchange Law of Japan, Law No. 25 of 1948, art. 127, no. 4 [hereinafter Securities Exchange Law], last visited July 8, 2005, available at http://www.japan law.info/f_statements/ PARENT/DX.htm.

Securities Exchange Law Ordinance, Law No. 321, September 30, 1964, Art. 13-1.

Securities Exchange Law, Art. 27-2.

Securities Exchange Law, Art. 27-2.

Securities Exchange Law, Art. 27-2.

Securities Exchange Law, Art. 27-2.

Seiyu homepage, last visited July 13, 2005, http://www.seiyu.co.jp/.

SoftBank Corp., last visited July 13, 2005, http://www.softbank.co.jp/.

Tokyo Stock Exchange, last visited July 11, 2005, http://www.tse.or.jp/glossary/gloss_t/tachiaigai.html.

Wal-Mart homepage, last visited July 13, 2005, *http://www.walmart.com/*.

Chapter 11

A Recent Reform of Banking Law — US and Japanese Comparative Study on Creation of Legal System for Banking Agencies[a]

Introduction

On October 4, 2005, an enactment intended to reform the Japanese Banking Law[1] ("Reform Enactment")[2] submitted by the cabinet was approved by the 163rd Special Session of the Diet and promulgated on November 2, 2005.

The reform was intended to create a legal system for banking agencies in order to improve depositors' benefits based on the required structural changes of Japanese financial and capital markets help to cope with the changes occurring in overseas financial situations.

This reform of the Banking Law in Japan is following in the footsteps of the US, and it is making it easier for general business firms to become banking agencies. This reform enables business firms to conduct banking business while they continue to do their original business. Banks may have to seek and study a strategy of alliance with business firms. The introduction of the banking agency system is urging Japanese banks to make better management decisions where selection and concentration are needed to increase their international competitiveness. The expected

---

[a] For this chapter, permission is granted to reprint by the Banking Law Journal, Mitsuru Misawa, "A Recent Reform of Japanese Banking Law-Comparison of The US and Japanese Legal Systems for Banking Agencies", The Banking Law Journal, June 2006, Volume 123, No. 6, pp. 536–552.
[1] Law No. 59, 1981.
[2] Law No. 106, 2005.

changes occurring in Japanese banks and how they adopt the new law under their traditional system are sure to attract the interests of US bankers.

Creation of System for Banking Agencies in Japan

Background

While there have been a number of system reforms in relation to banking agencies, including the change from a system requiring banks' approval to a system requiring only a report for creating or terminating a banking agency, the expansion of the scope of banking agency business, and the creation and expansion of the financial agency system, there still exist restrictions concerning these practices, e.g., (i) corporate agencies are approved only for 100% subsidiaries and (ii) the agencies are not allowed to be involved in other businesses than the agency business.[3] Therefore, although the agencies are effective manned channels, it is difficult for them to be created speedily enough as needed or to respond to various needs, so consequently they have not been used fully and there has always been strong desire among the financial institutions for abolishing or relaxing the investment regulation and further expansion of the scope of business.

Thoughts on Banking Agencies System

When general business operators try to invest in banking agency businesses, the law requires that they place their participations for review under a license system.[4] If they wish to operate banking agency businesses simultaneously with their original businesses, they are legally required to review it under an individual approval system.[5] The purpose of this reform is to secure and improve the users' access to financial services as well as to allow general business operators to participate in a broader form of banking agency businesses so that financial institutions can use wider varieties of sales channels.[6]

---

[3] Banking Law, Article 8.
[4] For the details, see Ministry of Finance, Financial System Council, Report of September 30, 2002, http://www.mof.go.jp/english/council.htm.
[5] Ibid.
[6] Ibid.

Banking Agencies System in US

Strict Control on Doing Other Businesses

In the United States, the businesses banks can be involved are strictly controlled, for example, by specifically itemizing them in case of a national bank in 12 USC 24 Seventh,[7] and a bank cannot be involved in other business than normal banking operations such as deposit, lending and exchange. It is strictly prohibited for general business entities to buy a bank and companies other than banks are generally prohibited from conducting banking or owning a bank as a subsidiary.[8]

The background of why banks and other business entities are so strictly separated in the US can be found in its unique history. In the United States, the central bank, FRB, was established relatively recently in 1913,[9] and bank notes were issued by commercial banks from the time when the US was founded until FRB was established. For example, in the president's room of Citizen Bank,[10] a well established old bank located in the outskirt of Baltimore, one can find a bank note issued by the bank approximately 100 years ago. In those days, it was not rare to see a bank go bankrupt, thus making the bank notes issued by the particular bank worthless, so that even today there is a strong suspicion and distrust among American people for banks in general. Therefore, strong regulations were formed restricting strictly what a bank can and cannot do in the US.

On the other hand, the central bank was established in 1882[11] and there was only a short period of time when commercial banks could issue bank notes so that it was considered unnecessary to control banks that

---

[7] The National Bank Act, 12 USC 24 Seventh. See http://www.fdic.gov/regulations/laws/rules/5000-1900.html.

[8] One of the few exceptions is state chartered industrial banks of the State of Utah, in which an industrial bank has an operational limitation that it cannot generally accept checking accounts; however, on the other hand, a general business company can own an industrial bank as a subsidiary. See http://www.dfi.utah.gov/IBSList.htm.

[9] In contrast, the Bank of Japan was established in 1882. See the web for the Bank of Japan, http://www.boj.or.jp/.

[10] The bank's founding was 1890. See the home page, http://baltimore.citysearch.com/profile/4857038/.

[11] See note 9.

do not have bank note issuing capabilities. However, because of a severe financial risk that occurred later, the Banking Law of 1927[12] was introduced to regulate banks strictly.[13]

Banking Agencies in US

There is a clear distinction between general business entities and banks, and both are strictly regulated in the United States, but there are not such strict regulations for "agencies," probably because they are thought to supplement the others essentially.

(1) Deposit

In the US, what is close to the "banking agencies system" in terms of deposit is "broker deposit." Although the brokers are normally major securities companies, it is not required to have any particular certificate to be a broker and even an individual can be a broker as well. Deposit brokers have traditionally provided intermediary services for banks and investors. Recent developments in technology provide bankers increased access to a broad range of potential investors who have no relationship with the bank and who actively seek the highest returns offered within the financial industry. In particular, the Internet and other automated service providers are effectively and efficiently matching yield-focused investors with potentially high-yielding deposits.[14]

A broker is entrusted with money from a client and deposits it to the most favorable bank, i.e., the bank that pays the highest interest. Customers

---

[12] In Japan, this period was ten years from 1872–1882.

[13] The Bank Law of 1927 (the pre-war banking law, Law No. 21 of 1927) set the minimum capital criterion for banks, which came to be a powerful measure for the government to promote consolidations. For details, see Tetsuji Okazaki, "Effects of bank consolidation promotion policy: Evaluating the Bank Law in 1927 Japan", http://ideas.repec.org/p/eti/dpaper/04004.html.

[14] Banks offer certificates to it (CDs) tailored to the $100,000 Federal Deposit Insurance Corporation (FDIC) deposit insurance limit to eliminate credit risk to the investor, but amounts may exceed insurance coverage. Rates paid on these deposits are often higher than those paid for local market area retail CDs, but due to the FDIC insurance coverage, these rates may be lower than for unsecured wholesale market funding. See, the press release of FDIC, May 11, 2001, www.fdic.gov/news/news/press/2001/pr3701a.html - 23k.

who focus exclusively on rates are highly rate-sensitive and provide less stable funding than do those with local retail deposit relationships. These rate-sensitive customers have easy access to, and are frequently well informed about, alternative markets and investments, and may have no other relationship with or loyalty to the bank. If market conditions change or more attractive returns become available, these customers may rapidly transfer their funds to new institutions or investments.

The deposit in this case is normally a negotiable deposit, or certificate of deposit (CD). From the standpoint of a bank, it gives the bank a means of relying on brokers to collect deposits in the areas where it does not have any branches, in case the bank cannot respond to high borrowing demands with its own deposits due to a high deposit/loan ratio. However, since many of the bankrupted S&L had collected huge amounts of deposits using broker deposits, which led to their bankruptcies during the S&L crisis of 1980s, Federal Deposit Insurance Corporation (FDIC) does not allow at this time for banks to accept broker deposits unless the bank has a sufficient amount of its own capital.[15]

Although one may see ATMs[16] located at non-bank institutions, such as convenience stores and gasoline filling stations in the US, those machines are cash dispensing machines, incapable of accepting deposits. For example, in the state of Illinois, a person other than a bank or an affiliate of a bank may establish or own, in whole or in part, a cash-dispensing terminal provided that the person establishing or owning the

---

[15] Under 12 USC 1831f and 12CFR 337.6, determination of "brokered" status is based initially on whether a bank actually obtains a deposit directly or indirectly through a deposit broker. Banks that are considered only "adequately capitalized" under the "Prompt Corrective Action" standard must receive a waiver from the FDIC before they can accept, renew, or roll over any brokered deposit. They also are restricted in the rates they may offer on such deposits. Banks falling below the adequately capitalized range may not accept, renew, or roll over any brokered deposit nor solicit deposits with an effective yield more than 75 basis points above the prevailing market rate. These restrictions will reduce the availability of funding alternatives as a bank's condition deteriorates. See, the press release of FDIC, May 11, 2001, www.fdic.gov/news/news/press/2001/pr3701a.html - 23k.

[16] ATM is Acronym for automated teller machine, a machine at a bank branch or other location which enables a customer to perform basic banking activities (checking one's balance, withdrawing or transferring funds) even when the bank is closed. For the details, see http://www.investorwords.com/308/ATM.html.

terminal shall file a notice of establishment or ownership of the terminal with the Commissioner within 60 days after the establishment of or acquisition of ownership of the terminal and file annually with the Commissioner.[17] The operators are only required to have ample lighting for security reasons.[18]

(2) Lending

Housing Loan

In the business of loans, the most popular operators are "mortgage brokers," who play an important role as brokers in making housing loans.

A mortgage broker is an individual or company which brings borrowers and lenders together for the purpose of loan origination, but which does not originate or service the mortgages. The broker might also negotiate with the lender to try to find the best possible financing deal possible for the borrower.[19] There are several ways for a bank to use mortgage brokers;

a. The bank buys the housing loan which is already executed by a mortgage broker. The bank will buy only those housing loans that fit its qualification standard.

b. The mortgage broker receives a housing loan request from a client and sends it to banks which offer favorable conditions. The banks then independently decide whether to offer the loan.

c. The mortgage broker, as an agent of the bank, accepts the housing loan application, examines it, and accepts the loan if it meets the bank's standard. However, it is the bank's responsibility to check if the broker is conforming to various housing loan regulations.

---

[17] See, Department of Financial and Professional Regulation, Division of Banking, State of Illinois, "Notice of Establishment or Ownership of a Cash Dispensing Terminal", IL505-0326 (8/2005), http://www.idfpr.com/FAQ/BRE/toggleBREnonbankatm.asp.

[18] See, note 17 on "What are the rights and responsibilities of an owner of a non-bank owned or a cash-dispensing only ATM?".

[19] For the definition of mortgage brokers, see http://www.investordictionary.com/definition/mortgage+broker.aspx.

Car Loan

It is a common practice in dealing with car loans for an automobile dealer to receive an application prepared by a client and fax it to a bank it is tied up with for loan approval. Such a loan is called "indirect lending" and is a popular practice in the US.[20] The indirect loan is transferred to a third party after being originated by a dealer, retailer or other seller of goods or services to finance the purchase of those goods or services. The loan is an indirect loan from the third party to whom it is transferred, to the consumer of the goods or services bought on credit.

Consumer loans provided by small institutions, which are often called community banks, mostly fall into the category of this indirect lending. However, a new tendency in the car loan business in the US is that the loans are provided more and more by financial subsidiaries of car manufacturers, and causing banks to be involved less and less. As a result, some of the banks are widening their scope of business to loans for pleasure boats, aircraft, and high-class recreating vehicles. These areas are niche markets and the margins on consumer loans are not as thick as in car loans but are still meaningful enough for banks to pursue.

In-Store Branch

Banks often have in-store branches in supermarkets these days. The branches offer full service to customers, ranging from check cashing to opening new accounts and loans. The number of employees varies, depending upon the size of the branch and the volume of business.[21]

In those cases, the supermarkets are not agencies of the banks, but rather lenders of spaces for the banks, and the branches are operated by the banks.

---

[20] For indirect loans, True yields are always concerns of the lenders and they are greatly dependent upon prepayments and charge-offs. See the details at, http://www.cunalendingcouncil.org/news/262.html.

[21] Wells Fargo Bank of US opened its first in-store bank branch inside a Vallejo, Calif. supermarket in 1990. That branch offered a scaled-down version of full-service banking as part of a strategy to take banking to where the customers are — in this case inside supermarkets. The success of that first branch inspired Wells Fargo Bank to roll out its "Anytime, Anywhere" banking program, a major expansion of in-store locations in the Sacramento, Calif. area. For the details, see Wells Fargo Official Site, http://www.wellsfargo.com.

Recent Reform of Japanese Banking Law Related to the Banking Agency System

Definition

According to the Reform Enactment,[22] it was defined that a "banking agency business" is a business of performing as an agent or intermediary in the act of either (a) accepting deposits or installment saving accounts, (b) lending of funds or discounting notes receivables, or (c) concluding contracts of exchange transactions,[23] a "banking agent" as a person who conducts the banking agency business under authorization,[24] and an "affiliated bank" as a bank which provides the services of receiving deposits or installment saving accounts, lending funds, or discounting notes receivables based on the actions of the banking agent.[25]

Authorization of the Banking Agency Business

(1) Introduction of the licensing system

The banking agency business is responsible for carrying out important functions such as settling of transactions and lending, and may cause problems in the settling system or protection of clients if the business fails to be properly managed. Because of this uniqueness of the banking agency business, a licensing system was introduced to examine applicants from a broad range of general business operators to see if each of them is fit to run the business before they are allowed to participate in the banking agency business.[26] In the case of an agent or intermediary for auxiliary business other than deposit, lending, and exchange,[27] there is no need to be licensed.

---

[22] See note 2.
[23] Banking Law, Article 2, Sec. 14.
[24] Ibid.
[25] Banking Law, Article 2, Sec. 16.
[26] Banking Law, Article 52, Sec. 36-1.
[27] Banking Law, Article 10, Sec. 2.

(2) Application of license

According to the Reform Enactment, the application shall accompany a document that shows (a) the institution's trade name, title, or a person's name, (b) name of officer(s) in case of a legal person, (3) name and address of the office where the banking agency business is conducted, and (4) trade name of the affiliated bank, and a description of the contents and method of the intended banking agency business.[28] If it is deemed necessary to do so for the sake of public benefits in reference to the examination standard, the institution shall be allowed to apply a certain restriction within the limit of necessity or modify it; for example, it shall be allowed to apply a restriction on the contents of the banking agency business depending on the contents of the business it is conducting additionally.[29]

(3) Standard of license

According to the Reform Enactment, a license for banking agency business shall be granted in accordance with the examination standard that (i) the institution has a sufficient financial base that is considered necessary to execute the banking agency business, (ii) the institution has a sufficient capability of conducting the banking agency business with accuracy, fairness and efficiency based on its personnel constitution, and (iii) the institution does not seem to have any problem conducting the banking agency business despite its operation of other businesses.[30]

(4) Change report

In order to secure the effectiveness of monitoring business operations, according to the Reform Enactment, a banking agent shall promptly report any change to the descriptions of the license application that occurred after the license was awarded, or if the licensee wishes to change the contents and method of conducting the banking agency business.[31]

---

[28] Banking Law, Article 52, Sec. 37.
[29] Banking Law, Article 52, Sec. 38-2.
[30] Banking Law, Article 52, Sec. 38-1.
[31] Banking Law, Article 52, Sec. 39.

Introduction of License for Side Business

According to the Reform Enactment, a banking agent shall be allowed to conduct side businesses that are different from the banking agent business or its auxiliary business only upon receiving a license from the government. This means that any side business the agent was already conducting at the time of the application for the banking agency needs to be examined by the government as well as any new side business to be added.[32]

According to the Reform Enactment, the application for approval of a side business shall be rejected if it is considered detrimental to a proper and secure operation of the banking agency business.[33]

It is considered unnecessary to obtain the license if the agent is to perform the affiliate bank's auxiliary business[34] as an agent or intermediary, as such a business is auxiliary business of the banking agency business.

Explanation to Client

(1) Clear indication to client

According to the Reform Enactment, when a banking agent conducts a banking agency operation,[35] the agent must clearly indicate to the client in advance the trade name of the affiliated bank and whether he is an agent or an intermediary.[36]

(2) Providing information to client

According to the Reform Enactment, similar to the bank's duty[37] to provide necessary information to its depositors, the banking agency agent shall provide the contents of the contract concerning deposits

---

[32] Banking Law, Article 52, Sec. 42-1.
[33] Banking Law, Article 52, Sec. 42-2.
[34] Banking Law, Article 10, Sec. 2.
[35] Operations listed at each subsection of Banking Law, Article 2, Sec. 14.
[36] Banking Law, Article 52, Sec. 44-1.
[37] Banking Law, Article 12, Sec. 2-1.

or installment saving accounts and other information that is useful to the depositors.[38]

(3) Measures of securing healthy and proper operation

According to the Reform Enactment, in addition to (1) and (2), the banking agent must provide explanation for important matters concerning its banking agency operation and take necessary measures to secure healthy and proper management, e.g., proper handling of the information concerning the client that is obtained through the banking agency operation, etc.[39]

(4) Prohibited actions related to banking agency business

The following acts are prohibited as they fail to provide adequate protections to clients, or because they affect the affiliated bank's healthy and proper execution of its business: (i) providing false information, (ii) providing a decisive judgement on matters of uncertainty or reporting information that can be erroneously construed as a matter of certainty, (iii) performing as an agent or intermediary in lending funds or negotiating drafts on the condition of performing another transaction thereby abusing one's dominant bargaining position, and (iv) performing as an agent or intermediary in lending funds or negotiating drafts at better conditions than the affiliated bank's normal transactions.[40]

Proper Way of Conducting Banking Agency Business

(1) Posting signs

Banking business agents are obligated to put up signs in conspicuous places declaring that they are licensed agents, prohibiting simultaneously those who are not licensed to put up signs of banking agencies or signs that could be mistaken as signs of that

---

[38] Banking Law, Article 52, Sec. 44-2.
[39] Banking Law, Article 52, Sec. 44-3.
[40] Banking Law, Article 52, Sec. 45.

banking agencies in order to prevent clients from conducting transactions with unlicensed parties by mistake.[41]

(2) Prohibition of name-lending

From the standpoint of preventing illegal actions from circumventing the purpose of licensing, licensed banking agencies are prohibited from lending their license to another party to allow the party to operate as a banking agent.[42] Banks are also prohibited from name-lending as well.[43]

(3) Separating management

It was stipulated that a banking agent must manage any money or assets received from a client separately from the agent's own assets.[44]

More specifically, when the agent receives money or other types of assets from a client, the agent must store them in a place clearly segregated from the agent's own assets and make sure that it can be quickly identified which affiliated bank they are related to. In the case of cash, the segregation can be achieved by books.

(4) Holidays and business hours of banking agent

From the standpoint of securing stability of the settling system, according to the Reform Enactment, the same rules of the holidays and business hours[45] of a bank are applicable to special banking agencies[46] in accordance with the Banking Law.[47] This rule does not apply to a branch or office which is not involved in the specific banking operations and it can be open on holidays or during hours outside of the business hours specified in the Banking Law.

---

[41] Banking Law, Article 52, Sec. 40.

[42] Banking Law, Article 52, Sec. 41.

[43] Banking Law, Article 9.

[44] Banking Law, Article 52, Sec. 43.

[45] 9 a.m. to 3 p.m.

[46] Special banking agencies perform agency operations for current deposits. See Banking Law, Article 52, Sec. 46.

[47] Banking Law, Article 52, Sec. 46.

Accounting

(1) Books and ledgers related to banking agency business

According to the Reform Enactment, banking agencies must prepare and preserve the books and ledgers related to banking agency business in order to clarify the processes and calculations of banking agency business.[48]

(2) Reports concerning banking agency business

According to the Reform Enactment, each banking agent must prepare a report on its banking agency business for each fiscal year which is to be submitted to the authority in order to make it available for public inspection.[49]

(3) Public inspection of affiliated bank's disclosure documents

According to the Reform Enactment, the banking agent must have the documents prepared by the affiliated bank or the bank holding company that holds the affiliated bank as its subsidiary for the purpose of public inspection based on the regulations of the Banking Law, i.e., the disclosure of documents at the banking agent's branch or office for public inspection.[50]

(4) Apply for voluntary closure

According to the Reform Enactment, a banking agent must apply for voluntary closure when the agent gives up the agent business, the agent dies, the agent institution ceases to exist due to a merger, or the agent is disbanded.[51] The license for banking agency business becomes ineffective when one of the above mentioned circumstances occur.[52]

---

[48] Banking Law, Article 52, Sec. 49.
[49] Banking Law, Article 52, Sec. 50.
[50] Banking Law, Article 52, Sec. 51.
[51] Banking Law, Article 52, Sec. 52.
[52] Banking Law, Article 52, Sec. 57.

Affiliated Bank

(1) Adoption of affiliated bank system

While two systems are possible for agency actions legally, i.e., (i) affiliated company system (dedication),[53] and (ii) brokerage system (non-dedication),[54] according to the Reform Enactment, a banking agent takes the form of (i) and it "shall not perform banking agency business unless it is assigned by an affiliated bank or re-assigned by a banking agent who is assigned by the affiliated bank,"[55] and the banking agency system shall be a system wherein a healthy and proper operation is secured by the affiliated bank.[56] A banking agent can operate banking agency business for a plurality of affiliated banks.[57]

(2) Affiliated bank's guidance for banking agent

According to the Reform Enactment, an affiliated bank shall provide guidance to a banking agent, and a banking agency reassignor[58] shall provide guidance to a banking agency reassignee[59] on how the business should be conducted in order to oblige them to operate a healthy and proper banking agency business.[60]

(3) Affiliated bank's liability for reparation

According to the Reform Enactment, the affiliated bank shall be held liable for repairing the damage the banking agent causes to its client. Similarly, the banking agency reassignor shall be held responsible for repairing the damage the banking agency reassignee causes to its client. It is also stated in the Reform Enactment that the liability

---

[53] Agent working for a specific company.
[54] Broker.
[55] Affiliated bank system.
[56] Banking Law, Article 52, Sec. 36-2.
[57] Ibid.
[58] Banking agent who reassigns banking agency business.
[59] Banking agent who conducts banking agency business under reassignment by a banking agency reassignor.
[60] Banking Law, Article 52, Sec. 58.

can be exempted if there was enough effort in preventing the client's damage. But no such example can be found in the employer responsibility of the Civil Law[61] in the past, proving that it is applied as a no-fault liability in reality, so that this exemption case seems to be severely limited.[62]

(4) Original register of banking agencies

According to the Reform Enactment, the affiliated bank must have an original register of banking agencies, and depositors' stakeholders shall have the right to ask the affiliated bank for inspections of said register.[63]

Supervision of Banking Agencies

According to the Reform Enactment, the Banking Bureau must be able to levy a report[64] from and conduct an on-the-spot inspection[65] at a banking agency as well as be able to order an improvement of business operations,[66] cancellation of the banking agency license, and be able to stop all or a part of the banking agency business[67] if the bureau sees any need for the purpose of securing healthy and proper operations at the particular banking agency.

Exclusion of Application

According to the Reform Enactment, a legal person who conducts financial business[68] such as a bank is permitted to conduct banking agency business without obtaining a license, which regulates what a banking agency business is permitted to do.[69]

---

[61] Law No. 89 of 1896.
[62] Banking Law, Article 52, Sec. 59.
[63] Banking Law, Article 52, Sec. 60.
[64] Banking Law, Article 52, Sec. 53.
[65] Banking Law, Article 52, Sec. 54.
[66] Banking Law, Article 52, Sec. 55.
[67] Banking Law, Article 52, Sec. 56.
[68] It includes financial institution for handling deposits and savings such as long term banks and credit unions. See Banking Law, Article 52, Sec. 61.
[69] Ibid.

Conclusion

Although the number of bank branches is decreasing in Japan, the number of bank branches in the US has been increasing despite the substantial reduction in the number of banks over the last 20 years.[70] This is due to the fact that in the US, there has been a substantial growth of branch operations that are aided by the banking agency system.

The regulation reform in Japan now is based on the recognition of the fact that in the US, flexible banking agency is quite effective in promoting its citizens' benefits concerning financial services, in particular, the improvement of accessibility to cash in remote areas. In that sense, the reform of the Banking Law in Japan is following the suit of the US, and it is making it easier for general business entities and individuals to become banking agencies. Not only that, it makes it possible for them to handle any kind of banking business.[71]

This reform enables business firms to conduct banking business while they continue to do their original business, thus causing a big hole in the regulation that prohibits banks from doing other types of business. Although it goes without saying that those business entities will be placed under similar regulations as banks, the objective of this reform is to make banking management more efficient by allowing new participants to enter banking business and promote development of new kinds of banking services.

---

[70] Although the number of banks reduced almost 50% in the last 20 years, the number of bank branches increased during the same period in the US. For example, while 909 banks disappeared in the last five years, the number of bank branches increased as many as 4746. On the other hand, 13 banks failed to exist and as many as 2087 bank branches disappeared during the same period in Japan. (Refer to: Japanese Bankers Association's home page on the Internet; http://www.zenginkyo.or.jp/.)

[71] On February 17, the Financial Services Agency proposed an amendment of the Cabinet Office Regulations that determined the decision of the Banking Agency System to lift the ban on a portion of the banking business for general business concerns as of April 2006. It has an upper limit of 10 million yen per case for the fixed format loan for business concerns in which the loan approval is mechanically determined based on the borrower's financial information. For detail, see February 17, 2006 issue of Nihon Keizai Shimbun, http://www.nikkei.co.jp/news/keizai/20060218AT1F1700S17022006.html.

This is good news for clients. However, it requires a mechanism for preventing the new banking agencies from conducting tie-in sales, conflict of interest operations, leakage of private information, etc.

Banks, on the other hand, can convert fixed costs to variable costs by breaking up the existing retailing branches and treating each employee as a branch. Making bank branches operate convenience stores will open up a way to diversify their business. Local banks of small to medium sizes can go for specialization by becoming an agency for another financial institution to sell their merchandizes. They can try to have best of breed items all the time. They can have the freedom to concentrate on business with local firms. Some of them may develop new types of financial business models.

In the meanwhile, general business firms can develop various new services by combining the flow of funds with the flow of products and services of their original businesses. It would make it easier to provide flexible, low cost, and speedier banking services if they apply the IT capabilities that they nurtured in their own businesses.

In such a new environment in Japan, banks can no longer survive unless they change their traditional mentality of waiting for clients to step up to their counters as they now have to compete with the creativity and speed of general business firms. They should give up the geocentric mentality. Otherwise, they will soon find themselves in a situation where a creative agency owner is controlling the bank.

The core business of a bank is no longer deposit. Banks may have to seek and study a strategy of alliance with business firms. Financial institutions that are incapable of forming such a strategy would be better off becoming agencies. The introduction of the banking agency system by the Reform Enactment is urging Japanese banks to make better management decisions where selection and concentration are key.

On February 20, 2006,[72] the Financial Services Agency disclosed a plan of the government/ministerial order to determine the detailed rules concerning the "Banking Agency System," which is supposed to lift the ban on general business firms for banking business. According to the

---

[72] See Nihon Keizai Shimbun, Feb. 21, 2000, p. 7.

proposed plan,[73] bans on most of the services and merchandizes intended for individual clients such as deposits, remittances, and housing loans will be lifted. Moreover, general business firms will be allowed to solicit and broker fixed type loans for firms (up to 10 million yen), which are automatically examined by machines.

According to the plan,[74] banking agencies require the license to operate from the Financial Services Agency. The Agency will approve corporations having a net asset (asset minus debt) of more than five million yen or individuals having three million yen, taking into consideration their social credibility to become banking agencies. Handling of loans requires the corporation to have a person with an experience of more than three years of experience in the case of personal loans and a person with an experience of more than one year of experience in the case of fixed type corporation loans stationed in each office.

The plan also establishes rules for client protection. It prohibits the use of a client's private information such as the amount of assets in custody for agent's business without the client's authorization and mandates written authorization in advance. It also requires agents to explain to their clients about the differences in fees depending on banks if they are agents of multiple banks.[75]

---

[73] Ibid.
[74] Ibid.
[75] Ibid.

Chapter 12

Japanese Shareholders' Lawsuits Concerning Political Donations[a]

In Japan, there is increased scrutiny over companies' political campaign contributions as well as their overall participation in the political process. Over the past decade, Japan has placed new restrictions on companies' political giving and has required greater disclosure of campaign contributions. Increasingly, shareholders are seeking to hold companies accountable for their campaign contributions.

However, political activities require a great deal of money and the situation in Japan is no exception. Consequently, political activities require donations from corporations and individuals for that purpose. In Japan, the political crisis and the challenge to the ruling Liberal Democrats in the 1990s and early 2000s centered on a series of scandals involving payments to politicians for their huge election expenses.

Political donations are classified according to donors, so that the donations fall into two groups: corporate donations and personal donations.[1] Under the current law, corporate donations are often viewed as collusion between business entities and politicians. Therefore, donations to individual politicians are prohibited, unless the donation is made to a single fundraising group managed by a particular politician.[2] An individual

---

[a] For this chapter, permission is granted to reprint by Columbia University School of Law, Columbia Journal of Asian Law, Mitsuru Misawa, "An Overview of Problems Concerning Political Donations in Japan", Columbia Journal of Asian Law, Columbia University, Spring 2008, Volume 21, No. 2, pp. 162–181.
[1] Seijishikin Kisei Ho, Political Donation Control Law, Law No. 194 of 1948, hereinafter PDCL, art. 3.
[2] *Id.*, art. 6.

politician can appoint only one organization as a single fund managing organization through which he can accept political donations from individuals and corporations. However, this exception is applicable only to personal donations and not corporate donations.[3]

Donations to political parties can be divided into two categories: (1) those made directly to political parties; and (2) those made to political funding organizations controlled by political parties.[4] Corporations and individuals may donate their money to either institution. However, there is a limit to the political donations of corporations; corporations that have lost money for three consecutive years cannot make any political donations.[5] A personal donation is a deductible item on an individual's income tax report.[6]

Political donations are always vexing for corporations in Japan. This study will examine the experiences of Japan pertaining to such donations in order to better understand the causes and consequences of money-driven politics in a democracy. This study will first define the current regulations of political donations in Japan. Next, it will survey past cases of political corruptions. These examples will provide a starting point for constructive discussion as to desirable regulations on this issue. This study will then introduce the recent trends on this issue in Japan.

Next, the study will provide information about, and insight into leading political donation lawsuits in Japan. The study will compare two leading cases — Kumagaigumi and Yawata Steel. Additionally, a related case, Kyushu Association of Accountants, will be discussed to see how the court came to a different decision from the leading cases above. Finally, the study discusses the current academic debate in Japan concerning corporate political donations. There are two different theoretical positions for the two different leading court cases. This study will examine them to show how these different positions emerged under Japanese laws, systems and practices.

---

[3] *Id.*, art. 21-3.
[4] *Id.*, art. 6.
[5] *Id.*, arts. 21-3 and 22-4.
[6] *Id.*, art. 32-3.

Government Regulation of Political Donations in Japan

Over the past decade, as companies' overall participation in the political process is facing increasing scrutiny, Japan has placed new restrictions on companies' political giving and has required greater disclosure of campaign contributions. Shareholders are seeking to hold companies accountable for their campaign contributions, as well as other forms of political involvement such as lobbying, support of trade associations, and issue advocacy campaigns. The lack of transparency and the ineffective enforcement mechanisms have led to many criticisms.[7] The regulatory regime of Japan relevant to political contributions consists of three laws. First, the most important law is the Political Donation Control Law (PDCL).[8] Second, the Political Party Subsidy Law[9] defines the system of distribution of public funds to political parties. Third, the Public Office Election Law[10] is also relevant in regulating the use of political funds during the election periods (see Table 1).

Table 1. Political Donation System in Japan

Recipient: Individual Politician (through the creation of a Fund Raising Group)

Donor	Allowed to Donate to Recipient?	Limit
Individual	Yes	10 Million Yen
Political Party	Yes	
Corporation	No	N/A

Recipient: Political Party and/or Fund Raising Group

Donor	Allowed to Donate to Recipient?	Limit
Individual	Yes	20 Million Yen
Corporation	Yes	7.5 Million Yen–1000 Million Yen (depending on the amount of capital the corporation has)

---

[7] For an example of criticism, see the case of Kumagaigumi in which the plaintiff, a group of shareholders, claimed that the management of Kumagaigumi, the defendant, did it against their duty of care. For details on the Kumagaigumi case, see *supra* n.58.
[8] Law no. 194 of 1948.
[9] Law no. 5 of 1994.
[10] Law no. 100 of 1950.

Contribution Limits

In terms of the contribution limits in Japan, the PDCL[11] sets quantitative controls through Article 21 and Article 22. These are very complex because this aspect of the regime has evolved in response to the changing public demands over the last 25 years. Article 3 of the PDCL deals with the contributor and recipient sides of donations. The categories of contributors and recipients are divided into different groups, and the quantitative limits imposed on different kinds of contributors and recipients vary considerably.[12]

Case 1: For individual politicians

Individuals can make political contributions to individual politicians only through Fund Raising Groups set up by the individual politicians.[13] The limit on such donations is 10 million yen.[14] Companies (and labor unions) are not allowed to contribute to individual politicians even through Fund Raising Groups set up by the individual politicians.[15] Political parties, however, are exceptions and can still make contributions to individual politicians.[16] There is no limit on contributions to individual politicians by political parties.[17]

Case 2: For political parties

Individuals and companies (and labor unions) are allowed to make contributions to political parties and Political Fund Groups set up by political parties subject to certain limitations.[18] For contributions from individuals, there is a 20 million yen limit[19] and for contributions from

---

[11] See *supra* n.1. For the details of arts. 21 and 22, see http://law.e-gov.go.jp/cgi-bin/idxsearch.cgi. This law is not yet translated in English by the Cabinet, Japan.
[12] *Id.*
[13] *Id.*, art. 21.
[14] *Id.*, art. 21-3.
[15] *Id.*, art. 21.
[16] *Id.*, art. 21-3.
[17] *Id.*
[18] *Id.*, art. 21.
[19] *Id.*, art. 21-3.

companies (and labor unions), the limit varies from 7.5 million yen to 100 million yen depending on the amount of the company's capital.[20]

Hence, the least restricted route of money flow is the route that originates from political organizations, especially political parties themselves. In other words, political parties can make donations to individual politicians and other political organizations, including individual fundraising groups, regardless of whether the transaction takes place during the election period or not. Political parties are thus largely treated as exceptions from an otherwise rigid regulatory regime. This treatment of political parties is regarded as the most serious flaw of the current regime.[21]

There are only a few minor qualitative control restrictions on who can make contributions for political purposes in monetary and other forms.[22] Under the current regime, foreigners, companies in deficit, and companies that are the recipient of government subsidies, are not allowed to make political contributions. Section 22 also stipulates that political contributions cannot be made anonymously or by using someone else's name.

Disclosure

In Japan, Article 9 and Article 10 of the PDCL[23] set out the procedures for disclosing financial statements of political financing. There is no requirement for individual politicians to file financial statements outlining the political contributions that they have received, invested, or used.[24] Political organizations, on the other hand, are required by Section 12 of the PDCL to make an annual report, listing the names and addresses of all contributors who made donations of more than 50,000 yen that year. The names and addresses of the recipients to whom the organization made a payment of more than 50,000 yen during that year must also be disclosed. Political organizations are also required to report various

---

[20] *Id.*
[21] *Id.*
[22] *Id.*
[23] See *supra* n.1.
[24] *Id.*

assets, including movable properties, savings, valuable securities, loans, debts, etc., that exceed one million yen.[25]

The PDCL stipulates that political organizations must file a formatted report on the earnings made from fundraising events. According to Section 12, the names and addresses of those who made a payment of more than 200,000 yen in return for services at a particular event must be disclosed. Section 20 of the PDCL stipulates that the gist of annual financial statements of political organizations be publicized in either the public register (Kanpo) or the prefectural bulletin (Koho). Section 20 also stipulates that these statements are to be made publicly viewable for a period of three years at the prefectural Election Administration Committee (Senkyo Kanri Iinkai) or at the Ministry of Home Affairs.[26] As discussed below, however, criticisms have been raised against the inconsistent and insufficient nature of these reporting requirements. The major criticism is regarding the difficulty of confirming the accuracy of reported numbers.[27] Under the current law, a politician is not required to report having received contributions from a single corporation as long as the amount paid to the politician's political organization amounts to less than 7.5 million yen per year for each group.[28] Also under the same law, the political organization files reports to different prefectures, as well as to the Ministry, depending on the location of the source and usage of political contribution so that it is difficult for any third party to grasp the entire picture of the money flow.[29] It was reported that many politicians could have tried to hide the money received from companies by having each company to pay in small sums so that none of the amounts were reported to the authorities. This method, whereby corporations make

---

[25] See art. 12.

[26] With the enactment of the Information Disclosure Act, Law no. 57, April 1, 2001, the right to "view" these financial statements now includes the right to "photocopy" them.

[27] The list of criticisms includes those presented by: 1) The Democratic Party of Japan, available at http://www.dpj.or.jp/news/dpjnews.cgi?indication=dp&num=10179 and 2) New Komei Party, available at http://www.komei.or.jp/. To secure transparency, both parties are claiming that the names of the recipients to whom the organization made a payment of more than one yen must be disclosed. For the details, see Sanyo News Paper of September 20, 2007, http://www.sanyo.oni.co.jp/newsk/2007/09/20/20070920010007201.html.

[28] See *supra* n.1, art. 12.

[29] *Id.*

contributions in small amounts to a number of political and fundraising organizations, all for a single politician, is a well-known practice in Japan's political world.[30]

Political Corruption in Japan

There has been a series of political corruption cases in Japan over the past two decades, some even involving senior politicians. This problem is quite serious and highlights the near incestuous relationship between politicians and the construction industry with regards to public works projects. The following are examples of such corrupt practices. These case studies help to define the current and central problems of the laws, regulations and court decisions on this issue. In turn, they provide a starting point for evaluating the efficacy of the current controls and regulations on political donations by corporations. This could hopefully lead to a constructive discussion as to desirable changes in the law.

1. Yoshihiko Tsuchiya, a former president of the House of Councilors, the upper house of the Diet from 1988 to 1991 and governor of Saitama Prefecture from 1992 to 2003, was suspected of violating the PDCL in 2003. He escaped indictment, but his daughter, who was in charge of his political fund management organization, was arrested and later pleaded guilty for misappropriating 113 million yen in funds from the organization.[31] She said she took the money for her own failing businesses. She had also sought, if not extorted, millions of yen from local firms, such as construction firms, and often tried to hide it by requesting that the donations be given in units smaller than the 50,000 yen limit. Governor Tsuchiya resigned from his position even though he claimed that he knew nothing about his daughter's activities.[32]

---

[30] Asahi Evening News, 24 September, 1993.

[31] For the details of this incident, see the official record of Saitama prefectural diet on June 10, 2003, http://www.pref.saitama.lg.jp/s-gikai/gaiyou/h1506/1506q010.html. For further details of the case, also see "Ex-Saitama Gov. Escapes Indictment, Daughter Charged", Japan Policy & Politics, August 4, 2003, http://findarticles.com/p/articles/mi_m0XPQ/is_2003_August_4/ai_106218800.

[32] *Id.*

2. In 1999, while Muneo Suzuki was the Deputy Chief Cabinet Secretary to the former Prime Minister Obuchi, he pressured the Foreign Ministry to fund the Japanese–Russian Friendship House, which became a scandal when it was revealed in 2002. This case revealed an appalling pattern of politico-bureaucratic collusion. Muneo Suzuki, as deputy chief Cabinet secretary in 1999, intervened in a construction project for a public lodging facility (Japan–Russia Friendship House, commonly known as "Muneo House") on Kunashiri Island, one of the Russian-held islands known as the Northern Territories.[33] He requested that the ministry only invite tenders from companies in Hokkaido's Nemuro district, which was his constituency.[34] The ministry then decided to limit eligible bidders to "those who have building experience in Nemuro."[35] Although the decision was made in consultation with the Assistance Committee, the implementing body for aid projects in the Northern Territories, Suzuki involved himself deeply in determining the bidding qualifications.[36] In 2004, he was sentenced to two years for accepting bribes from two Hokkaido companies. His secretary, Akira Miyano, was convicted of bribery in July 2003 and was given an 18 month suspended sentence for not reporting 100 million yen of donations in violation of the PDCL.

---

[33] For the details, see unpublished source in 2002, "A Foreign Ministry Investigation of Influence-peddling by Liberal Democratic Party Legislator Muneo Suzuki", http://www.japantimes.co.jp/shukan-st/english_news/editorial/2002/ed20020322.htm. The report concluded that it is abnormal for a member of the Diet to get involved with such details by using his influence and this is impermissible in light of commonly accepted norms. For this case see also, *Asian Times*, June, 2002, http://www.atimes.com/japan-econ/DF20Dh02.html. For further details on the Tokyo District Court sentence for him of two years in prison and 11 million yen fine for four charges including two counts of taking bribes from two Hokkaido companies in exchange for favors, see Japan Policy & Politics, Nov 8, 2004, http://findarticles.com/p/articles/mi_m0XPQ/is_2004_Nov_8/ai_n6343796. For the 1999 construction of the Japan–Russia Friendship House, an evacuation facility on Kunashiri Island in which Muneo Suzuki was allegedly involved in bid-rigging, see "Ministry's Affiliate for Russian-held Islands Not Functioning", Japan Policy & Politics, March 4, 2002, http://findarticles.com/p/articles/mi_m0XPQ/is_2002_March_4/ai_84260652.
[34] *Id.*
[35] *Id.*
[36] *Id.*

Suzuki and Miyano also helped to fix a 400 million yen public works projects for friendly construction firms.[37]

3. Many prominent Japanese politicians were forced to resign in 1988 as a result of the Recruit corruption scandal.[38] Recruit[39] is a real estate and telecommunications company based in Tokyo. Its former founder and chairman, Hiromasa Ezoe,[40] offered a number of shares in a Recruit subsidiary, Cosmos,[41] to business leaders and senior politicians shortly before Cosmos went public in 1986. Following the public offering, Cosmos's share price skyrocketed, and the individuals involved in the scheme saw an average profit of 66 million yen.[42] Although only 17 members of the Diet were involved in the insider trading, another 30 were later found to have received special favors from Recruit.[43] Among the politicians involved in the scandal was Prime Minister Noboru Takeshita.[44] As a result, Takeshita's cabinet was forced to resign.[45] After 13 years, the Tokyo District Court finally made its decision in 2003 and gave Ezoe, the former chairman of Recruit, a three-year suspended prison term.[46]

These case analyses and assessments reveal that the existing Japanese laws relevant to the regulation of political contributions are not effective. This ineffectiveness comes from a wide range of factors including the

---

[37] *Id.*
[38] For this case, see "Top Court Rejects Lawmaker's Appeal in Bribery Case," Looksmart, Find Articles, Oct. 25, 1999, http://www.findarticles.com/p/articles/mi_m0XPQ/is_1999_ Oct_25/ai_57163161. For further details this case, see also "Japan a Scandal That Will Not Die", Time, October 9, 2007, http://www.time.com/time/magazine/article/ 0,9171,957517,00.html. The politicians involved in the scandal were Prime Minister Noboru Takeshita, former Prime Minister Yasuhiro Nakasone, and Chief Cabinet Secretary Takao Fujinami. For the details on the case, see also, "Recruit Scandal" http://en.wikipedia.org/wiki/Recruit_scandal.
[39] For company information on Recruit, see http://www.recruit.co.jp/corporate/english/.
[40] For Hiromasa Ezoe's biographical data, see "Ezoe Hiromasa", Wikipedia, http://ja.wikipedia.org/wiki/%E6%B1%9F%E5%89%AF%E6%B5%A9%E6%AD%A3.
[41] For company information on Cosmos, see http://www.cosmos-flw.co.jp/contents/company.html.
[42] See *supra* n.38.
[43] *Id.*
[44] *Id.*
[45] *Id.*
[46] *Id.*

Japanese political culture and the Liberal Democratic Party's long one-party dominance, which has led to close ties with the bureaucracy, and loopholes in the related laws.

Recent Trend in Japan Concerning Political Donations

On September 25, 2003, Keidanren, the most powerful management association in Japan comprises of 1623 companies, published[47] an opinion paper titled, "On Preferential Policy Matters and Significance of Political Donations by Corporations" (hereinafter referred to as Preferential Policy Matters).[48] This paper is a summary of opinion polls Keidanren conducted canvassing 1600 major Japanese corporations as well as independent professionals, and is supposed to represent the most popular opinion of the economic circle in Japan. Prior to that, on May 12, 2003, Keidanren published a statement titled "Promotion of Donations by Corporations/Organizations Keyed Toward Policy-Oriented Politics,"[49] in which Keidanren disclosed its policy on promoting self-propelled political donations by corporations/organizations based on their own policy evaluations of political parties. Based on this policy, Keidanren compiled Preferential Policy Matters as a yardstick for policy evaluation.

The list of policies in Preferential Policy Matters consists of urgent and important items needed to realize an autonomous economic society led by the private sector. Keidanren desires organizations to use these policies to evaluate political parties on their own and then act accordingly. In conjunction with compiling Preferential Policy Matters, Keidanren evaluated the philosophy of political donations among

---

[47] *Keidanren* (The Japanese Federation of Economic Organizations) is a general economic organization consisting of 1,623 companies and other organizations, which include 91 companies with foreign capital affiliations and 1,306 major representative Japanese companies. It is the strongest interest group in Japan that applies pressure on the government as well as overseas organizations by collecting opinions from all corners of business communities on any important issues of business communities ranging from economic and industrial issues to labor issues urging speedy solutions.) See the Federation's website at http://www.keidanren.or.jp/Japanese/profile/pro001.htm.

[48] "Land of Hope, Japan" is included in Nippon Keidanren: Keidanren Priority Policies 2007 (2007-01-10) http://www.keidanren.or.jp/cgi-bin/estseek_en.cgi.

[49] Keidanren, "Promotion of Corporate Donation toward Policies Oriented Politics", May 12, 2003 http://www.keidanren.or.jp/japanese/policy/2003/040.html.

member corporations. The result revealed that political donations from corporations are extremely important in the three following ways:

1. *Policy-Oriented Politics.* As globalization continues, industries are trying very hard to help themselves by strengthening their international competitiveness. Meanwhile, institutional reforms, such as regulatory reform, tax reform, and foreign trade agreements need to be implemented by politicians to provide strength and incentives to private industries. Corporate donations and contributions based on policy evaluations should increase the competition among political parties and contribute to the realization of politics based on the selection of policies.

2. *Healthy Development of Parliamentary Democracy.* Parliamentary democracy is a cost-effective system that funnels people's ideas through a broad communication channel with the private sector while bearing the cost. This applies especially to corporations, which are expected to bear a reasonable share of the social responsibility as "good corporate citizens." Since the introduction of the public funding system for political parties, most of the political parties are expecting more public funding. We need to remember that donations from the private sector, including corporations, help to secure the independence and autonomy of political parties, which are two rights that make up the basis of democracy.

3. *Maintaining Transparency of Political Funds.* Donations to political parties that do not induce individual profit are considered to be the most transparent among all the sources of political funding at the moment. Enrichment of such donations can contribute to the transparency of the entire political fund. This can be further improved by asking corporations' political donations to be used specifically for the planning and promotion of policies.[50]

It is worth noting that there is a move toward the legalization of political donation from foreign sources. The PDCL stipulates that "[political organizations] are not allowed to receive donations intended for their political activities from foreigners or foreign organizations or

---

[50] *Id.*

institutions,"[51] in order to prevent Japanese politics and elections from being influenced by foreign countries. The Ministry of Internal Affairs and Communications acknowledged that "legal entities whose shares are more than 50 percent owned by foreigners are subjected to this restriction."[52]

None of the major political contributions scandals in Japan listed previously in this article involved foreign companies. The reasons for their absence in the list of scandals are as follow;

1. With Japanese politicians playing a role in the Japanese politics and administration, their decision-making processes are not easy for foreign companies to understand.[53]
2. Japanese politicians still present themselves as representatives of their constituency and thus do not usually develop an international profile.[54]
3. Key industries in which bribery scandals are more frequent are aviation, oil and energy, and defense. In these sectors, the Japanese economy is either still very strongly regulated or is closed to foreign firms.[55]

Due to internationalization of the Japanese economy, more foreign companies can be expected to enter the Japanese market. In the future, there is a high possibility that foreign firms will be seen as newcomers. However, access for foreign firms to the Japanese market has been and still is difficult. Specifically, the market access and participation of foreign firms in large public works bidding processes are big political issues. These will put foreign companies at a competitive disadvantage.

From the perspective of political contributions, foreign firms can be expected to do more political funding activities for Japanese politicians, in order to increase their influence on Japanese business.

---

[51] See *supra* n.1, art. 22-5.
[52] Acknowledged on Dec. 13, 2006.
[53] "Corruption through Political Contributions in Japan" by Verena Blechinger, working paper submitted for a TI workshop on corruption and political party funding in La Pietra, Italy. October 2000, p. 6 www.transparency.org/content/download/15514/167316.
[54] *Id.*
[55] *Id.*

Behind the move towards the legalization of political donations by foreign entities is Keidanren's intention to beef up its influence on the political scene through donations. When Fuijo Mitarai, the chairman of Canon Inc., was officially elected as the new chairman of Keidanren in January 2006, he stated that "Canon,[56] whose foreign investors own more than 50 percent of the company's shares, is prevented from legally making any political contributions under the current law" and that "such a law logically contradicts the trend of the times."[57]

Leading Political Donation Lawsuits in Japan

In Japan, it is questionable whether a company, in the same manner as a natural person who is a citizen, should be entitled to freely undertake political activities and whether donating to political funds is one aspect of this freedom, even if it will exert influence over political trends. There are two conflicting and leading cases in Japan: (1) the Supreme Court Decision of Yawata Steel (June 24, 1970) and (2) the Fukui District Court Decision on Kumagaigumi (February 12, 2003).

In 1970, the Supreme Court of Japan made a decision which permits corporations to make political donations. This case involved Yawata Steel, a predecessor of Nippon Steel. The court said that companies are free to engage in political activities and that donations to political parties are part of such activities. However, in 2003, Fukui District Court, the Nagoya High Court's Kanazawa branch, reversed a lower court ruling that said Kumagaigumi Co.'s political donations to the ruling Liberal Democratic Party between 1996 and 2000 were illegal. The author wishes to compare these two opposing cases.

The Fukui District Court delivered a judgement on February 12, 2003,[58] on a shareholder's action against Kumagaigumi,[59] one of the second tier

---

[56] For corporate information of Canon Inc., see http://web.canon.jp/corp/.
[57] For the profile of Nippon Keidanren (Japan Business Federation), see http://www.keidanren.or.jp/index.html.
[58] Kumagaigumi Kabunushi Daihyou Soshou (Kumagaigumi Shareholders' Derivative Suit) Fukui District Court, February 12, 2003, Civil Sec. Nos. 144 and 262, 2003 (wa).
[59] For the company's homepage, see http://www.kumagaigumi.co.jp/index2.html.

major general construction companies, in which shareholders claimed that the company, which was in the process of restructuring, made donations to the Liberal Democratic Party.[60] The shareholders accused three members of its management team, including its former president, of violating the Commercial Law[61] by ignoring their duty of care for the company's financial condition by allowing such donations to occur. The shareholders sought repayment and an injunction of a total of approximately 99 million yen paid out as political donations over the period from the year the Heisei 8 (1996) through 12 (2000).[62]

The judge accepted a portion of the plaintiffs' claims stating that "the fact that the defendants allowed the company's donations omitting strict examinations while the company was losing money exceeds a director's authority and constitutes a violation of the fiduciary duty of care as good managers." The court ordered Yoshio Matsumoto, who was the president during the period when the company was losing money, to repay the plaintiffs the amount of the political donations, which was approximately 28.6 million yen.[63] The judge rejected the request for repayment involving a former president Taichiro Kumagaya and the request for injunction for contributions involving a former president Kazutoshi Ugai.[64] This is the first ruling that ordered repayment from a director due to a violation of his or her duty of care relating to the Commercial Law or the Civil Law in Japan.[65]

The history of shareholders' lawsuits started with Yawata Steel's political donation in 1970,[66] which was the only case that questioned political donations[67] until Kumagaigumi's decision was delivered in

---

[60] For the history and constitution of Jiminto (Liberal Democratic Party of Japan), see http://www.jimin.jp/jimin/english/index.html.

[61] Law No. 48, enacted on March 9, 1899, amended 18 times (hereinafter cited as the Commercial Code). For details see wysiwyg://6/http://www.ron.gr.jp/law/law/syouhou1.htm.

[62] See *supra* n.58.

[63] *Id.*

[64] *Id.*

[65] Law No. 89 of 1902.

[66] In 1970, Yawata Steel and Fuji Steel merged to form Nippon Steel Corporation. For the details of the birth of Nippon Steel Corporation, see its annual report, http://www0.nsc.co.jp/shinnihon_english/company_profile/enkaku/index.html.

[67] Arita v. Yawata Steel, Tokyo District Court, April 5, 1960, 1958 (wa) No. 2825, Hanji No. 330, p. 29.

2003. The issue in the case was whether a corporation should be allowed to make a political donation. The Tokyo District Court, as the first trial court, ordered the related directors' repayment, reasoning that the particular political donation violated the directors' fiduciary duty.[68] The case was brought before the higher court in 1961,[69] and the appeal of the higher court was dismissed in the final appeal at the Supreme Court in 1970.[70]

Yawata Steel had made a political donation of 3.5 million yen to the Liberal Democratic Party in 1960. Shareholders sued the director of the company, claiming that the donation was outside the purpose of the corporation as stated in the articles of incorporation. Consequently, the act of donation was a violation of the director's fiduciary duty.[71] The defense claimed that the political donation was within the purpose of the corporation as well as being socially appropriate, and hence it did not constitute any violation of the director's duty.[72] During the first trial, the judge determined that the defendant's action was a violation of his fiduciary duty because the defendant's action was not a profit-making act and therefore was a violation of the articles of incorporation.[73] However, the court of appeal and the Supreme Court dismissed the complaint.[74–75] This was a notable case not just because it was the first shareholders' action that was brought to the Grand Court of the Supreme Court but also because it showed that the shareholders' action through the court system was used as a method of checking the corporate manager's actions relating to political donations.[76]

---

[68] *Id.*
[69] Arita v. Yawata Steel, Tokyo High Court, January 31, 1963, 1966 (ne) No. 791, Hanji No. 433, p. 9.
[70] Arita v. Yawata Steel, Grand Court, Supreme Court, June 24, 1970, Minshuu No. 24-6, p. 625 and Hanji No. 596, p. 3.
[71] See *supra* n.67.
[72] *Id.*
[73] *Id.*
[74] See *supra* n.69.
[75] See *supra* n.70.
[76] *Id.*

Comparison of the *Yawata Steel* and the *Kumagaigumi* Decisions

The Yawata Steel Decision

The current leading case in Japan concerning the issue of a corporation's political donation is the Supreme Court's decision on *Yawata Steel* in 1970.

Yawata Steel was a shareholders' lawsuit brought under the Commercial Law, Article 267[77] in which a group of shareholders of Yawata Steel Co., Ltd. (currently Shin Nippon Steel) claimed that the directors acted outside of business purpose[78] specified in the articles of incorporation and that they violated the fiduciary duty of directors as defined in the Commercial Law, Article 254-2 (presently Article 254-3).[79]

The first trial court, the Tokyo District Court, divided the corporation's act into transactional operations (business operations) and non-transactional operations (non-profit operations). The non-transactional operations "are operations that essentially are not anticipated in any consideration, so that they are to be considered as operations that are against the purpose of profit-making, therefore, ... all non-transactional operations are outside the business purposes, being contrary to profit-making."[80] On the other hand, exceptions were made for corporate donations (1) to raise funds for natural disasters and (2) for scholarship programs, since these are non-business purposes. But the management has to secure an agreement as to whether these donations from all shareholders and the donation amounts are reasonable.

The court concluded, however, that "because a political party assumes the existence of an opposing political party under a democratic political system, it can never be that all the people involved will

---

[77] Commercial Law, Article 267. For the case, see *supra* n.70.

[78] Article 2 of Incorporation: It is a purpose to be involved in the manufacture and sale of steel and all other associated businesses. See *supra* n.66 for the company's Web page.

[79] It provides that the directors shall be obliged to obey any law or ordinance and the articles of incorporation as well as resolutions adopted at a general meeting and to perform their duties faithfully on behalf of the company. For the translation of the Commercial Law of Japan by the Cabinet, Japan, see
http://www1.oecd.org/daf/asiacom/pdf/japan_commercial_code.pdf.

[80] See *supra* n.67.

unanimously feel that a political donation to a certain political party is socially responsible."[81] The court consequently entered its judgement that the donation to the political party in this case was like a donation to a certain religion and could not possibly constitute an exception to which all the shareholders could agree is a social obligation. Therefore the directors were liable for damages to the plaintiffs.[82]

The Supreme Court later reversed this ruling stating[83] that:

1. A corporation is "a social being similar to a natural person and a constituting unit of a nation, a local public organization, a local society and the like;" that "it can certainly respond to expectations and requests so long as those expectations and requests for the corporation are within the boundary of socially accepted notions even if a certain act is seemingly unrelated to the objects of its articles of incorporation," and it is also "an indispensable element that supports parliamentary democracy";[84]

2. "It is expected and understandable for a corporation to cooperate in the promotion of healthy development of, including donations of political funds to," a political party, which is "a most effective medium for the formation of the political opinions of the public";[85]

3. A corporation has the "freedom to be engaged in political actions including support, promotion of or objection to certain policies of the nation or a political party" as an exercise of the "right guaranteed in Chapter III of the Constitution[86] as a citizen being a natural person would";[87]

4. Even if a portion of the funds is used for corruptive purposes, it is simply a syndrome that occurs sporadically; and[88]

---

[81] *Id.*

[82] *Id.*

[83] See *supra* n.70.

[84] *Id.*

[85] *Id.*

[86] The Constitution of Japan was promulgated on November 3, 1946 and was put into effect on May 3, 1947. Chapter III defines the right and duties of the people. For the translation of the Constitution of Japan by the Cabinet, Japan, see http://www.kantei.go.jp/foreign/constitution_and_government/frame_01.html.

[87] See *supra* n.70.

[88] *Id.*

5. "A corporation has the freedom according to the Constitution to donate political funds unless the donation violates the public welfare and such a donation infringes on the public voting right, so that the plaintiffs' claim that such a donation violates Article 90 of the Civil Law[89] lacks its premise."[90]

The distinctive features of the Supreme Court's judgement in 1970 are as follows:

1. Although the central issue in the original action involved a violation of the directors' fiduciary duty, an issue specific to the Commercial Law, a private law, the Supreme Court discussed the legal capacity theory of corporations using the issues of a person's political freedom and the public voting right, which essentially belong to public laws;[91]

2. As a result, the Supreme Court concluded that a corporation is a social being that can constitute a unit of a society similar to a natural person. Therefore, it can respond to the expectations and requests of a society and it is not exceptional for a corporation to cooperate in the promotion of healthy development of political party through donations;

3. The Court further stated again that within the framework of the legal capacity theory, a corporation has the freedom to be engaged in political actions and to make political donations similar to a natural person.

---

[89] For the civil code, see *supra* n.65. Article 90 provides that a juristic act that has for its objective such matters as are contrary to public policy or good morals is null and void. For the translation of the Civil Law of Japan by the Cabinet, Japan, see http://www.cas.go.jp/jp/seisaku/hourei/data/CC_2.pdf.

[90] See *supra* n.70.

[91] Article 33 of the Civil Code of Japan provides the basis for existence of a juristic person — no juristic person can come into existence unless in accordance with the provisions of the present Code or of other laws. There are two associations: one is incorporated association and the other is corporate association. The difference comes from this article 33 of the Civil Code. Therefore, legal capacity theory (in German, Rechtsfhigkeit and in English, legal capacity, the ability, to be carriers from rights and obligations to) belongs to private laws. For the translation of the Civil Law of Japan by the Cabinet, Japan, see http://www.cas.go.jp/jp/seisaku/hourei/data/CC_2.pdf.

In this sense, the case established a new theory which states that corporations can act within the boundary of socially accepted objectives even if a certain act is seemingly unrelated to its articles of incorporation. And so, corporate management decisions regarding political donations gained more flexibility. This court decision was well accepted in the Japanese business world.

The Kumagaigumi Decision

The *Kumagaigumi* case exposed the cozy relationship between politicians and businesses, particularly public works contractors. In this case,[92] the plaintiff, a group of shareholders of Kumagaigumi,[93] claimed, relative to Kumagaigumi's donations to Kokumin Seiji Kyokai (The People's Political Association),[94] a political fund group,[95] in a shareholders' lawsuit based on the Commercial Law,[96] Article 267,[97] that the donations were

1. Against public order and morality;
2. Outside of the boundary of the purpose of the corporation;

---

[92] See *supra* n.58.
[93] *Id.*
[94] This is the political donation receiving organization for the Liberal Democratic Party, Japan. For the details, see its homepage: http://www.kokuseikyo.or.jp/jimin/.
[95] See PDCL, arts. 21 and 22.
[96] See *supra* n.61.
[97] It provides:
   1. Any shareholder who has at least held a share continuously for the last six months may demand, in writing, of the company to institute an action to enforce the liability of directors.
   2. In case the company has failed to institute such action within 30 days from the date on which the demand mentioned in the preceding paragraph may institute such action on behalf of the company.
   3. In case irreparable damage is caused to the company by the expiration of the period provided for in the proceeding paragraph, the shareholder mentioned in paragraph 1 may immediately institute the action mentioned in the proceeding paragraph, notwithstanding the provisions of the proceeding two paragraphs.
   4. When the shareholder has instituted an action mentioned in the preceding two paragraphs, the Court may, at the request of the defendant, order him to furnish adequate security.
   5. The provisions of Article 106 paragraph 2 shall apply mutatis mutandis to the request mentioned in the proceeding paragraph.
For the translation of the Commercial Law of Japan by the Cabinet, Japan, see http://www1.oecd.org/daf/asiacom/pdf/japan_commercial_code.pdf.

3. A violation of the Public Office Election Law,[98] Article 199, Section 1;[99]

4. A violation of the Political Donation Control Law,[100] Article 22-4, Section 1;[101]

5. A violation of the fiduciary duty of care as good managers under Article 298[102] of the Civil Code.[103]

The plaintiffs demanded damages in accordance with the Commercial Law, Article 266, Section 1-5 (damages equivalent to the political donations and delay damages calculated from the day after the date of delivery of the complaint related to the above until the day the repayment is completed)[104] and injunction of the political donations based on the Commercial Law, Article 272.[105]

---

[98] Law no. 100 of 1950.

[99] The article provides that donations from companies competing for or receiving public works orders must be banned.

[100] See *supra* n.1.

[101] The article prohibits donations from companies that have run deficits for three or more consecutive years.

[102] It provides: (1) a person having the right retention shall keep the thing retained with the care of a good manager, (2) a person having the right of retention may not, without the consent of the obligor, use or lease the thing retained or give it as security. However, this shall not apply to such use of the thing as is necessary for its preservation, and (3) if a person having a right of retention contravenes the provisions of the preceding two paragraphs, the obligor may demand the extinction of the right of retention. For the translation of the Civil Law of Japan by the Cabinet, Japan, see http://www.cas.go.jp/jp/seisaku/hourei/data/CC_2.pdf.

[103] Law no. 2100 of 1966.

[104] This article provides that directors who have done any one of the acts mentioned here shall be jointly and severally liable in effecting performance or in damages to the company. For the translation of the Commercial Law of Japan by the Cabinet, Japan, see http://www1.oecd.org/daf/asiacom/pdf/japan_commercial_code.pdf.

[105] It provides: When a director performs an act that is not within the scope of the objectives of the company, or an act against any law or ordinance or the articles of incorporation, and thereby gives rise to fear of irreparable damages done to the company, any shareholder who has held a share continuously at least for the last six months may demand the director to stop such an act on behalf of the company. For the translation of the Commercial Law of Japan by the Cabinet, Japan, see http://www1.oecd.org/daf/asiacom/pdf/japan_commercial_code.pdf.

The five issues in the case and the decision by Fukui District Court on February 12, 2003[106] can be summarized as follows:

1. Is the political donation in question against public order and morality?

A political party or a political organization is expected to perform a broad range of political activities for its promotion of political doctrines and policies as well as endorsement of specific candidates for certain public positions. So a donation to such an entity has a close relation with the execution of the donator's election right.

A corporation's donation is enormously more influential than the political donation of an individual citizen because the economic capacity of a corporation's donation is far larger than that of an individual citizen. This is even more noticeable when member companies of a certain industry make a joint contribution to a political party, in which case the influence to the political party is understandably enormous.

Therefore, one cannot deny the possibility of corporate donations essentially infringing upon the voting rights and suffrage of the people. Furthermore, if the political donations of a corporation or an industry are concentrated on a particular political party or organization, such a party would significantly increase its financial power and political activities. Thus corporate giving creates a decisive influence on the nation's policies, and may end up creating a hotbed for unhealthy collusions between the political elite and industrial leaders, as witnessed in the past.

Consequently, a corporation's or an industry's political donations have to be modest and constrained to a degree that will not cause any essential infringement on the voting rights and suffrage of the people. However, the degree of allowance, *i.e.*, the limit that a corporation should be allowed to donate to a

---

[106] See *supra* n.58.

political party, is something to be entrusted primarily to the legislature.

The law recognizes the danger of political donations to an individual politician by entities such as a corporation; this can create a hotbed for collusion between them and therefore, the law prohibits it as an antisocial activity. However, judging from the revision process of the PDCL,[107] it is obvious that the law does not regard corporate political donations as inherently antisocial since corporations are permitted to make donations to political parties and political fund groups. Hence, the court cannot declare that it is against public order and morality for a corporation or similar entity to make political contributions.

Ultimately, a corporation is not an organization to which one is forced to belong to; a stockholder is completely free to dissociate himself from the corporation by disposing stocks. It is unreasonable to equate a corporation making a political donation to a stockholder of a corporation who is expressing a specific political opinion. Due to these reasons, it is unreasonable to say that a political donation by a corporation causes infringements upon its shareholders' freedom of thoughts and beliefs.[108]

2. Does the political donation in question reside within the objects of the articles of incorporation?

Although a political donation by a corporation is different in its nature from general contributions to the society by the corporation, it is considered to be included within the boundary of the corporation's authority under the articles of incorporation. Since

---

[107] The problems concerning political donations have been getting worse. Most of these activities have been legal under the current unsatisfactory laws. But loopholes allowed some political contributions to go undisclosed or be disguised. So in the reform process, the disclosure rules have been tightened for more transparency. However, the basic position of the law is that political donations are not antisocial if they are made to a political party or political fund group by entities such as a corporation. This law was amended many times since its enactment in 1948. By the time the court said this, the law was amended 15 times. The last one was the amendment of July 31, 2002 (law no. 100). For the details of these amendments, see PDCL http://www.houko.com/00/01/S23/194.HTM.

[108] See *supra* n.58.

the PDCL permits political donations by these corporations, it is construed to be included within the boundary of the corporation's object even though there is no specific definition pertaining to donations in the articles of incorporation of these corporations.

Since the basic objective of political donations is for an individual to support a political party of his choice using his own assets, it is natural for a political donation to be intended for a specific political party. Hence, it is unreasonable to claim that the particular political donation in question deviates from the objective of the corporation.[109]

3. Does the political donation in question violate the Public Office Election Law?

The Public Office Election Law, Article 199, Section 1 prohibits a donation from a person who is a party to a national government contract or regional government contract related to a national or a regional election respectively. A donation related to an election is understood to mean donation with a motivation related to a particular election. More specifically, the donation related to an election is understood under the law to be (1) a donation made for an election after its public announcement or notification, or in such a temporal relation that an election is expected within a certain time due to the maturity of a public office's term, or the dissolution of the Diet, and (2) a donation made with the expectation that the particular political donation will be used as part of the election expense. This means that the Public Office Election Law simply prohibits donations for a specific election and it is irrelevant to whether the donations are eventually used for election expenses. The conclusion is that the political donation in question was made regardless of any specific election as a whole and therefore it is not violating the law.[110]

---

[109] *Id.*
[110] *Id.*

4. Does the political donation in question violate the PDCL?

The PDCL, Article 21-3 provides that a corporation that has lost money for three consecutive years cannot make any political donations. Under the PDCL, Article 22-4 and its Enforcement Order, Article 9, a corporation's loss is based on its balance sheet that is recognized as accurate by an audit unless there is an indication that the balance sheet includes untruthful statements. In this particular scenario, the contents of the balance sheet can neither be recognized as untruthful nor be proven with evidence to be fraudulent, and there is no other suspicious evidence.[111] The balance sheet of this company indicates that it has not lost money for three consecutive years and so it is not violating the PDCL.

5. Does the political donation in question violate the fiduciary duties of the company's directors?

To answer this question, it is necessary to do an overall evaluation of the following points;

(a) Because the nature of a political donation is not to seek compensation, a political donation does not contribute to the profit-making purpose of a corporation directly. It is not clear whether it can contribute to the profit-making purpose indirectly either. Not only that, as for the purpose of sustaining and developing a free economic system as the defendants claimed, major political parties coincide with reference to the point of adopting the free economic system, so that the particular political donation cannot be related to the purpose of sustaining and developing a free economic system. That being the case, its effect on the corporation's profit-making objective is extremely indirect and vague. It is difficult to conclude that this particular political donation is necessary or useful for the company.

---

[111] *Id.*

(b) Moreover, since the target of a political donation is a political party or organization, unlike donations for general social activities, it is not related to the execution of the corporation's contribution to the society or responsibility to the society. The corporation that donates a lot is not necessarily a good corporation. It has no effect in maintaining or elevating the society's evaluation of the corporation. Thus, political donations have little relevance to the realization of the objective of the articles of incorporation of the company.

(c) The intention of the PDCL that places the criterion of whether to allow a political donation depending on the specific financial and accounting status of the corporation is based on the concept (1) that the political activity of a corporation, which is subsidized by a public fund, regardless of whether such a public fund is a small portion of its total business fund, should be curbed because it is not purely a private corporation any more but rather a public entity and thus it cannot be allowed the same treatment as private corporations, and also (2) that a corporation with continuing losses should not be allowed to make political donations because political donations do not contribute to the reduction of the losses while the objective of a corporation is to make profits.

(d) According to the PDCL, Article 26-3, Section 1, a corporation that has created a deficit, even if it has not had a deficit for three continuous years, is required to examine rigorously the appropriateness, scope, amount, timing and other qualifications of any donation. In addition, the corporation must consider how a donation will affect the elimination of its losses, and whether there is a need to prefer the donation over the dividend payment to the shareholders; it should not be construed that a donation is allowed so long as the donation amount is below the upper limit stipulated by the law without going through such examinations.

Consequently, the court decided that since the political donations in question were executed without the company rigorously examining the appropriateness, scope, amount, timing and affect on current losses of the donation and considering the alternate benefits of dividend payment to the shareholders, the judgement was wantonly made and the directors violated their fiduciary duties.[112]

The judgement entered by the Fukui District Court is notable as it is their first decision to find such a donation illegal since the Supreme Court's judgement in the *Yawata* case in 1970. The judgement is also important because it denied the logic of the usefulness of political donation, although it did not explicitly refute the *Yawata* judgement. From the standpoint of effectiveness and usefulness for the business purposes, it stated that:

1. Donations to political funds do not directly contribute to the corporations' benefit because by their nature they do not accompany any consideration;[113]
2. It is difficult to consider that the political donation in question can contribute to the maintenance or development of the liberal economic system;[114]
3. As the receivers of political funds are usually political parties and other political organizations which have nothing to do with the company's contributions to society and the execution of its social responsibilities, political donations normally have very little to do with the realization of the purposes stipulated in the articles of incorporation of a company.[115]

Moreover, the district court judgement stated that in view of the PDCL, a company that receives any assistance of public funds, even if the ratio of the public fund in the business fund is small, bears a public

---

[112] *Id.*
[113] *Id.*
[114] *Id.*
[115] *Id*

nature, and it should be in its priority to eliminate its loss at the earliest possible time. The court further stated that the donations of political funds in this case were conducted without strict examination of necessity, range, amount and timing and without careful judgement if there were to be any impact on eliminating loss, and if such a political donation has any priority over dividend payments to shareholders. The court decided that it constitutes a violation of fiduciary duty of care as good managers according to the Civil Law.[116] This aligns with the concept of corporate governance, *i.e.*, the checking function against the corporate manager, so that the judgement is quite meaningful in this regard.

However, the Appeals Court, the Kanazawa Branch of Nagoya High Court, overturned the first trial decision by the Fukui District Court, which ordered the former president Matsumoto to pay approximately 28.6 million yen, and dismissed the shareholders' request.[117]

Stating the grounds for the decision, the Appeals Court's judge pointed out that "the directors were trying to improve the management and financial status"[118] noting, as to the violation of the fiduciary duty of care by the directors, that "there was a danger that, unless they accommodate the donation request by the industry association, the company would have lost the trust of the market and the stock price could have plummeted. The amount of the donation was within a reasonable range judging from the sales and the operating performance of Kumagaigumi."[119]

While the decision by the Nagoya Appeals Court overturned the first trial decision by Fukui District Court, the case is significant in that it highlights the arguments against political donations by corporations. There are strong criticisms over political donations from corporations in Japan.[120]

---

[116] See *supra* n.65.

[117] Kumagaigumi Kabunushi Daihyou Soshou Kousoshin (Kumagaigumi Shareholders' Derivative Suit, Appeals Court) Nagoya District Court, January 11, 2006 (ne), No. 63.

[118] Asahi Shinbun, January 14, 2006, see
http://blogs.yahoo.co.jp/abc5def6/folder/1177887.html?m=lc&p=3.

[119] *Id.* However, the defendants took the case to the Supreme Court on January 13, 2006 and the case is still pending. See "Kumagaigumi Case Jyokoku" (Kumagaigumi Case Goes to the Supreme Court), Mainich Newspaper, January 14, 2006.

[120] For example, see Political Donation Ombudsman, "Corporate Donations Should be Ended", October 27, 2004 http://homepage2.nifty.com/~matsuyama/0041.html.

Critics have called for corporate political donating to end, arguing that the donations are a gift and a form of bribery.[121] They say that corporate donations are a major threat to the political and democratic system.[122] These critics often use the first trial decision by Fukui District Court for Kumagaigumi as the legal basis for their claims. In 2003, political parties and their local chapters as well as political organizations collected a total of 319.6 billion yen mainly from corporations.[123] People in Japan are seeking to enhance the transparency of funds and journalists are supporting these efforts.[124]

Supreme Court's Decision in Southern Kyushu Association of Accountants

In the Southern Kyushu Association of Accountants case in 1970, the Supreme Court found that a political donation was unlawful. This is another case which took a different position from the Yawata Steel Supreme Court decision in 1970.

The Southern Kyushu Association of Accountants is a public interest entity which all the accountants in Kyushu are obligated to join. This case[125] occurred when a certain member of the association objected to the association's decision to collect, as a special member fee, funds intended for political donation to the Liberal Democratic Party to promote a political movement toward the revision of the Accountant Law. One member refused to pay the special member fee, and sued the association on the ground of violation of the freedom of thought.

A brief overview of the Supreme Court's Decision shows that the Court: (1) explicitly cited the argument that appeared in the *Yawata Steel* political donation case with reference to the scope of objective based on

---

[121] *Id.*
[122] *Id.*
[123] Yomiuri Online, "Enhancing Transparency of Political Funds", January 7, 2007 http://www.yomiuri.co.jp/kyoiku/learning/editorial/20050107/.
[124] *Id.*
[125] Minamikyuushuu Zeirishikai Seijikenkinn Soshou, Saikousai Hanketsu (Minamikyushu Association of Accountants Political Donation Suit, Supreme Court) Supreme Court, No. 3, Shouhan, March 19, 1998, Minshuu, 50-3, page 615.

the Civil Law, Article 43, which defined the rights of a legal person;[126] (2) stresses the difference between a corporation, which is a legal entity for profit, and the association of accountants, which is a legal entity for public interest with compulsory membership;[127] (3) construes the latter's action within the scope of object more restrictively;[128] and (4) thus concludes the political contribution to a political organization, such as a political party, as an act which falls outside of the boundary of the association's objective.[129]

The Supreme Court indicated in its decision that

> "it is natural to anticipate that there are members with different thoughts, beliefs, principles and claims so that there is a limit to what the association can ask its members to cooperate in, when judging the scope of the object in relation to the members' freedom of thoughts and beliefs."[130]

The Court further stated that,

> "it should be construed that a judgement whether to make the member's contribution or not, in particular, to a political organization such as a political party, which is the subject of the pertinent control law, is a matter closely related to the freedom of voting in the election, so that each member should make an individual decision as a citizen based on his personal political thought, opinion, judgement and others."[131]

Moreover,

> "a member's donation through such an association is an issue of choosing a certain political party or a candidate in the election" so that "for the association of accountants to make a political donation on behalf of its members to a

---

[126] *Id.*
[127] *Id.*
[128] *Id.*
[129] *Id.*
[130] *Id.*
[131] *Id.*

political organization, such as a political party, which is the subject of the pertinent control law, is an act that falls outside of the boundary of the object of the association of accountants even if the purpose is to realize a request for an amendment/abolishment of a law related to accountants."[132]

Compared to the Yawata Steel case, which found political donations by companies to be lawful, the scope of object according to Civil Law, Article 43 was construed more restrictively in this case since the issue in question was the freedom of thought and belief of the members of the organization and the association of accountants is a compulsory organization.[133] However, the Yawata Steel Case discussed the political donations by the company and the shareholders could leave the company at any time just by selling their shares. The court stated in this case that each member should make an individual decision for corporate donation as a citizen based on his personal political thought, opinion, judgement and others.[134] This recognition was central to distinguishing the case from Yawata Steel.

In comparison to the Kumagaigumi case which stated that a political donation by a company is unlawful, the court in this case took a position claiming that there is a limit to what the association can ask its members to cooperate in, when judging the scope of the object in relation to the members' freedom of thoughts and beliefs.[135] In the Kumagaigumi case, the court stated that a corporation's donation is enormously more influential than the political donation of an individual citizen and thus one cannot deny the possibility of essentially infringing upon the voting rights and suffrage of the people.[136]

Debate in Japan Concerning Corporate Political Donations

Just as there are two opposing court cases regarding political donations by companies, there are also two opposing academic theories on the

---

[132] *Id.*
[133] *Id.*
[134] See *supra* n.70.
[135] See *supra* n.58.
[136] *Id.*

same issue in Japan. The two opposing theories are: (1) that political donation is within the capacity of a corporation; and (2) that political donation is outside the company's business objective, and therefore it is invalid as it is outside the authority of a corporation.

Theories Upholding Corporate Donation

Among the theories based on the Civil Law and the Commercial Law, the prevailing theory is one that approves of corporate political donations based on advantages such as usability and efficiency for business purposes.[137] A view that approves corporate political donation stressing the social existence and real existence of a corporation is exemplified by the second trial decision and the Supreme Court's decision in the *Yawata Steel* political donation case, as well as the second trial decision of the *Kumagaigumi* case. These decisions identify corporate political donations as necessary and useful for the business purposes of a corporation based on the general position of profitability. Thus it does not constitute any violation of directors' responsibility.[138]

The typical opinion among those upholding this theory was that the violation of directors' responsibilities cannot be proven because political donations are, from a macro perspective, useful actions necessary for the profitability of a corporation.[139] In other words, "approval of a corporate political donation should be based on whether its economic effect is useful for the execution of the business, which is the purpose of the corporation."[140] This theory is frank and simple since it says that political donation is within the scope of the corporation's objective if it is useful for the business activities of corporation.

Admitting that political donations have a grave risk of corruption as undue influence, this theory probably takes the position that this problem should be cured by special laws for that purpose and it is difficult to deny corporate political donation under the commercial law.

---

[137] For example, Kazuo Mitsueda, "Kaisha no Sejikenkin Nituite" (Political Donations by Corporations), Houritsu Ronsou, 63-2, 1990, p. 31.

[138] See *supra* ns.58 and 70.

[139] For example, Takeo Suzuki, "Kaisha no Seijikenkin" (Political Donations by Corporations), Yuhikaku, 1971, p. 301.

[140] *Id.*

Another view that supports political donations, the juristic person's real existence theory, defines the essence of a juristic person as a thing that owns a social value suitable to be a subject of legal capacity similar to a natural person. This social value of a corporation should be evaluated from overall judgements, with the help of economics, sociology and other social sciences. So it is quite impossible to prove that corporate political donation is outside the scope of the objective of a corporation, based upon the current commercial law.[141]

Theories against Corporate Donation

There are a few opinions coming from different legal sources that argue against corporate donations. One can see that the theory denying political donations developed the most systematically and precisely in the arguments of the court cases as shown below.

(1) Civil Law Theory

This is a theory that denies a corporation's political donation:

"It is against the public order and morality specified in Article 90 of the Civil Law."[142,143]

Consideration of political donations is duplicitous in that they are first considered to be within the scope of the corporation's objective, but then further examination of appropriateness is needed after making a judgement on social appropriateness. It is found that they are not after all within the scope of the business objective.[144]

---

[141] For example, Sakae Wagatsuma, "Seijikenkin ni Kansuru Hanketsu Nituite" (Regarding the Court's Decisions on Corporate Donations), Jurist No. 341, 1966, p. 10.

[142] Article 90 of the Civil Law provides that a juristic act that has for its object such matters as are contrary to public or good morals is null and void. For the translation of the Civil Law of Japan by the Cabinet, Japan, see http://www.cas.go.jp/jp/seisaku/hourei/data/CC_2.pdf.

[143] For example, Kazuo Shinomiya, "Kaisha no Seijikenkin no Houritsu Mondai" (Legal issues on Corporate Political Donations), Jurist, No. 343, 1966, p. 36.

[144] *Id.*

According to this theory, what happens to the money is not an essential matter; political contributions should be controlled by the individual, such that corporate donations are a violation of Article 90 because they rob the individual of this privilege. Application of this theory to corporate political donations indicates that they are considered violations of public order and morality, which essentially takes them outside the scope of the corporations' objectives. The argument refers to an individual's political suffrage and the possibility of corporate donations being permitted only if every shareholder agrees. But such a possibility is something that is unrealistic because it is an impossible legal fiction to obtain political agreement of all the shareholders in a large corporation such as Yawata steel.

(2) Constitutional Law Theory

The theory states as follows:

"It is already invalid at the stage of the Constitution prior to the Commercial Law unless a corporation's donation is made after a unanimous decision by all the shareholders. It is based on a theory that such a donation should be made according to a citizen's own selection as a natural person and it is against such a theory for any director to use the corporation's assets, which are not the director's assets, for political purposes."[145]

This theory should agree with the viewpoint stated in the Supreme Court in Yawata Steel case. The logic of the Supreme Court was specifically intended to establish the legality of a corporation's political donations. However, as can be found in the Supreme Court's own statement that a political donation can affect political trends and the formation of political opinions of the public, a donation must be made with a unanimous vote.

---

[145] For example, Ichirou Kawamoto, "Gendai Kaishaho" (Modern Corporation, 8th edition), Shouji Houmu Kenkyuukai, 1999, p. 72.

(3) Another Constitutional Law Theory

It states that:

"It is too far-fetched and inappropriate to consider an act that has nothing to do with the objectives of a corporation under its articles of incorporation, in particular, of a corporation (especially a huge organization that is otherwise considered a social power) having an enormous economic power and social influencing capability, to act in response to expectations and requests (for the corporation) within the boundary of socially accepted notions or an expected act of a social being, and considering that the Constitution approves of unlimited freedom for corporation's political actions similar to that of a natural person."[146]

It is undeniable that a large donation can not only affect the outcome of an election but also enormously affect an "individual citizen's exercise of its voting rights and other political suffrage."[147] In the Kumagaigumi case, the court used the same logic to establish the illegality of political donations by companies. It stated that a corporation's donation is enormously more influential than the political donation of an individual citizen and therefore one cannot deny the possibility of essentially infringing upon the voting rights and suffrage of the people. Also the court stated that it creates a decisive influence on the nation's policies, and may end up creating a hotbed for unhealthy collusions between the political circle and the industry.

(4) Commercial Law Theory

The theory states that:

"The corporation's actions are divided, based on the corporation's profitability, into trading actions (profit-making actions) and non-trading actions (non-profit-making actions), the latter being considered

---

[146] For example, Sai Ashizawa, "Houjin to Jinken" (Corporation and Human Rights), Keibundo, 1995, p. 33.
[147] *Id.*

actions unrelated to the objectives of the corporation, including a tolerated exception for a social obligated action to which an agreement from all the shareholders can be expected."[148]

The view was taken by courts that denied the legality of political donations. They are exemplified by the first trial decision of the *Yawata Steel* case[149] and the first trial decision of the *Kumagaigumi* case,[150] in which the corporation's actions are divided, based on the corporation's profitability, into trading actions and non-trading actions, the latter being considered actions unrelated to the objectives of the corporation. Because the political donations in question do not fit the above exception, the directors' liabilities for damages were sought in both cases. One can see that the theory denying political donation developed the most systematically and precisely in the arguments of these cases.

Conclusion

A series of political corruptions and "structural scandals" occurred in Japan during the decades following WWII as the result of a hotbed of corporate donations. Voters in Japan are right to wonder why such large sums of money are donated when there is no benefit to be gained. It is fairly clear that if people give money to parties or individuals and then they can hide the fact that they have given that money, they are obviously expecting something in return.

As long as this powerful mix of money and politics remains loosely regulated, democracy will continue to be undermined because the potential for corrupt or undesirable influence in Japanese politics will continue. These views have led the Japanese government to impose restrictions on fundraising sources in the hope of eliminating perceived undue influence being given to money interests. In Japan, political and business accountability and transparency are on the rise.

---

[148] Koukichi Tomiyama, "Nihon Shoho no Mondaiten" (Current Problems of Japanese Commercial Law), Seibundo, 1975, pp. 72–73.
[149] See *supra* n.67.
[150] See *supra* n.58.

For corporate political donations, there are differing views on what is legal and what types of corporate donations to politicians and political parties are acceptable. Even courts' decisions are divided. Several disciplines other than law, such as economics, public policy, sociology, and other social academic theories should attempt to understand the dynamics of the political processes to find out the legality of this issue.

However, the legality and appropriateness of these corporate donations have been repeatedly justified in Japan by the premise that a corporation has the freedom to be engaged in political actions including the support, promotion, or objection to certain policies of the nation or a political party similar to a natural person and that political donations is essentially a part of that freedom.[151] The Supreme Court reiterated these ideas in the Yawata Steel decision. This is a leading position as to political donations by corporations, including the recent position of Keidanren, the most powerful economic organization in Japan.

One may wonder if this conclusion is correct, assuming that the existence of a juristic person is a technique for creating the existence of a thing that is not a person as a universal point of attribution for rights and liabilities. In other words, from a legal-technical point of view, a juristic person is a method of allowing the rights and liabilities of a social group, which belongs to a single entity, and not the constituting members of the social group.[152]

If the above technique is reviewed with reference to human rights, it has a very important significance that is related to the issue of legal protection, *i.e.*, how to protect the human rights of individuals against potential invasion by so-called social powers in a modern society, as human rights are essentially considered in regard to natural persons and not to juristic persons. As long as we continue to think of human rights in terms of natural persons, any human rights with respect to a juristic person will always carry only a secondary meaning in relation to the individuals.

Now that we have established the human right that a juristic person (or a corporation) can enjoy, the next issue is: When can a juristic person

---

[151] See *supra* n.70.
[152] Sai Ashizawa, "Juristic Person and Human Rights," Keibundo, 1995, pp. 33–34.

exercise his or her human rights? It is difficult to establish a uniform selection of human rights for this question and should be determined depending on the nature of the right in question. Because of the nature of each right, we should be able to conclude that certain rights, including the right to vote, the right to be elected, the right to life, the right to freedom of thought and conscience, and the right to freedom from slavery, are considered as human rights that a juristic person cannot enjoy.

Whereas rights related to state and economic issues, including equality under the law and the right of access to trial, property rights, and various other rights including freedom of expression, privacy of communication, and rights on criminal procedures such as proper procedures and non-invasion of address are the human rights that can be enjoyed by a juristic person. That leaves only one issue which is that it is possible to deduce freedom of making political donations straight from a corporation's freedom of conducting political actions. This is the decision that the court made in the Supreme Court's decision on the Yawata Steel's political donation case.

There are still two schools of thought as to this issue and no unanimous conclusion has been drawn in Japan yet. Even court decisions are divided. It is expected that a reasonable conclusion will come only after we have experienced a few more similar cases. The only conclusion left to make is whether corporations, as juristic persons, can make political donations. It is an issue that requires some patience and thought.

Chapter 13

Financing Japanese Investments in the United States: Case Studies of a Large and a Medium-Sized Firm[a]

Introduction

The volume of Japanese direct investment in the United States is steadily increasing. A recent case is the 400-million-dollar plant constructed by N Motor Company[1] to manufacture trucks in Tennessee is a recent case. Another case concerns a medium-sized enterprise that supplies components to larger firms, which has recently committed itself to an almost 10-million-dollar project in the United States. Indeed, there has been quite a large increase in the variety and number of Japanese investment activities in the American market. The financial aspect of these investments is of much interest since a range of techniques, including institutional financing, leasing, and tax-saving schemes, is being used. The purpose of this paper is to describe two examples that will shed some light on the financial techniques used in Japanese direct investment and to assess the potential for their continued use by both Japanese and American enterprises.

The author is solely responsible for the views expressed herein, which do not necessarily agree with the official views of the Industrial Bank of Japan.

[a] For this chapter, permission is granted to reprint by the Financial Management Association, Mitsuru Misawa, "*Japanese Investments in the United States: Case Studies of a Large and a Medium-Sized Firm*", Financial Management, The Financial Management Association, Vol. 14, No. 4, Winter 1985, pp. 5–12.
[1] N Motor is the second largest auto manufacturer in Japan. Its total sales amounted to 3,460 billion yen and its net profit was 61 billion yen in 1984.

Increasing Japanese Investment in the US

Table 1 shows that Japan's direct investment overseas has steadily increased. Investment in developing countries has slowed down, however. Table 1 also shows that investment in the industrialized countries, particularly in the United States, has had a sharp increase. There has been a discernable shift of emphasis in this investment from basic-resource sectors such as petroleum and coal to automobiles, electric machinery, electronics, and other manufacturing sectors. This has in turn translated into a shift in emphasis from the developing nations to the industrialized countries. The extent of concentrated investment in the manufacturing sector of the United States can be attributed to several factors.

First, a number of Japanese exports have succeeded in projecting a favorable product image in the marketplace, and this sort of foothold in the market is now secure enough to justify local production.

Table 1. Overseas Direct Investment by Japan, Overall and in the USA.

Fiscal Year	(A) Total (mil.$)	(B) U.S.A. (mil.$)	(B)/(A)
1975	3,280	846	26%
1978	4,598	1,282	28%
1979	4,995	1,354	27%
1980	4,693	1,484	32%
1981	8,931	2,354	26%
1982	7,703	2,738	36%
1983	8,145	2,565	32%
Accumulated Outstanding End of 1982	61,276	16,535	27%

Source: The Industrial Bank of Japan, Ltd.

Second, several Japanese manufacturing sectors now face a saturated demand for their products in the domestic market and manufacturers feel compelled to seek markets overseas.

Finally, some Japanese exports have gained an edge, both in qualitative and quantitative terms, over rival American-made products, causing unemployment in relevant sectors of the United States market. In order to stave off a backlash of protectionism, replacing direct exports with local production has become essential.

Case Studies in Investment Financing

The financing of these increases in Japanese direct investment in the United States deserves to be studied, since most of the financial arrangements adopted have been very different from those practiced in Japan by Japanese enterprises. It should be added that the arrangements for financing foreign direct investment differ somewhat between larger and medium-sized Japanese firms.

Let us now examine the cases of N Motor Company (N Motor) and N Plastic Company (N Plast) as examples of financing for large and medium-sized firms respectively.[2]

A Large Firm: N Motor

N Motor established a subsidiary in Smyrna, Rutherford County, in 1983. It then started producing trucks there at the rate of 10,000 units per month.

The Smyrna subsidiary now manufactures automobiles with its workforce of 2,000. Its equipment is completely modern and the level of productivity there is said to exceed that of any N Motor plant in the parent's homeland. It cost N Motor 400 million dollars to establish this

---

[2] The main difference between the cases of the large and medium-sized firms is their ability to raise funds through the Industrial Revenue Bonds (IRBs). Such bonds may be issued in amounts up to $10 million to build facilities that are deemed to be beneficial to the local municipality.

manufacturing subsidiary.[3] To finance this amount, N Motor exhausted practically all available means of financing know-how that seemed to promise legitimate merit of any sort. The overall structure of the financing is shown in Fig. 1. N Motor, the parent firm, raised 100 billion yen (400 million dollars) from a loan syndicate[4] formed by the Export-Import Bank of Japan and several commercial banks.

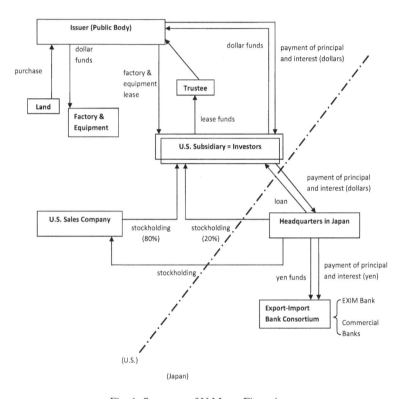

Fig. 1. Structure of N Motor Financing.

---

[3] The figures used in this article, such as the amounts of investment and the interest rates applied to N Motor and N Plast, are not identical to the actual figures. However, they are quite close.

[4] This arrangement belongs to a type known as an EXIM-syndicated loan. The EXIM-Japan offered 40 percent of the loan, while the rest was financed by a group of commercial banks managed by the Industrial Bank of Japan, Ltd. The long-term prime interest rate was only slightly above eight percent per annum at that time.

The interest on this yen loan was about 8.5 percent per annum. N Motor converted these yen funds to dollars and then relent the converted amount to its US subsidiary — N Motor Manufacturing Corporation, USA, or NMMC for short. NMMC then used these funds, which had been borrowed at a certain internal interest rate level,[5] to subscribe to a series of taxable bonds[6] issued by Rutherford County at a coupon rate of 13.5 percent per annum.

The location and design of the manufacturing plant were chosen by NMMC itself, but the entire plant and equipment were assigned to Rutherford County in terms of the actual sale. Rutherford County's purchase had been financed with the proceeds from the taxable bonds issue. The county then leased the plant and equipment back to NMMC.

This financial scheme has a number of advantages for N Motor's group as a whole:

First, N Motor, the parent firm, raised funds at 8.5 percent per annum and relent them at a higher rate, say 11 percent per annum. This spread helps to protect the parent firm from currency exchange losses, though to what extent is unknown.

Second, although the plant and equipment are leased back to NMMC, Rutherford County retains ownership. Since NMMC is thus not liable for fixed-asset taxes, the leasing fee is offset to that extent.

Third, the whole property is deemed to belong to NMMC when computing federal corporate taxes. In other words, NMMC can take full advantage of depreciation and investment tax credits.[7]

---

[5] The internal interest rate level is surmised to be around 11 percent per annum. It must be between the original funding cost of 8.5 percent and the taxable bond rate of 13.5 percent.

[6] The state and county may issue tax-exempt general purpose revenue bonds, but the bonds are not tax-exempt if the funds that are raised are used for the benefit of a third party, such as an investment company. In that case, the bonds are generally called "taxable bonds." The only exception is in the case of industrial revenue bonds that have a face value not exceeding $10 million (Internal Revenue Code, 1954, Section 103).

[7] IRS Revenue Ruling 55-540, 1955.

Fourth, NMMC must shoulder a heavy depreciation burden in its start-up phase, but for tax purposes, its losses can be used to cancel out part of the large income of N Motor Sales USA, the local sales company of N Motor Group, which operates on a consolidated accounting basis.[8] Thus, the N Motor group is able to pocket substantial tax savings in the US.

Fifth, after enjoying the benefit of off-balance sheet financing, NMMC is entitled to exercise an option to buy back the plant and equipment once the new firm gets past the start-up stage.

Sixth, NMMC used tax-exempt pollution-control bonds (PCBs) to finance part of the initial investment. At the time, the cost of financing using this method was just about six percent per annum. The county issued the PCBs and used the proceeds to purchase pollution-control equipment for NMMC. This equipment was leased back to NMMC. The bond issuer in turn used its leasing revenues to service the debt. The pollution-control equipment, which was financed through PCBs, must satisfy federal and state pollution control standards.

To get a quantitative estimate of the benefits from this financing arrangement, let us compare its after-tax net cash flows with those of conventional bank financing. The primary benefits that will be reflected in this comparison are the third, fourth, and sixth ones listed before. The comparison is made on the basis of

Land value	10 million dollars
Building value	90 million dollars
Machinery value	300 million dollars
(of which 20 million dollars is	
related to pollution control)	
Total investment	400 million dollars

---

[8] This sort of tax break on a consolidated basis is granted to a pair of firms, say A and B, provided that A holds 80 percent or more of the capital stock of B. In this example, N Motor Sales USA holds 80 percent of NMMC and the parent firm in Japan holds the remainder.

The net after-tax cash outflows associated with the taxable bond plus leaseback financing are shown in Table 2,[9] while those associated with conventional bank loan financing are shown in Table 3. It is important to note that the original project appraisal envisioned deficits for the first five years. The advantage of a tax shield (depreciation, interest payments, and the investment tax credit) is realized during this five-year period, therefore, only under the taxable bond plus leaseback arrangement. Under this arrangement, the project's early losses are consolidated with the profits of the US sales company, and all tax benefits are realized in a timely fashion. Under conventional financing, by contrast, the project stands alone and some of these tax benefits are lost, or at least postponed until after the five-year start-up period. Discounting the net after-tax cash flows from Tables 2 and 3 at the after-tax rate for conventional financing results in a present value of net cash outflows of $244.8 million for the taxable bond plus leaseback arrangement and $492.1 million for the conventional financing arrangement. The difference, which is $247.3 million, is a measure of the advantage of the taxable bond plus leaseback

---

[9] Although the county administration is the issuer of taxable bonds, the calculation of the net cash flow from the taxable-bond-plus-lease transaction is carried out as if NMMC itself had done the issuing. The leasing part of the transaction is ignored. As stated earlier, the Internal Revenue Service views the transaction in the same way (IRB Revenue Ruling 55-540, 1955). It allows NMMC to deduct the interest payment on the taxable bonds as if it had made those interest payments itself. In addition, the calculation assumes that NMMC's pretax cost of funds is 13.5 percent of the taxable bond portion of the financing and the 11 percent of the cost that is applicable to the intra-company fund transfer is not used. The reasons for using 13.5 percent are twofold. First, if the parent company had decided to lend dollar funds in the U.S., it could have realized a 13.5 percent pretax return; and second, all interest payments on the bonds to be paid by the county administration on a 13.5 percent basis must be fully reimbursed by NMMC.

For reference, the typical conditions at the time for the issuing of taxable bonds were as follows:

Maturity	10 years
Interest	13.5 percent per annum
Timing of payment	At the end of each six-month period
Repayment	The debt will be repaid in equal installments every six months, starting in the sixth year

Table 2. Cash Flow Analysis of the "Taxable Bonds Plus Lease-back" Method.

Period No. (Half-year Basis)	(1) Deprec. (Machine)	(2) Deprec. (Buildg)	(3) Interest Payment	(4) Deductible Expenses	(5) Tax Savings	(6) Invmt Tax Credit	(7) Debt Amortization	(8) Net After-Tax Cash Flow	(9) NPV of (8)
1	45.0		26.3	26.3	12.1		0	−14.200	−14.200
2		4.5	26.3	75.8	34.8	30.0	0	38.500	37.144
3			26.3	26.3	12.1		0	−14.200	−13.218
4	66.0	9.0	26.3	101.3	46.6		0	20.300	18.230
5			26.3	26.3	12.1		0	−14.200	−12.303
6	63.0	8.1	26.3	97.4	44.8		0	18.500	15.464
7			26.3	26.3	12.1		0	−14.200	−11.452
8	63.0	7.2	26.3	96.5	44.4		0	18.100	14.083
9			26.3	26.3	12.1		0	−14.200	−10.659
10	63.0	6.3	26.3	95.6	44.0		0	17.700	12.819
11			26.3	26.3	12.1		40	−54.200	−37.871
12		6.3	23.6	29.9	13.8		40	−49.800	−33.571
13			21.0	21.0	9.7		40	−51.300	−33.365
14		5.4	18.4	23.8	10.9		40	−47.500	−29.805
15			15.8	15.8	7.2		40	−48.600	−29.422
16		5.4	13.1	18.5	8.5		40	−44.600	−26.049
17			10.5	10.5	4.8		40	−45.700	−25.752
18		5.4	7.9	13.3	6.1		40	−41.800	−22.725
19			5.3	5.3	2.4		40	−42.900	−22.501
20		5.4	2.6	8.0	3.7		40	−38.900	−19.685
Total								−423.200	−244.837

* Formulas: (4) = (1) + (2) + (3); (5) = (4) × 0.46, where 0.46 is the federal income tax; (8) = − (3) + (5) + (6) − (7); (9) = N.P.V. of (8), discounted by 0.0365 on a half-year basis, or [0.135(1−0.466)]/2.

† The calculation here is based on the following numbers: General machinery depreciation, 5 years; Building depreciation, 15 years; Maturity of taxable bonds and PCBs (lower floater), 10 years (5 years as the grace period).

‡ Depreciation is applicable to all machinery ($300 million) including pollution-control equipment ($20 million).

§ Interest is payable on 13.5 percent taxable bonds ($380 million) and six percent PCBs ($20 million), which together finance the machinery, land, and buildings.

¶ ITC is granted for ten percent of the $300 million investment in machinery.

Table 3. Cash Flow Analysis of Conventional Financing.

Period No. (Half-year Basis)	Profit	(1) Deprec. (Machine)	(2) Deprec. (Buildg)	(3) Interest Payment	(4) Total Deductible Expenses	(5) Tax Savings	(6) Invmt Tax Credit	(7) Debt Amortization	(8) Net After-Tax Cash Flow	(9) NPV of (8)
1	−			27.0	27.0	0.0		0	−27.000	−27.000
2	−	45.0	4.5	27.0	76.5	0.0		0	−27.000	−26.049
3	−			27.0	27.0	0.0		0	−27.000	−25.132
4	−	66.0	9.0	27.0	102.0	0.0		0	−27.000	−24.247
5	−			27.0	27.0	0.0		0	−27.000	−23.393
6	−	63.0	8.1	27.0	98.1	0.0		0	−27.000	−22.569
7	−			27.0	27.0	0.0		0	−27.000	−21.774
8	−	63.0	7.2	27.0	97.2	0.0		0	−27.000	−21.008
9	−			27.0	27.0	0.0		0	−27.000	−20.268
10	−	63.0	6.3	27.0	96.3	0.0		0	−27.000	−19.554
11	+			27.0	27.0	12.4	30.0	40	−24.600	−17.189
12	+		6.3	24.3	30.6	14.1		40	−50.200	−33.841
13	+			21.6	21.6	9.9		40	−51.700	−33.625
14	+		5.4	18.9	24.3	11.2		40	−47.700	−29.931
15	+			16.2	16.2	7.5		40	−48.700	−29.482
16	+		5.4	13.5	18.9	8.7		40	−44.800	−26.166
17	+			10.8	10.8	5.0		40	−45.800	−25.808
18	+		5.4	8.1	13.5	6.2		40	−41.900	−22.779
19	+			5.4	5.4	2.5		40	−42.900	−22.501
20	+		5.4	2.7	8.1	3.7		40	−39.000	−19.735
Total									−707.300	−492.052

* Formulas: $(4) = (1) + (2) + (3)$; $(5) = (4) \times 0.46$, where 0.46 is the federal income tax; $(8) = -(3) + (5) + (6) - (7)$; $(9) = N.P.V.$ of (8), discounted by 0.0365 on a half-year basis, or $[0.135(1-0.466)]/2$.

† The calculation here is based on the following numbers: General machinery depreciation, 5 years; Building depreciation, 15 years; Maturity of taxable bonds and PCBs (lower floater), 10 years (5 years as the grace period).

‡ Depreciation is applicable to all machinery ($300 million) including pollution-control equipment ($20 million).

§ Interest is payable on 13.5 percent taxable bonds ($380 million) and six percent PCBs ($20 million), which together finance the machinery, land, and buildings.

¶ ITC is granted for ten percent of the $300 million investment in machinery.

arrangement.[10] Of this amount, $247.7 million represents the benefit of timely realization of tax shields (depreciation, interest payments, and ITC). The remainder, which is $4.6 million, reflects the advantage of PCB financing for the eligible expenditures of $20 million.

A Medium-Sized Firm: N Plast

N Motor's venture in Tennessee parallels Honda's deployment in Ohio. Both these Japanese ventures stick to the "just-in-time" inventory method[11] in order to keep inventories to a minimum. The adoption of this inventory method by Japanese automobile manufacturing ventures has prompted many Japanese automotive component suppliers to follow these makers to the United States.

The Ohio venture of N Plast[12] fits into this pattern. Therefore, let us take a closer look at the project's financing scheme.

The N Plast venture in Ohio required an investment outlay of two million dollars. This was small enough to qualify the project for Industrial Revenue Bond (IRB) financing.

---

[10] The net benefit from the N Motor transaction may be somewhat overstated. It is based on the assumption that the depreciation-tax shields lost in periods 1–10 will never be regained. It is implicitly assumed, therefore, that NMMC's taxable income is insufficient in periods 11–20 to use any tax loss carried forward from previous periods. An alternative and more conservative calculation would be to spread out these carryforwards in some ways over periods 12, 14, 16, 18 and 20. Suppose $120 million in carryforwards was used in each of these five periods. Under these conditions, the net advantage of the taxable bond plus leaseback arrangement will decrease to $68.8 million.

[11] The "just-in-time" inventory method (JIT), also known as the "kanban" method in Japan, was originally initiated by Toyota Motor Corporation. It has since been adopted by many other manufacturers of various products. The word "kanban" refers to small cards indicating assembly-line processes. When a stock of components is depleted, these JIT cards are relayed back to earlier stages in the assembly and to suppliers of components to call for replenishment. Thus the component stock can be reduced to a minimum. The JIT method, however, presupposes the existence of nearby suppliers and their readiness to respond quickly.

[12] N Plast, located in Shizuoka, is a manufacturer of steering wheels and other automotive parts. Its annual sales amounted to 30 billion yen and its income 330 million yen in 1984. N Motor owns 30 percent of the shares.

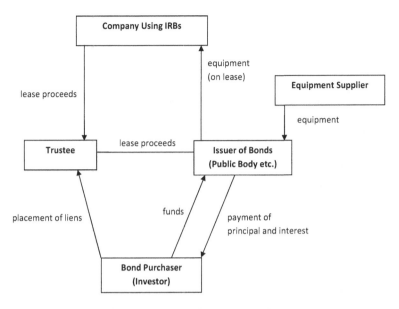

Fig. 2. Structure of N Plast Financing.

As illustrated in Fig. 2, the city of Eaton, Ohio issued IRBs amounting to two million dollars, which were purchased by an institutional investor in the United States.[13] The city of Eaton used the proceeds to purchase the plant and equipment of Eaton Auto Products Manufacturing, Inc. (EAPM), N Plast's subsidiary. EAPM, however, retained the use of the plant and equipment through a leaseback arrangement from the city of Eaton.

---

[13] The investor, in this case, is Industrial Bank of Japan Trust Company in New York. The term of the bonds is 10 years and the rate is about 70 percent of the US prime rate on a three-month floating basis. Theoretically, any institutional investor with a tax position in the United States may serve as a purchaser. Such investors include, for instance, banks or life or indemnity insurance companies. However, in the case of Japanese investments in the US, the bonds are usually privately placed in financial institutions that have close ties to the company undertaking the project. In fact, the financing ultimately comes from Japanese banks, since the long-lasting relationship established between the company and the bank in Japan is usually also extended to their operations in foreign countries. On the other hand, the typical US practice in this regard is different. The RIBs would typically be sold to the public at large if they were issued for the benefit of a US company.

The institutional investor purchasing the IRBs was exempted from the 46 percent federal tax on interest income. The investor was able, therefore, to offer a lower rate to the city of Eaton, which in turn could offer better terms when leasing the plant and equipment to EAPM. EAPM, in effect, was thus able to lower its funding cost to about 70 percent of the market interest rate on taxable bonds.

In order to better understand the advantage of IRBs, let us quantify it in net present value terms relative to some other conventional financing structure. The basis of the analysis of financial cost using conventional financing and IRBs is as follows:

	Conventional Financing	IRBs
Principle interest rate terms	$2,000,000	$2,000,000
	13.50%	9.45%
	10 years	10 years
	(20 payments)	(20 payments)
Semi-annual mortgage payment (interest plus amortization)	$185,133	$156,764

The advantage of IRBs is equal to the present value of the difference in after-tax cash flow, discounted at the after-tax interest rate on conventional financing. The present value of the difference in this case is equal to $201,537 on the 2,000,000 dollar investment.

Elements of Financial Engineering

The financial arrangements described upto this point represent a range of separate elements. Let us focus our attention on these elements, one by one:

Utilization of Government Financial Incentives

The United States, at its various levels of government, has institutionalized financial incentives to encourage regional investment. These measures include IRBs, taxable bonds, and PCBs. All these incentives have been fully utilized in the cases under study.

Utilization of Leasing

Leasing as a means of raising funds is not so well developed in Japan as in the United States, but Japanese firms engaged in raising industrial funds are quite willing to exploit leasing's potential as an instrument for off-balance sheet financing.

A Multi-Currency Mix

The financing of a direct-investment project is usually done in the same currency as the one in which the project proceeds are expected to accrue. This is considered necessary in order to hedge exchange risks. Recently, however, interest-rate differentials between countries appear to have been larger than the probable exchange risk levels. This is why hybrid-currency financing has become increasingly preferred. By combining financial techniques, we can achieve the following results.

First, the efficiency of a financial package can be increased by combining incentive financing and leasing with a combination of different maturity structures. In Japan, this aim is now being pursued under the name of "financial engineering."

Second, the available tax advantages are fully exploited. Under the influence of supply-side economics, the United States at various levels of government has granted a wide range of investment credits to firms undertaking investment. Leasing and institutional finance are also being used in combination with these tax-credit schemes. While US businessmen tend to focus their attention on after-tax profits, their Japanese counterparts divert more attention to pretax profits. This is because most Japanese businessmen consider taxation as purely a governmental matter, to which they have no choice but to adapt passively. Even in Japan, however, this attitude is changing, and Japanese businessmen are likely to pursue tax advantages more vigorously in the future.

Third, the potential of international finance is fully exploited. Though the area of project activities may be confined to the United States alone, such financing aims to optimize global possibilities. Funding can be carried out in various international markets that include Tokyo, New York, and the Euromarket.

Conclusion: Wider Application of Potential

What may be termed "global financial engineering" is now frequently being used by Japanese businesses when they invest in the United States. Japanese businesses are now very international in both outlook and activities. They can avail themselves of the most sophisticated financial techniques available, and they are in fact determined to make the best of such opportunities. Japanese financial institutions, in turn, are venturing into international markets and are engaged in fierce competition with foreign banks, mostly from America and Western Europe. The desire to outsmart one's competitors certainly lends a greater impetus to polishing up one's financial skills.

These recent developments in financial engineering have potentially wider applications.[14] US firms themselves have used and will continue to use similar techniques to invest in their homeland.[15] Other foreign enterprises contemplating investments in the United States may be able

---

[14] N Motor, in venturing into automobile production in the United Kingdom, is trying to make the best out of locally available tax preferences, just as it has done in the United States. For this purpose, N Motor concluded a leasing agreement in December 1984 with the Forward Trust Group (FTG), a subsidiary of Midland Bank. Under this agreement, FTG will construct an automobile plant on behalf of N Motor Manufacturing UK (NMM – UK) with an investment of 50 million pounds (400 million US dollars). FTG will lease this plant to NMM – UK, which will eventually acquire plant ownership when the leasing agreement expires.

This scheme is apparently modelled after N Motor's leasing arrangement in Tennessee. (See the article on this subject in *Nihon Keizai Shinbun*, page 8, December 4, 1984).

[15] Financial transactions, such as IRBs, PCBs, and leasing, have all been relatively widespread in use in the US. However, they tended to be utilized separately. Japanese efforts deserve study as an attempt to put all these techniques together into a financial package that ensures maximum benefit for the project in question.

to employ financial engineering.[16] Furthermore, foreign firms desiring to invest in Japan may be able to use such techniques, to some extent.

It is not too much to say that financial engineering in this sense is getting more refined, sophisticated, and internationalized day by day.[17] This is certainly one area being closely watched in the United States and Japan by business people, bankers, and academia.

---

[16] Various states in the US are eager to invite foreign firms to invest within their borders and they are ready to offer a range of attractive financial arrangements. They would surely want to know what other states are doing. The particulars of a financial scheme are not usually disclosed, however.

[17] The recently proposed changes in the US tax law would certainly have some effects on those financial packages that are oriented towards tax savings. If the ITC is eliminated and depreciation schedules are made less generous, as it appears to be quite possible now, this would reduce the benefits available for a financial transaction like that of N Motors, although its comparative advantage would not disappear. In any case, new techniques and methodologies are sure to be developed in the course of coping with the new changes in the tax laws.

Chapter 14

New Japanese-Style Management in a Changing Era[a]

The recent capital flow from Japan to the US has been quite remarkable.[1] Merchandize exports from Japan to the US have been so successful that their rapid increase in recent years has caused a range of problems known as "trade friction."[2]

Mitsuru Misawa is the General Manager of the International Investment Services Department of the Industrial Bank of Japan and the author of numerous articles.

[a] For this chapter, permission is granted to reprint by Elsevier, Mitsuru Misawa, "New Japanese-Style Management in a Changing Era", The Columbia Journal of World Business, Vol. XXII, No. 4, Winter 1987, pp. 9–17.

[1] Japanese direct investment in the US has been increasing since the 1970s. This investment amounted to $1.3 billion in 1978 and $2.6 billion in 1983. Direct investment doubled in this period. (JETRO, Foreign Direct Investment from Japan and to Japan, 1985, p. 13.)
The reasons for this remarkable increase are:

- Rapid growth is no longer possible for many industries located in Japan;
- Japanese firms have achieved a sufficiently high level of technological and managerial skill and have built up enough financial strength to be able to operate in the world market;
- Restrictions on capital outflows have been loosened and sometimes investment abroad has even been encouraged by the Japanese government as the surplus in the trade balance continues to grow;
- Recently, Japanese companies have been forced to invest more in the US to reduce trade friction with US Industries.

[2] Following textiles and color TV sets, the automobile surfaced as the major cause of trade friction between Japan and the US, as well as between Japan and Europe. Automobile manufacturing is an extremely competitive industry and criticism from abroad against Japan's export drive has intensified considerably. Trade friction subsided when Japan voluntarily regulated exports to the US and the EC member countries. For example, export to the US was limited to 16.8 million cars per annum. However, this conflict triggered other trade friction and Japan has been exposed to mounting demands

The high value placed on Japanese products has motivated many overseas managers to take a closer look at Japanese management. The internationalization of Japanese companies made it possible for Japanese-style management to increase the interface with its US counterpart. For example, the term "kanban method" (just-in-time method) developed by Toyota is now used in English in such expressions as "We have *kanbanized*" our factory."[3] This method for procuring parts was invented and developed by Japanese auto manufacturers and is now used by their American counterparts.[4] The phrase, "QC (quality control) circle," is often used not only in companies, but also in hospitals and schools in the US. Product quality control was introduced to Japan by Dr. Deming from the US after World War II, but it was more widely utilized and developed in Japan. A new QC method is thus being introduced to the US by Japanese companies.

---

to open its markets and to eliminate duties on agricultural products. It seems that future trade friction will not be limited to specific items, but will develop into a comprehensive and structural problem. If US business picks up further, Japan is expected to increase the export of products such as VCRs, household electric appliances, computers and industrial robots. In the meantime, the major import items from the US are products with low income elasticity, such as fruit, meat and raw materials for the textile industry. Given these circumstances, it is anticipated that the Japanese trade surplus with the US will continue to persist and that the trade friction problem will be protracted.

[3] Toyota is the largest auto manufacturer in Japan. Its total sales amounted to 6,100 billion yen and net profits to 285 billion yen in 1985.

[4] The aim of the method is to minimize the inventory of parts on hand and to be able to efficiently place orders for the procurement of parts with affiliated parts companies. The system has computerized all the information on parts at hand and the requests for them so that the necessary amount of parts procurement is calculated automatically on a continual basis. Thus the cost of carrying unnecessary parts in the inventory of the parent company is minimized. A look at the US auto industry reveals that the Big Three of Detroit have shown remarkable recovery in their profit performances. In 1980, they suffered a combined loss of $4 billion, but it is estimated that in 1981, they showed a combined profit of $5 billion (Toyo Keizai, September 10, 1983, p. 26). Their recovery is certainly due in part to the general revival of consumption in the US economy, but it is also due to their efforts to improve the quality of their products and reduce costs. The success of their Japanese competitors may also have stimulated the Big Three in their efforts in this direction. They have learned that the high quality of Japanese cars is the result of quality control exercised by the parts manufacturers. As a result, the Big Three in Detroit have requested their suppliers to raise and maintain the quality of their products. The observance of agreed-upon delivery dates by suppliers is a prerequisite to the introduction of the "kanban" method. Accordingly, the Big Three have requested their suppliers to meet the same standard with respect to the observance of delivery times.

It has also been reported that the creation of "*sogo shosha*" (general trading firms) is under serious consideration by businesses in the US This movement has resulted from an evaluation of the functions of Japanese "*sogo shosha*," which have contributed greatly to the rapid growth of Japanese exports.

American management methodology developed by US companies and business schools has enjoyed a dominant position in management all over the world. There has been an increasing interest in Japanese-style management, however. This is evident from the fact that several books of the subject, such as *Theory Z*[5] and *Japan as Number One*,[6] have become bestsellers.

The lifetime employment system, seniority system, paternalistic employee management and company union system, once considered defining characteristics of Japanese management are slowly becoming less relevant as the Japanese management system evolves over time. These characteristics were considered valuable in developing employee loyalty, improving productivity and maintaining a high standard of quality control.

Recently, however, the Japanese management system, which had previously supported Japan's economic progress, has gradually weathered in response to environmental changes in order to maintain corporate vitality. The Japanese managerial environment is undergoing major changes due to the development of highly advanced technologies and internationalization. No longer does the Japanese industry adhere rigidly to conventional Japanese-style management based on mass production systems and improved technologies developed elsewhere.

In this paper, we will first take a look at the existing Japanese management. We will clarify its characteristics by comparing it with the American approach to management. We will then examine the questions of whether the main features of Japanese management are necessarily unique to Japan and whether some American companies have introduced similar practices. A discussion is included on how the Japanese management is changing and will continue to change in the

---

[5] William G. Ouchi, *Theory Z: How American Business Can Meet the Japanese Challenge*, Addison-Wesley Publishing, 1981.
[6] Ezra F. Vogel, *Japan as Number One: Lesson for America*, Harvard University Press, 1979.

future. If the Japanese economy is now coming to an important cross-road, we must determine whether and how the Japanese management should respond to these new changes. The main issue is whether the Japanese propensity for homogeneity, which has been suited to the mass production system so far, will have an adverse effect on the development of creative technologies, which will be the driving force for the continued success of the Japanese economy. Finally, there will be a discussion of how the US and the Japanese management systems can be improved by incorporating each other's management techniques.

Existing Japanese Management

What images do the notion of Japanese management evoke? There are many characteristics of Japanese management, but the principles and rules found in a large number of Japanese companies are consistent. Below are phrases used in companies to bind workers and managers together for the good of the company.

Keiten aijin

This is a policy undertaken by Kyocera for example.[7] Whenever the opportunity presents itself, the staff will discuss the company motto, which means, literally, to respect heaven and love your fellow man. This is considered to be a way of fostering the spirit of participation. The goal of this is to achieve a unity that can be said to approach near religious intensity. In fact, Kyocera has an "employees' graveyard" at the Buddhist Enpukuji Temple on the outskirts of Kyoto. Clearly, Kyocera is an outstanding example of an approach that sees workers as part of a corporate family, even after death. Some commentators see this as a kind of corporate religion.[8]

---

[7] Kyocera is a leading Japanese high-tech company headquartered in the old Japanese capital of Kyoto. The company is best known as a manufacturer of ceramic packages for the electronics industry. Its total sales amounted to 283 billion yen and net profit to 32 billion yen in 1985.

[8] Seiichi Kikuchi, *Nigai America* (Bitter America), Japan Management Association, Tokyo, 1983, p. 122.

Zen no junkan

The company motto of YKK, the foremost zipper manufacturer in the world, is *zen no junkan*, which literally means "cycle of goodness."[9] Rather than spending all of today's profits, it is better for the company to reinvest the funds for tomorrow and generate new profits. By continuing this cycle, the company will flourish and workers' incomes will rise. The company will not only be able to contribute directly to society through the taxes it pays, but will also benefit consumers and its partner firms by offering them better products at lower prices. Added to this notion is the idea that this cycle will steadily grow wider, and you have *zen no junkan*. We expect this motto to be rather hard to understand outside the context of long-term stability offered by Japan's distinctive lifetime employment system.

Tanohkoh seido

Another instance where the concept of a corporate family can be seen is in the Toyota-GM joint venture in the US Toyota, together with General Motors, negotiated with United Auto Workers regarding a labor contract. A basic agreement was finally reached in September, 1983 that includes an extremely important clause, *tanohkoh seido*. This clause states that the joint venture will adopt a multiple-skills system under which workers' job classifications will be as flexible as possible, and a single worker will be able to handle a variety of different tasks.[10]

This, of course, is another element of Japanese-style management, and it stems from the idea of the company as one big household. In a family, there are clearly different job responsibilities for the father, the mother and the children. But when people are busy, or when there's a crisis of some kind, everyone pitches in to help one another.

Toyota hopes that by eliminating rigid work division, it can introduce some more flexible family-like elements into the US labor-management relations, which tend to be inflexible and frequently lead to confrontations.

---

[9] YKK's total sales amounted to 216 billion yen and net profit to eight billion yen in 1985.
[10] *Nihon Keizai Shimbun*, October 12, 1983, p. 6.

In this sense, the efforts of all three parties to reach a compromise were significant.

Nenkoh joretsu

Companies in Japan recruit fresh graduates from high schools and colleges every year, but the salaries for all employees hired at the same time are equal regardless of their differences in ability, dedication, and motivation. Individual differences do not take on significance until five to ten years after entering the company. Employees are entitled to regular pay raises according to seniority (*nenkoh joretsu*).

As is well-known, a Japanese salary is accompanied by many fringe benefits, which include company housing for all employees who want to have it. Employees all live in the same style of housing provided by the company and eat the same food for lunch at the company's cafeteria. This shared form of life style may promote the same ways of thinking and basic attitudes.

Sabetsu

Are there any discrimination (*sabetsu*) problems in Japan? The issues of sexual and minority group discrimination are not clear-cut. Of course, we can hardly claim that there is no discrimination in Japan. Article 14 of the Japanese Constitution states that, "All people are equal under the law and there shall be no discrimination in political, economic or social relations because of race, creed, sex, social status or family origin."[11] The very fact that this clause had to be included in the Constitution is an indication of the historical reality of discrimination in Japan. Moreover, as one Japanese saying goes, "The things that have gotten stronger since the war are nylon stockings and women." There has been a rapid influx of women into the workplace in recent years and it is now no longer possible to simply ignore problems of discrimination.

Even with these reservations, the Japanese are an extremely homogenous group of people racially, culturally and linguistically.

---

[11] *The Japanese Constitution*, 1946.

Despite occasional friction, it is not very difficult to build a sense of solidarity and unity.

Shohgaikoyoh

This policy refers to the lifetime employment system which is a common practice in almost all Japanese companies. Once someone joins a certain company, he or she rarely leaves that company for another, although the option of leaving is always open. The commitment of Japanese employees to their company in Japan is thus quite different from the situation in the US, where high labor mobility in the job market encourages people to move freely from one company to another.[12]

This difference in commitment leads to other important differences in the relationship between a company and its employees. One example of this involves company training. Under the lifetime employment system, companies do not hesitate to invest considerable time and expense in employee training on the assumption that all investment in training will prove an asset to the company since employees are not expected to leave.[13] Japanese companies in the US, where there is a highly mobile labor force, are often uncertain as to how much they should invest in educating and training their work force.

A second example is the difference between US and Japanese companies with respect to merit ratings. The Japanese approach is to keep an employee's performance evaluation confidential and not divulge it even to other members of the company. An evaluation is an extremely sensitive affair made with the employee's long-term potential in

---

[12] Psychological aspects of lifetime employment are emphasized in Chuichi Nakamura's, *Igirisu Byo, Italia Byo, Nihon Byo* (The British Disease, the Italian Disease and the Japanese Disease), Toyo Keizai Shinposha, 1982, p. 196. The author states that the real spirit of lifetime employment is loyalty to one's company and the patience to endure even low salaries.

[13] The Industrial Bank of Japan will serve as an example of the efficacy of investment in training in Japan. Approximately ten employees are sent to graduate schools in the US and Europe every year to study business, law or other subjects. There is not clear contract or agreement involved, but of the more than 180 employees who have received this special training over the past 20 years, only four have left the bank.

mind. In other words, most evaluations tend to be shaped by the requirements of the lifetime employment system.

However, the American approach to merit rating is to evaluate the employee's actual job performance during a given period, rather than evaluating his or her long-term potential and dedication. Since the American evaluation is an extremely specific affair that decides, for instance, the size of one's next pay raise, the rating process tends to be very open between the supervisor and the employee and is based on short-term performance. Once an agreement is reached, it is signed and formalized. This is the method that is most often used in the US to the dismay of Japanese companies.

Kigyohbetsu kumiai

In Japan, labor unions are organized on a company-by-company basis (*kigyohbetsu kumiai*).[14] As a result, the interests of the company and the union are the same to a large degree. If, for instance, the company can increase profits by installing welding robots, the union has no particular reason to protest because workers have the lifetime employment system to protect their jobs.

In contrast, many of the labor unions in the US are craft unions. Thus, the interests of individual companies and labor unions do not necessarily coincide. A welding robot may contribute to raising a given company's profits and may even help to raise the income of all its employees, but the industry-wide union of welders have no choice but to oppose it.[15]

---

[14] For details regarding the differences in trade unions in both countries, see the Industrial Bank of Japan, *Guide to Investment in Japan*, August 1983, pp. 25–31.

[15] This structural difference represents a large problem for Japanese manufacturers entering the US market. They would prefer a management style that dispensed with unions. The Industrial Bank of Japan recently interviewed executives from 27 of its client companies for a collection of case studies entitled, *Taking on the Challenge of Overseas Local Production* (The Industrial Bank of Japan, Tokyo, 1983). Based on the information obtained from these interviews, it appears that Japanese companies are adopting a number of management strategies in an attempt to forestall labor unions. These include:

- Providing better working conditions than the local norm;
- Locating in states where the extent of unionization is still low; and
- Introducing suggestion systems and workers' participation in decision-making.

The set of Japanese management techniques may be encapsulated into three categories: solidarity, homogeneity, and commitment. These three concepts, however, do not seem to be unique since they are also used in the US management. This point will be discussed in detail later on.

Difficulties in Understanding the Japanese Management

From the previous examples, one may have the impression that Japanese management strategies have been understood quite well by US companies. On the contrary, there remain aspects which seem to be filled with mystery. Why is this so?

The first complication is the language barrier. This can be traced back to Japan's insularity. Some statistics are available to illustrate this point. Japan's present population stands at about 118 million. Of these 118 million people, a scant 0.06 percent speak English. While there are about 774,000 foreign residents in Japan, more than 90 percent are Japanese-speaking Koreans and Chinese.[16] For this reason, the opportunities for a Japanese to come into contact with native English speakers are extremely rare. Similarly, the number of Japanese living abroad is very small — only some 464,000.[17] As a result of this insularity, one can imagine how difficult it is to get across to foreign managers the subtle essence of Japanese-style management, which·defies any clear written description or other precise documentation.

---

[16] Numbers of foreign residents registered as of December 31, 1979:

Korean	662,561	(89%)
Chinese	50,353	(7%)
American	21,651	(3%)
Filipino	4,757	(0.5%)
British	4,754	(0.5%)
Total	774,076	(100%)

(Source: *Hoso Jiho*, Vol. 21, No. 7).

[17] Number of Japanese living abroad as of October 1, 1982:

Long-term residents	215,799
Permanent residents	247,881
Total	463,680

(Source: Ministry of Foreign Affairs).

Another factor hampering communication is the tendency among Japanese to shun argumentation, and to frown upon giving clear "yes" and "no" answers. There is a cultural affinity for non-verbalized understanding, for an unspoken shared awareness and an implicit sense of "you know what I mean" in conversations. Even labor-management relations are handled in this tradition. No doubt Americans who have been brought up to prize the clear expression of honest opinion from an early age will find this aspect of Japanese behavior hard to understand.

Another difference is that the decision-making process in a Japanese company is based on the "bottom-up method," whereas the US process is a "top-down method." The Japanese method is very much related to the so-called *"ringisei,"* which literally means "reverential inquiry."[18] The following is an example of this process:

A low-level official who is confronted with a problem requiring a corporate decision prepares a recommendation draft. This draft is then circulated to all the parties concerned not only at the horizontal but also at the vertical levels to obtain approval, attested to by the stamp of official seals. Through this system, Japanese companies achieve a high degree of communication, consensus and coordination. Such differences in the decision-making process in Japanese companies make it difficult for US executives to understand the thought process in Japanese companies.

Unfortunately, good English literature on Japanese management is rather rare. There are a number of texts available but these guidebooks merely skim through the surface. When it comes to experience with real business practice in Japan, we can hardly expect much from the US scholars who have authored most of these books. The authors quote from one another and the inevitable result of this process of cross reference is common denominators masquerading as new discoveries. On the other hand, Japanese business executives have not taken the initiative to write a comparative study of Japanese management in English, although they are in a privileged position to secure ample sources of data. In this

---

[18] For details of "ringi-sei," see Dan Fenno Henderson, *Foreign Enterprise in Japan*, Charles E. Tuttle Company, 1975, p. 115.

regard, Japanese scholars are not of much help either since they are apt to be contented with their own status as inhabitants of the ivory tower.

We are beginning to see a light at the end of the tunnel, however, since quite a number of Japanese have recently graduated from US business and law schools. Their entry into business and academia gives rise to the hope that when they start writing in English, they will influence overseas studies of Japanese management.

Finally, and fundamentally, the reason to why Japanese management seems rather mysterious to outsiders lies in the secretive attitudes of Japanese companies. It is a small wonder that both the labor and management, who regard themselves as a corporate family, do not want to share with outsiders their knowledge of what they regard as internal family affairs.

Similarities in Management Techniques between Japanese and US Companies

So far, we have seen the principles of Japanese management. We have also seen how differences in language, social and cultural values, and national characteristics have sometimes led to differences in the management styles of the US and Japan. However, there is another important question which deserves our attention. Is the existing Japanese-style management really peculiar to Japan?

We have discussed the sense of unity and community based on the family approach as one of the distinctive characteristics of Japanese management. It is a commitment on the part of the management to treat everyone in the organization as a valued employee and to take into consideration everyone from the top to the bottom.

It is interesting that a book has recently been published in the US that gives case studies of leading companies along with descriptions of the managerial policies of these so-called "excellent companies." Entitled *In Search of Excellence*, the book lists eight points that are common to the management of these companies.[19] One of the points is

---

[19] Thomas J. Peters and Robert H. Waterman, Jr., *In Search of Excellence*, Harper & Row, New York, 1982, p. 48.

that management is keenly aware of the need for a sense of solidarity between the management and the labor.[20] The Japanese fondness for employee meetings and mass singing and chanting of company songs and mottos is apparently not under the exclusive Japanese patent. According to the book, Hewlett-Packard, the computer-maker holds beer parties for all employees, and the participants in IBM's sales training program sing the company song every morning.[21]

As we have seen, one characteristic of Japanese companies is their willingness to invest heavily in in-house training. But it would seem that among these American corporations, there are some that in one sense or another, are even more committed to investing in employee education than their Japanese counterparts. The book cites numerous examples of how enthusiastic such companies are about their staff education, for example, IBM and Caterpillar, as well as Disney and McDonald's with their "universities."[22]

The lifetime employment system and the no-layoff policy of Japanese companies have been cited numerous times. One may have the impression that these are practices found solely in Japanese companies, but is this in fact the case?

According to one recent survey of Japanese companies operating in the US, not all necessarily subscribe to a universal no-layoff policy.[23] On the other hand, in the US it is said that IBM did not lay off a single worker even during the Great Depression of the 1930s. Dow Chemical refused to lay off any of its workers even at the height of the recessions

---

[20] For instance, in one passage the authors quote the president of United Airlines. "Nothing is worse for morale than a lack of information down in the ranks." I call it NETMA — Nobody Ever Tells Me Anything — and I have tried hard to minimize that problem. Ibid., p. 449.

[21] *Id.* at p. 16.

[22] *Id.* at p. 445.

[23] A full 28 percent of the companies surveyed said that when necessary, they would lay off workers, just as any American company might. Only 5 percent said they had promised their workers no layoffs in the interest of stable employment. Another 64 percent replied that although as a rule they try to avoid layoffs, they could not promise that it would never happen. For details, see Toshio Shishido, *USA ni Okeru Nihon Kigyo* (Japanese Companies in the USA), ed. Nikko Research Center, Toyo Keizai Shinposha, 1980, p. 118.

following the two oil shocks. Procter & Gamble has reputedly never laid off an employee since its founding.

It seems that the many characteristics of Japanese-style management discussed so far are relative rather than absolute. Rather than labelling them as unique features of Japanese companies, it would be better for us to widen our horizons and say that they are characteristics shared by excellent companies.

Changing Environment for Japanese Management

To achieve efficient mass production, which has been a priority of Japanese post-war economic development, it was considered necessary to employ people who shared the same standards and modes of thinking and thus priority was placed on good teamwork. The system required high worker morale, which was maintained by the lifetime employment system, the seniority wage system and the individual company trade unions. However, under such a system, it is difficult for creative technological innovation to take place.

Generally speaking, Japanese economic progress so far was not achieved by creative innovation. The success of Japanese companies was brought about rather by the accumulation of improved technology, such as QC and total quality control (TQC), which were invented by someone else.[24]

Until now, Japanese companies introduced new technology from abroad as soon as it was developed. Then they immediately improved and modified it for mass production application, and in less than no time, outperformed the foreign company which originally invented the technology.

However, advanced technology can no longer be easily improved by companies unless they possess the capability for basic research. It is also likely that foreign companies will become more cautious in light of

---

[24] QC (quality control) technique is a management control method designed to maintain and improve product quality. TQC (total quality control) technique is a measure which is introduced into the entire production process in order to improve product quality. Both techniques were originally invented in the US.

Japanese practices and may impose a technological blockade. Therefore, Japanese companies should not merely concentrate on improving the existing technology invented by others, but also work on expanding their capability for developing basic technology themselves. Japanese companies have now realized that such technological capability is becoming an important requirement for continued success.

The Japanese people do not necessarily lack creativity. However, Japanese companies have recognized that there are some factors present which hamper the creative development of technological innovations. Japanese society tends towards homogeneity. There is a trend to ostracize those who are somewhat different from the majority. Unconsciously, people tend to assimilate and harmonize themselves with their peers, lest they be regarded as outsiders.

Until recently, it was not necessary for Japanese management, which encouraged inclination toward homogeneity, to seek for and accommodate creative people who can play a leading role in promoting technological innovations. Now Japanese companies have recognized the necessity of cultivating strong individuals who differ from the majority and allowing them to fully display their unique abilities.

Due to the traditional corporate climate, it is not easy for Japanese companies to suddenly encourage the creativity of employees. However, there are a few environmental reasons for why Japanese companies have become more inclined to accept heterogeneity in human resources. At present, many companies are promoting internationalization and are in the process of developing into multinational companies. This means that they do not simply export produced goods, but must also carry out research and development as well as production activities in other countries. In some cases, they must employ foreign personnel. Japanese companies have reached the stage where they must try to utilize all possible management resources available on a global basis.

In the past, Japanese companies have tried to secure management resources, including employees, from domestic sources if possible. However, since Japanese companies are now trying to develop creative talent, it has become necessary to collect human resources from more diverse sources.

In addition, young employees are now demanding interesting jobs which are more suited to their individuality. This attitude on the part of youth may lead to a new style of management which emphasizes the importance of creativity. It is important that companies do not ostracize such young employees, but rather employ the enthusiasm of youth to further the development of corporate strategies.

There is no doubt that after World War II, the Japanese management system supported the nation's economy during the periods of restoration, high economic growth and the two oil crises. As a result, the so-called Japanese-style management has been highly praised by other countries and is still enjoying much admiration and applause. However, it now seems that the Japanese management has reached an impasse which is not yet widely recognized.

We would like to further examine the reasons for why traditional Japanese-style management does not work efficiently in the current Japanese economy. The first reason relates to human resources. Although management resources are comprised of three elements, that is human resource, goods and money, human resource was the only thing that Japan could depend on at the end of the war. The educational level of the people was high; they were eager to make improvements; they worked hard; they were good at organizing teamwork and they had a strong sense of loyalty to their companies. These people studied foreign technology with great enthusiasm and worked hard to improve their technology. Eventually, they made the Japanese production system the most efficient in the world.

Now young people who have grown up in the "age of satiation" are entering the labor force. They do not wish to work as fiercely as their elders. They are ill-suited to jobs such as TQC, which are strictly bound to the work manual or job rules. Under these circumstances, Japanese companies cannot expect to maintain their superiority if they continue to adhere to the conventional management system, which depends excessively on the "persistency" of employees.

Another reason for the impasse is the change in the nature of the demand for goods. Until recently, Japanese products sold well because they were high in quality and cheap in price. The national income level was standardized and the general public gained purchasing power. After which, there emerged a series of products which enjoyed explosive demand. Due to the increase in volume, manufacturers could introduce mass production. High-quality and inexpensive products sold well not only in Japan, but also overseas.

Today, however, products do not sell explosively, even at slightly reduced prices and with new product designs. It has been suggested that people have come to own most necessities, and thus have become less attached to goods in general. The situation is not as simple as this. As many products have matured people to become satiated with these goods, it can be said that a simple dependence on conventional technology will lead to nowhere. Without innovative technology, such as integrated circuits and quartz, a new market cannot be exploited.

With fewer workers willing to work fiercely and old products that will not sell well even with the expanded use of improved technology, the strength of Japanese-style management will naturally diminish. No one expects the Japanese industry to collapse easily. However, if the situation remains the same, one must recognize that the Japanese industry will decline in the long run.

Necessary Changes in the Japanese-Style Management

Let us discuss how the Japanese management must change in response to these recent developments in the environment of Japanese companies. Corporate behavioral patterns are expected to undergo several changes. For example, Japanese companies will shift emphasis from operations to planning. In order to enhance mobility, they will use more resources from external sources rather than depending on in-house resources. They will no longer concentrate solely on their existing business but will try to diversify their operations to cover related business fields. They will emphasize innovation rather than efficiency.

It is also expected that the corporate structure will experience several changes. For example, the present stratified hierarchy system will change into a horizontal corporate network. The centralized control system will be replaced by a decentralized system. Large headquarters will be scaled down into smaller units. The decision-making process will change from bottom-up to from top-down. In addition, companies will place more emphasis on research and development than on production.

There will be changes in the systems and practices of Japanese companies. It is likely that the lifetime employment system will be maintained. However, the seniority system will gradually be replaced by the merit system. As mentioned earlier, QC and TQC should experience at least a partial modification. Although present systems such as the company union, company education and training and company welfare programs will be maintained, the value of such systems will be reassessed.

Furthermore, there must be changes in the employment of human resource. Companies will not only pursue homogeneity. Rather, they will try to employ an appropriate number of high quality employees. The present group-oriented structure will be changed to accept individualism. In this context, it is obvious that management must take a strong initiative. Meanwhile, employees will have to understand that society has entered a new phase of development. In spite of such changes, employees will probably continue to give a great deal of loyalty to companies. Japanese companies will change their behavior from accumulation and consciousness-oriented dynamism to entrepreneurship in the future.

We have tried to introduce a new definition of the Japanese management system. Japanese companies have already entered a new stage where they must modify, at least partially, major traditional management practices such as corporate solidarity, homogeneity and commitment. They must introduce individualism and the merit system, both of which characterize the American management approach. They must maintain the advantages of their present system while at the same time discard their weak points. They have realized the necessity of shifting away from their conventional management system and adopting some American-style management practices. Japanese companies are aware that the economy can take new steps toward progress only when a new style of Japanese management is established.

Today, Japanese companies feel the necessity to maintain their positive features while at the same time nurture management techniques oriented towards entrepreneurship and high-technology industries.

Directions for Improvement in the Future

In spite of differing traditions, Japan and the US have followed a path of convergence as far as management techniques are concerned. In coping with the rapid changes in the environment, Japanese management techniques continue to change, with the tendency to become more Americanized.

The directions of anticipated changes point to further convergence between Japan and the US By following this course, the business in both countries is expected to achieve progress in productivity, cost efficiency and profit maximization and maintaining good quality control. Managers in the two countries must be quite open-minded in evaluating management techniques, regardless of which country they come from, and must try to be both flexible and aggressive in experimenting with innovations.[25]

An example of innovation is found in the case of the US auto industry. The Big Three selected only those suppliers who can comply with the "kanban method" and they held special seminars on how to maintain quality control and meet delivery schedules. The Big Three emphasized the importance of modernizing equipment and motivating employees to increase productivity. These efforts are noteworthy in that the Big Three, being the first-class companies in the US, undertook a complete analysis of the Japanese-style management, distilled its essence to improve their international competitiveness, and then delivered this know-how to many of their suppliers.[26]

Bethlehem Steel Corp. has reportedly invested $60 million to construct continuous annealing equipment, and Jones and Laughlin Steel

---

[25] It has been said in recent years that traditional Japanese industries are now changing to become light, thin, short and small. This means that machines and products weight less, and are becoming thinner and smaller in size. Such changes have been brought about due to the fact that the oil price hike gave rise to the need to save energy and resources. Also, the improvement of IC density and the introduction of microcomputers made it possible to miniaturize machines and products. For example, the automobile industry reduced vehicle size, introduced the front engine and the front wheel drive system and began using lighter materials such as aluminum and plastic in order to produce smaller and lighter passenger cars. Calculators and stereo sets have become smaller and thinner in size due to the improvement of IC density and the reduced number of components and parts. The introduction of sheet coil has made it possible to make subminiature motors.

[26] *Business Week*, Nov. 1, 1982, p. 49.

Corp. has reportedly invested $160 million to construct continuous casting equipment in compliance with requests from General Motors Corp., which is the single largest corporate consumer of steel in the US.[27] It is interesting to note that this steel production equipment was all exported from the Japanese companies, Nippon Steel[28] and Nippon Kokan,[29] as a package system including both the equipment and the technical know-how.

There is a cost differential of some $2,000 between the US and Japanese manufacturers for a Chevrolet-type compact car. This difference is not due entirely to the Japanese management techniques, although it is certainly a big factor. In the Tennessee-based Saturn project, GM plans to achieve cost reduction within a short time by introducing a wide range of Japanese management techniques.[30] It seems that the very choice of Tennessee as the site of the project was motivated by the existence of part and component suppliers for the local subsidiary of Nissan Motor Company.[31] The Japanese inventory method depends, of course, on the existence of ancillary part and component manufacturers that are in close proximity to the plant.

The Tennessee subsidiary of Nissan Motor Company is headed by an American but uses Japanese management techniques.[32] The president meets with the employees every morning before the assembly line starts up and bonuses are given twice a year, even to blue-collar workers. The company cafeteria also follows the Japanese model in that both managerial and production staff use the same facilities. Furthermore, this operation uses a seniority system. It also holds company parties,

---

[27] *Toyo Keizai*, July 23, 1983, p. 44.

[28] Nippon Steel is the world's largest steelmaker. Its total sales amounted to 2,860 billion yen and net profit to 41 billion yen in 1985.

[29] Nippon Kokan is the second largest crude steel maker in Japan. Its total sales amounted to 1,500 billion yen and net profit to 20 billion yen in 1985.

[30] The comments were made by General Motor officials at Tennessee's 33rd Annual Governor's Conference on Economic and Community Development, held in Tennessee on Nov. 14, 1985.

[31] Nissan is the second largest auto manufacturer in Japan. Its total sales amounted to 3,618 billion yen and net profit to 74 billion yen in 1985.

[32] The president of Nissan Motor Manufacturing Corporation in Tennessee, Mr. Marvin Runyon, formerly with Ford, has shown a deep understanding of Japanese-style management.

athletic meets, and picnics in an effort to foster family-like relations and solidarity based on fundamental equality, particularly between the management and the line workers.

Provided that the business managers of both countries can be flexible and resourceful, management techniques will further advance and bring about higher productivity. Since direct investment from one country to the other is bound to increase, the area of interface between Japanese and American management techniques will enlarge and the convergence of these managerial methods will be further encouraged.[33] This is perhaps only one facet of the close and friendly relations between the two countries that have developed since the end of World War II. This trend is not surprising given the increasing similarity of the two countries in political, economic and social terms.

Conclusion

We have so far discussed Japanese-style management from various perspectives. The following can be concluded from this analysis:

- So-called Japanese-style management is not necessarily unique to Japan, although its concept is sometimes difficult for foreign managers to understand.
- Traditional Japanese management is undergoing significant changes.
- Japanese management has been introducing American-style management techniques.
- Japanese and American management practices share a similar nature. By influencing one another, the companies of both countries will achieve higher productivity while maintaining a high level of quality control.

---

[33] Direct investment in Japan by US businesses amounted to $6.8 billion in 1981 after recording constant growth during the 1970s (JETRO, supra note 1, p. 27). Further substantial increase is expected in the future due to the high growth rates of Japanese high-tech fields, the abundant opportunities for high profits and the positive government attitude towards foreign investment.

One final point is that as companies from both countries study each other's practices, they are refining and polishing the traditional techniques of their own styles of management. An analysis of these practices, based on a wide range of actual examples, would be valuable and worth pursuing. The efficacy and practicality of any management technique are put to a test only when transplanted from the soil in which they were nurtured to a new and different environment. There is a great deal to be learned from such a study by both Japanese and American managers. In this sense, the management techniques newly adopted by Japanese companies and the Japanese management techniques adopted by US companies are an area of research that fully deserves the attention of scholars and experts in both Japan and the US, since these practices constitute valuable test cases for the theory and practice of modern management.

Chapter 15

Successful Japanese Management Cases as a Contrarian

The analyses of two Japanese companies reveals an interesting and noteworthy common principle as the basis of their success, which was their position as "contrarian." "Contrarian" means someone who moves in opposition to others.

Introduction

When the world economy is facing serious difficulties, some corporations have realized successful results in the marketing, production, financing, and allocation of their resources in today's borderless environment. The author recently conducted case constructions of 11 Japanese companies from field studies consisting of numerous visits to and interviews with managers of those corporations.[1] Analyses of 11 cases revealed an interesting and noteworthy common principle as the basis of their success, which was their position as "contrarians". A "contrarian" means someone who moves in opposition to others.

For an example of contrarian behavior, let us look at the following illustration from our daily lives. (*See* Fig. 1.)

You are driving on the expressway and you come to a fork in the row. On Side A, the traffic light is crowded, and on Side B, the traffic light is not crowded. Which way would you choose? Most people would choose Side B, but a contrarian would choose Side A, counting on the fact that

---

[1] They are as follows: Tokyo Disneyland, Resona Bank, Fuji TV, Livedoor, Nireco, Ina Food Industry, OSG, Bank of Japan, J-Com, World Co., and Softbank.

most other people would select Side B so that Side B would become more crowded and Side A would become less crowded. This article examines the two success stories of Tokyo Disneyland, owned by Oriental Land Corp., Japan (hereafter OL), an international company, and Ina Food Industry Co. Japan, a small domestic company who acted as the "contrarian" against traditional international management techniques in today's borderless environment.[2]

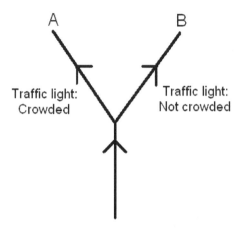

Fig. 1. A fork in the road.

While globalization of the Japanese economy has been advancing at an astounding pace, there remain significant cultural differences between the management philosophy and techniques used within Japanese companies and those used in American firms. Such differences have a momentous impact on the decision making processes within international companies, and this case study illustrates many of the key differences that exist in the realm of corporate management.

---

[2] During his time as an executive officer at The Industrial Bank of Japan (IBJ, now Mizuho Corporate Bank), the author acted as an investment banker in charge of the Oriental Land Corp. (Tokyo Disneyland) in Japan. He therefore had first-hand involvement and extensive dealings with this project. The author has had had considerable access to relevant information as well as a broad-based familiarity with the issues discussed. Due to this, the company gave him the permission to write about the case.

The Case of Tokyo Disneyland[3]

Tokyo Disneyland is one of the most prominent and successful examples of an American-Japanese partnership in Japan. This case allows readers to examine evidence indicating that the very foundation of Anglo-American and Japanese corporate management is different. Central to this difference are issues that include contrasting cultures, customs and values. As this case describes a project of international proportions, readers are given a unique opportunity to gain insight into the foreign party's and host's viewpoints. This article will be able to contribute a complete analysis for any multinational company which may be considering investing in Japan or running a joint venture with a Japanese company, and which may intend to raise money from Japanese banks.

Tokyo Disneyland is the result of a licensing agreement between Walt Disney (WD) of the United States and Oriental Land Corporation (OL) of Japan (*see* Table 1).

Table 1. Basic Oriental Land data (as of March 31, 2009).

Name	Oriental Land Group
Date of Establishment	July 11, 1960
Paid-in Capital	¥63,201 million
Sales	¥389,242 million
Net Income	¥18,089 million
President	Kyoichiro Jyonishi
Employees	2,196
Address	1-1, Maihama, Urayasushi, Chiba-ken, Japan
Main Banks	Mizuho Corporate Bank (Industrial Bank of Japan)
	Chuo Mitsui Trust (Mitsui Trust Bank)
Major Shareholders	Keisei Electric Railway Corp. 19.08%
	Mitsui Real Estate Corp. 15.95%
Tie-up Company	Disney Enterprises Inc. (US)

Source: Yukashoken Houkokusho (Annual Reports), Oriental Land Corp. 2008. See also http://www.olc.co.jp/en/company/profile/index.html (accessed October 30, 2009).

---

[3] This case is abstracted from the author's previously published article. For the details, see "Tokyo Disneyland – Joint Venture vs. Licensing," A Case Study, Asian Case Research Centre (ACRC), The University of Hong Kong, August, 2005.

Current Condition

Tokyo Disneyland is now a smash hit. It is a company that posted record profits on its 25th-Anniversary amid the global recession. Theme park operator OL reported a group pretax profit of slightly more than 37 billion yen for the year ending on March 31, 2009, up 34 percent that year and marking an all-time high. Parades and other events celebrating the 25th anniversary of Tokyo Disneyland helped attract a record turnout of 27.22 million visitors (*see* Fig. 2.) The figures show that OL theme

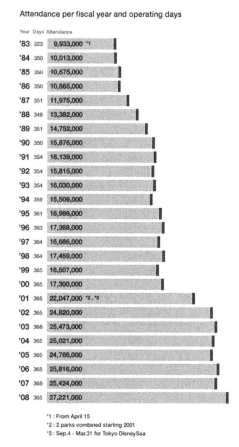

Attendance per fiscal year and operating days

Year	Days	Attendance
'83	323	9,933,000 *1
'84	350	10,013,000
'85	350	10,675,000
'86	350	10,665,000
'87	351	11,975,000
'88	349	13,382,000
'89	351	14,752,000
'90	350	15,876,000
'91	354	16,139,000
'92	354	15,815,000
'93	354	16,030,000
'94	359	15,509,000
'95	361	16,986,000
'96	363	17,368,000
'97	364	16,686,000
'98	364	17,459,000
'99	365	16,507,000
'00	365	17,300,000
'01	365	22,047,000 *2, *3
'02	365	24,820,000
'03	366	25,473,000
'04	365	25,021,000
'05	365	24,766,000
'06	365	25,816,000
'07	366	25,424,000
'08	365	27,221,000

*1 : From April 15
*2 : 2 parks combined starting 2001
*3 : Sep.4 - Mar.31 for Tokyo DisneySea

Source: Yukashoken Houkokusho (Annual Reports), Oriental Land Corp. 2008. See also http://www.olc.co.jp/en/company/profile/index.html (accessed October 30, 2009).

Fig. 2. Attendance records from 1983–2008.

parks filled with attractive products and services got consumers to loosen their purse strings amid the recession. Group sales appeared to have enjoyed year-on-year growth. The newly opened Tokyo Disneyland Hotel enjoyed strong demand, and the combined occupancy rate of this and two other directly run hotels came up to around 90 percent.

History

In April 1979, nineteen years after OL's establishment, the company signed a license agreement with WD, involving the design, construction, and operation of Tokyo Disneyland. (*See* Table 2.) In December 1980, the construction of Tokyo Disneyland began in the Maihama district, in the village of Urayasu (currently Maihama, in the city of Urayasu). Less than three years after construction had begun, Tokyo Disneyland opened its doors for business in April 1983. In December 1996, the company's stock was listed on the First Section of the Tokyo Stock Exchange. When Tokyo Disneyland opened, it started with an initial investment of approximately US$1.53 billion, and was injected with a similar amount over the next 18 years.

WD proved to be a tough negotiator when it negotiated the terms for Tokyo Disneyland. Although WD liked the location of Urayasu, its offer in 1979 was to provide only the know-how without shouldering any risk. It was not willing to pay anything for the construction of the park, but it wanted 10 percent royalty on the admission fee and sales of foods and beverages. OL strongly objected to this proposal, with its board of directors saying, "We have never seen such a lopsided contract condition and high royalty." From the very beginning in 1978, OL tried their best to make WD bear some risks, but their efforts were in vain.

Finally, an agreement was signed that stipulated a license fee of 10 percent on admission fees and 5 percent on food, beverages, and novelty goods. A big question at that time was whether OL would be able to make the project profitable despite hefty licensing fees that were an average 7 percent of sales. At the time of the negotiations, WD's financial position was weak. Disneyland and Walt Disney World were attracting approximately 10 million entrants each year, and WD could not raise the entrance fee to increase income. Also, the movie and TV

Table 2. History of Tokyo Disneyland.

1960 Jul.	Oriental Land Co., Ltd., is established with the aim of reclaiming land off the coast of Urayasu, developing commercial and residential land and constructing a major leisure facility, thereby contributing to the cultural life of the nation and the welfare of its citizens. (Capital: 250 million yen)
1962 Jul.	Oriental Land and Chiba Prefecture conclude the Urayasu District Land Reclamation Agreement, permitting Oriental Land to reclaim land off the coast of Urayasu and purchase the land for development.
1964 Sept.	Reclamation work begins off the coast of Urayasu.
1970 Mar.	Chiba Prefecture begins dividing reclaimed land into lots for sale to Oriental Land for construction of leisure facilities and houses.
1972 Dec.	Oriental Land begins sales of the residential section of the reclaimed land purchased from Chiba Prefecture.
1975 Nov.	Reclamation work is completed.
1979 Apr.	Oriental Land and Walt Disney Productions (currently Disney Enterprises, Inc.) conclude an agreement concerning the licensing, design, construction and operation of Tokyo Disneyland park.
1980 Dec.	Construction of Tokyo Disneyland park begins in the Maihama district of the town of Urayasu (now the city of Urayasu).
1983 Apr.	Tokyo Disneyland opens.
1996 Apr.	Oriental Land and Disney Enterprises conclude an agreement concerning the licensing, design, construction and operation of a new Disney theme park, Tokyo DisneySea, and the Tokyo DisneySea Hotel (now Tokyo DisneySea Hotel MiraCosta).
1996 Jun.	Wholly owned subsidiary Maihama Resort Hotels Co., Ltd., is established for management and operation of hotels.
1996 Dec.	Oriental Land lists its shares on the First Section of the Tokyo Stock Exchange.
1997 Apr.	Oriental Land and Walt Disney Productions (currently Disney Enterprises, Inc.) conclude an agreement concerning the licensing, design, construction and operation of Tokyo Disneyland park.
1998 Aug.	Construction of Maihama Station Area Development Project (IKSPIARI and Disney Ambassador Hotel) begins in Maihama.
1998 Sept.	Oriental Land and Disney Enterprises, Inc., conclude an agreement concerning the licensing, construction and operation of Disney Ambassador Hotel.
1998 Oct.	Oriental Land and Disney Enterprises, Inc., conclude an agreement concerning the licensing, design, construction and operation of Disney Resort Line. Maihama Resort Line begins construction of Disney Resort Line in Maihama. Construction of Tokyo DisneySea and Tokyo DisneySea Hotel MiraCosta begins in Maihama.
1999 Feb.	Wholly owned subsidiary Maihama Business Services Co., Ltd. is established.
1999 Mar.	Wholly owned subsidiary IKSPIARI Co., Ltd. is established for management and operation of a commercial complex.
1999 Oct.	Consolidated subsidiary RC Japan Co., Ltd. is established for management and operation of themed restaurants.
2000 Jul.	Ikspiari and Disney Ambassador Hotel open.
2000 Oct.	Wholly owned subsidiary Resort Cleaning Services Co., Ltd. is established for cleaning services.
2001 Jun.	Wholly owned subsidiary Maihama Building Maintenance Co.,Ltd. is established for building maintenance service and OLC Kitchen Techno Co., Ltd. is established for sales and maintenance of kitchen units.
2001 Jul.	Disney Resort Line opens.
2001 Sept.	Tokyo DisneySea opens. Tokyo DisneySea Hotel MiraCosta opens.
2002 Apr.	OLC acquired all issued shares of wholly owned WDIJ subsidiary Retail Networks Co., Ltd., and started operation of The Disney Store shops in Japan.
2002 Dec.	Wholly owned subsidiary E PRODUCTION CO., LTD. is established for management of entertainers.
2003 May	Wholly owned subsidiary OLC/Rights Entertainment Inc. is established for management of copyrights.
2005 Jul.	Wholly owned subsidiary M TECH Co., Ltd. is established for maintenance of theme park attractions, including ride vehicles and other attraction components.

Source: Yukashoken Houkokusho (Annual Reports), Oriental Land Corp. 2008. See also http://www.olc.co.jp/en/company/profile/index.html (accessed October 30, 2009).

production division was doing poorly. Under these conditions, collecting a fixed amount of money from their overseas partner, regardless of the theme park's success, was an attractive proposition for WD. This was a tough condition for the Japanese partner, but if WD could find a partner who would want to do the project under these terms, they would draft a contract, assuming the partner could build a Disneyland to their stringent quality standards. In 1984, a management change at WD created a powerful team, with Michael Eisner as the company's chairman and Frank Wells as its president. With the help of the license income from Tokyo Disneyland, Eisner's management team built hotels in Disney World. In turn, the income from the hotels helped to revive WD, whose performance had been at an all-time low under the leadership of E. Cardon Walker as chairman (1980–1983) and Ron W. Miller as president (1980–1984).

Positions of Various Stakeholders of OL

The mission of top management has been recognized in the US business world as needing to maximize profit and generate attractive shareholder returns. Traditionally, Japanese companies have not been primarily oriented towards increasing shareholder return, instead focusing on making profits for corporate enhancement. OL was not the exception, although it is widely recognized that Japanese companies facing global competition have no choice but to adapt to global standards and practices. Through the 1980s, top Japanese management had maintained the systems and structures that helped companies succeed in the past (e.g., a set of interlocking relationships with other companies and loosely interpreted corporate governance principles).

OL's directors had to make a tough decision, because OL had a number of stakeholders it had to please, including the parent company, the main bank, landlords, and shareholders, all of whom had their own representatives on OL's board of directors. The relationship among these parties determined and controlled the firm's strategic direction. OL's management had to incorporate all of these various interests in their decision making process to come up with an optimal decision.

The Parent Company

The Mitsui Real Estate Group (MREG), OL's parent company, owned 20.48 percent of OL's shares. Since the initial negotiations in 1979, MREG had been very critical of all the deals with WD. The first issue was the period of the contract. During a meeting between the American and Japanese companies in November 1978, Azuma Tsuboi, the MREC's president, objected to the terms of the contract. He said that while it is such a volatile period that there is no way of knowing what is going to happen 10 years ahead, how can one be expected to have a contract for as long as 50 years?

The second problem involved the license fees. WD originally demanded a 10 percent license fee, to which MREG strongly objected. The third issue was risk-sharing. From the start of the project in 1978, MREG had guaranteed the project borrowing up to 48 percent of its investment but no more, in which case the remaining balance would have to be borne by WD. Azuma Tsuboi said that this was such a humiliating contract and as a company of the proud Mitsui Group, they could not accept it.

The Main Bank

Tokyo Disneyland was financed by a group of 22 banks. The group was headed by the Industrial Bank of Japan (IBJ), and Mitsui Trust Bank was the second largest partner. WD's position in the Tokyo Disneyland contract—take no risk, just collect the fee—caused a lot of commotion among the Japanese banks. Kisaburo Ikeura, IBJ's president, called this policy "a very strange one" and stated that WD's position was that they would not offer any land or money, nor take any risk; IBJ must construct as they tell them to do, and they would collect 10% license fee for entrance fees and 5% license fee for beverages and novelty goods; such a policy was never heard of in Japan.

IBJ was a successful bank and often was referred to as the "Morgan Guaranty Trust Bank" of Japan. It dealt with many large Japanese corporations in many complex and delicate transactions. But because it used to be a government-owned bank, its borrowers were chosen in accordance with current government policies, or were traditional companies in the heavy industries sector, such as steel, ships and machinery, which supported the recovery of the Japanese economy after the Second World War. IBJ's top management, however, believed that the future of Japanese industries would shift toward the service industries, based on software and technology, and become much more international, with joint ventures and export industries becoming popular. So IBJ shifted its lending targets accordingly and was quite willing to lend to OL, as it considered OL to be a potential future leader. In August 1979, the group of banks decided to lend ¥65 billion (US $0.55 billion) to OL. The main banks in Japan were closely involved in companies' internal affairs, both in cross-ownership and as a prime lender. OL and the IBJ had a close relationship. Mitsuaki Mori, who was sent from IBJ, succeeded Masatomo Takahashi as the second president of OL. Mituaki Mori (1988–1992) passed away suddenly in 1992, and Masatomo Takahashi (1992–1995) returned as the third president.

Landlord

OL was granted a vast plot of reclaimed land by the government, which could be taken back if not used for the agreed purpose within a certain timeframe. In March 1962, Chiharu Kawasaki, president of Keisei Electric Railway Co., one of OL's largest shareholders, asked Masatomo Takahashi to approach the prefecture to negotiate a grant of one million *tsubo* of reclaimed land to OL. When Masatomo Takahashi went to the Chiba prefecture to negotiate the land grant, they said that they heard that even the Disneyland in Los Angeles was only 90,000 *tsubo* (73 acres) and they had never heard of an amusement park as large as 1 million *tsubo*, which is ten times that.

Eventually OL got 750,000 *tsubo*. Kawasaki later told Takahashi the reason he wanted a large piece of land was to have the ability to expand at a later date, and not fall into the same trap as Disneyland in Los Angeles. In his autobiography, Takahashi wrote that he later found that Kawasaki had shown foresight when suggesting the acquisition of a large piece of real estate to accommodate any future expansion. Because the land was public property, OL wanted to use it for something the public could enjoy. Moreover, OL's top management also was mindful of the fact that the plot of land was reclaimed from the sea, causing many fishermen to lose their jobs and way of life; they felt a social responsibility to help these people.

Contrarian Theory Worked for OL

Without WD's insightful advice and support, OL would not have achieved the success it has enjoyed thus far. This gargantuan investment in the midst of a poor economic climate led many to question the undertaking, creating doubt in the minds of not only the management but also the parent company, shareholders, and lenders. Their consensus was that the licensing arrangement wouldn't work. OL management made the "contrarian" decision, keeping in mind the vast differences in culture and principles that existed between Japan and the United States. WD, a prestigious licensor with great know-how, and OL, a licensee with a huge plot of land having great potential, were united. The success of investments would have been impossible if either of the factors did not exist. The relationship between the two companies changed from one of confrontation to one of the indispensable partners.

September 4, 2001 was the day of the grand opening of Tokyo DisneySea, the second project by OL and WD. The management teams of both WD and OL expressed their profound joy for the success of the project. Michael Eisner, president of WD said that he felt especially touched when he knew that Tokyo Disneyland and Tokyo DisneySea, which resulted from the cooperation between OL and WD, proved the success of collaboration between a US company and a Japanese company and that it was possible to sustain such success. Toshio Kagami, president of OL said that he had a hope of jointly developing an entirely different business, other than theme parks, in Japan and other areas of Asia, together with WD.

How could OL be successful as a contrarian in going against international rules and standards? The following differences in the Japanese and Anglo-American theories of corporate governance were relevant to OL's decision making process as a contrarian.

Maximizing Shareholder Wealth or Maximizing Corporate Wealth

The idea of maximizing shareholder wealth was realistic both in theory and in practice in the Anglo-American markets. Firms like WD had to strive to maximize the returns to shareholders, as measured by the sum of cash flow, capital gains and dividends, for a given level of risk. In contrast, Japanese markets worked on the theory that a firm's objective was to maximize corporate wealth. A firm like OL had to treat shareholders on par with other stakeholders, such as management, labor, suppliers, creditors, the local community and the government. The goal was to earn as much as possible, but to retain enough of the corporate wealth for the benefit of all stakeholders. The definition of corporate wealth was broader than financial wealth. It included the firm's technical, market and human resources.

Agency Theory

The study of agency theory examines the principal-agent relationship within a company. Agents (managers) are likely to have their own goals that do not directly accord with those of the principals. In Anglo-American firms like WD, the principals' (shareholders') goal is to maximize shareholder wealth. In order to reach this goal they can use positive or negative incentives to get agents on the same line as the principals. For example, liberal use of stock options in Anglo-American firms can get management to think like shareholders. In Japanese firms like OL, the principals (stakeholders) themselves can have different goals. The principal-agent relationship is therefore far more complex in Japan.

Long vs. Short Term Value Maximization

Instead of seeking long term value maximization, Anglo-American firms like WD tended to seek short term value maximization to meet the market's or shareholders' expected quarterly earnings. In contrast, Japanese firms like OL tended to be patient and focus on long term stakeholder wealth maximization.

Employees were important stakeholders in any firm in Japan. Although the permanent employment system in Japan was gradually changing, the traditional system was still used by many Japanese firms such as OL with little expectation of change. It was therefore natural for management to be more concerned with long term success instead of considering the interest of stockholders. The American concept, which analyzed investment success and profitability of stockholders, did not fit within this viewpoint.

The Case of Ina Food Industry[4]

This is another case of a Japanese company which acted as the "contrarian" against traditional Japanese management techniques and philosophy and is showing high profits even under the recent global financial crisis.

Ina Food Industry Co. Ltd was situated in the city of Ina, Nagano Prefecture, and surrounded by the soaring mountains of the Japanese Alps. It was established in 1958 to produce agar. (*See* Table 3.) This natural gelatin, derived from seaweed, was originally developed as an important ingredient used in traditional Japanese confectionery. Its manufacture was the product of a cottage industry by farmers, who used the natural cold during the coldest three months of the year for its production. As a consequence of (1) production being confined to only the three winter months of the year when the farmers were free, (2) the quantity and quality not being stable or reliable, (3) it appearing in both bars and a fibrous state, and (4) it being the victim of a seasonally fluctuating market, use of the product was avoided by large industry.

Ina Food therefore concentrated on producing powdered agar, developed sources from which the raw material could be imported and stored throughout the year, and through the consolidation of production into a highly efficient process, achieved a stable market that eliminated fluctuating prices to develop a stronger demand. Mr. Hiroshi Tsukakoshi, Ina Food's 68 year-old chairman led the company through an incredible 48 years of continuous revenue and profit growth up to 2008.

---

[4] This case is abstracted from the author's previously published article. For the details, see "Ina Food Industry: A New Management Philosophy For Japanese Businesses", A Case Study, Asian Case Research Centre (ACRC), The University of Hong Kong, November, 2006.

Table 3. Company profile (as of December 31, 2008).

Company name	Ina Food Industry Co., Ltd
Chairman and CEO	Hiroshi Tsukakoshi
President and COO	Osamu Inoue
Date established	June 18th 1958
Capital	¥96.8 million
Annual sales	¥15,937 million (2008)
Operating income	¥1,597 million (2008)
Head office address	5074 Nishiharuchika, Ina-City, Nagano, Japan
Plants	Sawando Plant, Kitaoka Plant, Fujisawa Plant, Inosawa Plant
Branches	Tokyo, Nagoya, Osaka
Business offices	Sapporo, Sendai, Nagano, Fukuoka, Okayama
Number of employees	385 (in 2008)

Source: Annual Reports, Ina Food Industry, 2008.

The company was a leading manufacturer of powdered agar.[5] In 2005, news about the medicinal benefits of their product led to a boom in demand. As a result, Ina Food experienced phenomenal growth in sales. Revenues for the six-month period ending in December 2005 amounted to 20 billion yen[6] with ordinary income for the same period at 3.8 billion yen. This was an increase in both sales and profits of approximately 40–50 percent from the previous year. The boom disappeared as quickly as it had come, and some of the distributors even asked the company to take back excess inventories. Therefore, the sales and profits of the company after 2005 come down slightly due to the adjustments.

Instead of celebrating, however, Tsukakoshi felt that this rapid growth was an unfortunate event. He would rather have had a 7 percent increase in both sales and profit. This was because Tsukakoshi believed that if a business grew too fast, a backlash would be inevitable. A sudden increase in business presented a problem for a small firm such as Ina Food, which had approximately 400 employees, since it had limited

---

[5] Agar was originally a product of a cottage industry by farmers, who utilized the 3 coldest months of the year to produce the product. As a result, both quality and quantity had historically been unstable.

[6] US$1 = ¥117.62 on 28 December 2005.

in-house talent to handle sudden change. This in turn could result in the hollowing out of efficient operations maintained by in-house talent due to vast outsourcing. It had therefore been his strong belief that sudden growth should always be avoided.

Growth Is Not the Target

During his time at Ina Food over nearly half a century, Tsukakoshi had developed his own unique philosophy on business and answer to the question "What is a company?". His cautious attitude towards quick growth was unique at a time when a company's return on sales and total market value were considered a management's key performance indices. Since the day he took over the management reins at Ina Food in 1958, he had experienced many tough situations in which all the employees had worked together to support the company and push it through the rough patch. Consequently, he began to think that the company did not exist for the management or even for itself; rather, it existed for the happiness of the employees. If all the employees were happy and had good morale, the communities they lived in would improve, thus making a contribution to society.

What Tsukakoshi strived for was the perpetual existence of the company; it was not quick growth that he wanted, but stable growth. He believed that history showed how rapid growth was always followed by quick decline. Decline, and the resultant restructuring, forced employees and suppliers out onto the streets, seriously damaging the community. His belief was that if management were not preoccupied purely with revenue, and focused instead on establishing steady growth, the company would continue to exist for a long time. This would, in turn, make happier everybody who was directly or indirectly associated with the company. He believed that his role as top management was to make employees happy at work. (*See* Fig. 3.)

Although Ina Food had fewer losses each year, it was not making profits. In those days, the demand for agar came primarily from industry, i.e., for the production of traditional Japanese sweet cakes such as *yokan* (a sweet cake made of agar and beans), or jelly, made by confectionary companies. The profit margin in these areas was very thin. In order to become profitable, Ina Food tried producing imitation powdered juice, a highly popular item in those days. Although the technique they used to make artificially flavored juices was incredibly labor-intensive in nature, they were able to generate more profit from it than from selling agar.

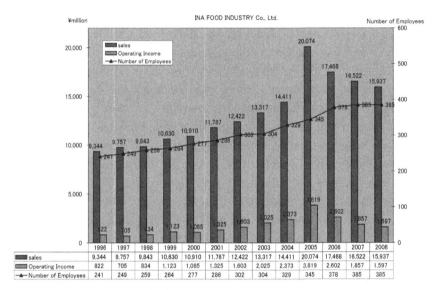

¥million   INA FOOD INDUSTRY Co., Ltd.   Number of Employees

	1996	1997	1998	1999	2000	2001	2002	2003	2004	2005	2006	2007	2008
sales	9,344	9,757	9,843	10,630	10,910	11,787	12,422	13,317	14,411	20,074	17,468	16,522	15,937
Operating Income	822	705	834	1,123	1,085	1,325	1,603	2,025	2,373	3,819	2,602	1,857	1,597
Number of Employees	241	249	259	264	277	286	302	304	329	345	378	385	385

Source: Annual Reports, Ina Food Industry, 2008.

Fig. 3. Financial records from 1996–2008.

After ten years of struggle, Ina Food finally began reporting profits. Just then, many factors came together to change the face of the agar industry. First, the price of agar swung violently up and down depending on the weather. For example, a warm winter caused agar to foul and no serious attempt was made to improve the situation, as agar was only a secondary source of income for farmers. This meant that agar would sometimes be in short supply, and its prices in the market would soar. Another problem that Ina Food faced was that the women who collected seaweeds from which agar was extracted were getting old, and it was becoming difficult to recruit young women divers. This caused the material price to go up. Agar producers and middlemen thus began using these unfortunate situations to their benefit by simply increasing the price while supplying less agar, which upset confectioners.

The Oil Crisis of 1973 brought out the problems of the agar industry in the extreme and agar prices tripled within a mere 12 months. Ina Food tried to keep its price low in the beginning, but with a barrage of orders from all over the country, they eventually raised their prices, following the market. As a consequence, they made a fortune. The high prices infuriated confectioners, however, and they cried that they would stop making *yokan* and switch to producing other cakes that did not contain agar. Hence agar producers lost credit overall. Tsukakoshi found the entire situation very stressful as he worried about the impact it would have on the industry and Ina Food in particular.

Tsukakoshi believed that their business would have no future if they continued to aggravate their clients by allowing the price to swing up and down violently. Consequently, he set out to find ways to stabilize the price, quality, and supply of agar. In order to store more agar, Tsukakoshi built four additional bays of storage buildings using the profit earned from the price hike. At the same time, the production facilities and the factory were enlarged to increase production capacity. Furthermore, he visited various countries to secure suppliers for raw materials needed in the production of agar in order to stabilize the flow inputs. He visited approximately 20 countries, including Chile, the Portuguese Azores Islands in the Atlantic Ocean, Morocco, China, South Korea, and Vietnam in search of partner companies.

His objective was not to find cheap supply sources based on cheap labor but to nurture local companies. He did not, however, want to invest in local companies or even establish resident representatives; his plan was to provide local firms with technology only. Local companies often were in need of technology, but did not want to be controlled by outsiders He aimed for mutual benefits: the local companies could improve their raw material qualities while Ina Food could secure an exclusive source of supplies. As a result of his travels, the company signed partnership agreements with suppliers from four countries, including Chile, Morocco, and South Korea. He believed any localization attempt that was simply seeking cheap labor costs in developing countries could not achieve the trust of the suppliers, and such an attempt would simply make the investor a deracinated wanderer, which would never grow in that country.

As a result of its new and stable supplies and its increased storage capacity, the company was able to release a large amount of agar to stabilize the price when market demand started to soar. On August 16th 1977, the company published an opinion advertisement in an industry paper (Japan Food Newspaper) declaring, "Agar is no longer a market-driven flamboyant merchandise."

Product Image

Immediately after he joined Ina Food, Tsukakoshi created an agar product branded "Pickel" (a German word for a rock climbing tool; an ice axe). He named it after his father who was nicknamed "Pickel" because of his sharply protruding chin. The product didn't sell at all. Tsukakoshi realized that perhaps it was necessary to increase consumer awareness of the very word "agar" (*kanten*) to make the product more popular. This led to the brand name "Kanten Papa," which he developed with the help of his employees in 1980. Kanten Papa was aimed at families and the domestic use of agar, which until then had primarily been used in industrial food manufacturing. The brand name was inspired by a popular TV program on NHK called Sweet Papa, in which celebrity fathers and their children appeared as couples. The name Kanten Papa thus aimed to invoke the popularity of the program with families when they bought agar. The company also created a product named "Kanten Cook" named after Captain Cook. The products were a big hit with consumers.

Kanten Papa was sold through stores in Nagano prefecture and nearby Yamanashi prefecture. The product made it easy for everyone to produce fruit jelly, and owing to its success, the following year Ina Food was approached by a nationwide supermarket store wanting to offer Kanten Papa through its network. Tsukakoshi, however, turned them down because he felt his small local company would not be able to follow up easily if something unexpected were to happen. Tsukakoshi felt that a product that shot to popularity would be quickly forgotten and that supplying Kanten Papa to a major, national, supermarket chain would deviate from his "Annual Growth Ring" management policy that sought a slow steady growth.[7]

However, the company soon started getting letters and phone calls from consumers living all over Japan asking for Kanten Papa. To serve these customers, Tsukakoshi set up a mail order department, which by 2005 had 250,000 regular customers. This allowed for an ideal relationship with their clients. As soon as Ina Food received a complaint or a thank you letter, they sent back a hand-written letter to the client. Although they sold the products via the Internet, relationships with their customers were such that when an employee handling client communications got married, he or she received numerous gifts from the customer congratulating him or her on the marriage. Had the company sold its product in large quantities to distributors, such a relationship with the customers would not have been possible. By 2008, the company also had sales offices throughout the nation and was selling some of its merchandise through supermarkets. Moreover, Ina Food had opened nine direct outlet stores and hoped to gradually increase them in a modest manner.

Contribution to the Community

Ina Food's headquarters were surrounded by nature. Originally built to provide a good working environment, it had since become an asset to the local community. The plot on which the headquarters stood measured approximately 100,000 square meters. Development of the plot started in 1987 with only the factory. Then when it came to building a parking lot for the employees, Tsukakoshi thought it would be nice if employees could park their cars in the middle of the woods, so he built one in the middle of red pine woods.

Subsequently, Tsukakoshi heard locals and visitors alike make comments such as "it would be nice to have a place to eat here." In response to this, he opened a health food restaurant serving agar and

---

[7] Annual growth ring is the layer of wood growth put on a tree during a single growing season. It is readily distinguished because of differences in the cells formed during the early and late parts of the season. In Japan this word is commonly used to show the "slow but steady" type of management style, philosophy and principle.

seaweed. The restaurant proved to be hugely popular, and soon he added a wild grass garden and a flower bed, as well as another restaurant. These developments were followed by relocating the headquarters there, and the building of a multipurpose hall to serve the community. The company called it Kanten Papa Garden, and it became a sightseeing spot for the community. Almost every year they organized a Kanten Festival where they served *tokoroten* (a sort of noodle made from agar) free of charge at food stands operated by Ina Food employees.

The company built a pedestrian bridge in front of the factory because Tsukakoshi thought it was dangerous for employees and visitors to cross the busy road on foot. The company also planted cherry trees along the road. It built a fountain using underground water that came to be favored by so many people that they had to stand in queue to get water, and so the company built another fountain. The area was cleaned every morning by the employees voluntarily. Tsukakoshi thought it was in people's nature to be attracted to a beautiful area. He believed that making their workplace beautiful contributed to a beautification of the community.

Moreover, employees parked their cars far from the store when they parked in the parking lot of a supermarket for the convenience of pregnant women and elderly people. The company also prohibited its employees from making a right turn when commuting to prevent traffic congestions caused by waiting to make a right turn. They were told to make left turns when coming to work even if it meant they drove further. He believed the employees' morale and morals went hand in hand. If a company's management thought about its employees' welfare first, the employees' morale improved and they ended up acting with high morals. That resulted in the company's contribution to the community.

IPO: Not Interested

Small and medium sized companies were going public one after the other during the Japanese bubble economy from the late 80s to the early 90s. However, Tsukakoshi kept away from such a trend. Toward the end of the 1990s, many securities brokerage companies came to visit Ina Food urging them to go public. Tsukakoshi was in favor of the idea at one point, but as soon as he heard about maximization of profits, total market value management, and an achievement-oriented policy in the IT boom that followed, he rejected the idea.

He felt that he would not be able to manage the company for the employees and for its contributions to the community if the company was listed. Tsukakoshi felt that if the stock market appreciated Ina Food's current management style and a rise in stock price was a result of that, he would not mind going public, but he suspected the stock market was only interested in how much profit the company made. He believed that the purpose of the company was the happiness of its employees. The market, however, seemed to reward companies who fired employees during restructuring rounds with higher stock prices. To Tsukakoshi, it seemed that the market was confusing the means with the object. His motto was for profit to be the means to make employees happier, and not the object.

Tsukakoshi believed that there was "an axis of progress" and "an axis of trend" in human society. The axis of progress was a straight line that led to an ideal society. The axis of trend was a movement of the society that swung constantly to the left and right, perpendicular to the axis of progress. He felt people should pay attention to the axis of trend, but not misunderstand it as the path to follow. American-style management that paid heavy attention to shareholders' profit was a trend in his eyes. If one wanted stability and long term existence of the company, one should not be influenced by it. To move steadily along the axis of progress with a thorough understanding of the optimum growth rate while keeping an eye on the trend was the kind of management he was aiming at.

For the Future

In the summer of 2008, Tsukakoshi was looking through the windows of his office in Ina City, Japan. The head office and Kitaoka plant which he was looking at were designed as part of the landscape. They had built their workplace with their own hands. The corporate garden, developed in 1988, displayed over 60,000 square meters of wild flowers and grasses containing mountain azaleas and hydrangeas which were voluntarily cared for by the employees who treasured their beauty. He aimed for his company to be a corporation that was conscious of the global environment. It had been his strong belief that no good company could exist independent of the surrounding communities. Employees tending flowers was no different from them wishing their town to be beautiful and the surrounding nature to be preserved.

He felt he had done a good job so far. Basically he has done all as a "contrarian". He attempted to manage his company in a manner that differed from the conventional wisdom, when the consensus opinion appeared to be wrong. The business had prospered and did not pose any urgent problems. But he also felt that he should not simply sit back and savor his success. There were tremendous growth opportunities and he knew operations should be improved before those opportunities could be targeted.

He had been thinking that real joy came from change and from going to the next level. His long-time belief had been that no company could get to the future by standing still. His vivacious personality, intelligence, and "can do" attitude had set the tone for the company.

Based on this, his attention had been directed towards various operational as well as management issues to identify any pressing matters that needed change. He was questioning himself about what changes needed to be made. He thought of the following possibilities, although he did not believe they would happen soon:

1. The company had not explored the possibility of exporting its products. Bearing various risks in foreign markets in mind, should the company export its products? What about production overseas?
2. Growth eventually would need financing. Small and medium sized companies were going public one after the other. Although Ina Food had managed to stay away from an IPO thus far, could it grow without going public?
3. Good quality agar products could not be manufactured without good materials, high quality water, and a good production process. It had been the company's practice to import high-quality materials from overseas suppliers. It also ensured a large stock of materials, thus contributing to the stability of agar markets around the world. However, Tsukakoshi wondered how much longer the company could continue to enjoy an overseas supply of materials. Should it try to

make extra efforts to secure longer term material supply contracts from foreign sources?

4. R&D had always aimed at further improving the company by seeking new possible uses for agar. They promoted their developments to customers for use in their corporate applications and actively proposed new products to meet predicted requirements in advance. To be able to do this, the company had made it a policy to have research staff that was equal to 10 percent of the total number of employees. Tsukakoshi wondered whether this investment in R&D would be sufficient in the future.

5. Tsukakoshi considered that in its quest to seek better profits and efficiency, the company must be wary of the following: not inconveniencing its suppliers, not discarding its regard for the environment and not forcing sacrifices upon its employees. He thought the company had to maintain a meaningful presence, and had to constantly strive to be a corporate entity with an endeavor that was lauded and appreciated by the stakeholders—all those around it. He was concerned that there might have been areas that had been overlooked and which had not been given adequate attention. If so, the company had to find them and improve in these areas.

6. He believed that the true corporate objective rested in seeking various ways in which the corporation might serve society while it ensured the livelihood of its employees. He also firmly believed that the pursuit of growth and profit were merely a means for attaining these objectives. He had done a lot in these areas, but wondered what else could be done for employees and society in the future.

Conclusion

When the world economy is facing serious difficulties, the management of Japanese corporations is once again attracting attention from all over the world. Many of these corporations have realized successful results in the marketing, production, financing, and allocation of their resources in today's borderless environment. However, these success stories are only partially known in the West.

This article is a case study concerning two Japanese corporations which acted as the "contrarian" against traditional Japanese and international management techniques and realized successful results in today's global economic crises environment. This success story encourages us to do something new as a contrarian against established standards and rules. It is very easy for companies both in Japan and foreign countries to get wrapped up in tradition and become resistant to change, but it is now necessary to shake them out of it for the future. Japanese management techniques are different from those of the Anglo-American companies. Having knowledge of these differences allows Anglo-American companies to do something new and different from what they have done previously. This article provides a unique perspective for analyzing the corporate cultures, customs, and systems exclusive to Japanese companies. It is advantageous for Anglo-American companies to know about new ways of doing things that are contrary to their way of thinking.

It is very easy to get stuck in a rut in the past. But if Anglo-American companies got to know more about Japanese companies, perhaps they too could change for the future. Any company can do something that has been done before by others, but the key to success is to stretch oneself in new directions both domestically and internationally.

.

The Center for Japanese Global Investment and Finance

Director: Professor Mitsuru Misawa
Address: Shidler College of Business
University of Hawaii, 2404 Maile Way, E-601e,
Honolulu, HI 96822
Tel: (808) 956-9713
Fax: (808) 956-9713
Email: misawa@hawaii.edu
Website: http://www2.hawaii.edu/~misawa

Background

The Center for Japanese Global Investment and Finance (the Center) was established in the College of Business Administration on April 3, 1997. Its purpose is to enhance knowledge of changes in the global investment policies and strategies of the Japanese financial sector by supporting and encouraging research, publication, international conferences and symposiums, faculty exchange and lecture series. Particular emphasis is to be placed on attracting Japanese investment to Hawaii and promoting mutual interests. The Center's activities strengthen the University of Hawaii's College of Business Administration's strategic thrust of Asia-Pacific teaching, research and public service.

The Center has been soliciting contributions from Japanese business organizations to provide support. The granting of Japanese tax exempt status for contributions by Japanese business organizations to the Center is under the jurisdiction of The Council for Better Corporate Citizenship

(CBCC) of the Keidanren (see "About Nippon Keidanren and CBCC" below).

On November 13, 1997, with the endorsement of the Honolulu Japanese Chamber of Commerce, the CBCC granted approval for tax exempt status for contributions made to the Center by Japanese business organizations.

From 1989 to 1996, Professor Mitsuru Misawa served as the U.S. Counselor on the CBCC of the Keidanren. On this basis, the CBCC decided to support the Center.

On September 1, 1997, Professor Mitsuru Misawa was appointed as the Director of the Center. The Center is now located at E305, CBA.

Mission and Objectives

1. To establish a Japanese investment research center in the Business School at the University of Hawaii. This idea is based on a suggestion from the Keidanren's Investment Study Mission to Hawaii in 1988, as well as the local community's strong request for well-balanced Japanese investment to Hawaii.
2. To study Japanese investment in the US mainland, and Asian countries' investment in Hawaii and the US mainland.
3. To promote university activities concerning Japanese investment:
   - Offer courses seminars on related subjects to train unique and effective individuals for international business;
   - Establish scholarships;
   - Foster faculty research and publishing;
   - Hold various international and local seminars;
   - Hold lectures by successful global business leaders;
   - Exchange personnel and information with other reputable universities and research institutions.
4. This is the first unique research center established in a university. As Hawaii is at the center of the Pacific, an active exchange of human resources and information is expected. The Center plays a significant role in deepening mutual understanding and promoting stronger ties between the US and Japan.

Publications in 2005–2010

1. Mitsuru Misawa, "Revitalization of Japanese Banks: Japan's Big Bang Reform," 2nd Revised and Enlarged Edition, Risk Management, edited by Michael Frenkel, Wrish Hommel, and Markus Rudolf, Otto Beisheim Graduate School of Management, WHU, Germany, March 2005, pp. 801–820.

2. Mitsuru Misawa, "Bad Loans: A Comparative Study of US and Japanese Regulations Concerning Loan Loss Reserves," The Banking Law Journal, November/December 2004, Vol. 121, No. 10, pp. 918–946.

3. Mitsuru Misawa, "Bad Loans of Japanese Banks –Directors' Civil and Criminal Liabilities–," Temple International and Comparative Law Journal, December 2004, Vol. 18, No. 2, pp. 101–127.

4. Mitsuru Misawa, "Laws and Regulations on Problem Loans in Japan — Is Application of International Accounting Standards Possible?" Columbia Journal of Asian Law, Fall 2004, Vol. 18, No. 1, pp. 1–45.

5. Mitsuru Misawa, "Japanese Issues and Perspective on the Convergence of International Accounting Standards," Journal of International Law and Business of Northwestern University School of Law, April 2005, pp. 711–745.

6. Mitsuru Misawa, "Bank Directors' Decisions on Bad Loans: A Comparative Study of U.S. and Japanese Standards of Required Care," The Banking Law Journal, May 2005, Vol. 122, No. 5, pp. 429–466.

7. Mitsuru Misawa, "Tokyo Disneyland — Joint Venture vs. Licensing," A Case Study, Asian Case Research Centre (ACRC), The University of Hong Kong, August 2005, Ref. 05/254C at ACRC, Case No. 1 at CJGIF, CBA, UH, 22 pages (Main Text) and 12 pages (Teaching Notes).

8. Mitsuru Misawa, "Shareholders' Derivative Action and Directors' Responsibility in Japan," Penn State International Law Review (The Dickinson School of Law), Summer 2005, Vol. 24, No. 1, pp. 1–57.

9. Mitsuru Misawa, "The Tokyo International Capital Market for Foreign Issuers and Required Disclosure," The Journal of Payment Systems Law, November/December 2005, Vol. 1, No. 7, pp. 699–753.

10. Mitsuru Misawa, "A Rogue Trader At Daiwa Bank: Management Responsibility Under Different Jurisprudential Systems, Practices And Cultures", A Case Study, Asian Case Research Centre (ACRC), The University of Hong Kong, November, 2005, Ref. 05/268C at ACRC, Case No. 2 at CJGIF, CBA, UH, 15 pages (Main Text) and 22 pages (Teaching Notes).

11. Mitsuru Misawa, "A Rogue Trader At Daiwa Bank: The Board Meeting on September 25th 1995 in Japan", A Case Study, Asian Case Research Centre (ACRC), The University of Hong Kong, November 2005, Ref. 05/269C at ACRC, Case No. 3 at CJGIF, CBA, UH, 4 pages (Main Text) and 6 pages (Teaching Notes).

12. Mitsuru Misawa, "Comparative Study of US and Japanese Bank Director's Duty of Disclosure", The Banking Law Journal, January 2006, Vol. 123, No. 1, pp. 39–79.

13. Mitsuru Misawa, "Tokyo Disneyland and the Disney Sea Park: Corporate Governance and Differences in Capital Budgeting Concepts and Methods Between American and Japanese Companies", A Case Study, Asian Case Research Centre (ACRC), The University of Hong Kong, March 2006, Ref. 06/281C at ACRC, Case No. 4 at CJGIF, CBA, UH, 26 pages (Main Text) and 12 pages (Teaching Notes).

14. Mitsuru Misawa, "Hostile Takeover Battle in Japan: Fuji TV vs. Livedoor for NBS", A Case Study, Asian Case Research Centre (ACRC), The University of Hong Kong, March 2006, Ref. 06/287C at ACRC, Case No. 5 at CJGIF, CBA, UH, 30 pages (Main Text) and 9 pages (Teaching Notes).

15. Mitsuru Misawa, "Case Note: The Long Term Credit Bank of Japan Litigation" Australian Journal of Asian Law, Asian Law Centre, University of Melbourne (paper accepted and forthcoming).

16. Current Business and Legal Issues in Japan's Banking and Finance Industry, 2006, World Scientific Publishing Company, Singapore.

17. "Nireco Japan: Introduction of the Poison Pill", A Case Study, Asian Case Research Centre (ACRC), The University of Hong Kong, September 2006, Ref. 06/294C at ACRC, Case No. 7 at CJGIF, CBA, UH, 26 pages (Main Text) and 11 pages (Teaching Notes).

18. "Bank of Japan's Meeting in March 2006: An End to the Quantitative Easing Policy?", A Case Study, Asian Case Research Centre (ACRC), The University of Hong Kong, November 2006, Ref. 06/301C at ACRC, Case No. 8 at CJGIF, CBA, UH, 21 pages (Main Text) and 8 pages (Teaching Notes).

19. "Ina Food Industry: A New Management Philosophy For Japanese Businesses", A Case Study, Asian Case Research Centre (ACRC), The University of Hong Kong, November 2006, Ref. 06/305C at ACRC, Case No. 9 at CJGIF, CBA, UH, 13 pages (Main Text) and 7 pages (Teaching Notes).

20. "OSG Corporation: Hedging Transaction Exposure", A Case Study, Asian Case Research Centre (ACRC), The University of Hong Kong, December 2006, Ref. 06/302C at ACRC, Case No. 10 at CJGIF, SCB, UH, 22 pages (Main Text) and 8 pages (Teaching Notes).

21. Cases on International Business and Finance in Japanese Corporations, 2007, Hong Kong University Press.

22. "World Co. Ltd, Japan: Why Go Private?", A Case Study, Asian Case Research Centre (ACRC), The University of Hong Kong, January 2008, Ref. 07/362C at ACRC, Case No. 11 at CJGIF, SCB, UH, 19 pages (Main Text) and 8 pages (Teaching Notes).

23. "J-COM: Share-Trade Irregularities on the Day of IPO". A Case Study, Asian Case Research Centre (ACRC), The University of Hong Kong, April 2008, Ref. 08/378C at ACRC, Case No. 12 at CJGIF, SCB, UH, 13 pages (Main Text) and 8 pages (Teaching Notes).

24. "SOFTBANK's New Strategy: The Largest LBO in Japan". A Case Study, Asian Case Research Centre (ACRC), The University of Hong Kong, December 2008, Ref. 09/399C at ACRC, Case No. 13 at CJGIF, SCB, UH, 22 pages (Main Text) and 9 pages (Teaching Notes).

25. "An Overview of Problems Concerning Political Donations in Japan", Columbia Journal of Asian Law, Columbia University, Spring 2008, Vol. 21, No. 2, pp. 162–181.

26. "Keidanren: Foreign Political Contributions in Japan". A Case Study, Asian Case Research Centre (ACRC), The University of

Hong Kong, October 2009, Ref. 09/429C at ACRC, Case No. 14 at CJGIF, SCB, UH, 18 pages (Main Text) and 5 pages (Teaching Notes).

27. "OSG Corporation: Hedging Transaction Exposure (Spanish)", A Case Study, Asian Case Research Centre (ACRC), The University of Hong Kong, November 2009, Ref. 06/302CSP at ACRC, Case No. 15 at CJGIF, SCB, UH, 25 pages (Main Text) and 8 pages (Teaching Notes).

28. Misawa, Misawa, *"Ina Food Industry: A New Management Philosophy For Japanese Businesses"* (Japanese) (ed., pp. 14 pages (Main Text, Asian Case Research Center (ACRC), The University of Hong Kong, 2010.

29. Misawa, Misawa, *"OSG Corporation-Hedging Transaction Exposure (Japanese)* (ed., pp. 22 pages (Main Text)). Asian Case Research Center (ACRC), The University of Hong Kong, 2010.

30. Misawa, Misawa, 2010, The 14 Cases written by Misawa, M. were listed in the US on Harvard Business Online (http://cb.hbsp.harvard.edu/cb/search/misawa?Ntk=HEMainSearch& N=0) under Misawa, on the European Case Clearing House (http:/www.ecch.com/) in Europe and on the Asian Case Research Center (ACRC) at University of Hong Kong (http:/www.acrc.org.hk/) in Asia. Through them, 5510 copies of these cases were sold (2060 in 2007, 1555 in 2008 and 1895 in 2009) to worldwide universities and business companies.

U.H. Professor Misawa — Honjo International Fellowship

1. Objectives of the fellowship:
    The Center for Japanese Global Investment and Finance
    • Encourages students of the University of Hawaii to study at Japanese undergraduate and graduate universities (Waseda, Keio and Hitotsubashi and other appropriate universities); and
    • encourages undergraduate and graduate students of those Japanese universities to study at the University of Hawaii

2. Fellowship Amount and Number of Recipients:
   A total fellowship amount of ¥2.4 million (about $30,000) shall be granted to four recipients a year. The average amount awarded per student is approximately $7,500. The Honjo foundation holds the right to make decisions on the number of recipients and fellowship amount granted to each recipient, based upon the applications it has received in that year.

3. General conditions for selection:
   This fellowship must be used for formal study in the visiting country. It may not be used for travel only. The student grantee must live in the visiting country at least for one regular academic semester (residency required and the summer session is considered as a regular semester).

4. This fellowship was initiated in 2003.

About Nippon Keidanren and CBCC

The center is supported by the Council for Better Corporate Citizenship (CBCC) of the Nippon Keidanren. The Nippon Keidanren (Japan Business Federation) is a comprehensive economic organization born in May 2002 by merging the Keidanren (Japan Federation of Economic Organizations) and Nikkeiren (Japan Federation of Employers' Associations). Its membership of 1,647 comprises 1,329 companies including 93 foreign-owned companies, 130 industrial associations, and 47 regional economic organizations (as of June 21, 2005).

The mission of the Nippon Keidanren is to accelerate the growth of the Japanese and world economies. It also aims to strengthen corporations to create added value to transform the Japanese economy into one that is autonomous and driven by the private sector, by encouraging the idea of individuals and local communities.

The Nippon Keidanren, for this purpose, shall establish timely consensus and work towards resolution of a variety of issues concerning the Japanese business community, including economic, industrial, social, and labor issues. Meanwhile, it will communicate with its stakeholders, including political leaders, administrators, labor unions, and citizens at large. It will urge its members to adhere to the Charter of Corporate Behavior and Global Environment Charter, in order to regain public confidence in businesses. It will also attempt to resolve international problems and deepen economic relations with other countries through policy dialogue with governments, business groups and concerned international organizations.

Index